W9-BBD-272

# COURTS, POLITICS, AND JUSTICE

**THIRD EDITION**

## Henry R. Glick

The Florida State University

**McGRAW HILL, INC.**

New York  St. Louis  San Francisco  Auckland  Bogotá  Caracas
Lisbon  London  Madrid  Mexico  Milan  Montreal
New Delhi  Paris  San Juan  Singapore  Sydney  Tokyo  Toronto

**COURTS, POLITICS, AND JUSTICE**

Copyright © 1993, 1988, 1983 by McGraw-Hill, Inc. All rights reserved. Printed in the United States of America. Except as permitted under the United States Copyright Act of 1976, no part of this publication may be reproduced or distributed in any form or by any means, or stored in a data base or retrieval system, without the prior written permission of the publisher.

2 3 4 5 6 7 8 9 0 DOC DOC 9 0 9 8 7 6 5 4 3

ISBN 0-07-023553-8

This book was set in Times Roman by Better Graphics, Inc.
The editors were Peter Labella and Fred H. Burns;
the production supervisor was Denise L. Puryear.
The cover was designed by Rafael Hernandez.
New drawings were done by Grafacon, Inc.
R. R. Donnelley & Sons Company was printer and binder.

Library of Congress Cataloging-in-Publication Data

Glick, Henry Robert, (date).
  Courts, politics, and justice / Henry R. Glick.—3rd ed.
    p.       cm.
  Includes bibliographical references and index.
  ISBN 0-07-023553-8
    1. Courts—United States.    2. Judicial process—United States.
  3. Political questions and judicial power—United States.
  I. Title.
  KF8700.G55      1993
  347.73′1—dc20
  [347.3071]                  92-30986

# ABOUT THE AUTHOR

HENRY R. GLICK received his Ph.D. degree in political science from Tulane University. He has taught at the Florida State University since 1968 where he also is a research associate in the Institute on Aging. Among his publications are *The Right to Die, Supreme Courts in State Politics, State Court Systems* (coauthor), and *Courts in American Politics* (author and editor). He also has published numerous articles and chapters on courts and the political process in political science and law journals and anthologies.

To I. David Glick

# CONTENTS

# PREFACE TO THE THIRD EDITION

In addition to bringing all of the materials up to date by discussing recent scholarly research and major events involving the courts, I have made a number of important changes and additions to this edition of *Courts, Politics, and Justice*. First, several reviewers have commented that the illustrative boxed inserts help to bring courts and politics to life, and they urged me to add more of them to each chapter. Therefore, I have increased the number of these inserts, and I have added tables, charts, and diagrams that also more vividly portray main points discussed in the chapters. Each chapter also concludes with a list of suggested additional readings directing students to more information. I also have expanded the table of contents to include the major elements of each chapter.

The third edition also includes several new topics and expanded discussion of others. A basic change concerns Chapter 2, Organization of Courts. This chapter has been enlarged to emphasize the distinctive role and work of federal and state courts in separate sections. Organization charts, illustrative tables, and inserts also illuminate the separate and interactive functions of federal and state courts in the judicial process. I also have expanded Chapter 3, Lawyers and Law Practice, to include discussion of lawyers' relationships with their clients, the availability of lawyers, lawyers' ethics, and their strategies in representing their clients. Chapter 6 includes a more complete discussion of sentencing within the context of plea bargaining.

Other changes include a discussion of the war on drugs, particularly its impact on the work of courts and the rights of criminal defendants. I also have added a discussion of the death penalty in the final chapter as part of the rights of criminal defendants. Also new are discussions of recent controversies concerning the election of state judges and the selection of the new conservative justices for the Supreme Court. I also have expanded the discussion of public interest law, public opinion and the Supreme Court, and the role of the Supreme Court and state supreme courts in judicial review.

Finally, I have brought the discussion of civil rights, rights of criminal defendants, and women's rights up to date with special emphasis on recent policy revisions by the Rehnquist Supreme Court. I also have enlarged the discussion of the politics of abortion—included as part of women's rights—to illustrate that the Supreme Court has an important, but not an exclusive, role in this and other controversial national policies.

I would like to thank the many reviewers who made numerous valuable suggestions for the third edition. I appreciate the comments of Professors Nathan Brown, George Washington University; Gregory A. Caldeira, Ohio State University; Bradley C. Canon, University of Kentucky; Melinda Gann-Hall, University of Wisconsin—Milwaukee; James L. Gibson, University of Houston; Sheldon Goldman, University of Massachusetts—Amherst; Steven H. Hatting, University of St. Thomas; Patricia Pauly, University of Kentucky; Neal Tate, University of North Texas; Michael Tolley, Northeastern University; and Diane Wall, Mississippi State University.

My wife, Joy, also has contributed mightily to this edition by putting up with my preoccupation in writing it.

I dedicate this edition of *Courts, Politics, and Justice* with love and high regard to my brother, Dave, professor of communications and education at the State University of New York College at Oswego. Although we work different parts of the liberal arts, we hear many of the same drums and ask many of the same questions.

*Henry R. Glick*

# PREFACE TO THE SECOND EDITION

It has been very gratifying to write the second edition of *Courts, Politics, and Justice,* reflecting the encouraging reception of the first edition among teachers of the judicial process and their students. I am especially pleased that I have had an opportunity to share my perspective of courts and politics with so many students beyond my own classroom. It has been good to learn that students feel that the text brings the judicial process to life and connects courts to politics. This is my main goal.

There are several important changes in the second edition that reflect student and faculty reactions. The discussion of judicial administration and court reform has been combined with the chapter on judicial organization, making structure and organization the central theme of the chapter. There also are two new chapters. A chapter on lawyers and the law profession examines the practice of law and legal education in the United States and links them to social structure and political behavior. A final chapter on courts and social change expands the discussion contained in the first edition and concentrates on the interactions between judicial decisions, political action, and social change. The second edition also updates factual information, illustrations, and recent scholarly research throughout the text. Especially important additions concern the impact of the Reagan administration on the selection of federal judges, concern with the litigiousness of American society, and recent changes in judicial policy and its impact.

I would like to thank the reviewers who carefully read the entire manuscript and made many useful suggestions and challenged as well as buttressed my own interpretations of courts and politics. Thanks go to Professors Sheldon Goldman, William P. McLaughlin, David Neubauer, Elliot E. Slotnick, G. Alan Tarr, C. Neale Tate, Lettie M. Wenner, and John Winkle. I also am grateful to my wife, Joy, for her consistent support and enthusiasm . . . and for relinquishing the word processor even when it was her turn to get her own work done!

This edition is dedicated to the memory of George W. Pruet, Jr., a recent graduate student and colleague at the Florida State University who was in the early years of his career in judicial politics at the University of Akron. It also is dedicated to Kenneth N. Vines, who introduced me and several colleagues during the 1960s at Tulane University to the new and emerging world of judicial politics. Both George and Ken have had a lasting impact.

*Henry R. Glick*

# PREFACE TO THE FIRST EDITION

Courts in the United States have growing opportunities to decide many new and unusual issues. As society and technology change at an ever faster pace, problems come to judges which most people have never thought much about or imagined before. However, judges often disagree on solutions to new and even customary disputes, and there are many differences in how similar cases are decided. Who uses the courts, what kinds of issues judges decide, how judges form their views, how they apply them to cases, and how their decisions affect society are important parts of *Courts, Politics, and Justice*.

But there is much more to courts. The number of disputes or conflicts that are decided by courts drops sharply at each stage of the judicial process. Most disputes never get to court at all but are settled informally. Many cases are settled before trials begin, and only a few trial decisions are appealed. Thus, while Supreme Court and other appellate decisions are important, most disputes are settled informally and locally. The first stop in the courts is usually the last stop.

This book has several objectives that reflect different aspects of courts. *First, it looks at the judicial process in all types and levels of courts in the United States.* Many books concentrate on the United States Supreme Court or the federal courts: but the odds are very high that when people go to court, they go to state court. Therefore, this book presents a broader perspective of the judicial process, and it covers state and federal and trial and appellate courts.

*The second objective is to explain what courts do, on the basis of recent social science research.* The text describes what goes on in court, but it also is important to explain *why* courts work as they do. There is a great deal of evidence that formal law cannot adequately account for judicial behavior and that social science research provides more complete and realistic explanations. Although the book rests heavily on social science research, it is included in ways that readers without special knowledge of the courts will understand and can use to develop an informed outlook on the judiciary.

The text also includes excerpts from news stories and summaries of actual cases and events involving the courts. They provide vivid examples of the operation of the judicial process and illustrate major points made in the chapters. These examples can also be the basis for class discussion of major topics.

*A closely related third objective is to link courts to politics.* Explaining judicial behavior means connecting courts to the broader social and political context in which they operate. But it also means seeing courts not just as formal legal institutions that are affected by an outside world of politics, but as major and integral parts of state and national politics.

A number of people have helped me along the way. I appreciate the hard work of George Pruet and Suzy Parker in collecting and organizing much of the background material. The staff of the Department of Political Science "word processor team" never faltered, and I thank Vicki Harley and Yulondia Wilson for their invaluable assistance. Professor Theodore Becker sent me interesting materials on mediation, and Professors Bradley Canon and Charles Johnson shared their latest ideas on the impact of judicial policy. I am especially indebted to Professors Sheldon Goldman, David Neubauer, and Elliot Slotnick, who read several drafts and commented extensively on the entire manuscript. Professors Leonore Alpert, Burton Atkins, I. Ridgeway Davis, David Gow, William P. McLaughlin, and Bruce Murphy read various parts of the manuscript and offered many other helpful suggestions.

*Henry R. Glick*

# 1

## COURTS, POLITICS, AND JUSTICE

Courts and the judicial process usually bring to mind a picture of a judge, draped in a black robe, overseeing a trial. When a judge enters a courtroom, everyone rises and stands quietly until he or she sits behind the elevated bench and raps the gavel to start the proceedings. In courts composed of a number of members, it is common for judges to march in together quickly as if choreographed on cue to take their seats in a flourish of flowing robes. Loud talking or even whispering among court spectators is not permitted.

At the U.S. Supreme Court severe-looking ushers holding long sticks roam the aisles, and they poke these sticks at individuals who talk too loudly or distract others from focusing on the front of the large courtroom. Called "the Marble Palace," the U.S. Supreme Court building is very ornate, with high ceilings and decorated walls, polished floors, and long benches that resemble pews in a church. Reverence and respect are expected and enforced. Other courtrooms are less magnificent, but the floor plan, furniture arrangement, and the judge raised above everyone else are similar and clearly show who is in charge and what goes on.

The odds are good that few of us picture a black or a woman presiding over a court. There is an increasing number of female and black judges in the United States, but chances are most of us still envision a middle-aged white man, perhaps slightly overweight, with thinning or silver hair. Judges are thought to be slightly aloof, but patient, understanding, and unlikely to lose their tempers. They also run their courts fairly but firmly. Judges are not too tall or too short or too thin, and they do not sport beards or styled haircuts. Of course, judges *do* come in all shapes, shades, and sizes, but Chief Justice William Rehnquist and Associate Justice Antonin Scalia *really look* like judges.

Most judges also do not hold press conferences, give speeches, or write for popular magazines or even law journals to explain their decisions or comment on public issues which may come before the courts. Even a judge who has held many other political positions prior to becoming a judge seems to change into a new person after donning judicial robes for the first time. The once very friendly and outgoing politician becomes a little distant, personally reserved, and removed from the day-to-day hustle and bustle of state or county politics. As the political role changes, the new judge prepares to perform different work according to different standards and expectations about appropriate behavior. Judges are public officials, but most of us expect them to be different somehow from other politicians and to take special care about how they act both on and off the court. Judges should act . . . well, like . . . judges.

Popular views of courts also include the belief that when a citizen gets her or his day in court, a good attorney can get any "nice" or "good" person out of trouble. TV programs, such as *L.A. Law, Divorce Court,* and the afternoon soap operas often focus on the intelligent, hard-working, and dedicated lawyer who represents glamorous, interesting, and usually white, middle-class people who are wrongly accused of murder or caught up in a nasty divorce—typically with plenty of adultery. Criminal defense lawyers always find the truth by the end of the program and just barely prevent conviction of the innocent, virtuous defendant. The police and prosecutors generally are portrayed as decent people, too, sometimes not quite as bright or as dedicated, but they do their job in a scramble for clues, culprits, and crime. Opposing attorneys are pictured as cordial adversaries who, like knights of old, joust before a judge and jury. The defense lawyer, often spurred on by a fair lady, always comes out on top. Justice triumphs in the end and the truly guilty get their just deserts.

Justice triumphs in the ideal judicial world because decision making is seen as objective and impartial. Unlike legislators or governors, who are expected to be partisan or to campaign for particular policies, judges are viewed as neutral referees and appliers of the law. Often in conjunction with juries, they review the facts, examine the law, and reach proper decisions without favoritism to anyone. Judicial decisions are based on what the law requires, not on political promises, policy preferences, or personal sympathy. Equal treatment before the law, justice according to law, a government of laws, not of men, are the watchwords of American justice.

## COURTS AND LEGAL CULTURE

Beliefs in equal justice and the rule of law, jousting lawyers (called the *adversary process*), and objective decision making are parts of legal culture.[1] Social scientists use the term "culture" to refer to basic values, beliefs, and expectations about social behavior. Legal culture deals with particular values and perspectives about how disputes are settled, how courts work, the content and role of law, and the behavior of people who manage the judicial process.

## The Distinctiveness of Courts

There are many sets of beliefs in legal culture that shape the major features of the judicial process and which *distinguish courts from other branches of government*. Although judges have some things in common with other public officials, such as being elected or appointed to office, judges usually behave very differently from other politicians and on the job.

Legal culture affects many features of courts, but it is especially visible in judicial decision making, selection of judges, public access to courts, and procedures involved in processing cases.

As indicated earlier, legal culture assumes that judges will be *objective and neutral in decision making*. They are expected not to take sides before a case is argued or be influenced by public opinion or the views of other political elites. They should remain open-minded throughout a trial or appeal. In contrast, legislators usually are elected partly on the basis of the policies they favor and the groups they support.

Legal culture also includes the expectation that society should *select the best qualified judges* regardless of their inborn personal characteristics, such as sex, race, or religion, and that judges with previous judicial experience and extensive legal careers ought to be selected over those with lengthy careers in partisan politics. Clearly, recruitment expectations for other politicians are very different, and many emphasize their previous political and governmental experience as qualifications for higher office. If judges must run in judicial elections, campaigns ought to be low-key and polite, in keeping with the aura and majesty of the judiciary. Campaigns for other public offices often are much rougher.

Legal culture also includes the idea that every citizen has a right to his or her *day in court* and that justice should be available to everyone without delay or extraordinary expense. In contrast, few citizens expect to have their personal day in a legislature. Legislatures are viewed as lawmaking bodies for the entire state or nation, not usually for individuals. Legal culture also has implications for the role of courts in making rules for society. Legal culture usually expects judges to limit themselves to making decisions that are clearly required by law and to leave new lawmaking to legislatures.

Legal culture also affects the specific *procedures* that courts use to reach decisions and distinguishes judicial decision making from processes commonly used in legislatures and the executive branch. For instance, lobbyists approach legislators and administration officials directly and personally in order to influence their decisions, and they probably call these officials by their first names after becoming personally acquainted and familiar with them. But a lobbyist who telephones a judge in order to influence a certain decision risks conviction for contempt of court! Influencing courts simply is not done that way. The only way that interest groups can legitimately influence a court is by taking part in a case that is handled like any other case, which means that there always is some distance and no private contact between the litigants and the judge. Like other litigants, an interest group will be represented by a lawyer, not a lobbyist, who will handle the case according to standard judicial procedure.

## Myths

While legal culture helps us to see the special characteristics of courts and to account for differences between courts and other government activity, legal culture also is filled with many myths, which makes the judiciary appear to be a totally isolated part of human activity. In this view, terms such as ''judicial politics'' are a hopeless contradiction. Judicial pomp and circumstance, public reverence, and the reassuring appeal of law and justice wrap the courts in a self-contained bubble or cocoon that separates and protects the judicial process from the larger context in which it really exists. Viewed as a television drama, it is as though the general public goes through life ''off camera'' but occasionally comes onto the stage of the judicial system to deal with crime or to handle a personal conflict or problem that is too big or difficult to manage privately. They turn their problems over to legal experts, who find the correct legal solution and then send the parties on their way.

Legal culture assumes that litigants and the rest of us are outsiders who cannot hope to understand the specialized and mysterious workings of the courts. Law has its own unique methods, procedures, and logic, and only those with proper training and experience can learn to unlock its secrets. This view was summarized well by a law school dean who once was asked to help arrange interviews with judges for a social science research project on the courts. He replied that it was not necessary for anyone to interview judges about their work, since everything a person needed to know about courts was contained in law books. Besides, it was improper for anyone to talk to judges about what courts did. But legal culture does not account for all of our attitudes or views of the judicial process.

## COURTS AND POPULAR POLITICAL CULTURE

To most Americans, the United States is the world's stronghold of democracy and representative government. From the early 1800s we have elected most public officials and required them to obtain voter approval to stay in office. We also have limited the number of terms a President or governors may serve, preferring turnover in office as a way of avoiding executive domination. Voting in many referendums to approve state constitutional amendments, special revenue bonds, etc., also is common throughout the nation. It seems that we are constantly being called to the polls. We also generally believe that public opinion should influence government decisions and that voting helps to shape future policy. Popular government, meaning government by the people and for the people, is the foundation of our political system. The popular political culture emphasizes democratic political values and making government responsible to the people.

Although courts are distinctive institutions heavily affected by legal culture, the popular political culture is intertwined with courts in two broad ways. First, popular political values have helped to shape the basic organization and operation of courts and the ways judges are selected. Second, courts often are enmeshed in political conflict because judicial decisions affect fundamental social and political beliefs, customs, and conduct.

### Organization and Operation of Courts

The impact of the popular political culture is clearest in the *selection of judges*. Voters in many states elect judges, as well as prosecutors, public defenders, and court clerks. Even when judges are appointed, it is by elected governors and Presidents, who regularly give most posts as rewards to people closely connected with the executive's political party and who supported the victorious campaign. Many political elites want to keep using elections or executive appointments for judges. Some groups believe that judicial elections permit periodic review of judges and their decisions and keep courts close to the people.

Judicial elections are the most visible procedures that make courts "political," but popular political culture operates throughout the judicial process. For example, the *organization and authority* of American courts are tied very securely to politics and society. Not only are judges chosen by various democratic methods, elected state legislatures and Congress largely determine the kinds of cases courts may decide (*jurisdiction*). Enlarging court jurisdiction increases judicial opportunities to become involved in new areas of public policy. This has been a crucial concern in the growth of federal courts during our 200-year history.

Courts also have limited geographic jurisdictions and usually hear cases only from relatively small and local regions. Georgia county courts hear only Georgia county cases, and courts in New York City hear only cases begun there. (Federal courts, however, hear some cases involving people from different areas.) This means that local economic and political systems and styles of life provide the setting for the kinds of cases that get to the courts. Disputes everywhere are put into a similar legal framework to fit the form of the judicial process, but the actual social or economic issues and the litigants involved are likely to vary around the country. For instance, courts in small towns and cities rarely hear cases involving corporations and the practices of big business, whereas courts in large metropolitan areas frequently deal with these kinds of cases.

The content of court decisions also is likely to depend upon the *social context* in which courts operate and the major values of people in the area. Many of us would guess that judges and juries, in small communities composed mainly of whites and Protestant fundamentalists, are likely to see divorce, homosexuality, crime, and other issues more traditionally than judges and juries in large cities, where more lenient or "live and let live" policies probably prevail. There probably are differences also among particular cities, depending on the values and lifestyles of the people who settled there, traditions built up over the years, and the kinds of people who are chosen as judges.[2]

### Decisions and Political Conflict

Courts also are included in the popular political culture because judicial decisions frequently conflict with popular beliefs and attitudes about important social problems. *Courts often create controversy.* For example, since the 1950s, the U.S. Supreme Court has made a number of decisions designed to protect criminal defendants from excessive police pressure and unfair judicial procedure. Requirements that criminals have access to lawyers shortly after arrest and that police not pressure defendants to confess, and limitations on obtaining evidence, are important examples of legal rules called "due process of law." During this same period, however, crime rates generally rose throughout the United States. The recent scourge of drug trafficking and crime associated with drug use has reinforced public fears of crime and increased demands on legislatures and the criminal justice system to get tough on criminals.

Many people believe the courts are responsible for increasing crime because judges "handcuff the police" by their rules and let criminals off because of "technical" violations of law. Popular beliefs link courts to the crime problem. These criticisms were a major part of Richard Nixon's presidential campaigns in the 1970s and frequently were voiced by Attorney General Edwin Meese of the Reagan administration.

With the appointment of four new conservative justices to the Supreme Court since 1985 by conservative Republican Presidents Reagan and Bush, the values of the Supreme Court have shifted to the right, and the Court has begun to expand police power to gather evidence and obtain confessions. Now, liberals have begun to worry about new limits on constitutional rights.

Links between crime and the courts also extend to the election of state judges, such as during the recent bitter and intense reelection campaign of liberal Justice Rose Bird of the California Supreme Court. Justice Bird and several other California judges were opposed by the governor and other conservatives because the judges oppose the death penalty. They had required new trials in nearly all criminal cases decided during their tenure on the court, including several involving brutal murders, because the judges believed the defendants' rights had been violated.[3]

Probably no issue in the United States is so divisive as abortion. Since granting the right to obtain an abortion in 1973, the Supreme Court has made a series of decisions that have further defined the circumstances under which an abortion can be obtained, and the Court has both approved and rejected various limits imposed on abortion by the federal government and the states. Recently, the Supreme Court has approved of federal regulations prohibiting doctors and others working in family planning clinics that receive federal funds from discussing abortion with their patients. Many doctors and others object to this policy and ruling as violations of free speech and restructions on the professional duties of physicians. Abortion-rights advocates and opponents quickly clashed in a struggle to overturn the decision. President Bush rescinded the rule regarding doctors but not other clinic employees. Court decisions involving civil rights, pollution control, the rights of AIDS victims, drug testing, and other issues also routinely involve the courts in political conflict.

Conflict frequently also occurs over *putting court decisions into effect*. Everyone is obligated to obey court decisions, but the actual extent to which people comply depends partly upon political and social environments and the attitudes of other elites. Despite U.S. Supreme Court rulings, for example, which require that public education and religious instruction be kept separate, there are many school districts where prayer, Bible reading, and religious pageants go on as before. Most of these have been small, socially similar communities where no one objects to religion in the schools and there is no outside enforcement of court rulings.[4] In larger cities, however, with a much greater variety of students in the schools and many different points of view about religion and education, there is likely to be much less religion in public education.

The same has been true of court-ordered desegregation. Most southern school districts remained segregated for about 10 years after *Brown v. Board of Education* was decided in 1954, and many cities resisted busing or other methods of achieving racial integration. In many instances, people rationalize their refusal to obey by attacking courts as undemocratic or for being insensitive to public opinion or local culture, or they argue that "everyone" is satisfied with existing arrangements, suggesting a sort of informal democratic consensus on what judicial policy should be. Whatever their explanations may be, they all reveal a close connection between courts and popular political culture.

## LAW AND POLITICS

The legal and the popular political cultures do not fit together very easily, yet both of them are basic parts of American courts. And, like lots of things in life, many of us would like to have our cake and eat it too. We often want both sets of values to apply to the judicial process at the same time. For instance, we want to elect judges and have them be responsive and concerned with community opinion and preferences, but we also expect judges to be independent and to make proper legal decisions. Various groups call on courts to make new policies in controversial areas such as abortion and discrimination, while others severely criticize courts for going beyond what they see as the proper judicial role of interpreting or applying existing law. We value due process of law, but also want to get tough on crime. These kinds of demands seem to go in opposite directions, and understanding courts requires careful consideration of the impact of *both* law and politics.

### Many Sources of Law

When people talk about "the law," they imply that there is a single set of authoritative rules created and enforced by a government. These rules are supposed to determine how people ought to behave, or what is permissible, and how judges should settle conflicts brought to them in cases. Law is seen as a body of logical, systematic, and clearly identifiable prescriptions, or a repair manual for solving social problems and disputes. We often speak glibly about "what the law requires" or "what the law says on this or that," etc., as if we could go to an encyclopedia and look up the single authoritative definition or solution. The legal system is seen as a kind of computer that is programmed to deal with any problem that litigants feed into it, and lawyers and judges are the technicians.

This view of law may be comforting and reassuring because it is so simple and sure, but law cannot be found in a single place or source. *There are many sources or bits and pieces of law.*[5] For instance, law includes the U.S. Constitution, state constitutions, legislative statutes, executive orders, administrative rules, and previous decisions of many courts (*precedents*). Federal, state, and local governments all produce their own laws. Moreover, these general sources of law include many individual laws or rules that often are vague and at odds with each other, and that contribute to confusion and conflict.

**Disagreement**  Relying on law and legal culture for information about the judicial process usually leaves many unanswered questions about courts. If everything we needed to know about courts were found in the law books, for instance, we indeed may wonder why there would ever be any disagreement on what the law is. Well-trained lawyers would save their clients a lot of expense and personal misery before a lawsuit is filed if they advised them exactly what the law requires. But many court decisions are difficult to explain through law, for it is clear that judges frequently disagree on what the law means and which sources of law to use.

Illustrations of such disagreement can be found in interpreting the meaning of federal and state constitutions by different courts, disagreement among judges on individual courts, and differences in the use of prior court decisions (*precedents*) as guidance in current cases.

It has been common in the fifty states since the early 1900s for government to pay for public education mostly with money raised locally through property taxes. However, in the early 1970s, several state supreme courts ruled that since property taxes produce unequal amounts of revenue because of local variations in the value of property, they also produce unequal education. This, they have argued, is forbidden by the U.S. Constitution. But, in 1973, the U.S. Supreme Court decided that taxation and education are unrelated and that the Constitution does not require a change in policy. Therefore, the law does *not* prohibit the use of local property taxes.

Since then, similar cases have been decided by twenty-four other state supreme courts. Thirteen courts have joined with the Supreme Court on this interpretation, but eleven others, relying on their reading of state—*not* the federal—constitutions, have declared that traditional funding methods do violate constitutional rights. Generally, courts with reputations for liberal policies have found state taxing methods unfair.[6] With both federal and state constitutions available to them, state courts have not produced consistent policy regarding the legality of state tax methods for public education.

Not only do various courts disagree on what the laws says, judges on appellate courts hearing the identical case frequently disagree among themselves and write dissenting opinions that reach conclusions exactly opposite from those of the majority. How do we explain dissents through law? Is it that some judges are right and others are wrong, that some read the law correctly and that others somehow miss the boat?

The use of precedents as law illustrates one of the sources of disagreement. The rule of precedent, or *stare decisis,* means that past court decisions that relate to a current case are to be used as guidance for settling the current controversy. The rule is part of the English legal tradition found in most of the nations originally colonized by the British. The principle of *stare decisis* is supposed to provide continuity in the law so that people can gauge their current behavior according to principles that have been followed in the past.

That is fine in theory, but we need to know more specifically how it affects particular judicial decisions. Major questions are: How do judges select from thousands of previous cases? How are old cases supposed to relate to current ones? The same facts: the same principles; the most recent cases? Which ones provide "true" guidance and which ones should be ignored? Should judges use cases from their own court or their region of the country only, or can they use any precedent anywhere that they believe fits the case currently before them?

Unfortunately for the predictive power of law, there are no precise standards or rules for using precedents, and different judges use various criteria as well as different precedents. Many lawyers and judges also believe that for any legal situation brought before a court and for any solution that judges might conceivably impose, there are dozens or even hundreds of previous court decisions that would justify and support their action.[7]

A study of southern state supreme court decisions in race relations cases during the early days of the civil rights movement found that many different sources of law can be used to support different decisions. State supreme courts in the border states of the south were likely to order desegregation of public schools, parks, and other facilities and to say that federal court decisions and the U.S. Constitution required them to do so. Deep south supreme courts that ordered desegregation often referred to state statutes and state constitutions to support their decisions rather than to national civil rights rulings, which probably would have been less acceptable in their state. However, other southern courts defied U.S. Supreme Court policy altogether and continued to rule in favor of segregation.[8] They based their decisions on state court decisions or state laws upholding segregation.

The key difference among the southern courts in this period is their civil rights policies. All of them had the same sources of state and federal law and court decisions available to them. However, they chose different ones to rationalize or support their rulings. The decisions in these cases strongly indicate that judges chose first to rule in favor of or against segregation and then selected the necessary legal rules to support their decisions afterward.

### General Principles of Law

In addition to having numerous and often contradictory sources of law, judges, lawyers, and other officials often have to interpret and use rules that are very general or vague and do not tell them specifically how to act. The U.S. Constitution, in particular, is a very general set of principles that have been interpreted and applied in many different ways throughout our history.

Some legislative and executive rules are vague because lawmakers cannot agree on more specific regulations. They often compromise by creating very general rules and allow others, often judges and lawyers, to interpret what the rules mean in particular circumstances. Other rules intentionally provide only general principles or guidelines so that they can be applied to many similar, but somewhat different, circumstances.

Criminal codes are examples of this kind of lawmaking. Criminal acts are defined by legislatures, but the penalties for the same crime may range from fines and probation to many years in prison. Judges are free to hand down sentences that fall within the range specified by the legislature and to make the punishment fit the crime and the criminal. It is possible and perfectly legal, therefore, for judges to sentence defendants convicted of the same crime to vastly different prison terms, and they often do. A particular decision depends on the personal values and choices of judges, prosecutors, and defense lawyers and the compromises that they produce among themselves. Whatever they decide within the broad range of sentences fixed by the legislature will be lawful.

**Equity**   Other vague legal principles also give judges plenty of room to make decisions they believe are proper or right. For instance, the principle of *equity* gives judges almost complete freedom to decide what is best. Equity generally means fairness or doing right. The rule comes from old England and the American colonies, where separate equity courts once heard certain types of disputes but also had the special power to ignore laws that judges believed were unjust in particular cases.

Today, separate equity courts are rare, but the equity idea still permits judges to acknowledge formal law but to avoid it selectively in the name of fairness. Who decides what is fair? Judges do. Box 1.1, "Formal Legal Rules

**BOX 1.1**

FORMAL LEGAL RULES AND EQUITY
IN CONFLICT

Fedo and Hattie Mae Kenon lived in a small, ramshackle frame house in rural north Florida. They had worked most of their lives picking tobacco for local farmers and existed now on about $400 per month in Social Security payments. Their house was worth $7500, and they were required to pay $3.05 each year in county property taxes. Fedo Kenon, aged 65, somewhat retarded and a patient in various mental hospitals over the years, paid the tax each year—except once. Mrs. Kenon was unaware of the missed tax payment.

John G. Barrow, a local investor, noticed the Kenon property listed in a legal advertisement containing property with overdue taxes. *Following a long-standing state statute and routine legal procedure,* he paid the tax himself and received a certificate from the county tax collector which gave Barrow the right to collect the back taxes from the property owner plus interest. The law stated that if the property owner failed to pay the amount due for 2 succeeding years, Barrow could apply for a tax deed giving him lawful ownership to the property.

After waiting 3 years instead of the minimum of 2, Barrow paid required fees of $102 to the clerk of the court and received a tax deed giving him ownership of the Kenon home. Barrow informed the Kenons that he owned their house and gave them notice to buy the property from him or to move within a specified time. The Kenons were unable to pay or to afford other housing and they refused to move. Their plight made the national news, and the Kenons began to receive financial contributions. They also obtained free legal services from a local legal aid organization. Barrow sued to assert his lawful right of ownership and to move the Kenons from the house.

The trial court judge decided that although Barrow had followed proper procedures sanctioned by state law, the doctrine of *equity* required that he be prevented from acquiring the Kenon home. Not only was the amount of money paid for the property very small, but giving Barrow title to the property would impose a terrible burden and hardship on the Kenons. Investor Barrow appealed, but the higher court affirmed the trial judge's decision. The Kenons kept their home and planned to use some of the $11,000 raised in contributions to make long-needed repairs. Barrow got nothing.

and Equity in Conflict,'' illustrates the use of equity even when formal legal rules seem very clear.

The general principle of equity also operates in many cases where there is little statutory law to tell judges how to decide a case or there are lots of precedents, but they lead in many different directions and provide no clear guidance or inescapable rule. In these cases, judges decide on their own what is the fairest, best, or most equitable way to resolve a conflict.

An example of this kind of decision making is found in thousands of divorce cases in which judges must decide how to divide property owned by the parting couple, how much child support and alimony to award, and which parent should receive custody of children. The judge has to decide how much a husband (or perhaps wife) can afford to pay, who would make the better parent, and other issues. Both sides in a dispute can be expected to put themselves in the best possible light, of course, and various experts may be called to testify, but the judge ultimately must decide. The judge will review the facts presented by both sides and the arguments attorneys make on their behalf, and decide what is right and proper. This also is law, but it is law created daily by judges according to their own values, beliefs, experiences, and customs.

**Personal Decision Making**   Numerous sources of law and vagueness in law do not simply permit, they *require* personal judicial decision making. Search as hard as he or she might for the required rule of law to use in a case, a judge still has to choose a specific solution. Although law does not predict the outcome of cases, few judges make decisions at random or without careful thought and consideration. However, the way they decide cases will be affected by factors other than law. Likely possibilities include judges' personal policy preferences and attitudes toward the parties (litigants) in a case, their personal backgrounds and experiences, and the impact of local political environments on the way they see social conflicts.

## JUSTICE AND POLITICS

Justice is the most general and widely interpreted legal concept. The definition of justice includes the idea of equity, but it has many additional meanings. Justice includes doing the right things in the right way. It also can refer to the many procedures that are followed in taking cases and people through the courts. Finally, justice also often refers to the content of court decisions and who wins or loses in the courts. Justice has a very positive ring to it, and it practically glows with respectability and virtue. But we also need to know if it is useful as an explanation of judicial behavior, or is but a shining political symbol that glorifies formal law and the courts.

### Justice as Process

**Judicial Systems**   Many social scientists and practitioners equate justice with anything that courts, lawyers, and law enforcement people do. Courses in law, political science, and criminology, for example, typically refer to the "criminal justice system" and include every activity and decision from arrest, prosecution, and trial to imprisonment and parole. All of the behavior of people in the system produces justice of some sort.

If justice means anything that legal institutions do, then "doing justice" can mean imposing the death penalty for violent murder as well as not prosecuting or giving lenient sentences to those accused of mercy killing. It can mean aggressive or lenient prosecution for possession of marijuana or treating child or spouse abuse as a purely domestic affair. It can mean "cracking down" on pornography or treating it casually as an element of big-city life. Since justice in this sense refers to the *activities* of decision making and the processing of cases, any decision or action does justice.

In a similar way, phrases such as "the administration of justice" refer to the management and direction of organizations and individuals who make judicial decisions. The administration of justice is concerned with a wide range of judicial activities, including the selection of judges and other judicial personnel, the processing of cases through the courts, obtaining operating funds for the courts, creating more efficient ways to manage judicial work, jury selection, and other issues.

**Procedural Justice** In addition to the organization and administration of judicial systems, concepts of justice focus heavily on proper procedures.[9] Procedural justice refers to the rules of the legal game—how cases are processed by the courts—and the rights guaranteed to litigants. Rules about when and which documents to file to get a case started in the trial courts or an appeal considered by a higher court, how trials proceed, the selection of juries, and other stages of the process are parts of procedural justice.

We usually think of procedural justice as due process. The most visible and controversial part of due process concerns the rights of criminal defendants, including the right to an attorney, protection from coerced confessions, protection from unlawful searches and seizure (illegal gathering of evidence), protections from self-incrimination (not having to testify against oneself), procedures to guarantee an unbiased jury, right to appeal, and others. These procedural rights are controversial because they sometimes seem to make the job of law enforcement more difficult, but they are fundamental features of criminal due process that distinguish justice in the United States from that in many other countries.

*Informal Judicial Settlements* The news media and popular television shows emphasize the formal judicial process by concentrating very heavily on arrests in lurid criminal cases, trials, and the maneuvers of opposing attorneys to gain advantage and public support.

Interesting or exciting as it may be, however, this image—which intertwines the thrills of a case with formal procedure—accounts for very few of the cases handled by the courts. Instead of trials, *approximately 90 percent of all cases in the United States are settled before a trial begins.* When cases are settled informally, formal procedure and due process do not apply, and the facts in dispute and the pertinent law are never considered by a judge or jury.

In criminal cases, most defendants plead guilty to some crime in exchange for a lighter sentence (*plea bargaining*). In noncriminal (*civil*) cases, both parties usually agree to compromise financial settlements in order to avoid the delays, expense, and uncertainities of a trial. Informal settlements often are preferred also because it is easier to collect part of what is owed early than it is after a formal trial, when the loser may disappear or resist until ordered to pay by the court. In the few civil cases that do go to trial, litigants who win may even compromise the actual terms of a court-ordered settlement in order to avoid further delay and a possible reversal of their victory should the loser decide to appeal.

Not only are most court cases settled without trials, but most legal work does not take place in the courtroom and rarely involves court cases. Most lawyers spend their time giving advice in order to keep people out of legal conflicts or to help a business or an individual get through a maze of government bureaucracy or negotiate successfully in a complex business deal. Conflicts and disagreements probably occur along the way, but court cases are rare.

Private decisions sometimes involve judges as negotiators, but they often involve them only after settlements have been worked out by others. Judges give official approval by imposing the negotiated sentence, or they write up the agreed financial or divorce settlement as an official court order. In these cases, the action takes place among attorneys and their clients and rarely involves judges or formal court procedures in any important way.

Strategies and procedures used to settle these conflicts rarely involve much consideration of formal law, but depend more on economic and psychological calculations of what might be won or lost, guesses about what judges are likely to think is fair if the case were to go to trial, delays in getting the case settled that occur in awaiting a trial date, skill at negotiation, ability to pay attorney's fees for a trial, personal sense of justice, and perhaps other values.

We cannot understand how these processes work if we rely on the law books or on formal descriptions of judicial systems because this activity is not part of formal law and court procedures, and it is rarely recognized in legal education. Still, it is how most judicial business is conducted. Consequently, equating justice to judicial systems and administration or to due process leaves a lot of unexplored territory.

*Procedure Does Matter* Although most disputes and cases are settled informally, we cannot dismiss formal law and procedure. Many social scientists and court observers have long assumed that winning is the only thing that matters to most opponents in a court case (*litigants*). For litigants in civil cases, winning means receiving all or most of a financial award they came to court to get. For criminal defendants, it means an acquittal or a light sentence.

Of course, winning is important, and losers sometimes proclaim that there is no justice, but recent research has found that procedure is equally or even more significant than winning in determining citizens' satisfaction with the courts and their sense of having received justice.[10] In the eyes of litigants, proper procedure covers all aspects of the judicial process, including how they are treated by police, prosecutors, judges, lawyers, and others. Getting justice means that people feel that officials are honest and unbiased, open-minded, fair, and listen carefully and treat them with respect and dignity. For criminal defendants, it also means having ample time to talk with their attorneys.

Litigants often feel more satisfied with the formal procedures of a trial than with informal negotiations and private dispute settlement because they believe that in court their grievances get a more complete hearing and are taken seriously, and that wrongdoing is clearly identified. In contrast, they feel that negotiations focus immediately on compromise and pressures to settle, and ignore assigning blame and determining right and wrong.

These findings indicate that the legal culture matters to people. Also, the findings strongly suggest that there is friction between achieving a sense of justice and the common practice of settling cases through negotiation. Consequently, some researchers suggest a compromise between informal negotiation and formal trials. More civil disputes might be settled through arbitration, in which both sides have a chance to tell their story and receive a binding decision, but the process is short and simple and does not require the time and expense of a formal trial. More criminal cases might be processed through quick nonjury (*bench*) trials in which the judge determines guilt as well as deciding the sentence. Arbitration and other methods for settling civil cases and criminal bench trials will be discussed in Chapters 5 and 6.

### Justice as Substance

Substantive justice differs from process and procedure. The focus of substantive justice is on the outcomes of cases or the bottom line of who wins and loses and what they get. It deals with the social, economic, and political content and possible consequences of judicial decisions. Issues in substantive justice include, for example, criminal sentences imposed on defendants, the amount of money awarded in auto accident or employee injury cases, which parent gets the children in a custody battle, whether or not busing will be used to integrate the schools, etc.

Legal scholars generally believe that substantive justice is less important than procedural justice since due process of law is the foundation of a free and open society, which somehow will produce substantive justice for all. If the rules of the game are followed, substantive justice likely will follow as well.[11]

While due process is extremely important in American courts and society generally, there is no guaranteed link between procedural and substantive justice. Critics of American justice often argue that complex and confusing procedures and the high cost of lawyers prevent many people from getting into the courts at all, or from operating equally in pursuing or defending a case.[12] If procedure makes it difficult or impossible for people to use the courts equally, then procedural justice has a direct substantive impact, since some people must suffer the consequences of social conflict or economic loss with no judicial recourse.

For instance, many Americans who can barely afford to meet their daily living expenses may have to suffer losses rather than spend more money to take their chances in court. Others with little education or who are not fluent in English do not understand court notices and lose cases by default because they do not appear on the right day. Poor criminal defendants are unable to hire lawyers of their own choosing and must depend instead on public defenders or court-appointed lawyers who often are so busy with other cases that they are unwilling or unable to challenge effectively the prosecutor's case.

Many court appointed lawyers assigned to represent poor defendants accused of murder often have not handled capital cases before, are poorly prepared, or receive so little money that they cannot spend much time on the case.[13] There also is growing evidence that prosecuting attorneys in the southern states, where most executions have been carried out, seek the death penalty up to three times as often in cases with white versus black victims, and that blacks who kill whites are up to four and a half times as likely to receive the death penalty. Challenges to prospective black jurors also have kept blacks off of many juries in death penalty cases. These are procedures which clearly have immediate and direct substantive impacts.[14]

**Disagreement on Justice**   There is considerable evidence that little agreement exists on what is substantive justice. From a criminal defendant's perspective, for example, justice may mean getting a light sentence in return for a guilty plea or getting a case dismissed altogether. But victims of crime and many other citizens probably believe that this is unjust because it does not impose punishment. For them, justice means an eye for an eye and a ban on plea bargaining.

Decisions that many people might believe are unjust can be produced with fair and impartial procedures. For instance, it once was common to burn or drown people for witchcraft or heresy so long as their trials were fair! Or, it is possible for trial and appellate courts to follow proper procedure while ruling that although vibration caused by jet planes makes a house uninhabitable, compensation should be denied since the planes do not pose a direct physical danger by flying *over* the house, but only take off and land *near* the house. Correct procedure also can be ignored to produce popular decisions, as in Box 1.1, ''Formal Legal Rules and Equity in Conflict,'' included earlier.

Box 1.2, ''Justice in Housing Court,'' and Box 1.3, ''Justice in Criminal Court,'' describe widely different but actual cases where there is possible conflict between procedural justice (using correct legal methods) and substantive justice (outcomes that people believe are fair or right)[15]. Most cases proceed according to established rules of legal process, but many people disagree about the justice of the final result.

Judges do many different and often contradictory things in the name of law and justice. Concepts of justice also seem to be catchalls used by judges and other officials to justify their actions and to increase acceptance of their decisions. Conflict and competition for government policies favorable to particular individual and group interests also often are presented publicly as involving basic issues of justice. Used in so many different ways, justice and other general legal principles cannot tell us why courts and legal officials make particular decisions or why differences occur in judicial behavior. Instead of a precise legal or scientific concept, justice and other similar ideals are better viewed as appealing symbols used to support particular political and social goals.

**BOX 1.2**

JUSTICE IN HOUSING COURT

The manager of a local supermarket owned a modest rental house which he leased to others for extra income. Before the end of a recent lease period, the tenant stopped paying rent and moved out, leaving the house dirty and damaged beyond the amount covered by the security deposit. After requesting additional rent and compensation for damages, which the tenant refused to pay, the landlord filed a case in housing court for $300. A hearing was set for about one month later, but the tenant ignored the legal summons and did not appear in court. Following usual court procedure, he lost the case to the landlord by default and the judge issued a court order stating that the landlord had the right to recover $300 from the tenant. The landlord mailed a copy of the court order to the tenant at his place of employment, but the tenant did not respond.

The landlord then asked the clerk of court how he was going to collect the $300 which he had lawfully won. The clerk gave the landlord a form which explained that the housing court was not a collection agency and could not give any assistance or legal advice on collecting judgments. The landlord was referred to the sheriff, who has the legal authority to enforce court rulings. The clerk in the sheriff's civil division explained that their office was not permitted to give legal advice on how to enforce judgments, but she offered to mail the landlord several additional forms. When properly completed, the forms would request the sheriff to seize personal property owned by the former tenant, which would be stored for four weeks and then sold at public auction to raise money to pay off the court judgment.

Before the sheriff could take any action, however, the landlord would have to pay a deposit to the sheriff to cover anticipated costs of property pickup, storage, and legal advertising for the sale, as well as the cost of holding the auction. The landlord also must be able to verify through serial numbers, bills of sale, etc., that the tenant really owned the property to be seized, or the actual owner could sue the landlord. The sheriff's clerk also could not guarantee that the sale would raise enough money to cover all of the enforcement expenses plus the $300 judgment. An alternative collection strategy would be to file the $300 judgment with the clerk of the county court as part of official public records. This would provide public notice of legal obligation (lien) against the tenant in the unlikely event that he owned (or bought) and then sold real estate. If he were to sell property, the court judgment would appear as a defect on the record of lawful ownership to the property (title) and may force payment of the $300 to clear the legal record. The landlord chose the second alternative, but he did not expect to collect anything.

## LAW AND POLICY

Although there are many different and often contradictory sources of law, there are consistent patterns of judicial decision making that provide continuity and regularity in law and society. But this is not due mainly to our reverence for particular laws. Instead, many laws seem permanent because society supports particular legal policies through custom, tradition, and expectations about proper behavior and correct social arrangements. In this sense, law is a result of political demands for particular policies.

It has long been customary, for example, that in cases of divorce, mothers receive custody of children and fathers pay child support and alimony. Mothers typically, and almost automatically, have been considered to be the most

**BOX 1.3**

JUSTICE IN CRIMINAL COURT

A jury found John not guilty of possession or sale of $10 worth of crack cocaine, but the police refused to release John's old Dodge van which they confiscated when he was arrested. The jury believed that the drug belonged to another man who ran from the van when police approached, but the prosecutor says that just because the jury acquits, " . . . doesn't mean we have to close our eyes to what really happened. What really happened was a drug deal." Even though John was not guilty, the state contraband forfeiture law permits the state to seize and keep any vehicle in which illegal substances have been found.

Several local defense lawyers believe that the forfeiture law is a convenient substitute for criminal prosecution, and a way to get something out of a weak case. "It allows them to do things that they can't with their arrest power," said a lawyer with the local legal services program and a member of the local chapter of the American Civil Liberties Union. "It's a shakedown," says another lawyer, arguing that the necessary link between a person's property and a crime often is missing in forfeiture cases. And, the legislator who sponsored the state forfeiture law believes the way it is being used exceeds the legislature's intent. For property to be seized, there should be a link between a crime and the property, and the value forfeited should be in proportion to the value of the drug found at the scene.

Prosecutors say that is not how the law reads, and other defense lawyers conclude that " . . . the interest of law enforcement outweighs the rights of private citizens in these cases," or " . . . it's a harsh law . . . and it seems unfair . . . but it's not unconstitutional." The local judge explains: "The way the law is set up is to say 'We know we've got people out there doing bad things we can't nail with the standard of proof in criminal court.' And they may walk out with their liberty intact. But if there's property involved, they're going to lose it."

Bernhard Goetz was charged with attempted murder, assault, and reckless endangerment after admitting to shooting on a New York City subway four young black men who approached him and asked for money. Believing that he was about to be robbed, Goetz pulled out a .38-caliber pistol and fired. Even after the men were down, Goetz fired again, saying: "You don't look so bad, here's another." One of the men was hit in the spine and is permanently paralyzed from the waist down.

No evidence was submitted at the trial that the four actually had tried to rob him, but the jury believed that Goetz was justified in shooting because he had been a victim of a prior mugging and was afraid. Law professors and sociologists concluded that the jury's verdict was a reaction to big-city life and the inability of the police to protect people from common crime. They say ordinary citizens can identify with Goetz's reaction and, while fear of young black males smacks of racism, the fact is that they have a crime rate exceeding that of young white males by a factor of ten.

Although he was acquitted of the shooting, the jury convicted Goetz of illegal possession of a handgun. He was sentenced to one year in jail and a $5000 fine, and, with time off for good behavior and credit for the time served in jail after his arrest, he was expected to serve only a few months. Several jurors said that Goetz should have been freed of all charges, but that the jury had no choice but to convict him of the gun charge. Local black leaders called the sentence a "tap on the wrist," and a lawyer for the paralyzed man said Goetz should have received a stiff sentence.

Of the four men shot by Goetz, one has disappeared; another is in prison for sodomy, robbery, and rape; another is on parole for grand larceny; and the fourth, who is paralyzed and suffered brain damage, lives with his mother. The family has filed a civil damage suit against Goetz.

suitable parent because they fill the traditional nurturing role and have been considered dependent upon men. There is no formal legal rule that requires this outcome, but the customary decision making of thousands of judges in millions of similar cases over the years has produced the same result. In this instance, judicial decision making is consistent with strongly held social beliefs and customs.

But times also are changing. Many women are altering their roles and no longer think of themselves as mothers and homemakers. Many are more interested in other careers and lives outside the home, and it no longer seems so obvious that mothers "naturally" make the best parents or that mothers always will want to obtain custody of their children. Popular journalism, the news media, and movies reflect these changing values.

Judges, like the rest of us, are involved with and become aware of changing social perspectives and conditions, and some are beginning to change their decisions. Mothers still obtain custody most of the time because both parents agree, but custody battles sometimes result in victories for fathers. Other families agree to joint custody in which both parents share the care and responsibility for their children. Many state legislatures also have changed provisions of family law which gave preference to mothers as the custodial parent. Now both parents are considered equal candidates.[16]

Other recent changes in family law endorsed by the courts include allowing the courts to hold fathers in criminal contempt for willfully refusing to pay court ordered child support, and allowing deductions of child support payments from paychecks. Some stepparents and homosexual parents are obtaining custody and visitation rights as well as child support obligations. As new generations of judges come to the courts, they will bring other new social values and assumptions with them.[17]

Our treatment of civil rights also reveals gradual social and judicial change. Segregation used to be an assumed national custom and the formal law in the southern states, and most court decisions supported it. However, in 1954 it appeared from a legal point of view that the Supreme Court suddenly discovered that all previous courts and judges had misread the Fourteenth Amendment to the U.S. Constitution and that segregation should not have been permitted. It was as though the Court had discovered a monumental legal mistake. But this view is much too narrow, for it ignores the long struggle for civil rights and even overlooks previous but less well-known court cases that whittled away at segregation before 1954. Decisions since the late 1950s are the result of major social and political changes in the United States, not the result of sudden judicial insight in which judges finally saw the true meaning of the law.

Social change does not have an immediate impact on law and judicial decisions, however. With some exceptions, most courts are slow to move in new directions. General respect for law, the principle of precedent, and links to tradition keep most courts oriented to the past. Judges often seem as though they are looking over their collective shoulder to see where courts have been rather than looking forward to what will be needed in new policymaking. Judges also are likely to believe that their proper role is only to interpret and apply law as they find it, not to innovate or to come up with new solutions to social problems. That is the job of legislatures, many judges believe, and it usually prevents the courts from taking major steps in policymaking.

Many judges on all levels of courts also hold their positions for life, and their views frequently do not change much throughout their judicial careers. Although changes may occur in the larger society, judges' decisions often reflect earlier perspectives, and they often seem out of date with legislatures and public opinion. While change is possible and even likely in the law, it often comes about extremely slowly and usually depends on clear shifts in social values as well as the selection of new judges with new ideas.

## JUDICIAL POLITICS

Sources of law are too vague and general to form clear explanations of what courts do and why. Since few trials and appeals occur, formal law also has little to do with most judicial and legal activity. Most lawyers do not spend nearly as much time searching out the meaning of the law as they do informally negotiating the terms of settlement in criminal and civil conflicts or giving advice on business transactions, wills, etc. A social science approach to the courts works to develop a more precise and complete description of what courts really do and explanations of why the judicial process operates as it does.

From this perspective, many social scientists are more interested in the *behavior* of judges, lawyers, and judicial organizations than in the formal legal content of court decisions or the official public explanations given for judicial actions. Social scientists also tend to place much more emphasis on decisions in large numbers of cases than on detailed analyses of individual decisions and the reasons judges give for their votes in written opinions. Comparisons of many decisions and perhaps many courts make it possible to discover whether certain common trends exist in judicial behavior that might explain judicial action.

For example, by looking at decisions in hundreds of cases involving the same type of issue (crime, employee injury, divorce, etc.), we can discover if certain judges consistently decide in favor of particular types of people. If so, a behavioral explanation of judicial decision making would lead us to speculate that judges have certain social attitudes toward groups of defendants or that they believe certain solutions to problems are better than others. In most instances we would find that the law(s) permits all of their decisions. Social scientists also are interested in interviewing judges, lawyers, and others about decision making and various aspects of the judicial process.

To learn more about courts, social scientists are interested in many behavioral questions, such as: Who are the judges? What political and economic attitudes do they have? What part do political parties and interest groups have in judicial selection and does it make a difference in judges' decisions? If we want to know something about the content and impact of judicial decisions, we also have to know who uses or cannot use the courts and why. We also want to know who wins and loses, and why, and what role courts have in affecting social and economic arrangements. But just as important are questions about why people settle out of court. Why do criminals plead guilty, and what consequences do they expect from a trial? Why does everyone *not* really want a "day in court"?

All these questions and more are the essence of judicial politics. Understanding courts as part of the political system means that we look at courts, judges, and lawyers in much the same way we look at legislatures or chief executives. We do not expect judges and other officials to behave the same way, but they all are parts of the same social, economic, and political systems and environments and must respond to many of the same political demands and social values that affect the behavior and policies of any agency of government. Therefore, we ask many of the same kinds of questions.

At the same time, though, we must keep in mind that courts are strongly affected by legal culture and that they operate differently from other political institutions. The task of judicial politics is to understand both aspects of courts and to describe and explain the behavior and operations of the judicial process.

## CONCLUSION

The central theme of this chapter is that understanding the judicial process requires us to think about more than formal law and procedure. Legal culture and popular political culture are competing sets of beliefs and expectations that we need to keep in mind at the same time to understand how courts actually work. The legal and popular political cultures appear again and again in the remaining chapters to demonstrate that while courts are part of the political process and larger social system, they also behave differently from legislatures and the executive branch.

Law is not adequate for understanding judicial decisions. Lots of law, vague principles of law, and loose concepts like justice do not pin down how decisions actually are made. Most cases also are settled through informal negotiation, not trials. Personal decision making and compromise are the keys to understanding how disputes are settled. Consequently, we have to approach courts from the perspective of judicial politics, not law.

## SUGGESTIONS FOR ADDITIONAL READING

Baum, Lawrence: "Judicial Politics: Still a Distinctive Field," in *Political Science: The State of the Discipline*, ed. Ada W. Finifter (Washington: American Political Science Association, 1983), chap. 7. A survey of research in political science on courts and the judicial process. Although research on courts shares many features with other contemporary work in political science, traditional links to law makes judicial politics probably the most distinctive sub-field in the political science discipline.

Frank, Jerome: *Law and the Modern Mind* (New York: Coward McCann, 1930). Written by an eminent federal district court judge, this early work emphasizes the myths and limits of formal law in explaining the judicial process.

Friedman, Lawrence: *Law and Society: An Introduction* (Englewood Cliffs, N.J.: Prentice-Hall, 1977). A compact introduction to the concepts, history, and role of law in society; law in different political systems; and social change through law.

Gates, John B: "Theory, Methods, and the New Institutionalism in Judicial Research," in *The American Courts: A Critical Assessment,* ed. John B. Gates and Charles A. Johnson (Washington: CQ Press, 1991), chap. 18. A survey of the most recent political science research on courts, and an assessment of new directions.

Janosik, Robert J. (ed.): *Encyclopedia of the American Judicial System* (New York: Charles Scribner's Sons, 1987), 3 vols. Includes eighty-eight original essays on legal history, substantive law, legal institutions and personnel, judicial process and behavior, constitutional law, and methodology in the study of law and the judicial process.

## NOTES

1 This discussion relies heavily on Richard J. Richardson and Kenneth N. Vines, *The Politics of Federal Courts* (Boston: Little, Brown and Co., 1970), pp. 8–9. See also Lawrence M. Friedman, *Law and Society: An Introduction* (Englewood Cliffs, N.J.: Prentice-Hall, 1977), p. 7

2 Martin A. Levin, *Urban Politics and the Criminal Courts* (Chicago: University of Chicago Press, 1977).

3 *New York Times,* October 23, 1982, p. 9; *Los Angeles Times,* November 23, 1985, p. 1; John T. Wold and John H. Culver, "The Defeat of the California Justices: The Campaign, the Electorate and the Issue of Judicial Accountability," *Judicature,* 70 (April–May 1987), 348–355.

4 Richard Johnson, *The Dynamics of Compliance* (Evanston, Ill.: Northwestern University Press, 1967).

5 See also the discussion in Harold J. Spaeth, *Supreme Court Policy-Making* (San Francisco: W. H. Freeman and Co., 1979), chap. 3.

6 Bill Swinford, "A Predictive Model of Decision Making in State Supreme Courts: the School Funding Cases," *American Politics Quarterly,* 19 (July 1991), 336–352.

7 Edward H. Levi, *An Introduction to Legal Reasoning* (Chicago: University of Chicago Press, 1948), pp. 2–3; Karl N. Llewellyn, "Remarks on the Theory of Appellate Decision and the Rules or Canons about How Statutes Are to Be Construed," *Vanderbilt Law Review,* 27 (February 1949), 192–193; Henry Robert Glick, *Supreme Courts in State Politics* (New York: Basic Books, 1971), chap. 4.

8 Kenneth N. Vines, "Southern State Supreme Courts and Race Relations," *Western Political Quarterly,* 18 (March 1965), 5–18.

9 Norman E. Bowie, *Towards a New Theory of Distributive Justice* (Amherst: University of Massachusetts Press, 1971), chap. 1; Lon L. Fuller, *The Morality of Law,* rev. ed. (New Haven: Yale University Press, 1964).

10 Tom R. Tyler, "What Is Procedural Justice: Criteria Used by Citizens to Assess the Fairness of Legal Procedures," *Law and Society Review,* 22 (1988), 103–135; Jonathan D. Casper, Tom Tyler, and Bonnie Fisher "Procedural Justice in Felony

Cases," *Law and Society Review,* 22 (1988), 484–507; and E. Allan Lind *et al.,* "In the Eye of the Beholder: Tort Litigants' Evaluations of their Experiences in the Civil Justice System," *Law and Society Review,* 24 (1990), 953–989.

11 Bowie, chap. 1, and Fuller.

12 Leonard Downie, Jr., *Justice Denied* (New York: Penguin Books, 1971); Richard Quinney, *Critique of Legal Order* (Boston: Little, Brown and Co., 1973).

13 "Firsthand Account of Capital Justice," *National Law Journal,* June 11, 1990, p. 40.

14 Raymond Paternoster, "Prosecutorial Discretion in Requesting the Death Penalty: A Case of Victim-Based Racial Discrimination," *Law and Society Review,* 18 (1984), 437–478; *New York Times,* July 10, 1990, p. 10.

15 *Tallahassee Democrat,* November 16, 1987, p. 1; *New York Times,* June 19, 1987, p. 11; January 14, 1989, p. 1.

16 *New York Times,* March 26, 1986, p. 17; *Newsweek,* January 10, 1983, pp. 43–44; Herbert Jacob, *Silent Revolution: The Transformation of Divorce Law in the United States* (Chicago: University of Chicago Press, 1988), pp. 134–144.

17 *New York Times,* March 2, 1987, p. 1; January 21, 1987, p. 13; April 28, 1988, p. 12.

# 2

# THE ORGANIZATION OF COURTS

There are fifty-one court systems in the United States: one for each state, plus the federal government. But this number is misleading because it oversimplifies the actual organization of courts. When we think of the national or state governments, we focus on Washington, D. C. or the state capital, and probably on the President or governor, Congress or state legislature, and on one court—the U.S. Supreme Court or the state supreme court. Were we to visit the national or state capital, we probably would have little difficulty locating these institutions among the government buildings.

But courts are everywhere. The federal and state courts include layers of courts from the highest appellate to the lowest trial courts, and most courts are located at the town, county, or district level. Nevertheless, they are parts of either the federal or state court systems. Courts also are connected to each other in a rank or hierarchy. Appeals go from trial to appellate courts, but there also is an expectation in court systems that the rules and policies set by appellate judges in their decisions will be followed by lower appellate and trial judges throughout the entire court system.

Although we frequently talk in terms of court systems as if courts were a set of precise and well oiled gears meshing together, each court—and often each judge—is a separate judicial authority, and there are thousands of semi-independent judges and courts conducting judicial business throughout the country. Consequently, court organization sometimes is quite complex.

To a great extent, the current structure and operation of American courts have been shaped by *strong traditions of local control of justice and judicial independence.* Local control stems from our rural and small-town origins and popular attachment to local government as "close to the people." The image of local justice endures despite the tendency to centralize other areas of government at the state and national levels.

Localism is reinforced by the legal culture, which includes the belief that courts should be free from "outside" influence that might threaten judicial independence and integrity. This usually has meant freedom from popular or partisan political pressure, but judges have interpreted or used the idea of judicial independence also to resist review of their decisions and procedures by appellate courts. Therefore, judicial independence has contributed to the fragmentation and variety that exist within state and federal court systems.

But there are contrary pressures for centralization and uniformity as well. Throughout American history, political conflict has shaped the courts. Advocates of national and state power have clashed over the authority of the federal courts. Within the states, disputes flare between those who see the need for an integrated or unified state court system and those who believe that each city and town is unique and needs its own distinctive set of courts.

Closely related to the historical development of courts is the politics of *court reform*, which calls for improving the efficiency of courts through new and simplified court systems and modern management procedures. But many judges, lawyers, and others object. They frequently are satisfied with how courts work, are reluctant to tamper with revered judicial institutions, or benefit from the existing system.

This chapter focuses on these main features of court organization: the basic structure and role of federal and state courts; the historical development of courts; and the politics of court reform.

## THE STRUCTURE AND JURISDICTION OF COURTS

There are two key elements to understanding court organization: the structure of court systems (the number and types of courts) and court jurisdiction (their legal authority to hear different kinds of disputes that people bring to court). The structure and jurisdiction of the federal courts are defined exclusively by federal law, and each of the fifty state court systems is established and regulated by state governments. These basic organizational features of courts provide the foundation for court involvement in public policy, and they affect judicial authority and ability to deal with important social issues.

This section begins with an overview of the types of courts and their jurisdiction. It is followed by description and analysis of the federal and state courts.

### Types of Courts

The federal government and about three-quarters of the states have *four basic types of courts: a supreme court, intermediate courts of appeal, trial courts of general jurisdiction, and trial courts of limited jurisdiction.* In all systems, these four types of courts are arranged in a hierarchy, with supreme courts at the top and trial courts at the bottom. Generally, litigants who are dissatisfied with the decision in a trial court may appeal to a court higher in the system, although there are special requirements and limitations on appealing cases.

The federal and state court systems are separate judicial systems. Once a case has been started, it normally remains within one judicial system. One important exception is the appeal of certain cases from state supreme courts to the U.S. Supreme Court.

Courts also have different names in different systems.[1] For instance, New York calls its highest court the Court of Appeals and refers to its major trial courts as supreme courts. In some states, the trial courts are called circuit courts, but in the federal system, the major trial courts are district courts. Although particular courts often have different names, their functions are roughly similar.

**Trial Courts**    Trial courts are the points of entry into the judicial process. Each side in a lawsuit or a case has an opportunity to state its claim or complaint, to present witnesses to prove its version of the facts and circumstances, and to cite the law relevant to the conflict. Each opponent hopes that the judge or jury will decide that its position is the correct one.

Court cases involve either *criminal or civil conflicts*. Criminal cases occur when a person has committed an act that is forbidden by state or federal law and is punishable, possibly by a fine payable to the government or a jail term. Crimes are illegal acts against "the people" or the state. Civil cases include all other cases and do not involve jail terms. Civil cases often pit a government against an individual or a group, but the issues usually concern the enforcement of various government policies.

Civil cases not involving the government are conflicts among private parties and usually involve personal injury or property damage resulting from an accident or other negligence (*torts*), debts, or some other conflict and claims for the transfer of money from one side to the other. In civil cases, sometimes neither side is seen as completely right and compromise financial settlements are imposed. Many states have separate divisions of the same trial court that specialize in civil or criminal cases.

The distinction between civil and criminal cases sometimes becomes very fuzzy when the federal or state governments are involved in cases. They sometimes sue individuals under civil laws that carry very heavy criminal-like penalties. In fact, suing in these circumstances often is called "prosecution," and it is similar to taking someone into criminal court. For example, an employer who turns a blind eye to employee negligence that causes death or injury to other employees or results in a bad chemical spill also may face heavy fines and may be responsible as well for employee compensation and the cost of cleanup. Governments are said to prefer these kinds of cases to straight criminal prosecution because it is easier to get judgments against wrongdoers.

In criminal court, the standards of proof, evidence, and defendants' rights make getting convictions more difficult.[2]

*General and Limited Jurisdiction*   Trial courts are divided into two groups: those with general and those with limited jurisdiction. *Limited jurisdiction* means that the particular court may hear only certain narrowly defined categories of cases. The federal government has courts which decide only tax disputes, and financial claims against the federal government and others. Certain state courts deal with traffic violations, juvenile crime, minor criminal cases (*misdemeanors*), small financial disputes, and so on. Trial courts of *general jurisdiction* have broader authority to hear a great variety of cases. Disputes involving large amounts of money and most criminal cases involving serious crimes (*felonies*) may be heard by a state trial court of general jurisdiction.

**Appellate Courts**   A person found guilty in a criminal case, and either party in a civil suit, if sufficiently unhappy about the outcome of a trial, may appeal to another court for review of the decision. Everyone is entitled to one appeal. Supreme courts and intermediate courts of appeals are the main appellate courts. Appeals courts determine if the trial judge made an important *error in procedure or interpretation of law* that would require the appeals court to reverse the decision and perhaps to order a new trial.

Appellate courts do not hold new trials, but only review the written record of the lower court and hear the arguments of opposing attorneys. Exceptions sometimes occur in cases appealed from trial courts of limited jurisdiction. Appeals from these courts may require new trials in trial courts of general jurisdiction. Certain other appeals are heard by intermediate appeals courts, while others, often involving more serious crime and more money, are reviewed by the highest court.

*Different Functions*   The basic purpose of all appellate courts is to correct errors of the lower courts, but both intermediate and the highest appellate courts have distinctive functions in judicial systems. Federal and state laws require intermediate appellate courts to hear most appeals. These courts have the widest *mandatory jurisdiction*, which means that most litigants have a right to appeal to these courts. The federal system and the system of most of the heavily populated states have several geographic divisions of intermediate appellate courts that hear many more cases than does the highest appellate court.

The highest appellate courts usually have less mandatory jurisdiction and broader *discretionary jurisdiction*, which means that they have some power to determine for themselves what cases they will decide. The U.S. Supreme Court has nearly complete control over its workload (*docket*). Therefore, the highest appellate courts often are described as *policymaking courts* because they can be selective in deciding the more significant disputes. This does not mean that other courts are unimportant, but that the highest appellate courts have a special role.

## FEDERAL COURTS

The basic organization of the federal court system and the ways that cases may be appealed from one court to another are found in Figure 2.1. The chart excludes several specialized trial and intermediate appellate courts that have very few cases.

Figure 2.1 shows the U.S. Supreme Court as the highest appellate court, several courts of appeals in the middle, and various trial courts. The major federal trial courts of general jurisdiction are the *district courts*; the major intermediate appellate courts are the *courts of appeals*. Also shown in Figure 2.1 is an arrow connecting the state supreme courts to the U.S. Supreme Court. State supreme courts are separated from the others by a dashed vertical line to show that they are not part of the federal court system. However, many U.S. Supreme Court cases come from the state supreme courts.

Although we think of the federal courts as part of the national government situated in Washington, D.C., most of the federal courts are distributed throughout the country. There is a minimum of one federal district court in each state, and the more populous states have two or more district courts for different sections of these states. Courts of appeals are located in one of twelve regional divisions called *circuits*. Therefore, despite their federal name tag, the major federal trial and appellate courts are organized on a local and regional basis so that cases destined for those courts enter a court in the area in which the dispute began. Consequently, federal courts often take on a distinctive local or regional flavor. There also is a thirteenth federal court of appeals (the U.S. Court of Appeals for the Federal Circuit). However, it is not a regional appellate court, and it has special limited jurisdiction, which will be discussed later.

**FIGURE 2.1**
The federal court system.

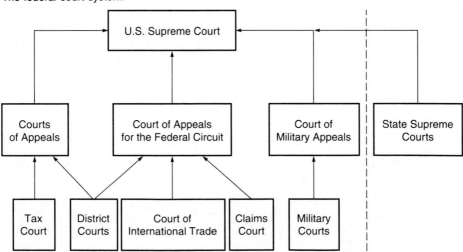

Figure 2.2 is a map of the federal court system. The heavy lines show the groupings of the states within the circuits, and the lighter lines within many of the states indicate the subdivision of these states into more than one judicial district. The U.S. Supreme Court and most of the specialized trial and appellate courts with limited jurisdiction shown in Figure 2.1 are located in the nation's capital. The Court of International Trade sits in New York City.

### Federal District Courts

The vast majority of cases that enter the federal courts begin in the district courts. In the early 1990s, there were ninety-four federal judicial districts with 636 judges. The map in Figure 2.2 shows that most of the eastern and southern states plus California and Washington state have been divided into more than one judicial district. California, New York, and Texas each has four. Most districts have several judges, but districts located in large cities in New York and California each have close to thirty judges. Each federal district judge presides over his or her own set of cases.

The number of districts has remained constant for a number of years, but in recent decades the number of judges has been increased by Congress every five to six years to serve growing populations and meet increasing caseloads in the busier districts. The latest increase occurred in December, 1990, when Congress authorized 65 new district court judgeships. Other large increases occurred in 1984, during the Reagan Administration (55 new judges), and in 1978, during the Carter years (113 new judges).

Increasing the size of the federal judiciary is important for handling increased amounts of litigation, but there are partisan political consequences of growth as well. Whenever the federal judiciary is enlarged, it provides the President with many new opportunities to fill the federal courts with judges from his own political party who share his political ideology.

Combined with filling vacancies, which occur regularly as judges resign, retire, or die, new positions provide a President, especially one who serves two terms, an enormous opportunity to influence the direction of court decisions well beyond his presidency. The impact of partisan politics on the selection of judges and on judicial decisions will be discussed in greater detail in Chapters 4 and 9.

**Jurisdiction**    The federal district courts have the broadest jurisdiction of all federal trial courts. This jurisdiction falls into three categories:

*Federal questions*    First, the federal district courts may hear any case involving a federal law, the Constitution, admiralty or maritime issues, or a ruling of an agency of the federal government.

*Federal government as litigant*    Second, the federal courts have jurisdiction over cases in which the federal government is a party to the case, either as plaintiff or defendant.

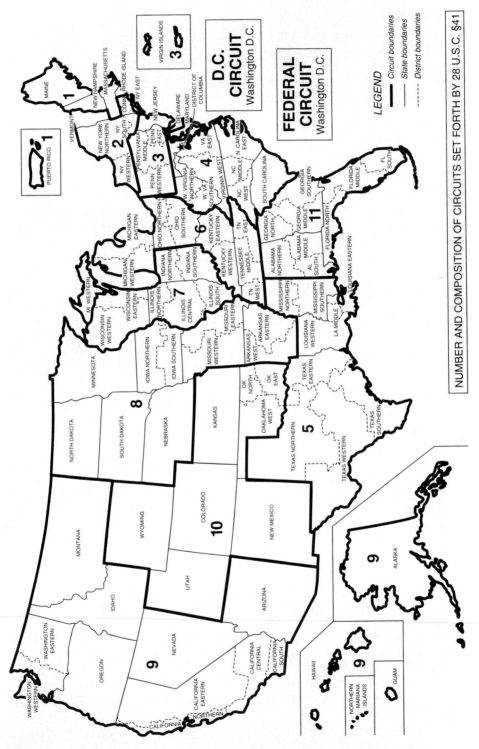

NUMBER AND COMPOSITION OF CIRCUITS SET FORTH BY 28 U.S.C. §41

LEGEND

Circuit boundaries
State boundaries
District boundaries

D.C. CIRCUIT
Washington D.C.

FEDERAL CIRCUIT
Washington D.C.

*Diversity*  The third major area of federal jurisdiction involves cases between litigants residing in different states in which the amount of money at stake is over $50,000.

Close to three-quarters of the work of the federal district courts concern federal questions and the federal government as a party to the suit. There are many cases in these two categories, including federal criminal laws, appeals by convicted criminals in state or federal prison based on Constitutional rights, civil rights, antitrust, labor-management disputes, Social Security benefits, the constitutionality of the state statutes, and many more. Diversity cases account for the remaining 25 percent.

When Congress and the executive branch create more law, the jurisdiction of the federal courts automatically increases. The most controversial area in recent years concerns growth in the number of federal drug offenses and court cases as part of the federal war on drugs.

**Changing Workload**  The variety of cases heard by the federal district courts is presented in Table 2.1. Criminal cases and petitions from prisoners in state and federal prisons top the list. Together, they account for slightly over one-third of all cases. The criminal cases involve prosecution in the federal district courts for federal crimes, while the prisoner petitions come from people already convicted of federal or state crimes and who are appealing their convictions and/or sentences based on the Constitution or other federal grounds.

Except for civil rights, Social Security, and some bankruptcy cases, most of the other categories in Table 2.1 involves business and commercial activities. Many of the personal injury cases also involve businesses and insurance companies.

Until recently, the work of the federal district courts had been steadily increasing. Caseloads grew approximately 60 percent between 1980 and 1985— from 197,000 cases to 313,000 cases. By the mid-1980s, it appeared the federal district judges would drown in a growing caseload. Since then, however, the annual number of civil and criminal cases filed in the federal district courts has decreased to just over 265,000. So, why is there concern about rising caseloads? The total caseload is not the complete picture.

*Civil Cases Down; Criminal Cases Up*  Figure 2.3 shows changes in the number of civil cases, drug cases, and other criminal cases brought to the courts from 1980 to 1990. The bar lines show that civil filings have come down while drug and other criminal cases have steadily risen.

Why have some cases declined while others have increased? Are Americans becoming less inclined to sue? Has crime increased dramatically? Violent crime has increased in many parts of the country, especially involving the sale

**FIGURE 2.2**
Geographical boundaries of United States courts of appeals and United States district courts.

**TABLE 2-1**
CASES FILED IN FEDERAL DISTRICT
COURTS

| Case type | Number | Percentage |
|---|---|---|
| Criminal | 48,904 | 18.3 |
| Prisoner petitions | 42,630 | 16.0 |
| Contract | 46,039 | 17.3 |
| Personal injury | 40,593 | 15.2 |
| Civil rights | 18,793 | 7.0 |
| Labor-management | 13,841 | 5.2 |
| Business regulation | 9,566 | 3.6 |
| Real estate | 9,505 | 3.6 |
| Social security | 7,439 | 2.8 |
| Property rights | 5,700 | 2.1 |
| Bankruptcy | 5,056 | 1.9 |
| Property damage | 3,166 | 1.2 |
| Securities | 2,629 | 1.0 |
| Taxes | 2,604 | 1.0 |
| Other | 10,362 | 3.4 |
| Total | 266,783 | 99.6[a] |

*Note:* Does not equal 100 due to rounding.
*Source:* Derived from *Annual Report of the Direc-tor,* Administrative Office of the United States Courts, 1990, Tables C-2A, p. 139 and Table C-3, p. 141.

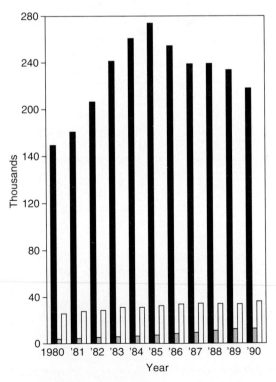

**FIGURE 2.3**
Changes in federal district court case-loads. (From the *Annual Report of the director* (*Administration Office of the United States Courts, 1990*), *Table 5, p. 8, and Table 8, p. 10.*)

and use of drugs. However, explanations for changes in the workload of the federal courts also are tied to *changes in the policies of the federal government*, which have increased the number of cases brought by the government and against the government.[3]

The increase in civil cases in the early 1980s was due largely to attempts by the federal government to recover disputed payments made to veterans and to students who had defaulted on federally guaranteed student loans. At the same time, the federal government tightened its eligibility for Social Security disability payments, and many thousands of citizens whose claims for coverage had been denied by the Social Security Administration sued. After 1985, following heavy Congressional and other criticism concerning its Social Security policy, the federal government loosened its policies and lawsuits declined.

Suits brought to federal court under the diversity jurisdiction also declined about 15 percent between 1989 to 1990. A likely reason for this drop is the higher dollar-threshold placed before litigants in these kinds of cases. Prior to 1988, diversity cases could be brought to the federal courts if the amount in dispute was $10,000 or more. By raising this amount to $50,000 or more, Congress shifted the smaller suits to the state courts.

While civil cases show an overall decrease, criminal cases are rising. Many categories of crime have increased, including weapons violations, fraud, and even drunk driving on federal lands and in Washington, D.C., but the category producing the largest number of new cases is that of drug offenses. This, in turn, reflects increased federal drug law enforcement. The Anti-Drug Abuse Act of 1988 increased the number of federal border patrol and alcohol, tobacco, and firearms agents by over 300 and the number of assistant federal prosecutors by 1240. Congress also raised the penalties for drug-related crimes. All of these policies promote federal investigation and prosecution of drug cases.

Although the work of the federal district courts has decreased overall, the increase in drug cases stands out. Judges complain that the federal speedy-trial law puts criminal cases at the front of the line, and that new federal laws requiring imprisonment and lengthy sentences for drug offenses lead many more defendants to insist on a jury trial, hoping for a chance at an acquittal, rather than quickly pleading guilty and receiving a customary shorter sentence. All of this crowds out the civil docket, which most judges and lawyers view as much more important than routine drug cases.

Consequently, many court reformers believe that drug cases should be shifted to the state courts to decrease the caseload burden on the federal courts. Although diversity cases have declined, these too are viewed as less important than cases involving federal law or the federal government, and reformers want to move these to the states as well.[4] These issues will be discussed further as part of the politics of court reform.

**Bankruptcy Courts**    Within the federal district courts, special bankruptcy courts with 300 additional judges hear a special set of cases. (These courts are not shown in Figure 2.1 because they are part of the district courts). Bankruptcy courts oversee the orderly liquidation of the remaining assets and supervise the financial obligations of individuals and businesses that no longer can pay their debts. Decisions of the bankruptcy courts may be appealed to the regular district courts, and the workload of the federal district courts includes some of these cases.

Although they are less visible to the public because of their narrow and special focus, the workload of the bankruptcy courts is much larger than that of the regular district courts. In 1990, during the depths of the economic recession, over 750,000 bankruptcy cases were heard in these courts, nearly double the number of filings in 1985. Personal bankruptcies account for about 90 percent of all cases. Defunct businesses account for the balance.

### Federal Courts of Appeals

The federal courts of appeals are the main intermediate appellate courts in the federal system. There are twelve regional circuits, including the circuit for the District of Columbia. (The thirteenth court of appeals is the special court for the Federal Circuit, also located in the capital.) Except for Washington, D.C., each circuit is a group of states (and territories) in a particular region of the country (Figure 2.2). There are a total of 179 courts of appeals judges, including those on the Court of Appeals for the Federal Circuit. Eleven new judges were added in 1990.

Each circuit contains an unequal number of states and judges, and receives different numbers of cases. The first circuit, for example, includes the states of Maine, New Hampshire, Massachusetts, Rhode Island, and the territory of Puerto Rico. It has only six appeals court judges and handles about 1200 cases each year. The ninth circuit is the largest. It includes nine western states, including Alaska and Hawaii, and the territory of Guam. It has 28 judges and receives approximately 7000 cases each year.

Unequal workloads periodically produce political pressures to increase the number of judges and occasionally to change the circuit boundaries. For example, partly in jest, the ninth circuit sometimes is called the "California Circuit" because approximately half of the cases that reach the court of appeals in that circuit originate in California (about 3500 cases). Fewer than 100 apiece come from Alaska and Idaho. The states in the fifth and eleventh circuits, which include the south and southeastern states, used to be included in one circuit. But in 1980, Congress split that circuit into two new circuits and added more judges. The politics of dividing the circuits will be discussed shortly as part of the historical development of the federal courts.

**Changing Workload**   Because the jurisdiction of the courts of appeals includes mainly appeals from the decisions of the federal district courts, the subject matter of cases before the appellate courts is largely determined by the cases that are filed at the trial level. Table 2.2 describes the major types of cases filed in the courts of appeals.

**TABLE 2-2**
CASES FILED IN FEDERAL COURTS
OF APPEALS

| Case type | Number | Percentage |
|---|---|---|
| Criminal | 9,493 | 23.2 |
| Prisoner petitions | 9,941 | 24.3 |
| Civil rights | 4,729 | 11.6 |
| Contract | 2,467 | 6.0 |
| Social security | 926 | 2.3 |
| Personal injury | 651 | 1.6 |
| Other | 12,690 | 31.0 |
| Total | 40,898 | 100.0 |

*Source:* Derived from *Annual Report of the Director,* Administrative Office of the United States Courts, 1990, Table B.3, p. 114, Table B.6, p. 127, and Table B.7, pp. 130–131.

Important differences between the district courts and the courts of appeals are the larger percentages of criminal and civil rights cases in the appellate courts. Criminal cases and prisoners' petitions make up nearly half of all cases in the courts of appeals but about one-third of the total in the district courts. Civil rights cases contribute over 10 percent of the appellate docket, but well under that number in the district courts (Table 2.1).

The significance of the work of the federal courts of appeals also lies in the heavy involvement of the federal government in its cases. The federal government is a party in over 15 percent of the cases, and federal laws, administrative rules, and the Constitution are at issue in approximately 40 percent. (Many of the cases in the "other" category concern disputes on the interpretation and application of various federal laws.) As will be discussed shortly, since very few cases are decided by the U.S. Supreme Court, the federal courts of appeals are the last stop for nearly all litigants in the federal system.

The Court of Appeals for the District of Columbia—not to be confused with the specialized Court of Appeals for the Federal Circuit—is one of the most important of the twelve regional circuit courts of appeals. It has the same jurisdiction as the other eleven courts of appeals, but because it is located in Washington, it hears a much larger percentage of cases involving rulings of various federal agencies. In recent years, all of the federal courts of appeals together heard approximately 2500 cases annually involving administrative appeals. More than 25 percent of them were in the District of Columbia circuit, and approximately 40 percent of the total docket of this circuit was composed of these types of cases. No other circuit has an administrative caseload this large.

The workload of the courts of appeals has been growing faster than in the district courts. From 1980 to 1990, the caseload increased over 75 percent, from 23,200 cases to nearly 41,000 cases. Criminal appeals, particularly drug cases, have increased the most.

### U.S. Supreme Court

The Supreme Court is the highest appellate court in the land. For over a century, it has had nine justices, but before 1869, a half-dozen acts of Congress varied the size of the Court from six to ten members.[5]

Until recently, certain cases could be appealed to the Supreme Court as a matter of legal right, but in 1988, Congress eliminated this avenue of appeal. Now, nearly all cases get a hearing before the highest court through the Court's discretionary jurisdiction. When the justices decide that a case deserves a hearing, they issue a *writ of certiorari* which allows the appellant to present the case. Although there are many requests to have cases decided by the Supreme Court, all but a few are rejected.

The Supreme Court serves as a trial court in a few cases required by the Constitution. These concern foreign diplomats and cases in which the states are named as parties to the case. But there are very few of these cases.

**Workload**  As in the other federal courts, the business of the Supreme Court has been increasing. In 1985, there were slightly over 5000 requests for *certiorari*, but the Court allowed less than 175 cases to be argued. By the end of the 1980s, requests for *certiorari* had increased to over 5700 and the Court heard fewer than 150 cases, or less than three percent of the requests.

A denial of *certiorari* means that the decision of the lower court is allowed to stand and it becomes the final decision in the case. Therefore, despite popular notions that anyone can "fight the whole way to the U.S. Supreme Court," the chances of this actually occurring are very slim. This means that state supreme courts and the federal courts of appeals are the final courts for the overwhelming majority of all appealed cases. They make final and binding decisions within the boundaries of their own judicial territory. How the Supreme Court selects cases for review will be discussed more fully in Chapter 7.

Since the justices determine for themselves which cases to decide, they often focus on controversial policies and on cases in which there is disagreement among lower appellate courts on the interpretation of law. In recent years, the Supreme Court has concentrated most heavily on cases involving the Constitutional rights of criminal defendants and on issues of civil rights and personal freedom (race, age, and sex discrimination; freedom of speech, press, religion; rights to privacy; political representation, and others). About half of the Court's workload concerns these kinds of cases. Others include various economic and business disputes and government regulations. The power to determine for itself which cases to hear as well as serving as the highest court in the nation give the Supreme court great power as a national policymaking court.

### Federal Courts of Limited Jurisdiction

In addition to the district courts, the 12 regional courts of appeals, and the Supreme Court, the federal court system includes trial and appellate courts of limited jurisdiction. The most important ones are included in Figure 2.1. Some of these courts have been part of the federal judicial system for more than a century, sometimes under other names, while others are recent additions. They include:

*Claims Court* Organized in 1855 to decide financial claims against the federal government. Most cases involve salaries, payments on contracts, property confiscation, and taxes.

*Court of International Trade* Organized in 1890 as the Board of General Appraisers. It hears cases involving the levying of customs and duties on imports.

*Tax Court* Organized in 1924 as the Board of Tax Appeals. It hears appeals from taxpayers from the Internal Revenue Service.

*Rail Reorganization Court* Organized in 1973 to determine value of properties transferred from bankrupt railroad companies to the federally supported Amtrak system. It hears very few cases.

*Foreign Intelligence Surveillance Court and Court of Review* These trial and appellate courts were organized in 1978 to hear government requests for wiretaps required for domestic surveillance related to national security.

*Courts of Veterans Appeals* Organized in 1988 to hear appeals from veterans who had been denied disability coverage and other benefits by the Department of Veterans Affairs.

*Temporary Emergency Court of Appeals* Organized in 1971 to hear matters related to energy conservation laws. It hears very few cases.

*Court of Appeals for the Federal Circuit* Organized in 1982 from the Court of Customs and Patent Appeals and the Court of Claims to hear appeals from the Court of International Trade and Claims Court as well as from the Patent and Trademark Office, International Trade Commission, and other federal agencies. It also hears certain cases involving these same issues from the district courts.

*Military Courts and Courts of Appeals* These special courts hear court-martials and appeals from convictions in the military courts.

**Politics and the Courts of Limited Jurisdiction** Throughout American history, arguments supporting the creation of federal courts of limited jurisdiction have been put in managerial terms—reducing the workload of the regular courts and providing new judicial expertise in highly specialized areas of law. In other words, new courts will make the judicial machinery run more smoothly and efficiently.

However, there always are political objectives behind these moves. All of these courts deal with disputes directly involving the federal government, and instead of being distributed regionally around the country—as are the district courts and the courts of appeals—they mostly are located in Washington. Members of the executive branch and Congress who supported the Claims Court, Court of International Trade, Tax Court, and others believed the federal government would win more cases if the disputes were taken out of the hands of "local" federal judges and centralized in one court in Washington. In the 1980s, the Reagan administration proposed a special Social Security court which would have removed appeals against the Social Security Administration from the federal district courts, where citizens had been winning heavily. Congress killed that proposal.[6]

Sometimes groups that are heavy users of a proposed court lobby for it because they believe that they will receive a larger number of favorable decisions than in the regular courts. For example, patent lawyers and their clients favored a special court to hear appeals from the Patent Office—now part of the jurisdiction of the Court of Appeals for the federal circuit—where they expected more patent grants to be upheld than by the regular federal courts. Veterans organizations, which became more politicized in the 1980s, supported the creation of the Court of Veteran's Appeals.[7]

## STATE COURTS

Each of the fifty states has its own separate court system. These courts hear criminal cases involving violations of state law, civil disputes occurring among individuals of the same state and others that involve less than $50,000, and other matters of state law.

Most crime is a violation of state law, so that serious crimes, including murder, rape, assault, and robbery, as well as minor offenses, such as public drunkenness, disorderly conduct, etc., and traffic violations are prosecuted in state courts. Civil disputes involving business contracts, divorce and child support, small financial claims, property damage and personal injury, government regulation of businesses and professions, and others also are heard in the state courts. State courts also rule on the constitutionality of state laws.

Many people think of the federal courts as "more important" because they hear many criminal appeals based on the Constitution, civil rights cases, and civil disputes involving large amounts of money and powerful litigants, such as large corporations and the federal government. And, of course, the U.S. Supreme Court gets maximum exposure because of its national policymaking role.

Many state cases involving traffic accidents and most crime and divorce *are* routine, but many others are not. Death penalty appeals, rules on recovering damages in medical malpractice cases, the right to discontinue medical treatment for dying and comatose patients, the constitutionality of state regulations of businesses and professions, and many others are decided by state courts. In addition, the volume of cases heard by the states vastly exceeds the caseload of the federal court system. Adding all of the federal cases together, including bankruptcy, produces a total of just over 1 million cases filed per year. In contrast, the total number of cases decided in the states is about 100 million. Many states handle millions of cases each year.[8]

## State Court Organization

Each of the states has its own distinctive court system, but they also have features in common. Generally, each state has a state supreme court situated in the state capital and one or more intermediate appellate courts. However, a dozen lightly populated states in New England and the northern plains plus Mississippi and Nevada do not have intermediate appellate courts. The states also have one or two trial courts of general jurisdiction and one or more trial courts of limited jurisdiction.

State court systems range from relatively streamlined and unified to complex and fragmented structures. Streamlined court systems have one court with clearly defined and separate or exclusive jurisdiction at each level. Complex systems have many courts with poorly defined and equivalent or overlapping jurisdiction in various courts.

As in the federal system, trial courts are distributed geographically throughout each state so that individuals can find a court fairly close to home that has jurisdiction over their dispute. Sparsely populated states often have less than a half-dozen trial court districts, but the large and populous states have several dozen districts. The larger states also have several of the same intermediate appellate courts for various sections of the state.

An example of the geographic distribution of state courts is found in Figure 2.4. It is a map of Florida that shows the boundaries of its twenty trial court circuits and its five intermediate appellate court districts. The smaller lines and names are counties. There is a county court of limited jurisdiction in each of the 67 counties.

State courts are more deeply embedded in local social and political environments than are the federal courts, since there are many more state courts, and they deal with the types of disputes that affect most people. In addition, selection procedures for state judges more deeply involve local and state politics (Chapter 4).

**Overlapping Jurisdiction**   Overlapping jurisdiction occurs when more than one state court may hear the same type of case. Generally, overlapping jurisdiction results from adding new courts over the years without much consideration to the role of the existing courts. Often, state laws spell out jurisdiction only vaguely so that overlapping authority practically is guaranteed. This results in a fragmented and confusing set of courts.

Courts in twenty-nine states have overlapping authority: in fifteen states, the trial courts of general and limited jurisdiction overlap with each other, and in fourteen others, several trial courts of limited jurisdiction have overlapping powers.[9] As part of judicial reform, certain states have revamped their state courts to reduce or eliminate overlapping authority.

Besides creating confusion, overlapping jurisdiction permits court shopping, in which lawyers try to locate a court in which they believe the rules of

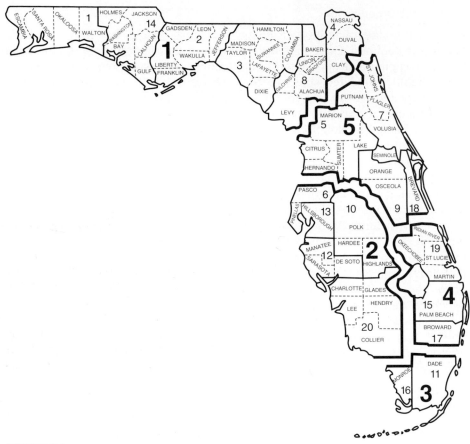

**FIGURE 2.4**
Geographic boundaries of the Florida district courts, circuit courts, and county courts. (*Source: State Court Administrator, Tallahassee, Florida.*)

procedure, workload, or the attitudes of judges and perhaps prosecutors will be most favorable to them. Criminal defendants, for example, may benefit from a court with a huge backlog of cases because the defendants may remain free on bail before their cases are called. Others look for courts in which judges have attitudes that favor one side or the other.

**A Streamlined and a Complex State Court System** Illustrations of a streamlined and a complex court system may be found in a comparison of the Florida and Indiana courts (Figures 2.5 and 2.6). Florida is a fast growing, increasingly urban state, with approximately 13 million people. The court system was reorganized about twenty years ago into a relatively streamlined system. Indiana is a more rural state with less than 6 million residents. Its court system retains its traditional complexity.

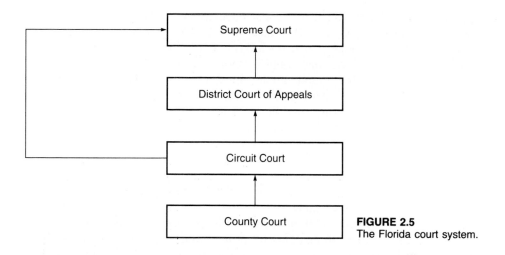

**FIGURE 2.5**
The Florida court system.

Florida has one court at four different levels: supreme court, intermediate court of appeals, trial court of general jurisdiction, and trial court of limited jurisdiction. The Supreme Court and the District Courts of Appeals both have mandatory and discretionary jurisdiction, but over different types of cases. Appeals to the Supreme Court may come from the Circuit Court and the District Courts of Appeals, but appeals from the intermediate appeals courts are largely discretionary with the Supreme Court. The County Court deals

**FIGURE 2.6**
The Indiana court system.

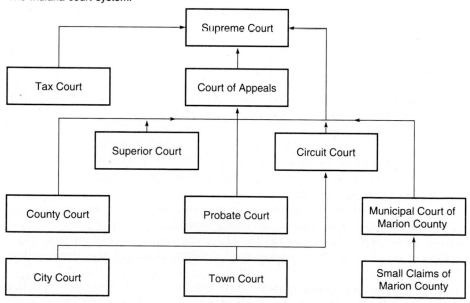

exclusively with small financial claims, misdemeanors, and traffic fines. Appeals from the County Court may be taken to the Circuit Court for a new trial.

Indiana has a supreme court, an intermediate court of appeals, two trial courts of general jurisdiction (superior and circuit courts), and seven trial courts of limited jurisdiction, including a special tax court. The Supreme Court has both mandatory and discretionary jurisdiction. The Court of Appeals has a large and general mandatory jurisdiction with additional discretion to hear a few additional cases. Appeals can be taken directly to the Supreme Court from tax court and the major trial courts when criminal sentences exceed 10 years.

Trial court jurisdiction in Indiana is confusing and overlapping. The two trial courts of general jurisdiction have the authority to hear the same types of cases, but they, as well as the trial courts of limited jurisdiction, also may hear small claims disputes. Six trial courts of limited jurisdiction also have overlapping roles. Several hear small claims cases involving the same minimum but slightly different maximum amounts of money, and all but probate court hear minor criminal and traffic cases. Appeals from these courts go to the Court of Appeals and both trial courts of general jurisdiction. Only the probate court, which deals with adoptions, estates, and juvenile cases, and tax court have clearly defined, exclusive jurisdiction over their cases.

These two examples do not exhaust the variations in state court systems. A few states have only three types of courts: supreme court, intermediate appellate court, and a trial court of general jurisdiction. Others have much more complicated systems. New York, for example, has one of the most confusing systems. It includes a supreme court, two intermediate appellate courts, two trial courts of general jurisdiction, and eight trial courts of limited jurisdiction. Understanding the jurisdiction of the New York courts requires a detailed road map and plenty of legal experience, for many of the cases and avenues of appeal may go to the same place.

### Trial Courts

As indicated by the Florida and Indiana examples, trial courts of general jurisdiction have the widest authority. They hear the most serious criminal cases and all civil cases that involve large amounts of money. In the dozen states, such as Indiana, with two or more types of these courts, court jurisdictions are defined in various ways, usually by the type of dispute, amount of money involved in the dispute, or by the seriousness of the crime. But their jurisdictions also may overlap.

Trial courts of limited jurisdiction hear more specialized and less serious types of cases, such as traffic violations, juvenile crime, and small financial claims. Some of the states, such as Florida, have consolidated many trial courts of limited jurisdiction into one county court, but with civil and criminal divisions.

As in the federal court system, state trial courts of limited jurisdiction usually have been created to deal with special problems, such as small claims

BOX 2.1

PART N . . . FOR NARCOTICS

Faced with a surge in narcotics cases that brought in more than twice as many defendants as the previous year, New York City has created a new court, called Part N, to move drug cases through the judicial system faster than before. Repeat offenders are urged to plead guilty quickly in order to move the cases, and are promised lighter sentences in return. In the regular court system, defense lawyers did not negotiate for guilty pleas (*plea bargaining*) until after the cases were presented to the grand jury, a process which took up to a year. Now, thousands of defendants are pleading guilty within a few days of their arrest and are sentenced within a few weeks. Sentence length is down, but the rate of convictions is up.

Defense attorneys complain that defendants are being pressured to plead guilty before attorneys can evaluate whether prosecutors have a good case. Says one: "People are taking felony pleas and getting state prison time with the same consideration that someone would get if they came in for drunken driving."

courts for the "common man" or juvenile crime, but they also serve political goals. They demonstrate that the government is taking action to deal with a problem and they increase the government's control over troublesome and politically visible cases. In the 1930s, for example, Chicago created a special Rackets Court to deal with organized crime.[10]

Similar problems surface today. Box 2.1, "Part N . . . For Narcotics," reveals the concern in many cities with the increase in drug cases and how one court system is dealing with it.[11]

**Workload**  Overall, filings in state trial courts of general jurisdiction are dominated by traffic violations (52 percent), followed by various civil disputes (31 percent), adult criminal cases (13 percent), and juvenile criminal cases (4 percent). In the trial courts of limited jurisdiction, three-quarters of the cases concern traffic violations with roughly equal remaining percentages of civil and criminal cases.[12]

The total workload of state trial courts has been increasing in all but a few states. From 1984 to 1989, various types of civil cases have increased by 25 to 33 percent. As in the federal courts, criminal cases show the sharpest rise, increasing by 50 percent in this 6-year period. Consequently, concerns with the size and management of caseloads and the impact of government policies on the work of the courts is a major issue in the states as well.

*Four States*  State courts hear the same types of cases, but there are many differences in the size of court workloads and the proportion of particular types of cases heard in the states. In order to illustrate these variations, Table 2.3 compares trial courts in four states with different sized populations and number of judges and in different regions. The table combines cases in trial courts of general and limited jurisdiction.

Table 2.3 shows that the volume of cases in relation to population varies tremendously. Connecticut, Kansas, and Minnesota have roughly similar populations, but the caseload of the Minnesota courts is more than double those in

**TABLE 2-3**
CASES FILED IN TRIAL COURTS IN FOUR STATES

|  | Connecticut | Florida | Kansas | Minnesota |
|---|---|---|---|---|
| Population | 3,300,000 | 12,700,000 | 2,500,000 | 2,700,000 |
| Number of judges | 298 | 611 | 482 | 230 |
| Total cases | 653,314 (100%) | 5,057,101 (100%) | 618,429 (100%) | 1,959,000 (100%) |
| Civil | 210,481 (32.2) | 873,650 (17.3) | 148,525 (24.1) | 208,062 (10.6) |
| Tort | 8% | 11% | 3% | 5% |
| Contract | 13 | 9 | 41 | 4 |
| Real property | 9 | 20 | 11 | 14 |
| Family | 14 | 28 | 20 | 22 |
| Estate | 23 | 8 | 9 | 7 |
| Mental health | 2 | 2 | 3 | 1 |
| Small claims | 30 | 23 | 13 | 46 |
| Criminal | 176,268 (27.0) | 621,618 (12.3) | 41,749 (6.7) | 178,580 (9.1) |
| Felonies | 3.5% | no data | 30.3% | 13.5% |
| Juvenile | 14,536 (2.2) | 108,013 (2.1) | 14,743 (2.4) | 34,989 (1.8) |
| Traffic | 252,029 (38.6) | 3,453,820 (68.3) | 413,412 (66.8) | 1,537,369 (78.5) |

*Source:* Derived from Court Statistics Project, *State Court Caseload Statistics: Annual Report 1989.* National Center for State Courts in cooperation with the Conference of State Court Administrators, Williamsburg, Va., 1991, Text Table 2, p. 11, Tables 8, 9, 10, 11, 12, Figure G, and Appendix D.

the other two states. Florida has four times as many people as Connecticut but it has nearly eight times as many cases. Workloads per judge also are very different. Kansas has the lowest ratio, with approximately 1300 cases per judge. Connecticut is next at 2200, but Florida and Minnesota have 8300 and 8500 cases per judge, respectively. However, the vast majority are traffic cases, which are routine and require very little court time.

The proportions of different types of cases also vary widely. Property damage and personal injury cases (torts) are more common in Florida, while contract disputes go to court often in Kansas. Small claims disputes are prominent in Minnesota. Differences also occur in criminal cases. Kansas ranks among the states with the lowest number of criminal cases per 100,000 population (1661), but a higher percentage of them than in the other states are felonies. Minnesota and Florida have 4103 and 4906 criminal cases per 100,000 population, but Connecticut is much higher at 5442 cases per 100,000. All of the states have similar percentages of juvenile cases, and the workloads in all but Connecticut are very heavily loaded with traffic cases. Most of the traffic and small claims cases are heard in trial courts of limited jurisdiction.

### Appellate Courts

The highest state appellate court usually is called the supreme court. However, in Maryland and New York it is the Court of Appeals and in several of the New England states, the court is the Supreme Judicial Court. Oklahoma and Texas each have two final courts of appeals: a supreme court with jurisdiction over civil cases and a final court of criminal appeals. A majority of the state supreme courts have seven members, others have five or nine judges.

Most states also have intermediate courts of appeals. However, four states have two intermediate courts, each with separate jurisdiction over civil and criminal cases or types of civil cases. Although a dozen rural states do not have intermediate appellate courts, the trend since the early 1960s has been to add intermediate courts as the states grow, in order to divert some of the supreme courts' increasing workload. Judges on most of the intermediate appellate courts sit in three judge panels, but others sit together as a group (*en banc*) to hear certain cases.[13]

**Jurisdiction and Workload**   Nearly all state supreme courts have both mandatory and discretionary jurisdiction. Three courts have only mandatory jurisdiction, but three others have complete discretion to select cases, similar to that of the U.S. Supreme Court. State intermediate appellate courts also have some discretionary jurisdiction, but it is not very broad.

As explained earlier, appeals from the trial courts of general jurisdiction go either to intermediate or to supreme courts. Supreme courts generally are required to hear the most serious criminal cases, and the more complex civil disputes, or those involving the most money, as well as certain appeals from government agencies. They also usually must hear cases involving the disbarment or disciplining of attorneys.

The large majority of criminal cases not involving the death penalty or life imprisonment go to the intermediate appellate courts as do most civil disputes involving relatively small sums of money, appeals to divorce decrees and others. Appeals from decisions of the intermediate appellate courts usually come to supreme courts only through their discretionary jurisdiction. However, in some instances intermediate appellate courts may pass on or certify certain cases to the supreme court which the intermediate judges believe require a decision at the top.

Toward the end of the 1980s, nearly 230,000 cases were filed in state appellate courts, and nearly three-quarters of them were routed to the intermediate appellate courts, mostly through their mandatory jurisdiction.

**Discretionary cases**   The policymaking potential of an appellate court is determined partly by the balance between its mandatory and discretionary jurisdiction and the percentage of its caseload composed of discretionary cases. The more discretion, the more opportunities a court has to select cases which may have a social impact. In order to capture some of the differences among state appellate courts, Table 2.4 presents the number of cases decided by state supreme courts and intermediate appellate courts and the percentage of them which are mandatory and discretionary.

The figures show that state supreme courts hear fewer cases than the intermediate appellate courts and that a larger percentage of them are discretionary appeals. Only the Louisiana intermediate appellate court has a significant discretionary caseload. But the supreme courts also vary. Several supreme courts derive one-third or more of their cases via their discretionary authority, and the Louisiana Supreme Court hears almost all discretionary cases. In contrast, the Connecticut and New Mexico supreme courts have relatively small discretionary workloads.

If the state supreme courts were mandated to hear fewer types of cases, some of them probably would have an even larger discretionary caseload and could play a more important role in state policymaking. Even the California Supreme Court, which already is a major force in state policymaking, probably could have an even greater impact. The court hears close to 400 cases per year

**TABLE 2-4**
MANDATORY AND DISCRETIONARY CASELOADS OF STATE
APPELLATE COURTS

| State/court name | Total number of cases | Percent mandatory | Percent discretionary |
|---|---|---|---|
| California | | | |
|     Supreme Court | 567 | 67 | 33 |
|     Courts of Appeals | 12,219 | 94 | 6 |
| Connecticut | | | |
|     Supreme Court | 312 | 88 | 12 |
|     Court of Appeals | 1032 | 95 | 5 |
| Louisiana | | | |
|     Supreme Court | 731 | 15 | 85 |
|     Court of Appeals | 4918 | 72 | 28 |
| Maryland | | | |
|     Supreme Court | 296 | 69 | 31 |
|     Court of Appeals | 1853 | 99 | 1 |
| Minnesota | | | |
|     Supreme Court | 378 | 66 | 34 |
|     Court of Appeals | 1860 | 95 | 5 |
| Missouri | | | |
|     Supreme Court | 306 | 74 | 26 |
|     Court of Appeals | 3659 | 100 | 0 |
| New Mexico | | | |
|     Supreme Court | 395 | 93 | 7 |
|     Court of Appeals | 792 | 98 | 2 |
| Ohio | | | |
|     Supreme Court | 696 | 77 | 23 |
|     Appeals Court | 10,771 | 100 | 0 |

*Source: State Court Caseload Statistics, 1991, Table 2.*

through its mandatory jurisdiction. It also receives over 4000 requests to hear discretionary cases, but it hears less than 190 of them, or under 5 percent. The Missouri, New Mexico, and Ohio supreme courts also grant relatively few requests for discretionary hearings. Other supreme courts, such as in Connecticut, receive many fewer requests, but these courts also grant relatively small percentages of them.

Therefore, while state supreme courts generally have more discretion to select cases than state intermediate appellate courts, the mandatory jurisdiction of state supreme courts prevents them from being as flexible as the U.S. Supreme Court in selecting cases for review.

*Rising Caseloads*    As in the trial courts, the caseloads of the state appellate courts have increased during the last six years. However, the increase is not uniform across the states. During the 1980s, about two-thirds of the state supreme courts experienced increased caseloads, while caseloads in a third of these courts have declined. However, all but a few intermediate appellate courts have received more cases every year. Overall, it appears that the broader mandatory jurisdiction of state intermediate appellate courts has absorbed most increases in litigation. Also, state legislatures have shifted more mandatory criminal cases and certain civil disputes from supreme courts to the intermediate appellate courts.[14] If litigation continues to increase, state supreme courts probably will gain discretionary jurisdiction and be required to hear fewer types of cases, and state supreme courts will become even more important state policymaking institutions.

## INTERACTION BETWEEN FEDERAL AND STATE COURTS

Once a case enters either the federal or state courts, it is unlikely to move from one court system to another. The main exception is the appeal of cases that involve issues of constitutional law, from state supreme courts to the U.S. Supreme Court. But there are other overlaps between the federal and state systems.

### Concurrent Jurisdiction

State and federal courts may hear some of the same types of cases. This is called "concurrent jurisdiction." In these instances, citizens find that it sometimes is possible to choose between federal or state courts as part of a strategy to win their cases.

*Diversity Cases*    As discussed earlier, Congress has given the federal courts the authority to hear cases involving citizens of different states when the sum of money involved is over $50,000. But state courts also may hear these same cases. State courts have the exclusive authority to hear cases involving less than this amount.

This concurrent jurisdiction gives the litigants in a case a number of options. For example, if the money involved is close to, but less than, $50,000, the person initiating the lawsuit (plaintiff) may claim $50,000 or more in order to get the case into a federal district court, or the plaintiff may keep the claim under $50,000 in the belief that state courts will be more favorable. Another example is a case in which the claim for money is over $50,000, but since the case is against an individual or corporation in a state far away from the plaintiff, the case may be filed in the home state court with hopes of making a defense expensive and inconvenient for the defendant and to gain the sympathy of a judge and jury from the plaintiff's home ground. Box 2.2, "Pete Rose and Diversity Jurisdiction," illustrates the legal strategies that may be used to get a case into a favorable court.[15]

**Federal Questions** The federal district courts have the authority to hear cases involving the Constitution, federal law, admiralty and maritime issues, and the actions of executive agencies, and they have the exclusive power to hear bankruptcy petitions. Cases involving numerous federal laws are likely to be heard in the federal courts, but the federal courts do not have exclusive jurisdiction over them, which means that state courts also may hear some cases involving federal law.

---

**BOX 2.2**

PETE ROSE AND DIVERSITY JURISDICTION

Commissioner of Baseball, A. Bartlett Giamatti, began an investigation of Pete Rose, legendary hitter and manager of the Cincinnati Reds baseball team, for gambling on baseball games, including those of his own team. This is a violation of Major League Rule 21.

Attempting to block the investigation, Pete Rose filed a lawsuit in an Ohio trial court in Cincinnati. The suit named the commissioner, whose office is in New York, as well as the Cincinnati Reds as defendants. The Ohio judge ruled that the commissioner's investigation revealed bias and that he had prejudged Rose. He issued an order temporarily halting the investigation. Pete Rose was enormously popular in Cincinnati, and the judge's decision was seen by many as a way of currying support for his later re-election. Pete Rose claimed that justice had prevailed.

The commissioner quickly filed his own suit in federal district court in Columbus, Ohio, contending that the case should be removed to federal court because of diversity of citizenship of the parties—the commissioner's office is in New York and Pete Rose is a citizen of Ohio. His attorneys also argued that Rose named the Cincinnati Reds as a defendant only to prove that the case was between two parties situated in the same state. The federal judge agreed with Giamatti. Citing diversity as the basis for federal jurisdiction, the judge ordered the case removed from state court to federal court and he dropped the baseball team from the case. The sixth circuit court of appeals affirmed the trial judge's ruling.

Previous federal court decisions concerning organized baseball have given the commissioner very wide latitude to investigate and punish its members for wrongdoing. When it was clear that the federal courts would hear the case, Pete Rose and the commissioner began negotiations. Rose was banned from baseball for life for illegal gambling.

Pete Rose later pled guilty in federal court to income tax evasion connected with other activities. His illegal gambling was not mentioned as part of the plea bargain.

If an individual argues that he or she has a right or claim under federal law, there are no financial or diversity of citizenship requirements to having the case decided by the federal courts. The possible laws involved in these cases are numerous and include civil rights, constitutional rights of criminal defendants, labor laws, Social Security, commerce, antitrust, and others. In many of these cases the federal government itself is a party. However, if a case involving the Constitution or federal law already has begun in a state court, federal judges are likely to defer to state authority and permit state courts to decide it unless there is a very compelling reason to intervene.

**Criminal Cases**  Besides overlapping in a variety of civil cases, both the federal and state court systems decide criminal cases. Most crimes only violate state law and can be tried only in the state courts. Certain other specialized crimes, such as counterfeiting, treason, and illegal immigration are federal crimes tried only in the federal courts. However, many other crimes violate both state and federal laws and could involve either court system. Examples are robbery and larceny, embezzlement, auto theft (primarily organized and interstate crime), forgery, and narcotics.

It also is possible for an individual to be prosecuted in both state and federal courts for a single *act* that violates different *laws*. For example, a person charged with murder or other crimes of violence usually will be tried in a state trial court of general jurisdiction, but he or she also could be charged and prosecuted in federal court for a different crime, most likely conspiracy to deny the victim's civil rights. Therefore, killing another person can be defined and punished differently in the state and federal courts.

An example of federal intervention involved the beating death of a Chinese-American by a Detroit automobile worker angry about foreign imports. The auto worker was convicted of manslaughter in state court and sentenced to 3 years probation and a fine. Asian groups condemned the sentence as too lenient, and federal prosecutors responded by filing a new case as a civil rights violation. They obtained a conviction and a 25-year sentence. However, a federal court of appeals overturned the conviction and the auto worker was found not guilty of the civil rights violation in a second trial.[16]

A more common and typical link between state and federal judicial systems occurs when convicted criminals held in state jails or prisons petition the federal courts for a review of their conviction and imprisonment, arguing that state actions violated their constitutional rights. They use a legal strategy based on federal habeas corpus laws.

*Habeas corpus* literally means "you have the body," and it requires a state government to show good reason for the imprisonment. It is an attempt by a prisoner to obtain a federal review of a conviction on constitutional grounds and a new trial or release from jail. Although it is relatively easy and common for prisoners to try to obtain a reversal of their conviction on these grounds, federal judges normally require that state prisoners appeal to other state courts before granting a release or a reversal.

### Consequences of Dual Courts

Federal and state courts exist side by side in separate but connected judicial systems. They are two parts of a dual court system.[17] This has a number of important consequences in American politics.

**Different Policies**   First, since both state and federal courts may hear similar cases, there is a great possibility that the direction of judicial decisions or the policies of the courts will differ at the state and federal levels. Actually, the fifty state and the federal court systems are so decentralized that trial and appellate judges in the same state or region as well as in different parts of the country respond to issues in various ways. Many major issues, such as desegregation, the rights of criminal defendants, abortion, school finance, and others, are decided differently. As a result, there rarely is a simple answer to what judicial policy is in the United States.

Some state courts also create or support constitutional and other legal standards that are more stringent than those of the federal courts. In recent years, the supreme courts of California, Hawaii, Michigan, New Jersey, and Alaska have relied upon extensive due process safeguards in their own state constitutions to move the rights of criminal defendants beyond the limiting decisions of the U.S. Supreme Court. Consequently, not only might state judicial policy be different from that in other states and the federal courts, it might also support higher legal standards created by state government. Faced with an increase in conservative Republican judges appointed to the federal courts by Presidents Reagan and Bush, gays, abortion rights advocates, environmentalists, civil rights groups, and others are increasingly looking to various liberal state supreme courts for favorable decisions.[18]

**Alternative Courts**   The existence of state and federal courts provides groups and individuals with alternatives in going to court and means that the advantages and disadvantages of state and federal courts can be weighed in developing a plan of litigation. Long-term experience in various kinds of cases gives some litigants and lawyers fairly clear signals about which courts are more favorable to certain claims and interests. Insurance companies, for example, generally believe that state juries are too generous in awarding damages to accident victims.[19] The history of the civil rights movement also illustrates the political alternatives that are available in using courts.[20] Most early civil rights rulings were made by the federal courts. But civil rights groups did not concentrate on the federal courts until it was clear that most state governments, including state courts, were unlikely to change traditional policies of segregation. Now, however, some state courts are providing additional opportunities.

**National Impact**   Finally, similar state and federal jurisdiction guarantees that local political and social issues are affected and often shaped by national policy.[21] By swearing to uphold the Constitution, federal and state judges are obligated indirectly to follow the policies created by the national Supreme

Court when it interprets the Constitution. Some judges are anxious to apply Supreme Court rulings to their own cases, while others only reluctantly follow the lead of the national court. Still, it generally is true that state and local governments and the judiciary in particular cannot blithely ignore national judicial policy. The huge transformation in civil rights and individual liberties that occurred during the 1960s and the 1970s was due largely to the leadership of the U.S. Supreme Court.

## THE ORIGINS AND DEVELOPMENT OF THE COURTS

Organization charts present an orderly picture of courts, and give the idea that court systems are carefully planned or that a full set of courts was created all at once. But this has not been the American experience. Instead, history reveals the intense political conflict that has surrounded the development of state and federal courts and which continues to affect courts today.[22]

### Early Courts

**Colonial and State Courts**    The original thirteen colonies were ruled individually by royal governors appointed by the British king. Under his rule, British courts and law generally were adopted, but colonial life in small towns and rural settlements was much simpler, and only a few county courts and justices of the peace were needed to deal with crime and personal disputes. Appeals could be taken to the governor or to his advisory council and theoretically to the courts of England, but few disputes were shipped across the Atlantic.

As towns grew into small cities and conflict increased and became more varied, the colonies added more of the same courts and created new ones to deal with growing litigation. The General Court of Massachusetts was a trial *and* appellate court as well as a colonial legislature, but as early as 1685 it had so many cases that it delegated some of its authority to county courts. In 1691, Connecticut created a special probate court to settle wills and estates, and in 1721, Pennsylvania created a special orphan's court to protect minor children and their property.

Complex court organization and overlapping jurisdiction also got an early start in the colonial period, since the early governments generally added courts but did not replace old ones. New ones simply became part of a lengthening chain of judicial institutions.[23]

*Limited Authority*    Although the number of courts gradually increased, judicial authority was limited in the colonies and the new states. In part, this reflected the simple social and economic conditions of the new world, but political factors contributed to keeping judicial authority in check. First, judicial power in the colonies was part of the governor's authority. The governor could create new courts and appoint and remove judges. As colonial rule became increasingly unpopular, courts and judges often were seen as mere extensions of British crown authority.

Second, Americans generally distrusted the professional practice of law, and some colonies and states prohibited a litigant from hiring another person to present a case. Few trained lawyers emigrated to the colonies, and many newcomers had left Europe to avoid criminal prosecution or civil suits and were not inclined to support the development of a trained and specialized class of lawyers and judges.

Following the American Revolution, former colonial courts became the foundation for the new state courts and judicial organization changed very little. In place of unpopular colonial governors, the new states placed most power in new state legislatures. Creation of courts and selection of judges shifted to legislative control in some states. Judges still enjoyed lifetime appointments, but early state legislatures also acted as appellate courts and overturned court decisions, ordered new trials, and occasionally even abolished or impeached judges who refused to follow legislative policy.

*Early Judicial Review* Despite legislative dominance, state courts gradually became more assertive and independent and sometimes declared acts of state legislatures unconstitutional, a practice that predated the famous *Marbury v. Madison* case by as much as 10 or more years.[24]

Courts became independent for several reasons. First, the new state constitutions contained provisions for three separate branches of government, and although early state legislatures freely interfered with the courts, the initial foundation of state government provided a legitimate basis for an independent judiciary. Second, when certain state legislators attacked court decisions, other legislators and interest groups defended them. For example, state laws providing for easy credit were supported by borrowers, but court decisions holding such legislation unconstitutional were supported by banks and other lenders.[25]

Finally, popular support for legislatures did not last very long. By the 1830s, for example, popular demands for broadening the right to vote and for giving voters the power to directly elect large numbers of state officials, including judges, began to erode the legislature's political monopoly. Charges of corruption and the inability of legislatures to manage state government effectively also encouraged the development of long and detailed state constitutions that sharply limited legislative power to make new laws. But state constitutions also are easily amended making them extremely long, complex, and internally inconsistent. This invites constitutional litigation and increases the policymaking power of state courts.

**Federal Courts** Independence also brought about the creation of national courts. The first national government under the Articles of Confederation relied on the state courts to handle all cases, including those involving the national government.[26] When delegates met for the Constitutional Convention in 1787, representatives from the southern states clung to the supremacy of state courts, for they believed as long as state courts heard all cases, including those that affected the national government, the power of state governments in the new federal system would be protected.

This arrangement was unacceptable to the northern Federalists who believed that the new national government needed a separate and complete court system to limit local prejudices and biases in court cases involving the national government and citizens from different states.

The Convention was stymied. Finally, the delegates compromised: the Constitution would include only the U.S. Supreme Court and a provision whereby Congress could create additional federal courts and determine their jurisdiction. In other words, the Convention agreed to postpone debate over most of the details of a federal court system. Creating only a Supreme Court was a victory for states' rights, but including the foundation of the federal court system in the Constitution was a victory for the Federalist forces. *This first skirmish over a new national court system signaled a long and intense conflict over the power of the federal government and the value of local control of justice.*

**New Courts**   The Federalists lost no time in advancing national power. The first Senate bill of the first Congress was the Judiciary Act of 1789, which created a new national judiciary composed of the Supreme Court, Circuit Courts, and District Courts. Both the circuit and the district courts were designed as trial courts with the circuit courts hearing diversity cases and the district courts deciding admiralty disputes. However, the circuit courts also had limited appellate authority over certain cases from the district courts. Despite the appearance of victory, however, the Federalists were forced to compromise with southern representatives. The jurisdiction of the new courts was extremely narrow and the circuit courts had no judges. The Supreme Court justices were required to be circuit judges too.[27]

The original organization of the district courts and selection of judges also combined state and national interests in ways that have guaranteed considerable local influence in the federal courts. The boundaries of each federal district were made identical to state political boundaries, and as states grew in population and were divided into more districts, each new district has been contained within an individual state. There are no federal districts that cross state lines, no districts in which the workload of the federal courts is drawn from any area other than an individual state or part of a state.

In addition, federal judges are required by law to reside within their district and their appointment must be approved by the United States Senate. This normally has meant that the senators from the state in which the appointment will be made have special influence in determining who the judges will be and that federal district judges typically are born, raised, and educated and "politicized" in their home state or region. Since they also hear cases coming only from their state, the work of the courts reinforce local values and loyalties in the operation of the national courts. This continues today.[28]

**Marbury v. Madison**   Following the compromised creation of the first federal courts, the Federalists immediately tried to change it. The Federalists had lost the election of 1800, but in the waning days of the John Adams administration, their lame-duck majority in Congress enacted the Judiciary Act of 1801. This new bill abolished circuit riding for Supreme Court justices by adding new permanent circuit judges, and the circuit courts were given the power to hear more cases, something state interests had tried to avoid.

But this did not last long. As soon as the Jeffersonian Republicans took their seats in the new Congress, they repealed the Federalist judicial reorganization. They believed it would be a place for Federalist judges to work against Republican policies and that the growth of the courts contained the seed for increased national power at the expense of the states.

This conflict also provided the setting for the most famous of Supreme Court cases: *Marbury v. Madison*. We remember this case best for the Supreme Court's pronouncement of its power to rule on the constitutionality of congressional acts, but the facts in the case concerned expansion of the federal court system, specifically the refusal of the new Republican administration to honor judicial appointments made by the Federalists under another law passed early in 1801.

William Marbury was to become a special justice of the peace in Washington, D.C., but he was not given his appointment papers by the time the Federalists left office. He sued James Madison, the new Republican secretary of state, for refusing to complete the appointment process.

In a shrewd political move, Chief Justice John Marshall—a Federalist—agreed that Marbury should have received the appointment, but stated that the congressional law that had required the Supreme Court to hear this particular type of case violated the Constitution.

Marshall's goals were to object to Republican policy but without ordering the administration to carry out the appointment, since it probably would refuse to comply. A confrontation between a new popular President and the Federalist-dominated Supreme Court would focus unavoidable attention on the Court's inability to enforce its own decisions. But at the same time Marshall proclaimed that the Court had the power to review acts of Congress.

The new Republican Congress scrapped the 1801 Federalist courts and restored the federal judiciary to the 1789 model, and it remained substantially unchanged until after the Civil War. After 1865, however, southern power in the Congress was discredited and temporarily silenced, giving northern and nationalist forces an opportunity to enlarge the federal courts.

### Modernizing Court Systems

**State Courts**   The inability of pronational groups to promote federal judicial power contrasts with the growth of state courts in the mid- to late 1800s. Limited federal jurisdiction meant that most cases were heard by state courts, and these grew mainly in the cities to meet a growing volume and variety of new litigation. Part-time and unprofessional state legislatures were unable to keep up with social and economic changes, and renewed executive power in the hands of governors had not yet developed, so it frequently fell to courts to create new policies to cope with an amazing variety of issues.

New industrial technology, such as the development of steam power and the growth of railroads, shipping, and commerce, and the creation and growth of corporations all created new problems and fundamental questions of public policy which were brought into the state courts. Faced with such cases, the courts began to create new rules regarding personal injury, lost and damaged property, shipping rates, business organization, and many other subjects.

Corporations and increased commerce also encouraged the development and professionalization of law practice. Experts were needed who could prepare necessary documents and contracts and who were familiar with the growing volume of court decisions that affected business transactions. Old restraints on law practice began to disappear. Although America remained a rural society for many years, the gradual growth of cities attracted many young lawyers who were anxious to work for the new corporations. Business opportunities were exciting and adventuresome and corporate law became the most glamorous and prestigious form of practice (Chapter 3).

The business lawyer also became a new factor in politics. In the 1870s business lawyers quickly began to form professional associations devoted to improving their status and political influence, regulating and limiting entry into law practice, and upgrading the quality of the courts. And they became active in the politics of court organization.[29]

*Social Change*   Changing from a rural and small-town country to a nation of cities also meant fundamental shifts in lifestyles and social and economic organization. Many of these changes produced numerous conflicts that were sorted out in court. New immigrants from all parts of the world settled in northern cities not far from other Americans who had migrated from rural areas after the Civil War to find new jobs and opportunities.

Unlike traditional societies, the millions of people in cities were much less able to depend upon themselves or their families. People no longer owned or worked their own land, but became dependent upon others for employment and for goods and services. The growth of industry led to labor unions and collective bargaining. Change also contributed to new social problems, including more juvenile and adult crime, alcoholism, divorce, and abandonment. Later, ownership of private automobiles produced more traffic violations, accidents, and personal injury, all presenting enormous problems for the cities and the courts.

The development of an urban, industrial, and complex society means that people interact with others more frequently—most often with strangers. Auto accidents, for example, occur between people who have never met before, and traditional private methods for settling disputes cannot be used often. Family elders or the local priest or rabbi is not known or acceptable to both sides. Consequently, formal courts and paid attorneys are called on much more to settle conflicts. Generally, in western societies, *traditional personal and nongovernmental methods for settling disputes have been replaced by impersonal, formal, and official mechanisms.*

*Specialized Courts*   For a time following the Civil War, existing state courts, particularly local justices of the peace, handled the growing volume of cases. If the courts were overloaded, new judges were added to the same structure. It was common for large cities to have dozens or even hundreds of identical courts with the same jurisdiction to meet the growing caseload of city life. But new problems also seemed to demand new kinds of remedies, and cities added many special courts of limited jurisdiction.

Confusion and overlapping jurisdiction abounded. Until recently in Philadelphia, for example, Municipal Court dealt with small financial claims, child support, abandoned children, and juvenile crime, but other city Courts of Common Pleas heard divorce cases and child custody disputes, while a third, Orphan's Court, had jurisdiction over the estates of minors. By the 1930s Chicago had over 550 independent courts, including approximately 500 justices of the peace, all with countywide jurisdiction. This meant that any case could be brought to one of over 500 different courts.[30]

Efforts to reform the courts began in the early 1900s. By the 1960s and beyond, the bewildering array of courts led many states to reduce the number and variety of courts and to create more streamlined and consolidated systems.

**Federal Courts**   The federal courts also began to change and grow in the late 1800s. With the defeat of the south in the Civil War, the pronationalists were able to enact a series of major new laws for the federal courts. In 1869, they added new circuit judges and reduced the obligation of Supreme Court justices to ride circuit. In 1875, Congress enlarged the jurisdiction of federal courts and shifted some of the Supreme Court's cases to the circuit courts, giving the high court greater opportunity to deal with more pressing issues.

In 1891, Congress created the Circuit Court of Appeal, a new set of intermediate appellate courts that would hear appeals from the district and old circuit courts. The act also permitted the Supreme Court to become more selective in deciding which cases it would hear. The old circuit courts were abolished in 1911 and their powers transferred to the district courts. After 1900, other bills further refined the role of each court in the federal judicial system.[31]

Generally, all new legislation tended to increase the importance of the intermediate appellate courts by shifting to the courts of appeals many cases that the Supreme Court previously had been required to hear. The specialized federal trial courts of limited jurisdiction also were established about this time.

The most significant benchmark in this trend occurred in 1925, when Chief Justice William Howard Taft persuaded Congress to pass a bill that gave the district courts all original general trial jurisdiction with the right of one appeal to the circuit courts. From then on, few types of cases could be appealed as a matter of right to the Supreme Court, and after 1988, most cases the Supreme Court decides are selected through the *certiorari* process in which the court decides on its own which cases are sufficiently important to deserve a hearing.

*Recent Federal Controversies*   The basic structure and jurisdiction of the federal courts has not changed much since 1925, but federal court organization is a continuing political issue. Various attempts have been made to limit court jurisdiction, redraw the boundaries of the circuits, and create new specialized courts. Efforts to change the federal courts often are angry and partisan reactions to unpopular court decisions, or attempts to promote particular policies.

Box 2.3, "Splitting the Circuits," illustrates intense political conflict over the organization and powers of the federal courts.[32]

Another recent effort to change the structure of the federal courts concerned various proposals in the 1970s and 1980s to create a new national court of appeals to be positioned between the courts of appeals and the U.S. Supreme Court.[33] Many lawyers and judges, including former Chief Justice Warren Burger and Chief Justice William Rehnquist, have maintained that a new court

---

**BOX 2.3**

SPLITTING THE CIRCUITS

Senator Slade Gorton, Republican from Washington state, argued in 1990 that splitting the large ninth circuit into two new ones would increase the efficiency of the courts. In his view, the present circuit is so large that the judges have to travel too much to hear cases, and there are too many judges and cases for one circuit to manage properly. The proposal would put Arizona, California, and Nevada into one circuit and Washington, Oregon, Idaho, and Montana into the other. The Justice Department and former Chief Justice Warren Burger favored the change.

But members of the Senate Judiciary Committee were doubtful. Opponents, which included California's two senators, nearly all of the circuit judges and environmental groups, maintained that the real reason behind the proposed split is to protect timber interests in the northwest from strict judicial enforcement of federal environmental laws. Recent decisions have prevented timber cutting in areas inhabited by the rare spotted owl. Splitting the circuit would require that environmental disputes in the northwest timber states be heard in the new "local" circuit, presumably with judges sympathetic to timber interests.

Then Senator Pete Wilson of California (now, governor) asserted that the split would be "environmental gerrymandering." The Senate has taken no action. In contrast,

Senator Gorton has been heard to complain that the ninth circuit is dominated by "California attitudes."

The only recent time a federal circuit has been divided was in 1980 when the fifth circuit, which included the deep south states, was divided into two new circuits. Florida, Georgia, and Alabama became the new eleventh circuit; Mississippi, Louisiana, and Texas became the revised fifth circuit.

The split has a long political history. In the 1960s, southern Congressmen proposed splitting the fourth and fifth circuits, which would have removed conservative southern judges from a minority voting position in the more northerly fourth circuit and thus allowed them to create a conservative voting majority with fellow conservatives in the deep-south fifth circuit. But civil rights groups and liberal members of Congress stopped this plan.

By the 1970s, all of the federal judges in the fifth circuit agreed that the circuit was so heavily loaded with cases that it needed to be reorganized. However, civil rights supporters remained suspicious that a split would dilute civil righs gains made in the fifth circuit court of appeals during the 1950s and 1960s. More delays followed. But after years of wrangling and with all of the judges in favor—and with new liberal, minority, and female judges appointed to the fifth circuit by President Jimmy Carter so that conservatives could not dominate—Congress agreed to the division.

is needed because the Supreme Court is so overloaded with petitions for *certiorari* that is cannot screen them properly. There also are many instances in which the federal courts of appeals have created conflicting policies on similar issues, but since the Supreme Court cannot grant *certiorari* to all of these cases, policy inconsistency inevitably exists and is permitted to stand. Different versions of the plan included giving the new court the power to screen *certiorari* petitions and jurisdiction over cases involving conflict among the circuits.[34]

The proposal for the new court encountered strong opposition from the very start. There was no agreement among lower court judges, lawyers, and Congress about whether the Supreme Court really was overworked and needed relief. Most important, they believed screening the *certiorari* requests is as important as actually making formal case decisions, because the Supreme Court determines which issues should receive national judicial attention. This power, they argued, should not be given to a lower court. Former Chief Justice Earl Warren and others charged that the new national court really was a maneuver by political conservatives to keep controversial civil rights and civil liberties cases from getting to the Supreme Court in the future.[35]

Despite continuing concern that the Supreme Court is overloaded with cases, no agreement on the new court or other solution is likely soon. Many judges, lawyers, and members of Congress are reluctant to support fundamental changes in the structure of the federal courts that would have unknown consequences for the role of the Supreme Court and the power of the lower federal judiciary. Change in court organization usually has come very slowly, and the federal courts, particularly the Supreme Court, have become venerable judicial institutions that few are willing to change very much.

## JUDICIAL ADMINISTRATION AND COURT REFORM

Judicial administration and court reform are closely related to organization and jurisdiction. Administration and reform are concerned with the day-to-day work of the courts and how it can be improved. However, the judicial process is not like mathematics or engineering; there are various ways that courts can be managed and major differences on what the goals of the judicial process ought to be. People do not agree on a single definition of court improvement.

Judicial administration includes a wide range of activities in two broad areas: *the management of court organization and personnel* and *the processing of litigation*.[36] Court management covers a number of specific areas such as the organization and jurisdiction of courts; the selection and tenure of judges and the hiring, training, and supervision of all other court workers; expenditures and budgeting for personnel and court operations; and routine clerical tasks. Processing of litigation usually concerns speed and cost and establishing uniform rules of court operation to reduce confusion and inequality in how cases are treated. Improved jury management and transferring judges to speed up trials also are aspects of organizing litigation.

As in court organization, the watchwords in judicial administration have been decentralization and local control, but there is much disagreement among those who feel that locally managed justice is best and reformers who believe that equal and efficient justice is produced by well-organized and centrally managed court systems. Competition for control over court operations is the politics of judicial administration and reform.

### Administration in the Federal Courts

The Chief Justice of the Supreme Court is the formal leader and manager of the federal court system. But actual power is divided among various federal judicial organizations. The system reflects past political compromise between supporters of national and local control of the federal courts.[37]

**Judicial Conference**   The main national decision-making organization is the Judicial Conference of the United States, which includes the Chief Justice as the presiding member, the chief judges of each of the federal judicial circuits, plus one district judge from each circuit. The conference meets twice each year for about two days to discuss various issues including judicial procedure, the transfer of judges within circuits, recommendations for congressional legislation required for creating new judgeships, increasing judicial salaries, budgets for court operations, etc. The conference also oversees the work of the *Administrative Office of the United States Courts*, which manages the day-to-day operations of the federal courts.

A two-day conference held twice each year cannot accomplish very much. Therefore, prior to conference meetings, as many as twenty-five committees, composed of various judges and lawyers from the twelve circuits, are appointed by the Chief Justice to analyze and make recommendations on issues that the conference will consider. Positions on the committees provide judges and lawyers with prestige as well as influence on the conference before it makes policy for the entire federal court system. Participation by so many judges also adds legitimacy to the work of the conference by drawing local lower court judges into policymaking and making them partly responsible for the success or failure of federal judicial administration.[38] However, the Judicial Conference and its many feeder committees are a loose organization and lacks the power to enforce its policy in the federal courts.[39]

Normally, proceedings of the Judicial Conference are relatively routine, and the Chief Justice obtains quick approval of his administrative proposals. Recently, however, political ideology has affected its activities. Partly to reduce the number of criminal cases coming to the federal courts, Chief Justice William Rehnquist has sought Conference support for a proposal, which would be recommended to Congress, that would limit the opportunity of death row inmates to appeal to the federal courts in hopes of overturning their state convictions or sentences. However, a majority of circuit chief judges, appointed under earlier and more liberal administrations, refused to go along.

They also wrote a separate letter to members of Congress opposing the Chief Justice's ideas. Clearly, the recent conservative shift in the Supreme Court has created conflicts with other, liberal, federal judges.[40]

**Administrative Office**   The Administrative Office of the U.S. Courts is the main national agency that manages the day-to-day affairs of the federal courts. It is the source of some ideas for the Judicial Conference and it supervises some judicial personnel. Its main function, however, is to collect and publish statistics on the work of the courts. It also is the official representative of the Judicial Conference in Congress, but it is out of the mainstream of political party and interest group politics and has not been very effective in obtaining money for the courts or congressional support for court proposals.[41]

**Regional Organizations**   In addition to the Judicial Conference, which makes policy for all the federal courts, each circuit has its own *regional Judicial Council* and *Judicial Conference*. The conference is composed of district and appeals court judges and lawyers and meets once each year to discuss issues and problems of interest to the judges. The judicial councils are more important organizations composed of judges of the courts of appeal. The councils provide leadership in proper judicial management, set examples for personal conduct for all judges in the circuit, and work to make the trial courts as efficient as possible. Enforcement of policy usually is through persuasion, peer group pressure, and occasional publicity directed at judges who are slow to go along with circuit policy.

The political significance of the circuit councils is that they reflect compromise in federal judicial administration between national and local control of the courts. They have been criticized, however, because they are unable to enforce uniform standards of judicial administration among the district courts. The circuit judges are likely to think of themselves as part of the brethren or professional colleagues of the district judges, not supervisors who direct the work of the lower courts. While the federal and other court systems look like hierarchies of authority on paper, actual administration is fairly loose, with much local independence. Rather than direct supervision, persuasion and compromise are the main ways in which changes in court procedures are accomplished.

### Administration in the State Courts

Administration in the state courts is more complex than in the federal court system since there are fifty separate systems, all with somewhat different procedures and practices for managing the judiciary.

**Court Administrator**   Nearly all the states have a full-time state court administrator, similar to the federal court administrator,[42] who is employed and supervised by the state supreme court and oversees certain functions of the state court system. The administrator's office does research on administrative problems, gathers statistics on caseloads, and may do some long-range budget and other planning. However, the job and the power of the supreme court are very limited in most of the states. A few states have granted the supreme court power to supervise the entire court system, but decentralization and local control still are typical in most states.[43]

The few states that have adopted centralized judicial management often are those that have been the first to adopt a wide variety of other governmental policies and have large centralized state bureaucracies. For them, adopting new patterns of judicial administration is not a unique development, since they are used to experimenting with many new programs and are more likely than most other states to abandon traditional ways of organizing state government. Topping the centralized judicial administration list are Alaska, Hawaii, New York, New Jersey, Rhode Island, North Carolina, and Colorado.[44]

**Limited Power**   There are two areas where state supreme courts are fairly influential in the state court system: the *power to transfer judges* to temporary assignments to help reduce case backlogs and the *power to make uniform rules for law practice and procedure* for all trial and appellate courts.[45] Supreme courts have become more powerful in these areas mainly because the control is seen as ''in- house,'' with few political implications for other elements of state politics. But even in these least controversial areas of judicial administration, the power of courts is not absolute or without political checks. In about one-quarter of the states, for example, the supreme court has no power to transfer judges, and almost half the states still provide for a veto of judicial rule making by a simple majority of the legislature. State legislatures are unlikely to become interested or involved in this specialized area of judicial power, but the potential for limiting the courts still exists.

Except for these two powers of administration, state supreme courts and state court administrators have little impact on local trial courts, where judges are free to run their own operations. In half the states, there is no required supreme court review of local court budgets and spending, no review of purchasing for new equipment, no review of case management procedures, and no supervision of court personnel and employment standards.

**Local Control**   Limited powers of state supreme courts and court administrators in judicial administration mean that most courts are locally managed and funded. But even local management is divided among various individuals with different interests in the courts. In most counties or judicial districts, management officially is shared by judges and the clerk of the court, an independently elected official who works part-time for the courts, but who also serves as county finance officer, treasurer, recorder of official documents, and secretary to county government.[46] The clerk of the court often has little interest in or allegiance to the court system.

Decentralized judicial administration also is maintained by the orientations of judges. Many judges think of themselves as legal and judicial professionals who should never become mere subordinates of court managers or appellate courts. But many also do not believe that their role requires them to be managers at all. One trial judge observes:

> Good judges know how to run a trial. They know how to write opinions. . . . They are workers and are not lazy. Now, when it comes to administration, there are a lot of things they don't think are their problems. . . . They don't think, for example, if the jail is overcrowded, that it's their problem. They don't think that if something is wrong with the [case] assignment system, that it's their problem . . . [or] that the idea of controlling their docket is their problem.[47]

### The Politics of Court Reform

Court reform involves policies that are designed to shift judicial administration from local control and independence to centralized court management. Historically, court systems have been loose and fragmented networks of separate courts with more local influence on them than state or national control. Under court reform the federal and state court systems would become *unified hierarchies of judicial authority* centered in Washington for the federal courts and in state capitals for the fifty states.

Reformers believe that tighter control will promote rational and efficient court operations and provide skilled professional leadership in new ways to manage the judiciary. Court reform also is championed by those who believe that popular political influence in the courts, which occurs through elections, political parties, and interest groups, detracts from proper judicial conduct and impartial decision making. In this area reforms concentrate on controlling the selection of judges to obtain qualified people for the courts. The politics of court reform is the competition between those who favor new ways over old ways and those who believe in centralized legal control versus local popular control of the courts.

**Goals**    Court reformers support a number of specific goals that together contribute to unified court systems.[48]

*Consolidated and simplified courts*    Reform would combine specialized trial and appellate courts so that each court system has no more than one court at each of three or four levels with each court having a clearly defined jurisdiction. This reform would increase the public's understanding and ability to use courts, and improve the image of the judiciary, and make the courts easier to supervise.

*Centralized management*    The federal and the state supreme courts, working through centralized court administrators, would have final authority over the operation and administration of their respective court systems and sufficient resources to manage and train court personnel.

*Centralized rule making*    Supreme courts would have final and complete authority to regulate the practice of law and to make rules of judicial procedure for their judicial systems.

*Centralized budgeting and financing*   Centralized budgeting would permit state supreme courts to create a budget for the entire court system and to submit it to the state legislature. This power exists at the federal level, but not in most of the states, where courts are included as part of city and county budgets and the governor's budget. Also, funds for the courts come from many different sources.

**Supporters**   The reform movement is based on legal values and the ideology of business efficiency that emerged as a powerful political force in the early twentieth century. There are many groups that have adopted this view and work in state and national politics to transform court management from decentralized, local operations to centralized administration and decision making.

State and national bar associations were early key supporters. Bar associations were first formed in the 1870s to improve the image, respectability, and quality of the legal profession (Chapter 3), including the courts, and getting judges out of partisan politics. The American Bar Association usually supports most reforms, and the American Judicature Society was formed in 1913 specifically to promote improvement in the courts. The Federal Judicial Center, the National Center for State Courts, the Institute for Court Management, and State Justice Institute are relatively new organizations which do research and propose changes in court organization and management.

Bar associations and judicial reformers have successfully lobbied the federal government to support court reform. The U.S. government has created many special agencies to do research and formulate plans for improvement. One of the earliest was the Law Enforcement Assistance Administration created in the late 1960s when the federal government's war on crime was at its peak. Other research organizations, particularly the Bureau of Justice Statistics and the National Institute of Justice, have taken its place.[49]

During the 1970s, former Chief Justice Warren Burger stimulated many changes in federal judicial administration, particularly new organizations to recruit and train court administrators. He also participated in dozens of conferences and meetings to encourage other federal and state judges to find ways to make the courts more efficient. Chief Justice Burger probably did more to stimulate judicial efficiency and modern management than any chief justice since William Howard Taft.[50]

*Party and Ideology*   High-status lawyers and other conservative Republicans often are especially active in promoting changes in the state courts.[51] In the states, they usually are aided by other middle-class reform groups such as Leagues of Women Voters and Chambers of Commerce, which also favor applying the ideals of business efficiency to the courts.[52]

The lawyers who lead campaigns to reform the courts usually are the most financially successful and prestigious attorneys, who also have the time and financial independence to become involved in bar association and other political activities. Often they are the senior or managing partners of law firms that represent large companies and other wealthy business clients. They usually have a "law office practice" in which they give advice on taxation, business organization, government regulation, etc. They rarely take cases to court.

This gives us an important clue to the political flavor of court reform, for these lawyers oppose Democratic political control and policies in many cities, including the selection of judges and local management of the courts. Since the Democrats are in control, Republicans often conclude that whatever is wrong with the courts is due to the influence of the Democratic party in urban politics. They also frequently believe that judges are biased by their ties to the Democratic party. They do not openly favor Republican justice, but they often oppose Democratic judges and speak of the general need to maintain judicial independence and integrity, constitutional government, improved judicial administration, and other abstract ideals.

At the national level, conservative Republicans seek to reduce the growing caseload burden on federal judges by limiting access to the federal courts, particularly by convicted criminals who have benefitted in the past from judicial policies that provided various means for challenging convictions and sentences. Liberals have a different view, believing that appeals should not be curtailed so long as there is evidence that defendants in state courts did not have an adequate legal defense or that jury selection was biased or that there were other defects in the way state courts handled their cases. Disagreement on the grounds for appeal indicates that judicial reform is not a neutral activity.

**Opponents** Not everyone agrees with the goals or assumptions of court reform. High-status business lawyers and bar association officers do not speak for all lawyers. The practice of law varies widely, and there are many other attorneys with different backgrounds, experiences, and political orientation.

*Trial Lawyers* Two groups of lawyers who often oppose court reform are trial specialists and general practice lawyers who work on their own or in small partnerships. Trial specialists may represent businesses or individuals, but they are known mainly for their trial expertise in personal injury, property damage, and sometimes criminal cases. Rural, small-town, and urban lawyers working on their own frequently have a general, nonbusiness law practice and handle a large volume and variety of cases including divorces, small debt collections, real estate transactions, and occasional criminal cases. They routinely file lawsuits, motions, and other documents and often go to trial. Unlike the high-status lawyers who seldom go to trial, trial specialists and generalists are frequently in court.

Lawyers who deal almost daily with local trial courts become accustomed to and dependent on existing court organization, procedures, and personnel. Their intimate knowledge of how local courts operate is an important key to their legal success. Changes in court structure disrupt their routine and create new uncertainties about how courts will behave. From their point of view, existing court operations are not out of date or inefficient, but are crucial parts of their legal work. Justice delayed is not necessarily justice denied, since delay may be part of a legal strategy to reach a negotiated settlement, to prepare a case more carefully, or to permit a lawyer to take on a larger volume of business than can be handled at one time.

Trial lawyers often oppose changes in jurisdiction, limitations on the right of appeal to state supreme courts, or limitations on the right to sue for personal injury.[53] Trial lawyers and generalists usually are suspicious of any suggestions which limit alternatives and opportunities to go to court.

The proposal to transfer all cases involving diversity jurisdiction to the states is among the most controversial judicial reforms. Box 2.4, "Eliminate Diversity Jurisdiction?" illustrates the intense disagreement among lawyers on court reform.[54]

*Party and Ideology*   Differences among lawyers often involve partisan politics as well. Many of the independent urban lawyers who handle a large

---

**BOX 2.4**

ELIMINATE DIVERSITY JURISDICTION?

Diversity cases account for about one-quarter of the federal civil docket. Many reformers want to shift all of these cases to the states, but others have proposed raising the threshold from $50,000 to $75,000 or $100,000, or allow diversity cases only in certain kinds of major, multi-party lawsuits. The debate includes the following opposing pro and con views.

**Pro**

• *No local bias*   The reason for creating diversity jurisdiction was to avoid local bias against out-of-state litigants. This no longer is a problem because the nation has become much more homogeneous. State and federal juries also are drawn from the same pool of citizens.

• *Huge increase in cases*   Cases are flooding the federal courts, but there are not enough judges. New federal laws increase the workload and the number of cases per judge is skyrocketing. Congress should provide money to the states to help them adjust to an increase in caseloads.

• *State law applies*   Federal judges are obligated to apply state law in diversity cases. Therefore, the cases belong in state court.

• *Federal questions*   The federal courts should be reserved for major issues involving federal law.

• *Easiest to eliminate*   Diversity cases are the most appropriate to shift to the states because there are no basic constitutional rights involved, as in civil rights or criminal cases.

**Con**

• *Local bias*   Local bias continues to undermine a fair trial for out-of-state litigants. Local juries are prejudiced against big corporations forced to defend themselves in state courts.

• *Add federal judges*   If the federal court dockets are crowded, fill existing vacancies and add more judges. Many state dockets are also crowded, and shifting cases to the states will add to the overload in those courts.

• *Quality of judges*   Federal judges generally are better qualified and equipped than state judges to hear complicated cases.

• *Big issues*   Many diversity cases involve interstate commerce and national economic development. They should be heard in federal court.

• *Eliminate other cases*   Civil rights laws are being abused by litigants, and trivial federal crimes and employee injury claims should be abolished.

• *Access to court*   Courts belong to the people and their lawyers, not to judges. The people should have a choice of forum.

volume and variety of cases for small economic interests are not wealthy. They typically make much less money than the business lawyer and generally occupy a lower rung on the socioeconomic and status ladder.

Reflecting the usual constituencies of American political parties, the independent city lawyer is more likely to be a Democrat. Conflict over court reform, then, involves differences in types of law practice as well as differences between the two major political parties. Democratic party leaders are apt to oppose court reform, particularly when it involves changing the method of judicial selection from election to merit plans where they suspect that Republican lawyers will have the upper hand (Chapter 4).

Urban-rural differences are important in some states. For instance, rural and small-town lawyers often are Republicans in the northeast and midwest, but because reform upsets the usual ways of doing legal work, they oppose other Republicans who favor court reform. They also are likely to believe that problems that trouble the big-city courts are not relevant to their smaller and less complicated communities.

Finally, many judges and other court personnel oppose court reform because they fear they will be transferred to new courts and will have to learn new procedures and perhaps new areas of law. Court officials who might be out of a job because of changes in court structure, such as nonlawyer justices of the peace, also fight hard to protect themselves.[55]

Since most court reforms have both supporters and opponents, the political outcomes of reform generally involve compromise. Reformers typically propose a far-reaching package of changes, such as merit selection for all judges, consolidation of all courts, and major shifts in jurisdiction. Various legislators, lawyers, and judges criticize and lobby against the package and reformers agree to withdraw some reforms, publicly stating their regret, but they also are pleased with what they can get. They settle for merit selection for some courts or win consolidation only when the incumbent judges are assured they will not lose their jobs. Certain other reforms are easy to obtain, such as the creation of special commissions or councils to study judicial management problems or assigning data gathering responsibilities to court administrators. Since none of these reforms threatens anyone or costs much, they pass legislatures easily.[56]

### Evaluation of Court Reform

The politics of court reform almost always creates so much smoke and noise that it is difficult to determine whether reforms accomplish their goals. Supporters of reform assert that justice will be improved, but they rely mostly on intuition or "common sense," simply asserting that reform works. Defenders of the status quo usually are too busy protecting their own interests and defending local independence to evaluate what reform might accomplish. However, most of the evidence gathered so far supports the conclusion that court reform has little or no impact on the outcomes of the judicial process or on judges and other individuals working in the system.

**Delay** A major concern in court reform efforts is reducing delay or back-logs in the courts. From the reform point of view, delay is produced by the ever-increasing number of cases that judges are unable to process in a reasonable period of time. As more cases are filed, already overworked courts become bottlenecks that back up the system and create more delay. The net result is that people have to wait months or even years before their cases are scheduled for trial. Some reformers believe delay pressures many litigants into negotiating settlements or pleading guilty to avoid the frustrations and other costs of waiting for trial. Solutions presumed to work include using pretrial conferences, adding more judges, changing the way cases are processed at the trial level, and shifting jurisdictions. Others include limitations on the right to sue or appeal, as in denying the right to appeal adverse administrative rulings regarding Social Security or worker's compensation benefits or criminal sentences.

There is no evidence that the size of a court's workload (the number of cases to be decided) is related to the time used to decide cases or to the percentage of negotiated settlements. Courts with heavy caseloads often are very efficient while those with few cases are very slow.[57] Adding more judges also is no cure. Requiring pretrial conferences in order to promote negotiation and to reduce the number of issues in contention also misses the mark since most lawyers already routinely try to negotiate settlements.[58] An example of case management reform concerns disagreement on whether one judge should preside from the beginning to the end of a single case (first appearance to final judgment) or different judges should handle the same stage of many cases. The evidence is that both methods are efficient in certain cities but not in others.[59] Overall, there is no evidence that any particular reform reduces delay.

However, surveys of judges show that when judges themselves decide that there is too much delay, they can speed things up by not allowing lawyers to drag cases on for weeks or months. Instead of granting motions to delay a trial, judges make the lawyers show up on the scheduled day and get the show on the road.[60]

It is interesting but somewhat mystifying that state and federal judges in the same city often differ from judges in other cities concerning how to handle delay. Even though state and federal courts meet in different buildings, use different procedures, hear many different types of cases, and have different caseloads, they all frequently require similar amounts of time to dispose of cases. This strongly suggests that various local legal cultures (beliefs and customs about how the judicial process should work) are more important in shaping how local courts handle the caseload problems than the formal procedures adopted by the courts.[61]

Mandatory reforms may not be necessary to end delay, but judges must decide that administration is important and that cases need to be speeded up. Judges can devise their own ways of making things go faster. On the other hand, if judges resent judicial administration and new rules that require greater efficiency, or if they believe that the judicial process is supposed to be slow, deliberate, and careful—meaning that a little delay is not a bad thing—they do not do much to encourage speed. For court reforms to work, they have to be backed up by new judicial attitudes. Also, short-term crash programs, even those involving cash rewards for improved efficiency, do not have a lasting impact.

Regardless of how inventive judges and others might be in developing new strategies for reducing delay in the courts, other policies frequently but unintentionally sabotage improvements. Tough law enforcement policies and stiffer sentences create more cases and trials in federal and state courts. Shifting diversity and drug cases from the federal to the state courts may reduce federal backlogs, but will probably also shift the caseload burden from one set of courts to another.[63]

## CONCLUSION

This chapter has described the basic structure of state and federal courts, the jurisdiction they have to decide cases, how cases move from one court to another, and the number of cases handled by state and federal courts. It is clear that in terms of people directly affected, the state courts have a much greater impact on most day-to-day disputes and crime in the United States. However, there is substantial concurrent jurisdiction between state and federal judicial systems. This has a number of important consequences for judicial policy as well as the strategies adopted by litigants in pursuing cases in the courts.

All courts appear on paper to be parts of judicial hierarchies with most power found in the appellate courts, but the origins and development of the courts and their administration underscore the view that courts usually are loose networks of judicial institutions with substantial decentralization and local control. Court systems have not developed in a logical or inevitable way, but have always been related to other political forces.

Reforms designed to end delay in the courts usually view the judicial process as a standardized mechanical operation and do not take into account the way that local legal values, traditions, and beliefs affect what judges and lawyers do. While there are many formal rules of procedure that affect how cases move through the system and numerous courts that handle legal business, judges and lawyers always have choices to make about how rules are interpreted and applied. Therefore, persons interested in court organization and management need to understand the psychological, social, and political forces that affect decisions about court structure and procedure.

## SUGGESTIONS FOR ADDITIONAL READING

Barrow, Deborah J., and Thomas G. Walker: *A Court Divided: The Fifth Circuit Court of Appeals and the Politics of Judicial Reform* (New Haven: Yale University Press, 1988). This is a careful political analysis of the history of the division of the fifth circuit court of appeals into two new circuits. However, it is even more valuable as an in-depth look at the intricate politics of judicial reform and its links to the interactions between federal courts, Congress, and presidents in civil rights policymaking.

Eisenstein, James, Roy B. Fleming, and Peter F. Nardulli: *The Contours of Justice: Communities and their Courts* (Boston: Little, Brown and Co., 1988). Three experts on criminal courts provide an intensive study of criminal courts in nine counties with an overview of the work of criminal courts.

Howard, J. Woodford: *Courts of Appeals in the Federal Judicial System* (Princeton: Princeton University Press, 1981). This is an in-depth study of the organization and role of the courts of appeals in the federal system. It emphasizes the position of these courts as the final arbiter for most federal cases.

Richardson, Richard J., and Kenneth N. Vines: *The Politics of Federal Courts* (Boston: Little, Brown and Co., 1977). A classic, this book provides an introduction to the history, development, and political role of federal courts in American politics.

Tarr, G. Alan, and Mary Cornelia Aldis Porter: *State Supreme Courts in State and Nation* (New Haven: Yale University Press, 1988). This is an introduction to the political role of state supreme courts in the federal system with detailed illustrations drawn from three states.

## NOTES

1 For detailed descriptions of court organization and jurisdiction, see various issues of the *Annual Report of the Director*, Administrative Office of the United States Courts; and *State Court Caseload Statistics: Annual Report 1989* (Williamsburg, Va.: National Center for State Courts, 1991).

2 Arie Freiberg and Pat O'Malley, "State Intervention and the Civil Offense," *Law and Society Review*, 18 (1984), 373–394.

3 The following relies in part on discussions in *Annual Report of the Director*, Administrative Office of the United States Courts, 1990, pp. 6–11.

4 *Annual Report of the Director*, 1990, p. 12; *Report of the Federal Courts Study Committee*, April 2, 1990, p. 36; *New York Times*, December 29, 1989, p. 1.

5 Henry J. Abraham, *Justices and Presidents* (New York: Oxford University Press, 2 ed., 1985), pp. 384–385.

6 Lawrence Baum, "Specializing the Federal Courts: Neutral Reforms or Efforts to Shape Judicial Policy," *Judicature*, 74 (December–January, 1991), 219; Robert E. Rains, "A Specialized Court for Social Security? A Critique of Recent Proposals," *Florida State University Law Review*, 15 (Spring 1987), 1–30; *Los Angeles Daily Journal*, March 11, 1986, p. 19; May 31, 1990; *New York Times*, November 16, 1988, p. 1; December 1, 1988, II, p. 6; January 8, 1989, I, p. 16; February 5, 1989, IV, p. 2; December 15, 1989, I, p. 20; November 19, 1990, p. 1; *Tallahassee Democrat*, May 20, 1991, p. 4A.

7 Baum, "Specializing the Federal Courts;" Barton F. Stichman, "The Veterans' Judicial Review Act of 1988: Congress Introduces Courts and Attorneys to Veterans' Benefits Proceedings," *Administrative Law Review*, 41 (1989), 365–397; "New Veterans Legislation Opens the Door to Judicial Review—Slowly," *Washington University Law Review*, 67 (1989), 889–922.

**8** *State Court Caseload Statistics*, 1991, pp. 1 and 102–107.

**9** *Ibid.*, p. 6.

**10** Albert Lepawsky, *The Judicial System of Metropolitan Chicago* (Chicago: University of Chicago Press, 1932), pp. 19–23.

**11** *New York Times*, February 6, 1988, p. 1.

**12** *State Court Caseload Statistics*, 1991, p. 5.

**13** *Ibid.*, pp. 24–26.

**14** *Ibid.*, pp. 50–54.

**15** *Tallahassee Democrat*, June 26, 1989, p. 1D; August 25, 1989, pp. 1C and 3C; *New York Times*, June 26, 1989, p. 38; August 18, 1989, p. A29; April 20, 1990, p. A1; July 20, 1990, p. A1; *Los Angeles Daily Journal*, July 11, 1989, p. 1; August 1, 1989, p. 1; August 30, 1989, p 7.

**16** *New York Times*, May 6, 1987, p. 12.

**17** Herbert Jacob. *Justice in America*, 4th ed. (Boston: Little, Brown and Co., 1984), pp. 169–170.

**18** Mary Cornelia Porter, "State Supreme Courts and the Legacy of the Warren Court," and Stanley H. Friedelbaum, "Independent State Grounds: Contemporary Invitations to Judicial Activism," in Mary Cornelia Porter and G. Alan Tarr (eds.), *State Supreme Courts: Policymakers in the Federal System* (Westport, Conn.: Greenwood Press, 1982), pp. 3–53.

**19** *The New York Times*, March 31, 1986, p. 1.

**20** Kenneth N. Vines, "Federal District Judges and Race Relations Cases in the South," *Journal of Politics*, 26 (1964), 337–357, and Kenneth N. Vines, "Southern State Supreme Courts and Race Relations," *Western Political Quarterly*, 18 (1965), 11–15; Clement Vose, "Litigation as a Form of Pressure Group Activity," *Annals of the American Academy of Political and Social Science*, 319 (1958), 20–31.

**21** Richard J. Richardson and Kenneth N. Vines, *The Politics of Federal Courts* (Boston: Little, Brown and Co., 1970), chap. 2.

**22** The political histories of state and federal courts are summarized in Glick and Vines, *State Court Systems*, chap. 2, and Richardson and Vines, *The Politics of Federal Courts*, chap. 2. See also Francis R. Aumann, *The Changing American Legal System* (Columbus: Ohio State University Press, 1940); Charles Warren, *A History of the American Bar* (Boston: Little, Brown and Co., 1950); Herbert Jacob, "The Courts as Political Agencies," in *Studies in Judicial Politics*; Herbert Jacob and Kenneth N. Vines (eds.), *Tulane Studies in Political Science*, 8 (New Orleans: Tulane University, 1962): Felix Frankfurter and James M. Landis, *The Business of the Supreme Court* (New York: Macmillan Company, 1927).

**23** E. H. Woodruff, "Chancery in Massachusetts," *Boston University Law Review*, 9 (1929), 169; Erwin C. Surrency, "The Evolution of an Urban Judicial System: The Philadelphia Story: 1683–1968," *American Journal of Legal History*, 18 (1974), 95–123; David Mars and Fred Kort, *Administration of Justice in Connecticut*, I. Ridgway Davis (ed.), Institute of Public Service, University of Connecticut, Storrs, Conn., 1963, p. 22.

**24** Charles Grove Haines, *The American Doctrine of Judicial Supremacy* (Berkeley: University of California Press, 1932), pp. 148–165.

**25** Jacob, "The Courts as Political Agencies," p. 18.

**26** *Ibid.*, p. 21.

**27** Hurst, p. 116; J. Woodford Howard, Jr., *Courts of Appeals in the Federal Judicial System* (Princeton: Princeton University Press, 1981), p. 4.

28 Richardson and Vines, chaps. 2, 3.

29 Jerold Auerbach, *Unequal Justice* (New York: Oxford University Press, 1976), pp. 22–23.

30 Hurst, p. 155; Surrency, p. 119; Albert Lepawsky, *The Judicial System of Metropolitan Chicago* (Chicago: University of Chicago Press, 1932), pp. 19–23.

31 Richardson and Vines, pp. 26–35.

32 *New York Times*, March 9, 1990, p. B6; *Los Angeles Daily Journal*, June 14, 1990, p. 5; Richardson and Vines, p. 17; plus fn. 28–31 in 2 ed. For a complete political history of the division of the fifth circuit court of appeals, see Deborah J. Barrow and Thomas G. Walker, *A Court Divided: The Fifth Circuit Court of Appeals and the Politics of Judicial Reform* (New Haven: Yale University Press, 1988); Final Report, *Commission on Revision of Federal Court Appellate System*, December 1973, in *Hearings Before Senate Committee on the Judiciary, on S. 2991*, 93d Cong., March 27, 28 and April 4, 10, 11, 23, 1974, pp. 25–60; reflected in President Jimmy Carter, *Statement on Signing H.R. 7665 into Law*, October 15, 1980; *Weekly Compilation of Presidential Documents*, 1980; *Congressional Quarterly Almanac*, 1980, p. 390; "Senate Passes Legislation to Split the Fifth Circuit," *Congressional Quarterly Weekly Report*, June 21, 1980, p. 1770.

33 *Report of the Study Group on the Case Load of the Supreme Court*, Federal Judicial Center, Washington, D.C., 1972; "The National Court of Appeals: Composition, Constitutionality and Desirability,"*Fordham Law Review*, 41 (May 1973), 863–886; Douglas A. Poe et al., "A National Court of Appeals: A Dissenting View," *Northwestern University Law Review*, 67 (January–February 1973), 842–856; "Creation of New National Court of Appeals as Proposed by Blue Ribbon Study Group," *American Bar Association Journal*, 59 (January 1973), 139–144.

34 "The National Court of Appeals . . ." *Fordham Law Review*, 41 (May 1973), 863; A Commission on Revision of the Federal Court Appellate System, Structure and Internal Procedures, Recommendations for Change, 75 F.R.D. 195 (1975); *The New York Times*, January 17, 1975, p. 1; Roman L. Hruska, "Commission Recommends New National Court of Appeals," *American Bar Association Journal*, 61 (July 1975), 819–824. A similar proposal for a national court to hear appeals from state courts also has been made. See James Duke Cameron, "National Court of State Appeals: A View from the States," *American Bar Association Journal*, 65 (May 1979), 709–712; *The New York Times*, February 13, 1983, p. E5.

35 *The New York Times*, January 7, 1973, sec. E, p. 6. See also Alan F. Weston, "Threat to the Supreme Court," *New York Review of Books, The New York Times*, February 22, 1973, p. 29; and Sidney Ulmer, "Revising the Jurisdiction of the Supreme Court: Mere Administrative Reform or Substantive Policy Change?" *Minnesota Law Review*, 58 (1973), 121–155.

36 Russell R. Wheeler and Howard R. Whitcomb (eds.), *Judicial Administration: Text and Readings* (Englewood Cliffs, N.J.: Prentice-Hall, Inc., 1977); Larry C. Berkson, Steven W. Hays, and Susan J. Carbon (eds.), *Managing the State Courts: Texts and Readings* (St. Paul, Minn.: West Publishing Co., 1977); and Larry Berkson and Susan Carbon, *Court Unification: History, Politics and Implementation*, National Institute of Law Enforcement and Criminal Justice Law Enforcement Assistance Administration, U.S. Department of Justice, Washington, D.C., August 1978.

37 A detailed political history of federal judicial administration is found in Peter Graham Fish, *The Politics of Federal Judicial Administration* (Princeton, N.J.: Princeton University Press, 1973).

**38** *Ibid.*, p. 274.

**39** *Ibid.*, p. 139; and Daniel J. Meador, "The Federal Judiciary and Its Future Administration," *Virginia Law Review*, 65 (October 1979), 1047–1059.

**40** *New York Times*, October 6, 1989, p. 1 and March 15, 1990, p. 1.

**41** Fish, pp. 206–227.

**42** *State Court Systems*, Council of State Governments, 1978.

**43** Berkson and Carbon, August 1978.

**44** Henry R. Glick, "Innovation in State Judicial Administration: Effects on Court Organization and Management," *American Politics Quarterly*, 9 (January 1981), 49–69.

**45** The following description of state court administrative powers relies on Berkson and Carbon, August 1978, chaps. 1, 2.

**46** Steven W. Hays, *Court Reform: Ideal or Illusion?* (Lexington, Mass.: D. C. Heath and Co., 1978), p. 28.

**47** Arlene Sheskin and Charles W. Grau, "Judicial Responses to Administrative Reform" (unpublished paper presented at the Southern Political Science Association Meeting, Atlanta, Ga., November 1980), p. 18. See also Beverly Blair Cook, "Role Lag in Urban Trial Courts," *Western Political Quarterly*, 25 (June 1972), 234–248.

**48** Berkson and Carbon, chaps. 1, 2; Henry R. Glick, "Supreme courts in State Judicial Administration," in Mary Cornelia Porter and G. Alan Tarr (eds.), *State Supreme Courts: Policymakers in the Federal System* (Westport, Conn.: Greenwood Press, 1982, chap. 5.

**49** Malcolm M. Feeley and Austin D. Sarat, *The Policy Dilemma: Federal Crime Policy and the Law Enforcement Assistance Administration, 1968–1978* (Minneapolis: University of Minnesota Press, 1980), pp. 137, 142–143; Nadine Cohodas," 'Think Tank' in Justice Department Earns Respect from Members, but Wins Passage of Few Bills," *Congressional Quarterly*, April 19, 1980, pp. 1049–1051.

**50** Edward A. Tamm and Paul C. Reardon, "The Office of the Chief Justice: Warren E. Burger and the Administration of Justice," in Mark W. Cannon and David M. O'Brien (eds.), *Views from the Bench* (Chatham, N.J.: Chathan House Publishers, Inc., 1985), pp. 100–119.

**51** Glick and Vines, chap. 2, and Richard A. Watson and Rondal G. Downing, *The Politics of the Bench and the Bar* (New York: John Wiley & Sons, Inc., 1969).

**52** Berkson and Carbon, pp. 157–163.

**53** *Newsweek*, May 22, 1978, pp. 78–79; Glick and Vines, p. 18; Linda F. Sweet, "Anatomy of a 'Court Reform'," *Judicature*, 62 (June–July 1978), 37–43.

**54** Victor Eugene Flango and Craig Boersema, "Changes in Federal Diversity Jurisdiction: Effects on State Court Caseloads," *University of Dayton Law Review*, 15 (Spring 1990), 405–455; Charles L. Brieant, "Diversity Jurisdiction: Why Does the Bar Talk one Way but Vote the Other Way with its Feet?" *New York State Bar Journal*, 61 (July 1989), 20–22; and Wilfred Feinberg, "Is Diversity Jurisdiction an Idea Whose Time Has Passed? *New York State Bar Journal*, 61 (July 1989), 14–19; Report of the Federal Courts Study Committee, April 2, 1990, pp. 38–42; *New York Times*, March 23, 1990, p. B10.

**55** Doris Marie Provine, *Judging Credentials: Nonlawyer Judges and the Politics of Professionalism* (Chicago: University of Chicago Press, 1986), especially chaps. 2, 3.

**56** Joel A. Thompson and Robert T. Roper, "The Determinants of Legislators' Support for Judicial Reorganization," *American Politics Quarterly*, 8 (April 1980), 221–236;

Berkson and Carbon, p. 136 and chap. 8; Beverly Blair Cook, "The Politics of Piecemeal Reform of Kansas Courts," *Judicature*, 53 (February 1970), 174–281; Glick and Vines, p. 16.

**57** Martin A. Levin, "Delay in Five Criminal Courts," *Journal of Legal Studies*, 4 (January 1975), 83–131; Malcolm Feeley, "The Effects of Heavy Caseloads," in Sheldon Goldman and Austin Sarat (eds.), *American Court Systems* (San Francisco: W. H. Freeman and Co., 1978), pp. 110–118; Church, chap. 3, See, generally, Malcolm M. Feeley, *Court Reform on Trial* (New York: Basic Books, Inc., 1983); Thomas Church, Jr., *Justice Delayed* (Williamsburg, Va.: National Center for State Courts, 1978), pp. 21–24.

**58** Jerry Goldman, "The Civil Appeals Management Plan: An Experiment in Appellate Procedural Reform," *Columbia Law Review*, 78 (1978), 1209–1240; David W. Neubauer and George F. Cole, "A Political Critique of the Court Recommendations of the National Advisory Commission on Criminal Justice Standards and Goals," *Emory Law Journal*, 24 (Fall 1975), 1023–1024; Raymond T. Nimmer, "Judicial Reform: Informal Processes and Competing Effects," in Herbert Jacob (ed.), *The Potential for Reform of Criminal Justice*, chap. 7.

**59** Raymond T. Nimmer, *The Nature of System Change* (Chicago: American Bar Foundation, 1978), chap. 6; Church, chap 4; James Eisenstein and Herbert Jacob, *Felony Justice* (Boston: Little, Brown and Co., 1977); Roy B. Fleming, Peter F. Nardulli, and James Eisenstein, "The Timing of Justice in Felony Courts," *Law and Policy*, 9 (April 1987), 179–206.

**60** Fleming, Nardulli, and Eisenstein, pp. 179–206.

**61** Church, p. 56; Thomas W. Church, Jr., "Who Sets the Pace of Litigation in Urban Trial Courts?" *Judicature*, 65 (1981), 76–85; and Charles W. Grau and Arlene Sheskin, "Ruling Out Delay," *Judicature*, 66 (1982), 109–121.

**62** Milton Heumann and Thomas W. Church, "Criminal Justice Reform, Monetary Incentives, and Policy Evaluation," *Law and Policy*, 12 (January, 1990), 81–102.

**63** Flango and Boersema, 405–455; *New York Times*, December 29, 1989, p. 1.

# 3

# LAWYERS AND LAW PRACTICE

It is difficult to imagine courts and cases without lawyers. A mental picture of a busy courtroom focuses on opposing attorneys examining witnesses and summarizing key arguments before a jury. The judge is a mostly quiet neutral umpire, and the litigants, who started the lawsuit, have a very limited role. They might testify, but they have little other influence on how the case unfolds or how it will turn out. Most litigants have no idea how to proceed in court and, left on their own, would feel very uneasy not knowing the right things to say or the correct order of events.

A trial dramatically illustrates the lawyer's strategic role. But, as suggested in Chapter 1, the practice of law involves much more than trials and appeals. A lawyer's major job is providing advice and information that prevents disputes from becoming lawsuits and keeps clients free from entanglements with government and other businesses and individuals. Lawyers often negotiate with other lawyers on behalf of their clients in order to reach settlements in disputes or remove snags in business deals. Even though it seems dull compared to a television legal drama, most law work is done in offices, not courtrooms.

When people go to lawyers for help in settling a dispute or to buy a house, write a will, or interpret the internal revenue code, they enter a specialized and unfamiliar world. Lawyers have the keys for unlocking doors and lights for finding the way. They know how to transform personal complaints into legal issues and possibly how to find remedies or strategies to prevent further trouble. Many also have the skills and knowledge to obtain information and to get answers from government officials or businesses. It is practically impossible to use the legal system or to go to court without having lawyers as guides, translators, and advisers.

The role of lawyers is examined in various chapters, especially in the discussions of the selection of judges (Chapter 4), civil disputes (Chapter 5), and criminal cases (Chapter 6). This chapter provides an overview of the role of lawyers, including: what lawyers do for a living and its relationship to society and politics; lawyers' relationships to clients and legal ethics; how people become lawyers; and the political and social characteristics of the legal profession.

## LAW WORK

The practice of law is a regulated profession, which means that it involves specialized knowledge and skills obtained only after a considerable period of study, successful examination, and formal licensing and admission to the profession by state government. Law also has several other things in common with other professions. Like doctors and dentists, for instance, lawyers expect to have considerable personal independence when making decisions for their clients, they expect high levels of social status and income, and they are governed by special codes of professional conduct.

### A Varied Profession

While law is somewhat similar to other professions, it is a much more general and varied line of work than such fields as architecture, engineering, medicine, or even teaching. Training in other professions usually includes a body of knowledge and skills that is designed more precisely for the actual jobs that their practitioners do. Engineers, for example, learn specific technical knowledge and its applications to appropriate problems and projects. A new civil engineer ought to be able to build a bridge without much additional preparation beyond formal technical education.

Law, however, applies increasingly to nearly every area of human life. We are increasingly inclined to translate difficult social problems into legal issues that require lawyers to handle them. For instance, in place of traditional doctor-patient communication and understanding for determining treatment, technical advances and medical specialization have produced new legal concerns with patients' rights and demands for particular procedures or the end of treatment. The spread of the disease AIDS (acquired immune deficiency syndrome) has produced disputes over employment, housing rights of homosexuals, and right of children who have the disease to attend public schools. Lawyers are involved in these and other new disputes. Environmental law has become routine, rather than the work of a few political reformers, and the increasing size of the elderly population has created a new specialty geared to their distinctive needs.

**More Rules**  But law concerns much more than unusual disputes and problems. Enactment of new legislation and administrative rules and regulations is the main way that modern big government tries to cope with problems and manage conflict. Businesses, schools, and other organizations also create rules and regulations and administrative procedures for their employees and clientele that have an impact similar to official law.

Many new rules are extremely controversial and receive a lot of public attention, such as required drug testing for athletes and the employees of various industries and government. Other regulations are much less visible and controversial but are just as important. For example, management review sessions for college administrators typically include lectures by the college attorney on proper procedures to be followed in faculty promotion and tenure decisions, policies on sexual harassment and discrimination, admissions and scholarship review procedures, and many other areas. All such matters used to be handled quietly, privately, and informally. Now they increasingly are public, legal issues with a focus on ensuring equal treatment.

Finally, law is both a hurdle and a tool for individual citizens when dealing with government in tax disputes, government regulation of business, and even everyday concerns such as home real estate purchases, marriage and divorce, wills, insurance claims, and more. Think of an area of human concern and activity, and the law and lawyers probably are or soon will be there.

The presence of law, rules, and procedure in nearly every phase of life means that law work covers a huge territory and lawyers earn their livings in many different ways. It also means that law training is only an introduction. Law students get a taste of what law includes, but they rarely get a full-course meal. New lawyers are not automatically ready to handle criminal cases as an assistant prosecutor or public defender, nor are they ready to take on IBM or the federal government in an antitrust case.

Law school training gives lawyers the basic technical knowledge for locating the body of laws and regulations that apply to particular problems, it teaches the special language of law, and it provides basic direction for getting a case into and through state and federal court systems or for making presentations before government regulators. But success at doing these and other tasks requires practice and experience in picking up details and learning the complexity of law, local procedures, and informal and customary ways of doing legal business.

## Specialization

The lawyers that most people use for buying a house or writing a will probably have a general law practice in which they handle a number of different but relatively routine personal matters. The procedures and paperwork may seem complex to most clients, but the law involved is relatively simple and clear. Finalizing a home purchase or settling an uncontested divorce involves similar repeated steps and standard legal forms that are available in reference books which legal secretaries learn to adapt to each case.

Lawyers doing this kind of work also are likely to be solo practitioners or to work in small law partnerships or three- or four-person firms. Since most of us use lawyers only for these kinds of things, it looks as though most lawyers are generalists who hang out their shingle and work for the general public. But this is not the complete picture.

A key development in law practice is that lawyers increasingly work in large law firms employing dozens or hundreds of lawyers. In 1960, nearly two-thirds of lawyers in private practice (not employed by government or corporations) were in solo practices. By the 1980s, lawyers employed by firms were in the majority—and increasing.[1] The growth of firms also means that lawyers specialize in particular types of law work. Specialization generally has resulted from the vast increase and application of law to nearly every area of human activity and from the growth and complexity of big business and big government increasingly concentrated in big cities.

**Levels of Specialization**    Lawyers specialize in two general ways, and each of these marks separate territories of law practice.

*Business or Personal Law*    First, most lawyers devote most of their time either to business matters or to the problems of individual personal clients, but not to both. A study of Chicago lawyers reveals that less than 10 percent of urban lawyers spend as much as 25 percent of their time and effort on business clients and on the needs of individuals. The overwhelming majority works exclusively in one area or the other. There is very little overlap between business law and personal law practice.[2] A much smaller number of lawyers work in public interest law, representing various organizations that use the courts, as well as the other branches of government, to obtain public policies which they favor (Chapter 5).

*Courtroom or Law Office*    Second, lawyers tend to concentrate either on courtroom or law office work. Most law practice involves legal research and negotiation, but when clients become involved in disputes that cannot be handled privately and informally, their lawyers sometimes pass them on to other lawyers who are more experienced and who specialize in going to court. Many courtroom lawyers specialize even further as trial or appellate advocates.

In small cities and towns, most lawyers handle their cases from start to finish, but in larger cities, where there is a larger volume of complex litigation and cases might go to either federal or state courts, special courtroom expertise sometimes is considered valuable for handling cases effectively in different arenas.

**Client Centered**    The specialization of law practice is dictated largely by the special needs of particular types of clients. Large corporations, for example, have a wide range of legal needs related to numerous aspects of their business activities, and they link up with large law firms or hire their own staff of lawyers that can meet all or most of their requirements. This kind of law work is steady and stable because big businesses repeatedly face the same kinds of problems and enter into the same kinds of transactions over and over again, year after year. Therefore, a large urban law firm will have a number of distinctive departments which devote all their energy and expertise to particular areas of law. In contrast, individuals encounter different types of problems, such as divorce, small financial disputes, real estate or perhaps criminal matters, and other lawyers develop specialties devoted to these needs.

An important consequence of the client-centered nature of law practice is that lawyers with different personal backgrounds tend to be concentrated in different specialties. Those with high social status tend to be selected for lucrative and high status business practice, while those with less social standing often have little choice but to concentrate on much less prestigious law work for individuals. This point will be discussed in greater detail in later sections of this chapter.

*Subspecialties*    Besides the major division between business and personal law work, law practice is separated further into even more distinctive categories and clients. Five major divisions of law practice with their subspecializations are listed in Table 3.1. They include: large corporate, general corporate, labor, government, and personal. Each of these types of law practice represents a separate kind of legal work.[3] The chances are small that lawyers working in one of these five areas will ever do much work in one of the others. In Table 3.1, personal law work is separated from all of the others by a vertical line to indicate that there is almost never any crossover between law work for individuals and the other forms of law practice. A banking or tax lawyer probably will never do any business litigation or civil rights work, and a tax lawyer never appears in criminal court.

Moreover, overlap among certain subspecialties is also rare. Asking an attorney in a large city what he or she does for a living could bring polite conversation to a stop when the lawyer replies that he specializes in patent law

**TABLE 3-1**
TYPES OF URBAN LAW WORK

| Large Corp. | General Corp. | Labor | Government | Personal |
|---|---|---|---|---|
| Antitrust | Bus. Litigation | Manag. | Criminal | General Litig. |
| Patents | Bus. Real Estate | Unions | Municipal | Criminal Defense |
| Bus. Tax | Public Utilities | | | Divorce |
| Stocks/Bonds | Personal Injury | | | Personal Injury |
| Banking | (defense) | | | (plaintiff) |
| Commercial | Civil Rights | | | Real Estate |
| | | | | Probate |
| | | | | General Family |
| | | | | Personal Tax |

*Source:* Adapted from John P. Heinz and Edward O. Laumann, *Chicago Lawyers* (New York and Chicago: Russell Sage Foundation and American Bar Foundation, 1982), p. 51.

for inventors of computer microprocessors or that she works on new stock offerings for bank corporations. The odds are smaller that a chance meeting will uncover a divorce lawyer for the super rich, or one who defends only drug dealers, although there are some of these as well. Patent law, in particular, is so highly specialized that patent lawyers do no other type of law work. Lawyers who work in business real estate and business litigation, including defending businesses against suits for personal injuries, are unlikely to work on antitrust problems, taxes, or stocks and bonds.

Labor law, government work, and representing private clients also are very separate areas of law practice. Labor lawyers usually work only for business or union clients, not for both. Large law firms may have a department for labor relations, but the lawyers working there will have little contact with other lawyers who work on taxes or other business matters.

In large cities, government lawyers are most likely to be prosecuting attorneys or public defenders. Other government lawyers work on the civil side, dealing with zoning, government reorganization, taxation, land condemnation, and other similar areas. In smaller towns, prosecuting attorneys may do some municipal work as well, but most big city prosecutors and public defenders are criminal law specialists.

Lawyers who represent private individuals are more likely than other lawyers to do a variety of law work, often because they do not have many repeat clients and have to take what they can get. But some experienced lawyers specialize somewhat because they are able to get new business through referrals or from their general notoriety as aggressive divorce lawyers or effective personal injury trial lawyers. Because of huge amounts of drug smuggling in certain parts of the United States, a few criminal lawyers in the biggest cities have developed a regular and exclusive clientele of big-money drug defendants. Other criminal defense lawyers are likely to do some divorce and personal injury work, probably because the courtroom and negotiating skills needed in each of these areas are similar, but they are not very likely to work in real estate, personal taxes, or other family matters. Other lawyers specialize in these areas.

**Community Size**  The types of law practice listed in Table 3.1 represent the broad range of law work done throughout the United States. However, the population size of a community affects the degree of legal specialization. Generally, the smaller the community, the less possible it is for lawyers to specialize narrowly. In smaller cities, there is very little large corporate or labor law work since most big businesses and unionized labor are located in the largest metropolitan areas. If an inventor needs a patent lawyer, he or she probably will have to find one in Washington, D.C., or some other large city.

But lawyers in small cities are likely to distinguish between business and personal work and perhaps between certain types of "personal plight"—criminal defense, personal injury, and divorce—versus taxation and real estate. However, the lines are likely to blur, for example, when lawyers handle real estate purchases for local businesses and home buyers or when local businesses and small real estate investors consult tax lawyers. However, in rural areas, nearly all law work involves a wide range of personal plight cases. Lawyers have large numbers of clients and cannot specialize.[4]

### Specialization, Prestige, and Politics

**Prestige**   Specialization and lawyer prestige go together. At the top of the legal heap are corporate lawyers in large business-oriented law firms and on the staffs of large corporations; such lawyers deal with high finance, stocks and bonds, corporate taxation, and banking. Some of these lawyers eventually become the directors or presidents of major corporations.

This kind of legal work is the most prestigious for several reasons. It brings lawyers into direct contact with high-status clients—the officers and directors of big corporations and wealthy individuals. Their high-status lawyers usually have upper-class personal backgrounds similar to the country's top business professionals. They often have gone to similar prestigious private colleges and law schools and frequently have come from very wealthy families. Big-business law work also is clean and quiet work. It rarely involves the courtroom and open conflict and never involves messy personal problems as in divorce, criminal defense, or personal injury lawsuits.

At the bottom of the prestige ladder are the lawyers who handle most of the divorces, criminal defense, wills, and minor real estate transactions. Slightly above them in the pecking order are personal injury lawyers (on the plaintiff's side) and others who do general litigation. Although some personal injury and a few criminal defense lawyers become very wealthy, the kind of law work they do relegates them to lower social-legal status than big-business law work. Much of their work is annoying, repetitious, and not very creative. Lawyers at this level deal with angry spouses, sick and injured employees and consumers, and minor criminals. Many of their clients do not appreciate them very much, nor do they understand why they probably have not won everything they wanted, and they are unlikely to return for repeat business. Some lawyers relish their expertise as divorce lawyers and even take special education courses to become certified experts at "family law," but most lawyers do not favor this line of work.

*Income*   Prestige law work pays much better than any other type of law practice. Experienced top corporate lawyers can count on hundreds of thousands and occasionally millions of dollars each and every year. Even starting lawyers at the top New York, Chicago, or Los Angeles law firms earn over $70,000 or $80,000 their first year.

However, most lawyers—beginners as well as veterans—earn much less. Average starting salaries for recent law school graduates is approximately $40,000, but starting salaries in smaller cities and rural areas, in the south and the west, and in small firms are well under $30,000 per year. Beginning salaries for state and federal government staff attorneys average only $30,000, and annual increases are not high.[5] Employment by the top big-city law firms, where the money and prestige are high, is the kind of law practice students dream about and to which many lawyers aspire—but which few achieve.

Personal plight lawyers generally do not make as much as lawyers in the large big-city law firms. A survey of criminal defense lawyers in the 1970s reported that half earned less than $34,000 per year. Similar surveys indicate that two-thirds to three-quarters of lawyers specializing in a variety of personal plight matters earn less than $40,000 annually.[6] Even allowing for inflation since the late 1970s, most lawyers are not high earners.

Box 3.1, ''Few Big Earners,'' illustrates the wide variation in lawyers' incomes. It also suggests there is a substantial gap between news media reports and public perceptions about lawyers' salaries and the economic realities of law practice.[7]

**Plantiffs' and Defendants' Lawyers**    The lawyer prestige ladder also parallels bar association and political party politics. Again, the main distinction is between corporate and big-business lawyers on one side and lawyers who represent individuals on the other. Lawyers who represent injured people or dissatisfied consumers against big businesses and insurance cmpanies often are called *plaintiffs' lawyers* because they initiate lawsuits that seek money damages. The lawyers who work for the insurance companies, doctors, and businesses being sued often are referred to as *defendants' lawyers* because they typically defend against suits for personal injuries.[8]

Corporate lawyers are sympathetic to the business point of view. They earn big salaries and, like the business people they work with, are likely to be conservatives and Republicans. Lawyers who represent individuals and go to court against businesses also identify with their clients' interests. This is

---

**BOX 3.1**

FEW BIG EARNERS

A recent issue of *Forbes*, a leading business magazine, lists seventy-one corporate lawyers with annual incomes of $1 million or more. The *Los Angeles Times* newspaper touts hourly fees of $400 for senior partners and starting salaries in New York City of over $80,000 and in Los Angeles up to $72,000.

But a Los Angeles survey showed that over 60 percent of veteran—not beginning—lawyers earned less than $75,000. Most lawyers work in small firms of fewer than ten members and many are sole practitioners who represent indiviuals, not businesses. Moreover, many lawyers in smaller towns and cities have problems making ends meet.

The American Bar Association also reported that the income of lawyers in solo practice and in small firms, adjusted for inflation, has fallen sharply over the last two decades and that only the elite law firms in the largest cities employing over 100 lawyers have experienced continued and leaping prosperity.

Because news about top earnings in law practice make the public angry at all lawyers, lawyers need to present a more complete and balanced picture of what most lawyers really earn.

clearest in the example of personal injury lawyers who make their living representing individuals who have been hurt by faulty products or while on the job. They take cases on a contingency basis which gives them perhaps 30 or 40 percent of the total award if they win the case, but little or nothing if they lose.

The contingency fee enables injured people who cannot afford to pay a lawyer by the hour a chance to get into court. Some of these plaintiffs' lawyers may have some conservative sentiments because of their own high income, but they are more likely to be Democrats because they represent individuals and underdogs against bigger economic interests and frequently oppose business groups that favor laws which would reduce allowable lawsuits, jury awards, and contingency fees.

Many other lawyers also are likely to identify with plaintiff underdogs and the Democratic party. Civil rights and labor union lawyers clearly have interests with the Democrats, but so do lawyers in solo practice who make modest incomes working on a variety of personal problems. Their clients and their own incomes have very little to do with big business and the Republican party.

*Broader Issues*  Business and personal legal conflicts spill over into other realms of politics. Opposing groups of lawyers try to influence the selection of judges who will be sympathetic to the sides they each represent in court (Chapter 4), and they work on opposite sides on the issues of court reorganization and attempts to limit jurisdiction which would make it more difficult to get cases into court (Chapter 2). They also lobby hard against each other in legislatures concerning proposals to limit the size of jury awards in personal injury cases or to limit the percentage in a lawyer's contingency fee.

Recently, insurance companies and their business and physician customers have lobbied in most of the fifty states and at the federal level to reduce awards for "pain and suffering," which in a few cases have been in the millions of dollars, to a few hundred thousand dollars or less. The companies claim that high jury awards and generous contingency fees motivate lawyers to sue and have raised liability insurance premiums for doctors and businesses. Lawyers representing the injured counter that the insurance companies are gouging their customers and have raised their premiums to offset other business losses due to their own poor business judgment. They claim the insurance companies are falsely blaming the injured and their lawyers for unnecessary increases in insurance costs.[9]

These conflicts are new wrinkles on old political issues. The contingency fee was invented by lawyers in the late 1800s in order to get poor injured workers into court against employers. This budding plaintiff's law practice often was handled by new immigrant lawyers who represented their fellow immigrant neighbors who labored in the growing industries.[10]

These lawyers usually had received their educations in low-prestige, part-time, or night law schools and had no prospects of working for business. Accusing them of ambulance chasing, business lawyers formed restrictive membership bar associations and wrote codes of professional ethics which prohibited advertising and soliciting for clients or encouraging litigation, and they opposed the contingency fee. Like their counterparts today, business lawyers sought to discourage litigation that threatened their clients' finances and business dominance, while their opponents tried to broaden opportunities to sue and to enlarge what is considered fair game in a legal battle.

The degree of solidarity or cohesion among lawyers has been a long-standing concern in American politics. Many commentators from the days of de Tocqueville to the present have worried particularly about lawyer-legislators, who often make up one-third to one-half of the membership of state legislatures and Congress. They have envisioned a legislature in which lawyer-legislators form a cohesive group that would promote laws in their own interest and prevent the passage of legislation which they oppose.

This concern assumes that there are interests that unite lawyers or that they have so much in common as a profession that they will stand together against all comers. However, except for the rare instance in which nonlawyers attack the entire law profession, much research shows there is no cohesion among lawyers in legislatures or in any other area of government. There are so many lawyers and so many positions that they represent in society that we almost never find lawyers grouped closely together against outsiders. In our large and diverse modern country, we find lawyers distributed over the entire political map.[11]

### Protecting the Profession

One of the important characteristics of a state-regulated profession is that it has the authority to do work that is prohibited to others. Only medical doctors can practice medicine, and anyone who acts as a doctor without a valid state license is subject to criminal penalties. The same is true of lawyers. No matter whether a lawyer works for a big law firm or handles divorces and debt collection in a solo neighborhood law office, a lawyer's work is protected by state law. Despite internal differences that frequently occur among lawyers, protecting the profession is the one issue on which most lawyers close ranks.

**Porous Boundaries**   Every profession tries to protect itself from outsiders. Medical doctors, for example, object to laws allowing optometrists, who are not licensed medical doctors, to prescribe drugs. Doctors argue that only highly trained ophthalmologists should treat eye diseases. Generally, medical associations have been successful in fending off infringements on their territory.

However, the problems for lawyers are more severe. First, lawyers have lower social status and get less respect than doctors and some other professionals. Despite decades of effort to improve the image of the bar, many people still think of lawyers as deal makers who really are out for themselves, not their clients. The shyster image still is common, and bar associations get a poorer reception in legislatures than many other groups.

Second, law work is not as easy to define and separate from other similar work that involves routine forms and set procedures. Many people can do simple law work without having a law degree, and they do not acknowledge lawyers' claims to special technical expertise.

Finally, medical doctors receive more deference and maintain their prestige because they have more control over their clients and can independently make professional decisions. Patients are unable to prescribe their own treatment, and they depend on their doctors to tell them what needs to be done. Lawyers, however, often are summoned by clients and told to file for divorce or to collect a debt or draw up a sales contract with the details having already been set by the businesses involved in the transaction. Lawyers are important and necessary, but they depend on clients to get things started and sometimes do not have complete control of "treatment" as a legal matter progresses.[12]

Bar associations generally have been successful in persuading state legislatures to write very general and vague statutes prohibiting the unlawful practice of law, leaving it up to lawyers and sometimes the courts to interpret what the statute means in particular circumstances. The purpose of general laws is to discourage other people from infringing on the lawyers' turf and their opportunities to make a living. Competition among lawyers is fierce enough; if others were allowed to do a lawyer's work, the exclusive control over law work would decline.

**Routine Law Work**   Lawyers do not worry about nonlawyers appearing in court representing a client. Judicial procedure is sufficiently complex and foreign to most nonlawyers so that few people would try to do this. The problem for lawyers is in law office practice, particularly drafting contracts or giving personal legal advice. One area of major concern has been property law, where real estate agents draft contracts for the sale of property and help to arrange financing. Mortgage company and bank employees also fill out legal forms for mortgages and other documents related to closing a loan.

In many states, bar associations were successful for years in preventing nonlawyers from doing this work, making it necessary to hire lawyers in all real estate transactions. But real estate groups fought back, arguing that the paperwork was routine and should be handled by real estate people. They managed in most of the states to exempt the writing of contracts for real estate from the unlawful practice of law.[13]

Currently, controversy over the unlawful practice of law surfaces most of the time in simple uncontested divorces, adoptions, name changes, and other routine matters that require legal papers, a judge's signature, and filing documents in the courthouse but do not require much expertise. Nevertheless, bar associations try to prevent nonlawyers from doing this type of work.

Recently, a Florida secretary who furnished and typed legal forms for individuals was challenged by the bar association for giving legal advice without a license. She claimed she only filled out forms upon request. She lost a lengthy court battle and was sentenced to serve one month in jail. But the

Florida governor and cabinet intervened and granted clemency, changing the sentence to probation.

Despite her guilt, several cabinet members were outraged that the bar association had sought a jail sentence since neither they nor the bar association lawyer could recall one time when the bar had gone to court to seek a jail term for a lawyer who had been convicted of serious offenses concerning the proper practice of law, such as using clients' trust account funds for his or her own purposes. In their view, the bar association was being very "political" in making an example of a secretary in order to protect its own business interests while typically winking at lawyers who violate the law.[14]

The California legislature recently considered, but did not pass, a proposal to permit individuals with non-law school legal training *(paralegals)* to advertise and offer their services directly to the public. They no longer would be required to work for lawyers nor to have lawyers supervise and bill for the work of paralegals. Like the convicted Florida legal secretary, paralegals perform routine law work at lower fees, but with formal legal protection. State laws continue to fend off encroachments on the practice of law, and non-lawyers dealing directly with the public occasionally are arrested. However, more proposals for independent paralegals like the one in California are likely to reach state legislatures.[15]

Boundary disputes between lawyers and laypersons arise also because of the high fees which, critics believe, lawyers collect for doing relatively simple work. An uncontested divorce can cost $500 or more but may take only an hour or two to arrange. Many people feel that if they knew which form to fill out, they could do it themselves and save lots of money. Of course, knowing what form to prepare and what to do with it is what lawyers have to sell. Nevertheless, some claim the cost is too high for the effort required.

*Do-it-Yourself* Dissatisfaction leads some people to try to do their own legal work. But this is difficult because court clerks and secretaries who work in the courthouse, and frequently know what forms are needed and how they must be processed, refuse to give nonlawyers much help or information. Courthouse employees work daily with lawyers and judges and frequently have adopted their professional perspective, which reserves law work for lawyers. They also have been counseled by their superiors that it is improper for them to provide help because it might constitute giving legal advice without a license.

Some interest groups, such as Help Abolish Legal Tyranny (HALT), seek legislation to limit lawyers' fees and to break the monopoly that lawyers have over law work. HALT and various publishers also provide to members information on how to handle their own divorces and how to avoid probate court when settling an estate, as well as other aids for legal do-it-yourselfers.

*Further Erosion* Some experts predict additional erosion of the boundaries of the legal profession. As will be discussed shortly, in the past decade the number of lawyers in the United States has increased enormously, producing more competition for available legal work. Many young lawyers have had to combine law work with other careers in order to survive or have given up law altogether. Having lawyers both in and out of practice weakens resistance to attempts to redefine what constitutes the practice of law.

The Supreme Court has outlawed fee fixing and prohibitions on advertising, which will lead to price cutting and more competition. Newer, younger lawyers also are less supportive of restrictive professional practices. There also will be more Florida secretaries and other entrepreneurs who are anxious to give legal advice and sell information to laypersons. Finally, the educated public is constantly becoming more sophisticated about buying services and products of all sorts so that it probably will be more difficult for lawyers to control and limit the availability and distribution of legal knowledge and information. All these factors threaten the exclusive control that lawyers have over defining the professional practice of law.[16]

## LAWYERS AND CLIENTS

Lawyers and clients need each other: lawyers make their living providing legal expertise and assistance, and clients need lawyers to help them negotiate and resolve legal problems or to find their ways through the courts. But various tensions and pressures between lawyers and clients sometimes make the practice of law as troublesome and controversial as the problems people bring to lawyers. Two major areas of concern are the public's access to lawyers and the ethics of law practice.

### Access to Lawyers

There is no absolute right to legal services or representation in the United States. An important exception is the requirement that poor criminal defendants be provided with free lawyers in any case in which a jail sentence is possible, but free or low-cost lawyers are not widely available for most civil disputes.

Wealthy individuals and larger businesses have little difficulty locating and using lawyers. Their legal problems become a routine part of their economic position and activities, and they have the money, information, and experience necessary to find lawyers who specialize in their personal or commercial needs. Therefore, access to lawyers by the wealthy is not an issue.

But the poor and middle class have greater difficulty finding and using lawyers. Because most people do not have many legal problems, they do not often look for lawyers. Therefore, finding a lawyer for an occasional problem is a difficult and confusing chore. Equally important, because most people cannot afford lawyers for routine legal needs, they do without, look for low-cost legal help, or muddle through themselves. Even when disputes involve substantial amounts of money, many people do not consult lawyers. (Using lawyers in civil and criminal cases is discussed further in Chapters 4 and 5.)

The poor, or people with modest incomes, have several low-cost options in obtaining legal help. These options include the contingency fee, legal clinics and legal insurance, and free or low-cost legal services for the poor.[17] However, none of them fully matches the ability of the wealthy or larger businesses to obtain whatever legal help they need.

**Contingency Fee**    As discussed earlier, the willingness of lawyers to accept cases on contingency—taking a portion of the financial award if they win; billing nothing of they lose—allows many people who suffer injuries in automobile or other accidents or due to medical malpractice or other negligence, to get into the courts. Since they cannot afford to hire lawyers on an hourly basis and pay costs in advance, signing over a portion of their awards gives them access to lawyers. This method goes a long way to putting injured plaintiffs on a level playing field with defendant insurance companies.

*Limitations*    But the contingency fee has a number of important limitations. Lawyers are gatekeepers to the legal system and the courts. If lawyers are unwilling to accept cases—if they refuse to open the gates—potential litigants have no access to the legal system.

The contingency fee is subject to legal gatekeeping and is not a guarantee of access to the law. Unless lawyers are very sure they can win a personal injury case and that there will be a substantial financial award in it, they are unlikely to accept contingency cases. Therefore, doubtful claims, those difficult to prove in court, or claims involving small amounts of money often will not get very far. As a result, some potential litigants will have no legal services and receive nothing for their losses.

Critics of the contingency fee also claim that the rewards for lawyers frequently are disproportionate to the work required to win compensation in big cases. For example, if a jury awards $5 million to a seriously injured and disabled plaintiff, the lawyer may receive up to $2 million (40 percent). Some argue such an amount is too much compared with the $3 million that the client receives and probably must stretch over a lifetime, with reduced or no earnings and continued medical problems and expenses. The problems are even more severe in the more common instance in which lawyers negotiate a settlement rather than take the lengthy, risky, and arduous route to trial. Instead of the potential $5 million, perhaps the injured client settles for $3 million. The lawyer still receives a hefty $1.2 million, leaving the client with $1.8 million.

In addition, critics worry that if lawyers can win a big fee without going to court, they may be more inclined to take the easier route to negotiated settlement—and to take on more cases—at the expense of their client. This is a potential problem in the ethics of law practice, discussed below, which requires lawyers to fully and faithfully represent the interests of their clients. But only the lawyers have the knowledge and experience to determine when it is best to negotiate rather than to take a chance on a trial.

Contingency fees also are not applicable to many important cases which have the potential for creating new law and policy, but which do not produce a lot of money. For example, cases involving the right to die—the desires of patients and/or their families to remove unwanted medical treatment in hopeless cases—produce no money for clients. Their victory simply is a court order requiring medical institutions and personnel to stop treatment. Cases like these may bankrupt individuals who must pay lawyers on an hourly basis. Otherwise, they require free legal help from charitable or social action organizations. Many other people suffer without relief because they are unable to pay for lawyers.

Box 3.2, "Suing Over Job Discrimination," illustrates cases that involve important issues but little money, the kinds of cases which lawyers frequently refuse to take on contingency, leaving litigants on their own. It reveals the gaps in access to legal services.[18]

**Clinics and Insurance**   Two sources of lower-cost legal assistance are available through legal clinics and prepaid legal insurance plans. These have become possible in the last dozen years since the Supreme Court has banned bar associations from setting minimum legal fees, prohibiting advertising, and limiting the solicitation of legal business. Now, the practice of law allows for much more competition and advertising of services through the mass media and direct mass mailing. Both legal insurance programs and legal clinics generally provide assistance in relatively routine matters—dealing with a landlord or tenant, writing a will or a contract, handling divorces and criminal cases.

Legal insurance is somewhat similar to a limited medical insurance policy in which a participant obtains legal help through a company or labor union program. The organization usually arranges with a panel or group of lawyers to

---

**BOX 3.2**

SUING OVER JOB DISCRIMINATION

Neither John Henry Smith nor Maurlean Edwards could find lawyers in Albany, Georgia, to take their cases of job discrimination against the county health department and the local hospital. Their only chance was to learn a few basics of court procedure so that they could present their cases in federal district court themselves.

Lawyers are reported to be unwilling for many reasons to take such cases. Most of the clients are poor and unable to pay a fee. Taking their cases on contingency is impossible because the cases are time-consuming, difficult to win, and bring in much less money than personal injury suits that permit punitive damage awards. In addition, the U.S. Supreme Court has discouraged lawyers from taking job discrimination cases by limiting large monetary awards in most cases and prohibiting class-action suits (cases in which one client symbolically represents a large group or class of people at the same time).

Local legal aid societies, which provide free legal help for the poor but which receive federal funds to support their work, are prohibited by federal law from taking employment discrimination cases.

Some lawyers also claim that increasingly conservative federal judges are hostile to racially based claims of job discrimination, and disputes occur with federal judges who determine the amount that lawyers may collect from an employer if their client wins.

Consequently, most clients are left on their own. But, says one civil rights lawyer, "They're getting killed in court. . . . It's like sheep to the slaughter." An analyst concludes, "What happens is that they end up not being able to enforce their rights. . . . They go out and find another job, and forget the whole thing."

offer services to employees or members. While legal insurance is available through some employers and other groups, this availability is not widespread. Legal clinics are more generally available, through local branches or offices of a national law firm, through long-distance telephone consultations with a staff of lawyers, or through local law firms advertising low-cost services.

*Advertising*    After the Supreme Court overturned bans on advertising by lawyers, the potential of national and local legal clinics to attract business mushroomed, and the amounts they spent on advertising increased dramatically. In 1978, all law firms in the United States spent a total of $900,000 on advertising, but by the end of the 1980s, lawyers were spending approximately $60 million annually. The big three in legal clinic advertising are Jacoby and Meyers ($7 million), Hyatt Legal Services ($5 million), and Injury Helpline (over $3 million). Branch offices of national firms are not available in every city or every state, but television viewers in medium-sized and large cities are likely to see advertising for national or local firms specializing in personal plight law. Hyatt Legal Services also sells computer software for drawing up routine legal documents.

Despite the greater freedom that lawyers have to advertise, state and local bar associations continue to limit the kinds of ads lawyers may run. In particular, local lawyers who run aggressive or inflammatory ads have been targeted by bar associations seeking to preserve a dignified image of legal professionalism. For example, to dramatize a divorce law practice, one ad showed a lawyer running a chain saw through the middle of a sofa and then towering over the family dog as the next to be divided—not too different from the flamboyant tactics of used-car dealers. However, state and local bar associations also have banned dramatic music or simplistic claims in legal advertising.

Many courts have upheld bar association curbs on the types of legal ads. Lawyers who rely on advertising complain that bar associations are trying to avoid Supreme Court rulings that permit advertising and promote competition. Despite the controversy, there is some evidence that advertising for routine legal work helps to keep legal costs down. In cities in which bar associations imposed the fewest limitations on advertising, legal fees tended to be somewhat lower than elsewhere.[19]

**Legal Services for the Poor**    Neither legal insurance nor legal clinics is available to help the poor. But the poor sometimes are considered better off in terms of access to lawyers than the near-poor or even the middle class, since public agencies provide legal assistance to the poor without cost. In the 1960s, after the Supreme Court mandated legal representation for the poor accused of crimes, public defenders' offices or court-appointed attorneys became common throughout the United States. Federally funded local legal services offices also became available in the 1960s to help the poor in a variety of civil law problems.

*Early Legal Aid*    Legal assistance for the poor has a long history in the United States. The nation's first legal aid was the Freedman's Bureau, which, for a short time during Southern Reconstruction after the Civil War, helped poor southern blacks in civil and criminal cases. Legal aid supported by private charities became more common toward the end of the nineteenth century, modeled on German-American legal aid societies set up to help new German immigrants avoid exploitation by landlords, merchants, and employers. But private support for legal aid declined during the Depression of the 1930s, and it did not substantially expand later, in large part because the American Bar Association in the 1950s worried about the socialization of law practice.

The early legal aid societies defined their role as providing legal assistance to the poor within the existing structure of law and institutions. Their view was that law and political institutions were neutral and available to anyone who had access to a lawyer. All that anyone needed was access to the playing field. Therefore, the legal aid societies were to operate like other law firms—providing legal help on an individual, case-by-case basis.

However, the belief in legal neutrality was eclipsed by the reality of privately funded legal aid. Mainly to avoid offending the organized bar, many charities prohibited legal aid societies from offering legal help in many areas of law served by private attorneys, but valuable to the poor as well as to other people: divorce, personal bankruptcy, personal injury, claims for wages, workman's compensation, and criminal cases. In fact, the few cases that the legal aid societies *did* accept generally were small financial claims too small to attract the interests of private lawyers.

In addition, many legal aid societies agreed to help only the "deserving poor"—those who were out of work due to no fault of their own, but not others who refused to help themselves. Little of the work of legal aid societies involved the courts, and most legal aid clients were referred to other social service agencies after their first visit to the legal aid office. Their problems were not defined as "legal" ones.[20]

***Legal Services Corporation***   Legal aid was transformed in the 1960s as part of President Lyndon Johnson's and the Democratic party's War on Poverty. New Great Society programs were devised by the federal government to erase poverty in the world's richest nation. In 1965, the federal government created the Office of Legal Services (OLS) as part of the then-new Office of Economic Opportunity. It was a federally funded national legal services program. It had two goals: to provide legal assistance to the poor and, unlike the early legal aid societies, to use law and legal institutions to reform society and government and help improve justice for those living in poverty. The early leaders of the OLS put their greatest emphasis on law reform, believing that little could be done to help the poor on a case-by-case basis.

However, conflicts between the two goals developed quickly. Lawyers in local legal aid offices faced the daily pressures of providing routine legal help to individuals as well as supporting the reform goals of the national administration. Local bar associations and public officials frequently became alarmed and angry when legal aid lawyers, using the federally funded program, challenged the procedures and policies of local governments. Nevertheless, during the 1970s, legal aid offices handled approximately 1 million cases annually, engaged in much more litigation on behalf of the poor than had the early legal aid societies, filed thousands of appeals in state and federal courts, and took over 100 cases to the U.S. Supreme Court.[21]

The reformist orientation of federally funded legal aid began to decline with the end of the War on Poverty, which occurred after the election of Republican President Richard Nixon in 1968.[22] In 1974, the Office of Legal Services was reorganized as the Legal Services Corporation (LSC), a federally funded but independent agency that provided federal grants-in-aid to local legal aid organizations. However, partisan politics has an important effect since the President appoints the agency's board of directors.

By the 1980s, the reform activity of the Legal Services Corporation had been substantially eliminated. President Reagan was particularly opposed to the LSC since, when he was governor of California, legal services offices attacked his efforts to reduce spending on welfare and Medicaid programs and LSC lawyers aided farm workers in their economic and legal battles against big growers. President Reagan wanted to eliminate the Legal Services Program entirely, but the Democratic Congress objected. However, he did succeed in reducing its budget and appointed conservative directors who substantially eliminated its mission of legal and political reform.

Local legal aid organizations now are much more dependent on state and local government funding and private charity to support their activities. President Bush has not declared a similar war on LSC, but he and his advisors agree that the emphasis of legal aid should be on case-by-case legal services, not on social reform.[23]

Box 3.3, "Limiting Social Reform," reports on the effects of national and state and local politics on the role of federally assisted legal aid.[24]

### Legal Ethics

Professional ethics are the standards, rules, and codes of conduct that the members of a profession are expected to follow and support. For lawyers, ethical standards affect their relationships with everyone with whom they interact—clients, fellow lawyers, the courts, and the general public. However, lawyers and others disagree about what the standards ought to be, and lawyers support certain standards but not others.

**Professional Codes**   The law profession has had codes of professional conduct since the early 1900s, but they have been revised several times to reflect social changes affecting the practice of law as well as court decisions which have made old standards obsolete. The American Bar Association's Canons of Professional Ethics, most recently revised in the 1980s as the Model Rules of Professional Conduct, once prohibited lawyer advertising, the direct solicitation of clients ("ambulance chasing"), and aiding the unauthorized practice of law (allowing or assisting nonlawyers to perform legal services). But, as discussed earlier concerning access to legal services, these rules were discarded

BOX 3.3

LIMITING SOCIAL REFORM

The reduction of federal funds plus the hostility of conservative Republicans to the Legal Services Corporation have made legal aid much more dependent on state and local government and private funding. These changes generally have created pressures on local legal aid attorneys to avoid suing local and state governments or powerful economic groups in order to change the social status quo. Typical cases have involved jail overcrowding, living and treatment conditions in public hospitals, and job discrimination. The poor often are of little political help because they are badly organized and their leaders have trouble mobilizing them for political action.

Local political and economic elites curtail legal aid in several ways: government threats to cut off state and local funding if lawyers sue government; a chummy legal culture emphasizes cooperation and negotiation to settle disputes; private lawyers who serve government and business clients—and who sit on the boards of directors of legal aid societies—discourage staff lawyers from bringing controversial cases; legal aid lawyers avoid controversy because they hope to move into private law practice in the same community; legal aid attorneys believe that lawsuits and the appearance of being unreasonable and uncooperative will hurt legal aid clients; legal aid lawyers fear that judges are conservative and hostile to reform efforts.

Restrictions on the reform activities of legal aid offices are greatest in small cities, suburbs, and rural areas where communities are homogeneous and there is little competition for political control. There, conflicts between legal aid lawyers and judges occasionally bring pressures for crusading legal aid lawyers to quit their jobs and leave town. In larger cities, with many different circles of political and economic power, legal aid attorneys are less affected by local government, bar associations, or other private organizations. They also can appeal to a number of charities to support their work if local governments or others reduce their funds. The poor also tend to be better organized in larger cities and to have political access to government so that a cutoff of legal aid funds is less likely. In larger cities, legal aid attorneys are more likely to file lawsuits that challenge the status quo.

after the U.S. Supreme Court interpreted them as unlawful limitations on competition among lawyers and the public's access to legal services.

Today, codes of conduct heavily emphasize lawyers' business relationships with clients, concerning such things as: keeping funds which clients have deposited with their lawyers separate from the lawyers' personal money; maintaining client privacy; fully and faithfully representing clients; and avoiding conflicts of interests with clients. Codes of ethics also call on lawyers to inform their clients of the progress of their cases or other work and to provide the needy public with a certain amount of free *pro bono publico* (for the public good) legal services.[25]

However, legal codes are vague and general statements that invite disagreement on interpretation, and the codes are difficult to put into effect. Certain violations of ethics, such as stealing from a client, are easier to prove and enforce, but misrepresenting how a legal matter is proceeding, or taking fees and not performing services are less clear. For instance, it is difficult for a client to show that a lawyer provided inferior or inadequate legal services for the fee that was charged. Often the client is not in a good position to know what are the appropriate legal steps to take in a dispute or other problem, how long it reasonably should take to resolve a claim, or whether negotiating a settlement is better than going to trial. The problems are most severe for individuals who have little experience dealing with lawyers, but large businesses also have trouble matching legal effort with the costs of legal services.

*State Enforcement*  Codes of professional conduct exert informal pressure on lawyers to conform to the standards of the profession, but they are important also because they generally become the basis for state regulation of the practice of law. Most of the states place regulation of the practice of law officially with the state supreme court, but the courts, in turn, give most of the responsibility to disciplinary committees of the state bar associations. State bar associations usually adopt the ABA standards as their own codes, and these codes become the basis for disciplining errant attorneys. Only rarely do state supreme courts become involved in very serious or criminal cases in which a lawyer might be disbarred.

Other than disbarment, penalties for violating the codes include reprimands, orders to make financial restitution to clients, or temporary suspension of the right to practice law. However, very few client complaints—less than 2 or 3 percent—result in any action by the disciplinary committees of state bar associations. Most professions are reluctant to closely regulate or chastise their own members, and state bar associations are no exception.

Clients also have the right to sue their attorneys for malpractice, but such suits are expensive and time-consuming, and it is difficult to prove lawyer wrongdoing. Only cases involving large amounts of money and clear evidence against lawyers are likely to be worth pursuing. Most clients do nothing or they resort to making complaints to state disciplinary committees, but their chances of recovering money or having their lawyer censured are slight.

*Improving Conduct*  Two-thirds of the states require lawyers to take continuing education courses, usually concerning new developments in the law. But California has become the first state to address problems in legal ethics by requiring lawyers to take continuing legal education courses concerning: improving lawyer-client relationships, eliminating all forms of personal bias toward clients and within law firms, alcohol and drug abuse among attorneys, as well as training in managing a law practice to avoid frequent complaints about unresponsive lawyers.

Critics suspect, however, that the new courses are designed only to improve the image of lawyers and are inadequate for substantially improving lawyers' ethics and their relationships with clients. The reforms also do nothing to improve the public's access to lawyers.[26]

**Representing Clients**  Most law work takes place in law offices, not in the courtroom. It involves research, giving advice and negotiation, not trials or appeals. Nevertheless, legal ethics become most visible and controversial in sensational criminal and personal injury trials where a lawyer's obligation to fully and faithfullly represent her or his client within the bounds of law often seems to conflict with other ethical obligations to serve as an officer of the court, work for the good of society, and promote justice. But these values seem to take a back seat to doing nearly anything to win the case. This issue surfaces in two major ways: the decisions to represent particular clients and in the tactics used during a trial. In addition, lawyers' relationships to each other raise additional concerns about ethics.

***Choosing Clients***    Legal ethics become controversial when lawyers represent extremely reprehensible or unpopular defendants accused of awful crimes of violence or unscrupulous business practices. Rapists, child molesters, serial killers, and others accused of monstrous crimes receive very little public sympathy. The same is true of members of organized crime or the former executives of banks or savings and loan institutions accused of unscrupulously bilking or defrauding their depositors. Banks, hospitals, and cigarette and insurance companies also often appear as heartless financial institutions when sued by an innocent injured plaintiff.

It is tempting to believe that a lawyer who represents such clients distorts the lawyer's proper role because the defendant's conduct clearly violates public morals or a common sense of right and wrong. The lawyer appears as a paid mouthpiece helping the defendant avoid his or her just deserts or responsibilities. This is especially true of lawyers who routinely represent members of organized crime. It may appear that the lawyer is as criminal as the client, or at least is a morally inferior person. Should lawyers accept these cases? Does a lawyer have a higher obligation to public safety, morals, and justice?

Despite these feelings about lawyers and their noxious clients, every person accused of a crime is entitled to a lawyer and a lawyer has an ethical obligation to provide a defense against criminal charges. Certainly every citizen who might be accused of a crime would cherish her or his right to an attorney. Along with other rights, the right to a lawyer is one of the ways that the public protects itself from an overly aggressive government or prosecutors anxious to please the voters. Also, any individual or organization that must defend itself against charges of negligence is entitled to hire a lawyer.

***Trial Tactics***    Even if unpopular defendants are entitled to a lawyer, further disagreement occurs concerning what lawyers should do for their clients during a trial. Are they obligated to do everything legal to win an acquittal or avoid a financial judgment against their client, including raising issues that seem to have little to do with guilt or liability? Or, if the evidence against their client seems clear, should they temper their defense strategy in order to see that justice is done? If a poor criminal defendant is represented by a public defender or court-appointed lawyer—who has no choice but to take the case—should the lawyer conduct a spirited and aggressive defense? Are there limits to the language and style used in their examination of witnesses and opening and closing arguments before juries?

The conduct of many highly publicized trials and occasional attempts to influence the public through pretrial publicity in cases involving public figures, such as the recent Kennedy-Smith sexual assault case in Florida, seems to show that most lawyers—prosecutors as well as defenders—do all that they can to win their case. For example, it is common for defense lawyers to raise questions in the press or aggressively cross-examine the victims of crime or the prosecutor's witnesses to create doubts either about the truthfulness or certitude of the victim and the authority, credentials, and accuracy of expert witnesses. Even if the lawyer has no reason to believe that the witnesses will lie or are incompetent, they become fair game in a criminal defense. Cross-examination tactics are very controversial in cases of rape, where the victim's personal conduct and sexual history often are attacked to undermine her credibility. Rape victims often must be prepared to defend themselves as much or more than the accused.

It is difficult to know the percentage of lawyers who use aggressive anything-to-win tactics, or the percentage of trials which involve these strategies. Most routine criminal cases and civil suits are fairly tame, but cases involving lots of money and abominable crimes may bring out aggressive competitive tactics.

Box 3.4, "Defense Tactics," illustrate the lawyer's widely recognized obligation to represent the client and the debate which rages over whether they have other obligations to see that justice is done.[27]

Lawyers use several reasons to defend their aggressive tactics. First, their primary obligation is to represent their client within the bounds of law. Although their cross-examination of witnesses may seem rough and aggressive, such tactics are not illegal. Second, many cases which go to trial involve

---

**BOX 3.4**

DEFENSE TACTICS

Dr. Veronica Prego sued New York City's Health and Hospitals Corporation and other doctors for $175 million for negligence when she accidentally contracted the AIDS virus by pricking her finger with a needle. She claimed that another doctor left a used syringe in a patient's bedding and that an AIDS researcher improperly divulged Dr. Prego's condition to others.

But defense lawyers challenged Dr. Prego's story. Not only did they suggest Dr. Prego was negligent in pricking her finger, but during seven days of cross-examination, they challenged Dr. Prego's honesty and truthfulness, stamina, and memory as well as her love life and previous abortions. Other witnesses were asked to estimate Dr. Prego's life expectancy while she and her relatives sat in the courtroom.

Dr. Prego's lawyers characterized the cross-examination as ". . . disgusting, out-rageous, desperate, ferocious, and venomous. He's beat up on her as if she was the villain. . . . The fact that Veronica Prego is on trial is a terrible indictment of the adversary system."

But the defense replied that delving into Dr. Prego's personal life was necessary to raise the possibility that she contracted the AIDS virus in some other way. Other observers agree, seeing the case as so many others where it is necessary to prove absolutely that an injured person has been harmed as a result of another's negligence, and to rule out that the plaintiff herself might have been at fault. Alternative theories about the cause of the injury must be presented in court.

The president of the New York State Association of Criminal Defense Lawyers agrees: "The lawyer has a role to play in the system, and his role is to bring out anything that can help his client's cause. He would be disbarred for not trying to do that. As a person, it's an unpleasant task. But as a lawyer, it has to be done."

reasonable doubt about guilt or responsibility, and the facts rarely point clearly in one direction. In a criminal case, there may be extenuating circumstances that point to a lesser degree of guilt than the most serious charges, or there may be problems in positive identification of the assailant that may exonerate the defendant entirely.

Moreover, it is not the job of the defense attorney to determine "truth." Rather, the adversary process, with one side pitted against the other, is the best way to uncover the available facts and give the judge or jury a basis for making a decision. Although general concerns with justice are important, legal ethics maintain that it is not the lawyer's role to sacrifice his duties to his client to promote social justice. That is a broader job for the judicial process and for society as a whole.

*Lawyer to Lawyer*   Concerns about lawyers' tactics go beyond their courtroom treatment of opposing witnesses. Recently, a special committee on *civility* organized by the U.S. Courts of Appeals for the Seventh Circuit, located in Chicago, concluded that lawyers' manners and their general conduct have become degraded in recent years. Based on a survey of 1400 judges and lawyers in three midwestern states, the committee found that respondents believe that lawyers have become more rude, belligerent, manipulative, and even dishonest in dealing with each other, both in and out of court. Lawyers in Chicago—a big, heterogeneous city with a competitive legal culture—were the worst offenders, but others in smaller communities also seem to have developed a rougher edge. Like their tactics in dealing with witnesses, lawyers seem increasingly inclined to behave roughly with their legal competitors as well.[28]

The committee speculated there are many reasons for the perceived decline in ethical conduct: clients increasingly demand a tough, bare-knuckled approach; aggressive lawyers in television dramas serve as role models for younger lawyers; liberalized rules of discovery that permit lawyers to obtain information about the other side in civil disputes encourage belligerent tactics; attempts to punish lawyers for outrageous behavior make lawyers even angrier with each other; and young lawyers, lured by high incomes in big-city law firms, are so highly competitive that they do not develop friendships with other lawyers who may become their courtroom adversaries.

More evidence is needed before we can conclude that lawyers are becoming more aggressive or antagonistic, but there are few signs that the profession is becoming a kinder or gentler one. Also, it appears that the core of legal ethics is representing the client's cause, but such an orientation probably encourages trial lawyers to strive to maintain their reputations for winning, even if their courtroom styles raise additional questions about lawyers' ethics.

## BECOMING A LAWYER

Becoming a lawyer has been one of the most popular goals of college graduates during the last 25 years. Until the mid-1960s, increases in the number of lawyers paralleled general population growth, but especially since 1970, the number of lawyers has grown tremendously. Competition for getting into law school and for making a living is fierce. There also have been many changes in legal education. Early in our history it was relatively easy to become a lawyer, but today it requires 3 years of postgraduate education and passing a state licensing examination. This section examines growth and changes in the profession and surveys the background and organization of legal education.

### Wanting to Be a Lawyer

Two important changes have occurred in the legal profession since the early 1970s which have no parallel in American history. First, the number of people entering the law profession expanded as never before. Second, a large part of the growth is due to huge increases in the percentage of women seeking a career in law. Women in law is a major example of a significant shift away from traditional women's work.[29]

In 1960, there was one lawyer for each 627 people in the United States, not far different from what it had been in the late 1870s. The total number of lawyers in 1960 was nearly 286,000. But in 1970 and beyond, the lawyer population set all-time records. In 1970, there was one lawyer for each 572 people and a total of 355,000 lawyers. By the 1990s, however, the population-to-lawyer ratio had dropped to 340/1 and the total number of lawyers had increased to over 725,000.[30]

Law school education also expanded in the last 20 years in order to meet rising demand. In 1960, the 134 American law schools graduated 9240 lawyers, or about 69 per law school. By 1980, the number of law schools had increased to 177, and they graduated over 35,600 lawyers, or 199 per law school.[31] Many also raised their admissions standards during this period, which reduced the relative ease of getting into law school.

Law school applications dipped in the mid-1980s, down to approximately 60,000 from the high of 70,000 in 1980–1982. This raised speculation that the population of lawyers had peaked. But applications were up again to approximately 83,000 in 1990–1991.[32] The number of law school graduates can be expected to continue to increase.

**Why Growth?**    There are several explanations for the huge increase in the legal profession during the last several decades. First, the growth of government and its expanded scope of policymaking have sharply increased the need for lawyers. There has been more government regulation of business, a vastly enlarged welfare system, and new policymaking and regulation in environmental protection and other areas, as well as greatly expanded areas of civil rights. This creates a demand for lawyers in both government and private practice. A second explanation is that industry and finance have grown and become more specialized and sophisticated, requiring more experts, including lawyers. In particular, some research suggests that much legal work has been produced in connection with advertising, consulting, selling, and other activities related to the automobile.

A related explanation is that expanded public higher education and increased specialization and sophistication in government and industry have made the bachelor's degree less attractive as a final college degree. Entry into high-level employment is more likely to require advanced and professional degrees. Since the 1970s, only a bachelor's degree in business or science provided many attractive opportunities. Many students who might have preferred graduate education in the humanities and social sciences also learned that college teaching jobs had diminished sharply with declining birth rates and economic decline of the states during the 1970s. So, instead of seeking M.A.s and Ph.D.s in political science, sociology, and related fields, many social science graduates looked to the law schools as providing better career opportunities. Although many law graduates find the road to a good job very tough and crowded, it seems to provide a better chance than the alternatives.

*Women and Minorities*    Law school has been especially attractive to women and nonwhites, groups which in the past rarely went to law school. Along with other opportunities that have opened in the period of equal rights and affirmative action, law is seen as a path to a professional career which previously was not available.

In 1970, there were only 800 female law students in the entire country. By 1980, 30 percent of all law students were women, and by the mid-1980s, this percentage had increased to 35 percent. These figures parallel a dramatic increase in the number of female lawyers. In 1970, female lawyers were fewer than 3 percent of the total, or about 9900 lawyers. By 1980, their number had increased to over 44,000, in 1984 to 83,000, and by the close of the 1980s, to nearly 140,000 or 20 percent of the total.[33]

More Blacks and Hispanics also have attended law school since the 1970s, but fewer than 4 percent of all lawyers are nonwhite: approximately 14,500 Blacks and 13,750 Hispanics.[34] Nonwhites are disproportionately poor, and fewer of them can afford tuition and living expenses to carry them through 3 years of law school. Some scholarships help outstanding minorities, but there is not much money to go around. Minorities also often are handicapped by poor quality early education and are less likely to gain admittance and to be able to graduate. Recently, the number of nonwhite law students has been declining, due largely to the inability of the poor to pay for law school, but also because fewer Blacks are attending college.[35]

## Early Legal Education

Today's legal profession is a different world from law in the 1800s. Many of the colonies had banned the practice of law (Chapter 2).[36] Jealous of their political control and motivated by religious dogma that held the Bible aloft as the only true and necessary law, many early colonial leaders feared and resented possible competition from lawyers. To be a lawyer meant that a man had to be able to read and write and to understand documents. Such knowledge could be dangerous to established authority. Lawyers might be an outside force for change and disruption, and they were not worth the risk.

Lawyers also were resisted because many of the colonists had fled England to escape debt collection, criminal prosecution, and other legal harassment from government and business. Lawyers were the agents of business and government and were not welcome in the new world.

However, as discussed earlier, the practice of law became inevitable as commerce and trade with Europe grew and people increasingly needed legal contracts and other documents and relied on prior court decisions to govern their transactions. Lawyers had to be tolerated and accepted. But colonial leaders also tried to control them as much as possible. Political power in the colonies was monopolized by educated and wealthy business and property owners and large planters, and they sought to control who and how people became lawyers.

The wealthy sometimes sent their sons to England to learn law. There were no formal law schools as we have today, but young men could associate with English lawyers, read cases, and study informally so that they became familiar with law. They returned to work for their family business and perhaps the businesses of friends and associates.

**Apprenticeships**    The most common way of learning law was through an apprentice system in which young men worked as clerks or assistants for other lawyers and hoped to pick up enough practical law to go out on their own. A clerk or apprentice became a lawyer by appearing before a local judge who had the authority to determine who was prepared and fit to practice law. The judge would ask the apprentice a few questions, satisfying himself that the fledging lawyer knew something about law, and the odds were good he would be allowed to call himself a lawyer. In the earliest days this was a fairly effective way of controlling who became a lawyer, since apprentices worked under older lawyers and were admitted to law practice by judges who generally represented the educated and propertied class.

The system was not foolproof, however, for as the number of lawyers increased, they were less easy to control and keep track of, and others who had learned a little law or had a natural knack for business and negotiation also offered themselves as lawyers, sometimes representing individuals who could not hire the official court-approved attorneys.

The apprentice system was the dominant way that people became lawyers until the early 1900s. However, the idea of formal law school training began in the early 1800s and grew out of the early apprentice system. Some lawyers rarely gave their apprentices much time or opportunity to learn law, but others liked teaching and attracted many apprentices and charged fees for a fundamental legal education.

**Formal Education**    The main shift in legal training occurred in 1870, when Harvard University created a law school and a particular type of education that continues to be the model for American legal education.[37] Instead of work-study arrangements in the old apprentice system or straight lectures, Harvard Law School created the technique of organizing sets of casebooks which focused on particular areas of law, such as contracts or criminal law, which students would read and study, searching for the guiding legal principles set down in appellate court decisions. The cases were arranged to take students from basic legal principles to more complex and varied circumstances in order to lay out the core of a particular body of law, much the way that constitutional law casebooks are used in political science classes.

Law classes consisted of question-and-answer sessions in which law professors called on various students to state the major principles of the case and to elaborate on the possible applications and expansion of the law for related situations. It is the general technique used today in most law schools.

**Changing the Profession**   The establishment of Harvard Law School and others which followed it were designed to *upgrade legal training*—to make law more a profession than a trade that could be picked up while clerking in a lawyer's office. No longer could anyone with a little practical experience easily pass as a lawyer.

However, raising educational standards had two additional effects. First, the advocates of formal law school education argued convincingly that *law was a science* that required specialized research and training that could only be done in a university setting. Law would be set apart from the rest of society, politics, and everyday life with new law professors dissecting court cases to discover legal principles that controlled particular types of situations. Soon, understanding law would be out of the reach of ordinary people.

Requiring a law school education also *limited access to the law profession* and channeled people into different kinds of legal careers. Generally, it ensured that only respectable and upright members of society—which usually meant mostly white Anglo-Saxon Protestant men from prominent and wealthy families—went to Harvard or similar prestigious law schools and took their expected places in the ranks of the largest, most prestigious corporate law firms in New York, Chicago, and other cities.

Social exclusion was rampant in the late 1800s and early 1900s, the period when millions of immigrants—mostly Catholics, Jews, Irish, Italians, eastern and southern Europeans, and Russians—came to the United States to escape poverty and persecution and to seek their fortune and a better life. Lawyers were not immune from national alarm about the impact of so many new and different people on American institutions and society, and they created new bar associations to regulate and uplift law practice and to protect their social, economic, and political supremacy.

Shortly after the founding of the American Bar Association in 1878, a new Association of American Law Schools (AALS) formed to include the most reputable law schools and to exclude night and part-time schools which catered mainly to immigrant law students who could not get into the prestigious schools or could not afford full-time law school. By today's standards, association-membership requirements are the absolute minimum we would expect, but in the early 1900s, they were astounding. Only law schools which required a high school diploma for entrance and a 2-year and later a 3-year program of law study could join. By the 1920s, some college experience was required for law school admission.

In time, attending a law school not accredited by the AALS carried a stigma that was hard to shake and limited a young lawyer's opportunities. By the 1900s, a clear distinction between high-status, prestigious law training and inferior, night law school was set.[38]

### Law School

Legal education has changed tremendously since the turn of the century. Bias against religious and ethnic minorities is largely gone, and applicants with superior qualifications and the means to pay the tuition have a chance of admission to a prestigious law school. The number and variety of law schools also have increased, especially through the creation of many state public university law schools.

Today, good law schools include a variety of nonprofit private colleges as well as many state universities. National and Ivy League law schools, including Harvard, Yale, Columbia, Chicago, Stanford, and a few others, are at the top. A close second group includes a few prominent state university law schools which offer a nationally oriented education, taking students beyond the limits of their own state. These schools include the University of California at Berkeley, Wisconsin, and Michigan. A third and much larger group of law schools includes the state universities and regionally prominent private schools. Still at the bottom are urban, proprietary (for profit), and night schools.

**Functions**   There are two general functions that law schools perform. First, law school provides the basics of a legal education and prepares new lawyers to make it on their own—to give them the fundamental tools to do law work. A second purpose of law school is to transform college graduates into law professionals who approach problems from a legal perspective and who adopt the core values of the law profession and its major clientele. The two goals are closely related.

The first year of law school is crammed with required basic courses and hard work learning how to approach problems from the legal rather than the philosophical, moral, or personal point of view. It often is called *learning to think like a lawyer*. Students have a dual task of learning the basics of law as well as shifting their own past orientations to the formal legal approach. Students are encouraged to think objectively about what the law requires in a particular situation rather than what they personally think is right or just.

Required classes include civil procedure (getting civil cases through the courts), constitutional law, criminal law and procedure, contract law, property law, torts (primarily damage suits and liability), and legal writing and research. The first-year classes in particular are conducted according to some variation of the classic Socratic dialogue. The professor poses a hypothetical legal problem or refers to a particular case and calls on a student to explain how the conflict should be settled according to law. An answer generates another question, and the process continues until the student has satisfied the professor or has given up and another classmate is put on the grill.

In the second and third years, students are required to complete additional hours for law school graduation, but nearly all the courses are electives that students may select at their own discretion according to their perceptions of what will be most useful to them. However, of the dozens of courses listed in most law school catalogs, about half deal directly with business or financial problems. A scattering of other advanced courses deal with criminal justice, family law, tenants' and borrowers' rights, legal history, international law, and others. Clearly, the business of law school is business.

*Business Law*   Law schools put heavy premiums on business law, with relatively little emphasis on other areas such as consumer law, civil rights, or environmental law. The major thrust is learning the basics of business problems and serving business clients.

The power of the business-oriented law school curriculum is mirrored in the attitudes and career expectations of most law students. Many students, perhaps as many as 50 percent, enter law school with the ideal that they will eventually do at least some public interest (*pro bono*) law work, such as that championed by Ralph Nader and others who claim to represent the broad general public and most consumers rather than narrow specialized business interests. *Pro bono* work is considered valuable to society generally and an attractive way to use a legal education.

However, the law school experience tends to erode these expectations. The curriculum and methods of teaching lead students away from thinking about values and social policies toward abstract legal analysis in which they learn specific rules that govern narrow legal situations. They have a tendency to become oriented to technical approaches rather than broader social interest points of view. Second, few, if any, required law courses focus on the public interest sector, conveying the silent message that it is not very important— certainly not important for graduation or for passing the state bar examination.

Economic laws also affect student orientations. All want to make a decent living and many aspire to riches. While they may have liked the idea of doing public interest work, they learn through faculty attitudes and cues, from the curriculum, and from other students that there are very few job opportunities in that field and that the pay is low. Consequently, many law students begin to adopt conventional business and law firm attitudes by the time they are in their third year, giving up many of their loftier goals of doing good works.[39]

**Case Method**   The law school curriculum and teaching methods have been heavily criticized in recent years by some students and faculty who object to the rigid casebook and class recitation method.[40] In their view, the question-and-answer sessions are demeaning games in which a few eager and competitive students excel while most others wait apathetically for professors to announce correct answers.

Most important, critics fear that the case method and the content of a law school education are irrelevant because they treat law as a world apart rather than an integral aspect of economics, politics, and culture. The bigger questions of how law relates to society are largely ignored. Students also learn little about how they actually will need to operate as a lawyer or what forces produce law or how law is used to change society.

Complaints about law school curriculum and student behavior have been made not only about state universities, which mainly prepare students to practice law in their own states, but about the most prestigious national law schools as well. The old-fashioned and impractical curriculum has been blamed mostly on tradition and faculty reluctance to change from the venerated Harvard model.

Increasingly, however, newer law faculty call for innovative courses that link law to other academic disciplines, such as economics and philosophy, and to real-world social concerns. Others call for new clinical courses that teach lawyers practical skills needed for successful negotiation, work for legislative committees, judicial administration, etc. But conflicts continue among faculty and administrators about which approach is most appropriate for the law schools of the future.[41]

*Bar exams*   The issue is further complicated by the conflicting pressure of state bar examinations. Many law schools are preoccupied with getting their students through the state bar examination, which places heavy emphasis on the first-year core courses. Many law firms also reportedly hire new graduates on the basis of their performance during their first year when they must do well in tough core courses. Finally, some students probably have become so accustomed to standardized and short-answer examinations from their earlier education that they are reluctant to take "impractical" or non-nuts-and-bolts courses such as legal history, law and social change, or public interest law.

But even if law school faculty and deans wished to change, they face other serious problems. Many prospective students evaluate law schools partly on the basis of how many graduates pass the bar exam, and schools with high pass rates are anxious to provide that information. State departments of education and legislatures also become suspicious of professional programs in public state-supported universities if their graduates fail to pass state licensing examinations. They frequently believe that money is being wasted if it does not produce clear, measurable success, as on an examination. Therefore, it is very difficult for most schools to radically change the law school curriculum or for students to stop giving their undivided attention to passing crucial examinations.

## Admission to the Bar

After completing 3 years of law study, students must pass a standardized state bar examination before being licensed to practice law. The exam is very long and usually is given over two days. Like many other exams students have taken in the past, it is composed of multiple-choice questions and a small amount of essay writing. In many states, the exam has three parts. The first tests students on their state's constitutional law and legal procedure and other material usually covered in the first year. The second part is standardized in over three-quarters of the states and covers similar basic material that is common in most of the states. It also deals mainly with civil, criminal, and business law. The third part covers legal and judicial ethics. Increased national standardization in the bar examination is the growing trend.

Many students take additional cram courses which fill them with minute detail and specific answers needed to get past this last major hurdle to law practice. Students at the national law schools, which do not concentrate so heavily on legal basics, are especially attracted to the cram courses as necessary insurance that they are ready for their state's bar exam.

In a few states, as many as half of all applicants fail the exam. However, pass rates in the 70 and 80 percent range are common. If students fail any of the three parts of the exam, they may retake that part within a certain period, often 2 years or more. Should they fail to pass all three parts within that period, they must retake the entire examination. There are plenty of opportunities to pass the examination, and the odds are good that anyone who persists will finally pass.

The final hurdle for a new lawyer is a "morals check." State boards of bar examiners require applicants to complete a very lengthy questionnaire listing past employers, credit references, personal references, criminal offenses, experience with alcohol or drug abuse, medical treatment, military service, and other information. The board contacts most or all of the references and checks with the FBI.

Usually, the only defect which automatically excludes an applicant is a felony conviction, but other problems such as recent substance abuse or a string of juvenile arrests will generate a more in-depth investigation and possibly a hearing. However, probably no more than one-half of 1 percent of all applicants are refused admission to the bar because of morals problems. For most applicants, filling out the lengthy application and remembering a long list of past contacts and references is the most difficult part of the process.

## ALL LAWYERS ARE NOT CREATED EQUAL

The practice of law is a public profession, meaning that anyone who obtains the necessary credentials can become a lawyer and do law work. However, the odds of becoming a lawyer are heavily weighted in favor of the middle and upper classes. Opportunities usually are limited to those who have developed strong education and career motivations and who can pay for college. Consequently, few people from poor and nonwhite families become lawyers.

While mostly middle-class white men and women become lawyers, there is additional social stratification within the bar. White, Anglo-Saxon Protestant lawyers are much more likely to find work in large firms and handle the legal business of big corporations and the wealthy, while minorities are most likely to end up as solo practitioners and deal with the problems of individuals. The firm depicted in *L.A. Law,* with its motley crew of white male Protestant, black, female, Hispanic, and Jewish attorneys, who handle criminal and divorce cases, as well as big-business legal matters, is *not* a typical big-city law firm.

### Roots of Stratification

An important reason for social stratification among lawyers is the close link between law practice and clients discussed at the beginning of this chapter, and the carryover of law into other social, economic, and political life. Law is not like medicine or dentistry, where a gall bladder or cavity is much the same in each patient. In medicine and dentistry relationships between professional and client (patient) are short-term and specific; they do not relate to other areas of a client's life. Doctors and dentists also possess precise, identifiable technical skills that are highly valued in themselves apart from the religion or social origins of the professional who practices those skills.[42] In contrast, law is a much more fluid profession where a lawyer's skills in business law often are very difficult to separate from his or her personal contacts, social status, and values. For business clients and wealthy individuals, relationships with lawyers also often last for many years and may affect a wide range of financial and possibly political activities. Such individuals prefer lawyers who are like themselves. Low-status lawyers have no high-status contacts and represent clients who pose a direct threat to social, economic, and political elites. They have always been viewed with suspicion by lawyers who head bar associations and who have prestigious positions in business and law.[43]

**Early Discrimination** Most contemporary discrimination dates from the late nineteenth century. Two related forces were at work in the country. As discussed earlier, millions of new non-English-speaking immigrants threatened the social status quo, and many sought to enter law practice as one way of improving their lot in life. In the 1900s, the threat from Germany and World War I and the communist revolution in Russia also generated fear and intense nationalism in a nation that had remained largely free from foreign wars and involvement.

A flood of patriotic, antiforeign fervor swept the country, often with white, Anglo-Saxon Protestant lawyers at the leadership. They frequently saw their role as keeping America pure and free from foreign influence and protecting American government and free enterprise from foreign ideas. They clearly saw law as a crucial part of maintaining the framework of American society. At the extreme end, Pennsylvania enacted a law requiring that only lawyers who could demonstrate that they were the grandsons of native-born Americans could practice law. Most other states settled for other more subtle ways to limit access to the bar, often requiring new lawyers to obtain employment as apprentice-like clerks with established lawyers for several years before they could be admitted to the bar. Naturally, many new immigrant lawyers could not find jobs.

Law schools also discriminated. Established, accredited law schools (and other professional schools as well) kept the number of Jewish students low by limiting the number who could enroll.[44] Throughout this period, women usually were not admitted to any law schools and blacks were prevented from enrolling in the south.

**Current Discrimination**   The remnants of past discrimination continue in many American cities. Numerous studies of lawyers in New York, Chicago, Detroit, and several other large northern cities consistently show that Protestant lawyers are much more likely to practice in large law firms which handle the business of corporations and the wealthy, while Catholic and Jewish lawyers are most likely to be solo practitioners handling divorces, criminal defense, and other personal business for individuals.

The most prestigious and best-paying sources of law practice are much less available to these groups.[45] Certainly, there are exceptions. Some Catholic and Jewish lawyers are members of large, prestigious firms, but their chances are considerably smaller than those of Protestant lawyers with Anglo-Saxon backgrounds.

The path to a particular law practice begins with a lawyer's early personal biography. Students from high-status, wealthy, Protestant families whose fathers are lawyers or self-employed professionals are most likely to gain admittance (and be able to pay the fees) of elite and other high-status private law schools. The large business-oriented law firms usually recruit people only from these schools and, most important, are likely to look at graduates who have the same personal background characteristics as most other lawyers in the firm and of the clients the firm represents. Even when minority students do attend a prestigious school and graduate near or at the top of the class, their chances of being recruited by a top firm are small. Thus, high status selects high status and the firm perpetuates itself.

Many minority lawyers and others who do not make it into the legal big time gravitate toward small partnerships or solo practices where they have a general or "personal plight" law practice. They also are very likely to remain in the same kind of law work and similar type of employment. Less than 5 percent of lawyers who start out in solo practice ever become members of a large law firm.[46] A few might find better jobs in government and small local firms or as house counsel to various businesses, but they are cut off from the elite law practice in the large cities.

This kind of selection process often is labeled ascriptive rather than achievement recruitment because it is based heavily on the inborn personal attributes of individuals rather than on their demonstrated skills and accomplishments. This does not mean that the lawyers hired by the big firms have been recruited only because of their personal pedigree. The ones selected for the top firms have excelled in law school and scholastically are a cut above the rest of their class. But it does mean that opportunities for other groups who are similary qualified are sharply reduced.

*Extent of Stratification*   It is difficult to determine how common this pattern of lawyer selection is throughout the United States. Most research on this issue reaches similar conclusions, but the studies mainly have examined the biggest northern cities where there are large concentrations of ethnic groups and histories of ethnic politics and sharp social divisions.

New York and Chicago, for example, have large concentrations of Catholics and Jews and many ethnic neighborhoods. Historically, ethnic lawyers in these and similar cities were the main targets of alarmist lawyers and local business elites. Patterns of close ethnic association and ethnic cohesion in local politics still are important in many large northern cities and carry over into the social structure of local bar politics and the recruitment of lawyers.

A national study of lawyers in a variety of large and small cities and towns does not reveal such sharp social divisions among lawyers. Religion, for example, does not account for the kind of work that lawyers do or the type of employment they obtain.[47] It suggests that different cities and perhaps regions of the country have distinctive histories and traditions and respond differently to social forces.

It is likely that cities with few minorities and no history of religious-based politics more easily absorb and integrate minorities into the social fabric of the city and encourage wider access to a variety of professional contacts. Possibly the legal professions of Atlanta, Tucson, Orlando, Albuquerque, and other cities place less emphasis on personal and law school pedigrees. Certainly, many lawyers in these cities have not attended prestigious national law schools, most likely because they are too far from home. Instead, they have graduated from the state universities and have opted to stay in their home state to practice law. Consequently, there may be fewer social differences among many lawyers throughout much of the nation. But more case studies are needed before we can be sure.

Most of what we know about lawyers also is based on male lawyers and religious minorities, groups on which there are enough historical data and sufficient numbers on which to do research. We know very little about female lawyers or about how blacks and Chicanos fare in the south and southwest. It would be a good bet, however, that relatively few nonwhites end up in corporate law practice. Part of the problem probably is simple racial discrimination, but since law work is very client-centered, white corporate law firms are probably reluctant to recruit racial minorities who have very little in common with other lawyers or other business clientele.

## Women in Law Firms

As we have seen, the number of female lawyers is increasing rapidly, and many of them attend and excel at top law schools and are recruited by the most prestigious big-city law firms. Nevertheless, there is some evidence that women do not do very well in the big firms. As many as 30 to 40 percent of the lawyers in big-city law firms are women, but only a few, usually less than 5 to 7 percent, become partners. (Partners are senior lawyers who are asked to stay on indefinitely, receive a share of the profits, rather than only a salary, and help to determine the firm's future directon.)

Things began to improve for women in the 1980s, when many more entered law school and professional practice. A female associate in a large Atlanta law firm also won a U.S. Supreme Court case, permitting women to sue over alleged law firm job discrimination.[48] Nevertheless, despite the increase in the number of female lawyers, women continue to find it more difficult than their male counterparts to establish themselves in big-time law practice.

A number of reasons have been offered to explain why women do not make it big in the prestigious law firms. One explanation is that it still is a man's world and male partners and clients stereotype women as being incapable of closing the big deal or holding onto business. Women also are frozen out of informal male socializing.

But recent studies of several state court systems, including New York and New Jersey, strongly suggest that simple bias also is involved and that some male judges and lawyers harass and disparage female attorneys.[49] However, some senior partners counter that women do not give the same 100 percent-plus commitment that young men give to the firm.

Conflicts between career and family interfere with sticking to a long and demanding schedule, and many women want time off for maternity leave or to care for sick children. While these needs are understandable—and are increasingly likely to be granted by law firms—male partners believe that such needs interfere with the goals of a hard-driving law firm that demands complete dedication from its employees.

Perhaps this also explains why female attorneys are more likely to be single, divorced, and without children.[50] Those desiring a full family life either drop out of law practice after a few years, or take somewhat less demanding jobs as corporate or government lawyers. An additional recent development is the so-called part-time mommy track, in which women lawyers with families work as staff attorneys for large law firms, but explicitly with no hope or expectation of becoming partners. Nevertheless, part-time often means working from 8:00 to 5:00, forty hours per week. Full-time means being available at all times to handle pressing legal problems.[51]

### CONCLUSION

Law and lawyers are involved in most aspects of modern life. Any private dispute, disagreement on government policy, or conflict in social values can be translated into a legal issue with lawyers taking any side of an argument. Lawyers also are essential in practically all complex business transactions or in personal financial and some family decisions.

Since law is practiced on behalf of any side in a case or for any cause or position, the law profession is split into a number of specialized subgroups. Unlike most other professions, lawyers are closely tied to particular types of clients and they usually represent the same kinds of economic and social interests over and over again. Legal battles also move easily into other realms of politics, with lawyers taking different sides to protect the interests they represent. Therefore, it is impossible to separate law practice from the larger social context in which it takes place.

Specialization and client-centered law practice are closely linked to legal education and the social divisions among lawyers. Higher standards for legal education and admission to the bar improved the quality of law practice, but they also reduced opportunities for many people to become lawyers. Prestige and quality differences among the law schools ensure that certain favored groups have more access to prestigious legal work. Those without the best grades and prestigious degrees and lacking other desirable personal backgrounds discover that many doors are closed to them, leaving most to work at the less prestigious and desirable types of law practice.

Although opportunities are greater for some lawyers than for others, big-business lawyers in the largest cities are not the only ones with successful law careers. As mentioned earlier, in most smaller cities, it is impossible to specialize in corporate law because there are not many corporations.

American life is sufficiently diverse that there are many career opportunities. Many lawyers work for national, state, or local governments, and others are extremely successful and financially secure with personal injury law, labor law, local real estate, and small business practices. In every state capital there also are large numbers of lawyers who work as lobbyists, representing business groups and others before state legislatures and administrative agencies. Other law graduates use their law degrees for other business or political careers.

And, of course, most lawyers do not go about worrying about their prestige and social status. They are busy doing their legal work, earning a living, and interacting with others in their local legal system.

## SUGGESTIONS FOR ADDITIONAL READING

Abel, Richard L.: "The Transformation of the American Legal Profession," *Law and Society Review*, 20 (1986), 1–17. Abel's article is an insightful examination of recent changes in the social structure and the practice of law in the United States.

Auerbach, Jerold S.: *Unequal Justice* (London: Oxford University Press, 1976). This book links the history of the legal profession to major social change in the United States. It examines how the organized bar and its leaders responded and attempted to shape American life.

Heinz, John P., and Edward O. Laumann: *Chicago Lawyers* (New York and Chicago: Russell Sage Foundation and American Bar Foundation, 1982). This is a carefully done study which explores the social organization of law work in a large city. Emphasis is on variations in legal specialization and divisions within the bar.

Wishman, Seymour: *Confessions of a Criminal Lawyer* (New York: Penguin Books, 1981). Although this is not a scholarly study, Wishman writes forcefully about his personal experiences as a defense lawyer and the conflicts between his duty to represent his clients and ethical obligations to society.

## NOTES

1 Barbara A. Curran, "American Lawyers in the 1980's," *Law and Society Review*, 20 (1986), 29.
2 John P. Heinz and Edward O. Laumann, *Chicago Lawyers* (New York and Chicago: Russell Sage Foundation and American Bar Foundation, 1982), p. 43.
3 The following is based on Heinz and Laumann, p. 51 and chap. 3.
4 Donald D. Landon, "LaSalle Street and Main Street: The Role of Context in Structuring Law Practice," *Law and Society Review* 22 (1988), 213–236.
5 *Lawyer's Almanac* (Englewood Cliffs, N. J.: Prentice Hall Law and Business, 1991), pp. 166–167; *National Law Journal*, June 3, 1991, S12; *Official Guide to U.S. Law Schools* (Newtown, PA: Law School Admission Service, 1991).
6 Paul B. Wice, *Criminal Lawyers* (Beverly Hills, Calif.: Sage Publications, 1978), p. 109; and Landon, 1988, p. 233.
7 Harry L. Hathaway, "Fueling the Fires of Discontent," *Los Angeles Lawyer*, December, 1989, 5.
8 Richard A. Watson and Rondal G. Downing, *The Politics of the Bench and the Bar* (New York: John Wiley & Sons, Inc., 1969).
9 *The New York Times*, March 31 and April 29, 1986, p. 1.
10 Jerold S. Auerbach, *Unequal Justice* (London: Oxford University Press, 1976), pp. 45–53.
11 Heinz Eulau and John D. Sprague, *Lawyers in Politics* (New York: The Bobbs-Merrill Co., 1964), pp. 26–27; David R. Derge, "The Lawyer as Decision-Maker in the American State Legislature," *Journal of Politics*, 21 (1959), 408–433; David Brady et al., "House Lawyers and Support for the Supreme Court," *Journal of Politics*, 35 (1973), 724–729; and Frederick D. Herzon, "Ideology, Constraint, and Public Opinion: The Case of Lawyers," *American Journal of Political Science*, 24 (1980), 233–258.
12 Robert L. Kidder, *Connecting Law and Society* (Englewood Cliffs, N.J.: Prentice Hall, Inc., 1983), p. 228.
13 Herbert Jacob, *Justice in America*, 4th ed. (Boston: Little, Brown and Co., 1984), p. 63.
14 *Tallahassee Democrat*, November 28, 1984, p. 1.
15 *New York Times*, October 12, 1990, p. B11.
16 Richard L. Abel, "The Transformation of the American Legal Profession," *Law and Society Review*, 20 (1986), 7–17.
17 Frances Kahn Zemans, "The Legal Profession and Legal Ethics," in *Encyclopedia of the American Legal System*, ed. Robert J. Janosik (New York: Charles Scribners' Sons, 1988), vol. 2, pp. 635–642.
18 *New York Times*, July 24, 1991, p. 1.
19 *New York Times*, March 21, 1988, p. 30 and June 30, 1989, p. 20.
20 Susan E. Lawrence, *The Poor in Court* (Princeton: Princeton University Press, 1990), p. 20; Auerbach, pp. 55–62.
21 Ibid., pp. 34–38.
22 Roger Billings, "Legal Services," in *Encyclopedia of the American Judicial System*, ed. Robert J. Janosik (New York: Charles Scribners' Sons, 1987), vol. 2, pp. 644–652.
23 *New York Times*, September 8, 1989, p. 20.
24 Mark Kessler, "The Politics of Legal Representation: The Influence of Local Politics on the Behavior of Poverty Lawyers," *Law and Policy Review* 8 (1986),

149–167; Mark Kessler, "Legal Mobilization for Social Reform: Power and the Politics of Agenda Setting," *Law and Society Review* 24 (1990), 121–143; Richard L. Abel, "Lawyers and the Power to Change," *Law and Policy Review* 7 (1985), 5–18; *New York Times*, July 1, 1986, p. 11.

25  Zemans, pp. 638–642.

26  *New York Times*, August 9, 1991, p. B7.

27  *New York Times*, January 23, 1990, p. A16.

28  *New York Times*, June 14, 1991, p. B9.

29  The following relies on Curran, pp. 19–25, and Terence C. Halliday, "Six Score Years and Ten: Demographic Transitions in the American Legal Profession, 1850–1980," *Law and Society Review*, 20 (1986), 53–78.

30  *Statistical Abstract of the United States* (Washington, D.C., 1990).

31  *Statistical Abstract of the United States* (Washington, D.C., 1986).

32  *New York Times*, March 3, 1989, p. 21.

33  Curran, p. 25, and *Statistical Abstract*, 1986 and 1990.

34  *Statistical Abstract*, 1990.

35  *New Jersey Lawyer*, December 2, 1987, p. 1.

36  See the detailed discussion in Lawrence M. Friedman, *A History of American Law* (New York: Simon and Schuster, 1973), pp. 81–88.

37  Lawrence M. Friedman, *American Law* (New York: W.W. Norton and Co., 1984), pp. 241–243. See also Robert Stevens, *Law School; Legal Education in America from the 1850s to the 1980s* (Chapel Hill: University of North Carolina Press, 1983).

38  Auerbach, pp. 87–101.

39  Howard S. Erlanger and Douglas A. Klegon, "Socialization Effects of Professional School," *Law and Society Review*, 13 (1978), 11–35; Robert V. Stover, "The Importance of Economic Supply in Determining the Size and Quality of the Public Interest Bar," *Law and Society Review*, 16 (1981–82), 455–480; and Robert V. Stover, "Law School and Professional Responsibility," *Judicature*, 66 (1982), 194–206.

40  David Margolick, "The Trouble With America's Law Schools," *The New York Times Magazine,* May 22, 1983, pp. 20–38.

41  *National Law Journal*, January 9, 1989, pp. 1.

42  Kidder, p. 228.

43  Auerbach, chap. 4.

44  *Ibid.,* pp. 125–126.

45  Jerome Carlin, *Lawyers on Their Own* (New Brunswick, N.J.: Rutgers University Press, 1962); Jack Ladinsky, "Careers of Lawyers, Law Practice and Legal Institutions," *American Sociological Review*, 28 (1963), 47–54; and Heinz and Laumann.

46  Heinz and Laumann, p. 195.

47  Howard S. Erlanger, "The Allocation of Status within Occupations: The Case of the Legal Profession," *Social Forces*, 58 (1980), 882–903.

48  *Newsweek*, June 4, 1984, p. 85.

49  *The New York Times*, April 20, 1986, p. 1; William Eich, "Gender Bias in the Courtroom," *Judicature*, 69 (1986), 339–343.

50  *New York Times*, December 23, 1988, p. 21; February 12, 1988, p. 14.

51  *New York Times*, August 8, 1988, p. 1.

# 4

# CHOOSING JUDGES

Except for the political conflict that sometimes occurs with the selection of a new justice for the Supreme Court, most Americans pay very little attention to the choice of judges. According to levels of voter turnout, for example, many judicial elections are no more important than voting for tax collector or registrar of voters. Judicial elections usually are such mild and formal affairs that many voters actually are unaware that an election has occurred.

The appointment of a new federal judge also may receive only a formal announcement in the local newspaper after the nominee has been confirmed. Neither instance is considered especially hot news, or even a human interest story, since so little conflict or passion is involved. Yet, when most of us think about courts and politics, how judges get into office is likely to be one of the specific connections that come to mind.

While it occasionally attracts news attention, judicial decorum and political insulation of the courts wrap judicial selection in the cloak of the law and soften its apparent partisan or public connections. Most of us have come to expect this kind of judicial ''nonpolitics,'' but making selection invisible also has its own special political impact. It muffles conflict, avoids widespread competition, and strengthens the hands of political elites. Legislators, governors, Presidents, and political party and interest group leaders frequently control most aspects of judicial recruitment.

The selection of judges also interests judicial reformers (Chapter 2), who believe that changes are needed to ensure that qualified and nonpartisan lawyers are put on the courts. Merit selection is one of the key features of judicial reform and mirrors concerns from the legal culture about the qualifications of judges and the qualities of the selection process.

This chapter deals with concerns that reformers have about the qualifications of judges as decision makers and the effect of popular political culture on staffing the courts. The two often are in conflict. Later, we will look at the effect of judicial selection systems, partisanship, and other factors on judges' decisions (Chapter 9).

All of these questions concern the effect of merit selection in judicial politics. To deal with them completely requires understanding how all selection systems operate. Whether changes in methods of recruitment are desirable involves political and personal choices, but such choices can and should be based upon informed views of the judicial process.

## ISSUES AND GOALS IN JUDICIAL SELECTION

Judicial selection is important to many political groups and individuals, but often for conflicting reasons. Frequently, disagreement over the selection of judges is expressed in terms of *judicial accountability versus judicial independence*.[1] Accountability calls mainly for judicial elections to make judges responsive to the will of the people. Judicial independence reflects the legal culture and calls for different recruitment methods, particularly merit selection, which insulate judges so that they can make decisions objectively and free from external pressures. But, judicial selection also involves *personal and partisan objectives* as well.

### Personal and Partisan Goals and Accountability

**Personal Goals**   There are over 1000 federal and nearly 30,000 state judges in the United States.[2] Salaries range upwards to $50,000 and $60,000 for many trial courts and even higher for the appellate courts. While these are not high compared with the six-figure incomes of the partners in some large law firms, most lawyers find these salaries attractive. Most important, unlike most other political jobs, a judgeship is a very secure position and perhaps the most prestigious an indiviual could hope to achieve. Many lawyers aspire to them.

Because they are attractive government positions, political parties use them frequently for rewarding their most active supporters (*patronage*). Because many states have more judgeships than legislators, there are many opportunities to reward the party faithful. State and federal judges often have participated previously in party politics and have held previous government positions. Many have "earned" their appointments to the courts.

**Support and Representation**   Besides interest in patronage, awarding judgeships sometimes involves building political support for other, nonjudicial policies and cementing broad political coalitions for future elections. For example, even though a governor can appoint judges without legislative approval, certain legislators may be permitted to pick judges for vacancies in their own legislative district. This creates goodwill and political obligations.

In a similar way, a governor or President may appoint members of certain social or economic groups to judgeships in an explicit attempt to win group approval and votes at election time. Such appointments also enable minorities to gain group representation and a share of prestigious political positions. During his first presidential campaign, President Carter promised to appoint more women and blacks to federal judgeships, positions historically dominated by white men. The replacement of retiring Justice Thurgood Marshall with Judge Clarence Thomas by President George Bush also signifies the presence of a black seat on the U.S. Supreme Court and recognition of blacks in American politics. Such appointments provide tangible rewards to very few individuals, but filling positions this way provides symbolic recognition and stature to these groups and encourages their support for the President.

Judicial elections also make it possible for particular groups to elect their own to the courts. However, as will be discussed shortly, blacks and Hispanics have found it difficult to elect their choice of judges.

**Accountability**   The selection of judges also is important because of its implications in judicial policymaking. Whether social scientists compile statistics in order to compare the backgrounds of many judges, or politicians review their list of candidates for a single vacancy, the questions they have in mind are roughly the same: Will judges with certain backgrounds and experiences tend to favor particular groups in court, and what policies are they likely to adopt to deal with various issues such as abortion, discrimination, crime, divorce, and other problems.

Is there Democratic and Republican justice? Will a trial judge from a business-oriented law firm be sympathetic to environmental protection and careful land use planning? Will a black judge be more lenient toward criminal defendants, many of whom are poor and nonwhite? A possible list of guesses about the effect of judges' backgrounds on decisions might be as long as the number of different cases. By electing or appointing judges with different personal backgrounds, judges theoretically are made accountable to the people. Judges' decisions are expected to reflect their backgrounds and attitudes and the values of the people who selected them for the courts.

### Judicial Independence

In contrast with the personal and partisan goals and accountability in judicial selection, judicial reformers emphasize judicial independence and the ideal role of judges. Their goals reflect maximizing the influence of the legal culture in judicial selection.

Role refers to expectations that judges and others have of how judges *ought* to behave in decision making as well as in their own personal conduct.[3] The conduct of judicial selection reveals that we often expect judges to be involved in partisan or popular politics in order to get elected or appointed. However, we also expect judicial campaigns to be quiet and courteous.

But, once judges are in office, we also expect them to be above politics and beyond any suspicion of personal misconduct, and even to erase their personal attitudes and sympathies. They are to be neutral and even-tempered in decision making and should appear to be neutralized off the court by staying out of the public eye—no trips to the night club or the racetrack or gathering with old political friends at the familiar spot.

**Merit, not Politics**   Critics of judicial selection frequently argue that it is impossible to satisfy popular political and legal expectations at the same time.[4] It is impossible, they argue, to expect judges who are selected by any popular or partisan method to behave objectively on the court or without some regard for old political attachments and policy preferences. Not that judges are openly or even consciously biased by their past, but it is inevitable that if popular politics plays a major part in determining who and how an individual gets to the court, it will have an impact on how judges see the facts in cases and how they interpret the law.

Moreover, partisan selection means that past political activity will be more important than legal skill in individuals being considered for judgeships. Good judges also may be voted out of office because they fall from favor with party leaders and voters. Consequently, reformers argue, new ways of choosing judges should be adopted to ensure that judges will be fully protected from popular or partisan influence and can perform their proper role of independent decision maker in court.

Emphasis must be placed on selecting individuals with legal experience, demonstrated skills and competence, a proper judicial temperament (personality), and proper ethical and moral conduct. The methods proposed by court reformers are commonly termed *merit* or *Missouri plans* (after the first state to adopt them).

*Mechanics of Merit*   In the states, merit systems are combinations of elections and appointments and provide much greater influence for lawyers than any other method of selection.[5] They are practical attempts to combine elements of the legal and popular political cultures.

The basic idea is that the governor will appoint a judge from several lawyers recommended by a nominating panel of five or more people usually including lawyers (often selected by the local bar), nonlawyers appointed by the chief executive, and perhaps a local judge with the greatest seniority. Either by law or by agreement, the executive must appoint someone from the list of recommended candidates, thereby limiting appointment options. The panel usually may consider any number of candidates before drawing up its final list.

After serving a short period of time, usually 1 year, the appointed judge stands for a special election. The voters are asked: "Shall Judge X be retained in Office? Yes—; No—." The judge has no opposition candidate running in this election and stands on his or her own record. If approved by the voters, he or she holds office for life or for a very long term.

The main idea behind this system is that the nominating panel, composed partly of lawyers, will be more interested in the legal skills and qualifications of potential candidates than in their prior political service and political beliefs. Therefore, it assumes that better judges will be chosen, and since there is no other candidate running against the judge, voters will have to focus on whether or not the judge has been good. They will not be distracted by personalities and irrelevant political considerations. With lifetime or long-term tenure in office, judges will be independent from outside pressure and able to make decisions required by law and the facts, not by popular politics.

*Most Favored*   The odds are overwhelming that any state that decides to change its method of choosing judges will move to the Missouri plan, not to any other selection system.[6] President Jimmy Carter also used a version of the plan to select some federal judges.

Shifting from traditional popular and partisan methods to merit plans usually requires approval by the other branches of government as well as state constitutional amendment. It also raises fundamental debate about the right of the people to select judges themselves, the proper role of judges, and the impact that changes probably will have on the political power of parties, governors, bar associations, and other interest groups that typically want to share in the plums of judicial politics.

The role lawyers should have in selecting judges is a critical issue, since their participation symbolizes and represents legal culture in judicial selection. Their influence in the politics of courts suggests a corresponding decline in the power of political parties, voters, and other competing groups that represent the idea of popular political culture in the judiciary.

Numerous issues are involved in this conflict. Should lawyers, as a special professional group, be given an advantage over others to choose judges? Are they accurate in claiming to possess special skills and concerns about the quality of the courts? Should political parties, traditionally viewed as representative of the popular will, be excluded from choosing judges? Should the governor or President have the greatest power in choosing judges, since he or she represents an entire state or the nation? Should judges, like other officials, be held accountable to the voters in regularly scheduled elections, or should they have special insulation from public opinion?

Deciding the "best way" to choose judges is a political and personal choice, but this chapter provides information and analysis that can help each person to answer these questions individually.

## THE SELECTION OF STATE JUDGES

### Five Methods

The fifty states use five different methods to select judges. They include *partisan election, nonpartisan election, appointment by the governor, legislative appointment,* and *merit selection* (the Missouri plan). Since many states are shifting to merit selection, at least for certain courts, there is considerable variation throughout the country in specific methods used. About 40 percent of the states use more than one method. Table 4.1 presents the method of selection used in each of the fifty states.

**Historical Trends**    Methods for choosing state judges generally have been part of other major developments in state politics.[7] There also is a regional orientation to selection systems, since states within particular regions tend to copy the policy innovations of neighboring states.

A few states, most of which are in the northeast, have used gubernatorial appointment since colonial times. However, with independence, some states

**TABLE 4-1**
JUDICIAL SELECTIONS IN THE FIFTY STATES

| Partisan election | Nonpartisan election | Gubernatorial appointment | Legislative election | Merit (Missouri plans) |
|---|---|---|---|---|
| *All or most judgeships* | | | | |
| Alabama | California | Maine | South Carolina | Alaska |
| Arkansas | Florida | New Hampshire | Virginia | Arizona |
| Illinois | Georgia | New Jersey | | Colorado |
| Mississippi | Idaho | Rhode Island | | Connecticut |
| New York | Kentucky | | | Delaware |
| North Carolina | Louisiana | | | Hawaii |
| Pennsylvania | Michigan | | | Indiana |
| Tennessee | Minnesota | | | Iowa |
| Texas | Montana | | | Kansas |
| West Virginia | Nevada | | | Maryland |
| | North Dakota | | | Massachusetts |
| | Ohio[a] | | | Missouri |
| | Oklahoma | | | Nebraska |
| | Oregon | | | New Mexico |
| | South Dakota | | | Utah |
| | Washington | | | Vermont |
| | Wisconsin | | | Wyoming |
| *Some judgeships* | | | | |
| Connecticut | Arizona | Alaska | Rhode Island | Florida |
| Indiana | Utah | California | | New York |
| Kansas | Wyoming | Hawaii | | Oklahoma |
| Maine | | New York | | South Dakota |
| Maryland | | South Carolina | | Tennessee |
| Missouri | | | | Utah |
| New Jersey | | | | |
| South Carolina | | | | |
| Vermont | | | | |

[a] *Note:* Ohio uses partisan primaries, but nonpartisan general elections.
*Source:* Derived from Sara Mathias, *Electing Justice: A Handbook of Judicial Election Reforms* (Chicago: American Judicature Society, 1990), p. 142.

changed to legislative election of judges in reaction to executive authority. By the 1820s, the new states were adopting partisan election of judges as part of Jacksonian democracy to make all of government closer and more accountable to the people. Initially, many states used partisan election, but today, it predominates in the south. Nonpartisan elections became popular during the Progressive movement of the early 1900s as reformers sought to remove the influence of political parties and bosses from many state and local elections. These methods were most popular in the midwest and west.

Merit selection has been used since the 1940s, and it is the most recent innovation in state judicial selection. It also has been a more distinctive judicial issue. Judicial reformers see political parties, elections, and unlimited executive appointment as blots on judicial decision making and proper judicial conduct. Even nonpartisan elections were dismissed as an improvement since parties in many states still endorsed candidates and heavily influenced voters to cast ballots for nominees supported by party leaders.[8] Like nonpartisan elections, merit systems have been adopted most often in the midwest and west, but they also have spread to states in other regions. Most recently, several northeastern states which formerly used gubernatorial appointment have switched to merit.

**Different Behavior?**   Since their formal procedures differ, it would appear that the five selection systems would operate very differently in state politics. In partisan and nonpartisan elections, for example, voters have a direct and obvious opportunity to choose judges, and political parties would seem to be extremely powerful. In legislative and gubernatorial appointment, the focus shifts to political elites in the executive and legislative branches, and merit selection directs our attention to nominating panels composed at least partly of lawyers and judges.

A hunch that political influence and responsibility vary according to the formal requirements of selection systems seems reasonable, but the actual operation of state judicial selection can produce political surprises about who chooses judges and why, and which participants have most influence.

### Judicial Elections

Although a majority of the states use either partisan or nonpartisan elections to choose some or all of their judges, half or more of the judges in these same states actually are *not* initially elected to the courts. Instead, governors appoint a large number of judges to vacancies that occur between elections, i.e., during the unexpired term of a departed judge (*interim or midterm appointment*).

This is how it works. A judge, once elected (or appointed to a previous vacancy), manages to win reelection term after term until death in office, or, more likely, a decision to resign or retire gives the governor an opportunity to appoint another judge. The process repeats itself again and again.[9] Why does a judge leave in the middle and not the end of a term? Some do, but others retain their party loyalty throughout their careers and give a governor from their political party an opportunity to fill the post with another party member. In addition, many judges oppose judicial elections, and we may speculate that they believe that a governor will be more responsible in selecting qualified people than voters and political parties.[10] In these instances the politics of elections really is the politics of appointment, and the role of political parties is channeled through the governor's office, not through the voters.

**Little Competition**    The most important reason judges are not defeated after obtaining their initial appointment is that they usually are not challenged for reelection.[11] Studies of individual states indicate that as many as nine out of ten judges who sought reelection ran unopposed, and only a mere handful of those with opposition were voted out of office.

Lack of competition is due partly to local bar associations, which follow a custom that might be termed the "sitting judge principle," meaning that incumbent judges should not be challenged for purely partisan or personal reasons if they are thought to be doing an adequate job as judge. Consequently, in many communities, there may not be many lawyers who are anxious to run against a judge.

These informal legal rules illustrate the overlap between legal and popular political culture in the courts. Candidates are discouraged from challenging an incumbent judge in a perfectly legal election, because unwritten legal custom brands the activity as improper. It would be difficult to find a parallel situation for other public offices. Candidates might choose not to run for mayor or the legislature for many politically understandable reasons, but violating legal niceties is not likely to be one of them.

Few judges are defeated when they face opposition. A main reason is that judicial elections are so quiet they are practically invisible to the voters.[12] About the most that judicial candidates promise is to improve the efficiency of the courts, to be fair and just, to avoid personal conflicts of interest, etc. Moreover, the candidates usually look alike: typically white, middle-aged men who dress in conservative business suits with respectable and unpublicized careers in law, business, or government. To most voters, they are not exciting and are hard to distinguish. Only 10 or 15 percent of the electorate bother to vote.

Given the general lack of information and interest in the election, incumbent judges have an enormous advantage.[13] They are the candidates with the prestigious title in front of their names, and the voters are more likely to remember or recognize them. Since the voters have heard so little about the judges before the campaign started, they are likely to assume that they must be doing a good job on the bench.

**Contested Elections**    There are some exceptions, of course, to this general pattern of mild, uncontested judicial elections. Once in a while, incumbents are opposed and voted out of office when they receive unusual amounts of negative publicity through the mass media, which targets a judge's advanced age, alleged incompetence, improper or immoral behavior, or other negative attributes.[14]

As a more general rule, we can conclude that *states that use partisan elections to choose judges are somewhat more likely to have incumbent judges voted out of office*. This is due to several related characteristics of state politics: the presence of two-party competition in state or local elections, the use of party labels on the ballot to designate judges as members of political parties, and the tendency of many voters to cast ballots for a party slate in partisan elections.[15]

Also, if both political parties seem to have a good chance of winning elections, more candidates are encouraged to challenge incumbents. The use of party labels serves as a major cue for distinguishing among policies and officials. If the voters are dissatisfied with the party in power, they are likely to vote against many or all candidates who share that label, and judges are not always immune to a party sweep from power.

In several states, judicial elections have none of the veneer of judicial decorum. Name-calling and personal accusations as well as political charges have been common. Recently, partisan elections for the Texas Supreme Court have been heavily criticized because several of the justices accepted hundreds of thousands of dollars in campaign contributions from lawyers representing the Pennzoil and Texaco oil companies, which later appeared before the court in a multibillion dollar court case. Judicial reformers increasingly worry about high campaign contributions and the image of justice for sale.[16]

Party identification and political competition also affect officially nonpartisan elections, and incumbents are at greater risk. In Michigan, for example, party conventions nominate judicial candidates for nonpartisan elections, and openly partisan campaigns have been common. In Ohio, which uses partisan primary elections but nonpartisan general elections, the party and policy positions of judicial nominees become clear and the voters select candidates largely according to the "hidden" party label.[17]

Election is the most controversial method for selecting state judges, and reformers target highly contested and brutal elections as proof that elections ought to be replaced by merit systems. Yet, many people defend elections because they permit judicial accountability and popular representation. The box "Abolish or Save Judicial Elections?" summarizes the pros and cons of one of the oldest methods of selecting state judges.[18]

**Unequal Representation and Accountability**   While judicial elections permit the will of the people to determine who will be selected for office, blacks and Hispanics recently have charged that their voices are excluded. Minorities claim that at-large elections, in which all candidates are elected by majority vote of all voters in the district, dilute the minority vote so that minorities cannot influence the outcome or select candidates they prefer.[19] Some districts are so large they encompass an entire city or county or, in supreme court elections, the entire state.

---

**BOX 4.1**

**ABOLISH OR SAVE JUDICIAL ELECTIONS?**

**Abolish elections**

• *Inflammatory campaigns* Candidates resort to flagrant personal and political charges and demean the integrity of the courts. Judicial campaigns are becoming similar to other elections.

• *Uninformed public* Voter turnout for judicial elections is low, and voters are poorly informed about the qualifications of the candidates.

• *Partisan influence* Party labels and endorsements by political parties and interest groups unduly influence the voters.

• *Campaign costs and favoritism* Judicial campaigns increasingly cost a great deal of money, even millions for state supreme courts, and judges decide particular cases in favor of contributors who appear in court.

• *Partisan decision making* Elected judges are likely to decide cases in ways which reflect the views of the electorate that voted for them. Elected judges are "too accountable."

• *Discourages candidates* Rough-and-tumble judicial elections discourage many excellent lawyers from seeking judicial positions, decreasing the pool of well-qualified people for the courts.

• *Good judges voted out* Well-qualified judges who face a partisan campaign or the winds of political change may lose their seats.

**Keep elections**

• *Few hotly contested elections* Although a few heavily contested and rowdy judicial elections occur, they are rare and critics overstate the problem. Political parties have limited influence and good incumbents normally win re-election.

• *Bad judges voted out* Candidates with tarnished integrity or judges who have shown obvious bias on the court are rejected by the voters.

• *Voters are informed* Voters in judicial elections are equally or even more informed than voters who vote in other high-visibility elections.

• *Equal turnout* Most judicial elections occur with other contests, so the electorate for judicial elections is about the same as for other elections. Partisan elections increase turnout the most.

• *Accountability* Since judges inevitably make policy and the law is an imperfect guide to decision making, the electorate ought to know where judges stand on the issues. Party labels give the voters the best way to make informed choices.

• *Control contributions* If campaign contributions taint the judiciary, impose limits on them.

---

In judicial, as well as in most other elections, white voters vote overwhelmingly for white candidates, and blacks and others vote heavily for black or ethnic candidates.[20] If blacks or Hispanics are in a minority in a judicial district, few or none of their number will be elected. This, minorities claim, results in racial discrimination. These complaints are similar to those raised in years past concerning at-large legislative elections.

Minorities have contested discrimination in judicial elections in the federal courts under the federal Voting Rights Act of 1965. In 1982, Congress amended the act to permit lawsuits when election arrangements *resulted* in discrimination, rather than requiring proof of *intentional* discrimination by government officials, which had been the previous interpretation of the law by the U.S. Supreme Court. Nearly all of the cases come from the south, where racial discrimination has a long history.

Minorities generally call for smaller single-member districts in which blacks and other ethnic groups will constitute the majority or at least a larger voting group. However, since the jurisdiction of most courts is larger than these new proposed sub or minidistricts, the judges elected under this plan would serve the entire court district.

Box 4.2, "Accountability and Representation," summarizes the opposing positions of minority groups and state officials on judicial redistricting. As in many other issues, the legal culture and the popular political culture are in conflict.[21]

With few exceptions, the federal courts have interpreted the Voting Rights Act to apply to judicial elections.[22] Increasingly, the states will be required to redraw their judicial election districts to allow minorities to have an opportunity to select candidates of their choice.

## Executive and Legislative Appointment of Judges

"A judge is a lawyer who knew the governor . . . or was a member of the state legislature." These simple and popular conclusions explain the final outcome of many judicial appointments, but they do not tell us how or why individuals become known to appointing authorities or why particular appointments are made. Only a handful of states officially use gubernatorial appointment, but because few judges are initially elected to the courts in the first place, judicial appointments are responsible for a large share of all judicial selections in most of the states.

Only three states continue to appoint judges in the legislature, and the key to success is past membership in the state legislature. Legislative selection of judges for state supreme courts sometimes involves many kinds of government experience, but appointment to the trial courts favors former state legislators about 80 percent of the time.[23]

---

**BOX 4.2**

ACCOUNTABILITY
AND REPRESENTATION

**Against redistricting**

• *Judges are not representatives* According to the attorney representing Louisiana in a judicial voting rights case, "The blindfolded lady with the sword and the scales, that's the constituency of a judge, no more and no less." Judges are not legislators.

• *Smaller districts produce bias* Judges elected in smaller districts with a majority of nonwhites will favor those groups or local residents against the residents of other minidistricts.

**For redistricting**

• *Discrimination* Since racial voting blocs are rigid, blacks and other minorities cannot influence at-large judicial elections.

• *Representation* Minorities have the right to elect candidates of their choice in order to gain group representation on the courts.

• *No evidence of bias* Courts frequently hear cases which involve litigants from other judicial districts. There is no evidence of local bias. If bias were a problem, it also exists in the big at-large districts where whites control election outcomes.

**Political Network**   Appointment by the governor is a little more complex. Governors cannot personally know every judge they appoint to all state courts. There are hundreds or thousands of judges in some of the states, and each governor usually has dozens of opportunities to make appointments during one or two terms in office. Consequently, appointment to the courts normally involves a network of political relationships.

Governors must depend on others for advice and information. While governors generally select well-qualified people for the bench, formal credentials alone do not significantly reduce the size of the pool of lawyers who are available and qualified. Therefore, governors usually pick individuals who have been involved in state politics and whose past activity either has been of personal benefit, or has benefited their political party or political allies.

When making appointments to the many trial courts around the state, governors often use judicial positions to bargain with mayors and state legislators whose support the governor needs for reelection or for the passage of important bills. For example, if a legislator requests that a particular lawyer be appointed to a court in the legislator's district, the governor is usually happy to go along, since it rewards the legislator, makes the legislator seem powerful in the eyes of the appointee and other local politicians, and obligates the legislator to support the governor. Governors also sometimes appoint legislators themselves to court positions as rewards for past loyalty and as an incentive to others in the legislature who might like to top off a political career with a secure judicial appointment.[24]

Appointment of state supreme court judges sometimes follows a similar pattern, but since it is the highest and most prestigious state court and there are so few vacancies filled during a 4-year term, governors give much more personal attention to these appointments. It also is more difficult for governors to use these positions for bargaining or rewards, since there are so few to give. Rewarding one political friend and supporter means snubbing others.

Governors sometimes appoint lawyers who have had long state political careers and who have become pesonally acquainted with the governor, perhaps as a state legislator, as a lawyer in the attorney general's office, or as a lobbyist for a large interest group.

Governors also give supreme court appointments to their friends and associates, including former law school or college classmates, personal friends, former law partners or bar association colleagues, or the governor's personal attorney. Instead of working up through the political ranks, these judges achieved special status or professional success and prestige *outside* the mainstream of state politics, and moved into the government through personal connections to the governor.[25]

**Symbolic Appointments**   Increasingly, governors also make symbolic appointments to state supreme courts. These usually are not rewards for party service but have broad political appeal and indirect benefit to a governor by recognizing a large group of voters. They are opportunities to hold political coalitions together and to reinforce group support for particular parties, candidates, and policies. They are risky, however, because they can alienate others.[26]

Box 4.3, "The Ultimate Symbolic Appointment," illustrates how governors can satisfy several constituencies at one time.[27]

Former Chief Justice Rose E. Bird of the California supreme court has been the most controversial symbolic appointment made in the state courts for many years.[28] She was appointed in the 1970s by liberal Demoratic Governor Jerry Brown, who had promised in his election campaign to place women and nonwhites in high state politial office.

A year after her appointment, Justice Bird won a retention election by a slim 52 percent of the vote. She had become the most controversial liberal justice, deciding heavily in favor of criminal defendants, and against Proposition 13— the famous constitutional amendment that limited taxation on real estate. Agricultural and other business interests campaigned against her.

Later, she and other liberal justices continued to decide in support of the poor, criminal defendants, injured individuals, and other underdogs. Chief Justice Bird voted against all death penalty sentences imposed by the trial courts and sometimes was the sole dissenter in death penalty cases. The Republican party, the consevative Republican governor, county prosecutors, and others opposed her and two other liberal justices in their 1986 retention elections. All three lost their posts, and the governor, reelected at the same time, appointed three new justices in their place.

---

**BOX 4.3**

THE ULTIMATE SYMBOLIC
APPOINTMENT

Former Florida governor Bob Graham appointed Rosemary Barkett to be the first female state supreme court justice in Florida. But, in addition to being female, Justice Barkett is a Mexican-born, former Roman Catholic nun. She served previously as a judge on the intermediate court of appeals in heavily urban south Florida.

Upon her appointment, one of her fellow appeals court judges noted: "With the addition of Justice Barkett, we now have a court which is comprised of justices who are young and old, male and female, black and white, Jew and gentile. Our Supreme Court reflects the rich religious, ethnic, and cultural diversity that is Florida's real treasure."

---

## Merit Selection (Missouri Plan)

As discussed earlier, merit selection now is the method most likely to be adopted in the states, and two out of five states use merit selection for some or all courts.[29] The exact procedures of merit selection differ among the states, but all of them place great significance on the nominating commissions that screen and limit the number of judicial nominees a governor may consider. In particular, lawyers on these panels are expected to play a crucial role, since, they have long argued, lawyers are most familiar with the skills, experience, and personality characteristics necessary for a qualified judge. They also claim to be familiar with many of the local lawyers who would like to be considered for the nomination.

**Who Are the Commissioners?** Table 4.2 provides a profile of the membership of state merit nominating commissions. The commissions are dominated overwhelmingly by older white males and lawyers, businessmen, and other professionals (mainly doctors and teachers).[30] However, women have greatly increased their representation in contrast to nearly two decades ago, when 90 percent of the nominating commissioners were men.[31] It is especially significant that most of the commissioners have been socially and politically active. Their activity level vastly exceeds the social and political participation of the general population. Overall, members of the nominating commissions are social, economic, and political elites.

The lawyers on the commissions also are legal elites. Most are above the average age of lawyers, and they come mostly from law firms—not from solo practices (not shown in Table 4.2). Moreover, lawyers from the biggest firms are more likely to serve on prestigious statewide commissions, which select

**TABLE 4-2**
CHARACTERISTICS OF MERIT
NOMINATING COMMISSIONERS

| Occupation | |
| --- | --- |
| Lawyer | 59% |
| Business, Professional | 22 |
| Other | 18 |

| Social and political activity | |
| --- | --- |
| Civic groups | 67% |
| Political Party Office | 26 |
| Public Office | 31 |

| Sex, race, religion | |
| --- | --- |
| Male | 75% |
| White | 93 |
| Protestant | 61 |

| Age | |
| --- | --- |
| 40 or younger | 17% |
| 41–50 | 32 |
| 51–60 | 24 |
| Over 60 | 27 |

*Source:* Adapted from Beth M. Henschen, Robert Moog, and Steven Davis, "Judicial Nominating Commissioners: A National Profile," *Judicature,* 73 (April–May, 1990), 329, 331–32.

intermediate appellate and state supreme court judges, than on local selection commissions that primarily screen trial judges.

Most states allow lawyer-commissioners to be elected by the bar, and lawyers in the smaller firms frequently are viewed as compromise candidates between the solo practitioners and the big firm lawyers. Nevertheless, since lawyers working in most law firms are more likely to specialize in business rather than personal plight litigation, and many other commissioners are businesspeople, business interests seem to be heavily represented on these bodies.

**Bar Politics**   Since many of the commissioners have been active in politics, it is likely that partisan politics will affect the way the commissions work. Detailed research on merit selection has found that merit selection is shaped by the major characteristics of state political systems and the social, economic, and political conflicts that occur among lawyers.[32]

Around the time of the Great Depression of the 1930s, urban lawyers often split into two political groups connected to different social and economic interests. Most of the time these divisions occurred within the same bar association, but in some cities conflict was so great that groups of lawyers formed their own separate organizations.[33]

In Missouri, for example, lawyers in the largest cities have formed two competing bar associations. One is composed mainly of plaintiff's lawyers— Democrats who work in small one- or two-person offices, earn modest incomes, and represent small economic or "have-not" interests. The other bar association includes generally defendants' lawyers—higher-income Republicans who work in large law firms and whose clients are likely to be banks, insurance companies, and other businesses (Chapter 3).

Each of these organizations has worked to elect their own members to the merit nominating panels and the lawyers try to select judges who they believe will lean toward the kinds of clients the lawyers regularly represent in court. Their interest in the expected policy or attitudes of judges is much greater than that of political parties, which are interested mostly in filling judgeships as rewards for party service.

Although they favor judges with different social and economic outlooks, it is impossible for lawyers on the commissions to confess their bias openly and honestly, for that would violate their claims to impartiality and the very reason they are supposed to be on the commissions. So, they masquerade their selections with vague references to each candidate's judicial temperament, experience, legal scholarship, integrity, etc.

**Lay Members**   The governor's nonlawyer appointees often have considerable power. The governor does not appoint representatives to these commissions by flipping randomly through the telephone book! Quite the opposite is true. They often have supported the governor's or another's election campaign, are sympathetic to the governor's political values, and usually are active in local politics. They are likely also to be members of the governor's political party or faction. They are attuned to the governor and are likely to support the governor's preferences for judges. *They are the same type of people a governor normally would consult in making judicial appointments in states without merit selection panels.*

There frequently is conflict among members of the commissions. Box 4.4, "Conflict on Merit-Nominating Commissions," summarizes some of the differences that occur.[34]

***Disagreement on Criteria***    A national survey of nominating commissioners shows that there is little agreement on merit criteria. Panelists mentioned over fifty mostly vague characteristics (integrity, fairness, knowledge of law, moral courage, industriousness, etc.) they believed were important in choosing good judges.[35] They did not rank all criteria the same way, nor did they reveal how the list could be used to distinguish objectively among the hundreds or thousands of lawyers in a large city who are eligible and who want to be considered for a nomination.

Criteria for appointment to the courts can be made more precise, such as requiring lawyers to have a certain number of years of legal experience or perhaps to serve in one or two other judicial posts. Selecting lawyers who graduated toward the top quarter of their law class also could become a rule.

However, there is no agreement among judges, lawyers, court reformers, and others on whether certain precise criteria produce better judges. Many U.S. Supreme Court justices, for example, have had no previous judicial experience, and several have said that trial court experience is irrelevant for a high appellate court. Graduating at the top of the class also may be irrelevant for the skills and competence that lawyers develop later on. Finally, even with

---

**BOX 4.4**

CONFLICT ON MERIT-NOMINATING COMMISSIONS

• *Lay commissions are novices* Lawyers complain that lay commissioners are unfamiliar with judicial qualifications, are too partisan, and are swayed by personalities during candidate interviews. Said one lawyer, "Lay people have no grasp of what it takes to make a good judge and are worthless additions to the commissions."

• *Lawyers freeze out others* But the nonlawyers have complaints of their own. Lawyers rely on their "old boy" networks for choosing nominees and they try to dominate commission meetings. Lawyers often behave as if the views of the nonlawyers are irrelevant, and in states where local judges

chair the commissions, judges are domineering and controlling. One nonlawyer concluded, "The attorneys were more interested in banding together to help fellow attorneys than listening to the evidence on all candidates."

• *Commissions are partisan* Some lawyers and lay commissioners believe that partisan politics has too large a role. Some commissioners are stand-ins for the governor and nominated only the governor's choices. One argued, ". . . the governor insisted the commission present him candidates of his choice; otherwise he refuses to appoint anyone. The system has become totally political." Others report that meetings are open and informal and commissioners openly discuss party politics.

these criteria, the selection process will only be narrowed somewhat. Many lawyers will qualify, and panels and governors still will have to choose among them.

How do merit panels actually narrow their choices? Members of nominating commissions—lawyers and nonlawyers alike—are likely to use concrete and familiar measures to select nominees. Political party affiliation, experience and service, social and economic status, type of law practice, political values and attitudes, religion, race, etc., are likely possibilities.

**Voters** Voters play a very small and generally insignificant part in the merit selection. They vote only in retention elections after a judge has served a short period in office, and national surveys of these elections have shown that less than 1 to 2 percent of merit selected judges are voted out of office.[36] Generally, voters are not interested in judicial elections in which only one nonpartisan candidate is running against a personal record. Turnout is low and voter acceptance of incumbents is routine.

These experiences with merit selection demonstrate that merit selection operates within the broader context of state politics and that elites who are important in other spheres of state and local politics have major influence in determining how the merit system actually will work. Although the official machinery of the judicial selection process can be changed, governors and political parties and even judges and lawyers will adapt to the new procedures and find ways of making them work to fulfill their political goals.

### Who Are State Judges?

A popular myth in America is that anyone can become President. Images of Abraham Lincoln studying by candlelight in a rustic log cabin come quickly to mind and are copied by presidential candidates who like to point to their humble beginnings as proof that they are "of the people." That may be all right for President, but there are no such myths for judges! The characteristics of state supreme court judges are presented in Table 4.3. Becoming a judge requires an individual to overcome a number of hurdles that are not typically required of candidates for other offices. In large part, these hurdles reflect the impact the legal culture has had on shaping the judicial job description and our acceptance of who judges ought to be. Increasingly, for example, there is emphasis on formal legal education and a period of legal experience before a lawyer is considered really eligible for most judgeships.[37]

Bar associations and law reform groups also have been campaigning for the recognition of trial court experience as a requirement for appointment to the state appellate courts. In some states, governors have adopted these standards informally and promote judges from within the ranks. About 60 percent of state supreme court judges have had prior judicial experience on a trial court, and they previously have practiced law an average of 15 years.[38] In terms of formal education and experience, most state judges are well qualified for the courts

**TABLE 4-3**
CHARACTERISTICS OF STATE SUPREME
COURT JUDGES

| Previous government experience | |
|---|---|
| Prosecutor | 21% |
| Legislator | 20 |
| Previous judicial | 63 |
| Other | 39 |

| Type of law practice | |
|---|---|
| Larger firm | 20% |
| 2–4 partners | 54 |
| Solo | 26 |

| Education | |
|---|---|
| Private/Ivy League Undergraduate | 45% |
| Private/Ivy League Law | 29 |

| Localism | |
|---|---|
| In-state birth | 78% |
| In-state undergraduate/law | 70 |

| Sex, race, religion | |
|---|---|
| Male | 93% |
| White | 96 |
| Protestant | 60 |
| Average Years of Law Practice | 15 |
| Average Age Upon Reaching Court | 53 |

*Source:* The information on sex and race is derived from M. L. Henry, Jr., *et al.*, *The Success of Women and Minorities in Achieving Judicial Office: the Selection Process* (New York: Fund for Modern Courts, 1985). Other data relies on Henry R. Glick and Craig F. Emmert, "Stability and Change: Characteristics of State Supreme Court Judges," *Judicature* 70 (1986), Tables 1 and 2, pp. 108 and 109.

and have a level of accomplishment that far exceeds our expectations for other political offices.

**Social Background**   Besides the legal requirements, there are various social and political requirements for the judiciary as well. More than most other political positions, for example, the courts are heavily dominated by men and whites. This usual pattern in American politics is even more important for tradition-bound courts. But women and blacks have begun to enter the nation's law schools in greater numbers, and some have been selected as state judges.

The number of female judges on the state courts has nearly doubled from the early 1970s to 1980, although their number remains small. In 1980, there were about 550 female state judges in the United States. Nearly all served on trial courts (nearly 60 percent on trial courts of limited jurisdiction). Less than 45 were members of any state appellate court. However, the number of female state supreme court judges increased from 10 in 1980 to 23 in the mid-1980s, or 7 percent of all state supreme court judges. A similar percentage of women also were on state intermediate appellate courts and the trial courts of general jurisdiction.

Female judges are most likely to label themselves as moderates or liberals, and they are found most frequently on courts in larger cities, where local politics is dominated by the Democratic party. This is not surprising since urban areas provide a political and social environment that is most likely to encourage the recruitment of women. Rural areas and small towns generally are more socially conservative and do not place many women on the courts.[39]

There are very few nonwhite state judges. In the mid 1980s, less than 5 percent of state judges were black and 1 percent were Hispanics. Most nonwhite judges have served on the state trial courts, especially trial courts of limited jurisdiction. Nearly one-fifth of the states had no black judges.[40]

The black judges have career patterns and personal credentials that are very similar to those of white judges. They are middle class, and have attended quality Ivy League or state university law schools, and many have graduated with honors. They also have held various governmental posts before going on the courts. Consequently, state judicial recruitment carefully selects black lawyers who are in the mainstream of the legal profession and, except for their color, fit traditional expectations of who judges ought to be. The courts are becoming integrated but still are limited to middle-class, politically experienced lawyers.[41]

**Political Credentials**  Most judges also are "local boys who made good." Recruitment politics generally requires a close tie to state and local politics, resulting in judges who have always been close to home. There are some exceptions, especially in the fast-growing states, but lawyers who leave home probably have a difficult time establishing sufficient ties to a new community to make them acceptable as local judges.

Winning an election or an executive appointment usually requires careful nurturing of a political career. This means developing contacts, establishing a record of service to a political party, holding lesser posts in the community, and being well known to fellow lawyers and other prominent groups.

Consequently, state judges normally have been born and raised in the same state as the court on which they serve, have attended law school in the same state or at least region of their court, and have held one or more nonjudicial political jobs such as state legislator and prosecuting attorney or have been a local judge (Table 4.3). They also are likely to be a member of the political party that dominates politics in their area. In short, they typically are political insiders and long-standing local residents.[42]

### Selection Systems and Judges' Characteristics

Despite the political rhetoric and competition for control of the courts, we need to know if selection systems make any difference in determining who becomes a state judge. Do selection systems produce judges with different personal characteristics, and, if so, can we agree that certain sets of judges are superior or inferior? Can a state government settle on one particular selection system and be reasonably confident that its method will produce the best judges possible? These are questions objective research can help to answer.

**Is Merit Superior?**    Whether selection systems make a difference is especially significant for the merit plan, since its promoters have long maintained that merit selection will produce decidedly superior judges. But, research on judicial backgrounds cast serious doubts on the ability of merit selection to recruit decidedly superior judges or to select judges who are significantly different from those in elective or appointive states. In fact, state selection systems do not make much difference in determining who becomes a judge.[43]

Studies of state supreme court judges have discovered that similar percentages of merit plan and other judges had been educated in the same state as their court appointment and that the educations of merit plan judges are nearly identical, but sometimes inferior to those of other judges. Moreover, the political careers of merit plan judges have been remarkably similar to the experiences of partisan election judges. For example, between 50 and 60 percent of both groups had been prosecuting attorneys, a local and usually partisan elective office that often is the first step in a state political career.

Over 60 percent of all state supreme court judges have had prior judicial experience, but, surprisingly, the percentage of merit plan judges with experience is *below* that of judges appointed by governors or legislatures or chosen in partisan election states. Only judges in nonpartisan election states have less judicial experience than Missouri plan judges.

**Discrimination**    Recent research also indicates that judicial selection under the merit plan seems to discriminate against religious minorities. Catholic and Jewish judges have been selected in significant numbers for state supreme courts only since the 1970s. Allowing for regional differences in their concentration in the population, they appear to be recruited in a relatively equal way in all selection systems except the Missouri plan, which heavily favors high-status Protestant lawyers.[44]

Discrimination also occurs in the selection of black judges. Merit systems lean toward selecting white judges, but judicial elections, especially in the south, also favor whites. Blacks do best in states in which governors or the legislature appoints judges, including having the governor fill midterm vacancies between judicial elections. In states that officially use elections, only 30 percent of the black judges actually were elected. The rest were appointed to fill vacancies. However, redistricting ordered by the federal courts of appeals is making a difference, and a few more black judges have been elected in recent years.[45]

Discrimination in merit selection should not be too surprising since the organized bar has greater influence in the Missouri plan and there are strong historical roots to discrimination within the bar. Overall, taking into account the record of different selection systems to choose judges solely on the basis of their legal credentials, merit selection fails to produce the results that are claimed for it. However, blacks are disadvantaged in southern judicial elections as well.

In making appointments, governors probably are interested in satisfying their diverse statewide constituency, and they appear to be more sensitive to producing a judiciary that, if not perfectly representative of the population, includes people of many different backgrounds.

**Choosing a Selection System**  All the research on state judicial selection points to several fundamental conclusions. First, while there are some differences among state judges, most differences do not result from the particular selection system used and the merit plan does not produce judges with superior formal credentials.

Second, the actual operation of the merit plan in state politics closely ties recruitment to other parts of the state political system, placing great emphasis on the power of the governor and the governor's links to political parties and local politics. Consequently, it is unrealistic to expect merit to be nonpartisan or separated from the forces of state politics.

Finally, it is clear that the major legal participants in merit selection—the lawyers and judges who serve on nominating commissions—are unable to apply general law reform goals to the specific task of selecting judges.

This does not mean that judges chosen by any selection system are inferior or unqualified for the bench. It means only that lofty and fuzzy conceptions of judges' personal characteristics are not helpful in trying to distinguish among many seemingly well-qualified people for the courts.

Some reformers are aware of social science research on the courts, since some of it is published in journals read by both academic researchers and practitioners, but it is not likely to make much difference on political campaigns to persuade government to add merit judicial selection. Law reformers believe in professional judicial management and recruitment, but like other interest groups and political parties, they also want to maximize their influence in politics.

Lawyers' support for merit selection often is closely related to their own political power. For example, judges and lawyers who are members of the locally dominant political party (Republicans in small towns and rural areas, Democrats in cities) often favor partisan election as the most appropriate way to choose judges. But lawyers and judges who are in the minority party that rarely wins elections often favor merit because they believe it will reduce the influence of the party in power and perhaps increase their own influence in local politics.

In addition, when lawyers rate the performance of judges in office, lawyers who favor the Missouri plan are somewhat more likely to consider merit selected judges best while lawyers who favor partisan election are likely to rate elected judges at least equal to or higher than Missouri plan judges.[46]

## THE SELECTION OF FEDERAL JUDGES

The selection of federal judges involves national as well as state politics. The major political actors and the values that are important in determining appointments differ according to the level of court involved. The President, for example, is personally involved with the selection of justices for the Supreme Court and is concerned most with choosing individuals who reflect the administration's political thinking.

For the courts of appeals and district courts, where there are so many more appointments made during a 4-year term, the President is likely to delegate authority to the government's lawyers in the Justice Department. The U.S. Senate also has a very powerful role in selecting judges for the lower courts. Senators represent their states by showing concern for choosing judges who will be acceptable to various state constituencies, but they mainly want to guarantee that appointments to federal positions in their states are used as rewards for deserving political party supporters.

In addition to the President and Senate, there are others who are concerned with the selection of federal judges. The American Bar Association (ABA) has lobbied for legal values in federal judicial selection since the early part of the century, and briefly, during the administration of President Jimmy Carter, merit selection became an element of senatorial and presidential power. Women, blacks, civil liberties organizations, business, and religious and labor groups also have lobbied for a share of judicial appointments or for the selection of judges whose attitudes toward major issues are similar to their own.

As in state judicial selection, we ask various political questions: How and why do certain people become federal judges? Who wins or loses influence through judicial selection and what difference does it make?

### The Roots of Judicial Appointments

The major judicial issue at the Constitutional Convention concerned the selection of Supreme Court justices, since political stalemate blocked the creation of a lower federal judiciary until the first Congress. Debate centered on which arm of the new national government should appoint other federal officers.[47]

Remembering the experience of colonial rule, many delegates to the 1787 Convention believed that a representative body—Congress—should choose the judges. Consequently, early proposals at the convention called for judicial selection by the Senate alone, or in combination with the House of Representatives. Trying to avoid domination by the larger northeastern states, the smaller states finally won a compromise: judges should be approved by the Senate alone where each state had two votes.

**Federal versus State Power** Conflict also centered on the political roles of the legislature and executive and on the overall power of the federal government. The Federalists maintained that national unification and defense required a strong central government with significant executive powers. They also argued that political experience in the states already had demonstrated the disadvantages of legislative government. Judgeships and other appointments frequently were used as rewards for personal and factional loyalty, service in the legislature, or as trade-offs for support for other legislation. Pressure for local representation on the state courts also meant that judges could not be selected according to legal competence and personal integrity.

Supporters of legislative appointment countered that U.S. Senators would be most familiar with the individuals who probably would serve on the Supreme Court, but the Federalists insisted that the President would maintain a national perspective and be more politically independent to select the most qualified men for the Court.

Toward the close of the convention, the current system of choosing Supreme Court justices (and later, all other federal judges) was accepted as a further compromise between legislative and executive power: *judges would be selected by the President with the advice and consent of the Senate and would have lifetime terms of office.*

Although this method has been used to select all federal judges, conflict over which branch of government should be most influential did not end. Reflecting the Jacksonian movement to make government more responsive to the people, early proposed constitutional amendments called for having the House of Representatives approve all judicial nominees. Efforts to make federal judgeships elective offices occurred in the Progressive era of the early 1900s. None of these was successful, however.

The exact meaning of senatorial advice and consent was not fully discussed or described by the convention, nor was it explained in the Constitution. Alexander Hamilton and other Federalists assumed that it meant that the Senate would not have any initiative in judicial selection, but would merely approve or reject presidential nominees. This usually has been the pattern in the selection of justices for the Supreme Court and to some degree the courts of appeals, but the selection of judges for the federal district courts has involved much more senatorial power and independence.

### The Supreme Court

The selection of Supreme Court justices occasionally has involved fierce political conflict and competition. Issues of party patronage, senatorial power, and judicial competence all have been involved, but the most important factors determining appointments are visibility to the President and the ideology or political attitudes of judicial nominees. The importance of ideology is due to the Supreme Court's far-reaching power to review the constitutionality of congressional and state laws and presidential decisions, and to make national policy whenever the Court rules on controversial social or economic issues.

The Constitution does not refer to judicial qualifications, but beginning with the first appointments to the Supreme Court, justices typically have been chosen with care and have had outstanding legal credentials and strong records of personal accomplishment. As if to set the tone for most future appointments, George Washington was highly regarded for selecting judges only after extensive and careful screening of many individuals who generally were considered worthy and capable.[48]

**Visibility**  There is no single path that ensures an appointment. Usually the President and the attorney general, who normally is a close political ally of the President, gather names of prospective nominees from many sources, including congressional leaders of their own party, major interest groups that support party programs and candidates, other Supreme Court justices, and state and federal judges as well as political and personal friends.

Throughout their careers and campaigns Presidents make many personal contacts who may suggest individuals having the social and political stature for the Supreme Court and who also share the values of the administration. In many cases, a President nominates political friends and advisers known for years. State and federal judges, deputy attorneys general, and a few U.S. senators also have been selected.[49]

Most Supreme Court justices have held other prominent state or federal political positions, but have further distinguished themselves in some special way—perhaps through personal service in the administration or to the President personally, or as lower court judges whose decisions reflect the President's own attitudes and impress the President with the judges' legal and political qualities.

**Ideology and Political Goals**  Members of the President's political party usually are appointed, but party membership and patronage are not key variables, since there are thousands of qualified Democrats and Republicans but so few who can be so highly rewarded. However, appointing a justice who shares the political views of the administration *and* who represents or is identified with a group of party supporters helps to maintain party solidarity, provides symbolic recognition to significant groups of voters, and perpetuates administration policy.

Finding candidates who fill all of these requirements is like killing three birds with one stone. In 1967, liberal Democratic President Lyndon Johnson appointed Thurgood Marshall, a liberal and the nation's first black justice. Close ties between party, symbolism, and ideology were maintained in 1991, when

Republican President George Bush selected a conservative black Republican, Judge Clarence Thomas of the District of Columbia Court of Appeals, to replace retiring Justice Marshall. In 1981, Republican President Ronald Reagan accomplished several political objectives by appointing Republican Sandra D. O'Connor, a noncontroversial conservative judge from Arizona, as the first woman justice of the Supreme Court, and in 1986, he appointed Judge Antonin Scalia, an Italian-American Catholic with nine children, to replace Chief Justice Warren Burger.

**Confirmations and Rejections**   Presidents normally are successful in obtaining Senate approval of their choices, but about 20 percent of Supreme Court nominations have been rejected. However, only a few nominations have been rejected or withdrawn since 1900. In contrast, about one out of three was rejected or withdrawn in face of heavy Senate opposition during the 1800s.[50]

Presidents are most successful when they propose nominees with uncontroversial backgrounds and moderate political attitudes—neither too liberal nor too conservative. Presidents also are more successful when they and a majority of the Senate are of the same political party and generally agree on major goals and direction of domestic policy. In addition, Presidents normally have more success in the early part of their terms. Presidents in their fourth year sometimes appear weaker since an election is due. It is then that the opposition tends to resist their appointments.[51]

*Legal Veneer*   Supreme Court appointments become controversial when a nominee's past actions and anticipated future decisions are seriously opposed by senators or a major interest group.[52] As early as 1795, for example, Senate Federalists rejected John Rutledge as Chief Justice. Rutledge already had served on the Supreme Court and at the time of his nomination was Chief Justice of South Carolina, but he earned Federalist hostility by making a public speech against their foreign policy and the Jay Treaty with England. Similarly, Roger B. Taney, President Andrew Jackson's Treasury secretary and attorney general, was temporarily kept off the court in 1834 by a Senate Whig majority that objected to the administration's national monetary and banking policy.[53]

Although the main reason for opposition to Supreme Court appointees is ideology and conflict over policy, strategies of opposition frequently use legal qualifications and ethics as a more legitimate and respectable way to try to block an appointment. Legal criteria were used by senators before lawyers were plentiful in the United States and became well organized into professional associations. For example, besides being attacked as a danger to the Federalists, senators labeled John Rutledge mentally incompetent and unfit for a judgeship. Then as now, such charges are very subjective and usually cannot be proved or disproved. They typically are part of an overall political strategy to defeat the President and the President's nominee.

A recent example is the elevation of Justice William Rehnquist to Chief Justice by President Reagan in 1986. Justice Rehnquist is among the most conservative members of the Supreme Court (Chapters 9 and 10), and liberal

U.S. senators and interest groups sought to block his appointment. Opponents scoured Justice Rehnquist's career from the 1960s for ammunition against him, and various ethics charges were raised, including his conduct in previous elections, his role in the Nixon administration, and conduct in family legal matters.

However, several senators revealed that ideology was their true concern. Senator Edward M. Kennedy and others stated openly that Rehnquist was "too extreme to be Chief Justice." Republicans countered that the Democrats opposed Rehnquist only because he was a conservative and that they sought to smear Rehnquist's reputation to block the appointment. Senator Robert Dole, the Republican majority leader, added, "The people voted for Ronald Reagan in 1980 and 1984, and they expect the President to carry their mandate all the way to the Supreme Court." Although the hearings and debate went on for weeks, Justice Rehnquist was easily approved by the Senate.

*Supremacy of Ideology*  Appointments to the U.S. Supreme Court (and to the lower federal courts as well) have become increasingly driven by ideology. There are many reasons for this. First, there is no doubt that the U.S. Supreme Court is a policymaking court, and that the justices make law. Second, the Supreme Court increasingly deals with extremely sensitive issues which arouse many groups of Americans—abortion, minority and women's rights, personal political freedom and civil liberties, the death penalty and rights of criminal defendants, environmental protection, and many, many more. There now are many more interest groups—liberal and conservative alike—which have become alerted to the crucial role of the federal courts in making civil rights, civil liberties, and other policies.

Third, and perhaps most important, the U.S. Supreme Court recently has undergone a major partisan and ideological shift that has generated intense political conflict. With the exception of the single term of President Jimmy Carter—who had no Supreme Court vacancies to fill—conservative Republican Presidents have been elected since 1968, and President Richard Nixon, but especially Presidents Ronald Reagan and George Bush, have appointed new conservatives to replace retiring liberals.

With the departure of Justice Thurgood Marshall in 1991, recent Republican Presidents have appointd ten justices to the Supreme Court. These appointments gradually have replaced all of the justices who contributed to the liberal Warren Court majority of the 1950s and 1960s. The only justice appointed by a Democrat still serving is Justice Byron White, appointed by President John F. Kennedy in 1962.

Although the Senate accepts most nominations, liberal Democrats have resisted the appointment of the most extreme conservatives, and they have defeated a few of them. Judge Robert Bork, nominated by President Reagan in 1987, has been the most controversial nomination in recent decades, but President Bush's nomination of Judge Clarence Thomas also aroused substantial opposition. Box 4.5, "The New Conservative Justices," analyzes the political conflict over recent nominations to the U.S. Supreme Court and highlights the backgrounds of the recent appointees.

**BOX 4.5**

THE NEW CONSERVATIVE JUSTICES

### Judge Robert H. Bork is defeated

Retiring Justice Lewis F. Powell had been a moderate—voting with the liberals on abortion and civil rights, but with the conservatives on the rights of criminal defendants. Republican President Ronald Reagan planned to replace him in 1987 with a strong, consistent conservative who would vote to overturn the right to an abortion, rule against affirmative action, oppose gay rights, and uphold the death penalty. The administration's agenda was framed in terms of appointing a justice who believed in judicial restraint and the original intent of the framers of the Constitution.

Judge Robert H. Bork filled the job description perfectly. He had clearly expressed his strong conservative views on these and other issues in numerous law review articles and public speeches. He also was eminently qualified for the Court, having graduated from the University of Chicago Law School, been a professor of law at Yale, and solicitor-general in the Nixon administration. At the time of his appointment, he was serving as a judge on the prestigious Federal Court of Appeals for the District of Columbia.

Democrats in the Senate were poised to resist since Bork had long been a favorite of the Reagan administration. Also, the appointment of Judge Bork would give Supreme Court conservatives a clear majority for the first time in decades and change the content of judicial policy for years to come. Finally, the Democrats recently had regained control of the Senate and had a good chance of lining up a majority against him.

Civil rights, women's and abortion rights groups, and many others quickly opposed the nomination. The American Bar Association endorsed Judge Bork, but in a divided vote. Other bar groups and many prominent law professors opposed him. Liberal organizations bought full-page ads in *The New York Times* and other big city newspapers denouncing Judge Bork as a right-wing danger to women, blacks, consumers, and workers as well as to all Americans who valued their privacy. Never before in American history had a judicial nominee been the subject of such an intense advertising campaign.

Judge Bork had supporters as well, including former Chief Justice Warren Burger and former Republican President Gerald Ford, as well as the former attorney general in the Jimmy Carter administration. But none of them represented broad public concern with Bork's conservative views, which grew as the hearings progressed.

The Judiciary Committee initially was divided along party lines. Five conservative Republicans favored Bork from the start while five Democrats were opposed. Crucial undecided votes included a moderate Republican and four conservative southern and southwestern Democrats, who were increasingly worried about the opinions of the large number of black voters in their states.

The hearings went on for weeks with Bork defending his extensive public record and trying to show that his views had changed from his earlier writings and speeches. He declared loyalty to the principle of judicial precedent and promised to support previous Supreme Court rulings. But Democrats challenged his positions as "confirmation conversion," and Bork sounded legalistic, formal, and aloof.

The Judiciary Committee voted 9 to 5 against the nomination and Bork was defeated in the full Senate by a vote of 58 to 42.

### Judge Douglas H. Ginsburg subs for Bork

Stung by Judge Bork's defeat, President Reagan changed strategies and quickly nominated a judge with no public visibility. Instead of having a lengthy record on abortion and civil rights, Judge Douglas H. Ginsburg, who also was a member of the District of Columbia Court of Appeals, mostly had decided cases involving government regulation and antitrust issues. He was a conservative, but the administration hoped his Jewish background might deflect some liberals from questioning the nomination.

Judge Ginsburg probably would have been confirmed, but it was learned that he previously had smoked marijuana, perhaps as recently as 8 years before his nomination, and conservatives pressed him to withdraw.

**BOX 4.5 continued**

### Judge Anthony M. Kennedy is confirmed

Judge Anthony Kennedy of the Court of Appeals for the Ninth Circuit had been considered at the same time as Judge Ginsburg as a possible replacement for Bork. When Ginsburg was forced to withdraw, Judge Kennedy was quickly nominated. Unlike Judge Ginsburg, Judge Kennedy had given a number of speeches, but all of them portrayed him as political moderate.

At the hearings, he deftly portrayed himself as a judge without a political agenda, whose mind was open to many points of view. Unlike Ginsburg, there were no skeletons in his closet. Liberal interest-groups generally did not object to his appointment, and the American Bar Association unanimously gave Judge Kennedy its highest recommendation of "well-qualified." The Senate quickly confirmed him.

### President Bush appoints Judge David H. Souter

When Justice William J. Brennan, one of the remaining steadfast liberals, retired in 1990 at age 84, Republican President George Bush selected Judge David H. Souter of the New Hampshire Supreme Court to be his replacement. Just a few weeks before his nomination, Judge Souter had been appointed to the First Circuit Federal Court of Appeals.

Judge Souter had been practically invisible. He was a lifelong bachelor who lived a secluded and very private life, and he too had not expressed himself on controversial public issues, although his few state supreme court decisions in criminal cases were in the conservative direction. Judge Souter became known to the President through former New Hampshire governor, John Sununu, who had become President Bush's chief advisor.

At his conformation hearings, he avoided revealing much about his views, including abortion, and he too was easily confirmed.

### Judge Clarence Thomas is confirmed, but with a fight

Following Justice Brennan, liberal Justice Thurgood Marshall retired in 1991 at age 83.

This time President Bush took a more controversial path to finding a replacement.

He selected Judge Clarence Thomas, who recently had been appointed to the Federal Court of Appeals for the District of Columbia Circuit. Like Justice Marshall, Judge Thomas is black, but unlike Justice Marshall, Judge Thomas is a Republican and a conservative who publicly had opposed affirmative action and other civil rights policies. As head of the federal Equal Employment Opportunity Commission, which hears complaints concerning job discrimination, Judge Thomas was accused of being insensitive to claims from women and the elderly.

At his hearings, Judge Thomas replied to liberal criticism that his speeches were tailored to his conservative audiences, and did not necessarily reflect his current views. But he was careful not to reveal what those views were, and he refused to take a stand on abortion, claiming he had never discussed it with others. Judge Thomas also claimed that delays at the EEOC involved an increasing workload, and did not indicate insensitivity to legitimate claims. He also appealed to blacks by speaking often about his growing up poor and black in the south.

The senators complained about Judge Thomas's Bork-like "confirmation conversion," and they accused him of confusing and obscuring the issues. Several also emphasized his lack of judicial experience and doubted his qualifications. By the time of this fourth conservative nomination since Bork, Democrats on the Judiciary Committee had grown restive, and believed that Judge Thomas was "doing a Souter" by not revealing anything about his attitudes and policy views.

However, liberal groups were divided. Many, including the National Association for the Advancement of Colored People (NAACP) and the National Organization of Women (NOW), opposed him, but others, such as the National Urban League and the Southern Christian Leadership Conference (SCLC), were neutral. Many blacks identified with Judge Thomas despite his conservative Republicanism, and they did not anticipate that President Bush would appoint another black and certainly not a liberal if Judge

**BOX 4.5 concluded**

Thomas were defeated. At this stage, liberals were not as passionate as they were in the Bork fight.

After a week of hearings, the Judiciary Committee tied 7–7 along party lines. One Democrat voted with the Republicans. But Judge Thomas seemed to have ample support on the Senate floor.

However, a few days before the Senate was scheduled to vote on his confirmation, Anita F. Hill, a black law professor at the University of Oklahoma, notified the Senate Judiciary Committee that Judge Thomas had sexually harassed her on the job. Judge Thomas was her boss at the Department of Education and the Equal Employment Opportunity Commission in the early 1980s.

When her charges were leaked to the mass media, pressure from women's rights groups and others led the Senate to delay its vote and the Judiciary Committee to hold public hearings on her charges. Republicans accused the Democratic committee staff of looking for dirt on Judge Thomas and informing the press after the committee had promised Professor Hill anonymity and planned to deal with the issue in a private session.

Both sides questioned Judge Thomas, Professor Hill, and co-workers and friends during several full days of televised hearings. Republicans anxious to save the nomination sharply challenged Ms. Hill's truthfulness and suggested before the Senate vote that she was lying, fantasizing, or had emotional problems. Judge Thomas vehemently denied the charges and claimed holding the hearings was racist and a high-tech lynching and that the charges reinforced racist sexual stereotypes of black males.

Despite intense questioning, which scoured the details of their relationship, and the seeming sincerity and honesty of Ms. Hill, Judge Thomas, and the other witnesses, the committee was unable to determine if the charges were true. Public opinion pollsters reported that men and women supported Judge Thomas, and talk shows suggested that blacks rallied to him after he claimed he was a victim of racism.

The Senate voted and Judge Thomas was confirmed by a slim margin of 52 to 48, with eleven conservative Democrats joining the Republicans.

But both sides were disturbed by the publicity which forced the committee to hold public hearings and the sordid and bitterly partisan "soap opera" which followed. Several senators and President Bush called for reforming the confirmation process, but with the stakes so high in ideologically motivated appointments, neither party is likely to agree on what the changes should be.

**The American Bar Association**    Before the 1900s, conflict over Supreme Court appointments mainly involved the President and the Senate, but as the practice of law grew and became organized and achieved higher social status, the American Bar Association became the main sponsor of legal values and emerged as a major political force in federal judicial selection.

The ABA has explicitly stated that it is not concerned with policy, but with obtaining the best possible federal judges. It has demanded a legitimate, semi-official mission of vetoing judicial candidates it rates unqualified for office. The ABA has campaigned tirelessly for recognition of this view, and it gradually achieved exceptional significance as a watchdog of the federal courts.

Early in the 1930s, the ABA organized a committee to screen and suggest nominees for the federal courts. Candidates were ranked on a four-point scale as: "Exceptionally Well Qualified," "Well Qualified," "Qualified," and "Not Qualified." This scale has been unchanged until very recently.

However, as discussed earlier, choosing the "best" judges leaves room for interpretation and political maneuvering, since there are so many legal-like indicators of a good judge that can be used to help or hinder a nominee. This has been true of the ABA's behavior as well.

ABA leadership comes predominantly from wealthy, business-oriented corporation lawyers, and for most of its history, they have viewed conservative nominees as better qualified than liberal ones. Critics complain that the ABA procedures are highly elitist, since the committee mainly consults prominent lawyers and presidents of local bar associations in producing its judicial ratings. This slants the evaluation toward wealthy, conservative, and Republican lawyers.[54] Consequently, Republican presidents generally have paid more attention to ABA recommendations than have Democratic chief executives.

The ABA's conservative tilt existed until the tense years of the Watergate scandals during the Nixon administration. Since then, the ABA has loosened its ties to Republican administrations, and the ABA has been able to evaluate Supreme Court nominees only after the President and his people have settled on their candidates. The ABA has not influenced the President's initial choices. Nevertheless, many liberals continue to perceive the ABA as a conservative influence on federal judicial selection. However, as will be discussed shortly, the ABA recently has been attacked by conservative Republicans as well.

*ABA Evaluations*    Several Supreme Court nominations illustrate the partisan influence of the ABA throughout history, and how legal values and standards frequently have been intertwined with partisan political purposes.

In 1916, President Woodrow Wilson nominated Louis D. Brandeis for the Supreme Court. Brandeis had been a crusading lawyer against child labor and other injustices in industrial working conditions, and he became a campaigner and advisor to the President. Corporations and railroads feared and hated him, and seven former presidents of the ABA testified that Brandeis was unfit for the Supreme Court because he lacked personal integrity and engaged in unethical legal practices.[55] A friend serving on the federal district court had warned Brandeis: "By your zeal for the common good you have created powerful enemies. They will do their utmost to defeat your confirmation in the Senate. . . . You will be accused of everything from grand larceny to a nonjudicial temperament.[56]

Brandeis was narrowly supported by the Senate Judiciary Committee, with the ten Democrats voting in favor of and the eight Republicans opposed to confirmation. On the Senate floor he won by a comfortable, but partisan margin of 47 to 22: all but one Democrat and three Progressives voted in favor and all Republicans were opposed.

Recently, the ABA has behaved almost identically in its treatment of other Supreme Court justices and nominees.[57] Toward the end of his term in 1968, Democratic President Lyndon Johnson nominated Justice Abe Fortas to become chief justice. Fortas had been a mainstay of the Warren Court liberal majority, and was opposed by conservative Republicans. He became a political target because he was head of a charitable foundation whose main contributor was a friend of Fortas and a possible litigant before the Supreme Court. Fortas also had accepted fees for giving public talks, and he had served as an informal advisor to President Johnson while on the Court.

The ABA claimed that Fortas had violated its ethical standards. The nomination was withdrawn, and in 1969, under increasing fire and threats of investigation from the newly elected Republican administration, Fortas resigned from the Court.

Then, President Nixon nominated conservative Republican Clement Haynesworth, the chief judge of the Fourth Circuit Court of Appeals, to replace Fortas. The ABA and sixteen former ABA presidents quickly announced their unanimous support for Haynesworth. However, shortly after Senate hearings had been held, further investigation revealed that Haynesworth had purchased stock in companies that were actively involved in litigation before him and that he had not fully reported his financial activities during Senate confirmation hearings. Despite these more serious violations of judicial ethics than those levied aginst Justice Fortas, the ABA leadership barely wavered in supporting his appointment. Nevertheless, Haynesworth was defeated by the Senate.

President Nixon fought back in 1970 with another conservative, Judge G. Harrold Carswell, a federal district court judge in north Florida. The ABA endorsed Carswell's appointment too, but the Senate rejected his nomination after it became evident that Carswell had a clear segregationist past, behaved roughly toward civil rights lawyers appearing in his court, and had a reputation as a mediocre judge and legalist. Many lawyers and law professors opposed Carswell despite the ABA endorsement.

It is unclear how the ABA would behave today toward liberal Democratic selections for the Supreme Court, since there have been no Democratic nominations since the 1960s. The recent leadership of the ABA is much less conservative than in earlier years.[58] Nevertheless, the ABA probably always will be criticized by extreme partisans who disagree with its evaluations. For example, right-wing Republicans were very unhappy with the ABA's split evaluation of Judge Bork. Following this episode, Attorney General Dick Thornburgh was able to convince the ABA to agree to avoid considering a nominee's political views as part of the rating process. Otherwise, the Bush administration would refuse to give the ABA advance lists of potential nominees. The ABA also agreed to drop its highest rating "Exceptionally Well Qualified," leaving three categories: "Well Qualified," "Qualified," and "Not Qualified." The reduced number of categories presumably would permit more nominees to appear to be of high standing.[59]

### The Lower Federal Courts

For most of American history, political views or ideology have ranked below other requirements, particularly political party patronage, in the selection of lower federal court judges.[60]

There have been several important reasons for this difference. First, as in the state trial and intermediate appellate courts, there are many more lower court positions to be filled. The President cannot devote much time to the details of lower court selection and relies on subordinates in the White House and the Justice Department to carry out judicial selection.

More important, the United States Senate has had a historically important role in influencing lower federal court selection, and senators typically use judicial positions as high-level political party or personal patronage rewards for individuals active in state or regional politics.

Finally, judicial ideology has been less important in the lower courts because those courts were not widely perceived as being deeply involved in policymaking, as is the Supreme Court. The lower courts were seen mainly as screening devices which decided the less important cases.

**Ideology**  Recent political changes have affected the selection of lower federal court judges, and ideology now is equally or even more important than patronage. It is difficult to pinpoint when the changes began, but they became more visible during the administration of Jimmy Carter and have been particularly prominent during the Reagan years. Since the 1960s, like the Supreme Court, the lower federal courts have become much more active and visible in significant policymaking. Many decisions have galvanized supporters and opponents of liberal judicial policymaking to work for the selection of judges with the "correct" attitudes and values.

President Jimmy Carter generally chose liberal Democrats, as have past Democratic Presidents, but the Reagan administration explicitly created new procedures in order to be certain that conservative Republicans who closely share the beliefs of the administration were appointed to all the federal courts. Judges with a track record of opposing abortion or favoring prayer in the public schools have an inside edge. With a few modifications, President Bush has maintained the Reagan tradition.[61]

Concern with ideology and patronage does not mean that judicial qualifications are insignificant in judicial selection. Well over 90 percent of all judicial appointments have received at least qualified support by the ABA, and there is no evidence that Presidents have actively considered many nominees who were obviously poor choices for the federal courts.[62]

**The U.S. Senate and the District Courts**  Through the routine operation of *senatorial courtesy* or consultation with other state party leaders, Presidents typically have permitted or encouraged the use of the federal courts as vehicles for sustaining political party organizations. The bond between state party politics and judicial appointments has been nearly automatic in the district courts, all of which are contained within the borders of individual states. Here senators usually are presumed to have tremendous power that cannot easily be challenged.

*Senatorial Courtesy*   Senatorial courtesy became fairly well established in the United States about 1840. It is a custom in which all federal appointments that occur within a particular state will be substantially influenced by the senators from that state when they and the President are of the same political party. In particular, it means that a senator of the President's party can ask his or her Senate colleagues not to approve a nominee from the senator's state that does not meet with the senator's approval. All other senators will support another senator's request, expecting similar treatment in return.

In most administrations, this means that federal patronage is made available to senators to reward state party supporters, contributors, and other allies in state politics. The President often acquiesces in the choices made by individual senators, substantially shifting the nomination process from the President to the Senate.

The Senate Judiciary Committee holds formal hearings on judicial nominations and makes a recommendation to the full Senate, but it routinely goes along with a senator's choice. In those rare cases in which senators and the Justice Department cannot agree on an appointment, senators usually have been successful in forcing acceptance of their nominees.

*Reagan-Bush Influence*   The Reagan and Bush administrations have asserted greater Presidential influence over the selection of lower federal judges. Senatorial courtesy still is in effect, but both administrations have created new procedures which guarantee that the White House staff and the President's key advisors substantially influence the selections. The Bush administration has required senators to submit three names for every vacancy, and reserves the right to reject a senator's recommendations which do not fit the administration's criteria.

Initial screening is done within the Justice Department. Potential nominees are interviewed by the deputy attorney general and the solicitor general. At about the same time, White House advisors review the candidates' records. Following initial screening, a new organization created by President Reagan—the President's Committee on Federal Judicial Selection—meets to make final recommendations for the President.

The committee includes powerful members of the President's administration. In addition to the assistant attorney general and the assistant White House counsel, who are in charge of initial screening, the committee includes the attorney general, deputy attorney general, assistant to the President for personnel, and assistant to the President for legislative affairs. The White House chief of staff also is a member, but rarely attends committee meetings. Although there is the possibility of tension between the White House and the Justice Department, both groups have been politically well synchronized under the Reagan and Bush administrations.[63]

The White House staff does not simply react to suggestions from the Justice Department or from individual senators, but suggests names of potential nominees themselves, and actively works for the appointment of people they favor. An expert on federal judicial selection concludes that under Reagan, the Committee produced a "consistent ideological or policy-orientation screening of judicial candidates."[64] The Bush administration has retained most of the Reagan administration procedures and continues to select conservative judges.

Senatorial courtesy does not operate when the President and the senators of a particular state are from different parties. In this circumstance, the President has more freedom to make district court appointments. Nevertheless, the President may still reach compromises with senators to obtain their support for other programs or votes for national appointments that are not controlled by senatorial courtesy.

Faced with a Democratic Congress, for example, President Richard Nixon appointed several Democratic judges to enlist Democratic support for his programs. During the Carter administration. Vice President Mondale recommended that one-third of the forthcoming judicial vacancies in his home state of Minnesota be filled with Republicans. In contrast, Presidents Reagan and Bush have appointed only a few Democrats.

Appointments across party lines create an image of bipartisanship, but the image often is only a thin charade. Less than 10 percent of a President's appointments generally go to the opposition, and in these cases Presidents often try to appoint judges whose political views are similar to their own.

**Courts of Appeals**   The selection of federal courts of appeals judges generally has followed similar procedures as those used for the district courts, but the outcomes have not been as clear-cut or as predictable. The most important difference is that *senatorial courtesy does not operate*, since the appointments affect several states and no single senator or state political organization is automatically involved.

*State Representation*   Nevertheless, appointment to the court of appeals often is rotated among the states in a circuit in order to maintain state representation. Consequently, there is a certain amount of predictability to appointments, since the senators from a particular state anticipate having a special role. Instead of senatorial courtesy, which implies considerable senatorial initiative and control, observers refer to the need to obtain "senatorial clearance" or approval before making an appointment. Senators may still suggest names, but they have less influence than in district court appointments.

A particular senator's influence depends on seniority, position on key committees, particularly the Senate Judiciary Committee, and ability to affect other appointments or administration programs and legislation. A senator who could affect a President's success in the passage of important bills in the future sometimes achieves considerable influence in court of appeals selections as a trade-off for support on other policies.

But other officials are important too. The Justice Department and the President's committee usually actively seek the names of qualified individuals from

**BOX 4.6**

JUDGE DANIEL MANION TAKES
THE COURT

In 1986, President Reagan nominated
Daniel A. Manion, a lawyer from South
Bend, Indiana, to become a judge on the
Seventh Circuit Court of Appeals, which sits
in Chicago. The screening panel for the
American Bar Association ruled that Manion
was qualified for office, but the nomination
raised a storm of protest, including opposition from forty law school deans, from,
among others, Harvard, Yale, the University
of Michigan, Northwestern, the University of
Chicago, and the University of Pennsylvania. The deans stated that Manion lacked
"scholarship, legal acumen, professional
achievement, wisdom, fidelity to the law, and
commitment to our Constitution." Fifty labor
unions, other liberal organizations, and various judges also joined in opposing the nomination.

As a lawyer, Mr. Manion had practically
no experience before the federal courts and
no prior judicial experience. He had not written an article for any law review, and legal
briefs which he submitted to the Senate for
review contained grammatical and spelling
errors. As a state senator he once proposed
posting the Ten Commandments in the public schools, two months after the Supreme
Court had banned such practices. He also
was linked to the John Birch Society, a right-
wing political organization once headed by
Manion's father.

President Reagan, Attorney General Edwin Meese, and Senate Republican leaders
defended Manion, stating that his qualifications were sound and that he was no worse
than some other federal judges. The only
reason for the opposition was Manion's conservative ideology, which, they argued,
should not be debated in the Senate.

The Senate was controlled by a slim majority of Republicans, but a few of them were
inclined to vote with the Democrats against
the nomination, so the outcome was in doubt
until the very end. President Reagan made
several bargains to get a favorable vote, including promising two Republican senators
that individuals they were supporting for
other federal judgeships would receive nominations. The vote was 47 to 47 along clear
party lines until Senator Robert C. Byrd, the
Senate Democratic minority leader,
switched his vote to give Manion a 48 to 46
victory. This was a political maneuver to acti-
vate Senate rules which permitted Senator
Byrd to call immediately for a reconsideration of the vote.

Another vote was put off for several
weeks. During this period, both sides tried to
hold their forces together, and President
Reagan personally lobbied doubtful senators. The vote for reconsideration was a 49
to 49 tie, another party vote, broken by Republican Vice President Bush in Manion's
favor.

numerous sources, such as state party heads, members of Congress, law school
deans, state bar association leaders, and other interest groups. A senator
cannot simply name the candidate, and it is advantageous to reach an agreement with the administration to avoid a confrontation that might be lost. In the
Reagan and Bush administrations, ideology has been very important in the
selection process, as in the choice of federal district judges.

Typically, compromises on judicial nominees may involve senators and even
congressional members from several states within the circuit. Sometimes, in
order to maintain their influence and avoid a public squabble, all the participants agree on long-term arrangements in which each of them is guaranteed an
opportunity to suggest a candidate for a judicial vacancy over the next several
years, or as soon as positions become available.

---

**BOX 4.7**

JUDGE RYSKAMP IS REJECTED

President Bush has submitted few controversial nominations, and the Democratic controlled Senate has approved most of his choices. But Judge Kenneth L. Ryskamp was an exception. Judge Ryskamp was a federal district court judge in Miami, and the Bush administration proposed that he be elevated to the Court of Appeals for the Eleventh Circuit, which hears cases in Florida, Georgia, and Alabama. The ABA had given Judge Ryskamp its highest rating.

Senate Democrats gave several reasons for rejecting this nomination. First, Judge Ryskamp lacked sensitivity to minorities. He remarked during a trial that the black litigants—who were suing the West Palm Beach Police Department, claiming they had been mauled by police dogs—deserved to carry some scars from their crimes. He likened it to countries which cut off the hands of thieves. To make matters worse, two of the four black litigants had never been charged with a crime.

Second, Judge Ryskamp was a member of a country club which was widely known in south Florida to have no Jewish or black members and which temporarily enacted a rule against permitting Spanish to be spoken at the club.

Rather than repudiating his offensive and inappropriate remarks and charges that he was biased, Judge Ryskamp told the committee that he did not believe that criminals should have the right to sue the police for damages. Concerning discrimination, the judge added that he was unaware of club discrimination but added that Miami was like a foreign city and that the club members simply wanted a place where they did not have to listen to Spanish. He reported that his wife disliked shopping in grocery stores with Cuban clerks and Cuban-style food. The judge also had resigned from the club just a few days before his Senate hearings, which offended several Judiciary Committee Members.

Many ethnic and civil rights organizations in south Florida communicated their opposition to their senator, Democrat Bob Graham, who, while not a member of the committee, notified the committee of his opposition to the nomination. The Senate Judiciary Committee rejected the nomination on a party vote. The eight Democrats voted no and the six Republicans voted yes. The nomination was not sent to the full Senate.

Democrats explained that Ryskamp was rejected because of his insensitivity to minorities and civil rights. Republicans dismissed the complaints against Judge Ryskamp and claimed the Democrats were motivated by ideology.

---

Other federal patronage may be included in the arrangement if an insufficient number of judicial vacancies is expected during the life of a current administration. Senators try to exert as much influence as possible without openly forcing a choice between their own and other candidates. They give a little and take a little to be sure of winning something in the appointment process.

The boxes ''Judge Daniel Manion Takes the Court'' and ''Judge Ryskamp Is Rejected'' illustrate the intense political conflict and bargaining that sometimes occurs in these appointments and the crucial importance of ideology as a judicial qualification in the Reagan and Bush administrations.

**The ABA and the Lower Courts**   As in Supreme Court nominations, the ABA's ultimate goal is to have the power to veto nominations to the lower federal courts before final commitments are made either to nominees or to their sponsoring senators. It had this power during the Republican Eisenhower administration of the 1950s and during the Nixon years. But Democrats and Presidents Reagan and Bush have not extended this power to the ABA.

The ABA's approval still is sought because it is the most prestigious legal organization, which carries some weight with the public and politicians alike, but it does not have exclusive control. However, since it compromised with the Bush administration on procedures, it does receive advance notification of potential nominees, which gives it some advantage over other interest groups in influencing judicial selection. Nevertheless, since there now are many more active interest groups seeking to influence judicial selection, the ABA faces much stiffer competition than in years past. When there is controversy on particular nominees, a high ABA rating is not enough to save the nomination.

*ABA's Power*    Although the ABA claims to safeguard the federal judiciary from bad appointments, it is difficult to measure actual ABA influence in federal judicial selection. It is doubtful the ABA can justifiably take most of the credit for ensuring quality federal judicial appointments. The stakes involved for the President, the Justice Department, and individual senators are so high that they also want respectable appointments.

Presidential concern with ideology and political party patronage does not mean that poor appointments are made. It means only that either Republicans or Democrats, usually with active party and other public experience, will receive most of the posts, and there always is an abundance of qualified people. There is no reason, then, why politicians should carelessly or routinely select poorly qualified individuals for the courts. Poor appointments may not always attract publicity, but there is little reason to take risks that may damage a President's or a senator's prestige by inviting a charge of cronyism or crass party politics.

If the ABA and government officials *both* publicly support quality merit appointments, it is very difficult to distinguish the ABA role from the policy of the politicians. Therefore, even when there is rare public disagreement over appointments, it is not clear that the ABA is "right" and the government is "wrong." The chances are that several candidates have above-average formal credentials, but there is disagreement on which candidate is "best" for the vacancy.

**Affirmative Action**    In recent years, women's organizations, civil rights groups, and others have become more involved in federal judicial selection. They demand a share of judicial appointments and want to contribute their evaluation of other nominees whose judicial decisions may affect their political rights and social opportunities. Such groups were recognized by President Carter in the 1970s, and he promised to apply merit criteria and affirmative action policy to the federal courts. In particular, he sought to give women and minorities special consideration for appointments in order to overcome past inequities in judicial selection. He was able to create merit panels only for the federal courts of appeals since the Senate refused to give up senatorial courtesy for the district courts. However, about half the senators voluntarily created their own district court nominating commissions.[65]

The commissions included many women, blacks, and nonlawyers and recommended more women and nonwhites for the courts than had ever been appointed by any previous administration. However, as in most judicial appointments, the commissions also served partisan political interests. Nearly 90 percent of the commissioners and the judges selected were Democrats, many of whom had been active in President Carter's election campaigns. The lawyers on the commissions did not represent the ABA but also were Carter Democrats.[66]

The ABA opposed Carter's affirmative action innovations, claiming that most women and minorities would have very little legal experience and would not be qualified for the courts. But the Carter administration counterclaimed that both merit and affirmative action goals could be achieved, a claim which is supported by social science research. Overall, the educations and legal and judicial experience of women and blacks selected during the Carter administration are equally or more outstanding than those of the white males selected in any previous presidency.[67]

However, these changes were very short-lived. When the Republicans won control of the U.S. Senate in 1980, conservative Republican Strom Thurmond of South Carolina became chairman of the Judiciary Committee and announced that he favored a return to traditional Senate methods for selecting federal judges. President Reagan abolished the merit selection panels used by President Carter for the courts of appeals and abandoned affirmative action for the federal courts.

### Who Are Federal Judges?

Becoming a federal judge requires political visibility, involvement in political activity, party loyalty, and sharing the political values or ideology of the administration making the appointments. These kinds of political requirements are revealed in the backgrounds of judges who have been appointed over the years by different Presidents and political parties.

An examination of the backgrounds of judges also clarifies the qualifications issue. By examining who the judges are, we can obtain an objective idea of the kinds of experience judges have had and how well qualified they are to serve. It also shows us generally the types of people preferred for the courts.

**Supreme Court**   Remarkable similarity describes the characteristics of justices of the U.S. Supreme Court.[68] Until very recently, this most prestigious judicial institution has been filled with men who ranked at the very top of the American social order. Nearly all of the justices have been white, Anglo-Saxon, Protestant (WASP) men around 50 years old.

*High Status*   In the 1800s, they typically were drawn from America's landed gentry, the early aristocrats of American society. As America changed, their backgrounds became largely upper middle class and their fathers were likely to be lawyers, doctors, clergymen, or other professionals. They also were very likely to have come from families where involvement in politics was expected and customary.

About one-third of the justices had relatives who had served on a state or federal court. Most of the justices also held a variety of government posts before going on the Supreme Court. Over half had been judges. The judges' educations also took place mostly in prestigious universities. Nearly two-thirds either were undergraduates or attended law school at Ivy League colleges.

The collective portrait of the justices demonstrates that upper-middle-class individuals have an advantage in selection for the Supreme Court. The occasional appointment of Catholic, Jewish, or black justices is a recent and rare event. President Reagan's appointment of Sandra D. O'Connor is the most recent change to occur in recruitment to the Supreme Court.

Table 4.4 summarizes some of the characteristics of the current justices of the Supreme Court. The members of the current Supreme Court also have exceptional backgrounds. All of the justices graduated from prestigious law schools. All but Justice O'Conner also held high-level positions in the U.S. Justice Department or were federal judges before their appointment.

**TABLE 4-4**
CHARACTERISTICS OF SUPREME COURT JUSTICES

| Justice | Political party | Year appointed | Major prior experience | Law school attended |
|---------|-----------------|----------------|------------------------|---------------------|
| Byron White | Democrat | 1962 | Deputy U.S. Attorney General | Yale |
| Harry Blackmun | Republican | 1970 | Federal Court of Appeals judge | Harvard |
| William Rehnquist | Republican | 1971 | Assistant U.S. Attorney General | Stanford |
| John P. Stevens | Republican | 1975 | Federal Court of Appeals judge | Northwestern |
| Sandra D. O'Connor | Republican | 1981 | State judge; state legislator | Stanford |
| Antonin Scalia | Republican | 1986 | Federal Court of Appeals judge; law professor at University of Chicago | Harvard |
| Anthony M. Kennedy | Republican | 1987 | Federal Court of Appeals judge | Harvard |
| David H. Souter | Republican | 1990 | State judge; recent Federal Court of Appeals judge | Harvard |
| Clarence Thomas | Republican | 1991 | Federal Court of Appeals judge; Chairman, EEOC | Yale |

Recently, only former Justice Thurgood Marshall had come from a lower-status family. Justice Marshall's father was a steward on passenger trains, and the justice graduated from Howard University in Washington, D.C., a predominantly black university that has been attended by many black civil rights lawyers. Of course, he had done much since his early days. Justice Marshall was chief lawyer for the National Association for the Advancement of Colored People (NAACP) and became a federal judge and solicitor general of the United States (the government's chief lawyer in the Supreme Court). Until the appointment of Justice Scalia, former Justice William Brennan had been the only Catholic for many years, and currently there are no Jewish justices on the Court.

If education and legal, governmental, and judicial experience are considered the necessary qualifications for appointment to the U.S. Supreme Court, then it is difficult to point out any justices who were not well qualified to serve. For those who may be inclined to equate social status with qualifications, it also is clear that Presidents generally could do no better in their choices for the high court. Even nominees who were rejected share most of the characteristics of the chosen. Disagreement over appointments, then, can best be understood as conflict over the policy preferences of judges, with legal qualifications used as a tool to achieve political success.

**Lower Federal Courts**   A description of the backgrounds of federal district and court of appeals judges appointed by Republican Presidents Bush and Reagan and Democratic President Carter is presented in Table 4.5.[69] The figures for Presidents Bush and Reagan are combined because they are similar, and President Bush had not yet made as many appointments as Presidents Reagan and Carter. The table shows that there are many similarities but also some differences among judges appointed by different Presidents.

*Judicial and Legal Experience*   As a group, the federal judges are well-qualified for office. Most of them either were recruited from other courts or had held some other judgeship during their career. Overall, appeals courts judges are somewhat more likely to have held prior judicial office, often as a federal district court judge. The emphasis on prior judicial experience as part of the career ladder to the federal courts has been greater since the Carter administration, and federal district judges in particular now are more likely to have had prior judicial experience than before the early 1970s. Many judges also had served as prosecuting attorneys at some point.

Most federal judges not serving in government at the time of their appointment were recruited from large or medium-sized law firms. Many of the judges found in the "small firm, solo, other" category were law professors. There are very few solo practitioners placed on the federal courts by any President.

The educational backgrounds of federal judges also indicate that they are at the top of social, economic, and legal strata. Except for the Carter district judges, well over half of the federal judges attended private or Ivy League undergraduate and law schools. Relatively few have attended public state universities and almost none have gone to low-status proprietary (for profit) law schools.

*Party Differences* Although there are many similarities among federal judges in all recent administrations, Presidents appoint individuals who tend to be more typical of their party's constituency. Generally, the Democrats are inclined to appoint a larger percentage of judges who have attended public undergraduate and law schools. In Table 4.5, this fact shows up in the fewer prestige appointments to the federal district courts under President Carter. Nevertheless, given that most Americans who attend college go to public

**TABLE 4-5**
CHARACTERISTICS OF FEDERAL DISTRICT AND COURT OF APPEALS JUDGES

| | Bush/Reagan (1980–1990) | | Carter (1976–1980) | |
| --- | --- | --- | --- | --- |
| | District N = 338 | Appeals N = 96 | District N = 202 | Appeals N = 56 |
| **Occupation at appointment** | | | | |
| Politics/Government | 12.4% | 7.3% | 4.4% | 5.4% |
| Judge | 38.8 | 55.2 | 44.6 | 46.4 |
| Law practice | | | | |
|    Large firm | 17.4 | 13.5 | 13.8 | 10.8 |
|    Medium firm | 19.2 | 11.5 | 19.8 | 16.1 |
|    Small firm, solo, other | 12.1 | 12.5 | 17.3 | 21.4 |
| **Previous government experience** | | | | |
| Judicial | 47.0% | 59.4% | 54.5% | 53.6% |
| Prosecutor | 43.2 | 29.2 | 38.6 | 32.1 |
| **Political Party[a]** | | | | |
| Democrat | 4.7% | 0.0% | 92.6% | 82.1% |
| Republican | 93.2 | 96.9 | 4.4 | 7.1 |
| Party activist | 59.2 | 68.8 | 60.9 | 73.2 |
| **Education** | | | | |
| Private/Ivy league undergraduate | 63.6% | 74.0% | 42.6% | 69.6% |
| Private/Ivy league law | 56.8 | 63.5 | 49.5 | 60.7 |
| **Sex, race, religion** | | | | |
| Male | 91.4% | 93.8% | 85.6% | 80.4% |
| White | 92.9 | 95.8 | 78.7 | 78.6 |
| Protestant | 60.9 | 55.2 | 60.4 | 60.7 |
| Average Age at Nomination | 48.8 | 49.7 | 49.7 | 51.9 |

*Note:* [a] Several judges were political independents.
*Source:* Derived from: Sheldon Goldman, "The Bush Imprint on the Judiciary: Carrying on a Tradition," *Judicature* 74 (1991), Tables 1 and 2, pp. 298–299 and 302–303.

schools, all administrations lean heavily toward making appointments from a small group of candidates with exceptional and elite educational credentials. Another difference is that Republicans appoint a larger number of very wealthy lawyers to the federal courts (not shown in Table 4.5). Democratic nominees tend to come from somewhat more modest means.

It is clear from Table 4.5 that Presidents almost always appoint members of their own political party to federal judgeships. As discussed earlier, these positions are highly desirable jobs which can be used effectively for patronage—rewards to party supporters and career politicians. Well over half of all of the judges also have been active in party politics at some point in their careers. They have campaigned for party candidates, held official party posts, or made financial contributions to campaigns.

Generally, the federal courts still are dominated by white males. Most administrations have appointed very few women and nonwhites. However, as discussed earlier, President Jimmy Carter appointed a larger percentage of women, blacks and Hispanics to the federal courts than any other President. There are very few differences between the parties concerning the religions of judges. Although there have been some variations among individual Presidents, overall, neither the Democrats nor the Republicans appoint different percentages of Protestants, Catholics, and Jews.

*Federal and State Judges Compared*   There is a widespread belief in the legal culture that federal judges are more highly qualified for judicial office than are state judges. The supporters of federal diversity jurisdiction, for example, frequently argue that complex multistate commercial litigation needs to be heard in the federal courts because the judges are better equipped to handle those kinds of cases. The judges have had better educations and wider and more varied experience and are more sophisticated in complex legal matters.

What differences are there among judges? In some respects, federal and state judges are very similar (Tables 4.3 and 4.5). Both sets of courts still are dominated by white males of about the same age, and both have roughly equal percentages from each of the major religions. Many federal and state judges also have had substantial prior political and governmental experience.

However, there are some differences which suggest that federal judges do have an edge over their state brethren. First, although most state supreme court judges have had extensive prior political experience, including prior judgeships, most of their experience is limited to the states and the lower courts. Just slightly over 10 percent of the state supreme court judges held any prior federal post (not shown in Table 4.3).[70]

In contrast, many of the federal district judges previously had distinguished themselves on state supreme courts or occasionally other state courts of appeals. And, it now is common for many of the federal courts of appeals judges to have served previously as a federal district judge. It is rare for judges to have "stepped down" from the federal to the state judiciary. Therefore, there seems to be an informal hierarchy in judicial mobility—from state positions to the federal courts, not in the other direction.

If private and Ivy League educations are rough indicators of a high quality education, then the federal judges, particularly those on the courts of appeals, outdistance the state judges. This is clearest in the difference between the percentage of federal and state judges who attended private and Ivy League law schools. Finally, federal judges are recruited more often from medium and large law firms. Almost none of the federal judges have been solo practitioners. In contrast, a majority of state supreme court judges have practiced in very small firms or were solo practitioners. As discussed earlier, these are the least prestigious types of law practice and the ones least likely to provide a lawyer with extensive experience in complex business legal affairs—the types of cases often handled by the federal courts.

This comparison does not mean that state judges are poorly educated or unqualified. They have law degrees and a number of years of prior judicial experience, law practice, and service in other state government jobs. Most have graduated from accredited state universities, and some have attended private or Ivy League schools, especially as undergraduates. Nevertheless, in terms of prestigious formal credentials, there is a pecking order in the judiciary, with the ladder pointing toward the federal courts.

## CONCLUSION

Choosing judges always has been an important part of state and national politics, since it involves political patronage, judicial policy, and the proper role of judges. The selection of federal judges illustrates long-standing conflict between national and state political power and the use of lower federal courts to satisfy political demands in the states.

Much conflict about judicial selection concerns how we can obtain the best possible people for the courts. Merit selection, or the Missouri plan, currently is seen as a way of combining traditional popular political control with a heavy dose of guidance from the legal profession. Many states have adopted merit selection, and President Carter and many U.S. senators used a version of it to select federal judges.

Reformers usually contrast the ideal operation of merit selection with "worst-case" examples of partisan election and appointment by governors and Presidents. However, comparisons of judicial elections, executive appointment, and merit selection clearly show that differences among them are not great. But there also is evidence that merit selection is not favorable to the selection of minorities. In all types of judicial selection, legal criteria for selection are vague and fuzzy, leaving lawyers and political executives alike searching for specific political and social factors to determine who will get judgeships.

The heavy influence of partisan politics in the selection of state and federal judges does not mean that the United States has poor judges. The opposite is true. The backgrounds of nearly all federal and state judges indicate that they have acceptable or superior legal training, and most have much legal and government experience before they reach the bench. There is very little evidence that governors, Presidents, state legislators, or U.S. senators give judgeships to just anyone in return for service in political campaigns. Examples of incompetent or corrupt judges are hard to find.

Partisan politics narrows the field of eligible candidates so that only those who are active in politics are likely to get positions. However, there always are highly qualified individuals who meet educational, experiential, and political criteria. The *real* political battle in judicial selection is over which groups will be rewarded with judgeships and what are the political values and likely policies of judges who are going to be appointed to the courts.

It probably is not possible to create a selection system that separates judicial selection from partisan politics. The national and state constitutions and our political traditions have guaranteed a substantial amount of partisan politics in judicial selection. Unless we create a career service for judges beginning with young lawyers, which is unlikely, we will continue to see conflict and compromise between popular political culture and legal culture and competition among political parties and interest groups in choosing American judges. The states probably will continue to adopt merit selection because it looks good on the surface, but state politicians and lawyers will not change their political and social goals in trying to get the judges they want on the courts.

## SUGGESTIONS FOR ADDITIONAL READING

Henry J. Abraham: *Justices and Presidents* (New York: Oxford University Press, 2d ed., 1985). This is a political history detailing appointments to the U.S. Supreme Court.

Philip L. Dubois, *From Ballot to Bench* (Austin: University of Texas Press, 1980). A comprehensive analysis of state judicial elections, this study also considers some of the frequently made charges about electing judges.

Sheldon Goldman, "Reaganizing the Judiciary," *Judicature*, 68 (1985), 313–25; and "Bush's Imprint on the Judiciary," *Judicature* 74 (1991), 294–306. These two articles describe and analyze recent changes in the politics of selecting federal judges and the special impact of recent Republican administrations on securing judges with conservative views.

Richard A. Watson and Rondal G. Downing, *The Politics of the Bench and the Bar* (New York: John Wiley and Sons, Inc., 1969). This is the most complete analysis of the operation of state merit selection in a single state (Missouri), and it links judicial selection to an array of political forces in state government and bar associations.

## NOTES

**1** Charles H. Sheldon and Nicholas P. Lovrich, Jr., "State Judicial Recruitment," in John B. Gates and Charles A. Johnson, eds., *The American Courts: A Critical Assessment* (Washington, D.C.: CQ Press, 1991), chap. 6.

**2** *Annual Report of the Director*, Administrative Office of the United States Courts, 1990, pp. 1–12; *State Court Caseload Statistics: Annual Report 1989* (Williamsburg, Va.: National Center for State Courts, 1991), Figure G, p. 259.

**3** Henry Robert Glick, *Supreme Courts in State Politics* (New York: Basic Books, 1971).

**4** Glenn S. Winters (ed.), *Judicial Selection and Tenure: Selected Readings* (Chicago: American Judicature Society, 1973).

**5** Richard A. Watson and Rondal G. Downing, *The Politics of the Bench and the Bar* (New York: John Wiley & Sons, Inc., 1969).

**6** Henry R. Glick and Kenneth N. Vines, *State Court Systems* (Englewood Cliffs, N.J.: Prentice-Hall, Inc., 1973), p. 41; American Judicature Society, "Judicial Selection and Tenure: A State-by-State Compilation," January 1979. Also, contrast *Book of the States* (Lexington, Ky.: Council of State Governments, 1982–1983) and Sara Mathias, *Electing Justice: A Handbook of Judicial Election Reforms* (Chicago: American Judicature Society, 1990), p. 142.

**7** Glick and Vines, pp. 41–42.

**8** Watson and Downing, p. 8.

**9** James Herndon, "Appointment as a Means of Initial Accession to Elective State Courts of Last Resort," *North Dakota Law Review*, 38 (1962), 60–73; Philip L. Dubois, *From Ballot to Bench* (Austin: University of Texas Press, 1980), chap. 4.

**10** William J. Keefe, "Judges and Politics: The Pennsylvania Plan of Judge Selection," *University of Pittsburgh Law Review*, 20 (1959), 621; Burton Atkins, "Judges' Perspective on Judicial Selection," *State Government*, 49 (Summer 1976), 180–186; John M. Scheb, II, "State Appellate Judges' Attitudes Toward Judicial Merit Selection and Retention: Results of a National Survey," *Judicature*, 72 (October–November, 1988), 170–174.

**11** Jack Ladinsky and Allan Silver, "Popular Democracy and Judicial Independence: Electorate and Elite Reactions to Two Wisconsin Supreme Court Elections," *Wisconsin Law Review* (1967), 132–133; Bancroft C. Henderson and T. C. Sinclair, *Judicial Selection in Texas* (Houston: University of Houston Public Affairs Research Center, 1965); Kenneth N. Vines, "The Selection of Judges in Louisiana," *Tulane Studies in Political Science*, 8 (1962); Herbert Jacob, "Judicial Insulation: Elections, Direct Participation and Public Attention to the Courts in Wisconsin," *Wisconsin Law Review* (1966), 801–819; Lawrence Baum, "The Electoral Fate of Incumbent Judges in the Ohio Court of Common Pleas," *Judicature*, 66 (1983), 420–430.

**12** Philip L. Dubois, "Voter Turnout in State Judicial Elections: An Analysis of the Tail on the Electoral Kite," *Journal of Politics*, 41 (1979), 865–887.

**13** Philip L. Dubois, "The Significance of Voting Cues in State Supreme Court Elections," *Law and Society Review*, 13 (Spring 1979), 757–779.

**14** Philip L. Dubois, "Voting Cues in Nonpartisan Trial Court Elections: A Multivariate Assessment," *Law and Society Review*, 18 (1984), 426.

**15** Herndon, pp. 60–73; Dubois, "The Significance of Voting Cues in State Supreme Court Elections," pp. 757–779; Dubois, *From Ballot to Bench*, p. 50.

**16** Glick and Vines, pp. 42–43; Lawrence Baum, "Explaining the Vote in Judicial Elections: The 1984 Ohio Supreme Court Elections," *Western Political Quarterly*, 40 (1987), 361–371; *New York Times*, January 22, 1988, p. 9; Jeffrey M. Shaman, "Texas Supreme Court Justice Publicly Reprimanded, Admonished," *Judicial Conduct Reporter*, 9 (1987), p. 1.

**17** S. Sidney Ulmer, "The Political Party Variable in the Michigan Supreme Court," *Journal of Public Law*, 11 (1962), 352–362; Baum, "Explaining the Vote . . . ," pp. 361–371.

**18** Dubois, "The Significance of Voting Cues in State Supreme Court Elections," pp. 757–779; Baum, "The Electoral Fate . . . ," 430; Mathias, 1990.

**19** There has been much discussion of this issue. For a good summary, see the several articles on this issue in *Judicature*, 73 (1989). Also, Barbara Luck Graham, "Federal Court Policy-Making: An Analysis of Judicial Redistricting," *Western Political Quarterly*, 44 (1991), 102–117.

**20** Burton Atkins, Mathew Dezee and William Eckert, "State Supreme Court Elections: The Significance of Racial Cues," *American Politics Quarterly*, 12 (1984), 211–225; Nicholas P. Lovrich, Jr. and Charles H. Sheldon, "The Racial Factor in Nonpartisan Judicial Elections: A Research Note," *Western Political Quarterly*, 41 (1988), 807–816; Richard L. Engstrom, "When Blacks Run for Judge: Racial Divisions in the Candidate Preferences of Louisiana Voters," *Judicature*, 73 (1989), 87–89.

**21** *Judicature*, 73 (1989); *New York Times*, April 23, 1991, p. A11.

**22** April D. Dulaney, "A Judicial Exception for Judicial Elections: 'A Burning Scar on the Flesh of the Voting Rights Act,'" *Tulane Law Review*, 65 (1991), 1223–1259; Pasquale A. Cipollone, "Section 2 of the Voting Rights Act and Judicial Elections: Application and Remedy," *University of Chicago Law Review*, 58 (1991), 733–767; *Chisom, et al., v. Roemer* (1991), 59 LW 4696.

**23** Herbert Jacob, "The Effect of Institutional Differences in the Recruitment Process: The Case of State Judges," *Journal of Public Law*, 13 (1964), 104–119; Bradley C. Canon, "The Impact of Formal Selection Process on the Characteristics of Judges— Reconsidered," *Law and Society Review*, 6 (May 1972), 575–593; Henry R. Glick and Craig F. Emmert, "Selection Systems and Judicial Characteristics," *Judicature*, 70 (1987), 228–235.

**24** James Eisenstein and Herbert Jacob, *Felony Justice* (Boston: Little, Brown and Co., 1977), pp. 78–140.

**25** Based on the author's interviews with state supreme court judges.

**26** Rick Karl, "Hatchett Becomes First Modern Black to Win in Florida," *Judicature*, 60 (1977), 291–296.

**27** *Tallahassee Democrat*, November 16, 1985, p. 1.

**28** "Judge Bird on Trial," *Newsweek*, October 23, 1978, p. 53; *Los Angeles Times*, September 10, 1985, pt. I, p. 19, and November 23, 1985, p. 1; John H. Culver and John T. Wold, "Rose Bird and the Politics of Judicial Accountability in California," *Judicature*, 70 (August–September 1986), 81–89; John T. Wold and John H. Culver, "The Defeat of the California Justices: The Campaign, the Electorate and the Issue of Judicial Accountability," *Judicature*, 70 (1987), 348–355. See also Kenyon N. Griffin and Michael J. Horan, "Merit Retention Elections: What Influences the Voters?" *Judicature*, 63 (1979), 80.

**29** For a discussion of the politics of adoption, see Philip L. Dubois, "Voter Responses to Court Reform: Merit Judicial Selection on the Ballot," *Judicature*, 73 (1990), 238–247.

**30** Beth M. Henshen, Robert Moog, and Steven Davis, "Judicial Nominating Commissioners: A National Profile," *Judicature*, 73 (1990), 328–334, 343.

**31** Alan Ashman and James Alfini, *The Key to Judicial Merit Selection: The Nominating Process* (Chicago: American Judicature Society, 1974), pp. 62–66.

32 Watson and Downing.

33 *Ibid*. See also Kathleen L. Barber, "Ohio Judicial Elections: Non-Partisan Premises with Partisan Results," *Ohio State Law Journal*, 32 (1971), 762–789. The following discussion relies mainly on Watson and Downing.

34 *Ibid*.; Henshen et al., pp. 333–334.

35 Ashman and Alfini, pp. 62–66.

36 Griffin and Horan, August 1979, and William Jenkins, Jr., "Retention Elections: Who Wins When No One Loses?" *Judicature*, 61 (1977), 79–86; Susan B. Carbon, "Judicial Retention Elections: Are They Serving Their Intended Purpose?" *Judicature*, 64 (1980), 221.

37 Henry R. Glick and Craig F. Emmert, "Stability and Changes: Characteristics of State Supreme Court Judges," *Judicature*, 70 (1986), 108.

38 *Ibid*.

39 Beverly B. Cook, "Women Judges: The End of Tokenism," in Winifred L. Hepperle and Lora Crites (eds.), *Women in the Courts* (Williamsburg, Va.: National Center for State Courts, 1978); Larry Berkson, "Women on the Bench: A Brief History," and Susan Carbon et al., "Women on the State Bench: Their Characteristics and Attitudes about Judicial Selection," *Judicature*, 65 (1982), 286–305; Glick and Emmert, "Stability and Change: The Characteristics of State Supreme Court Judges," p. 109, and M. L. Henry, Jr., et al., *The Success of Women and Minorities in Achieving Judicial Office*, (New York: The Fund for Modern Courts, 1985).

40 Henry, 1985; Barbara Luck Graham, "Do Judicial Selection Systems Matter? A Study of Black Representation on State Courts," *American Politics Quarterly*, 18 (1990), 316–336; Graham, "Judicial Recruitment and Racial Diversity on State Courts: An Overview," *Judicature*, 74 (1990), 28–34.

41 Thomas M. Uhlman, "Race, Recruitment and Representation: Background Differences between Black and White Trial Court Judges," *Western Political Quarterly*, 30 (1977), 457–470.

42 Jacob, "The Effect of Institutional Differences . . . ." pp. 104–119; Canon, pp. 575–593; Glick and Emmert, "Stability and Change," p. 108.

43 Canon, pp. 575–593; Glick and Emmert, "Selection Systems and Judicial Characteristics"; Watson and Downing, p. 210; Larry L. Berg et al., "The Consequences of Judicial Reform: A Comparative Analysis of the California and Iowa Appellate Court Systems," *Western Political Quarterly*, 28 (1975), pp. 263–180.

44 Craig F. Emmert and Henry R. Glick, "The Selection of State Supreme Court Justices," *American Politics Quarterly*, 16 (1988), pp. 445–464.

45 Graham, "Do Judicial Selection Systems Matter? . . ," pp. 316–336; Graham, "Judicial Recruitment and Racial Diversity. . . ."

46 Watson and Downing, p. 51; Keefe, p. 621; Atkins, pp. 180–186.

47 On the selection of Supreme court justices, see Joel Grossman, *Lawyers and Judges* (New York: John Wiley & Sons, Inc., 1965); Joseph P. Harris, *The Advice and Consent of the Senate* (New York: Random House, 1953), pp. 7–35; John R. Schmidhauser, *Judges and Justices* (Boston: Little, Brown and Co., 1979), chap. 2.

48 Harris, pp. 1–35.

49 Henry J. Abraham, *Justices and Presidents* (New York: Oxford University Press, 2d ed., 1985).

50 Howard Ball, *Courts and Politics* (Englewood Cliffs, N.J.: Prentice-Hall, Inc., 1979), p. 167.

**51** Jeffrey Segal, "Senate Confirmation of Supreme Court Justices: Partisan and In-stitutional Politics," *Journal of Politics*, 49 (1987), 998–1015; Lawrence Baum, *The Supreme Court* (Washington, D.C.: CQ Press, 1989, 3d ed.), pp. 47–49; Charles M. Cameron, Albert D. Cover, and Jeffrey A. Segal, "Senate Voting on Supreme Court Nominees: A Neoinstitutional Model," *American Political Science Review*, 84 (1990), 525–534.

**52** Donald R. Songer, "The Relevance of Policy Values for the Confirmation of Su-preme Court Nominees," *Law and Society Review*, 13 (Summer 1979), 927–948.

**53** Sheldon Goldman and Thomas P. Jahnige, *The Federal Courts as a Political System*, 2d ed. (New York: Harper & Row, Publishers, Inc., 1976), pp. 62–74.

**54** In addition to Grossman, see Elliot Slotnick, "The Changing Role of the Senate Judiciary Committee in Judicial Selection," *Judicature*, 62 (1979), 502, 508; Schmidhauser, pp. 28–33; and Elliot E. Slotnick, "The ABA Standing Committee on Federal Judiciary: A Contemporary Assessment—Part I," *Judicature*, 66 (1983), 352, 360.

**55** Harris, pp. 99–114; Alpheus T. Mason, *Brandeis: A Free Man's Life* (New York: Viking Press, 1946); Schmidhauser, pp. 24–26; A. L. Todd, *Justice on Trial* (New York: McGraw-Hill Book Company, Inc., 1964).

**56** Harris, p. 103.

**57** Schmidhauser, pp. 28–36.

**58** Goldman and Jahnige, p. 53; *The New York Times*, August 8, 1981, p. 43; Sheldon Goldman, "The Bush Imprint on the Judiciary: Carrying On a Tradition," *Judi-cature*, 74 (1991), 295.

**59** Goldman, "The Bush Imprint . . ."

**60** See, generally, Goldman and Jahnige, pp. 49–86; Grossman, Harris, pp. 314–324; Harold Chase, "Federal Judges: The Appointing Process," *Minnesota Law Review*, 51 (1966), 186–218; Sheldon Goldman, "Judicial Appointments to the United States Courts of Appeals," *Wisconsin Law Review* (1967), 186–214; Donald D. Jackson, "Federal Roulette," in Sheldon Goldman and Austin Sarat (eds.), *American Court Systems* (San Francisco: W. H. Freeman and Co., 1978), pp. 261–269; Richard J. Richardson and Kenneth N. Vines, *The Politics of Federal Courts* (Boston: Little, Brown and Co., 1970), chap. 4; Harold W. Chase, *Federal Judges: The Appointing Process* (Minneapolis: University of Minnesota Press, 1972), pp. 66–71, 128–138, 169–185.

**61** Goldman, "The Bush Imprint . . ."

**62** Richardson and Vines, p. 66; Sheldon Goldman, "Reaganizing the Judiciary," *Judicature*, 68 (1985), 319, 325; Goldman, "The Bush Imprint . . ."

**63** Goldman, "The Bush Imprint . . ."

**64** Goldman, "Reaganizing . . ." 315.

**65** Executive Order No. 12.059, *3 C.F.R.* 180 (1979). See also Susan Carbon, "The U.S. Circuit Judge Nominating Commission: A Comparison of Two of Its Panels," *Judi-cature*, 62 (1978), 233; "Report Card on Judicial Merit Selection," *Congressional Quarterly*, February 3, 1979, pp. 191–192; Richard E. Cohen, "Choosing Federal Judges—The Senate Keeps Control," *National Journal* (March 3, 1979), 355.

**66** Martin Tolchin, "Testing the Merit of Carter's Merit Selection," *The New York Times*, December 31, 1978, sec. 4, p. 4; Elliot Slotnick, "The Carter Presidency and the U.S. Circuit Judge Nominating Commission" (paper presented at the 1978 Meeting of the American Political Science Association).

67 Sheldon Goldman, "Should There Be Affirmative Action for the Judiciary?" *Judicature*, 62 (1979), 493.
68 John R. Schmidhauser, *The Supreme Court: Its Politics, Personalities and Procedures* (New York: Holt, Rinehart and Winston, 1960); Schmidhauser, *Judges and Justices*.
69 The following relies on Goldman, "Reaganizing . . . ," and "The Bush Imprint . . . ." For data on previous administrations, see Goldman, "Carter's Judicial Appointments: A Lasting Legacy," *Judicature*, 64 (March 1981), 348, 350, and Sheldon Goldman, "Characteristics of Eisenhower and Kennedy Appointees to the Lower Federal Courts," *Western Political Quarterly*, 18 (1965), 755, 757–761.
70 Glick and Emmert, "Stability and Changes."

# 5

# SETTLING CIVIL DISPUTES

The judicial process is started by people who bring disputes or conflicts to court. Unable or unwilling to settle them privately and informally, they ask lawyers and judges to create official solutions to their seemingly insoluble problems. Unlike legislatures and executive officials, who pass laws or issue orders on their own initiative, courts must wait for people to bring cases to them for decision. Courts technically are available to anyone who has a dispute requiring official judicial settlement, but in reality, courts are not used equally by everyone or all groups of people. Using courts depends a lot on alternative ways people can deal with conflicts, what they hope to accomplish by going to court, their ability to pay for lawyers, and other factors.

## ALTERNATIVES IN COPING WITH DISPUTES

If all of us went to court over conflicts with other people, many citizens would be involved in litigation full time. The number of people who have grievances against others is very high. One survey discovered that about 40 percent of all households had significant personal or financial grievances involving $1000 or more during the previous 3 years. The number of people having smaller gripes is much larger.

Yet, most people do not ask lawyers, courts, or others to intervene in their private quarrels. Less than 25 percent of those surveyed hired lawyers and only 11 percent filed cases in court. However, nearly three-quarters of those with major grievances contacted the person or organization they felt was responsible for their loss or problem, and nearly 70 percent got some settlement. Most disputes were settled without starting up the formal judicial process.[1]

Equally important, of the 10 or 11 percent of disputes that become court cases, only about 10 percent go all the way to trial. The vast majority are abandoned by the litigants or are settled through negotiation. Therefore, of all serious civil disputes, *only about 1 percent* are settled through formal judicial decisions. Court decisions as settlements in civil disputes are only the tiny tip of the iceberg.

There are many alternatives to going to court that people are likely to try before even considering filing a case.[2] They include various individual methods, mediation, and arbitration.

### Individual Methods

**Lump  It**    Some conflicts are not worth the time, effort, and cost to pursue at all. Therefore, one of the most frequently used alternatives in coping with disputes is to simply suffer small losses or grievances rather than make a fuss or demand satisfaction. It is a lot easier, for example, not to return to a restaurant that provides poor food or service at high prices than to demand a refund or another meal. Or it may be a lot easier to buy new tires than to go through the procedures required to get reduced, prorated satisfaction from a dealer.

Businesses take their lumps too, for example, when tenants disappear without paying their last month's rent or when a manufacturer cannot pay suppliers because of a business slump. Suing often will not recover any money, so the loss is chalked up to experience with the hope of making it up some other time.

All of us have these kinds of experiences, and we take our lumps or suffer losses rather than add to our inconvenience and expense by filing official complaints, hiring lawyers, or asking others to help resolve the issues. Suing probably is only wishful thinking or a fleeting thought most of the time.

Some people also flee the scene of conflict or trouble that cannot be settled satisfactorily. For example, tenants who are dissatisfied with a landlord's maintenance of a building probably will put up with inconvenience or move rather than go through awkward formal procedures of withholding rent until repairs are made. Even housing authorities and others who might be called for advice and assistance are likely to advise that it is simpler and perhaps more effective to move than to face continuing hassles or to go through the red tape of filing complaints.

Fleeing may be used for many problems. For instance, many poor people who cannot afford lawyers to handle divorces simply abandon their spouses and families as the only available alternative.

**Negotiation**    Suffering losses and fleeing are things that individuals can do totally on their own, without becoming further involved with those who have caused them grief and without calling in outsiders to help resolve differences. Other methods involve positive steps to resolve disputes and require greater effort and other emotional and financial risks.

A common theme that runs throughout most dispute settlement is the narrowing of grievances to specific problems or claims for compensation.[3] Narrowing issues transforms disputes from generalized dissatisfaction, anger, frustration, or dislike to manageable problems.

Most disputes are settled through private negotiation and compromise. For example, rather than pay a bill for home repairs done unsatisfactorily or at too high a price, a property owner may make a specific complaint to the contractor and try to work out an informal settlement. Maybe a contractor will agree to make repairs or to lower the charges in order to reach a quick and satisfactory solution to a problem. But perhaps that contractor will refuse, and a cordial discussion may turn nasty and uncomfortable.

A decision to seek satisfaction through negotiation requires assertiveness, some communications skills, and a willingness to risk the prospect of conflict and emotional stress. Very few people welcome it, and only some will risk it or feel capable of working through negotiations.

*Lawyers*  Some disputes are so important or involve so much money that individuals or groups hire lawyers to negotiate for them. Larger businesses, for example, that routinely deal with a variety of disputes almost always employ experienced lawyers as negotiators. Many personal injury cases for individuals also are handled by lawyers. Individuals who face an experienced insurance company lawyer or claims adjuster in a big claim usually are no match in negotiations unless they have their own experienced lawyer.[4]

Lawyers are valuable because they are expert evaluators of claims. They know the going rate for a variety of injuries and property damage and what specific losses are worth. They are sought after, not for their winning courtroom style, but for the substance of their knowledge and information and their effectiveness in negotiation.

Most individuals are unlikely to know what is a reasonable settlement and may accept too little or demand too much. For example, a person badly injured in an accident might settle for medical expenses, but experienced lawyers are likely to demand and get compensation for loss of employment and income, pain and suffering, and future, uncertain medical expenses. They also know the probabilities of winning a case in court and whether a negotiated settlement is a reasonable alternative to the risk of a trial.

Hiring a lawyer also may encourage serious negotiations and settlements, because it notifies the opposite side that an individual feels strongly enough about the issues to hire outside help. Hiring lawyers is a signal that an individual does not intend to suffer losses or to flee without a fight.

**Violence**  Instead of negotiation and compromise, some people, usually in lower-class neighborhoods, resort to harassment and violence to manage civil disputes. Verbal abuse, spreading rumors, vandalism, and assault are used to get back at others for various slights or to settle the score from earlier conflicts. Although much of this behavior is criminal, it often is not reported to the police and is the customary way of dealing with many conflicts.

## Mediation

If individual methods do not work or cannot be used, people frequently ask others to work out settlements through mediation. Mediation is an informal procedure in which a third person serves as a middleman between two opposing sides. Unlike lawyers who are hired to represent one side, mediators are neutral negotiators who try to work out a settlement satisfactory to both sides. Mediators often try to get each person to understand the other's point of view and agree to give up an ''I'm right, he's wrong'' attitude. Anyone who seems capable of working with the opposing sides might be asked to serve as a mediator.

Mediation is *voluntary*, and the solutions reached are *not legally binding* on the opposing parties. Mediation works, however, when mediators are skillful in using various strategies to lead the opposing sides to a settlement.

Mediators present themselves as trained experts, and when disputes have been referred to them by the courts, mediators assert their legitimacy and authority by linking themselves to the law. They frequently improve the chances for a negotiated settlement by stressing that the alternative is to go to trial, and they emphasize that this may have unforseen and unfortunate consequences. Mediators also work toward settlement by controlling the interaction and discussions between opponents and getting the opposing sides to make commitments on the terms of a settlement. Finally, mediation often is a blend of bargaining on concrete issues and therapeutic counseling, which allows the opponents to vent their feelings and move toward restoring peace.[5]

**Disputes for Mediation**   Mediation can occur in many different settings and involve minor or major disputes. People living in apartment buildings or other housing developments, for example, frequently take minor disputes involving loud stereos, parties, strewn garbage, and even personal conflicts to landlords or management offices in the hope of resolving differences or obtaining compliance with house rules. In city neighborhoods with concentrated ethnic or religious populations, religious or other leaders, such as Chinese elders, also may be asked to resolve differences among local residents.

The federal government recently has adopted mediation as a way of resolving disputes between farmers and the government concerning the collection of delinquent loans. Two hundred thousand people are affected involving $25 billion. An example of a big mediation case is the $41 million settlement reached in a dispute in which twenty-eight construction workers were killed when a high-rise building under construction collapsed. The settlement involved a federal and a state judge serving as mediators who dealt with nearly a hundred lawyers representing the victims' families and forty contractors and subcontractors.[6]

*Police*   Police often act as mediators in the sense that they are asked to intervene in various personal disputes and to help people with other problems. Police involvement does not fit the ideal image of calm, give-and-take mediation, since police situations often are heated and even dangerous, and the police have considerable formal authority and power. Nevertheless, the function of the police, even in violent disputes, often is similar to mediation.

A large portion of police time and energy is devoted to keeping the peace and providing information and assistance mostly to poor and uneducated people who often have no other way of coping with routine problems. Sometimes, the police are the only visible and handy source of information about city services.

Also, many people do not understand the differences between civil and criminal conflicts and what to do about them. In fact, many conflicts seem to involve both elements of the law. For example, is an argument with the landlady a criminal or civil matter? What if she forms a fist and raises her arm while demanding late rent or insisting on quiet during the evenings? What about noisy children playing ball in the street? Should the police be called?

Thousands of calls are for disturbances in homes or bars or other public places. Officially, disturbances could be considered criminal matters, as many people believe they are, but police typically try simply to restore relative peace and calm and quickly leave the scene. Few arrests are made, no formal complaints are filed, and life goes on as before.

Studies of police work in large cities show that about 60 percent of all citizen calls to the police are to report crime, but that police treat less than 25 percent of these incidents as criminal matters, and they make very few arrests.[7] There are many reasons why so few citizen requests for help are treated as criminal issues by the police. In many fights and assaults it is impossible to determine who, if anyone, has committed a crime. Many thieves also cannot be identified or apprehended, and police often do not encourage filing reports and complaints when the culprit cannot be found. In many cases of domestic and neighborhood violence, husbands and wives and other relatives and friends refuse to file charges or will not testify once a case has begun.

Many of these kinds of cases do not provide "good collars," since convictions are hard to get. Consequently, police prefer to view much "friends-and-neighbors" crime as civil disputes. In most instances, citizens do not intend to go to court, but only want the police to restore order or to take their side in an argument.

**Mediation Services**    Although much mediation is informal and circumstantial, it also is becoming increasingly organized in local mediation services.[8] The idea of mediation has been endorsed by the American Bar Association, the U.S. Justice Department, and other judicial reform organizations as an alternative to going to court. More than 100 cities in over half the states have a local public mediation service that will try to settle disputes that are brought or referred to them.

Mediation services usually are supported with private donations and some local government money, and many of the mediators are unpaid volunteers. Congress and several states have passed laws that encourage mediation, but they have not provided much money to get local centers started.

Mediation services have various names (neighborhood justice centers, citizen dispute settlement programs, private complaint programs, etc.), but they all generally focus on private interpersonal and small commercial disputes. Slightly over half of all disputes are family or neighborhood squabbles among poor people. The others also involve the poor who have disputes with small businesses, usually landlords, local merchants, and employers. Some centers handle 1000 or more cases per year.

When mediation first became a popular reform in the early 1970s, mediation centers were connected with a variety of volunteer community groups, including legal aid societies, housing authorities, and other social service organizations. Over half of all their "cases" were referred to them by various other organizations, including the police and the courts.

But these private organizations have been only partially successful. They received mostly interpersonal disputes but only when both parties were willing to submit to mediation. Only about 25 percent of grievances against businesses received a hearing, probably because businesses refused to cooperate. Businesses almost never bring disputes to mediation services, preferring other ways to collect debts or enforce contracts.

Another problem is that relatively few people are aware of mediation centers and still are likely to believe that they must call a lawyer or go to court to settle a dispute. Lawyers also are accustomed to traditional judicial procedures and want to retain control over their cases. They also do not welcome the loss of their livelihood. Mediation offered by formal organizations now appears to be giving way to arbitration.

### Arbitration

Arbitration is a nontrial technique for settling disputes. It is somewhat similar to mediation, but it is more formal and the decisions of arbitrators are *legally binding*, like those in a trial. Entering into arbitration can be voluntary or involuntary. When it is voluntary, both sides agree in advance to be bound by the decision of the arbitrator. It is a form of contract, and if one side reneges, the other side can ask a judge to enforce the ruling.

An arbitrator is an umpire who meets in private with the opposing sides to hear the plaintiff and defendant and then reaches a decision about the dispute. Settlements tend to be compromises that recognize both sets of demands. Some arbitrators are lawyers, but others can perform the same function. Economists, business school faculty, and other experts in labor-management relations or various other aspects of business, for example, also serve as arbitrators in commercial cases.

**Voluntary** Arbitration seems to be outpacing mediation in popularity. It has the advantage of providing binding results while saving time and money that ordinarily would be spent on a full-length trial. In addition to its traditional conference table format, arbitration now has many forms.

California permits individuals to hire a retired judge, including Judge Joseph Wapner of *People's Court* fame, who will hear cases in short form and render a judgment quickly. Certain state and federal judges hold minitrials, sometimes with juries, who advise the parties how the case likely will come out if they go to trial. Although not a pure form of arbitration, there is considerable judicial pressure on both sides to settle along the lines spelled out by the judge or jury.

In various other states, arbitration is an alternative to litigation that is suggested by the courts, especially in small financial claims. The method seems to be attractive to many litigants, possibly because they recognize that both sides have legitimate claims which they both would like to settle, but they also fear the costs and a possible complete loss in a trial.

Arbitration has been used for years by some businesses and labor unions as a faster, less expensive, and more effective way of dealing with commercial and labor-management disputes that recur during years of business and work relationships. Recently, it has been reported that as many as 200 of the nation's largest corporations have taken a formal pledge to use arbitration or other similar short-cut settlement techniques rather than resort to litigation to resolve disputes with another company that also has signed the pledge.[9]

**Court-Annexed Arbitration**   In addition to voluntary arbitration, a recent development is the increased use of *mandatory arbitration* in the trial courts. It sometimes is called court-annexed arbitration. Judges often view arbitration as a way to relieve heavy caseloads. Since it increasingly is viewed as a new method of case management, we probably will see it adopted by many more courts.

Court arbitrators are lawyers, and their decisions have the same legal force as a judge's decision. Courts in nearly half the states and several federal districts require certain cases to go to arbitration but with the option of returning for trial if either side will not accept the result.

Financial claims in cases which go to arbitration range from a few thousand to one hundred thousand dollars, but most cases in the state courts average between fifteen and fifty thousand dollars. Lawyers and litigants generally seem satisfied with the fairness of the procedures and outcomes, and believe they save money over the cost of going to trial. Most cases are settled before they go before the arbitrator and very few go on to trial.[10]

## DECIDING TO GO TO COURT

Most methods of coping with conflict are not terribly expensive nor do they require extensive personal commitments. Fleeing to a new neighborhood and hiring lawyers may be costly, but most methods are informal, require no fees, and can be invoked relatively quickly and without much fanfare. Going to court, however, is an alternative that usually involves much more expense and personal inconvenience. But sometimes there seems to be no other way to settle a dispute.

## Obstacles

Courts are the most formal public agencies available for resolving conflicts. Their procedures, official language, and reliance on special legal knowledge make them almost impossible for laypersons to use on their own. Some small claims courts operate informally, and each person is free to "tell it to the judge" in his or her own words, but forms and instructions for filing cases, responding to summonses to appear, and arranging evidence are unfamiliar and make many do-it-yourselfers unsure and uneasy. The novice litigant probably feels as if he or she is groping to find the way in strange and hostile territory.

Figure 5.1 illustrates the forms that litigants must use to pursue their cases. Filling out the form is not very difficult, but the attached *Information Sheet for Small Claims Litigants* describes many other hurdles that litigants must get over if they expect the court to hear their case. These instructions are likely to discourage the timid and the fearful and many others who do not believe their claims are worth the trouble.

**Court Costs and Lawyers**   The costs of filing cases, sending notices to opponents and witnesses, possibly paying for the time of expert witnesses, as well as hiring lawyers and paying other costs, make going to court expensive. Often attorney's fees, running at $60 to $75 per hour or more, quickly exceed what a litigant can hope to recover in court.

Lawyers are always necessary in the trial courts of general jurisdiction and appellate courts, but people sometimes employ them in small claims cases as well, especially when their opponents use lawyers, which puts them at a disadvantage, or generally when they do not feel capable of managing on their own.

As discussed in Chapter 3, the availability of lawyers is very uneven. Large businesses and corporations easily can afford to hire lawyers as part of their own staff, or they retain private law firms to represent them in a wide range of business matters. But the poor and the middle class have far fewer resources and may have to abandon legitimate claims because costs mount more quickly than results and they cannot compete with business or wealthy opponents who can outlast them. Neither the contingency fee nor lawyers provided the poor by the Legal Services Corporation are true equalizers.

**Emotional Costs**   Going to court costs more than money. It creates psychological burdens as well.[11] For businesses, government, or other organizations that use courts as part of their regular activities, psychological costs probably are not much of a problem, but for individuals who are rarely involved in court cases and who will be personally affected by the proceedings and outcome, the psychological load may be equal to or heavier than the financial one.

Several features of litigation create emotional stress. First, litigation usually takes much more time than informal ways of settling disputes. Even in small

𝕮𝖔𝖚𝖓𝖙𝖞 𝕮𝖔𝖚𝖗𝖙, 𝕷𝖊𝖔𝖓 𝕮𝖔𝖚𝖓𝖙𝖞 𝕱𝖑𝖔𝖗𝖎𝖉𝖆
𝕾𝖚𝖒𝖒𝖆𝖗𝖞 𝕮𝖑𝖆𝖎𝖒𝖘 𝕯𝖎𝖛𝖎𝖘𝖎𝖔𝖓
1920 Thomasville Road, Tallahassee. FL 32303

Case No._____

PLAINTIFF: **Green Leaf Tree Co.**          DEFENDANT: **Ms. Holly Budd**

ADDRESS: **452 Shady Ln.**                ADDRESS: **3625 Maple St.**

                                 Sues

CITY: **Pineview, FL**      ZIP: **32325**      CITY: **Pineview, FL**      ZIP: **32325**

TELEPHONE: **904-427-0972; 427-0972**      TELEPHONE: **904-777-3927; 344-9642**
          WORK & HOME NO.                           WORK & HOME NO.

**PLEASE, PRINT OR TYPE**

And claims the amount of $ **850.00** _____ as being from the defendant, together with

$ **45.00** _____ for interest plus court costs of $ **60.50** _____, which all totals $ **955.50** _____, and alleges:

**Defendant agreed to have trees trimmed for $850.00 and refuses to pay.**

**All work was completed on October 23, 1992.**

_____

_____

_____

_____

☐   Plaintiff further states the suit is based on a written instrument, a copy of which is attached.
    The Defendant is/is not in the Military Service of the United States.

STATE OF FLORIDA, COUNTY OF LEON: The undersigned, being duly sworn, says that the foregoing is a just and true statement of the amount owing by the Defendant to said Plaintiff, exclusive of all set-offs and just grounds of defense: and this suit is brought in good faith, with no intention to annoy the Defendant subscribed before; and that the action has been brought in the County in Venue is proper pursuant to Chapter 47, Florida Statutes.

PLAINTIFF or BUSINESS Name: **Green Leaf Tree Co.**

SIGNATURE AND TITLE: *Harry Oke, Prop.*

                     The foregoing instrument was acknowledged before me on
_____**January 4**_____ , 19 **93** by the above named Individual, Officer
Partner, Agent, Attorney in Fact, Trustee, Personal Representative, who is person-
ally known to me or who has produced __**driver's license**__
(Type of I.D.) as identification and who (did/did not) take an oath.

PAUL F. HARTSFIELD, CLERK

By: *Clara Clerk* _____ Deputy Clerk (or Notary)

    __**Clara Clerk**__ _____ Printed name of acknowledger.

This is carbonless paper: **Do not xerox these forms**

**(See Reverse Side for Important Information)**

**BOTH PARTIES MUST KEEP THE COURT INFORMED OF THEIR CURRENT ADDRESS FUTURE NOTICES WILL BE BY REGULAR MAIL**

CCC-1508

**FIGURE 5.1**
Documents and Instructions for Small Claims Court. *The filing page.*

### NOTICE TO PLAINTIFF AND DEFENDANT

PRETRIAL CONFERENCE: **YOU MUST BOTH APPEAR** at the time and place set for the pretrial conference, **with full authority to settle the case, and be prepared to mediate in good faith.** If plaintiff fails to appear, the case may he dismissed. If the defendant fails to appear, the plaintiff may be awarded a judgment by default. A **written motion or answer** to the court by the plaintiff(s) or defendant(s) **does not excuse personal appearance.** The purpose of this pretrial conference is to determine the nature of the dispute, if any, to the claim, and to set the trial date if the case cannot be resolved by mediation. **Do not bring witnesses.** If a defendant does not dispute the claim, but desires additional time to pay, the defendant must come and state the circumstances to the judge who may or may not approve a payment plan and withhold judgment or execution or levy. If settlement is reached prior to the pretrial date, the plaintiff must file a voluntary dismissal with the clerk and furnish a copy to the defendant. The case can then be removed from the court docket.

**BOTH PARTIES MUST KEEP THE COURT INFORMED OF THEIR CURRENT ADDRESS. FUTURE NOTICES WILL BE BY REGULAR MAIL.**

### HOW TO FILE CLAIM

NOTE: You will need the original of this form for the court, one copy for each defendant, one for each sheriff's service, and one copy for yourself. This is carbonless paper: **DO NOT XEROX THESE FORMS.**

1. First, make sure that you fill in the name, address and telephone numbers of yourself and the defendant.

2. Fill in the amount of your clam, including interest if appropriate, and state the basis for your claim in the blanks provided.

3. If your suit is based on a written instrument, note, check, etc., place an "X" in the proper space provided. (NOTE: You must furnish the court with a copy of the written instrument and a copy for each defendant).

4. If the defendant is or is not a member of the Military Service, so signify by striking through the wording that does not apply.

FILING FEE: For all claims less than $100.00 . . . . . . . . . . . . . . . . . .$24.50
For all claims of $100 but less than $2,500 . . . . . . . . . .$48.50

In addition to the filing fee, Certified Mail, Restricted Delivery Charges in serving each defendant are $5.15 for the 1st ounce and $.12 for each additional ounce. (**service by mail <u>is not</u> available for <u>out-of-state</u> defendants**).

SERVING PAPERS ON DEFENDANT(S): Service can be obtained on the defendant(s) by either Certified Mail, Restricted Delivery, or by Sheriff's Service. The Sheriff's Service Charge is $12.00 for each defendant served. If you serve the papers through the Sheriff ,make a separate check payable to the Sheriff of the County where the defendant lives. (A defendant must be served with papers before judgment can be entered against him). Do not use post office box addresses for Sheriff service.

**FIGURE 5.1** (*Continued*) *Instructions on back of filing page.*

# County Court, Leon County Florida

CIVIL DIVISION - 1920 Thomasville Road, Tallahassee, Florida 32303

Green Leaf Tree Co.

CASE NO.

_____
Plaintiff

vs.

Ms. Holly Budd

_____
Defendant

## SUMMONS
(Notice to Appear)

THE STATE OF FLORIDA

TO ALL AND SINGULAR THE SHERIFFS OF THE STATE OF FLORIDA:

YOU ARE HEREBY COMMANDED TO SERVE THIS SUMMONS and a copy of the complaint upon the defendant: Ms. Holly Budd

YOU ARE HEREBY NOTIFIED that the above named plaintiff has made a Claim and is requesting Judgment against you as shown by the foregoing Statement, together with Court costs and any further costs which may accrue. The Court will hold a PRE-TRIAL HEARING on the Claim on:

Wednesday, January 27, 19 93, at 9, A.M., o'clock

in Courtroom #  2B , Leon County Courthouse, 301 South Monroe Street, Tallahassee, Florida 32301.

If you desire to file any counterclaim or off-set to plaintiff's said claim, it must be filed in this Court by you or your Attorney in writing at least five (5) days prior to the above date. You should also serve a copy to the plaintiff, by mail.

RIGHT TO VENUE: The law gives the person or company who has sued you the right to file suit in any one of several places as listed below. However, if you have been sued in any place other than one of these places, you, as the defendant, have the right to request that the case be moved to a proper location or venue. A proper location or venue may be one of the following: Where the contract was entered into; if suit is on unsecured promissory note, where note is signed or where maker resides; if suit is to recover property or to foreclose a lien, where the property is located; where the event giving rise to the suit occurred; where any one or more of the defendants sued reside; any location agreed to in a contract. If you, as a defendant, believe the plaintiff has not sued in one of these correct places, you may appear on your court date and orally request a transfer or you may file a written request for transfer, in affidavit form (sworn to under oath) with the court seven (7) days prior to your first court date and send a copy to the plaintiff or plaintiff's attorney, if any. A copy of the statement of claim shall be served with said notice.

YOU ARE REQUIRED TO BE PRESENT AT THE PRE-TRIAL HEARING IN ORDER TO AVOID ENTRY OF A JUDGMENT BY DEFAULT. IT IS NOT NECESSARY TO BRING WITNESSES TO THIS CONFERENCE.

IN WITNESS WHEREOF, I have hereunto set my hand and seal this 4th day of January, 19 93.

PAUL F. HARTSFIELD, CLERK

BY: _Clara Clerk_
_____
Deputy Clerk

TO THE PLAINTIFF: This is also your memorandum of PRE-TRIAL HEARING. You are required to be present at the time, date and place set out in the foregoing summons.

**BOTH PARTIES MUST KEEP THE COURT INFORMED OF THEIR CURRENT ADDRESS FUTURE NOTICES WILL BE BY REGULAR MAIL.**

CCC-1506

**FIGURE 5.1** (*Continued*) *Summons.*

## INFORMATION SHEET FOR SMALL CLAIMS LITIGANTS

The following Information Sheet has been prepared to acquaint you with procedures that are followed in Small Claims cases filed in Leon County Court. By following these procedures you will be able to assist the Court in its fact-finding function and insure that the trial process is conducted as fairly as possible.

**PRE-TRIAL DOCKET CALL AND MEDIATION**: Upon the filing of the initial complaint with the Clerk of the Court, the Plaintiff will be given a date, time and location to appear for a pre-trial docket call. The Defendant will be notified of the court date when served the Complaint and Summons or Notice to Appear. Please arrive in the courtroom at least 15 minutes prior to the time set for your appearance. As each case is called by the Clerk, both parties, their representatives, or their attorneys will be referred to a trained certified mediator who will attempt to facilitate them in making a good faith effort to settle the case. **ALL PARTIES, THEIR REPRESENTATIVES OR THEIR ATTORNEYS MUST COME TO THE PRE-TRIAL DOCKET CALL WITH THE AUTHORITY NECESSARY TO SETTLE THE CASE AND PREPARED TO PARTICIPATE IN A GOOD FAITH EFFORT TO MEDIATE THEIR CASE SUCCESSFULLY. FAILURE OF ANY PERSON TO PARTICIPATE IN GOOD FAITH WILL RESULT IN THE IMPOSITION OF APPROPRIATE SANCTIONS.** In addition, the failure of the Plaintiff to appear for pre-trial docket call will result in dismissal of the case; failure of the Defendant to appear will result in a default judgment for and in behalf of the Plaintiff.

**THINGS TO DO BEFORE THE TRIAL DATE**: If mediation is unsuccessful the case will be set for trial. It is important that you note the trial date on your calendar and to plan for the availability of yourself <u>and your witnesses</u>. The Clerk will complete a Notice of Trial and provide a copy to the parties. Because hearsay testimonial evidence is generally not admissible at trial, it is imperative that you arrange for your witnesses to personally attend the trial. A witness may appear voluntarily or may be compelled to appear by issuance and service of a witness subpoena. Witnesses may appear at trial by telephone if prior notice has been provided to the opposing party and arrangements have been made with the presiding judge's judicial assistant. **NOTE: THIS CONVENIENCE IS NOT AVAILABLE TO THE PARTIES. THE PARTIES MUST ATTEND THE TRIAL IN PERSON UNLESS THE OPPOSING PARTY AND PRESIDING JUDGE WAIVES THIS REQUIREMENT IN WRITING**. If you need to subpoena any witness to appear for trial, go to the County Clerk's Office for assistance.

**EXCHANGE OF DOCUMENTS AND INFORMATION**: If any Order of the Court requires you to exchange copies of documents or lists of exhibits and witnesses, please make sure that you do so promptly. It is your obligation to comply whether or not the other side complies. If you fail to comply as directed by the Court's Order, the Judge may refuse to accept your evidence, continue the case, and impose costs against you.

**SETTLEMENT**: If you and the other party have agreed to settle your case prior to trial, you must notify the Court of the settlement. It is the responsibility of the <u>Plaintiff</u> to immediately call the Judge's office to advise of the settlement. Also, written notice of the settlement must be filed with the Clerk of the Court so the case file can be closed and the computer updated.

**ADDRESS CHANGES**: You must furnish every party in your lawsuit as well as the Clerk of the Court with your proper and most current mailing address. If you change your mailing address, you must immediately notify the Clerk and <u>all</u> other parties.

**FIGURE 5.1** *(Continued) Information sheet (first page).*

**IF YOU NEED HELP**:  After the case has been set for trial and, if you are unsure how to proceed, do not hesitate to speak with the Court Clerk's Office. While no deputy clerk of court can give you legal advice, a deputy clerk may refer you to certain provisions of the Small Claims Rules which may apply as well as advise you as to what custom and practice the judge generally follows. For legal advice, you should consider consulting an attorney. While the assistance of an attorney is not required in Small Claims Court, many litigants find such professional assistance to be very helpful.

**PROCEDURES FOLLOWED AT TRIAL**:  At trial each side will have an opportunity to make an opening statement. Thereafter, the Plaintiff will testify and be subject to questioning by the Defendant. Plaintiff's witnesses will then be heard, subject to questioning by the Defendant. The Court will consider receiving documents or exhibits into evidence as they are referred to by the Plaintiff or witnesses. The Defendant will then have a corresponding opportunity to testify, present defense witnesses and offer exhibits. The Defendant and the defense witnesses will be subject to questioning by the Plaintiff. After all of the evidence has been presented, both sides will have an opportunity to present a brief closing argument. The judge will then decide the case.

**TELECONFERENCING**:  There is only one trial and you must have everything ready and be on time. Occasionally, witnesses will be reluctant to appear to testify at trial. Such witnesses may either be subpoenaed to appear personally or they may be subpoenaed to be available to have their testimony taken over the telephone. Telephone testimony is admissible and the Court will provide a speaker telephone so that both parties will be able to hear and question the witness to be telephoned. A party should arrange to have a witness telephone the conference call telephone number (904-922-2185) at the scheduled time for the trial. On occasion, the Judge will place the call to the witness during the time allotted for trial. All long distance calls made by the presiding judge must be placed collect or charged to the party who wishes to call such witness. If a witness is not subpoenaed to stand by the telephone to be called and that witness is not available when the presiding judge calls, the party calling such witness will have lost the benefit of that witness' testimony.

**SKILLED OR EXPERT TESTIMONY**:  At the pre-trial docket call or during mediation, you may be advised that your case would benefit from the testimony of a skilled or expert witness. If you choose to use such a witness, please make sure that you have that type of witness available, either telephonically or in person, at the time of trial. Failure to do so may result in your losing the case. **SECOND HAND TESTIMONY OR INFORMATION, WRITTEN ESTIMATES AND NOTARIZED STATEMENTS ARE NOT ADMISSIBLE AT TRIAL**.

**CONTINUANCES**:  All requests for continuances must be filed in writing with the Clerk of the Court and a copy sent to all parties. Stipulations (agreements) between the parties to continue a case must be included in the written request for a continuance and will be ruled on without a hearing. Motions for Continuance which are contested will be heard by the Court and therefore, the moving party must contact the presiding judge's Judicial Assistant to reserve a time for the hearing on a contested Motion for Continuance. If for some reason a party cannot personally come to court to argue or to respond to a Motion for Continuance, arrangements may be made with the presiding judge's judicial assistant for the party's presentation to be made over the telephone.

**IN CONCLUSION**:  The quality of justice that you receive in Small Claims Court is directly affected by your compliance with Florida's Small Claims Rules, these procedures, and any others that are specified by the presiding trial judge. If you have any questions concerning how the Florida Small Claims Rules or these procedures apply to your case, you may contact the Clerk of the Court who may, subject to certain limitations, be able to assist.

D:\WP\CLAIMS\INFOSHEE.F

**FIGURE 5.1** (*Continued*) *Information sheet (second page).*

claims courts, which are geared to quick hearings, a month or more may pass between filing a case and a trial. Cases in other courts may wait several months or years for trial. During that time, people temporarily suffer their losses, since they cannot obtain cash settlements from the other side and important witnesses may move away or die.

Litigants also may begin to lose confidence in their side of the story and the evidence needed to convince a judge or jury. Anger and moral certainty frequently give way to doubts and fears and thoughts that there are always two sides to every story.

For some individuals, hiring lawyers also creates a sense of loss of personal control over their own dispute. Some attorneys welcome litigant participation in building a case, and active clients usually receive more attention and can influence the development of their case. Other lawyers limit client involvement and prefer that they be passive and dependent on their lawyers for expert advice and direction.[12]

Trials impose their own special emotional burdens. Instead of litigants telling their side of the story in their own words, lawyers take charge and ask questions designed to portray their side favorably and to tear down the legal position and image of the opposition. The motives and honesty of both sides are dredged and challenged, and litigants are likely to feel that all sides of the issues are grossly blown out of proportion in order to win.

Contested divorces, for example, may provoke charges of extramarital sexual relations and financial cover-ups on both sides. Even disputes over the terms of a sales contract may escalate into major charges of conspiracy to defraud when a dispute becomes a court case. Unused to the rigors of a trial, novice litigants are likely to feel dirtied and dissatisfied with court—even if they win.

### Why Use Courts?

With all of these apparent obstacles, why do people go to court? There are many different reasons, depending upon individual and social needs. Surveys of litigants in small claims courts show that close to 40 percent of plaintiffs who were unable to reach an out-of-court settlement but who still did not bother to appear for their trial had filed a case only to "*let off steam*" and to harass someone who had wronged them.[13]

Others file cases because they feel they have *something serious at stake* and suing may promote informal negotiation and settlement. Still others permit themselves to be sued and go to trial because they have *nothing to lose* by not paying a bill or repaying a loan until a judge orders them to do so. In many small claims cases, signed loan and sales agreements provide no defense for not paying, but it does not cost a person already in debt to wait for a court order.

Some observers of courts also believe that many people go to court because they *overestimate their chances of winning*.[14] Seeing the case from their own point of view only, they believe right is on their side and that judges or juries will agree.

**Strangers**   People are likely to go to court most often in certain kinds of social circumstances. Studies of litigation consistently show that disputes are likely to be taken to court when individuals are strangers prior to a conflict, such as in automobile accidents, and when they do not intend to maintain a relationship following the court case. In contrast, individuals who have known each other a year or longer and who intend to continue to interact are more likely to use other, more informal methods that promote negotiation, give-and-take, and the possibility for mending relationships at the end of the conflict. For example, people in low-income urban neighborhoods seem most likely to file criminal charges against their neighbors when they plan to move from the area following a fight or disagreement. They use other methods, however, including violence, when they plan to remain in the neighborhood.[15]

Businesses in disputes with other businesses also rarely go to court when they expect to do more business with each other in the future.[16] However, businesses and other organizations often use the courts to collect debts, to enforce sales agreements, or to contest government policies.

Nearly all these kinds of cases are very impersonal and involve people who are unknown to each other and probably will not deal with each other again. Equally important, such cases concern the success and power of organizations, not individuals, and the people working for large organizations usually are not personally affected by the proceedings or the outcomes of going to court.

**Last Resort**   Going to court sometimes is the last resort or only way that individuals and groups have to deal with personal disputes and political conflicts. Civil rights organizations and other interest groups sometimes go to court as an alternative to lobbying in other locations of government where they have not been successful in influencing policy. There also is some evidence that women and the elderly in particular sometimes file criminal complaints against neighbors in poor urban ghettos because they cannot fight back any other way. Clearly, few of these kinds of disputes are treated as crime or come to trial, but when they do, the opportunity to present a case using the same rules of the game available to the opposition sometimes makes the weak stronger.

People who contemplate going to court have to weigh the pros and cons of the legal process. If they decide to pursue a claim, they have to be prepared for many frustrations along the way.

Box 5.1, "Frustrations of Going to Court," illustrates many of the pitfalls of litigation. The people who brought these very different cases must have felt strongly that they had something important at stake, and they pursued their cases despite frustrating delays and lack of concrete results that often come even with court victories. But, there probably was no other way for them to get anything from the other side.[17]

**BOX 5.1**

FRUSTRATIONS OF GOING TO COURT

### Burnette v. State

[William M. Burnette unwound a fire hose from the wall and strung it through the fifth-floor suite in the state Department of Transportation.]
Next, he swung his arm from left to right and sprayed water from the high-pressure fire hose everywhere. The unexpected gush, which witnesses said lasted about five minutes, left in its wake streaked wood paneling, a soggy couch, squashy carpeting, splattered paperwork, standing water in the hallway, and startled secretaries. . . .

Burnette has been locking horns with the department for four years over a drainage problem that has flooded eighty-five acres of his land in Madison. . . .

In 1973, the Department of Transportation diverted the natural flow of water off the north side of U.S. Highway 90, dumping the water on Burnette's planned housing development on the south side.

In December 1978, Burnette brought a successful lawsuit against the highway department that would force the state to either condemn and buy his southside property or pump the water off.

The Department of Transportation appealed that ruling.

In July 1980, the Court of Appeals affirmed the lower court's decision and levied a $1000-a-day fine against the department until it solved the drainage problem.

After ninety days, trial court Judge Declan O'Grady found the state in contempt of court for not taking any steps to correct the flooding. Again, the state appealed the ruling.

On Wednesday, Burnette's temper broke loose, and he called the state's appeal "just a stalling technique."

"They know they've been guilty since December of 1978 and here it is March 1980. Where is the damn end of it? When am I going to get the money? I want to get paid. I've struggled all this time paying my bills. By God, it's time to come to a damn end. For four damn years they've been flooding me and nobody cares."

After spending more than $100,000 in court costs, Burnette now faces a felony charge of criminal mischief.

[Note: Several months later, the appeals court overruled the trial court that had fined the Department of Transportation $1000 per day. Burnette has asked the appeals court to rule that the DOT is in contempt of court for not ending the drainage problem. Burnette also was found guilty of a misdemeanor for damaging government property.]

### Marsha v. John

John and Marsha were divorced after 17 years of marriage. Their three children lived with Marsha, and John agreed to pay Marsha $225 per month for their support. John managed a store and earned $22,000 per year. Marsha had no special skills and went to work for the first time in her life as a grocery store checkout clerk, earning about $6000 per year.

At first John paid regularly, but suddenly he stopped. After calling John and waiting two months for a payment, Marsha looked for help. After contacting several state and social agencies, she learned that the sheriff employed a child support counselor who collected support payments for the receiving parent. But a formal court order was needed to open an account. Marsha needed a lawyer.

After a fifteen-minute hearing, a judge signed an order opening a child support account. Marsha's lawyer charged her $145.

During the following year, John paid haphazardly and gradually fell $1000 behind in his payments. The counselor issued a summons for John to appear in court, but he made another payment and the summons was withdrawn. But with more payment interruptions, John finally had to appear before the judge. He lectured John, threatened him with jail, and ordered him to pay $50 per month extra toward the back payments.

John paid for a while, but soon he was $1500 in debt to Marsha. Marsha decided to try her lawyer again, who suggested withholding (garnishing) John's wages to get the money. This required another court order and the cooperation of John's employer. The judge signed the required court order, and

---

**BOX 5.1 continued**

John's employer received a notice to send John's next paycheck to the court. The employer refused, however, and he too was summoned to court along with John, Marsha, and her lawyer, who filed another request to get the money. The employer finally sent $900 to the counselor. The lawyer charged Marsha $300.

When John stopped paying again, Marsha decided not to use the lawyer again, but to rely on the sheriff's office. This time the judge ordered the sheriff to arrest John if he failed to make any future payments on time.

But when John stopped again he was not arrested. The counselor explained to Marsha that the sheriff had to order the arrest. Another court appearance would find out if the judge *really* meant to have John arrested. But John quickly made several payments and the judge decided he should not be jailed.

In a year, the third child reached 18 and John's obligations ended. He paid his debt to Marsha in bits and pieces, and she finally received all her money (without interest) 4 years after the case had begun.

---

## SETTLING CASES WITHOUT A TRIAL

Even after people have filed cases and are getting ready for trial, negotiations and compromise settlements still are likely. In fact, planning to go to trial and using formal court procedures usually are part of settlement strategy.

### Civil Procedure and Negotiation

There are several preliminary steps to a trial that help to promote negotiation and settlement.[18]

**Complaints, Responses, and Motions**   To start a case, the plantiff files a formal complaint with the trial court in which the case will be heard. As explained in Chapter 2, the plaintiff chooses a court based on legal jurisdiction and litigation strategy. Complaints state the specific claims the plaintiff has against the defendant and how the court should remedy the problem or compensate the plaintiff.

In many cases, receiving the complaint is enough to produce a settlement, since many defendants, especially in small claims cases, are unfamiliar with court procedures and do not want to become involved in a lawsuit. They either settle or flee the scene to escape further conflict and uncertainty.

If the defendant does not choose to settle, he or she probably will consult with an attorney, who will prepare a response to the complaint. In the response, the defendant may deny part of or the entire claim, charge that the plaintiff really is at fault, and present a list of counterclaims against the plaintiff.

Filing complaints and responses are formal legal ways that each side accuses the other and indicates that each will pursue his or her interests. While the intensity of the battle seems to increase with claims and counterclaims, the process also may provide a basis for compromise as each side stresses the issues that are most important to it. Going to trial remains a possibility, but it does not occur right away.

In complicated commercial disputes or personal injury cases, exchanging claims and responses usually takes much time and gives each side ample opportunity to gather evidence, consider the strength of their case and that of the opposition, and weigh the possible costs and benefits of going to trial. There also is time to negotiate. In small claims cases, however, cases are heard more quickly. Defendants have only a few days or weeks to respond to claims, and most complaints delivered to defendants also include a date for a court hearing. If settlements are going to occur, they get started quickly.

In addition to charges and responses, the defendant may submit legal re-quests (*motions*) asking judges to dismiss the plaintiff's suit. Some motions to dismiss are based on technical claims, such as improperly prepared documents or not filing motions on time. Other motions state that the plaintiff's claims are unsupported by evidence or are too flimsy or vague to deserve a hearing. The plaintiff also has a chance to respond to these motions and to explain why the case ought to be heard. Although some motions to dismiss are granted, judges are reluctant to sidetrack most lawsuits this way.

Deciding on motions also may contribute to a settlement. Once a judge decides not to dismiss a case, it moves one step closer to trial. The pressure increases on both sides to decide whether to negotiate or to invest more time and money and to take a chance on the outcome of a trial.

**Depositions**   If the opposing sides do not settle after the claims, responses, and motions, they often begin to gather pretrial depositions in which each side may require the other to answer a list of factual questions and to furnish other evidence that pertains to the dispute. Depositions are very similar to formal trial testimony, but they are obtained in private with both attorneys present, and the questions and answers are recorded for later use.

Gathering depositions is permitted under judicial *rules of discovery* in which both sides have a right to obtain advance information to use in preparing their case and which may provide the basis for other questions to be raised at the trial. Pretrial discovery also saves trial time, since the same questions do not have to be repeated in court.

Sometimes the number of issues that are contested in a trial also can be reduced through early depositions, saving more time and expense. In a com-mercial case, for example, pretrial depositions may include questions concern-ing the financial status of the plaintiff and defendant, their types of business activities, their job responsibilities and decisions in various business transac-tions, identification of business documents, etc. All of these are fairly routine and straightforward factual questions that can be answered in advance.

Most cases are settled before the deposition stage, but depositions may contribute to later settlements. Each side learns more about the other and about the line of questions that supports the claims and the defense. Depositions are additional bits of information to use in weighing the strengths and weaknesses of each side and their chances in court. Having more of the cards face up on the table may lead to frank discussions and compromise.

**Pretrial Conference**    Finally, with all the preliminary information in hand, both sides may be required to attend a pretrial conference with the judge who will hear the case. Some reformers believe that pretrial conferences provide an important opportunity to negotiate and settle cases (Chapter 2). However, by the time a pretrial conference is held, both sides probably have considered the possible grounds for a settlement and have invested a lot of time, energy, and money in preparing their case. If attorneys are likely to settle cases, it probably will occur before this late meeting. But, negotiations always are possible and some cases are settled at the tail end of the process, sometimes moments before a trial is scheduled to begin.

## How Negotiations Work

Most cases are settled shortly after the plaintiff files a complaint. Often, defendants immediately agree to settle, but sometimes they hire lawyers to negotiate for them and to file responses to show that they are not going to cave in with the threat of a lawsuit. Several common types of cases illustrate the course that negotiations may take.

**Debt Collection**    The first is *wage garnishment* to pay debts.[19] Wage garnishment is a formal legal procedure in which a merchant or other person who cannot collect a debt (as in *Marsha v. John*) files a case to establish a right to payment. It also asks a judge to send a court order to the debtor's employer requiring the withholding of a portion of the debtor's wages and sending it to the court. A formal trial will be held to determine whether or not the plaintiff should receive the money to cover the debt.

However, with their wages substantially reduced through garnishment, as many as 75 percent of debtors quickly contact their creditors to promise repayment or to work out arrangements for extended time payments. If satisfactory agreements are reached, creditors often withdraw their suits and the money is returned to the debtor.

It seems surprising that a creditor would agree to return a debtor's wages simply in return for a promise to resume payment. But informal settlements benefit creditors as well as debtors. Many creditors do not take all the money they can get in order to keep the debtor financially afloat. Forcing a debtor into bankruptcy does not put any money into the cash register, and slow or partial payments are better than none at all. Creditors also are likely to prefer a steady flow of cash payments to repossession of furniture, televisions, or automobiles in used condition which they have to sell to recover their losses. Mortgage companies and banks also prefer to see payments resumed on real estate rather than resort to lengthy and cumbersome foreclosure procedures. Winner-take-all is avoided: winnings may not be great and taking them may be a lot of trouble.

Debtors also are encouraged to settle up for several reasons. First, they usually have no defense for not paying. A trial or their failure to appear in court will cost them all of their garnished wages. Many debtors also report that their employers threaten to fire them or are angry at being drawn into the personal problems of their employees. Many employers also are merchants who probably sympathize with the creditor, not with their debtor-employee. Even with a settlement, debtors often face serious financial burdens, but at least they have an opportunity to keep their goods and restore their credit.

Informal and negotiated settlements are the outcome in most of these cases, but the formal garnishment procedure and plans to go to trial often are necessary to get the disputes settled.

**Rent**   A landlord usually informally requests payment for late rent before going to court. If no payment is forthcoming from a tenant, the landlord may go to housing court or the landlord-tenant division of small claims court to file a case. This consists of filling out a form listing names, addresses, payment due dates, and a brief description of the dispute. This form also serves as a summons to the tenant to appear in court for a trial. In some cities, procedures are even simpler. A landlord first obtains a short form from the court which is filled out and posted on the tenant's door. It demands payment or giving up the property within a specified few days. If a tenant does not comply, the landlord goes back to the court and fills out a formal complaint and asks for an early trial date. A sheriff's deputy delivers the summons. Faced with a formal court notice taped to the door or a police officer striding up the walkway, nearly all tenants pay or move. Few of these cases to trial.

**Insurance Claims**   Insurance claims also usually are settled without trials. Like other disputes, most insurance claims are settled without cases being filed at all. Insurance company claims adjusters have to keep the financial interests of their employers in mind, but their job performance also is evaluated mainly by the number of claims they settle in a certain period of time, so they usually try to settle claims quickly. But when early settlements are not possible and people hire lawyers and file cases, most suits still are negotiated before a trial.

Some people believe that holding out for a trial is a major advantage for insurance companies because they can postpone payments for a long period, use the money for other purposes, and pressure plaintiffs into settling for less.[20] This sometimes occurs, but if a case goes to trial, insurance companies also will have substantial legal expenses and cannot predict what a judge or sympathetic jury might award an injured plaintiff. Trial decisions may cost more than the money temporarily saved by the delays in going to court.[21]

Most insurance cases are settled after complaints have been filed. Lawyers who specialize in personal injury cases know what financial settlements are customary, and adjusters realize that the lawyers are experienced and have to earn their fees. Both of them may counter with estimates of actual damages as well as claims of what pain and suffering caused by an accident are worth. However, except when plaintiffs insist on making exorbitant claims, both sides are likely to reach agreement on how much the insurance company should pay.

### Cases for Trial

Although most cases are negotiated, some cases are likely to go to trial. Some litigants go to trial for the same reasons they file cases in the first place. Some are angry and overestimate their chances of winning, and others have nothing to lose by being required to pay a debt. However, many litigants make rough calculations of the potential benefits and costs of going to trial. An individual is likely to go to trial when he or she already has lost or might win a lot, the comparative expense of going to trial does not seem very great, and the opposition refuses to bargain or offer an attractive settlement.

For instance, an investor who lost $150,000 believed it was reasonable to gamble a few thousand dollars more to sue the investment company, hoping to pressure it into refunding at least some money. The company, guessing it could win the case, refused to pay anything. However, it had to pay its own attorneys' fees to defend itself.

Insurance companies faced with huge claims may see no reason to settle without taking a chance on a trial, since they probably will not have to pay more as a result of a jury verdict. Even when the money claimed is not very great, plaintiffs may go to court if the costs and inconvenience of suing are low, such as in small claims court.

Finally, some cases that involve major government policies important to large businesses or various social and economic interest groups may be taken to trial in order to obtain a binding ruling toward the policy. Governments are involved in lots of disputes, but like other litigants, government lawyers pick and choose those that are most worthwhile according to their impact on government policy. Interest groups also select cases that contain important policy questions and go to trial to try to get judicial support for their demands.

### WHO GOES TO COURT?

Courts are open to anyone, but they are consistently used more heavily by certain groups of people. Also, any conflict can be brought into one court or another, but particular kinds of disputes regularly appear in certain courts. Choosing a court depends on jurisdiction, strategies of litigation, and the ability to hire lawyers. Certain appellate courts, such as the U.S. Supreme Court and some state supreme courts, also have substantial leeway or discretion to determine which cases they will agree to decide. There also are differences in the use of trial and appellate courts and state and federal courts.

### People and Issues in Court

**State Court**   State courts deal with the kinds of disputes most people are likely to encounter during their lives. As described in Chaper 2, the federal courts are more likely to hear cases involving large sums of money, citizens from different states, and various issues affected by federal law and the U.S. Constitution. Most disputes, however, fall outside those categories. Divorce, most debt actions, property sales, contract disputes, and many others are heard mostly by the state courts.

With the exception of divorce (family law) cases, which are plentiful in some courts, most courts deal mainly with commercial cases. Typical disputes include: loan collections, suits for payment of goods and services, rent collection and security deposits, property damage and auto accidents, and personal injuries. In addition, some cases involve contested wills, trusts, and estates. Even small claims courts, which often have been viewed as havens for the average person, also are used heavily to collect loans and debts for goods and services.

*Repeat Players*   Individuals and organizations both use the civil courts, but there is a clearly lopsided pattern of litigation in almost all courts. Generally, we find that various organizations usually file suits against individuals. Organizations also are *repeat players* who use the courts regularly as part of their business activity.[23] Individuals tend to be *one-shotters* who probably never have been to court before.

A typical case is one in which a bank or commercial loan company, hospital, or home construction business has lent money or provided services to an individual who fails to pay as agreed. Taking a signed contract, note, or other evidence to court, various businesses ask judges to rule that they are entitled to payment and to order defendants to pay up. In addition to businesses, various divisions of governments also are frequent organization plaintiffs in the courts. Their suits usually involve attempts to collect taxes that are past due or obtain court approval for filing tax liens against property owners.

When individuals sue other individuals, it also usually is to collect debts, money damages for contract violations, or money compensation for personal and property damage. The number of cases filed by individuals in money matters is less than the number of organization claims.

Most commercial cases involve men. Women go to court most often for divorce. As the traditional position of women in American society changes, however, we would expect more of them to become involved in money issues, too, but today courts still deal most often with organization financial interests and suits by and against men.

**Federal Court**   State and federal courts hear some of the same kinds of cases owing to their concurrent jurisdiction. However, there also are important differences in the number and kinds of issues and the people who appear in the federal courts.

As discussed in Chapter 2, many civil cases get into the federal courts through federal diversity jurisdiction. Typical cases include personal injury and property damage, contract disputes, real estate disputes, and bankruptcy. Other federal cases involve disputes over the application of federal law, such as labor-management conflicts, social security, patents, taxation, and others.

Prisoner petitions are a separate and distinct category of federal civil cases. Prisoner petitions come mostly from state and some federal defendants who already have been convicted of a crime and are serving time in a state or federal prison. They use the federal courts to contest the constitutionality of state and federal judicial procedures, sentences, or the conditions of prison life. In order to get into the federal courts, prisoners have to claim that their constitutional rights were violated during previous trials and appeals or in prison.

Other important federal cases discussed in Chapter 2 include civil rights and civil liberties claims—disputes involving fundamental liberties and freedom guaranteed by the Constitution. Cases involving race relations, women's rights, abortion, affirmative action, freedom of speech, press, religion, and others routinely are taken to the federal courts.

***Repeat Players*** As in the states, except for criminal defendants and prisoners, most of the litigants in the federal courts are organizations and repeat players. The most prominent litigant is the *federal government* itself. Agencies or departments of the U.S. government are the plaintiffs in nearly one-quarter of all civil cases in the federal district courts and the defendant in another 15 percent of litigation. The federal government is a party in one-third to one-half of appeals court and Supreme Court cases.

In most of these cases, the federal government goes to court to obtain court approval and support for its policies in numerous areas of business regulation, relations with state governments, and other policies. The heavy use of courts by the federal government differs from the relatively light use of courts by state and local governments. Many more private cases are litigated by individuals and organizations in the state courts.

There are other repeat players in the federal courts. State governments are involved in many U.S. Supreme Court cases where state policies in criminal procedure, prison conditions, control of individual constitutional rights (freedom of speech, press, and religion), and occasional conflict with the federal government are fought out.

Corporations also frequently use the federal courts and the Supreme Court. Big businesses compete with each other for various commercial rights regulated by federal law, contest government regulation of their activities, face stockholder suits, oppose employee compensation claims from injuries, and do battle with consumer organizations.

Excluding criminal defendants and prisoners, individuals litigate about 25 percent of Supreme Court cases. Many of these individuals are not average citizens, however, but are themselves involved in large business transactions or are members of large private organizations.

## Social Environments and the Courts

The description of people and issues in the state and federal courts provides a snapshot of the current work of the courts, but the amount of legal activity and the issues brought to court vary throughout the country and change over time. Changes in court jurisdiction account for some of the differences, but the social, economic, and political makeup of the country probably has a greater effect on the kinds of disputes that go to court.

**Social Complexity**    There are a number of theories about the changing work of courts. One key idea is that as societies become more urban, industrialized, and generally more complex and impersonal the amount of formal legal activity and litigation is likely to increase.[24] Lawyers are used more frequently to draw up formal documents, agreements, and financial obligations, and new and different kinds of disputes develop and are apt to be brought to the courts.

This theory helps in part to explain the work of courts in the United States. After the Civil War and continuing into the early 1900s, the state and federal courts were confronted with new cases stemming from industrialization and development. Cases involving railroads and corporations became commonplace, and labor-management conflicts, property cases, contract disputes, and debt collections began to flow into the courts. But around the 1930s, these kinds of cases began to decline in favor of more criminal, personal injury, property damage, and divorce cases. In the federal courts, appeals of criminal convictions and civil rights cases have increased dramatically in recent years.[25]

Possibly certain areas of policy and law become settled and routine over time and more disputes are settled out of court. In the early days of business and industrial development, most conflicts were not covered by legal rules, but with a growing number of court decisions and legislative enactments, the rules for settling disputes became clearer and more standardized. The costs of going to court also increased, encouraging people to settle disputes informally.

**New Issues**    As some areas of policy became routine, others emerged. Civil rights and the rights of criminal defendants, for example, are issues that have emerged largely since the 1950s. Years ago, divorces were much more difficult to obtain, and social values often prevented people from ending a marriage. But divorce has become common and more cases now come to the courts. In addition, getting a divorce still requires official judicial approval. Therefore, even if a judge only rubber-stamps a private agreement, courts still must officially deal with a divorce "case."[26]

Auto accident cases have risen steadily in the state courts since the early 1900s. Recently, however, the percentage of motor vehicle accident cases has declined somewhat. This may be due to state no-fault insurance laws that reduce the opportunities and need for litigation as well as increases in private negotiation of losses by insurance companies to avoid jury trials. Finally, the content of other business cases has changed. For example, patent and copyright cases are down, but labor relations, tax cases, and other government regulation cases are up.

*Regional Differences* Besides changes over time, the present work of the courts varies around the country. The best explanation for the differences is that the social and economic characteristics of the state produce different kinds of disputes that go into the courts of each state or region. Generally, the urban, highly industrialized states have more disputes involving business relations and government regulation of the economy. There also are more criminal and civil liberties cases in these states, which reflects the competitive and often violent nature of urban life. The more rural, agricultural states tend more often to deal with a wider variety of noncommercial cases including divorce, property damage, personal injury, real estate disputes, and other private cases that are brought by individuals.[27]

## TOO MUCH LITIGATION?

Different types of cases come and go over the years, but the overall amount of litigation is much higher today than ever before. The statistics are absolutely clear. In 1977, there were approximately 67 million cases filed in the fifty states. By the 1990s, this figure had increased 50 percent to 100 million cases. Some states had whopping increases. Michigan's civil caseload went from 167,000 cases to 687,000, or a fourfold increase. Even sparsely populated Utah had 129,000 cases, up from 63,000 a decade earlier, more than a 100 percent jump.[28]

Sharp increases also have occurred in the federal courts, although civil caseloads in the district courts are down from their all-time highs. In the mid-1970s, there were about 131,000 cases in the district courts; but, by 1985, the figure had more than doubled to nearly 274,000 cases. By 1990, however, the number of cases had decreased slightly to 267,000. However, the rate of appeals is higher than ever. In the mid-1970s, only 18,400 appeals were filed. In 1985, there were slightly over 33,000 cases in the federal courts of appeals, or an 81 percent increase. But by 1990, the number was nearly 41,000 cases, or an additional 25 percent growth.[29]

## A Litigious Society?

The statistics seem to support claims by many legal experts and commentators that the nation has become more litigious—a tendency to resort to the courts rather than other more informal and personal methods of resolving conflicts. Taking note of the increases, former Chief Justice Warren Burger has characterized the population as suffering from "an almost irrational focus—virtually a mania—on litigation as a way to solve all problems."[30] Others refer to our increasing tendency to sue each other as *hyperlexia*.

This perception is reinforced by a continuing stream of newspaper and television news stories about new and unusual types of cases that seem to be flooding the courts. The insert "Cases in the News" provides a sampling.

Although the number of cases has increased, and new and unusual issues reach the courts, we need a broader and more complete overview of litigation in the United States before we can conclude that there is "too much" litigation or that Americans have become too prone to run to court. Newspaper stories alone are misleading because they concentrate on new, controversial, and often bizarre cases that do not represent most litigation. For every case involving controversial drug testing by employers or a multimillion dollar divorce or medical malpractice settlement, there are thousands of relatively modest small claims cases and personal injury suits that are settled for a few thousand dollars.

---

**BOX 5.2**

CASES IN THE NEWS

• More than 1000 AIDS-related lawsuits have been filed since 1988, many involving blood transfusions

• Mother of young child with AIDS sues school for requiring youngster to be separated from her classmates by a glass booth

• Intoxicated customer—who later was hit by an automobile while crossing a busy street to beg a quarter for a pay telephone—sues the bar which refused to allow him to use its phone to call a cab

• Patient with kidney failure sues several physicians who declined to give her treatment, because they claimed she was a quarrelsome and difficult patient

• Driver sues state driver's-license division for its refusal to allow him to use a hyphenated last name (his and his wife's last names) on his driver's license without officially having his name changed

• California wife sues celebrity husband in divorce for a share of the future value of his "celebrity good will"—his earnings power as an entertainer

• Lifelong smoker sues tobacco companies for industrywide conspiracy to mislead smokers and potential smokers about the dangers of smoking

• Surrogate mother sues divorcing couple to gain joint custody with the father of the child

• Minority parents sue local school board to require taxes to be raised in order to improve standards at the school and to attract more white students

• Parents of terminally ill daughter sue to prevent forced caesarean delivery to remove a viable fetus

• College student sues her university because she was forced to dissect a frog in biology class, despite her request for an alternative assignment

• White mother sues sperm bank, charging she was mistakenly inseminated with sperm from a black donor

• Neighbors band together to sue owners of nearby buildings in small claims court for damage caused by violence, noise, and crime related to drug use and sales by the occupants

• Gays sue housing authority, claiming that long-term gay relationships constitute a family unit, thereby qualifying for rent-controlled housing

• Driver injured by a Domino's Pizza delivery man sues, claiming the pizza delivery company encourages careless driving in order to deliver pizzas within the guaranteed time

• Parents and high school students in rural Missouri sue school board to permit dances in the high school, claiming that its refusal supports a religious belief that dancing is immoral

• Family of depressed suicide victim sues church, claiming clergy who provided counseling should have sent the young man to a psychiatrist

Newspapers also often report cases which have been filed in court but not yet decided. As we have seen earlier, most cases are abandoned or negotiated long before they get to trial, but newspapers almost never report when litigation has been withdrawn or when judges dismiss trivial lawsuits.

Some of the major repeat players in litigation also frequently serve their own interests by dramatizing litigation horror stories. For example, insurance companies frequently advertise huge multimillion dollar jury awards in medical malpractice or other personal injury cases as proof of a crisis in the insurance industry and the reason for high premiums.

But broader surveys indicate that when patients have grievances against their doctors, only one-third contact lawyers and approximately 25 percent sue. Most either lump it or flee by changing to another physician. In addition, most malpractice lawsuits are decided in favor of doctors.[31] Injured patients actually do less well than other litigants in personal injury litigation. Most malpractice plaintiffs receive modest awards in jury trials, ranging from a few thousand dollars to less than $100,000. Only rarely do juries award hundreds of thousands or a million dollars. The big cases are the big exceptions.[32]

### Litigation Rates

The numbers are also misleading because they do not take into account changes in the population nor do they compare current rates of litigation (number of cases per 1000 population) with earlier rates.[33] It also is useful to compare rates of litigation in the United States with those in other countries as another way of understanding and evaluating the use of courts in America. One of the problems with the debate over litigiousness in America is that good data has not been available. Until the last few decades, court systems generally have not kept statistics so that researchers have had to painstakingly count earlier cases in order to make historical comparisons.

Their research often shows that while the raw number of cases has increased nearly thirty times from the early 1800s to the present, the rate of litigation actually has fallen. For instance, in St. Louis in the 1840s, there were about 36 cases filed per 1000 people. The rate dropped sharply during the early 1900s to about 8 cases and increased to only about 17 cases in the 1970s.[34]

The federal district courts had a low rate of litigation in the early 1900s— only 0.20 case per 1000 people. It rose to 0.44 in the 1930s, dropped to around 0.30 in the early 1960s, and has only recently climbed back to about its 1930s level. It appears that more cases are settled through negotiation and that cases take less time to go through the courts.

**U.S. Rates Compared to Others**    Litigation rates in the United States are not dramatically higher than in many other western countries. The overall rate in the United States is estimated at 44 cases per 1000 people compared with 47 in Canada, 62 in Australia, 41 in England, and 53 in New Zealand. Litigation rates in various other countries are much lower: Spain—3.5, Japan—12, Italy—10, and West Germany—23. While the U.S. rate is not low, it is lower than or about equal to that of many other highly industrialized and urban nations.

It is especially interesting to contrast the American and Japanese rates of litigation, since Japan has become the west's favorite model for everything from new cars and technology and ideal labor-management relations to low-fat diets. Japan often is pictured as a society which places a premium on close family and organizational ties and shuns conflict and contention. Presumably, its low rate of litigation is evidence of an ideal society that knows how to solve disputes in a quiet, informal manner. But what about the even lower rate of litigation in Italy, a nation never known for its quiet and uncontentious ways?

More recently, Japan's low rate of litigation has been attributed to official government policy which keeps the court system small and drastically limits the number of lawyers, both of which discourage litigation. But grievances and disputes are not necessarily low. A Japanese lawyer who represents a crime syndicate states that Japanese organized crime fills a need slighted by the small judicial system. Since lawyers are not widely available, gang members, he asserts, are hired to collect damage payments resulting from traffic accidents in return for a percentage of the take.[35] In addition, Japan has a large mediation service which settles several hundred thousand disputes every year.[36] Clearly, we have to be very careful before drawing quick conclusions about American, Japanese, or other people's litigiousness, and the presence of disputes. Although many disputes in the United States end up in court, in other societies, other institutions and arrangements—some of them less desirable than litigation—may be used to resolve claims that people make on one another.

**What Is Too Much?**    Finally, there is no agreement on what is too much litigation or whether increases are necessarily harmful. Those who are alarmed by the increases tend to see them as a sign of social or moral decay and blame greedy and unreasonable litigants and lawyers for bleeding others through the courts. But there are other explanations that are more firmly rooted in the growing complexity of American society and parallel changes in the legal system.

The United States increasingly produces a bewildering array of high-technology products and services, including talking cars, personal computers, space shuttles, chemicals, fast food of every description, automatic bank tellers and money machines, new medical devices, and much more. There are bound to be more injured and dissatisfied consumers and businesses in conflict going to court. Advances in science and technology also improve detection of pollution and its links to personal injury. The courts also have created stricter rules of liability for manufacturers and providers of other services and have given more legal rights to consumers.

Since the 1960s, the courts also have dramatically expanded the realm of individual constitutional rights, and issues that never would have reached the courts in an earlier age—abortion, rights of criminal defendants, racial and sexual equality, and many others—now are part of regular court business.

People also have become much more aware of their opportunities to go to court. The provision of lawyers for poor criminal defendants and the poor in civil cases has added to the list of litigation. To some people, expanded rights and use of courts are a bad sign of the times; to others, they constitute a long overdue reform of the legal system.

Finally, more Americans now live in cities—and are probably under more stress—and work and interact in more impersonal relationships, where disputes are more likely to lead to lawsuits than informal give-and-take.

While there is no consensus on the good or evil of the increase in litigation, there have been several important changes in the legal system and in society which account for the recent increases. When we also recall that litigation rates have been much higher in our history, when there were fewer people, fewer cities, a simpler economy, and far fewer legal rights and opportunities to go to court, current rates of litigation may not seem quite so high.

## INTEREST GROUPS IN COURT

Many of the organizations and repeat players that use courts have continuous and long-term political objectives. Going to court often is part of a broader group strategy to obtain government policies favorable to the group or that group leaders believe are good for society. However, courts are not as easy to lobby as legislatures or the executive branch, because the legal culture requires distance between partisan political interests and judges. Few lobbyists would consider contacting a judge about a case, and few judges would react favorably. Lobbying the courts has to be done indirectly and through litigation.

Interest groups in court provide a vivid illustration of courts as part of the political process. Interest groups usually are concerned with policy issues that are larger and more general than the conflict in particular cases. Like other litigants, interest groups often go to court as a last resort. Suing may be an alternative to closed doors in the legislature or executive branch. But interest groups sometimes use courts aggressively to protect political victories they already have achieved. For example, if an industry has succeeded in presuading Congress or a state legislature to enact a vague environmental protection law, it may sue executive officials who interpret the law to permit tighter regulation of pollution.

Groups in court may involve any social, economic, or political interests. We often think of interest groups in court as social underdogs—blacks, prisoners, homosexuals, welfare recipients, women—but *any* group that is unsuccessful in influencing government policy elsewhere or needs to continue the fight may wind up in court.

### Strategies for Influencing the Courts

Organized interest groups use a number of strategies or methods to influence judicial decisions. All the methods are perfectly legal and are authorized by court rules. Some judges and lawyers believe that organized litigation is contrary to the traditional legal ideal of individuals using courts to resolve private disputes, but lobbying in the courts almost always is done in ways that meet official judicial standards of how group interests may properly enter the legal process.

Lobbying the courts generally involves supporting litigants and managing their cases so that they contribute to the group's objectives, and making presentations to the courts through oral and written legal arguments (*briefs*).

**Test Cases**   One of the most important strategies of lobbying in the courts is to approach a problem as a test case.[37] A test case is one in which an interest group challenges the fundamental constitutionality of a particular government policy or private action. It focuses on the broadest possible principles of law and policy in order to obtain wide and general application of a court ruling. For example, rather than seek racial integration of a particular school or public building, litigants in a test case try to establish a very broad principle that racial segregation anywhere is unconstitutional and illegal. Another illustration concerns laws that provide federal funds to private organizations and religious groups that counsel teenagers against having sexual relations, but prohibit federal funding of agencies that discuss abortion. Civil liberties groups have argued that such laws violate First amendment prohibitions on government established religion.

By obtaining a favorable court ruling in a single test case, an interest group achieves a broad statement of court policy on an important issue, which also goes well beyond the particular circumstances of the immediate case. It is a way of killing many birds with one stone, since a ruling in a test case can be expected to be applied to similar circumstances in cases occurring in the future. Many test cases also attract considerable news attention, and they are written about in law journals, which quickly inform other judges and lawyers of new court policy.

*Group Support of Individuals*   Interest groups organize, manage, and pay the costs of test cases, but most cases have been started in the name of individual litigants. This is done to comply with legal rules concerning standing to sue. Rules concerning standing to sue generally require that only people who have suffered a real loss or have a genuine grievance may file a case.

Many interest groups, such as civil rights organizations, environmental protection groups, or business associations, do not suffer direct losses themselves, and they have been prevented from suing on their own. To get over this legal obstacle and to get a substantive social or economic issue before a court, they must locate individuals who have suffered discrimination or some other loss, or obtain the cooperation of individuals who purposely will violate a law and be convicted. This sets up a genuine conflict that makes it possible to test a law in court.

Therefore, while the titles of many test cases are in the names of private citizens and individual government officials, the cases do not really concern only individuals. They have implications for the interests of many people and the government as a policymaker and enforcer of laws. Test cases are legitimate ways of getting group social and political demands into the legal system.

*Moot Cases* Obtaining individual litigants to test policies gets a group into the courts, but other legal requirements may still prevent cases from being decided. Besides requiring real controversies, usual judicial procedure demands that the issues and circumstances presented in a case must still exist when a case comes before a court. A major change such as the death of a litigant or a change in the factual situation or settlement of the dispute makes a case moot. It is no longer a genuine controversy fitting the ground rules of what is required to get into court. When a case becomes moot, judges usually refuse to decide the issues and will dismiss the suit. After carefully preparing the case, awaiting court dates, and probably going from trial to appellate and possibly from state to federal courts, a moot case frustrates group objectives.

Exceptions to this practice have occurred in abortion cases and those involving the removal of life support systems from the terminally ill. By the time such cases reach appellate courts, litigants either have had a baby or an abortion or sometimes have died and the cases actually are moot. However, judges believe the issues are so important and would affect so many people that they want to deal with the issues. To declare the cases moot would prevent any such cases from reaching appellate courts in time. These cases also illustrate that well-established legal principles can be interpreted and used in many different ways.

**Class Actions** A way to get around the general problem of a case becoming moot is to file a case as a class action. These are cases in which a plaintiff claims to represent the interests of many people who are in the same social or economic boat even though they are not named as parties to the case. They are part of the same class or group as the plaintiff, however, because the dispute affects them in essentially the same way. In civil rights cases, for example, a single black litigant can claim to represent all blacks who have been discriminated against in the same way, or a female employee who sues her employer for job discrimination can claim to represent all women working in the same kind of position or in the same industry. Class actions have been part of the federal judicial process since 1955.

When a judge agrees to consider a case as a class action, the chances of a case becoming moot are greatly reduced, because the litigant officially named in the case is not the main focus of the controversy. In fact, if the circumstances have changed so that the conflict is no longer personally relevant, the court decision will not apply to the named litigant. However, the circumstances of the case continue to exist for most people in the class or group. Class actions keep a case alive and the group in court.

*Noncontroversial Class Actions* Some class actions also are test cases because an interest group questions the fundamental legality of laws or social practice. Cases in race relations, sex discrimination, fundamental constitutional freedoms, and rights of prisoners and criminal defendants often are both test cases and class actions.

Many other class actions, however, are not test cases, because they deal with very narrow issues or the specific application of a law. For example, a stockholder who charges that company officials manipulated the price of stock, causing him or her to lose money, may represent everyone who owned stock during the same period of time. He or she may claim compensation for everyone in the stockholder class. To be considered a member of the class in this kind of case, stockholders may simply have to fill out a form swearing that they owned stock during the period covered by the suit. If the company loses, it probably will have to pay damages to each stockholder plus the cost of attorneys' fees for the plaintiff.

Recently, only about 25 percent of all class action suits in the federal courts have involved discrimination, civil rights, and civil liberties. The large majority involve stockholders and other business related claims.[38]

Similar to a class action is a state *taxpayer's suit*. Taxpayer suits generally are not permitted against the federal government. In these kinds of cases, individuals claim to represent all taxpayers who are affected in the same way by state spending or particular administrative procedures. Since many state constitutions are very long and full of detail, taxpayers' suits can contest practically any decision to spend money that is not specifically permitted by state constitutions. Suits against new garbage dumps or incinerator plants, decisions of state governments to reimburse church-related schools for certain education costs, increases in tax rates, the use of property taxes to fund public education, and many others have occurred in the states.

The term "taxpayer suit" often conveys an image of a group of concerned citizens who band together to fight for good government, but taxpayers can be anyone, including associations of businesses, labor unions, or other groups who contest policies that go against their interests.

Class actions and taxpayers' suits are an important part of judicial politics, because they provide legitimate ways for organized interests to use the courts for the same reasons they use other branches of government. Class actions also make it possible for very large groups of people, often millions, to receive benefits indirectly from court policy without having to file their own cases.

It is impossible for every black person or every member of a religious minority or every stockholder to file and fight a court battle. It simply is too expensive and inconvenient and most people would take their individual lumps. One or several cases brought on behalf of many others, however, can be the judicial policy equivalent of a legislative statute that affects many citizens.

**Brandeis Briefs**    Test cases and class actions are important vehicles for arriving in court, but interest group strategy also requires careful consideration of the kind of case presentation that will be most persuasive.

If an interest group is trying to change the status quo, it probably will prepare a kind of legal argument known as a Brandeis Brief. This style of presentation was initiated by Supreme Court Justice Louis D. Brandeis during his early years as a crusading lawyer. It stresses social and economic conditions relevant to the case rather than formal law and precedent. Since the written law reflects past thinking on an issue, promoting change requires newer ideas and information.

Many test cases rely on this kind of material to make judges aware of the need to make new policies. For example, civil rights cases have emphasized the psychological and social harm and injustice caused by racial or sexual discrimination, and suits against manufacturers often have drawn attention to the quality of goods or to management practices that permit costly or dangerous errors. Opponents to the death penalty have tried unsuccessfully to convince the Supreme Court through statistical evidence that the death sentence is discriminatory because blacks who kill whites are much more likely to receive a sentence of death than other murderers.

Brandeis Briefs are not the legal sensation they were decades ago, since many groups and individuals use a variety of information from the social and natural sciences, and courts are becoming more accustomed to the blend of law and other knowledge. While they are becoming more routine, Brandeis style arguments are crucial for bringing social conditions into the courts as the basis for creating new law.

**Amici Curiae Briefs**    In addition to taking their own cases to courts, interest groups often participate in cases begun by other groups or individuals by filing additional written briefs as an amicus curia, or "friend of the court." Friends of the court may not give oral arguments.

The purpose is to provide judges with additional information that might be used to decide a case and to draw judicial attention to themselves as being interested in the outcome. Their interests frequently are very close to those of the main litigants. If a state government is involved in a case involving the death penalty, for example, it is common for other states to file their own amici curiae briefs, because their policies and practices are likely to be similar and will be affected by the decision. In other cases involving constitutional rights such as freedom of speech, religion, etc., various civil rights and liberties organizations likely will ask permission to submit arguments.

The decision of one group to file a brief may encourage organizations on the other side to become involved, too. The entry of many briefs provides a vivid picture of group conflict in the courts. In the famous 1977 case of *University of California Regents v. Bakke*, in which medical school admissions policies reserving a small number of seats for racial minorities were contested, 120 organizations filed fifty-seven amici curiae briefs. Thirty-two groups opposed the admissions policy, eighty-three were in favor, and five others dealt with different issues. Teachers' organizations, religious, racial, and ethnic organizations, professional and business associations, universities, students' organizations, veterans groups, labor unions, and others filed briefs.

This record was broken in 1989 in *Webster v. Reproductive Health Services*, a Missouri case involving state regulation of the right to an abortion. Over 400 groups filed seventy-eight briefs on both sides, including the Bush administration, which unsuccessfully urged the Supreme Court to use the case to overturn the right to an abortion.

*Other Reasons to File*  Besides hoping to influence the Court's decision in an important case, interest groups file briefs for additional reasons. Groups believe they must file briefs because their opponents do and they must present a counterweight. Also, the issues in particular cases are important to the group's members and the leadership must file to keep them satisfied. Finally, groups seek to build political coalitions by joining together in one amicus brief.[39]

### Public Interest Law

Much interest group involvement in the courts concerns public interest law (PIL). Groups acting in the public interest claim to represent large numbers of average citizens or even the entire population. They are altruistic interest groups in the sense that they go to court not to pursue specific economic or political goals that benefit only the organization but to obtain governmental policies that they believe benefit the entire general public.

For example, the Sierra Club has sued to prevent the cutting of trees on public lands even though it owns no trees and has not suffered any particular economic loss. It has claimed only to represent aesthetic values held by many citizens. The Consumers Union sues corporations and government officials regarding product safety, public information on products, and import policies on behalf of the general consuming public. Common Cause pursues a number of liberal political objectives in court. Since it seeks membership and financial support from *anyone* identified as a supporter of liberal policies, it has an extremely broad constituency.

Probably few or none of the supporters of these and other similar organizations have a specific personal claim in any public interest case. The organization, however, challenges various policies in the name of everyone—the general public interest.

The issues raised in public interest cases deal with important government policies or the actions of other large organizations, frequently businesses or corporations. Also, rather than sue for compensation for specific past wrongs or injuries, the plaintiffs often urge judges to look to the future to prevent further harm and to develop a comprehensive course of action that is best for a state or the nation.

Although trial and appellate decision making follows standard judicial procedures in these cases, the issues and outcomes are as important as legislative programs or various executive decisions. A professor of law has suggested that, compared to the "traditional model of [a case], the proceeding is recognizable as a lawsuit only because it takes place in a courtroom before an official called a judge."[40] Public interest law is the ultimate in interest group politics and the courts.

**PIL Profile**   Litigation in the public interest has grown and developed since the 1960s, when the civil rights movement made people more aware of the policymaking power of the courts and the ability of people without money and political experience to organize and compete politically. Public interest law got another boost partly through the work of politically active young lawyers in the federal Legal Services Program. In addition to handling individual civil cases, lawyers in the early years sued state and local governments as well as businesses regarding programs and actions that affected large numbers of poor people.

However, as reported earlier, state and local governments objected to federal funds being spent on lawsuits against them. The Nixon administration persuaded Congress to limit the range of lawsuits that legal service lawyers could handle, and funding was reduced during the Reagan years.

A profile of public interest law groups is presented in Table 5.1. The greatest growth of public interest law organizations occurred in the 1970s, as more groups of Americans became aware of the potential for winning important policy gains in the courts. In 1970, there were approximately 50 public interest law groups in the United States, but this number increased to approximately 225 by the end of the decade. However, by then growth had slowed and flattened.

Public interest law groups support their goals in two ways. Groups either argue for particular social causes, such as environmental protection and civil rights, or they are advocates for particular groups of people, such as the poor, minorities, women, and others. Nearly all groups represent social and political underdogs and causes that challenge the status quo.

The number of PIL attorneys also grew substantially from fewer than 50 nationwide before 1970 to approximately 900 in the 1980s. Poverty, civil rights, and environmental groups employ most of them. Few public interest lawyers earn large salaries. The median salary in the 1980s was $40,000 per year, but approximately 20 percent earned less than $21,000.

The largest and most politically active groups are the American Civil Liberties Union (ACLU), the National Association for the Advancement of Colored People Legal Defense and Education Fund (NAACP/LDF), the Natural Resources Defense Council, and the California Rural Legal Assistance.

Most public interest law groups have very limited funds, which prevents all but a few from being very active in politics and litigation. The budgets of most groups ranged between $100,000 to $1 million annually with a median of approximately $500,000. Even the budget of the ACLU, which was over $10 million in the 1980s, is very small compared with the tens of millions of dollars of many other interest groups active in politics.

Financial support for public interest law groups comes from many different

**TABLE 5-1**
PUBLIC INTEREST LAW PROFILE

| | |
|---|---|
| Number of Groups | 222 |
| Types of Groups | |
| "Causes" | 41% |
|     Civil rights/civil liberties | 10% |
|     Environmental | 8 |
|     Consumer Advocacy | 4 |
|     Media/communications | 4 |
|     Other | 13 |
| "Clients" | 59% |
|     Poor | 15% |
|     Women | 10 |
|     Disabled | 9 |
|     Children | 8 |
|     Minorities | 7 |
|     Prisoners | 4 |
|     Others | 6 |
| Number of lawyers | 900 |
| Lawyers' salary | |
|     Range | $15,000 to $60,000 |
|     Median | $40,000 |
| Organization budgets | |
|     Range | $16,000 to $10 million |
|     Median | $500,000 |
| Sources of Funds | |
|     Foundation Grants | 24% |
|     Contributions | 20 |
|     Federal government | 18 |
|     Dues | 11 |
|     Court-awarded fees | 9 |
|     Other | 18 |

*Source:* Derived from Nan Aron, *Liberty and Justice for All: Public Interest Law in the 1980s and Beyond* (Boulder, Colo.: West-view Press, 1989).

sources. Following reductions under the Reagan administration, less than 20 percent of public interest law activity is funded by the federal government. The remainder comes mainly from membership dues, individual contributions, and grants from private charitable contributions. Court-awarded lawyers' fees account for some group income.

**Liberal and Conservative Groups** Most public interest law activity is begun by liberals on behalf of people without other effective political representation.[41] Supporters of public interest suits argue that businesses, corporations, and government do not need public interest organizations to represent them because they have ample legal and financial resources to fight their political battles. Other citizens, however—blacks, women, the poor, people in mental hospitals, and consumers—have no such resources. Liberal interest groups, acting in what they believe is the public interest, provide a new opportunity for the previously unrepresented to get their day in court. Public interest organizations try to be the great equalizer by providing experienced legal guns to fight for people who are no match for established organizations and experienced repeat players.

Although most public interest law organizations represent the powerless, conservative groups claiming to represent the public also have begun to use the courts. There are early predecessors of conservative public interest law firms, such as the American Liberty League which opposed the New Deal of the 1930s, but modern conservative public interest activity dates from the early 1970s and was a reaction to the rapid growth of liberal organizations.

They appear to have become active first in California when then Governor Ronald Reagan sought to make conservative reforms in the state welfare system and ran into liberal opposition in the legislature. The conservative Pacific Legal Foundation organized to lobby on behalf of his policies. Later, the National Legal Center for the Public Interest organized to develop other regional conservative groups that would lobby and go to court for conservative causes.

One of the most prominent is the Mountain States Legal Foundation, which goes to court on behalf of businesses and other groups who favor greater use of public lands for mining, oil drilling, and other commercial ventures. They oppose many state and federal environmental protection policies. The founder of the organization is political conservative Joseph Coors, brewer of Coors Beer. James Watt, first secretary of the interior in the Reagan administration, was once the chief lawyer for the foundation.[42]

Opportunities for groups to use the courts increased during the 1970s, when the U.S. Supreme Court eased legal requirements through a broader interpretation of standing to sue.[43] As new conservative justices came to the Supreme court in the 1980s, however, the Court tightened its requirements somewhat so that groups found it more difficult to bring cases in their own names. But groups continue to file many amici curiae briefs and there is little evidence that the Court wants to cut off access.[44] It is likely that active group participation in litigation will continue.

**State Agencies**   Most public interest law is sponsored by private organizations. In the mid-1970s, however, New Jersey created a new Department of Public Advocate to respond to citizen complaints and file lawsuits, if necessary, against private businesses and other agencies of state and local government. The department may deal with rates charged by public utilities, housing, mental health facilities, nursing and boarding homes, auto insurance, unemployment benefits, environmental protection, and other issues. The department also runs a statewide public defender system for poor criminal defendants, represents prison inmates in class action suits against the state prison system, and responds to complaints about the treatment of juvenile criminal defendants.

Several other states have consumer protection and other agencies, sometimes termed "ombudsmen" (Norwegian origin), who perform some of the functions of the public advocate, such as looking into specific complaints against government officials and agencies, challenging public utility rates, and providing public defenders in criminal cases.

**Public Interest and Politics**    Public interest law has considerable political appeal because it seems to include and represent everyone. Also, unlike most interest groups, public law organizations usually do not seek direct benefits for themselves but are motivated by altruistic social beliefs.

Nevertheless, the United States is much too complex and varied to be reflected in a single public interest or opinion. When a group claims to represent the public interest in court or in another branch of government, it can only represent *part* of the public. It may not even represent the opinions of all of an organization's members, especially if it is a large association. Instead, it may adopt goals that its few directors have decided are good public policy. Each of us might agree or disagree with those goals.

For instance, there is no single opinion on the safety and value of nuclear energy facilities, yet some public interest law organizations have claimed to represent the general public interest in opposing nuclear energy. Likewise, not everyone agrees that tree cutting on federal land ought to be limited.

To understand public interest law, we need to look at it as we would any other interest group activity. We need to be informed about who its organizers are, the kinds of policies it wants government to adopt, the groups of people who support the organization, and who contributes money to it. This will provide some of the same kind of information we get when labor unions, businesses, doctors, civil rights groups, and others go to court to win favorable court policies for themselves.

### How Much Lobbying?

Organized interest groups and sensational cases make the news. However, we need to know how often groups actually are involved in litigation and in what kinds of cases. Are most court cases individual disputes, or is it common to find interest groups behind lots of conflicts? What is the overall role of interest groups in court? It is not easy to answer these questions, because there are lots of courts that people can use as well as different group strategies.

*Amici Briefs*    Group activity has been measured most often by the number of amici curiae briefs submitted in cases. From this research it appears that most lobbying is done in cases that reach the U.S. Supreme Court. Less than 5 percent of the cases decided by the federal courts of appeals have any amicus participation. In addition, class action suits usually account for less than 3 percent of all cases filed in the federal courts and there are very few taxpayer suits in the states. It seems that organized groups use their resources for cases that will have an important national effect.[45]

The picture of interest groups and litigation is different for the Supreme Court. During the 1950s and 1960s, amici briefs were found in about 25 to 35 percent of all cases involving race relations and civil liberties (freedom of speech, press, and religion, right of association, voting, legislative and judicial procedure, etc.). Only 10 percent of all criminal cases were accompanied by amicus curiae briefs. Overall, about 20 percent of all nonbusiness cases attracted amicus support.[46]

Most commercial cases did not involve much organized group activity and were handled mainly by the litigants themselves. Attorneys in these cases rarely developed any cooperative strategy with other attorneys or organizations, and they received no financial assistance from outside groups. Most of these cases involved large businesses and government, so the main litigants needed no help and viewed the cases as purely private disputes.[47]

***Burst of Activity*** The low rate of participation by interest groups in Supreme Court litigation has changed dramatically since the 1960s.[48] During the 1970s, *over half* of the noncommercial cases attracted one or more amici briefs, but the rate of group participation still is climbing. Table 5.2 shows that groups recently have submitted amici briefs in approximately 80 percent of all cases decided by the Supreme Court, including commercial and noncommercial issues. The most active groups are federal, state, and local governments;

**TABLE 5-2**
INTEREST GROUP PARTICIPATION AND
SUCCESS IN SUPREME COURT CASES
(PERCENT OF CASES)

| Participation | |
| --- | --- |
| Groups submit amici briefs | 80% |
| Types of organizations | |
| Governments | 24 |
| Businesses/Commercial | 24 |
| Legal | 13 |
| Civil liberties | 11 |
| Religious | 5 |
| Women's | 4 |
| Others | 19 |
| **Success** | |
| Obtaining writs of certiorari | |
| Cases with amici briefs | 36% |
| Cases without amici briefs | 5 |
| Winning discrimination cases | |
| Cases sponsored by groups | 67 |
| Cases not sponsored by groups | 41 |

*Source:* Derived from Lee Epstein, "Courts and Interest Groups," in John B. Gates and Charles A. Johnson (eds.), *The American Courts: A Critical Assessment* (Washington, D.C.: Congressional Quarterly Press, 1991, pp. 356, 358, and 361; and Gregory A. Caldeira and John R. Wright, "Organized Interests and Agenda Setting in the U.S. Supreme Court," *American Political Science Review*, 82, 1116 (1988).

individual businesses and commercial associations; followed by bar associations and other legal groups; civil liberties organizations; and others.

Cases at the top of the amici list included church-state relations, environmental protection, government procedures, labor-management disputes, business finance, disputes over government benefits, freedom of speech and press, and discrimination. Criminal cases attract some amici participation, but not nearly as much as other areas of policy.

*Conservative Groups* Another notable change in interest group activity is that conservative interest groups are much more active now than ever before in Supreme Court cases. In the 1960s and 1970s, liberal organizations were very prominent, either supporting litigation directly or filing numerous amici curiae briefs. But conservative groups have steadily increased their presence, while liberal group participation has declined. Increased conservative participation— and declining liberal activity—probably reflects the improved access of conservative groups to the Reagan administration and to the conservative majority on the Supreme Court.

There are important differences in the emphasis which conservative and liberal groups put on litigation before the Supreme Court. Conservative groups file close to half their briefs in economic cases, while liberal organizations are involved in very few of these cases. Reflecting their traditional concerns, liberal interest groups file nearly all of their briefs in civil liberties and criminal rights cases. However, conservative groups also file nearly half their briefs in civil liberties and criminal rights cases in support of conservative positions involving abortion, obscenity, employment discrimination, and law enforcement issues. The new, wide-ranging conservative lobbying at the Supreme Court is a major change from its earlier minor participation.[49]

### Winning

Groups invest much money and expertise in preparing amici briefs or sponsoring litigation, but does it pay off? Are groups successful in court? There is evidence that groups do better than individuals in Supreme Court litigation. Table 5.2 shows that cases in which groups file amici briefs are much more likely to be granted a hearing by the Court (receive a writ of certiorari) than cases in which no amici briefs have been filed.

Other case characteristics are important, too, in determining whether the Court will agree to hear a case, but the addition of an amici brief adds to the likelihood of getting a hearing. In particular, cases in which there is a conflict among the lower courts and the federal government is also a party to the case are likely to be granted certiorari. However, if these cases also include just one amicus curiae brief, the chances of their being heard by the Supreme Court increase by 40 to 50 percent.[50]

Groups also are more likely to win cases than individuals. Table 5.2 shows that groups which sponsor discrimination cases win approximately 67 percent of the time; individuals win 41 percent. These percentages include cases in which groups are claiming discrimination or defending against claims of discrimination. Many studies of individual lawsuits also strongly suggest that carefully engineered legal and political strategies are successful in winning favorable judicial and other governmental policies.

## CONCLUSION

Going to court usually is the last thing that people do to settle disputes. Courts are remote, formal, and expensive, and the legal process prolongs stress and uncertainty. Trials also emphasize blame and winners and losers rather than reconciliation, and victories in court may not produce concrete results. For people who know each other and will continue to interact, such as family and neighbors, there probably are better ways to manage conflict. Many urban court systems encourage people to use mediation or arbitration as alternatives to standard court procedures.

Except for divorce cases, where judges must put their official stamp of approval on a final settlement, most cases concern money and business. Social change and environments have an impact on the kinds of cases that courts hear, but the overwhelming majority of cases involve large or small commercial activities.

In a complex urban society where most people are strangers, many people go to court. However, most cases are settled without trials. Many of the same doubts that make individuals reluctant to file cases also lead them to negotiate their differences. The outcomes of trials are uncertain, and most litigants compromise to reduce their costs and risk of losing. For businesses that use courts to collect debts, filing cases may stimulate settlements, because trials always are available to impose settlements. Instead of a nation of trials, we are a nation where going to court is an extension of social conflict and one of many strategies that people use to cope with disputes.

Organized interest groups also use courts to make political, social, and economic demands on others and to influence broad government policies that affect many people. They often use courts as alternatives to other parts of government, but they also sometimes must defend their victories against other group challenges.

Lobbying the judiciary demonstrates the political significance of courts as clearly as any other aspect of the judicial process, and interest group activity is increasing in the Supreme Court.

## SUGGESTIONS FOR ADDITIONAL READING

Nan Aron: *Liberty and Justice for All: Public Interest Law in the 1980s and Beyond* (Boulder, Colo.: Westview Press, 1989). This book reports on the result of a survey of public interest law firms operating in the 1980s. It discusses their characteristics and political strategies.

Lee Epstein: "Courts and Interest Groups," in *The American Courts: A Critical Assessment*, ed. John B. Gates and Charles A. Johnson (Washington, D.C.: CQ Press, 1991), pp. 335–371. This is an overview of current research on the roles and strategies of groups in litigation. It contains a good bibliography for further investigation.

Marc Galanter: "The Day After the Litigation Exposition," *Maryland Law Review* 46 (1986), 3–39. An analyst of the relationship between law and society studies litigation rates and argues that there is no huge increase in litigation in the United States.

Richard Kluger: *Simple Justice: The History of Brown v. Board of Education and America's Struggle for Equality* (New York: Alfred A. Knopf, 1976). This is an in-depth case study of the NAACP and school desegregation litigation.

H. Laurence Ross: *Settled Out of Court: The Social Process of Insurance Claims Adjustment* (New York: Aldine de Gruyter, 1980). This study of settling insurance claims provides an excellent introduction to the process of private negotiation.

Linda R. Singer: *Settling Disputes: Conflict Resolution in Business, Families and the Legal System* (Boulder, Colo.: Westview Press, 1990). This book provides an overview of the growth of mediation and arbitration and the processes used to lead opponents to a settlement, in small private disputes as well as in larger issues involving government policy.

Clement E. Vose: *Caucasians Only: The Supreme Court, the NAACP, and the Restrictive Covenant Cases* (Berkeley: University of California Press, 1959). This is an early and classic case study of the role and strategy of the NAACP Legal Defense Fund in pursuing civil rights in the Supreme Court.

## NOTES

1 Richard E. Miller and Austin Sarat, "Grievances, Claims and Disputes: Assessing the Adversary Culture," *Law and Society Review*, 15 (1980–81), 537.
2 Alternatives to going to court are discussed in a number of sources. See, for example, Vilheim Aubert, "Courts and Conflict Resolution," *Journal of Conflict Resolution*, 11 (1967), 40–51; Sally Engle Merry, "Going to Court: Strategies of Dispute Management in an American Urban Neighborhood," *Law and Society Review*, 14 (Summer 1979), 891–925; Austin Sarat, "Alternatives in Dispute Processing: Litigation in Small Claims Court," *Law and Society Review*, 10 (Spring 1976), 339–375; Austin Sarat and Joel B. Grossman, "Courts and Conflict Resolution: Problems in the Mobilization of Adjudication," *American Political Science Review*, 69 (1975), 1200–1217.
3 Lynn Mather and Barbara Yngvesson, "Language, Audience and the Transformation of Disputes," *Law and Society Review*, 15 (1980–82), 778.
4 H. Laurence Ross, *Settled Out of Court* (Chicago: Aldine Publishing Company, 1970).
5 Susan S. Silbey and Sally E. Merry, "Mediator Settlement Strategies," *Law and Policy*, 8 (1986), 7–32; Linda R. Singer, *Settling Disputes: Conflict Resolution in Business, Families and the Legal System* (Boulder, Colo.: Westview Press, 1990).
6 Farmers Home Administration, U.S. Department of Agriculture, *FmHA Roster, Farmer-Creditor Mediators, 1989; New York Times*, November 16, 1988, p. 12.

7  Albert J. Reiss, Jr., *The Police and the Public* (New Haven, Conn.: Yale University Press, 1971), pp. 77–80.

8  The following relies on *Neighborhood Justice Centers Field Test: Final Evaluation Report* (Washington: U.S. Department of Justice, National Institute of Justice, February 1980), pp. 5–7 and 22–23; *National Justice Centers* (Washington: U.S. Department of Justice, National Institute of Justice, Policy Briefs, May 1980), pp. 6–8; and "Alternative Dispute Resolution and the Courts: A Symposium," *Judicature*, 69 (1986), 252–300. See also Christine B. Harrington, *Shadow Justice* (Westport, Conn.: Greenwood Press, 1985).

9  *The New York Times*, March 4, 1986, p. 34.

10  Deborah R. Hensler, "What We Know and Don't Know about Court-Administered Arbitration," *Judicature*, 69 (1986), 272; Raymond J. Broderick, "Court-annexed Arbitration: It Works," *Judicature*, 72 (1989), 217–225; Craig Boersema, Roger Hanson, and Susan Keilitz, "State Court-annexed Arbitration: What Do Attorneys Think?", G. Thomas Eisele, "The Case against Mandatory Court-annexed ADR Programs," and Raymond J. Broderick, "Court-annexed Compulsory Arbitration . . . ," *Judicature*, 75 (1991), 28–33; 34–40; 41–44; John P. McIver and Susan Keilitz, "Court-Annexed Arbitration: An Introduction," and Keith O. Boyum, "Afterward: Does Court-annexed Arbitration 'Work'?", *Justice System Journal*, 14 (1991), 123–132 and 133–137.

11  Thomas P. Jahnige, "A Note on the Implications of Legal Rules and Procedures," in Thomas P. Jahnige and Sheldon Goldman (eds.), *The Federal Judicial System: Readings in Process and Behavior* (New York: Holt, Rinehart and Winston, Inc., 1968), pp. 94–99; Bruce Campbell and Susette M. Talarico, "Access to Legal Services: Examining Common Assumptions," *Judicature*, 66 (1983), 313–318.

12  Douglas E. Rosenthal, *Lawyer and Client: Who's in Charge?* (New York: Russell Sage Foundation, 1974).

13  Sarat, p. 345.

14  Aubert, p. 44.

15  Merry, p. 893; Sarat, pp. 357–358; Donald J. Black, "The Mobilization of Law," *Journal of Legal Studies*, 2 (1973), 134.

16  Stewart Macauley, "Non-Contractual Relations in Business: A Preliminary Study," *American Sociological Review*, 28 (1963), 55–67, and Marc Galanter, "Reading the Landscape of Disputes," *UCLA Law Review*, 31 (1983), 25.

17  *Burnette v. State* is based on *Tallahassee Democrat*, March 19, 1981. p. 1, *Marsha v. John* is based on county court records.

18  A useful and readable description of legal procedure can be found in Blair J. Kolasa and Bernadine Mayer, *Legal Systems* (Englewood Cliffs, N.J.: Prentice-Hall, Inc., 1978). See also William P. McLauchlan, *American Legal Processes* (New York: John Wiley & Sons, Inc., 1977), chap. 3.

19  The following is based on Herbert Jacob, *Debtors in Court* (Chicago: Rand McNally & Company, 1969), pp. 16, 34, and 99–101.

20  Leonard Downie, Jr., *Justice Denied* (Baltimore: Penguin Books, Inc., 1971), p. 122.

21  Ross, pp. 140–170.

22  Barbara Yngvesson and Patricia Hennessey, "Small Claims, Complex Disputes: A Review of the Small Claims Literature," *Law and Society Review*, 9 (Winter 1975), 237–238; John C. Ruhnka and Steven Weller, *Small Claims Courts* (Nationl Center for State Courts: Williamsburg, Va., 1978), pp. 41–44. For additional discussions of the work of the state courts, see: Sarat, 1986; Lawrence M. Friedman and Robert V.

Percival, "A Tale of Two Courts: Litigation in Alameda and San Benito Counties," *Law and Society Review* (1976), 281–282; and Burton M. Atkins and Henry R. Glick, "Environmental and Structural Variables as Determinants of Issues in State Courts of Last Resort," *American Journal of Political Science* 20 (1976), 100–101.

23 Marc Galanter, "Afterword: Explaining Litigation," *Law and Society Review*, 9 (Winter 1975), 347–368; Craig Wanner, "The Public Ordering of Private Relations," *Law and Society Review*, 8 (Spring 1974), 421–440; Yngvesson and Hennessey, 237–241.

24 Friedman and Percival; Joel B. Grossman and Austin Sarat, "Litigation in the Federal Courts: A Comparative Perspective," *Law and Society Review*, 9 (Winter 1975), 321–346.

25 Robert A. Kagan et al., "The Business of State Supreme Courts," *Stanford Law Review*, 30 (November 1977), 121–156; Friedman and Percival; Wayne V. McIntosh, "150 Years of Litigation and Dispute Settlement: A Court Tale," *Law and Society Review*, 15 (1980–81), 823–848; Lawrence Baum, Sheldon Goldman, and Austin Sarat, "The Evolution of Litigation in the Federal Courts of Appeals, 1895–1975," *Law and Society Review*, 16 (1981–82), 291–309.

26 Friedman and Percival, pp. 296–301.

27 Atkins and Glick.

28 *State Court Caseload Statistics: Annual Report, 1989* (Williamsburg, Va.: National Center for State Courts, 1991).

29 Administrative Office of the United States Court, *Annual Report of the Director*, Washington, D.C., various years.

30 *Newsweek*, November 21, 1983, p. 98.

31 *Newsweek*, February 17, 1986, p. 75.

32 Marilynn L. May and Daniel B. Stengel, "Who Sues their Doctors? How Patients Handle Medical Grievances," *Law and Society Review*, 24 (1990), 105–120; Stephen Daniels, "Tracing the Shadow of the Law: Jury Verdicts in Medical Malpractice Cases," *Justice System Journal*, 14 (1990), 4–39.

33 The following relies on Galanter, "Reading the Landscape of Disputes," pp. 4–71.

34 Wayne McIntosh, "Private Use of a Public Forum: A Long Range View of the Dispute Processing Role of Courts," *American Political Science Review*, 77 (1983), 991–1010.

35 *New York Times*, August 29, 1991, p. A11.

36 Joel Rosch, "Institutionalizing Mediation: The Evolution of the Civil Liberties Bureau in Japan," *Law and Society Review*, 21 (1987), 243–166.

37 Clement E. Vose, "Litigation as a Form of Pressure Group Activity," *Annals of the American Academy of Political and Social Sciences*, 319 (September 1958), 20–31; *Caucasians Only* (Berkeley: University of California Press, 1959); Lee Epstein, "Courts and Interest Groups," in John B. Gates and Charles A. Johnson (eds.), *The American Courts* (Washington, D.C.: Congressional Quarterly Press, 1991), pp. 335–371.

38 Administrative Office of the United States Courts, *Annual Report*, 1990, Table X-5, pp. 311–312.

39 Epstein, pp. 348–349.

40 Abram Chayes, "The Role of the Judge in Public Law Litigation," *Harvard Law Review*, 89 (May 1976), 1302.

41 Mitchell Rogovin, "Public Interest Law: The Next Horizon," *American Bar Association Journal*, 63 (March 1977), 335; Sanford M. Jaffe, "Public Interest Law: Five Years Later," *Amerian Bar Assciation Journal*, 62 (August 1976), 984.

**42** Lee Epstein, *Conservatives in Court* (Knoxville: University of Tennessee Press, 1985.

**43** Karen Orren. "Standing to Sue: Interest Group Conflict in the Federal Courts," *American Political Science Review*, 70 (September 1976), 723–741.

**44** Epstein, p. 352.

**45** Administrative Office of the United States Courts, *Annual Report*, Washington, D.C., 1985; Wayne V. McIntosh and Paul E. Parker, "Amici Curiae in the Courts of Appeals" (a paper presented at the 1986 Annual Meeting of the Law and Society Association, Chicago, May 29–June 1, 1986).

**46** Nathan Hakman, "The Supreme Court's Political Environment: The Processing of Non-Commercial Litigation," in Joel B. Grossman and Joseph Tanenhaus (eds.). *Frontiers of Judicial Research* (New York: John Wiley & Sons, Inc., 1969), pp. 209–210.

**47** Nathan Hakman, "Lobbying the Supreme Court—An Appraisal of 'Political Science Folklore,'" *Fordham Law Review*, 35 (1966), 15–50.

**48** Karen O'Conner and Lee Epstein, "Research Note: Amicus Curiae Participation in U.S. Supreme Court Litigation: An Appraisal of 'Hakman's Folklore,'" *Law and Society Review*, 16 (1981–82), 311–320.

**49** Karen O'Conner and Lee Epstein, "The Rise of Conservative Interest Group Litigation," *Journal of Politics*, 45 (1983), 480–489.

**50** Gregory A. Caideira and John R. Wright, "Organized Interests and Agenda Setting in the U.S. Supreme Court," *American Political Science Review*, 82 (1988), 1122.

# 6

## COURTS AND CRIMINAL CASES

One of the most persistent beliefs about American justice is that when persons are arrested and charged with a crime, they get their day in court. With an attorney by their side to maintain their innocence, they go to trial. The trial discovers the truth; the guilty are punished and the righteous go free.

However, as in civil disputes, very few criminal cases go to trial. In fact, many cases do not go further than an arrest. Prosecutors decide to drop as many as half of all cases brought to them by the police, and they dismiss even more as they prepare their cases for formal court hearings. Judges also dismiss some additional cases early in the judicial process. In the remaining cases, nearly 90 percent of criminal defendants across the country plead guilty before their cases come to trial, leaving only a handful who choose to face a judge or jury. This chapter describes the people and process that settle criminal cases without trials.

Especially important are early decisions to prosecute and how and why defendants plead guilty and go directly to sentencing. Procedures for settling criminal cases rarely are governed by formal law, but are based on tradition, concerns for court efficiency, and informal social interactions among the people who work in the courts.

### CRIMES AND CRIMINALS

Just as there are many ways for dealing with civil disputes, resorting to the criminal courts is only one way of dealing with crime. The criminal courts do not deal with all crime for a number of reasons.

### Reporting and Investigating Crime

Most victims do not report crime. Much crime takes place among family and friends, and victims often want to keep it quiet or do not want to get the assailants in trouble. Others do not believe that the police can catch the perpetrator or recover stolen items. Much other crime takes place in private, and police come upon little crime on their own. Unless people report crime, there is little that the police can do.

The huge increase in the illegal sale and use of drugs illustrates the difference between obvious and hidden crime and the power of the police. Informed observers estimate that up to 80 percent of illegal drug users are whites with a high school or college education, but the vast majority of those arrested are poor and black. The head of Chicago's police narcotics division explains:

> [White sellers and users] are harder to catch. Those deals are done in office buildings, in somebody's home, and there's not the violence associated with it that there is in the black community. [T]he guy standing on the corner . . . almost [has] a sign on his back. These guys are just arrestable.[1]

Reporting or observing crime is not the entire story. The large majority of the crimes that are reported to the police also do not result in arrests. In 1990, nearly 15 million serious crimes were reported to the police, including violent crimes against individuals and major property crimes. However, the police made arrests in only 20 percent or about 3 million of these cases.

Often, the police cannot find a suspect, but in very large cities, where the police have a great deal of crime to investigate, even much of the obvious crime is not investigated very carefully. The Chicago police department recently acknowledged that for two decades, detectives routinely dumped victims' complaints if the victim knew the assailant (friends-and-neighbors crime), if the victim was not easy to contact for police interviews, and if the property involved in the crime was not worth much. As many as 40 percent of all valid cases were not properly investigated. In Boston and New York and, probably, other big cities, crimes other than murder do not receive in-depth police attention.[2]

Unless a victim can clearly identify the criminal and is willing or eager to press a complaint, the police apparently do little to solve the crime. Skillfully planned crime carried out by intelligent professional criminals, organizations, or middle-class criminals is much more difficult to detect and rarely leads to arrests. Subtle bribery of public officials or embezzlement or stealing trade secrets through computers is very difficult for local police or even the FBI to uncover.

Consequently, defendants in the criminal courts usually are uneducated, lower-class criminals and juveniles who commit unsophisticated, obvious, common crime and leave a trail of evidence—but only a small percentage of these perpetrators are caught.

**Discretion**   Even when there is ample evidence that a law has been broken, arrests are not automatic, for there are various other ways that police deal with possible crime and suspicious people. Issuing warnings to motorists and loiterers, harassing prostitutes or young toughs on the streets, or ordering people to "move along" are ways of controlling crowds and informally punishing offenders.

Police most often arrest young, lower-class men who are disrespectful, hostile, or violent toward the police. Individuals who are deferential and who respect a patrol officer's authority and power are much more likely to avoid arrest or other harassment.[3] This also means, then, that the people who end up in the criminal courts most often are lower-class young men. They are the criminal courts' "regular customers."

### Crime and Criminal Profile

A profile of criminal defendants and the crimes they commit is presented in Table 6.1. Criminal defendants in the United States clearly are not a cross section of the general population. Over 80 percent are males and nearly half are 24 years old or younger. Contrary to popular belief, most criminals are not black; however, a much higher percentage of blacks are charged with crime than the proportion of blacks in the general population. Close to 30 percent of criminal defendants are black.

**TABLE 6-1**
PROFILE OF CRIMES AND CRIMINALS

| Who are the criminals? | |
|---|---|
| Males | 82% |
| Whites | 69% |
| Age | |
|     Under 18 | 16% |
|     18 to 24 | 30 |
|     25 to 34 | 32 |
|     35 and over | 22 |

| What are the crimes? | |
|---|---|
| Total number of arrests | 14,195,000 |
|     Drunk driving | 13% |
|     Drunkness; disorderly conduct | 12 |
|     Larceny; theft | 11 |
|     Assault | 10 |
|     Drugs | 8 |
|     Liquor laws | 5 |
|     Burglary | 3 |
|     Other | 38 |

*Source:* Derived from *Uniform Crime Reports for the United States* (Washington, D.C.: Federal Bureau of Investigation, U.S. Department of Justice, 1990), pp. 173–174.

In 1990, police made over 14 million arrests (excluding traffic violations), up from 9 million in the mid-1980s. The largest number were for drunken driving, public drunkeness, and disorderly conduct, followed closely by larceny, theft, assault, and drug violations. Nearly 70 percent of the drug arrests are for possession with others for the sale and manufacture of illegal drugs, mostly heroin or cocaine (arrests not shown in Table 6.1). Added together, arrests involving alcohol and drugs were approximately one-third of all arrests.

The most serious violent crimes, including murder, rape, and manslaughter; are listed separately in Table 6.1 because they are a tiny percentage of the total arrests. But in 1990, approximately 62,000 arrests involved these crimes, or one-half of one percent of all arrests.

There is comparatively little federal criminal law. Therefore, certain types of criminal cases are rare in the federal courts while others are a federal specialty. For instance, the federal courts decide only a few hundred murder cases each year (many of them from Washington, D.C.) compared with thousands in the states. However, the federal courts are much more likely to deal with other types of cases, including fraud, forgery and counterfeiting, narcotics, immigration violations, and larceny. Other common federal crimes include income tax evasion, liquor violations, denial of civil rights, and several others. State and federal laws overlap in certain cases, such as narcotics and liquor violations, but generally, most criminal laws and, consequently, most crime belong to the states.

## PROSECUTORS, JUDGES, AND LAWYERS

Settling cases in the criminal courts involves three main sets of people with different jobs and influence in how cases are handled.

### Prosecutors

**The Job**   Prosecuting attorneys have many different official titles. They may be called prosecutors, state's attorneys, district attorneys, solicitors, or, in the case of the federal government, U.S. attorneys. In the states, prosecutors typically are elected to a 2- or 4- year term of office and can run for additional terms. Federal prosecutors are appointed by the President. Senatorial courtesy and political decisions similar to those involved in the appointment of federal district judges usually shape their appointment. A prosecutor normally has authority over the same geographic area or district as the trial court of general jurisdiction.

The prosecutor usually is an office administrator who sets general policy concerning how cases are to be treated, and he or she is concerned with the productivity and efficiency of the office. In larger towns and cities, prosecutors usually hire a number of assistant prosecutors, who actually handle most of the criminal cases. Assistant prosecutors often are young attorneys or recent graduates of local law schools. In big cities, there may be dozens or a hundred or more assistant prosecutors. A few are interested in developing a political career, but most want experience before going into private law practice.[4]

Upon receiving arrest reports from the local police, the FBI, or other law enforcement agency, the main job of a state or federal prosecutor is to decide whether or not to initiate criminal charges against a suspect. The prosecutor also must determine which criminal laws have been violated and the exact charges to file. He or she also manages the progress of a case against the defendant through the courts. Prosecutors generally have much freedom to make whatever decisions they consider appropriate. They rarely face any external review or controls concerning which cases they bring into the courts and how they manage their work.

Some state prosecutors in small towns and rural areas also have an additional responsibility of giving legal advice to local government officials in noncriminal matters. Frequently, there is such little criminal or government legal work that prosecutors are part-time officials who have a private law practice on the side. U.S. attorneys also serve as lawyers for the federal government in civil cases, such as in motor vehicle accidents involving postal vehicles. About 40 percent of their work involves noncriminal matters.[5]

Federal prosecutors are formally obliged to follow policies set by the Justice Department in Washington, but since they usually think of themselves as local law enforcement officials, and there are so many of them nationwide (one for each federal judicial district), it is difficult for officials in Washington to influence their routine operations. In cases with national implications, such as major civil rights litigation or organized crime, local federal prosecutors are subject to national influence, but in most other crimes, they generally manage their own affairs.[6]

**Politics** State prosecutors in particular are symbols of law and order and crime control. Their elections and behavior in office often attract considerable public attention. Since they are elected to local offices, often on a partisan ballot, they may be closely identified with local political parties or other groups and may receive endorsements from other politicians. Their political campaigns often emphasize high conviction rates that their offices achieve (often 90 percent and above). By convicting most criminals, they show that they are effective crime fighters.

Prosecutors also can attract considerable news attention and exposure by their policies to fight crime. Sometimes prosecutors select certain categories of crimes, which they push prominently in the courts. Moral issues such as pornography and prostitution, or other issues such as drug sales, frequently attract prosecutors with particular beliefs or hopes for a future political career. Other prosecutors seek publicity and visibility as a head start in obtaining an attractive job in private law practice. Whatever their goals, their freedom to make decisions in prosecution gives them a unique opportunity to determine the kinds of crimes to prosecute and how to manage individual cases.

*Management Styles*   The independent political power of state prosecutors allows them to vary their management styles to achieve various political and personal goals. Two factors are important in determining how prosecutors manage their offices. The first concerns prosecutors' satisfaction with their relationships with judges and lawyers on two issues: how cases are processed—trials or plea bargains; and the "going rate"—the typical sentences imposed for particular crimes. Second, prosecutors' styles depend on their personal taste for political conflict.

Prosecutors who are satisfied with the status quo tend to adopt a *conservator* role and concentrate on routine management. They do not battle others. Those who are moderately dissatisfied with the prosecutor's influence over criminal cases, but who do not relish personal conflict, become *reformers* and try to make modest changes. But prosecutors who are very unhappy with their lack of control of the criminal justice process become *political insurgents*. They happily do battle with judges, public defenders, and other defense lawyers in order to gain the upper hand and control the disposition of cases and sentencing. Their political dominance in the local criminal justice system also may help them advance their own political careers.[7]

## Judges

**The Job**   Judges often appear to be passive in processing criminal cases. In most trials, for example, they quietly referee between the prosecutor and defense attorney. Even when they perform one of their most important jobs in sentencing defendants, judges often rely on information and recommendations from prosecutors and probation officers.

Despite their relatively inactive appearance in trials, judges have a number of important functions and leadership opportunities throughout the judicial process.[8] One of their most important jobs is to decide in preliminary hearings whether a prosecutor has sufficient evidence to justify prosecution. If witnesses are uncertain, or there are many fingerprints in addition to those of the defendant, or the defense argues that the police did not have sufficient reason to search a car or building for evidence, a judge has to decide whether the case should continue. Another important early decision for judges is whether to grant bail, if money bail is required, and how much, or if the defendant can remain free without money bail before trial. Judges also make decisions to grant delays to give one side or the other additional time to prepare their case, to attend to other legal business, or to give a defense lawyer time to persuade a client to plead guilty or even to pay part of the lawyer's fee.

**Power**   Some judges do not merely respond to sentencing recommendations from prosecutors, defense lawyers, or probation officers. Instead, they may take a central role in conferences on the progress and likely outcomes of cases and the appropriate sentences that ought to be imposed. In a few cities, they largely shape negotiations that determine how cases will be settled. Federal judges generally do not consider recommendations from prosecutors on sentencing, but retain full power to impose sentences themselves.[9]

Finally, judges have special status and receive great respect from everyone in court. Judges do not hire or pay prosecutors and defense lawyers or control their decisions to bring cases to court, but their lofty position gives them an opportunity to lead others. If judges choose to exert themselves, they have practically unchallenged opportunities to influence the outcome of cases.

### Lawyers

**Perry Mason?**   Contrary to popular conception, there are only a few Perry Mason types such as F. Lee Bailey and Edward Bennett Williams. Every large city is likely to have several local stars who appear in highly publicized criminal trials. These lawyers also sometimes handle big personal injury cases in civil court. In criminal cases, they generally represent relatively few clients for exceptionally high fees and frequently plan to combat a prosecutor in a dramatic and emotional trial. Their clients normally face very serious charges and want lawyers who will use rules of procedure extensively to challenge the evidence, the witnesses, and sometimes the criminal law to obtain an acquittal.

Their strategies include making various motions to dismiss the case, to delay the trial, or to prevent certain evidence and testimony from being considered. Generally, their goal is to create obstacles for the prosecutor and to make the criminal court into an unpredictable and contentious battlefield. Sometimes they win their highly publicized cases, but they also lose many of them. The prominent position of these cases in the news makes it clear that they are the exception and not the rule in the criminal courts. Over 99 percent of all criminal cases involve different kinds of lawyers and defense styles.

**Low Status**   Criminal law is not especially attractive or prestigious to most lawyers, and few plan to make it a career.[10] As discussed in Chapter 3, law schools normally give little emphasis to criminal law and concentrate instead on business and property law. Law professors do not dismiss criminal law as unimportant, but the lack of many courses and their own specialties and interests reveal that they do not expect young lawyers to take up criminal defense work. It also is difficult to make money in criminal law. Most defendants are poor and cannot pay much of a fee. Charging on an hourly basis quickly exceeds the resources of all but a few defendants, and most lawyers are likely to choose more lucrative ways of making a living.

There also is little social support for criminal court work. Despite legal values that every defendant is entitled to legal representation, popular feelings go against lawyers who make a practice of defending unsavory characters. We often assume that lawyer and client are cut from the same cloth. If a lawyer frequently represents accused mobsters, for example, people believe he or she is a member of the gang or a paid mouthpiece who will say or do anything to get a client off the hook. If a lawyer frequently represents common criminals, his or her own values and morals are questioned. Most lawyers hope for other kind of work.

Certain lawyers take most criminal cases.[11] As discussed in Chapter 3, lawyers are divided into several distinct socioeconomic levels. High-status, high-income business lawyers rarely appear in any court, especially criminal court. General practitioners, who take on a greater variety of legal work for individuals, sometimes take criminal cases, too. However, it is common for lawyers to refuse certain types of cases as their legal practice grows and becomes more lucrative. Cases that lack legal prestige and social respectability, especially criminal law, divorce, and small financial claims, often are abandoned in favor of more rewarding and prestigious business law work.

**Regulars** The bulk of criminal cases falls either to *public defenders* or to a small group of private criminal lawyers frequently known as *courthouse regulars*. Public defenders are full- or part-time salaried lawyers employed by state or county governments. Their job is to represent in a particular judicial district criminal defendants who cannot afford to pay a fee to a private attorney.[12] Their territory generally is the same as the jurisdiction of the trial courts.

Public defenders have increased in recent decades due to rulings by the U.S. Supreme Court that all criminal defendants are entitled to legal representation beginning with police interrogation and extending to an appeal to a higher court. Public defenders deal exclusively with criminal cases and are the official counterpart of prosecutors. Poor defendants usually are assigned a public defender at their earliest hearing before a judge, which is shortly after arrest and when prosecutors have decided to press charges.[13]

In some states, public defenders are locally elected to office, but generally they are appointed by a local supervisory board. Like the prosecutor, the chief defender is an administrator and general supervisor who employs assistants to deal with clients and individual cases. Like assistant prosecutors, public defenders usually have considerable independence in managing their cases. Some assistants make a career in the public defender's office, remaining for many years, but most of them consider public work an opportunity to gain experience and to make contacts before going into private law practice or perhaps seeking some other political job.

Public defenders are not used universally in the United States. They tend to be found in most large cities where there is a large number of criminal cases. In less populated areas and some smaller cities, courts use court-appointed lawyers for some or most poor defendants.

Judges select lawyers in various ways from among those practicing in the area. In some cities, there are small groups of attorneys who have little other legal work and are happy to get assignments in criminal court. Known to judges and court employees, they are selected on a regular basis to represent the poor. They usually receive small fees from the county or a state fund for their work.

Usually the fees are so modest that assigned lawyers are encouraged not to take cases to trial but to seek quicker solutions. Other cities avoid assigning most cases to a small pool of court regulars and rotate appointments among all practicing attorneys in the area. Most lawyers are selected occasionally to represent a poor defendant as part of their professional obligations. They usually receive a small fee, which does not compare with what they can make in their private practice.

Besides public defenders and assigned counsel, most cities have a group of criminal law regulars who spend most of their time representing defendants who are not sufficiently poor to qualify for a public defender or who choose to hire their own attorney. Some of these lawyers work in the criminal law because they are unsuccessful in attracting other business, or they use criminal cases to supplement other trial work in personal injury and similar cases.[14] A few of the regulars specialize in taking many criminal cases and make a fair living due to the rapid and continuous turnover of business. They rely on recommendations from police, jailers, bail bondsmen, and other defendants to steer business to them.

These lawyers normally do not plan to go to trial since none of their clients has much money. Rather, they represent criminals in plea negotiations with prosecutors. The size of their caseloads gives these criminal court regulars a great deal in common with public defenders who handle large numbers of cases every year. More than most other private lawyers, the regulars are a customary part of local courts and interact daily and routinely with prosecutors and judges.

## DECISIONS TO PROSECUTE

Court cases go through many stages before they are ready for trial. Each one presents alternatives for settling or dropping cases and involves the personal decisions of police, prosecutors, lawyers, and judges.

### Arrest and Charges

Criminal cases begin with an arrest, but as discussed earlier, police frequently decide that conflicts really do not involve crime or that arrests are not necessary or worthwhile. If information about a crime is fuzzy or contradictory, or witnesses and victims are unwilling to cooperate, police are unlikely to make arrests. If suspects cannot be identified and located quickly, arrests also are unlikely. Very few arrests are the result of judges' orders (warrants) to bring in a particular individual, and police supervisors also rarely control on-the-scene arrest decisions.

Therefore, individual police officers make quick personal judgments about whether or not to take an individual to the station house. Few arrests are made compared with the total number of citizen-police contacts, and more potential criminal cases are ended by the police at the arrest stage than at any other step in the criminal justice process.

**Screening**    Following arrest, prosecutors generally have the greatest influence in criminal cases. In some cities, police have the authority to prosecute defendants accused of minor crimes. They also bring other cases before judges in the preliminary stages of the judicial process. However, in most cities, and generally in most serious crimes, prosecuting attorneys make all decisions concerning prosecution. Prosecutors also are permitted to change the charges suggested by the police and may decide to drop cases altogether even though they have gone through various additional judicial steps.

Prosecutors have enormous power due to *assumptions of guilt* that run throughout the criminal justice system. Despite legal rules and ideals that defendants are to be presumed innocent until proven guilty, most criminal court regulars assume that anyone arrested by the police must be guilty of something. Not only do prosecutors and police assume guilt, but judges, defense lawyers, and the general public also share this view.

This stems from conceptions of common crime and police work. It is important to bear in mind that police make arrests mostly in simple and clear-cut criminal situations, when they can catch criminals in the act or there are victims or witnesses who can clearly identify and help locate offenders. The trail of evidence usually is abundant and leads to a lower-class male near the scene of the crime who seems to be avoiding the police or behaves in some other unusual or suspicious manner.[15]

Many suspects are repeat criminals who have been arrested for the same kind of crime before. Even if they are not found near the location of a crime, local people familiar to the police are suspects. In turn, their criminal record makes them vulnerable to future suspicion and arrest. They fit the pattern of typical lower-class criminals committing crime that is normal and routine in the area.[16] Consequently defendants are assumed to be guilty of something.

### Factors Affecting Prosecution

Despite assumptions of guilt, many cases are not prosecuted. The decision to prosecute a case hinges on a number of factors.

**Crime Seriousness**    An important one is the prosecutor's view of serious crime and the press of other business. For example, nonmarital sexual relations (fornication) and homosexuality are illegal in many states, but arrests and prosecution in these cases are rare. In some states, possession of any amount of marijuana is a serious offense which can land an offender in state prison, but in other locations, sometimes university towns, possession of small amounts of pot assumed to be for personal use is not considered a serious crime and often is not prosecuted. Even shoplifting, writing bad checks, and minor assaults often are not prosecuted in large cities, where district attorneys have many more cases involving major thefts or murder cases to prosecute.[17]

**Police Work**   Decisions to prosecute also depend on the prosecutor's interaction with police.[18] Prosecutors rely on the police to provide the raw materials for the criminal courts, and police need prosecutors to transform arrests into convictions. There frequently is conflict between the two, however, concerning the quality of police work needed to obtain convictions.

Prosecutors reject certain cases brought by the police in which they believe there are serious legal flaws or the evidence will not be persuasive if a case were to go to trial. For instance, if an officer becomes excited while chasing a purse snatcher and smears all the fingerprints on the discarded stolen pocketbook, it may be difficult to obtain a conviction only on the basis of uncertain eyewitness testimony. Even though the officer thinks the catch is good, the prosecutor may decide that the evidence is not persuasive. Sometimes prosecution is foiled by police who fail to include complete information in their arrest reports. Full names and addresses of victims and witnesses may be omitted, for example, making it impossible for a prosecutor to verify testimony and to get willing citizens to cooperate with prosecution.

Prosecutors and police also may disagree on what is a serious crime. Like most people, police like to see the fruits of their labors and are likely to urge prosecutors to push all arrests toward conviction. In cities with many assistant prosecutors, police officers may even shop for particular prosecutors who agree with their views of serious crime. But sometimes chief prosecutors make an office policy regarding the crimes that should receive most attention in order to block or control police influence.

Prosecutors may try to prevent certain kinds of cases from getting to their office by influencing police procedures. For example, in one city, police frequently made arrests in family fights to restore order, but they also referred the person who made the call (usually the wife) to the prosecutor if she wanted to press charges. Swamped with tales of marital woe and victims who later wanted to drop the case, the prosecutor finally sent a memo to the police instructing them to make their own investigation to support their arrests and to stop referring wives to the prosecutor.

With the full burden of the case back on the police and faced with the sorry task of listening to many husband and wife grievances themselves before they could make an arrest, most police officers stopped making arrests to settle family disputes. The prosecutor's decision accomplished two objectives. It stopped a set of cases the prosecutor considered unworthy of prosecution and it cut down on the volume of work for the prosecutor's office.[19]

**Victims**   An important additional consideration is the social status and credibility of victims. Cases in which the victims are clear social outcasts, such as prostitutes who claim they have been robbed, often are not prosecuted. In some cities, sexual assaults among family and friends or among minorities are considered unimportant or even normal behavior by police and prosecutors and receive little official attention.

Even when prosecutors agree to press charges, their perceptions of the credibility and status of the victims affect how serious they view the crime and the specific charges they decide to file against the defendant. A "stand-up victim" is an ideal witness for the prosecution—totally credible, with higher social status, and very convincing before a judge or jury. When the evidence and the police work are good, higher-status victims are likely to increase the likelihood of prosecution.

Box 6.1, "The Credibility of Victims," reveals how important a prosecutor's quick and perhaps unwarranted stereotyping of victims affect their early screening of cases.[20]

Prosecutors may agree to take doubtful cases if victims insist on prosecution and will identify and testify against the offender. The loser in a fist fight, for example, may demand and receive legal satisfaction though prosecutors, judges, and lawyers agree that the case is not important and the assailant should not be punished. But since prosecutors are elected public officials who believe they should respond to legitimate citizen demands, they proceed anyway. Failure to do so may invite charges that the prosecutor is not performing properly, and few officials look forward to that kind of popular political hassle.

*Murder*    Early screening decisions are crucial not only for how victims are viewed and treated by prosecutors but also—the other side of the coin—for

---

**BOX 6.1**

THE CREDIBILITY OF VICTIMS

**The stand-up robbery victims**

- Two white, articulate graduate students from a local university. Charge against the defendant is robbery in the first degree.

- Elderly woman victim of purse snatching who chased the 16-year-old assailant through the park. Charge against the defendant is robbery in the first degree.

- Professional man, but characterized by the prosecutor as homosexual. Prosecutor considers lowering charge to a misdemeanor, but reconsiders because evidence is clear and victim is certain of the events.

**The doubtful victims**

- Young black male victim of two males who demanded money. Despite clear evidence of possession of victim's money, prosecutor reduces charge from robbery in the first degree to grand larceny in the third degree. Says victim probably could not prove force in the robbery attempt.

- Young black male victim robbed by a former female acquaintance. Prosecutor considers dropping the case because he assumes there still is a close relationship between the two.

- Young white couple robbed at knife point by three men after being taken into a building. Woman was uncertain about the events and was visibly distressed. Prosecutor sets charge at first-degree robbery, but shortly thereafter, the male victim returns to tell prosecutor that he was in the area to buy drugs and does not want his girlfriend to know. Prosecutor lowers charge against defendants to a misdemeanor.

how different types of defendants fare in the courts. Many of these decisions literally involve life and death.

There is growing evidence that prosecutors upgrade charges to first-degree murder and seek the death penalty when black assailants murder whites. They rarely downgrade these types of cases to lesser felonies or to nonfelony status. However, cases in which blacks murder blacks are much more likely to be downgraded to less serious felonies and least likely to be upgraded to more serious crimes.[21]

This research has implications for the fairness and constitutionality of the death penalty. Most concerns about the death penalty have focused on jury recommendations and judges' sentencing decisions, but if there are clear differences in how prosecutors classify cases which they bring to court, there are new constitutional issues for the courts to examine. However, the U.S. Supreme Court has not accepted these research findings as sufficient to condemn the death penalty (*McClesky v. Kemp*, 1987).

**Other Policies**   Prosecution also depends on patterns of court decisions and other local policies. Judges who are very lenient in sentencing or who frequently dismiss minor drug cases or simple assaults indirectly signal a prosecutor that it is not worthwhile to bring these cases to court. Sheriffs and jailers often worry about overcrowding in local jails and may try to persuade prosecutors to recommend easier bail or probation so that more people can stay out of jail and prevent overcrowding from worsening. Prosecutors often have to juggle a variety of pressures in making and modifying prosecution policy.[22]

### Prosecution and Law

A prosecutor's discretion to select cases for prosecution has not gone unchallenged over the years. Proponents of strict or full enforcement of the laws maintain that a prosecutor is obligated to take *all* cases to court that are brought in by the police. But most statutes or state constitutions giving prosecutors their authority are not particularly clear about their obligations, and state and federal courts generally have concluded that full enforcement is a myth and that discretion is a necessary part of doing justice.

Prosecutors are expected to use the power and responsibility of their office, but also to use their own judgment and good sense about which cases to bring to court.[23] Judgment and good sense, of course, are subject to wide and varied interpretation.

Instead of relying on formal law, the decision to prosecute should be seen as reflecting personal values and informal relationships in the criminal justice process. All the states have many criminal laws and huge amounts of crime, so there are many opportunities to bring charges against defendants. But not all crimes produce arrests and prosecution, and many cases are dropped along the way to trial. Understanding criminal courts means understanding the decisions that prosecutors and others make and the cases that are likely to stay in or be removed from the system.

## THE MOVEMENT OF CRIMINAL CASES

Initial decisions to prosecute generally are made very quickly, since defendants must be brought to court early in the criminal justice process. They cannot be held in jail indefinitely or unnecessarily and they are entitled to a prompt bail decision. Most states had interpreted the right to a prompt hearing to mean within twenty-four hours of arrest, but the Supreme Court recently ruled that a hearing held within two days is satisfactory. Many states probably will continue to require a hearing within twenty-four hours.

If police write up the charges, the defendant is ready immediately for a court hearing. In other instances, prosecutors must review the case first. This may require interviews with the arresting police officer and the victim or other key witnesses. Prosecutors then decide quickly what the official charges will be. In either situation, decisions to prosecute are made very rapidly, and defendants are ready for their first court hearing within hours or a day of their arrest.

### Arraignment

The first hearing is called the arraignment or the initial appearance.[24] At this hearing, a judge will officially charge the defendant with the crime designated by the prosecutor, ask the defendant about the need for a court-appointed lawyer, and may set bail. Arraignments often take only a minute or two and are handled one after another, sometimes even while other court business is going on.

Arraignments for minor crimes (misdemeanors) and serious crimes (felonies) usually are handled differently by local courts. Misdemeanors are heard by trial courts of limited jurisdiction (such as county or magistrates courts), and felonies are processed by trial courts of general jurisdiction. Procedures in limited trial courts are likely to be more informal and often are very rushed. Defendants accused of misdemeanors may plead guilty at their arraignment, while felony defendants do not enter pleas until a later hearing.

**Quick Guilty Pleas**   *Most minor crimes that carry only fines or short jail sentences (misdemeanors) end at the arraignment.* Many repeat drunks, drug addicts, traffic violators, and others plead guilty to the original charge and are immediately sentenced, often in less than five minutes. They may be required to pay small fines, serve a few days in county jail, or perform some sort of community service work. Requiring reckless drivers to assist at the hospital emergency room or having teenage drinkers clean up the grounds at a public park are some of the nonjail sentences judges sometimes impose in minor offenses.

Box 6.2, "Fighting Traffic Court," shows that the cost of defending against minor violations often quickly outweighs the benefits.

Most minor crimes are considered so insignificant by judges that they often are very casual about informing defendants of their constitutional rights or sometimes do not bother to do it at all. Often, arraignments are held with

**BOX 6.2**

FIGHTING TRAFFIC COURT

Seventeen-year-old Andy was driving home from visiting a friend in a neighboring state when he was arrested in a small town for speeding. Andy protested that he was not going too fast and was in line with the rest of traffic. The police officer replied that he was radared at 15 miles over the limit and to follow him to the station. Andy did and was given a $50 fine, but Andy insisted he had not been speeding, so the magistrate set a court date and gave Andy a receipt for his driver's license, which would be kept with the police report. Andy drove 75 miles home and told his parents about his misfortune.

Andy's father believed him and added that a special governor's commission re-

cently had concluded that radar was inaccurate. Andy was notified of his court appearance, set for six weeks later, but Andy telephoned to ask for a delay because he had a high school baseball game to play that day. Two months later, Andy drove back to the little town in the neighboring state, prepared for his day in court. But Andy learned that his court appearance was only for him to plead guilty or not guilty. If he pled not guilty, he would have a trial later on. A police officer standing nearby added, "radar doesn't lie." Andy protested that he had driven two hours to see the judge, but he got nowhere. The public defender overheard the conversation and chimed in, "Pay the ticket, kid. You'll never win." Andy swallowed hard and paid.

groups of defendants hearing their rights at the same time. Defendants facing minor penalties also usually plead guilty without consulting attorneys. Defendants in misdemeanor cases do not seem to be pressured toward conviction, but the penalties are so light and guilt is so obvious that they see nothing else to do than get the case over with quickly.[25]

**Lawyers and Bail**   Decisions on appointing an attorney or requiring the defendant to hire a lawyer and setting bail are very important judicial matters. They can have substantial benefits for defendants and affect their chances in court. Some judges have very strict requirements for obtaining a court-appointed attorney or public defender. A defendant who is unemployed and has no cash may still be required to hire a lawyer even though it means selling personal possessions. Other judges, however, may permit defendants to obtain free legal help simply by stating that they cannot afford to hire their own attorney. Therefore, the right to an attorney is interpreted in different ways.

Defendants usually are granted bail in all but very serious felonies, but the nature of the bail varies. Judges may release defendants on their *own recognizance*, which means that they permit the defendants to await trial out of jail based on the defendant's pledge to appear voluntarily for trial. But money bail may be required instead. Then, defendants must pay hundreds or thousands of dollars as a fee to a bondsman who provides the court with a financial deposit against the defendant's failure to appear in court.

Awaiting trial out of jail has advantages for defendants.[26] The most important one is that they do not have to sit idle for weeks or months in an often crowded and dangerous county jail. Bailed defendants may continue to live with their family, work, and live as before. Some, but not all, research on bail shows that bailed defendants receive lighter sentences, possibly because they were able to work on their case with their attorneys and were not depressed and bedraggled from a long stay in a county jail.[27]

Some writers also believed that defendants awaiting trial in jail were more likely to plead guilty to get their cases over with and move to better living quarters in state prison. Figures vary widely, but one-quarter to three-quarters of all defendants cannot pay a bail bondsman's fee and must stay in jail.

In some cities, judges permit many defendants to be released on their own personal promise to appear for trial while others almost never agree to anything other than money bail.[28] Although the decision seems routine and is made very quickly, bail policy varies among judges and across the country and has consequences for all criminal defendants.

Judges are inclined to set high bail for serious crimes and to make their decisions partly in response to the prosecutor's bail recommendation. Prosecutors normally encourage high bail, defense lawyers argue for low bail, and judges often set bail somewhere in the middle, but on the high side. In this way judges and prosecutors share the responsibility for releasing a defendant on bail.[29]

Judges sometimes set very high bail to prevent dangerous defendants from getting out of jail before their trials. Using bail this way is informal *preventive detention* to keep bad actors off the streets. However, this is very controversial in the United States, because most defendants are presumed to have a right to ''reasonable'' bail used only to guarantee their appearance at trial.

High bail also sometimes has been used against unpopular defendants, such as civil rights demonstrators and other protesters. In addition, high bail is not uniformly effective and fair because some very dangerous defendants manage to find the money to pay their bail. But if a defendant makes bail and fails to appear for trial or commits more crime while awaiting trial, prosecutors and judges can defend themselves by insisting that bail was set at a high level.

### Preliminary Hearings

Following arraignment and bail setting, felony cases in many states are scheduled for *preliminary hearings*. They are usually held within a few weeks of arraignment. These court appearances are short minitrials to determine if there is probable cause or good reason to hold a defendant for trial. Prosecutors present witnesses and evidence, and defense attorneys have the right to cross-examine witnesses and to demonstrate the weakness of the prosecution's case. The proceedings take place before a judge alone. The judge has the sole responsibility for determining whether a crime was committed and if the defendant is the likely culprit.

**Dismissals and Pleas**   Outcomes of preliminary hearings vary tremendously. Generally judges dismiss relatively few cases at this stage if prosecutors have reviewed and screened their cases beforehand in order to remove the weak and insignificant ones. However, in cities where the police determine the initial charge and decide on prosecution, there usually is very little early screening. In these situations, judges often dismiss 25 percent or more of all cases in which the evidence is weak or the violations are considered unimportant.[30] Other cases in which victims have been paid for their stolen or damaged property or have reconciled with their attacker (family and friends) also usually are dismissed.

In some cities a majority of remaining cases that have not been dismissed also end at the preliminary hearing. Faced with clear evidence against them, possibly a prior criminal record and no chance of winning a dismissal, defendants plead guilty in the hope of getting a lighter sentence or just to end the strain of going to court.

**Grand Juries**   Over half of the states use grand juries in addition to or in place of preliminary hearings in serious cases. Grand juries consist of twenty-three citizens who hear the charges presented by the prosecuting attorney. Unlike preliminary hearings, defense attorneys do not have an opportunity to cross-examine witnesses or question the state's case. In addition, legal standards are much lower than in trials. Prosecutors normally need little evidence to persuade a grand jury that prosecution should proceed (indicting defendants), and decisions are reached by majority vote rather than unanimity as required in most jury trials.

The purpose of the grand jury also is to determine probable cause and to prevent overly eager prosecutors from bringing charges that are unsupported by the evidence gathered by the police. However, grand juries normally support prosecutors and pass cases on to the trial stage. Grand juries have been criticized for meekly rubber-stamping the prosecutor's decisions and permitting indictments in flimsy cases for political advantage or to begin a moral crusade against unpopular individuals and groups. Some reformers want to abolish grand juries.

## Prosecution as Punishment

A common conception about the criminal courts is that an individual who avoids prosecution or has a case dismissed early avoids punishment or the other consequences of going to court. However, this view oversimplifies the impact of the early stages of the judicial process on defendants. It does not take into account the financial costs, the uncertainty, and the personal disruption and emotional stress that arrest and preliminary decisions have on a suspect.

Many cases are not dropped by prosecutors within hours or days of an arrest, but may be abandoned weeks later only when prosecutors become concerned with more important cases or witnesses fail to appear in court. Judges might dismiss some cases, but their review probably will not occur for weeks after arrest.

In the meantime, defendants may have to spend a few hours, days, or weeks in a crowded and dangerous jail, worrying about their ability to raise money for bail and how to pay for a lawyer. Arrest also carries a permanent social stigma. Stress on family, fear of losing a job, and the trauma of being ordered about, photographed, fingerprinted, and handled by police and jailers is a short experience that lasts a lifetime. Being arrested and going through the mill has led some observers to conclude that a defendant "might beat the rap, but he won't beat the ride," or "the process is the punishment."[31]

There are thousands of defendants who are released by prosecutors and judges without being convicted of a crime. Most court regulars have very little sympathy for these defendants, however, since they believe that they are guilty of something and get off very lightly if their cases are dismissed. Even if the process is the punishment, in their view it is lenient compared with being convicted and sentenced.[32] Therefore, even though many defendants have only been accused of crime and are legally innocent, going to court is the penalty for being considered guilty.

Box 6.3, "Punishment First; the Verdict Later," illustrates the many ways that criminal procedures punish defendants waiting for arraignments, who have not been convicted, and who plead guilty rather than wait for a trial.[33]

## PLEA BARGAINING

Once a prosecutor decides to pursue a case and a judge refuses to grant motions to dismiss, the chances of conviction are overwhelming. Usually the crimes involved are serious or the evidence against defendants is so clear that the chances of being acquitted of a crime are extremely remote. Some readily plead guilty because they recognize the odds are against them and want to put an end to the stress and disruption. They simply want to get out of the system. Others plead guilty because they expect leniency or have negotiated specific bargains with prosecutors and judges.

The mechanics and details of bargained guilty pleas vary considerably. Arrangements may involve reducing criminal charges to less serious crimes, dropping certain charges altogether, promising light sentences for guilty pleas to original charges, and possible combinations. Whatever the arrangement, *the key element to any bargain is that in return for pleading guilty and avoiding a trial, cooperative defendants expect to receive lighter sentences.* Through plea bargaining, almost all cases end with convictions, but not with trials.

Until recently, plea bargaining was not especially visible to the general public, and most judges and lawyers refused to acknowledge that it was the way most cases were settled. Plea bargaining was an official secret, because it does not square with perceptions of the way that courts and justice are supposed to work. But plea bargaining gradually became a poorly kept secret as social scientists and the mass media became more aware of the informal workings of the courts and the widespread use of plea bargaining.

**BOX 6.3**

PUNISHMENT FIRST;
THE VERDICT LATER

On a typical summer day in New York City, forty female prisoners sit on hard benches or the concrete floor in a 400-square-foot cell in the basement of the criminal court building. There are no windows and no air conditioning, and only one toilet and one sink. A repetition of bologna and cheese sandwiches is served every eight hours. Cells like these are supposed to be temporary holding pens while prisoners wait up to twenty-four hours for arraignment, but backlogs have increased the waiting time to 34 or even 40 hours in some courts.

Prosecutors are so busy that police wait in line for six or more hours to explain the arrest charges, and if the fingerprints are botched, or the defendant's record does not come through quickly from state computers, prisoners are shuffled out of the court and back to the precinct station and placed in yet another holding pen until the paperwork is completed. "You don't even know where you are—it's like being kidnapped," complains one legal aid lawyer.

The way inmates get out of the overcrowded jail in Capital City is to plead guilty and be sentenced to the time they already have served while waiting out the process. Critics claim the prosecutor intentionally moves slowly following arraignment in order to pressure defendants to plead guilty and to be sure that every defendant who cannot make bail serves some time.

In the past, prosecutors could pressure defendants to plead guilty by threatening them with long prison terms, but that threat has become hollow because prison overcrowding means that many prisoners get out earlier and earlier. Now, a long wait in county jail serves the same purpose.

Public defenders are so overloaded with cases that weeks go by before they consult with their jailed clients, and defenders have no time to pressure prosecutors to plea-bargain or take the case to trial. Defendants gain nothing by insisting on their innocence because they will serve even more time waiting for a court date.

County commissioners want the prosecutor to screen cases more quickly, and drop charges for minor crimes and where the evidence is weak. But the tough prosecutor, a former policeman, says his job is to prosecute wrongdoers and satisfy victims, including large department stores with many shoplifting cases. One liberal commissioner retorts that "Lock 'Em Up, Willie," the prosecutor, would fill the jail even if it were the size of the old southwood Plantation.

In 1971, the U.S. Supreme Court also acknowledged plea bargaining as a fact and a necessity of judicial life (*Santobello v. New York*). However, many people oppose plea bargaining and argue that it provides few benefits for courts, criminal defendants, or the public.

This section examines how plea bargaining works in most cases. Since nearly all cases are settled short of a trial, plea bargaining is a central feature of the judicial process and we need to carefully evaluate its place in American justice. Box 6.4, "Pros and Cons of Plea Bargaining," summarizes the arguments in favor and against this common procedure.[34] Keep these opposing points of view in mind as you read how plea bargaining works and why most criminal cases end with a guilty plea. Also note that many of the arguments in favor of plea bargaining concern efficiency and managing cases, while those opposed focus mostly on the rights of defendants.

**BOX 6.4**

PROS AND CONS OF PLEA BARGAINING

**Pro**

• *Efficiency* Plea bargaining is necessary to move cases quickly. Trials require hours, days, or weeks, and if more cases went to trial, state and local governments would have to add more judges, prosecutors, public defenders, and courtrooms to prevent a huge backlog.

• *Unnecessary burden* Trial preparation requires prosecutors, judges, defense attorneys, and court personnel to spend extra time and public money on a case.

• *Spare victims* Trials create emotional stress for victims, especially those harmed in brutal assaults and sex crimes. Plea bargaining shields them from sensationalism.

• *Cooperative defendants benefit* Weak cases are screened out early, so that guilt is obvious in most other cases. Trials are unnecessary and cooperative defendants are rewarded with reduced sentences.

• *Tailored punishment* Legislatures continually create more crimes and harsher penalties, but plea bargaining allows less dangerous offenders to escape excessive harshness while assuring that hardened criminals are adequately punished.

**Con**

• *Cheap justice* Instead of a search for truth through a trial, prosecutors "sell" bargains to defendants who accept the best deal. As a result, the used-car business has a better image.

• *Defendants pressured* Defendants are uninformed outsiders, pressured to plead guilty by their own lawyers who are anxious to cooperate with prosecutors and reduce their own workload.

• *No constitutional rights* Once a defendant pleads guilty, he or she has no right to challenge police or court procedures, or the right to appeal. In addition, plea bargaining amounts to a coerced confession.

• *Unequal treatment* Sentences imposed after plea bargaining and trial are unequal. A defendant who insists on his or her right to a trial takes a big gamble, in that conviction may well produce a very harsh sentence.

• *Too lenient* Plea bargaining may produce sentences that are too lenient. Bargained sentences return criminals to the streets where they commit more crime.

## How Plea Bargaining Works

Plea bargaining is widespread and is the typical way in which cases are settled. But there is no single method or pattern to the way that cases are handled. A few cases involve extensive discussions and shrewd wheeling and dealing, but plea bargaining in most cases is very quick and routine and involves only one or two short meetings between prosecutors and defense lawyers. There also are differences in the control that court regulars have in plea bargaining and the extent to which plea bargaining is used in various towns and cities.

**Prosecutor Dominance** Prosecutors normally dominate the settlement of cases. Judges and defense lawyers have secondary roles. Shortly after a defendant has been formally charged and has obtained a lawyer or public defender, the defense attorney usually approaches the prosecutor to determine if and what kind of bargain can be reached. If defense lawyers believe there is a chance the case could be dismissed, bargaining may wait until after the preliminary hearing, but if the defense is fairly certain the defendant cannot avoid conviction, bargaining may begin early and the defense may even give up the right to a preliminary hearing.

In most courts, plea bargaining is very quick and informal, with prosecutors and defense lawyers talking about cases as they move through the courthouse on other business or over coffee during a break in their appointments. Some prosecuting attorneys and public defenders have offices next to each other or even share space in the courthouse. They can talk to each other through the workday. With many cases to be settled, defense attorneys sometimes line up outside the prosecutor's office waiting their turn to get the best offers they can and they quickly put the deals to their clients.[35]

*Charges and Sentences*   Prosecutors have two main items they can negotiate in return for a guilty plea: criminal charges and sentencing recommendations to judges. Charges and prison sentences usually are related. As charges increase in seriousness, the severity of the penalty also usually goes up. Therefore, reducing the charges probably will lower the maximum sentence a judge can impose.

Defendants often are charged with several different crimes stemming from the same incident or multiple violations of the same law, such as a dozen counts of writing bad checks for each of twelve checks passed at local stores. If convicted on all of the original charges, defendants would face many years in prison. In return for pleading guilty, the serious charges may be reduced to less serious crimes, some charges may be dropped altogether, or numerous counts could be consolidated into one or two.

Besides reducing charges, prosecutors bargain on sentencing. Judges have the authority to hand down sentences on their own, but they often ask prosecutors and defense lawyers for their recommendations. There are several reasons for this. Judges typically know much less about a case than either prosecutors or defense attorneys. The prosecutor has the advantage of having all the information obtained by the police and may have a staff that has conducted an additional investigation. Defense lawyers also usually gather some additional information about the character of the defendant and the family situation. Experienced prosecutors and defense lawyers typically share this and other information as they discuss a case. By the time sentencing occurs, the prosecutor and defense are likely to know more about the facts, the law, and the social context of the crime than anyone else. Consequently, judges usually depend on them for information and sentencing recommendations.

*Basis for Bargains*   Prosecutors and defense attorneys usually focus on three big issues in most cases as the basis for their negotiations. The elements they generally consider are *the strength of the case against the defendant* (physical evidence, witnesses, police procedures), *the seriousness of the crime* (amount of money stolen, injury to a victim, use of a gun, etc.), and *the criminal record of the offender*. Prosecutors are likely to begin discussions by emphasizing the strength of the case against the defendant and insisting that the crime is a serious one.

In some cities, it is common for prosecutors to overcharge or "throw the book" at a defendant, which means that the prosecutor officially charges practically every conceivable crime the police report seems to permit. Then, as part of a bargain, there is agreement to drop or reduce some of the charges.[36]

This strategy makes the criminal act, which involves many separate and individual crimes, much more serious than it might otherwise appear. For example, breaking into an automobile to steal a stereo may be defined as burglary, but in addition, the defendant might be charged with possession of burglary tools, vandalism, possession of stolen property, possession of a weapon, possibly possession of illegal drugs, even violating curfew, if a juvenile, and possibly fleeing to avoid arrest. Most of these charges probably will be dropped if the defendant agrees to plead guilty to something.

Critics of plea bargaining maintain that overcharging is unrealistic and unfair, since a prosecutor probably could not obtain a conviction on all the charges in a trial and that the bargain offered is no real discount at all. It is only a reduction to a more realistic charge that might be made to stick in court. A defendant is led to plead guilty through fear of conviction on all the charges and a heavy prison term. Sometimes charging a defendant with serious crime even when the evidence is weak is a way of holding him or her in jail or keeping the case alive until the police have an opportunity to obtain additional evidence.[37]

Although overcharging seems improper, other observers of the courts believe that determining when a prosecutor is overcharging is extremely difficult, since there are so many criminal laws and many are so vague and general that practically any suspect who has committed even a minor crime can be charged with something more serious with the same set of facts. Some prosecutors also stress that they do not overcharge, but only make the charges fit the facts and the requirements of the law.[38]

Determining if a prosecutor is overcharging depends heavily on a defense lawyer's own experience and knowledge in bargaining. If most cases are settled with charges far less serious than those originally filed or judges and juries fail to convict on most of the charges, the defense attorney probably would conclude that charging is a ploy in the bargaining process.

**The Response of Defense Lawyers**   In most cases, there is overwhelming evidence of guilt with little or no chance of obtaining a dismissal. Many defense lawyers consider filing motions for dismissal when they believe the police have improperly gathered evidence or where their client was not clearly identified, but many of these kinds of cases also are dropped by prosecutors or dismissed by judges very early in the process.

*Mitigation*   The only thing a defense lawyer usually can do is try to reduce the charges or the sentence by stressing a client's redeeming characteristics, such as a light criminal record, stable family life, steady employment, etc. The defense also may suggest that the circumstances of the crime justify giving the defendant a break. Perhaps the victim provoked an attack or the defendant was drunk. Usually, the prosecutor and the defense attorney can come to a quick agreement on what "the case is worth."[39] Many lawyers also agree with prosecutors and judges that there is no need to burden the courts with open-and-shut cases.[40]

*Pressure?*  The speedy settlement of many cases creates the impression that lawyers are unconcerned with defendants and pressure them to plead guilty.[41] But guilt is certain in most cases, and there is little reason to spend a great deal of time on them. Frequently, prosecutors have a consistent policy on what certain crimes committed by particular types of defendants are worth, and they refuse to deviate much from their regular routine. It does not take a lot of time to make a deal. However, if defendants are reluctant to plead guilty, insist on a trial in the face of terrible odds, or want probation for serious offenses, lawyers may have to spend some time convincing them about the facts and their chances. In these kinds of situations, there is a fine line between pressure and education.

Defendants are likely to believe they are pressured by their lawyers for several reasons. Most defendants have more meetings with their lawyers than with anyone else and lawyers most often suggest the guilty plea. Many defendants, especially first offenders, initially resist the idea and have to be persuaded that it is the best thing to do.[42] There also is a great social gap between lawyers and criminal defendants. Most defendants are young, poor, and uneducated, and many are minorities. Their lawyers, however, usually are white and middle class and have college and professional educations. Trust and communications are likely to be strained in most of these encounters.

Some black and minority defendants refuse to plead guilty to "white man's justice" and demand a trial. Many others cannot distinguish the roles of police, prosecutors, judges, and lawyers and believe the entire court organization is against them.

This is especially true of their views of public defenders. Many defendants assume that since public defenders and prosecutors are paid a salary by the same government, they work together. As many as 80 percent of defendants with public defenders did not feel their lawyers were "on their side" compared with no defendants with privately retained lawyers and 30 percent with lawyers obtained through legal aid offices.[43]

Finally, most repeat criminals are suspicious and are accustomed to deceiving others. They are not inclined to cooperate with anyone in the courts or to tell their lawyers the whole truth. They also are suspicious of advice given. Consequently, lawyers often report that their biggest problem in plea bargaining is their client.[44]

**Various Roles of Judges**  Traditionally, judges have not participated in plea bargaining. The main reason is that it violates the ideal legal role of the trial judge as neutral and impartial umpire. The police and prosecutor may seek convictions and the lawyer defends, but the judge is supposed to be above the battle.

*Charade*    Before plea bargaining received its Supreme Court stamp of approval in 1971, trial courts played out a sentencing game. Knowing that bargaining was common, trial judges would ask defendants if they were pleading guilty freely and of their own accord and to affirm that no one had made any deals or promises in return for their admission of guilt. To have a guilty plea accepted, the defendant had to give the "correct" answer, which was that there had not been any pressure and that no bargains or promises had been made. Judges then would usually impose their customary reduced sentence or the one agreed to in advance. Judges sometimes would say that a lenient sentence was a reward for a defendant who felt remorse and was on the first step of a journey toward rehabilitation.

Usually this judicial charade went off according to the script, but defendants sometimes became confused during the ritual and would admit in open court that a bargain had indeed been made or that the prosecutor had promised leniency. Judges would abruptly stop the proceedings and have the defendant talk privately to counsel, who would once again explain what the necessary responses were so that the guilty plea could be accepted and the sentence imposed.

Since 1971, plea bargaining has become more legitimate, and the fiction of nonjudicial involvement is beginning to fade. The Santobello decision accepts the need for plea bargaining, but also requires that deals must be honored. To ensure that bargains are kept, judges must be sure that agreements are made explicit and that defendants understand what they will receive as a result of pleading guilty. The details of agreements often are written into court records as well.

Although trial judges have a more legitimate opportunity to participate in plea bargaining, it appears that the large majority of them still are not actively involved. One national survey suggests that only 25 percent participate in plea bargain negotiations, but many of these judges as well as others still rely mainly on recommendations by prosecutors and defense attorneys.[45]

*Active Judges*    There are some circumstances where judges are more active in plea bargaining and may have more influences than prosecutors. As mentioned earlier, where police file criminal charges, judges dismiss many cases at preliminary hearings. They also frequently reduce felony charges to misdemeanors and may suggest appropriate sentences if defendants plead guilty. In some cities, judges also preside at compulsory pretrial conferences or informally discuss cases with prosecutors and defense lawyers before trials are scheduled.

Judicial involvement also depends upon judges' personalities. Some judges are very assertive and like to control as much of the process as they can. Others are passive and do little other than handle their courtroom duties. Most probably fall in the middle and work with lawyers, but do not control every aspect of a case. When judges are active, attorneys are very likely to defer to them, permit them to shape discussions, and present their own views as the basis for decisions.[46]

*Sentence Bargains* Judges also can have a dominant role in plea bargaining when prosecutors do not appear to overcharge and will not negotiate on reductions. Many observers of plea bargaining have assumed that a prosecutor who refused to negotiate on charges would produce a flood of trials. However, most defendants continue to plead guilty for several reasons. One is that judges take on the bargaining role by offering sentence reductions. Believing that they must make concessions to prevent their court from becoming overloaded with trials, judges become the new focus of bargains. But even where judges refuse to agree to reduced sentences, most defendants still plead guilty. Most lawyers believe that judges sentence more harshly if defendants insist on trials and so they urge their clients to plead.[47] Rather than obtain an explicit deal, lawyers and defendants rely on unspoken, implicit assumptions of leniency for guilty pleas.

The role of judges in plea bargaining may increase in the future, since plea bargaining is becoming more visible and is often unpopular. Few prosecutors are defeated for reelection, but plea bargaining has become an issue in some of their campaigns. Some prosecutors also are uneasy about the conflict between strict law enforcement and their own discretionary power to select cases for prosecution and plea bargaining. Consequently, some states and individual prosecutors have banned negotiation on criminal charges. The only possible room for negotiation is on the sentence, and that is controlled by judges. Therefore, judges could become more important in plea bargaining.

**Cases for Bargains and Trials** All cases are not treated the same way. Some are fairly obvious candidates for plea bargaining, while others seem likely to go to trial. Still others fall in the middle and lawyers are unsure how they will be settled. There are several factors that account for the way cases generally are decided.

As in negotiating for a guilty plea, deciding which cases to take to trial and which ones to bargain depends largely on *the strength of the evidence and the seriousness of the crime*.[48] Serious cases are those in which the criminal law and judges and prosecutors are likely to favor longer sentences. Additional elements that affect decisions to bargain or to choose a trial are *the criminal record of the defendant and the sentencing reputation of the judge who is scheduled to hear the case*.[49] These factors do not have equal importance everywhere, but they figure prominently in most courts.

Table 6.2 summarizes the major conditions that determine whether cases are bargained or go to trial. However, there are exceptions to each of these conditions as defendants, lawyers, and prosecutors calculate their chances and the likely outcomes in individual cases.

*Dead-Bang* Cases that are most likely to be plea-bargained are those in which the evidence is very solid but the charges are not very serious (cell 1 in Table 6.2). These sometimes are called *light dead-bang cases* (sure convictions but with light penalties). Defendants are urged to plead guilty in these cases, because they have no chance of acquittal but a prison sentence is very unlikely.

**TABLE 6-2**
CASES FOR BARGAINS AND TRIALS

| | Strength of the Evidence | |
|---|---|---|
| Seriousness of crime | Dead-Bang (most cases) | Reasonable doubt (fewer cases) |
| Light | **1** Plea bargain likely | **3** Trial likely, plea bargain possible |
| Serious | **2** Plea bargain likely; trial possible | **4** Dilemma: Plea bargain—long sentence; trial—longer sentence, but possible acquittal |

Probation, time already served in jail while awaiting trial, or some other light sentence is the likely outcome. First offenders also usually are assured leniency.

Plea bargains also are likely, but perhaps not quite as frequent, in *serious dead-bang cases* (cell 2). These are major crimes in which the evidence also is very good. Cases in which a repeat criminal is caught in the act of committing a felony, for example, are very serious for the defendant, and sure convictions for the police and prosecutor.

These kinds of cases often are plea-bargained because the defendant realizes the state has good evidence. However, since the penalty is likely to be a heavy one, negotiations may be lengthy and perhaps will not produce a deal that is sufficiently attractive to make it worthwhile to plead guilty. If the prosecutor holds out for a lengthy prison term or local judges are known to be severe, a defendant may take a chance on a trial.

Some prosecutors do not bargain in serious dead-bang cases, because they feel very confident they can win at trial. Defendants have to either plead guilty and hope for leniency or take their chances with a jury.[50] Mitigating circumstances, strength of the evidence, a defendant's record, and other factors also affect the outcomes of individual cases differently across the country. As a general conclusion, research on plea bargaining shows that cases of serious crime are more likely than others to go to trial.

*Reasonable Doubt*   Cases likely to go to trial are those in which there is reasonable doubt about whether a crime was committed or whether the defendant was involved. As in dead-bang cases, those involving reasonable doubt can be either light or serious, and the particular circumstances of the case can influence the decision to plead guilty or to go to trial.

If a defendant appears to be not guilty of any crime and the penalties are very light, the lawyer may decide to go to trial, since pleading guilty means having a criminal record and perhaps serving a short jail sentence (cell 3). Going to trial in the hope of getting off free is an attractive alternative. Some of these cases do not reach trial, however, because prosecutors also are willing to drop them. However, if a defendant looks a "little bit" guilty and already has a criminal record in similar kinds of cases, or associates with other criminals, the case is less doubtful and plea bargaining may seem the wisest thing to do.

Serious cases in which there is reasonable doubt seem to pose the greatest problems for defendants and their lawyers (cell 4). In these few cases, the chances of a heavy sentence are high and asserting a defendant's innocence at a jury trial is very risky, since few can predict what a jury will do. Therefore, a defendant takes a big risk whether the decision is to bargain or to go to trial. Neither alternative looks good to a defendant who insists he or she is innocent.

Most cases appear to be dead-bang situations. Everyone knows defendants are guilty of something, and they usually can be convinced that their chances of escaping conviction are poor. Taking a chance on a jury trial usually is done when there seems to be nothing else to lose. In some communities, though, taking a chance on a jury is preferable to a bench trial if judges are extremely harsh sentencers. These kinds of cases are rare, however, and most defendants plead guilty.

### Why So Much Plea Bargaining?

Besides understanding how plea bargaining works, it is important to learn why it is so common in the United States. Judges, prosecutors, and defense lawyers are likely to tell us that most defendants are clearly guilty and everyone benefits from a quick end to cases. If defendants believe they get lenient sentences, we can understand why they agree to plead, but it is less clear what prosecutors and judges have to gain. After all, if defendants clearly are guilty, why do prosecutors not go to trial and seek lengthy sentences? These explanations also do not account for why amounts of plea bargaining vary and why trials are about as likely as plea bargains in a few cities. Explaining amounts of plea bargaining requires broader and more general theories. There are several that need to be considered.

**Caseloads** The most frequent and widely accepted explanation for plea bargaining is that it is necessary to prevent courts from becoming hopelessly backlogged with cases and creating enormous delays. More trials would mean that defendants either would languish in jail awaiting trial or be free on bail perhaps for years before their cases could be tried.

Related to the heavy caseload explanation is a widely held assumption that plea bargaining is a relatively recent development. This view is that as the nation grew and more people began to crowd together in cities, crime increased and police and prosecutors were faced with a rising tide of cases. Plea bargaining was the answer to the heavy caseloads and the need to battle crime.

As reasonable as these explanations for plea bargaining may seem, they do not hold up under careful analysis. *Workloads do not cause plea bargaining.* Historical studies indicate that plea bargaining is at least 100 years old and became the routine way of handling criminal cases before the rapid growth of

American cities occurred.[51] Comparisons of rates of plea bargaining over time in particular courts and comparisons of courts in various cities consistently show that plea bargaining is unrelated to the amount of work facing the courts. Courts that are heavily loaded with cases and those with lighter caseloads, including rural areas, use plea bargaining to a similar degree.

Although heavy caseloads do not cause plea bargaining, trials regardless of their number take much time and effort, and most cases simply do not seem worth the trouble. In addition, in poor rural counties with low caseloads and low-paid part-time prosecutors and public defenders, county governments often must pay extra lawyers' fees for cases that go to trial. Therefore, silent or informal pressures lead to more bargains and fewer trials. Overall, there is little incentive to go to trial, even if court dockets are not overloaded.[52]

**Career Goals**    Prosecutors and regular defense lawyers have a variety of career goals that they try to satisfy through plea bargaining. First, work in the criminal courts often involves high political stakes for chief prosecutors and some of their assistants who hope to build a political career. Many state prosecutors run for reelection to keep their jobs. For others, a stint as a state or federal prosecutor is the first step to another political post such as state or federal judgeship, legislator, or even governor.[53] Part of their public image as a successful prosecutor includes their success in achieving very high conviction rates. What most voters do not realize, however, is that high conviction rates are obtained through plea bargaining.

Public defenders also prefer plea bargaining, because they are not rewarded for winning cases. They are appointed in many states and must answer to an outside supervisory agency, which usually expects efficient, routine, and low-cost office procedures. However, elected public defenders also do not pledge to battle the local police and prosecutor. That kind of campaign would make them appear to be "soft on crime." Their clients are expected to be convicted, but in a fair way. Getting the best deal possible through plea bargaining is the closest that public defenders (and most other defense lawyers) come to winning.

Plea bargaining also helps assistant prosecutors and public defenders to establish reputations for reliability and moderation and a willingness to behave as others expect. Lawyers who refuse to follow the accepted rules of the game or who take extreme positions become visible as nonconformists or eccentrics, making them unattractive for later positions in most local law firms. Since plea bargaining is the usual and accepted way of settling cases, most lawyers go along.

Lawyers also do not have the resources necessary to take most cases to trial. Neither prosecutors nor public defenders have unlimited funds or human resources, and they must find ways to handle their cases quickly. Private lawyers also cannot afford to take cases to trial for small fees. This is not another version of the caseload argument, for even if there were fewer cases, there still are too few resources to take more than a few of them to trial.

**Courtroom Work Groups**  A court is not simply a bundle of formal rules and procedures with a judge acting as master of ceremonies. It also includes many informal and continuous relationships among everyone who has a regular role in settling cases. Judges, prosecutors, defense lawyers, clerks, and assistants who work every day in the criminal courts make up courtroom work groups. They deal personally with each other and cooperate in many ways to settle cases. The outsiders are the defendants. They come and go, but the cases and the jobs of courtroom work groups remain the same.

*Close Groups    The more closely particular sets of judges, prosecutors, and lawyers (usually public defenders) work together, the more likely they are to settle cases through plea bargaining.*[54] The closest interactions occur when a particular judge, assistant prosecutor, and assistant public defender are assigned to the same courtroom for a long period, perhaps a year or more, and handle all stages of all criminal cases assigned to their group.

Since the group works together every day, the members get to know each other well and grow to depend on each other for simple courtesies and cooperation. In a short while, they approach cases informally and discuss them around a table in the judge's office, over coffee, or in the halls. They quickly begin to understand each other's attitudes and rules of thumb about the seriousness of certain crimes, the relevant characteristics of defendants, and appropriate sentences. Discussions generally are friendly, informal, and routine.

Instead of concentrating only on the plea, a close work group is likely to engage in broader "preplea" discussions, which include social as well as legal factors in cases. There is little uncertainty, conflict, or tension about the outcomes of cases. Plea bargains become the routine way of settling all but a few cases.[55]

Close courtoom work groups are likely to develop in cities in which the same teams of lawyers and judges work together on many cases. But cohesive work groups are especially likely to develop in smaller counties where there are few assistant prosecutors, judges, and defense lawyers. There, all the players tend to form a tight legal community where no one rocks the boat, people work together, have similar attitudes about crime, and even develop informal language and implicit ways of understanding each other.[56]

*Fragmented Groups    There are some cities where court work groups are not close. Instead of having a particular judge, prosecutor, and public defender assigned to one courtroom, work groups are constantly split up. Individuals may work for a week or two with a certain group and then move to another and never have an opportunity to get to know the other people well. Judges, prosecutors, and public defenders also may be given responsibility for parts of many cases and never have an opportunity to see a case through from start to finish.

In this kind of environment, it nearly is impossible for stable and informal work groups to form. There is little reason, then, for judges, prosecutors, and public defenders to use plea bargaining, since none of them know if they will be working on the same case or with each other the following week. Informal agreements made at one stage of a case may not even be communicated to the new prosecutor or public defender or considered binding by those who take over the case at a later stage. As a consequence, courtroom work groups are more likely to rely on formal judicial procedures to settle cases. This means more cases go to trial.

Most cities and towns have informal and close courtroom work groups rather than a constant rearrangement of judges, prosecutors, and public defenders. Consequently, most cities are cities of plea bargains rather than cities of trials.

## Sentencing

Following a plea bargain or a trial, judges sentence convicted defendants. In minor criminal cases, judges frequently sentence defendants at the conclusion of the trial or when they plead guilty, but in more serious cases, sentences are imposed days later, after probation officers complete presentence investigations and reports. These reports include various social and psychological information about the defendant (family history, current family circumstances, previous criminal record, job prospects, etc.); and they may emphasize circumstances that justify leniency, or alternatives to prison that give a defendant a chance to redeem him or herself.

**Judicial Discretion**    Judges have very wide discretion in sentencing.[57] However, they are limited by legislatures. Legislatures define acts that constitute crimes and the sentences that may be imposed, but usually allow judges to impose a range of punishments—often ranging from fines or probation, which means no jail time, to a number of years in state prison.

Judicial discretion is even wider than the choice between incarceration and the length of a prison term. As part of imposing probation, judges often require offenders to abide by certain rules, such as reporting to a probation officer on a regular basis, abstaining from alcohol or drug use, obtaining mental health counseling, etc.

**Sentencing Laws and Goals**    Several different types of sentencing laws and theories about the purposes or goals of sentencing co-exist in the United States. The importance of these laws and goals has varied in different historical periods, and they rise and fall in popularity as dissatisfaction with one law calls forth another.

*Indeterminate Sentence*    Many states and the federal system have long used indeterminate sentences in which an individual is imprisoned for a minimum to a maximum period, but may be released before the maximum time is served. Deciding when the prisoner should be released is subject to periodic review of the criminal's conduct by a parole board.

The indeterminate sentence is linked to the theory of correction or *rehabilitation*, in which criminals are perceived as disturbed and in need of treatment. When they have improved, they may be released.

***Determinate Sentence*** But indeterminate sentencing has become suspect, and starting in 1975, some states began to abolish parole in favor of determinate or fixed sentencing. A determinate sentence designates a set or flat prison term without early parole. However, there may be compromises with the indeterminate sentence, in that early parole is possible after a certain part of the fixed sentence has been served. Legislatures also continue to give judges leeway in setting the exact term of the sentence.

Determinate sentencing is not new. It was the common form of sentencing prior to the 1920s, but was abandoned in favor of indeterminate sentencing and the rehabilitation model. Reasons for the shift back to determinate sentencing include skepticism about rehabilitation and psychological pressures on convicts. Many researchers in the 1970s argued that prisons do not rehabilitate and may even contribute to crime. The indeterminate sentence also creates psychological stress, because prisoners never know when they will be released and they constantly must be careful to avoid violating prison rules and thus jeopardizing parole. The indeterminate sentence also produced wide variation in minimum and maximum sentences for similar crimes and criminals.

Determinate sentences with rigid and fixed terms are less common than those which include a range of possible sentences and preserve judges' flexibility. But to reduce sentencing variation, judicial discretion has been limited somewhat by state and federal sentencing guidelines. According to these rules, judges are expected to impose sentences within a narrow range determined by the seriousness of the crime and the defendants prior criminal record.

Theories of sentencing that go along with various forms of determinate sentencing include a traditional view of *punishment or retribution*, in which sentences are imposed because criminals deserve them. While in prison, criminals also are *isolated* from society and *deterred* from committing more crime. Determinate sentencing also is believed to serve an additional goal of *general deterrence*, which means sending a message to all members of society that crime does not pay.

**Alternatives to Prison** Judges increasingly are devising unusual and innovative conditions of probation as an alternative to prison for many first or minor offenders. Such action further increases their power to determine the outcome of a criminal case.

For example, a judge required two white teenagers who burned a cross on a black family's lawn to help rebuild a century-old black church destroyed by arson in a separate and unrelated incident. A dozen states have passed laws that allow judges to eliminate or shorten the period of a driver's license suspension if drivers convicted of drunk driving will install a device in their cars that prevents the car from being started if it measures alcohol on the driver's breath. Another innovative sentence for drunk driving is a modern version of the scarlet letter—placing a sticker on the car which reads: "CON-VICTED DUI—RESTRICTED LICENSE" (driving under the influence), which permits the driver to use the car for business purposes only.[58]

Requirements to perform a specified number of hours of community service in the public schools, hospital, or other public agency and making restitution also are becoming common. Others include confinement at home, in which offenders wear electronic bracelets that signal their whereabouts to a central transmitter. If they move beyond 150 feet of their home, the signal is broken. Judges also have given some defendants a choice of jail or of completing high school degree-equivalency programs.[59]

*Why Alternatives?*    Alternative sentences are a product of several factors. First, as mentioned earlier, many criminologists and judges believe that sending minor criminals or first offenders to prison is unlikely to rehabilitate them. Rather, imprisonment with career criminals will contribute to hardening their criminal attitudes and behavior and contribute to their committing more crime (*recidivism*). Perhaps keeping these offenders out of jail while still limiting their freedom and imposing other obligations also will make them into better citizens and serve society at the same time.

Second, violent crimes, especially rape and assault, and larceny, motor vehicle theft, and drug violations have increased sharply since 1980. Legislators have responded to public fears of crime by lengthening prison sentences and requiring a minimum of some prison time for many more crimes. Consequently, the prisons are overloaded.

Prison overcrowding is a serious problem. Federal prison populations in the United States have more than doubled since 1980 (from 20,600 to about 43,000) and state prison populations have increased 90 percent (from 295,000 to over 560,000). In addition, thirty-eight states are operating prisons over their designed capacity levels.[60] Prison overcrowding has produced judicial orders to reduce crowding, creates pressures in nearly every state to build more prisons, which costs millions of scarce tax dollars, and leads to releasing prisoners early—sometimes before they have completed fifteen to twenty percent of their sentences.[61]

**Sentence Variation**    Each state's criminal law gives judges discretion in individual cases. But since each of the states defines and punishes similar criminal acts differently, sentencing variation is very likely across—as well as within—the states.

The law of rape is an illustration. Idaho has separate penalties for the rape of a female under and over age 18; Tennessee distinguishes between rape of those under and over age 13; and in New York, different penalties are imposed for rape of a female under and over ages 11, 14, and 17. In Idaho, the penalty ranges from a minimum of one year to life. In Tennessee, for rape of a person under age 13, the penalty ranges from 15 to 60 years plus fines, but over age 13, it is a minimum of 8 years to a maximum of 30 years plus fines; in New York, penalties increase as the age of the victim decreases, from one year or less to a maximum of 25 years.[62] Therefore, among these three states, sentences for rape can vary widely. Similar variations in authorized sentences can be found for many different crimes.

The actual sentences handed down by judges in similar or even identical cases often reflect nearly the full range of permissible sentencing possibilities. Judges in the same city or county often gain reputations as tough or lenient because they sentence different percentages of defendants to prison, even though all of them handle similar types of cases. A few judges may sentence 80 or 90 percent of all defendants to prison while others incarcerate only 30 or 40 percent. Recently, the average sentence in Florida for armed robbery was 9.8 years in prison, but individual judicial circuits ranged from an average of 4.87 years to 18.5 years. All of the circuits had a mix of cases involving first offenders as well as career criminals.

Differences in these patterns of sentencing were explained best by local crime rates: the higher the crime rate, the *lower* the average sentence. Court regulars in high crime districts probably viewed armed robbery as routine, whereas murder, rape, and other assaults were viewed as more serious crimes worthy of the most serious sentences.[63] Similar variations in sentencing have been found in the federal courts. For example, sentences for illegal entry into the United States with one prior deportation or conviction for illegal entry have ranged from: a fine to five years probation (22 percent of defendants); a few weeks to five months in jail (46 percent); more than five months to nearly three years in prison (32 percent).[64]

Sentencing disparity is controversial because many believe it produces unfair and unequal treatment. But it also illustrates the enormous discretion and power that judges have, as well as the importance to defendants of knowing in advance a prosecutor's sentencing recommendation as part of plea bargaining.

## Effects of Plea Bargaining

The previous sections have described how plea bargaining works and why it is so widespread. The discussion of sentencing also demonstrates that judges have enormous latitude in determining the sentence for individual offenders. This section examines the effects of plea bargaining on sentencing and arguments over whether defendants are treated properly. Several key questions deserve special attention. They include:

Do defendants receive sentencing benefits from plea bargaining?

Are constitutional rights violated and are defendants coerced into pleading guilty?

Do defendants receive equal treatment through plea bargaining?

Are sentences too lenient as a result of plea bargaining?

What changes might be made in plea bargaining to improve its image and the work of the courts? Should plea bargaining be abolished?

**Sentencing**   There is disagreement and confusion concerning the sentencing benefits of pleading guilty. There are two closely related parts to the problem: the effect of trials and guilty pleas on sentences and the effect of charge reduction on sentences.

*Trials and Guilty Pleas*   It is clear that people who are convicted at a trial go to prison more often and for longer periods. However, it also is true that serious rather than light cases, such as murder rather than possession of drugs or shoplifting, are more likely to go to trial, so that we would expect sentences resulting from a trial to be harsher.

It is necessary to separate apples from oranges—to look at cases in which the criminal charges and the defendant's records are similar. Then, it turns out that whether cases are disposed of through bargains or trials makes much less difference than other factors.[65] These other factors are: the actual seriousness of the crime and the original charges determined by the police; whether the defendant had committed previous crimes; and whether the defendant previously had served a prison term.

However, even though other factors are more important in determining the sentence, case disposition still makes some small additional difference. Jury trials are likely to result in harsher sentences than either plea bargaining or a quick trial before a judge acting without a jury (*bench trial*). Bench trials may be similar to plea bargaining because they occur within stable criminal court work groups and usually take just a few minutes. In some cities, quick bench trials substitute for informal plea bargaining.

*Charge Reduction*   Prosecutors frequently reduce charges in order to persuade defendants to plead guilty. However, as just mentioned, the seriousness of the crime defined in terms of the *original charges* filed against a defendant has more to do with the final sentence than the reduced charges.[66] Prosecutors may reduce criminal charges to get defendants to plead, but this concession does not have a large effect on sentencing.

For example, a defendant who pleads guilty to a reduced charge of simple robbery, but who actually threatened a convenience store clerk with a gun (armed robbery), often receives a sentence that is more similar to others who committed armed robbery than to those who actually committed and were originally charged with simple robbery. Therefore, disposing of the case through plea bargaining or a trial has more effect than charge reduction.

In sum, most research confirms that jury trials produce harsher sentences than plea bargains, although the differences are not as large as might be expected when other characteristics of the defendant and the crime are taken into account. But for individual defendants and their lawyers, a little difference is very important if it translates into a prison term versus county jail or probation, or a few more months or years rather than less time. To most lawyers and their clients, pleading guilty usually will look like the best deal.

**Constitutional Rights**   A major issue in plea bargaining concerns the constitutional rights of criminal defendants. Some critics fear that plea bargaining prevents defendants from making use of due process to protect themselves from the steamroller effect of the criminal courts. Pleading guilty leaves no room for cross-examining witnesses, questioning the evidence, or challenging police decisions in arrest and interrogation. A defendant gives that up in agreeing to plead guilty and has no protection against conviction nor any right to an appeal. A trial, it is argued, puts those protections into play and insulates the innocent from a pressured conviction.

Constitutional concerns probably are irrelevant in most criminal cases. The due process ideal sees criminal courts filled with reasonable doubt rather than dead-bang cases, and with defendants who are arrested with circumstantial evidence, not with sure identification and solid physical evidence.

Most defendants, however, do not seem to be innocent. The evidence or witnesses used to convince them to plead guilty are the same as those that enabled the police to catch them in the first place. For most defendants, there seems to be no point in going to trial to simply affirm what is already obvious to themselves, the police, prosecutors, and defense lawyers.

For most defendants, the punishment is much more important than due process since their guilt is obvious and they have no legal basis for challenging their arrest and later treatment. This does not mean that procedural guarantees are luxuries that we can just as easily live without, but only that most defendants do not wish to invoke them in the criminal courts.

**Adequacy of Defense**   Assuming that most defendants are guilty of a crime and will plead guilty, an important remaining issue is the role that defense attorneys play in the courts.

It is easy to assume from the close relationships that exist in courtroom work groups that public defenders in particular merely play along at providing a defense and that they are part of the inevitable road to conviction. Defendants seem to believe this is true. But most defendants who hire their own lawyers also rarely go to trial. They may feel they got a better deal because they paid for their lawyers, but this is not necessarily so.

Some critics have argued that only well-paid private lawyers will challenge a prosecutor. But the nature of their cases and their clients may be more important than aggressive strategies in affecting case outcomes.

Some public defenders maintain that their office represents a much larger number and percentage of repeat criminals who are caught in dead-bang cases with no chance of a dismissal. Repeaters plead guilty more quickly than first offenders.[67] However, where public defenders' offices are large and well financed, public lawyers seem to be just as vigorous and equally successful in challenging cases.[68]

Most privately retained defense attorneys who handle a large number of cases for small fees, and court-appointed lawyers who often are paid small fixed fees by the state or county probably are less able than public defenders to challenge the prosecutor effectively. Not only do public defenders not have to concentrate on collecting fees, they usually have some resources to conduct an independent investigation of the case, something that most private lawyers cannot afford.

Public defenders and most court regulators favor guilty pleas or bench trials, and their clients often receive shorter sentences. When public defenders go to trial, they obtain acquittals as often as or more frequently than other lawyers. The overall conviction rates of defense lawyers of all types are about the same.[69]

The best explanation for their success is that their familiarity with local courts and their membership in close courthouse work groups give them an advantage over lawyers who are outside the network of the criminal courts. Perhaps judges pay more careful attention to a case brought to trial by a public defender, since they know that a fellow regular will not inconvenience everyone with a trial in an obvious dead-bang case.

In areas where public defenders are not used, a local attorney is appointed to represent poor defendants. Sometimes these are courthouse regulars who handle the case like any other, but sometimes defendants are assigned lawyers from the local bar who are unfamiliar with criminal law or the local courts. Sometimes they are the newest members of the bar, who have not yet "paid their dues" by taking on a few free or low-paying criminal cases.

Since they have dealt with very few criminals or criminal cases, they sometimes believe that their case is unique and ought to go to trial. In many instances, plea bargaining would be the wisest choice, since they often lose at trial. If local judges are severe in dead-bang cases that go to trial, their clients are apt to suffer the consequences.

***Resources*** Overall, there is an imbalance in public support for prosecution and defending the poor. Many states do not require public defender systems statewide, and many smaller cities and counties rely on fixed-fee court-appointed lawyers.

Not all public defenders' offices are well funded. Many states began the 1980s and the 1990s with economic recession, high unemployment, and rising crime. Budgets for paying court-appointed counsel were totally depleted in some states, and lawmakers were reluctant to raise taxes or divert state money from other projects to defend the poor—never a popular or especially visible political issue.

Some criminal defendants were sentenced to jail without ever having seen a lawyer, a clear violation of their constitutional rights. Many inmates on death row have trouble locating legal representation beyond their first appeal, for which a paid attorney is provided for the mostly poor defendants.

It is difficult to generalize about the adequacy of defense for the poor since policy and budgets vary widely. Public defenders can be equally or more effective than private counsel and probably are more effective than most court-appointed lawyers who have little economic incentive and little experience with the criminal courts. However, overall, defense of the poor is not a high priority for state and local government.

**Equal Treatment**   While plea bargaining is informal and most defendants do not assert their constitutional rights to trial, an important issue is whether they are treated equally and fairly in plea bargaining. Equality and fairness are difficult to achieve in the best of circumstances, since they are subject to numerous interpretations, often according to individual self-interest. But we can consider some basic issues.

Prosecutors do not offer plea bargains in all cases, nor do they always offer deals to all defendants accused of similar crimes. A survey of prosecutors revealed that about 25 percent would refuse to bargain if cases involved particularly violent or serious crimes, such as the murder of a child or police officer, crimes committed with weapons, or political corruption. About the same number stated they would not bargain if a particular case had received news media coverage, and about 20 percent said they would not bargain if the evidence against a defendant was very strong.[70]

Prosecutors also often offer plea bargains to accomplices in serious crimes in order to have an eyewitness who will testify against the others at a trial, ensuring convictions but often very different sentences for all. In murder cases, accomplices frequently receive life imprisonment or less, while their partners in crime get the death penalty.

It may not be difficult to justify refusing to bargain in very serious crimes where maximum punishment seems appropriate, but it is more difficult to reconcile a refusal to bargain to fear of the press or the strength of the evidence. In terms of roughly equal justice, it seems that similar defendants accused of similar crimes ought to be treated the same way. Forcing them to go to trial seems designed to assure that they are punished more harshly because they got caught red-handed or because the press may be hostile and a threat to a prosecutor's career.

*Fair Bargains?*   Even if prosecutors offer bargains, the deals may seem so unattractive to defendants that they feel they must take a chance on a trial. But it is a huge gamble. While case disposition is not as important in determining the sentence as the characteristics of culprits and their crimes, there always are some cases in every city that deliver a much stronger message: judges give the maximum in a jury trial. In addition, defendants who commit crimes which vary enormously in seriousness and violence sometimes receive very similar sentences.

Consider the sentences offered in plea bargains and those imposed after a jury trial in Box 6.5, "Bargained and Trial Sentences."

**Leniency**   Law-and-order critics of plea bargaining often assume that bargained sentences are too light. Most people who think sentences are too short are interested in punishment as retaliation or vengeance. There is no scientific

---

**BOX 6.5**

BARGAINED AND TRIAL SENTENCES

• A defendant rejected a 15-year sentence in return for pleading guilty to lewd and lascivious assault for trying to rape his young cousin. At his trial, the victim's mother pleaded for mercy, medical experts testified that the victim suffered only minor scratches, and the jury recommended a life sentence. But the judge imposed the death penalty.

• The prosecutor offered to recommend a life sentence for a brutal serial murderer and multiple rapist, but the defendant refused and, following his trial, received the death penalty.

• Charged with sexual battery of a minor, the defendant insisted on his innocence and demanded a trial. However, he sat in county jail for 3 years because a succession of public defenders obtained delays since they strongly believed he should plead guilty. The prosecutor offered a 12-year sentence, but the defendant finally was convicted at a trial and received the maximum of 25 years.

• The prosecutor offered a sentence of 7 years to a defendant who had written bad checks, but at the trial the evidence showed he had bounced numerous checks over a 10-year period and had been convicted of thirty-seven other crimes. He received 100 years in prison.

---

or objective way to determine the proper length of sentences. These decisions depend on personal values or public policy such as what a legislature or a prosecutor or judge believes a crime deserves. Sentencing also varies throughout the country, reflecting local political and social values. Therefore, definitions of leniency have to vary according to what local criminal courts are doing.

Discussion of leniency also needs to include a broader concern with the entire criminal justice process. While trial sentences usually are longer, trials also produce acquittals. In some cities, there are many of them. In contrast, plea bargaining always guarantees a conviction and some punishment. Even defendants whose criminal charges are dropped suffer some punishment just by going through the system.

Prosecutors also dismiss about as many cases as they prosecute, and police fail to make nearly as many arrests as they could. Between the two of them, many more people suspected or accused of crime are allowed to go free than are dismissed or sentenced lightly by judges. Most city jails and state prisons also are terribly overcrowded, and prisoners frequently are released early to make room for new convicts. Leniency through plea bargaining is one small piece of the criminal justice puzzle.

### Abolish Plea Bargaining?

The drawbacks of plea bargaining lead many observers to call for its abolition and replacement with trials. But the odds for that are nearly zero. Plea bargaining has been used for over 100 years and is a well-established part of standard judicial practice, even if it is not in the official rules. Close courtroom work groups and the strain of going to trial reinforce its widespread use. Most cases also are dead-bang ones and trials seem unnecessary. Plea bargaining is here to stay.

Attempts by various state governments and local prosecutors to abolish plea bargaining show that either the reform is quietly abandoned in a short while or that prosecutors begin to drop many more cases or judges begin to offer sentencing bargains.

**Sentencing Reform**   Other reforms also produce few results. In the 1970s, many states and the federal government enacted new criminal laws that required *mandatory minimum sentences* for certain crimes. These were designed to partly limit the discretion that prosecutors and judges have in plea bargaining. If a defendant is found guilty of a crime carrying a mandatory sentence, such as the use of a handgun in committing another crime, the judge must impose the required minimum sentence. He or she has no discretion and the sentence cannot be bargained away.

However, many prosecutors refused to charge defendants with a crime requiring a mandatory sentence, because it limits their bargaining power; or prosecutors agree not to charge a mandatory crime in return for a defendant's pleading guilty to a related charge, such as unarmed robbery.[71] Mandatory laws are not used or they are part of other bargains; they do not limit discretion.

Another popular reform, discussed earlier, is *sentencing guidelines* for judges. Reform organizations have sponsored seminars and round-table discussions for judges to develop a consensus on the criteria that judges should use in sentencing. But judges rarely have voluntarily agreed on specific sentencing policies, and many jealously guard their independence to do what they think is right.

Recently, many states and the U.S. Congress have passed new laws creating judicial commissions to set sentencing guidelines for the various state and federal courts. However, as before, many judges have objected, claiming that the new laws violate the separation of powers since it mixes judicial with legislative and executive functions. Nevertheless, these laws generally have been held constitutional by state supreme courts and the U.S. Supreme Court.

While they may narrow the range of judicial discretion, sentencing guidelines do not take plea bargaining into account since the guidelines only apply to the judicial side of the sentencing equation. They do not cover deals or recommendations promised by the prosecutor. In addition, judges may override the guidelines if they write opinions justifying their departure from the rules.

**Political Reform**   Despite the limitations of reform, plea bargaining probably can be made more fair and equal. The U.S. Supreme Court helped end the hypocritical position that court regulars normally took in order to get a guilty plea. The 1971 decision also helps to protect defendants from prosecutors or judges who refuse to honor a deal that was arrived at in secret but was officially disavowed in public as part of the old sentencing ceremony.

Plea bargaining could be improved further if it were less a political issue. Encouraging state legislatures to recognize plea bargaining officially as part of a prosecutor's legal discretion, for example, might reduce partisan and media attacks on plea bargaining and give prosecutors more freedom to bargain equally in all cases.

Encouraging prosecutors to become full-time, permanent, and professional state and federal employees also would remove the temptation of prosecutors to use cases selectively for their own personal or political advantage. It is unfair to make an example of a particular defendant or to force a defendant in a serious dead-bang case to select a jury trial in order for the prosecutor to gain publicity as a tough crime fighter.

All defendants should have a similar opportunity to bargain and should receive comparable deals. A written policy on charge reduction, sentencing recommendations, and other deals might help, but no written policy can cover every case, and there are loopholes and ambiguity in general policies.

A more effective way of ensuring general equality is to assign cases to small, continuous work groups of judges, prosecutors, and public defenders.[72] Each work group that stays together for months or years would be more likely to produce similar punishment for similar crimes. Overcharging and sentencing surprises are likely to be reduced, because others in the stable work group could anticipate a prosecutor's or judge's decisions and informally influence them to include their own views on charges and sentences.

Although individual courthouse work groups may develop some internal consistency, some variation in sentencing is likely to exist from one group to another and certainly from one city and state to another. Each state has its own criminal laws and sentences, usually with wide discretion available to local judges. Therefore, we are not likely to see national or even statewide consistency in judicial sentencing, regardless of reforms made in plea bargaining.

## CONCLUSION

This chapter has looked at the settlement of criminal cases from start to finish, including the basic character of crime and the activities of people in the courts who deal with defendants. The most important figure in criminal cases is the state prosecutor, who has substantial personal discretion to press charges, to determine what the charges will be, and to take the lead in plea bargaining. Defense attorneys and judges usually respond to the prosecutor's initiatives and ground rules for settling cases.

More serious cases generally go to trial, but there is no sure-fire way of knowing exactly when a particular case will be negotiated or will go to a jury. Defense lawyers have to decide when to take a chance on a trial. A few judges also are becoming more active in plea bargaining, partly because bargaining now has official status and because some prosecutors refuse to negotiate, leaving judges with the major trump card to determine the sentence.

There have been lots of explanations for why there is so much plea bargaining. Prosecutors and defense lawyers often claim that most cases are open-and-shut and that there is no need to go to trial. However, more general explanations are needed to account for variations in bargaining around the country.

More general theories emphasize the "sociology of the courthouse" with accent on the individual career goals of lawyers and prosecutors and the close working relationships that develop among stable teams of judges, prosecutors, and public defenders. Close, congenial contact and smooth working relationships probably are more important than mechanical theories for accounting for why there is so much plea bargaining.

Probably the thorniest issue in plea bargaining is the fairness and equality of the deals. Constitutional rights are not critical in most criminal cases, since defendants are clearly guilty and the police have not violated their rights. Most defendants want to get out of the ordeal of prosecution, and the big question is the kind of deal they get. Prisoners sometimes find that cellmates have similar sentences for very different crimes or different sentences for similar crimes.

There is no easy solution for those who search for equality in plea bargaining. With general sentencing statutes, judges and prosecutors have many opportunities to juggle the charges and the penalties. There also is nothing to prevent a prosecutor from refusing to bargain or going to trial with maximum charges when a defendant rejects a deal. Close courthouse work groups help, but do not ensure equality. Perhaps in addition to Supreme Court rulings that require judges to enforce deals, every defendant ought to have a "constitutional right to deal" according to specific bargaining policies. Bargaining is here to stay and the search for improvement will continue.

## SUGGESTIONS FOR ADDITIONAL READING

Blumberg, Abraham: *Criminal Justice* (New York: New Viewpoints, 1974). This is a classic in criminal justice and one of the first to examine plea bargaining as a system of informal interactions among prosecutors, defense lawyers, and clients.

Casper, Jonathan D: *American Criminal Justice: the Defendants Perspective* (Englewood Cliffs, N.J.: Prentice-Hall, Inc., 1972). One of the few books based on interviews with criminal defendants which explores their perspectives of criminal justice, including plea bargaining.

Eisenstein, James, and Herbert Jacob: *Felony Justice* (Boston: Little, Brown and Co., 1977). One of the earliest, but still one of the most thorough studies of the behavior of criminal courts in America's large cities, with emphasis on plea bargaining and the work groups which develop among judges, prosecutors, and defense lawyers.

Scheingold, Stuart A: *The Politics of Law and Order: Street Crime and Public Policy* (New York: Longman, 1984). The author analyzes conflicting social theories about the causes and cures of crime, how crime became a major political issue, and the possibilities of criminal justice reform.

Skolnick, Jerome. *Justice Without Trial* (New York: John Wiley and Sons, Inc., 1967). Another classic which focuses on the organization and behavior of police in big cities. Emphasis is on police discretion, the policeman's personality, and police attitudes toward criminal justice.

# NOTES

1 *Los Angeles Times*, April 22, 1990, A1.

2 *Newsweek*, May 16, 1983, p. 63 and February 18, 1985, p. 34; *New York Times*, November 7, 1982, Sec. I, p. 34.

3 Albert J. Reiss, Jr., *The Police and the Public* (New Haven: Yale University Press, 1971), p. 136.

4 Herbert Jacob. *Crime and Justice in Urban America* (Englewood Cliffs, N.J.: Prentice-Hall, Inc., 1980), pp. 76–78.

5 James Eisenstein, *Counsel for the United States* (Baltimore: Johns Hopkins University Press, 1978), p. 40.

6 *Ibid.*, pp. 12–20.

7 Roy B. Flemming, "The Political Styles and Organizational Strategies of American Prosecutors: Examples from Nine Courthouse Communities," *Law and Policy*, 12 (1990), 24–50.

8 On the various roles of trial judges, see Maureen Mileski, "Courtroom Encounters," *Law and Society Review*, 5 (May 1971), 473–538; and Austin Sarat, "Judging in Trial Courts: An Exploratory Study," *Journal of Politics*, 39 (1977), 368–398.

9 Eisenstein, p. 181.

10 Abraham S. Blumberg, *Criminal Justice* (New York: New Viewpoints, 1974), chap. 5.

11 David W. Neubauer, *Criminal Justice in Middle America* (Morristown, N.J: General Learning Press, 1974), pp. 68–71; James Eisenstein and Herbert Jacob, *Felony Justice* (Boston: Little, Brown and Co., 1977), pp. 48–52, 119–121, 157–160.

12 Anthony Platt and Randi Pollock, "Channeling Lawyers: The Careers of Public Defenders," in Herbert Jacob (ed.), *The Potential for Reform of Criminal Justice* (Beverly Hills, Calif.: Sage Publications, Inc., 1974), chap. 8; Jacob, *Criminal Justice in Urban America*, pp. 78–79.

13 David W. Neubauer, *America's Courts and the Criminal Justice System* (North Scituate, Mass.: Duxbury Press, 1979), p. 193.

14 Martin Levin, *Urban Politics and the Criminal Courts* (Chicago: University of Chicago Press, 1977), pp. 65–67, 73–80.

15 Jerome H. Skolnick, *Justice Without Trial* (New York: John Wiley & Sons, Inc., 1967), pp. 45–48.

16 "Prosecutorial Discretion and the Initiation of Criminal Complaints," *Southern California Law Review*, 42 (1969), 519; David Sudnow, "Normal Crimes: Sociological Features of the Penal Code in a Public Defender Office," *Social Problems* (1965), 255–274.

17 Pamela J. Utz, "Two Models of Prosecutorial Discretion," in William F. McDonald (ed.), *The Prosecutor* (Beverly Hills, Calif.: Sage Publications, Inc., 1979), p. 110.

18 George F. Cole, "The Decision to Prosecute," *Law and Society Review*, 4 (February 1970), 313–343; Neubauer, *Criminal Justice in Middle America*, chap. 6.

19 Neubauer, *Criminal Justice in Middle America*, pp. 130–131.

20 Elizabeth Anne Stanko, "The Impact of Victim Assessment on Prosecutors' Screening Decisions: The Case of the New York County District Attorney's Office," *Law and Society Review*, 16 (1981–82), 225–239.

21 Michael L. Radelet and Glenn L. Pierce, "Race and Prosecutorial Discretion in Homicide Cases," *Law and Society Review*, 19 (1985), 587–621; and Raymond Paternoster, Prosecutorial Discretion in Requesting the Death Penalty: A Case of Victim-Based Racial Discrimination," *Law and Society Review*, 18 (1984), 437–478.

22 Cole, *passim.*

23 Mortimer R. Kadish and Sanford H. Kadish, *Discretion to Disobey* (Stanford, Calif.: Stanford University Press, 1973), pp. 80–85.

24 Descriptions of the various stages of the criminal justice process can be found in many sources. See Neubauer, *America's Courts and the Criminal Justice System*, chap. 2, and George F. Cole, *The American System of Criminal Justice* (North Scituate, Mass.: Duxbury Press, 1975), chap. 2.

25 Mileski, p. 487.

26 The literature on bail is extensive. See, for example, President's Commission on Law Enforcement and Administration of Justice, *Task Force Report: The Courts* (Washington, D.C.: U.S. Government Printing Office, 1967); Ronald Goldfarb, *Ransom: A Critique of the American Bail System* (New York: Harper & Row Publishers, Inc., 1965); Charles Ares, Anne Rankin, and Herbert Sturz, "The Manhattan Bail Project," *New York University Law Review*, 38 (1963), 84–85.

27 John S. Goldkamp, "Effects of Detention on Judicial Decisions: A Closer Look," *Justice System Journal*, 5 (Spring 1980), 234–257.

28 Eisenstein and Jacob, p. 197.

29 Frederic Suffet, "Bail Setting: A Study of Courtroom Interaction," *Crime and Delinquency*, 12 (1966), 318–331.

30 These figures vary considerably around the country. See Neubauer, *America's Courts and the Criminal Justice System*, pp. 226–230.

31 William F. McDonald, "The Prosecutor's Domain," in William F. McDonald (ed.), *The Prosecutor*, p. 43; Malcolm M. Feeley, *The Process Is the Punishment* (New York: Russell Sage Foundation, 1979).

32 Eisenstein and Jacob, p. 274.

33 *New York Times*, July 11, 1987, p. 13; *Tallahassee Democrat*, February 26, 1989, p. 7A.

34 The pros and cons of plea bargaining are discussed in a variety of sources. See Albert W. Alschuler, "The Prosecutor's Role in Plea Bargaining," *University of Chicago Law Review*, 36 (1968), 50–112; Donald J. Newman, *Conviction: The Determination of Guilt or Innocence without Trial* (Boston: Little, Brown and Co., 1966); Arthur Rosett and Donald R. Cressey, *Justice by Consent* (Philadelphia: J. B. Lippincott Co., 1976), especially chaps. 1 and 8; Russell R. Wheeler and Howard R. Whitcomb, *Judicial Administration* (Englewood Cliffs, N.J.: Prentice-Hall, Inc., 1977), pp. 170–172; The President's Commission on Law Enforcement and Administration of Justice, *Task Force Report: The Courts* (Washington, D.C.: U.S. Government Printing Office, 1967); William P. McLauchlan, *American Legal Processes* (New York: John Wiley & Sons, Inc., 1977), pp. 125–130; Abraham S. Blumberg, *Criminal Justice* (New York: New Viewpoints, 1974).

35 Milton Heumann, *Plea Bargaining* (Chicago: University of Chicago Press, 1977), pp. 35–40, and Douglas W. Maynard, "The Structure of Discourse in Misdemeanor Plea Bargaining," *Law and Society Review*, 18 (1984), 75–104.

36 Blumberg, pp. 56–57; Rosett and Cressey, pp. 20–21; Alschuler, pp. 85–105.

37 "Prosecutorial Discretion and the Initiation of Criminal Complaints," p. 519.

38 Pamela J. Utz, "Two Models of Prosecutorial Professionalism," in William F. McDonald (ed.), *The Prosecutor*, p. 104; Martin A. Levin, *Urban Politics and the Criminal Courts* (Chicago: University of Chicago Press, 1977), p. 71; Lynn M.

Mather, "Some Determinants of the Method of Case Disposition: Decision-Making by Public Defenders in Los Angeles," *Law and Society Review*, 7 (Winter 1973), 201–202.

39 William F. McDonald et al., "The Prosecutor's Plea Bargaining Decisions," in William F. McDonald (ed.), *The Prosecutor* (Beverly Hills, Calif.: Sage Publications, Inc., 1979), pp. 192–194.

40 Levin, p. 73; McDonald. "The Prosecutor's Plea Bargaining Decisions," pp. 176–178, 192.

41 Abraham S. Blumberg, "The Practice of Law as Confidence Game: Organizational Cooptation of a Profession," *Law and Society Review*, 1 (June 1967), 15–39.

42 In addition to Blumberg, "Practice of Law . . . ." see Donald J. Newman, "Pleading Guilty for Considerations: A Study of Bargain Justice," *Journal of Criminal Law, Criminology and Police Science*, 46 (1956), 780–790.

43 Jonathan D. Casper, *American Criminal Justice: The Defendant's Perspective* (Englewood Cliffs, N.J.: Prentice-Hall, Inc. 1972), p. 105 and chap. 4.

44 Heumann, pp. 59–61.

45 John Paul Ryan and James J. Alfini, "Trial Judges' Participation in Plea Bargaining: An Empirical Perspective," *Law and Society Review*, 13 (Winter 1979), 479–507.

46 Mather, p. 190.

47 Thomas Church, "Plea Bargaining, Concessions, and the Courts: Analysis of a Quasi-Experiment," *Law and Society Review*, 10 (1976), 387–389; Michael L. Rubenstein and Teresa J. White, "Alaska's Ban on Plea Bargaining," *Law and Society Review*, 13 (Winter 1979), 367–383.

48 Mather, pp. 197–211; Neubauer, *Criminal Justice in Middle America*, p. 233.

49 Eisenstein and Jacob, p. 271; McDonald, "The Prosecutor's Plea Bargaining Decision," p. 193.

50 Juanita Jones, "Prosecutors and Public Defenders: Cooperative Relationships and Non-Negotiable Cases," in Burton Atkins and Mark Pogrebin (eds.), *The Invisible Justice System* (Anderson Publishing Co., 1978), pp. 200–202.

51 Albert W. Alschuler, "Plea Bargaining and Its History," and Lawrence M. Friedman, "Plea Bargaining in Historical Perspective," *Law and Society Review*, 13 (Winter 1979), 231–238 and 247–259.

52 Milton Heumann, "A Note on Plea Bargaining and Case Pressure," *Law and Society Review*, 9 (Spring 1975), 517; Malcolm Feeley, "Pleading Guilty in Lower Courts," *Law and Society Review*, 13 (Winter 1979), 111; Philip Revzin, "Richard McQuade Gets Prestige, Little Crime as a Rural Prosecutor," *Wall Street Journal*, May 6, 1976, p. 1; Eisenstein and Jacob, chap. 4, James Eisenstein, Roy B. Fleming, and Peter F. Nardulli, *The Contours of Justice: Communities and their Courts* (Boston: Little, Brown and Co., 1988), pp. 263–265.

53 James Eisenstein, *Counsel for the United States* (Baltimore; Johns Hopkins University Press, 1978), p. 230.

54 The most complete discussion of work groups is found in Eisenstein and Jacob. Most other research on the criminal courts confirms these patterns.

55 Mather, p. 199. For an example of extremely close work groups, see Henry R. Glick, "The Judicial Firm," *Judicature*, 63 (February 1980), 328–337.

56 Eisenstein, Fleming and Nardulli, pp. 28–36.

57 The following relies on Elyce Zenoff, "Sentencing Alternatives," in *Encyclopedia of*

*the American Judicial System* (ed.) Robert J. Janosik (New York: Charles Scribner's's Sons, 1987), vol. II, pp. 915–923; James A. Inciardi, *Criminal Justice* (Orlando, Fla.: Academic Press, Inc., 1984), pp. 505–525; Michael H. Tonry, *Sentencing Reform Impacts* (Washington, D.C.: U.S. Department of Justice, National Institute of Justice, February 1987).

**58** *New York Times*, December 19, 1988, p. 9, and December 24, 1988, p. 16; "Sentenced to Wear the Scarlet Letter: Judicial Innovations in Sentencing—Are They Constitutional?" *Dickenson Law Review*, 93 (1989), 759–788.

**59** Michael Brennan Getty, "Alternative Sentences for the Alcohol/Drug Defendant," *Southern Illinois University Law Review*, 14 (1989), 1–26; J. Robert Lilly and Richard A. Ball, "A Brief History of House Arrest and Electronic Monitoring," *Northern Kentucky Law Review*, 13 (1987), 361–374; Ed Austin, "We Will Throw the Book at Them," *The Prosecutor*, 21 (1988), 16–18.

**60** *Statistical Abstract of the United States* (Washington, D.C.: 1990), pp. 187–189.

**61** *New York Times*, April 25, 1988, p. 1, and July 3, 1989, p. 1.

**62** Idaho Code, vol. 4, section 18, chapter 61, 1987, 1991; Tennessee Code Annotated, vol. 7 and 7a, sections 39 and 40, 1990; McKinney's Consolidated Laws of New York, Annotated, Book 39, Penal Law, sections 70 and 130, 1987, 1992. Also, Inciardi, pp. 512–513.

**63** Henry R. Glick and George W. Pruet, Jr., "Crime, Public Opinion and Trial Courts: An Analysis of Sentencing Policy," *Justice Quarterly* 2 (1985), 329.

**64** Anthony Partridge, Patricia A. Lombard, and Barbara Meierhoefer, *Punishment for Federal Crimes* (Washington, D.C.: The Federal Judicial Center, 1986), pp. 7–8.

**65** Eisenstein and Jacob, pp. 269–287; Thomas M. Uhlman and N. Darlene Walker, "A Plea Is No Bargain: The Impact of Case Disposition on Sentencing," *Social Science Quarterly*, 60 (September 1979), 218–234; William Rhodes, "Plea Bargaining: Its Effects on Sentencing and Convictions in the District of Columbia," *Journal of Criminal Law and Criminology*, 70 (Fall 1979), 367; David Brereton and Jonathan D. Casper, "Does It Pay to Plead Guilty? Differential Sentencing and the Functioning of Criminal Courts," *Law and Society Review*, 16 (1981–82), 45–70; Levin, p. 73.

**66** Maureen Mileski, "Courtroom Encounters," *Law and Society Review*, 5 (May 1971), 511–513; Uhlman and Walker, p. 227.

**67** Dallin H. Oaks and Warren Lehman, "Lawyers for the Poor," in Abraham S. Blumberg (ed.), *The Scales of Justice* (Hawthorne, N.Y.: Aldine Publishing Co., 1970), pp. 91–104; Neubauer, *Criminal Justice in Middle America*, p. 206; Newman, "Pleading Guilty for Considerations."

**68** Utz, pp. 115–116.

**69** Eisenstein and Jacob, p. 285; Oaks and Lehman, pp. 99–102.

**70** Jones, p. 200.

**71** Milton Heumann and Colin Loftin, "Mandatory Sentencing and the Abolition of Plea Bargaining: The Michigan Felony Firearm Statute," *Law and Society Review*, 13 (Winter 1979), 393–430; and Henry R. Glick, "Mandatory Sentencing: The Politics of the New Criminal Justice," *Federal Probation*, 43 (March 1979), 3–9.

**72** Eisenstein and Jacob, p. 309.

# 7

# TRIALS AND APPEALS

As we have seen in previous chapters, nearly all civil and criminal cases are negotiated and settled informally and privately. There are few trials and opportunities to appeal to higher courts. In settlements requiring official judicial approval, such as criminal plea bargains and divorces, judges also usually rely on informal settlements reached earlier by others as the basis for a court's official action.

Despite their small number, trials and appeals are the most visible parts of the judicial process. Many of them, however, involve routine disputes and occur only because opposing sides would not reach a settlement. The few cases we usually see in the news are a much smaller percentage of the total that go to court. They involve controversial social and political issues, lots of money, powerful individuals and groups, or terrible crime. They are especially dramatic and fascinating as testimony and evidence unfold in a long trial or as attorneys argue fundamental points of law and policy before supreme courts.

## SIGNIFICANCE OF TRIALS AND APPEALS

Trials and appeals are more significant, however, than as spectacles or for stimulating news stories. For litigants who do not negotiate settlements, trials and appeals are a *final and authoritative way to settle conflicts*. Certain kinds of disputes, such as neighborhood and family fights, continue regardless of the techniques used to stop them, but for many litigants, trials and appeals mark the final episode in conflict. Win, lose, or draw, the disputes are finally ended.

Trials and appeals also are opportunities for judges to affect society and the lives of many people. Trials and appeals are full-scale judicial hearings. They provide the widest opportunities to air and consider conflicting viewpoints, contrary evidence, thorny social issues, and procedural rights. Judges have an opportunity to state their views on the law and to *define social policy*. Some decisions are widely reported and influence the behavior of others besides the immediate litigants in the case. In contrast, cases that are negotiated or bargained usually are forgotten among the stacks of official records filed in courthouses across the nation.

Besides providing the setting for judicial policymaking, trials and appeals attract attention because they are almost sacred symbols *of law and justice* in the United States. The legal culture is most apparent in the conduct of trials and appeals. The first ten amendments to the Constitution include provisions designed to ensure a fair judicial process for persons accused of crime. The right to a trial by jury, the right to remain silent (not to be forced to testify against yourself), the right to confront opposing witnesses, the right to legal assistance, and other protections are the basic parts of American criminal justice. The Bill of Rights also includes a provision calling for due process of law, which was designed to protect citizens from arbitrary and unregulated judicial and other government power.

Americans rely on constitutional and other legal rights when dealing with officials at all levels and departments of government, but judicial trials and appeals are at center stage in focusing our attention on legal and constitutional issues. They explicity reflect our national concern with *fair and proper procedure, equality before the law, and impartiality*. Unlike negotiated and bargained settlements, where there are few controls on how decisions are reached, trials and appeals are public forums in which proper procedure is very important.

This chapter examines the structure and operation of trials and appeals. It includes a discussion of the major procedures as well as the behavior of lawyers, judges, and juries in courtrooms. This chapter concentrates on what goes on in court. How judges make decisions and the impact of court rulings are discussed more fully in later chapters.

## TRIALS

A trial is a fact-gathering forum governed by rules on how information is presented and the kinds of facts that can be used to support the claims made by each side. A trial requires the plaintiff to prove a claim against the defendant, meaning guilt in a criminal case or liability in a civil dispute. In plea bargaining and civil negotiation, the people involved usually assume that defendants are guilty or have done something that they have to pay for, but when a case goes to trial, legal procedure requires that defendants be presumed innocent until proven guilty or found liable.

### Jury and Bench Trials

**Right to a Jury**  The Constitution guarantees the right to a jury trial in criminal and civil cases (Sixth and Seventh Amendments). However, the right to a jury generally has *not* meant an absolute or unlimited right to a trial by jury.

The Supreme Court has stated that adult criminal defendants are entitled to a jury trial if their imprisonment might exceed six months (*Baldwin v. New York*, 1970). Juvenile defendants are not automatically entitled to a jury. The states and the federal government also have limited use of juries to certain sets of civil disputes. Generally, if money damages are sought in a civil case, either the plaintiff or the defendant may request a jury.

Juries are honored and revered for several reasons. Juries have been part of western judicial tradition for hundreds of years. Juries once were the witnesses at a trial and did not render verdicts, but with the signing of the Magna Carta in England in 1215, juries became trial decision makers. A trial by a jury of one's peers was a part of early English political liberty and the basis for American practice since the Colonial period.[1]

Juries are especially important because they tie the legal culture and the popular political culture together. When judges make all judicial decisions, all judicial authority is in the hands of government, but a jury of local citizens offsets judicial authority by permitting the people to make decisions themselves. When juries were new, citizen participation was seen as an important safeguard or check against arbitrary executive or judicial power. It still does that today, but it also may encourage general respect and support for courts, since decisions are made by fellow citizens.

**Bench Trials**    Since juries are not guaranteed for all cases, many trials take place before judges alone. Trials of criminal misdemeanors, where fines and probation or short jail terms are typical, and certain civil cases, such as small financial claims, divorce, and landlord-tenant and various other disputes, are decided by judges.

These trials usually require only a few minutes or occasionally a few hours, and there are few or no witnesses and little mystery about the outcome. Lawyers and litigants either gather before the judge's raised bench and quickly present their case or they all sit around a table in the judge's office or in a conference room. Cases still proceed according to standard legal procedure, but since there are no juries or spectators, the setting is somewhat more relaxed and casual. Sometimes defendants in serious criminal cases also waive or give up their right to a jury, hoping for greater leniency from a judge, but jury trials in felony cases are more common. Box 7.1, "The Three-Minute Divorce," illustrates how routine "trials" can be.

As mentioned in Chapter 6, a few cities use bench trials as *slow pleas of guilty* in criminal cases. In these cases, defendants do not plead guilty immediately following negotiations between prosecutors and defense lawyers, but are found guilty by a judge after a quick trial.[2] Slow plea trials are based largely on the written record of the preliminary hearing. Like other forms of plea bargaining, guilt is assumed and the trial focuses almost exclusively on the defendant's personal characteristics or other circumstances that defendants hope will reduce the sentence.

---

**BOX 7.1**

THE THREE MINUTE DIVORCE

At 7:45 a.m., Laura and her best friend, Mary, met Laura's lawyer outside of his office, a few blocks from the county courthouse. They were on their way to get a judge's signature on a document prepared by Laura's lawyer granting an uncontested divorce. (Laura's husband had agreed to a division of their few belongings several weeks earlier.) Mary was needed to testify that Laura had lived in the county for at least six months. While they walked, the lawyer explained that they would sit before the judge's desk and answer a few routine questions about names and dates.

The lawyer added, "Now, don't laugh when the judge says, 'Is there anything other than waving a magic wand that I can do to save this marriage?' The right answer is no.

Then he will say, 'Well, you know better than I because you have lived it.' Next, he'll sign the order I have prepared granting the divorce."

They arrived on the fourth floor to find that there already were three other people waiting before them. Laura's lawyer impatiently paced up and down the dimly lit hall. "What's taking these people so long?" he exclaimed. "I can do these things in three minutes. They've been in there ten already!"

When it was their turn before the judge and Laura and Mary had answered the questions, the judge said, "Is there anything other than waving a magic wand that I can do to save this marriage?" Laura laughed and said no. Then the judge said, "Well, you know better than I because you have lived it." Then he signed the paper and the divorce was granted.

The entire procedure took three minutes.

---

Short trials appear to benefit defendants in several ways. First, they do not have to be convinced to plead guilty and the formal trial preserves their right to an appeal. Most important, however, they also receive the benefits of a negotiated guilty plea. One defense lawyer explained the benefits this way:

> I want [trials] to be short and fast; I try to get my clients in and out with as little said as possible. Most of my clients are guilty and the more the judge hears about them the worse it is for them. If you move your case in and out quickly, it looks "unimportant" to him and it does not appear to merit an "important" [i.e., severe] sentence.[3]

Slow pleas are short, cooperative trials with the judge having most influence in determining the anticipated lenient sentence.

In contrast, jury trials are much more formal and involve the complete inventory of legal procedure. Jury trials emphasize proving criminal guilt or civil liability. The opposing lawyers act like true adversaries and try their best to convince the jury of their version of the facts and surrounding circumstances. In a jury trial, the judge referees to keep both sides playing by the rules, but juries determine who wins and loses. They also usually state the financial compensation that should be paid to the plaintiff in a civil case, and they may have an opportunity to recommend criminal sentences, as in cases requiring the death penalty or life imprisonment.

**Presiding Judge**   The role of a judge during a trial is very important. Besides often deciding who wins and loses, judges interpret rules of evidence and testimony and make decisions about which information may legitimately be considered during the presentation of a case. Examples of important rulings that may shape the outcome of a case are: ordering the lawyers and witnesses in a notorious rape case not to talk to the mass media in order to preserve a fair trial; allowing the racist comments made by police about blacks to be admitted as evidence in a police brutality case as an indication of motive; or ordering the President of the United States to give testimony via videotape in the Iran-Contra case. As will be discussed shortly, judges also instruct juries on how to consider the evidence in reaching their verdicts. Judges are not mere figure-heads; they play an important and active role in governing the trial.

Most judges recognize their supervisory role in trials as an important part of their job, and many relish their leadership opportunities. Their feelings are described well by judges who say:

> I really enjoy conducting hearings and trials. I guess that is when I feel most like a judge. You know, when you get the contest between people with competing view-points and very different interests, when you have to be awake and on top of things to make sure that everyone plays by the rules and everyone gets a fair deal. . . .
>
> The judge is in control. It is up to him to run the show both in the courtroom and out. I am not sure that I always do it well, but I always try to make sure things do not get out of hand. The judge must make sure that whatever happens happens according to the rules.[4]

Judges, lawyers, and juries occupy separate territory in the courtroom. The judge is the central figure. He or she sits behind a raised desk (the bench) in the front and center. In most courtrooms, judges wear black robes to distinguish their superior status. Lawyers sit at separate tables placed next to each other just in front of a railing that separates courtroom spectators from the main participants. They face the judge. Criminal defendants and litigants in civil cases sit beside their lawyers. Juries also are seated at the front of the court-room, but in a separate boxed compartment to the side. Juries only listen to the presentation of the case. They may not ask questions, nor may they take notes in most courts as the trial proceeds. They usually appear as impassive as the spectators behind the rail.

### Selection of Juries

Except in bench trials, jury selection marks the beginning of a trial. Although juries symbolize the public in court, they are not supposed to translate local values or beliefs into judicial decisions. Jurors are not like legislators, who often think of themselves as representatives of the will of the people. Instead, jurors are amateur judges called on to determine the facts and to make a fair and objective decision consistent with the facts.

**Who Sits?**   If juries performed according to these ideals, there would be very little controversy over how juries were selected and the way they go about reaching verdicts. Any group of citizens could be expected to judge a case in the same way. But like others in the judicial process, juries have considerable discretion. Also, there often are many conflicting facts and unclear laws in a case and a jury has to do the best it can in a sometimes confusing but critical situation.

The issue of who sits on a jury is extremely important to litigants and lawyers and to others who are interested in how juries perform their job. Ideally, juries are to be selected in ways that assure a fair and equal representation of all adults living in the local area. Getting a jury of one's peers does not mean that only people similar to the defendant may serve. Rather, it means there should be no systematic bias that overselects certain groups or excludes others from jury duty. The drive for broadly representative juries emphasizes equality of opportunity to participate in government. Every citizen, no matter how high or humble, should have an equal chance to serve on a jury as part of his or her right to participate in public affairs. Serving on a jury is part of American democracy.

The search for broadly representative juries also has a practical side. It assumes that everyone's attitudes and decisions are shaped by who they are and the kinds of experiences they have had. For example, women, blacks, the young, and the poor are expected to have views that are different from men, whites, and older or more affluent citizens. Often, hunches about an individual's attitudes are incorrect, but assumptions that social background affects attitudes shape jury selection.

This belief also quietly assumes that it is impossible to find a truly impartial jury. A juror who comes to court with certain attitudes will look at a case in a certain way even if there has not been a lot of pretrial publicity. Therefore, getting a jury that reflects the views of society requires selecting people with many different social characteristics. The link between personal attributes and attitudes also implies that certain types of jurors will be more favorable to one or the other side in a case. This practical consideration is crucial to lawyers and their clients.

**Biased Selection Procedures**  Jury selection procedures usually guarantee that juries will *not* be broadly representative of the local population. Some bias creeps in as a result of the methods used to choose from the large pool of potential jurors.

Jurors usually are selected from local voter registration lists, and the federal district courts are required to use the voter lists. This is the most convenient and plentiful source of names readily available to the courts. Although it is convenient, it is not very representative of the population, since certain groups of people are much more likely than others to register to vote.

Voter registration procedures and requirements vary considerably in the fifty states, and they have an impact on overall voter registration. For example, where residence requirements are longer and the office hours of the registrar of voters are shorter, fewer people register to vote and they are excluded from the jury pool.

Jury selection based on voter registration lists generally produces a disproportionate number of middle-aged, educated, and employed men as jurors.
Owners of businesses, professional people, and other higher-status individuals
are overrepresented. In contrast, women, blacks, the poor, the unemployed,
and young people are least likely to register to vote and are not represented
equally for jury duty.[5] Some judicial districts use other lists of names for jury
service, such as the property tax rolls, but these also bias jury pools in favor of
the better-educated, middle-class individuals who own homes or other real
estate.

Recognizing the limitations of these lists, some counties have broadened the
base for jury selection by using lists of city utility customers or the telephone
directory. These lists include many more people than voter registration lists or
the property tax rolls.

Certain occupational groups are legally excluded from jury duty in some
states. Doctors, nurses, teachers, and various others are dismissed because
their services are needed more critically elsewhere in the community. Lawyers, police officers, and other court employees frequently are not permitted on
juries because they possibly have attitudes that could bias them in some way.
Other individuals who have pressing personal needs or who cannot afford to
take off from work or leave small children to serve on a jury may be excused by
asking the judge presiding over jury selection to dismiss them. Most requests
are routinely honored.

**Lawyers' Tactics**   Additional bias in jury selection occurs through the tactics that lawyers use to get a jury favorable to their side. After the jury pool has
been selected, the lawyers have additional opportunities to screen each potential juror to determine his or her suitability for jury duty in a particular case.

Both opposing lawyers usually ask questions about jurors' occupations,
education, or other background, their familiarity with the case, knowledge of
the litigants, or relationship to court employees or police. These initial questions are designed to discover if individual jurors might have attitudes that
could prevent them from having an open mind about the case or from being able
to judge the litigants and the facts fairly.

*Cause*   An attorney who believes a juror should be disqualified asks the
judge's approval to challenge the juror for cause. The judge must be convinced
that the juror is incapable of performing as an impartial decision maker. In
highly publicized cases, it may be very difficult to find a juror who is unfamiliar
with the case or who has not already formed an opinion about the guilt of the
defendant. Inability to select a jury in a few days may lead a judge to grant a
defense request to move the trial to another city (*change of venue*) where a
more neutral jury might be selected.

A special situation in which judges themselves remove jurors for cause is in
capital (mainly murder) cases where the death penalty can be imposed. Long-
standing judicial policy, confirmed by the Supreme Court, permits judges to
remove jurors who are so opposed to the death penalty that they could not vote

for it if the defendant were found guilty. Opponents to this policy argued that removing anti-death penalty jurors heavily loads the jury with conviction-minded people, but the Supreme Court rejected this position and added that the requirement for representative juries extends only to including a cross section of population groups—men, women, whites, blacks, Mexican-Americans, etc.—not a cross section of political or social attitudes (*Lockhart v. McCree*, 1986).

*Peremptory Challenges*   In most routine cases, few jurors are dismissed for cause. Most are removed as a result of peremptory challenges, which do not have to be supported by reasons or approved by the judge. Each side has a certain number of these challenges, usually depending on the seriousness of the case. In criminal cases, for example, the more serious the charge, the larger number of challenges that are given to the prosecutor and defense lawyer. In theory, providing peremptory challenges is a way of giving each side ample opportunity to select a jury that is free from bias or that could be attacked later as stacked against one side or the other.

*Hunches*   Most jurors are selected according to the personal insight or guesses of the attorneys in the case. Since they usually have very little advance information about jurors, they use pseudosociology or psychology based on their own experience or stories told by other attorneys over the years. They may react to the way a potential juror looks at the defendant, or the way he or she answers questions, or some other clue.

Several defense lawyers have given the following reasons for dismissing a juror:

> He gave his last name first, sounded as if he were in the Army and liked it; looked mean and grim; foreign born, looked afraid, easily intimidated; catered to the judge in response to questions; German extraction, too bossy.[6]
>
> If a juror's feet are crossed, he is not accepting what you say. . . . The juror with poor posture is thinking off balance. . . .[7]

Plaintiffs' lawyers in civil cases are said to believe the following:

> Athletes lack sympathy for fragile, injured plantiffs; accountants and "engineering types" are insensitive to emotional factors; cabbies are good plaintiff jurors unless the injured party is a pedestrian.[8]

Prosecutors rejected jurors because:

> Worked in criminal law in college; a drifter, no community ties; not married; membership in a large number of liberal organizations reflects prejudice against government; juror appeared too anxious to serve.[9]

Certain occupational or social groups often are suspected of being favorable to one side or the other. In a murder case, for example, a college professor who teaches social science courses is very likely to be rejected by the prosecutor, who assumes the professor is biased against the criminal justice system or the death penalty. The prosecutor may be wrong, but does not want to take the chance.

Some convicted black defendants have appealed their sentences, claiming that prosecutors have used peremptory challenges to systematically remove blacks from the jury in their case and that this constitutes racial discrimination. In the past, proving racial bias in jury selection required defendants to show that prosecutors had removed blacks repeatedly in case after case, but the Supreme Court has changed this policy, ruling that if blacks are systematically removed in any individual case, it creates sufficient grounds to appeal the conviction. Now, if prosecutors use their challenges to strike blacks from a jury, they must explain their challenge in court and it must be on some basis other than a supposed link between the race of the juror and their possible bias toward the defendant (*Batson v. Kentucky*, 1986 and *Powers v. Ohio*, 1991).

**Scientific Selection**    Since the 1970s, jury selection has taken a new scientific turn in a few highly publicized criminal trials involving political notables. Rather than relying on personal hunch, attorneys have employed social scientists or public relations firms to try to determine before the trial the kinds of people who would be likely to favor the defense.

This requires conducting surveys with hundreds of local residents to identify groups of people who hold particular social and political beliefs. Interviewers usually obtain background information for each person regarding his or her occupation, religion, income, etc., and his or her outlook on major public issues and political and social activities. This will be used to create a profile of different segments of the local population.

During the actual jury selection, defense attorneys will try to select those types of people who have been identified in advance as most sympathetic to their side. They also will challenge those who have been identified as hostile to the defense. Another approach is for lawyers to select mock juries before the trial to try out their arguments and refine their technique in order to make the most effective presentation in court.

Many different kinds of defendants have benefitted from scientific jury selection, including Vietnam war protestors accused of destroying draft registration records, defendants accused as masterminding the coverup of the Watergate burglary during the Nixon years, the publisher of *Hustler* magazine accused of pornography, and even large corporations in commercial cases. The FBI also has used the technique in important federal trials.[10] In the several dozen cases in which scientific jury selection has been used, litigants win more often than they lose. Box 7.2, "Scientific Jury Selection," describes the new legal industry which has developed to guide litigants through a trial.[11]

*Fairness*    Scientific jury selection may help a litigant, but it also conflicts with legal ideals. In theory, jury selection is supposed to produce an unbiased jury that considers a defendant innocent until proven guilty. It is not supposed to wire or stack a jury in advance of the trial.

But jury stacking is not new. Scientific pollsters have added new sophistication and exposure to the lawyers' art of guessing about the attitudes of jurors. Polling to predict juror decisions also makes it clear that *no lawyer or litigant*

---

**BOX 7.2**

SCIENTIFIC JURY SELECTION

Jay Schulman is a maverick sociologist credited with being the founder of scientific jury selection. He began this work for Vietnam war protestors after being dismissed from a college teaching job for supporting black and Puerto Rican students demonstrating for admissions changes.

He has advised prison inmates, radical war protestors, battered women, and other defendants. However, he occasionally works for corporations and wealthy individuals so that he can donate his time or work for a reduced rate for social underdogs who have little money. In a change from his normal work, he recently volunteered to assist the prosecution in the Howard Beach murder case, in which several whites were accused of killing a black man.

Schulman specializes in identifying jurors who are likely to be dominant in jury proceedings and to decide whether that person will be sympathetic to his side in the case. He claims the "authority factor" proves effective more often than not.

Litigation Sciences, Inc., claims to be the nation's largest legal consulting firm. It employs more than 100 psychologists, sociologists, marketers, graphic artists, and technicians. An estimated 300 smaller companies offer similar services.

The firm provides pretrial polls, creates profiles of "ideal" jurors, holds mock trials, selects "shadow" juries, coaches lawyers and witnesses, and designs courtroom graphics. (Shadow jurors have personal characteristics similar to the real jury. They sit in on the trial and provide feedback to the attorney.)

LSI represents mainly corporations in personal injury cases, and it concentrates on finding jurors who believe that victims get what they deserve. These potential jurors also usually have negative views of the physically handicapped, the poor, blacks, and women. Others claim to have found that people likely to vote for acquittal in a typical rape case believe . . . "when women go around braless or wearing short skirts and tight tops, they are just asking for trouble. . . ."

In addition to finding jurors sympathetic to their clients, LSI develops strategies and visual aids which lawyers can use to shift responsibility for an accident from the corporation to the injured plaintiff.

LSI claims it loses only one in twenty cases.

---

*really wants a truly impartial jury*, even if one could be found. Both sides want to win and one way is to try to get the right people to decide the case. It is not much different from considering a bench trial on the basis of the sentencing record of local judges.

However, scientific jury selection is not available to everyone. Interviewing a cross section of the local population is very expensive and can be done only for very rich clients or for those who can enlist a score of sympathetic volunteers. Most criminal defendants do not fall into either category. It strikes some people as unfair that some defendants can obtain an edge at trial that is not available to others or that generally is not available to the prosecution.

However, others downplay the importance of scientific jury selection in most cases where the facts are simple and not seriously in doubt, and where there is little reason to be concerned about bias because a litigant's political attitudes or actions rarely come up or are relevant in most trials. Others doubt its importance because the opposition will use its peremptory challenges to remove jurors who obviously are the ideal type for the other side.[12] The issue is likely to remain controversial as scientific jury selection is used in more cases and liberal critics of the courts worry about jury bias against poor, nonwhite defendants.

### Conduct of Trials

After the jury is seated, the trial gets under way. In most cases, the opposing attorneys begin with an opening statement to the jury in which they briefly summarize their side of the case and outline what they hope to show through the presentation of witnesses and evidence. The opening statement is informal and in lay language. It does not qualify as evidence or as sworn testimony, but only presents an outline of the case from the point of view of the plaintiff or defendant.

**Witnesses and Testimony**  Opening statements are optional to both sides. In place of an opening statement, the lawyers for the plaintiff may begin the trial by calling witnesses, who testify under oath concerning facts that relate to the case. As witnesses are called, the circumstances of the conflict are pieced together. In a criminal case, for example, the first witness might be the police officer who was assigned to investigate the complaint or who made the arrest. The prosecutor usually asks for a description of the events that occurred or were observed or the circumstances that led to the arrest. The police officer's testimony is designed to establish that a crime has taken place and to describe other evidence that led to the arrest of the defendant. Police and other criminal investigators also may be asked to identify physical evidence such as weapons, clothing, photographs, etc., which provide concrete physical support for the state's case.

In a similar way, plaintiffs in civil cases may call on witnesses to identify signed documents such as sales agreements, mortgages, contracts for services, etc., which establish a business relationship between the plaintiff and defendant.

In complex civil cases or criminal cases involving reasonable doubt, the plaintiff or prosecutor may present many witnesses to prove the case. Sometimes trials are slow, and even boring and confusing, because witnesses provide only bits and pieces of information that contribute to the overall picture that lawyers try to create. Often, more than one witness is asked to provide the same information in order to make a convincing argument about the essential facts.

To a casual spectator, it may seem easy to establish that the defendant is guilty of a crime, but a lawyer whose case is at stake often wants to be doubly and triply sure to furnish the judge or jury with plenty of reinforcing evidence. In criminal cases, this involves detailed and repeated questioning about times, places, personal identification, physical evidence, and the credentials of expert witnesses.

In civil cases involving complex business transactions, such as business mergers or the sale or leasing of expensive commercial property, sales contracts, leases, letters, and records of telephone calls and personal conversations have to be unraveled and analyzed through the testimony of many people who may be involved in the dispute. Presentation of this kind of information may take hours, days, or weeks, and without attending all sessions of the trial and carefully following the testimony, it often is difficult to see how it all relates to the central issue.

**Cross-Examination**  After prosecution of plaintiff witnesses testify, the defense has an opportunity to ask questions that challenge their statements or cast a different light on what they say. This is cross-examination and satisfies the constitutional requirement that a defendant has the right to confront accusers. When all of these witnesses have been questioned, the defense presents its witnesses and the other side has an opportunity to question them.

The purpose of cross-examination is not necessarily to show that a witness is lying or is hostile, but to suggest ways in which the same information might be interpreted or used in other ways. For example, medical or laboratory experts testifying for the prosecution may state that blood samples, cloth fibers, or dental impressions belonging to the defendant match stains, fragments, or marks found at the scene of the crime and imply that there is little doubt that the defendant and the victim are connected.

But a defense lawyer may try to show that many blood samples could match the same stain or that many pieces of clothing contain the same kinds of fibers and that the methods used to match dental impressions to bite marks are unreliable. Defense lawyers also frequently try to discredit the testimony of victims and eyewitnesses by rigorously questioning them about details of the crime, hoping they will not remember clearly or will become confused. Defense lawyers also may seek trial delays, expecting time to blur recollections. This is reported to occur frequently in cases involving elderly victims. Older victims and witnesses often are physically and psychologically frail and afraid, and they do not withstand the rigors of cross-examination well. They are easily led into contradicting themselves and confusing the facts, and they generally appear unreliable to judges and juries.[13]

When the defense presents its side of the case, it often tries to reinforce doubts that it created during the cross-examination of the opposing witnesses. For example, a defendant in an auto accident case may be able to produce a witness who testifies that the injured plaintiff was speeding when the defendant made an illegal turn, which was the primary cause of the accident. This may reduce the defendant's liability. Of course, the other side will cross-examine to question the witnesses reliability or ability to judge speed.

Criminal defendants in serious dead-bang cases cannot simply deny the state's case. Since there is no doubt that they committed the crime, they try to mitigate their involvement, throw some blame on the victim, or show self-defense, insanity, or other duress.

*Overcoming Hostility*   Most criminal defendants are unpopular people with few chances of an acquittal, so defense lawyers have to be careful how they conduct cross-examination and present their own witnesses. They usually have to overcome a hostile climate in order to win, and aggressive trial tactics may actually make their chances of winning smaller.

A lawyer can alienate a judge, for example, by filing lots of motions, trying to delay the trial, or constantly challenging the relevance and accuracy of testimony and evidence. Such tactics make a trial unusually long and tax the patience of everyone who normally expect a quick verdict. If the defendant loses despite the attorney's theatrics and the judge believes the case was weak or frivolous in the first place, the defendant might suffer the consequences. A judge of an urban trial court explained the situation this way:

> If someone has a trial and it's apparent that there is some question of a good defense . . . then the sentence is probably no harsher than it would have been if he'd entered a plea. It's a delight to have a good trial, handled by a good attorney. He knows what he is doing and comes up with sharp things during the trial. . . . But I think there are times when you see a completely frivolous trial which . . . is a waste of everyone's time. Take the guy who is caught with his hand in the till, and there's no question but that he's guilty. And the case is still tried, and his hands are still in the till, and he hasn't been able to get them out, and you wonder why he's wasted everyone's time.[14]

**Facts and Hearsay**   An important aspect of trials is that only verifiable facts supported by the personal knowledge of witnesses are permitted as evidence in a case. This means that witnesses may testify only concerning what they personally know about the circumstances and the parties to the case. They may not report what they have heard from others or what they believe is true. This kind of information is called hearsay and can be challenged by the opposing side.

Other facts may be considered irrelevant in a trial even though witnesses can testify that they are true. A defendant's prior criminal record, for example, may be factual, but it is irrelevant concerning guilt (but not the sentence) in the current case. A litigant's past unemployment is irrelevant to current ability to pay creditors if he or she now has a steady job.

While this kind of information may be excluded from a trial, it is ironic that virtually any information and beliefs can be considered in bargained or negotiated settlements. For example, a prosecutor's belief that the defendant is a "real bad actor" or perhaps not really into crime, etc., may affect the decision to prosecute or the kind of sentence that will be recommended. But in court, such beliefs and opinions are not allowed.

Sometimes attorneys try to get hearsay or other inadmissable testimony before a jury even though they know that the opposing side will object and that the judge will tell the jury to ignore it and will not permit the statement to go into written transcript of the trial. Once it has been presented, however, it is difficult for the jury to act as if the statement had never been made. The entire episode may even highlight and emphasize the statement in the minds of the jurors.[15]

For example, defense witnesses sometimes are coached in advance by defense attorneys to say that they have heard from other reputable people that the defendant is a solid citizen or has never lost his or her temper, etc. This is hearsay because a witness can only testify to personal knowledge about the defendant. In theory, too many attempts to get improper information in front of a jury can lead a judge to declare a mistrial. The trial stops and the case has to start over again with a different jury. Very few of these occur, however.

*Loaded Questions*   Lawyers also may ask questions in a hypothetical or opinionated manner designed to trap a hostile witness or the opposition in an unattractive or misleading answer. For instance, a parent who sues a former spouse to have child support payments reduced may be characterized through questioning as cheap or lazy. The dialogue goes as follows:

*Lawyer:* Why are you not making as much money as you did last year?

*Parent:* Well, we're in the middle of a recession and business is down. People cannot afford to buy, so there are fewer sales.

*Lawyer:* Maybe you are not trying as hard as before. Is that right?

*Parent:* No, sir.

*Lawyer:* Is everyone affected the same way, or are you simply not working as hard?

*Parent:* Other people are having the same problems.

*Lawyer:* You also have said in your deposition that your child now spends over ten days per month with you and that the amount of your child support ought to be reduced because you support the child at your home. Is that correct?

*Parent:* Yes.

*Lawyer:* We can conclude, then, that you want to be paid for taking care of your own child. Is that correct?

*Parent:* That is not true and you know perfectly well that it is not!

In a case of drug smuggling brought against a county official, the dialogue went as follows:

*Prosecutor:* Isn't it true you just had to sell the office of the board of county commissioners? Isn't it true money got to you, greed got to you, and you just had to have some of that drug smuggling?

*Defendant:* God has been good to me for 39 years. I do not have to smuggle drugs to make a way.

*Prosecutor:* Isn't it true you are a monumental liar?

*Defendant:* No, I am not a monumental liar.[16]

Unless a defendant decides to plead guilty or give up the case on the witness stand, TV style, we should not expect affirmative answers to these questions! They are not designed to get at the truth, but to project an image of the defendant to a judge or jury.

**Closing Statements**   After both sides have presented and cross-examined all the witnesses, each side has a chance to make a closing statement and to sum up the case for the judge or jury. Each side will refer to testimony and evidence that best supports its position and will try to cast further doubt on the opposition.

In criminal cases, prosecutors usually argue that the state has made a clear case against the defendant and that the jury ought to bring in a verdict of guilty. The defense will remind the jury that a defendant is entitled to be considered innocent unless proven guilty and that there is reasonable doubt about the state's case. If the evidence does not look good for the defendant, a lawyer might try to mitigate the crime by arguing that the victim was partly responsible for the crime or is a person of low morals, or that the case should not even have been prosecuted at all because the circumstances are so cloudy.

Closing statements in civil cases follow similar lines. The plaintiff summarizes in a way that shows that the defendant is liable and that the plaintiff has suffered significant losses and should be compensated. In accident cases, lawyers emphasize physical injuries, disabilities, and financial losses and appeal to empathy for the injured plaintiff. A defense lawyer has to respond to jury sympathy, but also may claim that the plaintiff is partly responsible for the accident or other loss that has occurred, or that the compensation claimed is too high.

In American folklore, the closing statement or summation is a time for orators to harangue the jury with appeals to emotion, loyalties, and sympathy. Anything that could not be presented strictly as evidence and fact is brought out now by the opposing lawyers in a final effort to swing the jury their way.

Sometimes the summation is pictured as the high point in a trial, with lawyers appealing to higher values and morals. Images of country lawyer Abraham Lincoln winning an acquittal for an innocent but unpopular defendant are part of American lore. The summation cannot be a lawyers' free-for-all, however, for legal rules of procedure forbid statements that are clearly biased against a criminal defendant. Prosecutors who use racial, ethnic, or political slurs, for example, face the possibility of having a conviction overturned on appeal.

**Jury Instructions**   Following the closing statements by both sides, the judge will charge or instruct the jury, explaining the rules of law that govern the case and the conditions under which the jury can find a defendant guilty or assess financial responsibility against the defendant in a civil case. Often there are several different degrees of guilt or guilt to different charges that a jury could select, or there are various amounts of money that a jury can award to a plaintiff to compensate for physical injuries or other losses. A judge will explain the kind of evidence needed to convict a defendant of certain crimes. In some cases, such as a slander suit against a newspaper, a jury also can award damages to punish the defendant for its behavior against the plaintiff (*punitive damages*).

A judge's instructions to the jury are very important in a trial, because their purpose is to influence the way that a jury looks at the evidence and how it fits the law and the facts together. Jury instructions are important also because they are among the possible points on which an appeal may be based. Incorrect instructions or statements that seem to bias the jury may provide an opportunity to challenge the verdict.

Court reformers have been critical of jury instructions which usually are presented in legalese that most jurors cannot easily understand. They urge judges to translate their instructions into everyday English so that jurors will be able to use them more effectively in their deliberations. Research on mock juries has demonstrated that jurors understand and retain more of a judge's instructions if they are presented in lay language.[17]

### Jury Decisions

After both sides have presented all their witnesses and have summarized their arguments and the judge has instructed the jury, it is up to the jury to render a verdict. (In bench trials judges render verdicts, sometimes immediately after the testimony or later if they need more time to consider the issues.)

**Popular Justice**   Juries are called on to determine the facts and to reach a verdict that is consistent with them. But juries sometimes pay more attention to certain facts and ignore others. They also often view criminal and civil conflicts as social as well as legal disputes. Their decisions fit their sense of justice as well as their determination of the facts and the requirements of law.

For example, juries sometimes are sympathetic to criminal defendants who are injured more than their intended victims and acquit them or find them guilty of less serious charges. Juries sometimes do not punish black defendants who have attacked black victims, believing that the morals and culture of lower-class blacks condone violence and aggression.[18]

There is substantial evidence that juries often produce such popular justice decisions. A criminal conviction or acquittal, where overwhelming evidence points to the opposite conclusion, or especially high compensation for an injured worker or other accident victim, reveals that jurors often are sympathetic or hostile to a particular party in a case.

Examples include the acquittal of a Florida man who fatally shot his father for continuing to molest a 13-year-old relative. The father, a career criminal, earlier had stood trial for sexually abusing the same girl, but had been acquitted. A California jury acquitted radical anti-abortion protestors of illegally blocking women's health clinics despite instructions from the judge that their defense (laws can be broken to prevent greater harm) had no legal standing. Finally, in Detroit, two neighbors who admitted in court that they burned down a crack house near their homes were acquitted of arson.[19]

Occasionally, jury decisions that seem to defy or nullify the law and the evidence have widespread and dire social consequences. Examples concern the acquittals of white police officers accused of beating or using excessive force toward black motorists. In 1979, black insurance salesman Arthur McDuffie died from a severe police beating with nightsticks and flashlights after failing to stop his motorcycle when signaled by a patrol car. The police tried to cover up the crime by claiming McDuffie was injured when his motorcycle crashed into a curb. Five police officers were tried for second degree murder but were acquitted by an all-male, all-white jury. Riots immediately erupted in Miami's black neighborhoods, two whites were killed, and property damage exceeded $100 million

In similar circumstances in 1992, four Los Angeles police officers were tried for assault for using excessive force by continually clubbing and kicking Rodney King after he was stopped by the police after a high-speed chase. In this incident, a local resident captured the beating on videotape, which was played repeatedly over national television and at the trial. The trial had been moved from Los Angeles to a nearby community in hope of finding an impartial jury. As in Miami, a jury with no blacks on it acquitted the police and rioting followed, causing the deaths of nearly 60 people and property damage close to $600 million. Thousands of armed military troops and police patrolled the city for several days. It ranks as one of the worst riots in American history, and the verdict and the riot are viewed by many as symbolic of deep racial and economic divisions in the United States.

Sometimes, consistent patterns of jury decision making occur, for example, when a particular criminal law is considered so unfair that many juries repeatedly acquit defendants charged with a particular crime. During the 1920 Prohibition era, for example, juries often refused to convict bootleggers of producing and selling illegal liquor.[20]

Popular justice decisions can be seen in a study of several thousand jury verdicts and questionnaires from judges who presided in the cases. The research shows that judges and juries disagreed in about 25 percent of criminal cases. Most of the disagreement occurred in cases in which the jury voted not guilty and judges said they would have convicted the defendant if they had been deciding the case in a bench trial.

In about half the cases where the judge and jury disagreed, judges believed they differed on the strength of the evidence against the defendant, but in about 30 percent of the cases the jury apparently ignored the law because they felt it was unfair. In about 10 percent of the cases, the jury either was very sympathetic or hostile to the defendant.[21]

Two main conclusions can be drawn from these results. Juries tend to acquit criminal defendants more often than judges, and the apparent reasons for disagreement reflect the jurors' own sense of justice and their attitudes toward the formal law or the parties in the case.

**Complex Decisions** Trial decision making is not an easy task. In many cases, juries must decide guilt to several entirely different criminal charges, such as assault and robbery, or must determine the degree of guilt in a particular kind of crime, such as first- or second-degree murder or manslaughter. In civil cases involving complex business decisions such as corporate mergers, contracts, patents, or compliance with government regulations, juries may be asked to decide a number of extremely complex and unfamiliar issues.

Judges' instructions also usually are expressed in legal language that few jurors fully comprehend. Some trials also last for weeks or months, and there is a great deal of evidence and testimony to remember and consider. Since jurors often are not permitted to take notes or to ask questions while the trial progresses, they have to do the best they can with what they are able to recall and understand. Jurors may deliver written questions to the judge during their deliberations and can ask to have certain testimony read to them, but keeping track of everything brought out during a trial is a huge job.

*Lay Justice*   Juries generally translate legal issues, evidence, and a judge's instructions into terms and meanings that are more relevant to their own experiences and personal values.[22] This does not mean that they are foolish or prejudiced. It means they are unfamiliar with vague laws and legal phrases and are unable to fully digest all the trial material. In order to comprehend everything that is presented to them, they have to deal with it in terms that they can understand and fit into their own sense of right and wrong. They make decisions according to the methods people use in ordinary personal conflicts.

In civil cases, jurors may talk about the amount requested by the plaintiff and decide whether it is too high or about right, or about their personal feelings about the injuries the plaintiff has suffered. They may come up with a figure that is a compromise for all of the jurors.[23] In criminal cases, jurors react to the defendant, the victim, and the crime, not just to whether the facts support a conclusion that a particular crime was committed.

Box 7.3, "Jurors Compromise," reveals the influence of personal differences and social interactions which are important in reaching verdicts.[24]

*Limit Juries?*   The tendency of juries to follow their hearts, as well as the law and the evidence, leads some judicial reformers to favor reducing the use of juries.[25] But juries have much in common with other judicial decision makers. Judges, prosecutors, and defense lawyers also are affected by their own personal evaluations of cases. In plea bargains and negotiated civil cases, they informally evaluate what a crime or an injury is worth and what the penalties or awards should be. These decisions often are reached very quickly and are based on personal experience and attitudes. In most cases, jury decisions are not much different from the negotiations and rough justice meted out by the courthouse regulars.

A related complaint is that juries do not have the competence and knowledge to decide complex commercial cases. They know nothing about contracts, mergers, insurance, etc., and should not be permitted to decide these kinds of cases. Decisions should be made by judges alone.

Years of judicial experience may give judges an edge, since they probably preside over some similar cases. But new issues constantly arise, and it is unclear how judges' experience or skills in running a trial or the knowledge

---

**BOX 7.3**

JURORS COMPROMISE

The 14-year-old boy was paralyzed after diving into shallow water from a rope swing at a summer camp sponsored by the state Division of Forestry. His lawyer contended that the state was at fault for allowing such a dangerous activity, but the state countered that hundreds of children used the swing safely and that counselors told the boys not to let go until they were over deep water.

The judge instructed the jury to makes its decision on the evidence, but to the jury there was no indication how much sense a young teenager should have. Using state rules of comparative negligence, the jury decided that the youngster was 65 percent at fault while the state was 35 percent responsible. It was a compromise among jurors who favored 90-10 in favor of the state and others who wanted 70-30 in favor of the injured boy.

Jurors also could not agree on what a broken body was worth. Everyone agreed that he should be compensated for "pain and suffering" and missing the joys of life, but the law did not set specific amounts. One juror said $100,000 was too low; another argued $200,000 was too much. They compromised at $150,000. They awarded additional money after squabbling over the costs and responsibilities of taking care of a paralyzed family member. One juror said a mother should do it without pay, but admitted that she would not want to give up her career to feed, bathe, dress, and care for a totally dependent family member. She went along with the majority.

After eight days, the jury convicted Joel Steinberg of first degree manslaughter in the beating death of his 6-year-old daughter. The possible charges ranged from more serious second-degree murder to less serious second-degree manslaughter.

One juror believed the case was clear and that the jury would reach its verdict in a day, and he was shocked to find the jury divided into three groups: one believed Steinberg's long-term companion had killed the child and that he was only partly to blame; another believed Steinberg was guilty of murder; and the third was in the middle.

Steinberg had been using cocaine for days, and some jurors believed he should not be held fully responsible. But others argued that Steinberg repeatedly had battered the child and his companion and that he should be held fully accountable. Cocaine was no excuse. The jury seemed deadlocked.

The standoff was eased by a juror who suggested they change their seats at the table. She had learned in a communications course that people in conflict often sit opposite one another, and she noticed that the jury foreman, who refused to budge, was sitting directly opposite the other unyielding member. When the jury foreman switched chairs and allowed others to lead the discussion, the jury relaxed and quickly compromised on first-degree manslaughter.

---

they learned prior to becoming judges is relevant for most decisions they have to make. They would have to be jacks-of-all-trades to decide many cases, and personal values affect judges and juries alike.

Criticism of juries usually contrasts the realities of jury behavior with an abstract ideal of how trial decisions ought to be made. Compared with that ideal, juries are deficient. However, compared with the real world of how judges and lawyers actually operate in trials and in civil negotiation and plea bargaining, juries appear to be about as well qualified to render verdicts. In addition, juries are a long and revered part of American legal and political tradition, and it is unlikely their role will be substantially lessened for the sake of judicial professionalism.

## Sentences and Orders

After the jury decides guilt or innocence in a criminal case or liability in a civil case, it announces its verdict or decision. In criminal cases, the verdict may be guilty or not guilty to one or several criminal charges. In civil cases, the jury may find the defendant liable or not for injury or damages to the plaintiff and may set a dollar amount for compensation. In bench trials, judges announce their own verdicts. Defendants are brought before judges who publicly announce their sentence. If jail terms are required, defendants are turned over to sheriffs and state prison officials.

Decisions in civil cases usually are contained in written statements (*orders*) that judges deliver to the opposing lawyers in the case. Court orders briefly summarize the decision in the case and state what the two sides should do, such as how family property in a divorce should be divided, or how much money the defendant should pay to the plaintiff. If the defendant wins, judges state that there is no remedy or other action required by the decision. Orders also usually specify whether each side is to pay its own attorney's fees and other expenses or if one of the parties shall pay all the costs. Courts depend upon the parties to the case to make the necessary arrangements to carry out judges' orders.

## Issues in the Trial Courts

A number of current issues involving the trial courts are being debated by legal reformers and various interest groups. They concern substantially different features of a trial. Two issues that have been prominent in recent years are the size of juries and televised trials.

**Jury Size**   There are two related issues concerning the size of juries. The first is the number of people required for a jury and the second is whether a jury is required to reach its verdicts through a unanimous or less than unanimous vote.

Most people are familiar with the twelve-person jury and the need for unanimity in reaching decisions. The image of the lone holdout causing a jury to deadlock in an important case is part of the lore of the judicial process. But in reality, the size of juries in criminal and civil cases varies around the country. Many states have used six-person juries for years, and some have enacted state laws permitting a jury to decide a case by a certain size majority. Twelve-person juries are still required in federal criminal cases, but six-person juries are used in civil cases.

The reason given for small juries and nonunaminous verdicts is to save time and money, which appeals to judicial reformers looking for more efficient trial courts. Nonunanimous verdicts also would prevent a hung jury caused by one vote, which creates the need for a new trial.

Beginning in 1970, the U.S. Supreme Court has made a series of decisions permitting six-person juries as well as majority rule in twelve-person juries.

The Court has required, however, that decisions of six-person juries be unanimous. Juries composed of less than six people have been ruled to be too small to provide a defendant with a fair trial.[26]

*Wrong Verdict*  There has been a good deal of debate over whether small juries and nonunanimous decisions are competent to give a defendant a fair trial. Opponents of the changes believe that in small juries or those governed by majority rule, jurors interact less, remember and consider less information, ignore various points of view, and are too hasty in reaching a verdict.[27] Supporters have countered that there are few differences in the deliberations of six- and twelve-person juries and that a large majority such as 10 out of 12, approved by the Supreme Court, is enough to make a decision. Considerable time and money also can be saved by smaller juries.

There is reason to be concerned about the justice of nonunanimous juries. One extensive experiment divided over 1000 jurors chosen from a regular jury pool into dozens of mock juries governed either by a unanimous or nonunanimous decision rule. Each jury was shown an identical, carefully constructed criminal case. Several dozen lawyers and judges who viewed the case all agreed that second-degree murder was the correct verdict.

Over half of the juries turned in verdicts of second-degree murder, another 30 percent decided in favor of manslaughter, and 6 percent was for acquittal. However, 10 percent decided the verdict should be first-degree murder. *All these decisions were produced by nonunanimous juries. Unanimous juries never produced a first-degree murder verdict.*

Compared with those in unanimous juries, jurors in the nonunanimous panels rated their group's deliberations as less thorough and less serious, and the group less likely to work hard toward agreement on the verdict. They also rated their fellow jurors as less open-minded. It seems that the nonunanimous juries were more likely than the unanimous ones to begin with a vote rather than discussion of the evidence and the law and, since total agreement was not necessary, not to delve deeply into everyone's perceptions of the case.

While some unanimous juries produced verdicts that were lighter than what the experts deemed correct, these researchers are more concerned about verdicts that are too harsh, and believe nonunanimous juries deserve reconsideration.

Other research shows there are few differences in the decision-making behavior or the verdicts of six- and twelve-person unanimous juries. Large and small juries decide most cases relatively quickly and with little disagreement. Few trials end with hung juries requiring another trial. Consequently, reformers' expectations that small juries will save court time do not appear valid.[28]

**Televised Trials**  Trials involving brutal crimes or famous people are news leaders. The parade of witnesses tells a tale of emotion, events, and evidence that rivals many functional mystery stories. The news media has always covered arrests and attended trials and other judicial proceedings as part of regular news reporting.

In recent years, however, commercial and public television have sought permission to film trials for later broadcast. This has created much controversy among those who favor giving TV maximum access to trials as news events and others who believe that taking motion pictures of a trial is disruptive and prejudicial to defendants and other participants.

***From Flashbulbs to TV***   In 1965, the U.S. Supreme Court banned all picture taking in the courtroom (*Estes v. Texas*). Most states had similar bans in effect. Many judges and lawyers believed that cameras make witnesses uncomfortable and prevent the free flow of testimony. A large knot of reporters, crowded together on the front row of the spectator's section with cameras clicking and flashbulbs popping, is distracting and intimidating. Cameras also may sensationalize a case in the newspapers and make all participants highly visible to the public and the targets of pressure and abuse. In particular, opponents fear that picture coverage could produce a climate of hostility against a criminal defendant and lead a jury to convict more readily.

The advocates of TV in the courtroom reject these arguments. They maintain that modern equipment is quiet, small, and unobtrusive and can be used from the back of the courtroom where few people even notice it. Moreover, since our political system is based on the right of the public to know what goes on in government, television ought to be permitted. There also is no danger of harmful pretrial publicity, since televised trials begin after a trial has started and simply record what actually takes place.[29] Finally, there is no evidence that camera reporting affects local public opinion.

By the mid-1970s, many states began to revise their rules of procedure to permit photography and television at a trial if all of the participants agreed.[30] Some states, however, have given trial judges sole power to determine whether TV coverage should be permitted. Certain kinds of crimes or certain testimony in rape, child molesting, or other lurid cases might qualify for a restriction of camera coverage, but the decision is left to the judge. In 1981, the U.S. Supreme Court supported this policy (*Chandler v. Florida*). Since then, most states have allowed TV coverage.[31]

During all of this debate, federal judges resisted allowing TV into federal court. But as of 1991, Chief Justice Rehnquist and the Judicial Conference bowed to what they termed the inevitable movement toward televised trials, including pressure from Congress, and they allowed a few district and appeals courts to experiment with television in the courtroom over the next few years.[32]

***Effects of TV***   Research on the effect of television on trials tends to support TV. Very few participants surveyed after their televised trials report feeling that TV had any effect. Witnesses may even be more alert and accurate knowing that they are being filmed. A survey of local residents done after a highly publicized televised trial showed that few people remembered many of the names or details in the case, suggesting that most viewers are not especially drawn to televised cases and that unbiased jurors could be found if a case were retried. Finally, about three-quarters of state judges favor TV in the courtroom.

Few who have presided over televised trials have any reservations about them.[33]

While TV may not affect the fairness of particular trials, critics worry that television will perpetuate myths about crime and the courts and that public understanding of the judicial process will not be increased. Opponents believe that only unusual or especially lurid criminal cases will be broadcast and that editing to fit TV time slots will sensationalize a case. The process will create the impression that regular TV crime shows reflect reality (violent crime, white victims, crime-busting police, and rich lawyers). In addition, televised trials generally ignore the millions of civil cases.[34]

There is some support for this concern about sensationalism. A few civil cases have been televised, but most have involved very serious and lurid crime. Several famous televised trials are the Florida cases of young Ronny Zamora, found guilty of beating an elderly neighbor to death, and Theodore Bundy, convicted of murdering and sexually mutilating several college coeds. Another televised trial which received enormous publicity was the New Hampshire case of Pamela Smart, a 23-year-old high school teacher who seduced one of her young students and persuaded him to kill her husband.

Zamora's case was unique because his attorney tried to convince the jury that Zamora should be found not guilty because he was drugged and duped into committing crime by overdoses of television violence. The Bundy and Smart cases drew much interest because of their sexual content. Bundy also had a long and widely publicized criminal record, for brutal crime. Other televised cases with explicit sexual testimony involving gang rape and child molestation in day care centers also have been shown, lending support to critics who believe broadcasters use sensational cases to improve ratings.

Supporting televised trials as part of freedom of the press or the public's right to know may be undermined also by commercial television's use of courts as game show and soap opera. *The People's Court* features real litigants, retired California Judge Joseph Wapner serving as arbitrator, and a set designed to look like a real courtroom. The litigants present small claims disputes and have agreed to be bound by the decision of the judge-arbitrator. But instead of the loser having to pay damages and court costs, the show's producers pay the damages and even give the loser a consolation prize. The show is accompanied by appropriate music.

Instead of the pain and trauma of going to court in the "real world," these trials seem like fun, especially since everyone wins.[35] However, a few small claims judges believe that litigants have improved their presentation in court as a result of watching *The People's Court*.

Recently, a new cable TV channel, the Courtroom Television Network, began televising trials live and unedited, but with commentary and analysis. While complete coverage of real trials may counteract the game show image, the network emphasizes unusual issues and stimulating cases, including the disorderly conduct trial of AIDS demonstrators who loudly protested in favor of condoms in New York's Catholic cathedrals, suits against rock group and record company brought by the parents of teenagers who committed suicide after listening to heavy metal, the trial of Marlon Brando's son for the murder of his sister's lover, and excerpts of the Pamela Smart trial.[36]

It is unclear whether television greatly increases the public's awareness and understanding of the judicial process. It probably is also true, however, that television does not interfere with getting a fair trial, although some criminal defendants have used the presence of television as the basis for appealing their convictions. However, as mentioned earlier, most judges who have presided over televised trials believe TV does no harm, and many are convinced it is good for the public to have an opportunity to see what goes on in court.

## APPEALS

There is a major formal difference between trial and appellate courts. Trial courts determine what occurred in a conflict (the facts) and make decisions that are permitted or required by law. Appellate courts accept the trial court's determination of the facts and are concerned with *how* decisions were made and the laws that were involved in trial decisions. In theory, an appeal is designed to catch legal errors that may occur in trials.

Appellate courts hear no new testimony and consider no new evidence. There are neither witnesses nor juries. The trial itself is the main issue and judges alone make the decisions.

Every losing litigant is entitled to one appeal. The litigant seeking review (appellant) hopes the appellate court will reverse or modify the first ruling. Criminal defendants who win in appeals courts often are granted a new trial. In many civil cases, appellate courts may overturn the trial or require the trial judge to modify the verdict to produce a different result.

The vast majority of all appealed cases end with one appeal. However, certain cases are so important to the parties and raise such controversial legal or policy questions that they are successfully appealed to another court, particularly the U.S. Supreme Court and some state supreme courts.

### Importance of Appeals

Although appellate courts catch some errors, correcting trial mistakes is *not* the main importance of appellate courts. Compared with the number of trials, few cases are appealed and most higher courts reverse only a tiny percentage of trial decisions. For instance, 2 percent or less of the verdicts in the Kansas and Florida trial courts of general jurisdiction are appealed to higher courts. The federal courts of appeals receive about 15 percent of the cases decided in the district courts. Appellate courts generally reverse less than 10 or 15 percent of these decisions. The U.S. Supreme Court, however, reverses lower courts in half or more of its decisions. Its special jurisdiction largely accounts for its high rate of reversal.

**Policy Making**    The greatest significance of appellate courts is that appealed cases create opportunities for courts to make broader policies. When lawyers appeal cases, they usually concentrate on larger, more general issues of law and policy in addition to the details in their particular case. Appellate cases often consider the bigger picture. Lawyers try to persuade appellate judges that the way the law was used was incorrect or that the law itself should be changed, and this usually requires greater attention to the general meaning of law, what legislators or judges intended when rules were developed, and the consequences of law.

*New Issues*    Legal issues also may change when cases move to the appellate courts.[37] In criminal cases, the issues often change from determining factual guilt to questions of constitutional law and due process. For example, it is common in criminal cases for police to seize evidence such as drugs, weapons, or suspected stolen property. The question for appellate courts is not whether certain material is a drug or whether it was found in a suspect's home, but whether the police had the legal right to take it. Did they need a search warrant or did they have to act quickly to prevent the suspect from escaping and/or destroying the evidence?

Other cases raise additional fundamental questions about when attorneys should be provided to a poor defendant in a criminal case, whether jury selection procedures prevented a fair trial, and other procedural questions. These issues deal with the basics of the criminal justice process and affect judicial policy for processing defendants.

The transformation of issues can occur in civil cases, too. For example, various states have laws that limit the amount of money that an injured person can obtain in a lawsuit against a state or local government. These laws were enacted by legislatures because cities and counties objected to paying high premiums for accident insurance and believed that government treasuries would be depleted by an expensive lawsuit. Despite these laws, juries sometimes have awarded more than the amount permitted by state law, and trial judges have reduced the amount to the maximum set by the legislature, perhaps $100,000.

State supreme courts have been asked by the injured person to decide whether placing a top limit on the amount is proper. The issue in the case is transformed from a dollar amount awarded in a personal injury case into a much broader issue dealing with due process of law in terms of every citizen's right to sue a party that has injured them. Appellate courts have more opportunities than trial courts to deal with these broader and often thornier issues.

*Reversal*    The policymaking role of appellate courts stands out in certain types of cases. While the percentage of trial court decisions reversed by appellate courts generally is low, they sometimes reverse large numbers of decisions in particular areas of policy. One study of the federal courts found that courts of appeals reversed about 40 percent of district court decisions in labor relations cases, but reversed less than 25 percent of other civil appeals.

The appellate courts also affirmed over 80 percent of all criminal convictions. Some state supreme courts are likely to overturn trial decisions in cases involving the constitutionality of state statutes.[38] This suggests that there sometimes are major differences in views about what policy ought to be and that the appellate courts can have the last judicial word in determining policy.

### Getting to Appellate Courts

Since litigants have the right to one appeal, getting into state intermediate appellate courts and the federal courts of appeals is relatively easy and automatic if appeals are filed correctly. However, getting to the U.S. Supreme Court and certain state supreme courts is a different matter. These courts have some power to determine for themselves which cases they will decide, so something more than proper papers is necessary to get their attention.

**Procedures**    The loser in a trial usually begins the appeal. Appellate procedures are specialized and complex so that the opposing sides always need an attorney to handle the case. Most courts permit a week or more for the appellant to file a *notice of appeal* with the trial court that originally decided the case. Like the complaint that starts the trial process, a copy of the notice of appeal is sent by the court to the other side (*appellee*).

The appellant also has the responsibility for paying for other necessary documents for the appellate court, including a transcript of the trial, court exhibits, and a written legal argument called the *brief*. Preparing the brief is the main job of the appellant's lawyer. The brief states the reasons for the appeal, the relevant facts, and the legal basis for reversing or modifying the trial court decision and legal citations to support it. The appellee's lawyer also prepares a brief, which usually argues in favor of the trial court decision. (Poor criminal defendants do not have to pay for these or for their lawyer for one appeal.)

In many cases, attorneys also request time to argue their case personally before the appellate court (*oral argument*), but not all appealed cases receive time for oral presentation. This is subject to the discretion of the appellate court.

Documents for appeals must be put in proper form and submitted on time or judges are inclined to dismiss appeals as improperly brought to court. An important exception to this general rule are requests for hearings (*petitions for certiorari*) that come to the U.S. Supreme Court from poor litigants, mostly criminals in state and federal prisons who do not have attorneys to prepare their cases. The right to a lawyer does not include an appeal to the Supreme Court, so many prisoners prepare their own petitions. They rarely conform to any specifications and often are only a page or two long. If their petitions are accepted, the Supreme Court appoints an attorney to prepare their case.

**Slim Chances**    Most litigants are discouraged from appealing because they must pay more money for attorney's fees and other court records for transfer to the higher court. The odds against their winning also are very high, since few disputes involve substantial legal or policy questions, and appellate judges are very unlikely to substitute their own view of the facts for those of the trial courts.

Even with these limitations, thousands of people appeal to higher courts. If they can afford lawyers or have free legal help, the additional stress of going to court probably seems worthwhile, especially since the alternative is accepting a trial decision that went against them. Many litigants probably believe also that their cases are unique and that justice is on their side.

But judges on intermediate appellate courts and some state supreme courts see most appeals as routine, uninteresting, and even boring last-ditch legal efforts. Appeals by convicted criminals are most likely to be seen as worthless. One state appellate judge said: "If 90 percent of this stuff were in the United States Post Office, it would be classified as junk mail."[39]

Sometimes lawyers in these cases do not request time for oral argument or prepare extensive briefs, but are satisfied to have the appeals court decide them on the basis of the transcript of the trial. Most of these cases probably were not very exciting or important in the trial courts either, and since they already have been decided once, the appeals are even less important and provide appellate judges with very few opportunities to announce innovative policies or changes in the law.

## Getting to the Supreme Court

Many cases taken to the U.S. Supreme Court and to many of the state supreme courts are not heard automatically since these courts have varying amounts of discretion to determine which cases they will decide. Selecting cases for review is just about as important as deciding them, for unless an issue is on a court's agenda, it cannot be considered. Decisions not to review a case automatically affirm rulings by lower courts, and the rejected cases do not receive the extra visibility or have the impact that often comes from being decided by the highest appellate courts.

**Discretion** The importance of discretion to hear cases is most apparent in the U.S. Supreme Court. In recent years, the Court has been asked to review nearly 5000 decisions annually, but grants *certiorari* well under 10 percent of the time. In addition, the Supreme Court decides only about 150 cases with full written opinions after oral argument. Another 75 to 100 or so are not given time for oral argument and are decided after very brief consideration, a quick decision, and no written opinions. The judgment of the Court is stated simply as "affirmed" or "reversed" or some other order, often with *per curiam* noted underneath, which means "by the court." Many other appellate courts also use the *per curiam* phrase for many cases they are required to hear but which the judges consider relatively unimportant and not worth separate written opinions.

**Reversal**   The chances of a case being decided by the U.S. Supreme Court are extremely small, but once a case is accepted for review, *the odds are good that the appellant will win*. During the past 10 years, the Supreme Court has reversed the lower federal and state courts in as many as 75 to 90 percent of its cases. However, recent rates of reversal are under 60 percent. The Rehnquist Supreme Court has affirmed a larger percentage of conservative lower court decisions than have previous Supreme Courts.[40]

The Supreme Court's reversal of lower courts is very different from the routine approval that the federal courts of appeals and the state appellate court's normally give to the trial courts in their areas. It reflects the Supreme Court's opportunity to substantially select its own agenda and to use its power to shape national judicial policy. Occasionally, the justices have said that granting *certiorari* is not designed to give a losing litigant another chance, but to select cases for review that have substantial importance beyond the immediate parties to the case.[41]

### Reasons for Granting Certiorari

The Supreme Court has provided a little information about its reasons for granting *certiorari* in its rules of procedure (*Rule 17*). The court says that if there is *conflict* among the lower courts or disagreement about the law throughout the nation or with the Supreme Court itself, the Supreme Court will be inclined to decide a case. It also adds that if the issue is an important one that the Supreme Court has not yet decided, it may grant *certiorari*.

Very few of the Court's written opinions offer much additional insight other than to say the issues are important. Since the Supreme Court considers so few cases and reverses most lower court decisions, it is intriguing to note how and why cases are able to win a review by the Court and what leads the justices to decide that certain cases are special.

**Discuss List**   It has been customary for some time for *certiorari* to be granted if four of the nine justices decide a case deserves to be reviewed. Normally, all requests for review are considered more carefully by the Chief Justice and his law clerks, who make up a list of cases that the Chief Justice believes ought to be discussed by the full Court. The other justices also have copies of summaries of the petitions and may add cases to the Chief Justice's "discuss list."

Recently, the conservative justices have pooled their law clerks to broaden their contribution to the discuss list, but the few liberal justices continued to screen cases on their own.[42] The recent replacement of the liberals with additional conservative justices may broaden the full court's participation in the discuss list pool.

**Cues**   Political scientists have developed an explanation for how the Supreme Court works in selecting cases for review. With thousands of cases to consider each year, along with actually deciding several hundred, the justices have to make their selections rapidly. Most petitions are a dozen or more pages long, so the justices or their clerks cannot read them all or spend a lot of time discussing the issues included in them.

Instead, the justices probably develop shortcuts to evaluate a case. Many cases contain certain characteristics or *cues* that catch the eye of the law clerks and the justices. Studying *certiorari* decisions made during many sessions of the Supreme Court, researchers have found that cases involving particular cues were granted a hearing much more often than cases in which there were no special cues.

*Finer Screening*   As many as 30 percent of the cases get on the discuss list. Many of the cues which are responsible for a grant of *certiorari* also are responsible for getting the cases on the earlier discuss list, but further paring is done as the justices consider all of the characteristics of the cases more carefully.

For example, as will be discussed shortly, the existence of conflict among the courts is a cue which places an item on the discuss list as well as results in *certiorari*. But there is a difference between an early perception of an *alleged* conflict argued by the parties seeking review and *actual* conflict as determined later by the justices. Alleged conflict becomes much less important than actual conflict in granting *certiorari*. In a similar way, dissents among judges on the lower appellate courts is a cue for the discuss list, but the presence of dissents are insufficient cues for a case to win *certiorari*.[43]

Since the Supreme Court rejects over 90 percent of all requests for *certiorari*, discovering which cues increase the odds of having a case decided adds considerably to our knowledge of the priorities of the Supreme Court. Box 7.4, "Cues That Get Certiorari," lists and describes the features which make cases stand out and gain the justices' attention.[44]

When the federal government, which is the biggest repeat player of them all, asks the Court to review a case, it often is successful for several reasons. The federal government is involved in a great amount of litigation and takes many cases to court, but the government weeds out litigation that is not worth an appeal. Therefore, the Supreme Court is likely to take special notice when the government decides that a high court review is in order. In addition, government lawyers are especially experienced and skillful at phrasing the issues and law in ways that alert the justices.

Cases in which the lawyers make a convincing case that there is a conflict between the lower court's decision and a Supreme Court precedent or where there is conflict between two or more circuits on a similar legal issue also are likely to get special attention by the justices. Some of the justices are very concerned that a criminal act in one circuit results in a violation of one law, but in another it might be a violation of several different criminal laws, or that the internal revenue code means different things in different judicial circuits.[45]

Other forms of judicial conflict are not cues. The Supreme Court, as well as certain state supreme courts, is more likely to hear a case when an intermediate

---

**BOX 7.4**

CUES THAT GET CERTIORARI

• *U.S. Government* When the federal government is a party to the dispute and seeks review (50 to 75 percent of cases)

• *Conflict among courts* When the decisions of the federal courts of appeals conflict with each other or with Supreme Court decisions (33 percent of cases)

• *Civil liberties* The importance of civil liberties varies with the changing ideology of the justices (33 percent of cases in 1950s; 21 percent in 1960s; 11 percent in 1970s)

• *Ideology* When the prevailing ideology of the Supreme Court conflicts with the ideological direction of the lower court decision

(e.g. a conservative Supreme Court seeks to review and overturn liberal lower court decisions, or a liberal Supreme Court plans to reverse conservative decisions—16 percent of cases)

• *Interest groups* Amici curiae briefs filed either in favor or against granting *certiorari* (36 percent of cases with one brief filed)

• *Multiple cues* When two or more cues exist in the same case, the chances of obtaining *certiorari* are very high. If the federal government is a party and seeks review in a case involving conflict among courts or in which several amici briefs have been filed, the chances of obtaining *certiorari* approach 100 percent.

---

appellate court *affirms* a trial court. This probably occurs because the justices disagree sharply with the consistent direction of judicial policy in the lower courts and want to alter it. However, if an intermediate appellate court already has corrected a trial court along the lines of existing Supreme Court policy, there is no need for the highest court to grant a review.[46]

Other cues which account for some of the *certiorari* decisions involve various *social issues* which are important to the justices. When the civil rights movement was building in importance (1950s), the Supreme Court, under the leadership of Chief Justice Earl Warren, paid special attention to cases involving civil liberties violations, and during the 1960s various underdog appellants, such as aliens, minorities, criminal defendants, laborers, and other have-nots, were more successful than others in getting *certiorari*. However, as the Supreme Court has shifted toward the conservatives, upperdogs such as governments at all levels and businesses have received more attention by the Supreme Court.[47]

This is consistent with the impact of ideology as a cue. The Court frequently grants *certiorari* when it disagrees with the ideological direction of a lower appellate court, and granting *certiorari* is an indicator that the Court likely will overturn the decision. A conservative Supreme Court majority is more likely to grant *certiorari* in cases involving business if the lower court has decided against business interests.

As the insert explains, when there is more than one cue in a case, the odds of its winning *certiorari* jump. These cases practically leap out of the large pool of cases on the discuss list because they contain so many ingredients that make them worthy to the Supreme Court for national judicial policymaking.

*Personal Strategies*   Most of the concern with cues centers on how the entire Supreme Court reacts to petitions for review. However, individual justices also tie their own policy goals with their votes on *certiorari*.

For example, liberal justices are likely to try to prevent cases from being granted *certiorari* if they believe the Court as a whole will elevate a local conservative policy, such as in women's rights, race relations, or some other case affecting underdogs, into a national judicial policy through a Supreme Court ruling.

If a certain bloc of justices is in the majority, however, they are likely to vote to grant *certiorari* if they are confident they can hold their majority together when the case is decided.[48] Since the Court now has a solid conservative majority, the few justices with liberal attitudes toward certain types of cases are unlikely to be able to put a coalition together to block conservative preferences. Similar strategies appear to exist on state supreme courts that have discretionary jurisdiction.[49]

With so much discretion to grant or deny *certiorari*, and few narrow legal rules to shape their decisions, it is clear that policy priorities, personal attitudes, and strategy are extremely important in determining the agenda of the Court and serving as a preview of the Court's final decisions.

## Deciding Appeals

Appeals are decided on the basis of written materials and sometimes after oral arguments from both sides. Appellate judges may review parts or all of the transcript of the testimony at the trial, the trial judge's rulings, instructions to the jury, and the verdict. They also read the written briefs prepared by each of the opposing attorneys and may consider any amici curiae briefs. Appellate judges and their law clerks also usually do additional research into previous decisions that pertain to the case (*precedents*) as well as other sources of law, such as legislative statutes and the actions of other government officials.

Hearing oral arguments is about the only time appellate judges are visible in appellate decision making. The rest of the decision-making process takes place in private. In court, the judges sit beside each other on their raised platform, which stretches grandly from one side of the courtroom to the other. The opposing lawyers take turns standing before them at a lectern to explain why the law should go their way.

Unlike a jury, appellate judges are legal experts and receive much respect and deference, so a lawyer's appellate style is much different from that at a trial. Lawyers do not pace about, talk informally, use anecdotes, or appeal to emotion. The lawyers are apt to be deferential, but also cool and professional, and to stick very closely to a discussion of the legal grounds of their position. Trial work and appellate work are so different that different lawyers may represent a litigant at each stage of a case. The judges may listen impassively to the lawyers or may interrupt at any time to ask questions, challenge a lawyer's interpretation of the law, or probe the broader implications of the argument. Sometimes judges are rough on lawyers who have not anticipated questions or whose position conflicts sharply with the judges' own view.

**Preliminary Vote**   Decisions in appellate cases can come quickly or very slowly. Sometimes an appellate court announces its decisions immediately, because the case seems simple and the judges quickly agree. Other cases receive more time and careful consideration.

After hearing oral arguments, the judges meet in a private conference to discuss the current crop of cases. On the U.S. Supreme Court, the Chief Justice speaks and votes first and the other justices take their turns in order of seniority, with the most junior judge speaking and voting last. This procedure is different from the one used in the past. The date of the shift is not clear, but it seems that until the 1970s, the Court used a two-stage process with the chief justice speaking first but voting last.[50] This procedure was thought to allow the chief justice to shape the discussion, but to permit him and perhaps other senior justices to gauge the way the voting is going and possibly cast their votes in a strategic way to influence the outcome.

The state supreme courts operate in a variety of ways. Some use the current as well as previous procedures of the U.S. Supreme Court, while others have the most junior justice speak and vote first.

The conference after oral argument does not end or settle a case. It is used to determine the initial majority and minority factions and to assign the writing of the tentative majority opinion. Only after much additional consideration of the majority opinion and possible dissents do the justices take a second and final vote that determines which side wins and whether the majority opinion becomes the final opinion of the Court.

After the judges have made their final changes in the opinions and the majority and minority positions are set, the decision is announced by the court and copies of the judgment are sent to the lawyers in the case, and the formal court opinions are published in official court reports.

## Writing Options

After the initial discussion and vote, the judges are fairly sure which way the case will go and which groups of judges agree with others. Then the court prepares to write an official court opinion which states and explains the decision. Court opinions may range in length from one to two paragraphs to dozens of pages. Opinions are something like legal briefs and may borrow heavily from them. They include summaries of the issues in dispute, the existing law, references to previous court cases, and other materials. Occasionally, they even include discussions of articles in legal journals.

**Opinion Assignment**    Determining which judge will write the opinion for a court is an important part of decision making, for the author of an opinion has a special opportunity to influence the content of the decision. On many appellate courts and the U.S. Supreme Court, the chief judge or justice assigns the writing of opinions if he or she is a member of the tentative majority that developed at the conference. The chief judge may give the job to anyone in the majority or can assign the case to himself or herself. If the chief judge is not in the majority, the senior associate judge assigns the case to a member of the majority.

*Strategies*    Chief justices of the U.S. Supreme Court use a number of strategies in assigning opinions. First, they generally are concerned with distributing the workload fairly equally among all of the justices. Second, chief justices tend to assign themselves a higher proportion of opinions in important, ground breaking constitutional cases. The symbolic prestige of the chief justiceship is used to give these decisions greater judicial gloss.[51]

When majority opinions are assigned to associate justices, a common strategy is to assign them to the justices who are on the fringe or the margin of the majority, i.e., ideologically closest to the minority position. The idea behind this strategy is that the majority opinion will reflect an "average" point of view and will keep the winning coalition together, and it might even bring in one of the justices from the minority. However, there is no evidence that this strategy works. Majority coalitions sometimes break up regardless of which justice writes the majority opinion. Also, the strategy is risky because, if the marginal justice switches sides, he or she takes the majority opinion along.[52]

Some judges prefer to write opinions in particular kinds of cases. Sometimes, their earlier law practice made them experts in state insurance law or the federal tax code, and their brethren are glad to have them take on these cases. Others are especially interested in particular areas of law and they soon become the court experts on certain issues. Their expertise gives them special influence and it saves the court time. This kind of opinion assignment occurs both on the U.S. Supreme Court as well as other appellate courts. However, issue specialization is not as important as other strategies, particularly building majority and minority coalitions which occur along ideological lines.[53]

Some state supreme courts, federal courts of appeals, and state intermediate appellate courts rotate the assignment of majority opinions among all of the judges on the court, and frequently all of the judges vote to support that opinion. In addition, some courts assign judges to smaller rotating panels which decide different cases. For example, all but one of the thirteen federal courts of appeals have ten or more judges each (one has six), but, except for rare occasions, they all divide into changing three-judge panels to decide the cases. Forming stable blocs is impossible and dissents are rare as well, possibly because one judge would have to stand alone.

However, since the judges often have different political party affiliations and ideologies, the direction and content of their majority opinions vary according to which group of judges is sitting on a particular panel and which judge writes the opinion. Therefore, even though the judges often appear to be in total agreement, there really are divisions among them that surface in the content of their unanimous majority opinions.[54]

**Getting Agreement**   Most courts appear to decide cases as a group with all the judges participating in the conference and having some voice in the final decision. In courts with many members, the writer of the majority opinion may have to satisfy four or five other judges in order to hold the majority together for the final count. A judge may write many drafts of an opinion before being satisfied with it and before other judges see it.

Appellate judges have one or several legal assistants (*law clerks*) who do legal research and who help to develop and structure decisions. In addition to doing the legal legwork, they often serve as a judge's backboard or devil's advocate to develop and test ideas and to prepare written opinions. In the U.S. Supreme Court, the law clerks work for individual justices. They usually are recent top graduates of the most prestigious law schools, and they consider their 1- or 2-year post as a great honor and a way of building personal prestige and experience before going into law practice. Law clerks in the state and the federal courts of appeals sometimes are career court employees. Some are hired as a result of their law school standing, while others get their jobs through personal social connections or political patronage.

After a judge is satisfied with a draft of the majority opinion, it is printed and circulated among the other judges on the court. Most of the other judges in the tentative majority probably will write memoranda suggesting changes in the opinion, which they send to the author of the opinion. Judges on state and federal appellate courts sometimes live in different cities, and they may discuss cases in conference telephone calls as well as by mail.

Sometimes judges are only partially satisfied with the final draft of the majority opinion, and they write their own separate *concurring opinions* in which they state their agreement with the majority's decision but also explain their own different or additional reasons for supporting the majority decision.

**Dissents**   Judges who disagree with the majority also may write one or more *dissenting opinions* to express their reasons for not going along with the decision. Occasionally, the initial decision of an appellate court is changed as a result of early dissents. One or more judges who initially voted with the majority may really be in the middle and uncertain about which side should win the case. Dissatisfied with the emerging majority view, they may be persuaded to join with the minority to produce a new majority coalition. Then, the early dissents might be consolidated into a new majority decision.

The percentage of cases with dissents varies very much on appellate courts. *Dissents in the U.S. Supreme Court are very common*, often occurring in 60 percent or more of the total decisions. This is due to the power of the Court to choose its own cases, the uncertainty and controversy involved in much Supreme Court litigation, and the firm views that many justices with different backgrounds and experiences have toward the issues.

Frequently, several dissenting justices support the opinion written by one of them. Often the dissenting justice whose ideology is furthest from the majority writes the dissenting opinion, but when there is a close 5-4 or 4-3 split, a dissenting justice closest to the majority frequently writes the opinion in the hope of attracting one of the fringe votes from the majority.[55]

Only a dozen state supreme courts produce dissents in 25 percent or more of their decisions. Ideology affects the tendency of state judges to dissent as well, but many additional factors influence these courts.[56] First, states with complex and heterogeneous economies and political systems produce more unusual and complex cases that evoke conflict, including among judges on appellate courts. Second, dissents are more likely in states that have intermediate appellate courts which hear most of the mundane appeals, leaving the complex and controversial cases involving government regulation of the economy, civil rights, the death penalty, and others for the state supreme court. Since more states are adding intermediate appellate courts, dissent rates probably will rise. Third, judges in states that use judicial elections are more likely to dissent than appointive states, probably because the popular political culture surrounding elections nourishes conflict. Judicial elections also produce judges with more varied backgrounds, and this also may lead to dissent.

However, differences in the structure and procedures of state supreme courts are even more powerful predictors of the tendency of judges to dissent. Random opinion assignment produces higher levels of dissent. It seems that stable coalitions are not formed, and there are few incentives for judges to logroll, i.e., support each other's majority opinions in return for future support. But, on courts where the chief justice speaks first and votes last, there are fewer dissents. Possibly, the chief justice shapes discussion and maintains court solidarity.

## CONCLUSION

Trials and appeals are important because they symbolize the rule of law and administering justice equally and fairly to all. "Getting your day in court" to "tell it to the judge" and expecting objective and fair treatment in return are hallmarks of American justice. But popular political culture also has a role in court. Juries, in particular, combine traditional legal procedure and popular participation. The ideal search for an objective jury is filled with practical strategies for getting a sympathetic jury.

The conduct of trials also blends formal procedure and popular beliefs. Trials tell a story by piecing together evidence and testimony from various witnesses, but lawyers also try to create mental pictures of plaintiffs and defendants for the judge or jury, believing that more than the facts presented in court are important in determining trial decisions. Juries often make decisions by fitting the facts and the law into their social perspective of the conflict and may reach compromises that fit their sense of right and wrong. This is much like judges and lawyers in plea bargaining and civil negotiation who decide what a case is worth.

Numerous current issues also are important in the trial courts. The size of juries and televised trials are two issues discussed in this chapter. The size of juries interests reformers who want more efficient trial courts, and trials and television reveal a concern with due process and the right of the public to see what goes on in trials.

Appeals are very different from trials. There are no juries or new evidence and testimony. Lawyers present the entire case, and judges have the sole responsibility for making decisions. However, few cases are appealed and most trial verdicts are upheld.

Appeals are important to society, however, not because they correct trial errors but because they provide judges with their greatest opportunity to make policies having wide impact on society. This is most important for the U.S. Supreme Court and state supreme courts, which may limit their caseloads. How cases get to these courts is an important part of the judicial process. Deciding which cases to hear reveals the issues that are most important to high courts and often forecasts a reversal of the lower court decision.

## SUGGESTIONS FOR ADDITIONAL READING

Hastie, Reid, Steven D. Penrod, and Nancy Pennington: *Inside the Jury* (Cambridge, Mass.: Harvard University Press, 1983). This is a comprehensive discussion of the history and importance of juries as well as a careful empirical study of jury behavior.

Lawrence, Susan: *The Poor in Court* (Princeton: Princeton University Press, 1990). Besides its focus on legal services for the poor, this research describes and explains the huge success of lawyers for the poor in obtaining *certiorari* before the U.S. Supreme Court.

Perry, H. W: *Deciding to Decide: Agenda Setting in the United States Supreme Court* (Cambridge, Mass.: Harvard University Press, 1991). Based in part on interviews with Supreme Court clerks, this is the most recent comprehensive examination of *certiorari*.

Woodward, Bob, and Scott Armstrong: *The Brethren* (New York: Avon Books, 1979). Based heavily on interviews with former clerks, two leading journalists take an insider's look at the interpersonal relations among Supreme Court justices.

## NOTES

1 Henry J. Abraham, *The Judicial Process* (New York: Oxford University Press, 1980), p. 107; Herbert Jacob, *Justice in America* (Boston: Little, Brown and Co., 1978), p. 125.

2 Lynn M. Mather, "Some Determinants of the Method of Case Disposition; Decision-Making by Public Defenders in Los Angeles," *Law and Society Review*, 8 (Winter 1973), 190; James Eisenstein and Herbert Jacob, *Felony Justice* (Boston; Little, Brown and Co., 1977), p. 251.
3 Martin Levin, *Urban Politics and the Criminal Courts* (Chicago: University of Chicago Press, 1977), p. 81.
4 Austin Sarat, "Judging in Trial Courts; An Exploratory Study," *Journal of Politics*, 39 (1977), 377–378.
5 Edward N. Beiser, "Are Juries Representative?" *Judicature*, 57 (1973), 196; Hayward Alker, Jr., Carl Hosticka, and Michael Mitchell, "Jury Selection as a Biased Social Process," *Law and Society Review*, 11 (1976), 10; Gordon Levine and Claudine Schweber-Koren, "Jury Selection in Erie County: Changing a Sexist System," *Law and Society Review*, 11 (1976), 50.
6 Hans Zeisel and Shari Seidman Diamond, "The Jury Selection in the Mitchell-Stans Conspiracy Trial," *American Bar Foundation Research Journal* (1976), 169.
7 L. S. Katz, "The Twelve Man Jury," *Trial*, 5 (December–January 1968–1969), 39–42, quoted in Cookie Stephan, "Selective Characteristics of Jurors and Litigants: Their Influence on Juries' Verdicts," in Rita James Simon (ed.), *The Jury System* (Beverly Hills, Calif.: Sage Publications, 1975), p. 98.
8 Saul M. Kassin and Lawrence S. Wrightsman, *The American Jury on Trial* (New York: Hemisphere Publishing Corp., 1988), p. 54.
9 Zeisel and Diamond. "The Jury Selection in the Mitchell-Stans Conspiracy Trial," p. 169.
10 Jay Schulman et al., "Recipe for a Jury," *Psychology Today*, May 1973, 40–41; Zeisel and Diamond, "The Jury Selection in the Mitchell-Stans Conspiracy Trial," p. 161; Amitai Etzioni, "Science: Threatening the Jury Trial," in Walter F. Murphy and C. Herman Pritchett (eds.), *Courts, Judges and Politics* (New York: Random House, 1979), pp. 467–471; Morton Hunt, "Putting Juries on the Couch," *New York Times Magazine*, November 28, 1982, pp. 70–88; Lawrence S. Wrightsman, "The American Trial Jury on Trial: Empirical Evidence and Procedural Modification," *Journal of Social Issues*, 34 (1974), 147.
11 *New York Times*, September 9, 1987, p. 14; *Wall Street Journal*, October 24, 1989, p. 1; Kassin and Wrightsman, p. 37.
12 Etzioni, pp. 469–470; Hunt, pp. 87–88.
13 *The New York Times*, March 13, 1983, p. 1.
14 Milton Heumann, *Plea Bargaining* (Chicago: University of Chicago Press, 1977), pp. 142–143.
15 Jonathan D. Casper, Kennette Benedict, and Jo L. Perry, "The Tort Remedy in Search and Seizure Cases: A Case Study in Jury Decision Making," *Law and Social Inquiry*, 13 (1988), 279–303.
16 *Tallahassee Democrat*, November 13, 1981, pp. 1, 12.
17 Amiram Elwork et al., "Toward Understandable Jury Instructions," *Judicature*, 65 (1982), 432–443; Walter W. Steele, Jr. and Elizabeth G. Thornburg, "Jury Instructions: A Persistent Failure to Communicate," *Judicature*, 74 (1991), 249–254.
18 Hans Zeisel and Harry Kalven, Jr., "The American Experiment," in Walter F. Murphy and C. Herman Pritchett (eds.), *Courts, Judges and Politics* (New York: Random House, 1979), pp. 462–466.
19 *New York Times*, October 22, 1988, p. 1; *Tallahassee Democrat*, September 15, 1989, p. 5A and January 19, 1990, p. 1B. See also, Irwin A. Horowitz and Thomas E.

Willging, "Changing Views of Jury Power," *Law and Human Behavior*, 15 (1991), 165–182.

20 Mortimer R. Kadish and Sanford H. Kadish, *Discretion to Disobey* (Stanford, Calif.: Stanford University Press, 1973), pp. 55–56; Harry Kalven, Jr., and Hans Zeisel, *The American Jury* (Boston: Little, Brown and Co., 1966), p. 291. Also, Lawrence M. Friedman and Stewart Macaulay (eds.), *Law and the Behavioral Sciences*, 2d ed. (New York: Bobbs-Merrill Co., Inc., 1977), pp. 363–364, 428–433.

21 Kalven and Zeisel. *The American Jury*, pp. 106–115.

22 Joan B. Kessler. "The Social Psychology of Jury Deliberations," in Rita James Simon (ed.). *The Jury System* (Beverly Hills, Calif.: Sage Publications, 1975), p. 83.

23 Wrightsman, pp. 152, 154; Jacob, pp. 131–132.

24 *Tallahassee Democrat*, November 24, 1980, p. 4D; *New York Times*, February 1, 1989, p. 46.

25 Warren E. Burger, "A Judge Is Better?" in S. Sidney Ulmer (ed.), *Courts, Law and Judicial Processes* (New York: The Free Press, 1981), pp. 173–180.

26 *Williams v. Florida*, 399 U.S. 78 (1970); *Apodaca v. Oregon*, 406 U.S. 404 (1972); *Ballew v. Georgia*, 435 U.S. 223 (1978); *Burch v. Louisiana*, (1979).

27 Hans Zeisel and Shari Seidman Diamond, " 'Convincing Empirical Evidence on the Six Member Jury,'" *University of Chicago Law Review* 41 (1974), 281–295; Reid Hastie et al., *Inside the Jury* (Cambridge; Harvard University Press, 1983).

28 Diane L. Bridgeman and David Marlowe, "Jury Decision Making: An Empirical Study Based on Actual Felony Trials," *Journal of Applied Psychology*, 64 (1979), 91–98; D. W. Broeder, "University of Chicago Jury Project," *Nebraska Law Review*, 38 (1959), 747–748; Kessler, p. 76; Robert T. Roper, "Jury Size: Impact on Verdict's Correctness," *American Politics Quarterly*, 7 (October 1979), 438–452; Wrightsman, 153.

29 Kermit Netteburg, "Does Research Support the Estes Ban on Cameras in the Courtroom?" *Judicature*, 63 (May 1980), 467–475; George Bergner, "Trial by Television: Are We at the Point of No Return?" *Judicature*, 63 (April 1980), 416–425.

30 James L. Hoyt, "Prohibiting Courtroom Photography: It's Up to the Judges in Florida and Wisconsin," *Judicature*, 63 (December–January 1980), 290–295.

31 Steven Abrahams, "New Efforts in 17 States to Expand Camera Coverage of Courts," *Judicature*, 65 (August 1981), 116–118; *Tallahassee Democrat*, September 21, 1984, p. 3A.

32 *Los Angeles Daily Journal*, September 13, 1990, p. 1.

33 Netteburg, pp. 470–473.

34 Bergner, pp. 419–421.

35 "Reality Strikes Again," *Newsweek*, June 29, 1981.

36 *New York Times*, July 3, 1991, p. B3.

37 Richard J. Richardson and Kenneth N. Vines, "Review, Dissent and the Appellate Process," *Journal of Politics*, 29 (1967), 599–603.

38 J. Woodford Howard, "Litigation Flows in Three United States Courts of Appeals," *Law and Society Review*, 8 (1973), 41; Craig F. Emmert, "Judicial Review in State Supreme Courts: 1981–1985," unpublished Ph.D. dissertation, The Florida State University, 1989.

39 John T. Wold, "Goind Through the Motions," *Judicature*, 62 (August 1978), 62.

40 Stephen L. Wasby, *The Supreme Court* (New York: Holt, Rinehart and Winston, 1978), pp. 151–152; "Statistics," *Harvard Law Review*, 104 (November 1990), 363;

Jeffrey A. Segal and Harold J. Spaeth, "Rehnquist Court Disposition of Lower Court Decisions: Affirmation Not Reversal," *Judicature* 74 (1990), 84–88.

**41** Wasby, p. 147.

**42** Gregory A. Caldeira and John R. Wright, "Organized Interests and Agenda Setting in the U.S. Supreme Court," *American Political Science Review*, 82 (December 1988), 1124.

**43** Gregory A. Caldeira and John R. Wright, "The Discuss List: Agenda Building on the Supreme Court," *Law and Society Review*, 24 (1990), 807–836.

**44** Joseph Tanenhaus et al., "The Supreme Court's Certiorari Jurisdiction: Cue Theory," in Glendon Schubert (ed.), *Judicial Decision-Making* (Glencoe, Ill.: The Free Press, 1963). See also Donald R. Songer, "Concern for Policy Outputs as a Cue for Supreme Court Decisions on Certiorari," *Journal of Politics*, 41 (1979), 1185–1194; S. Sidney Ulmer. "The Supreme Court's Certiorari Decisions: Conflict as a Predictive Variable." *American Political Science Review*, 78 (December 1984), 901–911; H. W. Perry, Jr., "Indices and Signals in the Certiorari Process" (paper presented at the annual meeting of the Midwest Political Science Association, Chicago, Ill., April 9–11, 1986); S. Sidney Ulmer, "Selecting Cases for Supreme Court Review: Litigant Status in the Warren and Burger Courts" (paper delivered at the Annual Meeting of the American Political Science Association, Washington, D. C., September, 1979), excerpted and reprinted in S. Sidney Ulmer (ed.), *Courts, Law and Judicial Processes*, pp. 284–298. See also S. Sidney Ulmer, "Selecting Cases for Supreme Court Review: An Underdog Model," *American Political Science Review*, 72 (1979), 902–910; Caldeira and Wright, 1988, pp. 1109–1127; Jeffrey A. Segal, "Amicus Curiae Briefs by the Solicitor General During the Warren and Burger Courts: A Research Note," *Western Political Quarterly*, 41 (1988), 135–144; Jeffrey A. Segal and Cheryl D. Reedy, "The Supreme Court and Sex Discrimination : The Role of the Solicitor General," *Western Political Quarterly*, 41 (1988), 553–568.

**45** Ulmer, "The Supreme Court's Certiorari Decisions," pp. 901–911.

**46** Lawrence Baum, *The Supreme Court* (Washington, D.C.: Congressional Quarterly Press, 1981), p. 88; Richardson and Vines, "Review, Dissent and the Appellate Process," See also Lawrence Baum, "Policy Goals in Judicial Gatekeeping: A Proximity Model of Discretionary Jurisdiction." *American Journal of Political Science*, 21 (1977), 13–35.

**47** Tanenhaus et al.

**48** Saul Brenner, "The New Certiorari Game," *Journal of Politics*, 41 (1979), 649–655; Baum, pp. 89–90; Saul Brenner and John F. Krol, "Strategies in Certiorari Voting on the United States Supreme Court," *Journal of Politics*, 51 (1989), 828–840.

**49** Lawrence Baum, "Judicial Demand—Screening and Decisions on the Merits," *American Politics Quarterly*, 7 (January 1979), 109–119.

**50** *Law, Courts, and Judicial Process Section Newsletter*, American Political Science Association, 7 (Fall 1989), pp. 8–9.

**51** Elliot E. Slotnick, "The Chief Justices and Self-Assignment of Majority Opinions," *Western Political Quarterly*, 31 (1978), 219–225.

**52** Saul Brenner and Harold J. Spaeth, "Majority Opinion Assignment and the Maintenance of the Original Coalition on the Warren Court," *American Journal of Political Science*, 32 (1988), 72–81.

**53** Saul Brenner and Harold J. Spaeth, "Issue Specialization in Majority Opinion Assignment on the Burger Court," *Western Political Quarterly*, 39 (1986), 520–527;

Saul Brenner, "Issue Specialization as a Variable in Opinion Assignment," *Journal of Politics*, 46 (1984), 1217–1225; Burton Atkins, "Opinion Assignment on the United States Courts of Appeal: The Question of Issue Specialization," *Western Political Quarterly*, 27 (1974), 409–428; Henry Robert Glick, *Supreme Courts in State Politics* (New York: Basic Books, Inc., 1971), pp. 110–111.

54 Robert J. Sickels, "The Illusion of Judicial Consensus: Zoning Decisions on the Maryland Court of Appeals," *American Political Science Review*, 59 (1965), 100–104; Burton M. Atkins and Justin J. Green, "Consensus on the United States Courts of Appeals: Illusion or Reality," *American Journal of Political Science*, 20 (1976), 735–748; Philip L. Dubois, "The Illusion of Judicial Concensus Revisited: Partisan Conflict on an Intermediate State Court of Appeals," *American Journal of Political Science*, 32 (1988), 946–967.

55 Saul Brenner and Harold J. Spaeth, "Ideological Position as a Variable in the Authoring of Dissenting Opinions on the Warren and Burger Courts," *American Politics Quarterly*, 16 (1988), 317–328.

56 Paul Brace and Melinda Gann Hall, "Neo-Institutionalism and Dissent in State Supreme Courts," *Journal of Politics*, 52 (1990), 54–70; Melinda Gann Hall, "Constituent Influence on State Supreme Courts: Conceptual Notes and a Case Study," *Journal of Politics*, 49 (1987), 1117–1124; Henry R. Glick and George W. Pruet, Jr., "Dissent in State Supreme Courts: Patterns and Correlates of Conflict," in Sheldon Goldman and Charles M. Lamb (eds.), *Judicial Conflict and Consensus: Behavioral Studies of American Appellate Courts* (Lexington, Ky.: University of Kentucky Press, 1986), pp. 199–214.

# 8

# LAW AND DECISION MAKING

How judges decide is one of the most fascinating but mystifying parts of the judicial process. Judges usually insist on absolute privacy while they decide cases, be it the U.S. Supreme Court meeting in conference with a guard at the door or a state trial judge working alone on a divorce decree. Unlike legislatures, no one is permitted to watch a court while it creates a decision.

For lawyers, litigants, and many social scientists, how courts decide is what the judicial process really is all about. Plans to go to court often hinge on a lawyer's hunch about the views of local judges and how a case probably will come out. Many trials end with a suspenseful wait for a judgment or a sentence. Announcements of controversial Supreme Court decisions also are eagerly anticipated by the mass media, lawyers, scholars, and politicians as the latest word in national judicial policy.

The secrecy that enshrouds judicial decision making makes it all the more intriguing. There are lots of good questions. What goes on behind closed doors? What do judges think and talk about? How do appellate judges work with each other? What leads them to decide cases in a particular way?

As in every part of the judicial process, there are two points of view about judicial decision making. One is the *legal* perspective, which sees courts as unique legal institutions where judges' behavior is explained by law and formal procedure. The second is a *political* approach, which focuses on judges as personalities operating within the broader society. In the political view, law provides judges with tremendous discretion, leaving plenty of room for personal values and social factors to influence decisions. This and the following chapter look at the legal and political approaches as ways of understanding the courts.

## THE LEGAL PERSPECTIVE

The legal approach maintains that since judges are trained and experienced in law, they all will use similar methods and information to decide cases. The legal view focuses on sources of law, techniques of legal decision making, and the explanations that judges give for their decisions in written court opinions. The legal approach also tends to examine closely individual cases with emphasis on the wording of opinions and the logic that judges use to create their decisions.

The legal view of decision making also sees judges as removed and detached from the everyday world around them. Judges are cloistered in their courts or chambers and have little contact with others. Their special role in society also forces them consciously to wash out the influence of previous political or social experiences that affect everyone's behavior.

Because of their formal legal training and personal orientation to their job, they are expected to separate their own personal opinions and views of world events and people from their legal obligations to decide cases objectively and on the basis of law. Judges who have had prior government or partisan political experience are expected to transform themselves into insulated, aloof, and objective arbiters.

Many people believe a transformation does occur. Being a judge is considerably different from the work of other politicians in several ways. Judges no longer have many contacts outside of court and they are substantially insulated from the threat of hostile public opinion. They spend most of their time in law libraries or personal offices and can give all their attention to the law and the specific facts in each case. Even if judges have to run for reelection, the odds are excellent they will win easily, so they really do not have to worry very much about pleasing anyone outside of court with their decisions. They can be their own person, substantially free from influence and pressure.

A state judge who had been very active in partisan politics explained his transformation this way:

> . . . when you go on the bench a chemical reaction takes place. [A judge] only wants to do the right thing within his limitations. When they put on the robe, they become a different type of man. When I was a senator, I wanted to make everyone feel good. I cut corners, I hedged in order to make me come out on top. I wanted to do the thing, in short, that would get me the most votes. When I got on the bench I felt that I'm not beholden to anyone. . . . I just decided to do the right thing.[1]

A legislator who becomes a judge takes on new tasks and obligations, changing outlook and behavior to perform according to personal and outsider expectations. He or she decides to do the "right" thing rather than, say, the politically expedient thing. The legal approach to judicial decision making tries to portray what the right thing is and how judges arrive at it.

## FACT FINDING

*Fact finding is the major legal task of the trial courts.* Judges, sometimes with juries, have to decide what events took place before a conflict became a court case. This is done through the presentation of testimony and evidence, as described in the previous chapter. When the trial courts have determined that a particular event or situation occurred, they are supposed to apply the appropriate law to produce a remedy or to redress a wrong. For example, if a court decides that a particular crime took place or that a buyer or seller failed to live up to an agreement, the court is supposed to impose lawful punishment in criminal cases or require the transfer of money from one party to another in most civil cases.

Appellate judges normally accept the facts as determined by the trial courts because they have no additional or workable means to obtain other information. Unless their review of the trial court record clearly shows that the judge or jury evaluated the facts so poorly that the outcome of the trial should have been different, trial court fact finding usually is allowed to stand.

### "Fight Theory"

Fact finding seems simple and straightforward if we assume that trial courts search for verifiable truth. But *the adversarial nature of trials, sometimes called the "fight theory" of justice, does not assure an impartial search for objective reality.*[2]

Trial courts are not laboratories where scientists carefully and dispassionately gather evidence or conduct experiments to verify a chemical reaction or where they observe and record animal behavior in a controlled environment. Trial courts are arenas where opposing lawyers present witnesses and ask questions designed to make the strongest impression possible for their own side.

A trial lawyer's skills are measured partly by the ability to ask only those questions that provide information that is beneficial to one's own side and damning to the opposition. They are careful not to ask loose or open-ended questions that give witnesses an opportunity to explain in detail or talk at length, possibly providing information that lawyers do not want anyone to hear. If the opposition lawyer is unable to obtain the information desired through testimony, the other lawyer is not obligated to help. Lawyers select and stress facts that help their case and try to ignore those that are harmful.

The objective search for truth is hampered also because certain facts are declared legally not relevant and because witnesses can tell the truth only as they see it or remember it. Since they often are sympathetic to one side or the other, their recollections are apt to be affected by what they would like to remember. Intentional lying sometimes takes place too, but even honest witnesses tend to shade their testimony to fit their own sense of justice. Consequently, fact finding is not as straightforward or as precise and reliable as legal theory suggests. With lawyers intentionally working at cross-purposes to justify their side, trials are not likely to discover the full or objective reality of a conflict.

**What Are the Facts?**   Even when lawyers are careful and skilled at extracting only the facts they want a judge or jury to hear, trials produce many facts that are used to support both sides in a case. Judges and juries always have to choose which ones they believe are most important. Therefore, fact finding gives judges and juries substantial discretion in decision making.

For example, in the famous Claus von Bulow case, in which the doctor was accused of trying to murder his wife with overdoses of insulin, the trial judge emphasized in his instructions to the jury that the fact that the doctor had a medical bag in his home containing syringes and insulin was important. However, the defense argued that the bag was a normal part of a doctor's equipment and, therefore, was unimportant. The wife also was portrayed in court as depressed and occasionally suicidal. The prosecution also explored the doctor's extramarital affairs in court to show he had plenty of motive for murdering his rich wife. But other people have extramarital affairs and do not commit murder.

The parents of six-year-old Adam Walsh, who was murdered following his disappearance from a mall department store, sued the retailer and the mall for negligence, claiming that a store security guard had improperly ordered their son to leave the building. In order to discredit the mother's testimony about her shopping trip, defense lawyers raised additional facts—the mother was having an affair with a family friend and both parents had used drugs. The judge agreed that these facts were relevant and admissible because the lifestyle of the family was important to the case.

A seller who tries to get out of an agreement by citing technical legal errors in the written contract may discover that the judge and jury believe these are less important than the fact of an original intent to sell property. As discussed in the previous chapters, other legally irrelevant facts such as hearsay or even a defendant's appearance in court may be important facts that juries consider.

Therefore, a search for facts is not the scientific or totally objective enterprise suggested by legal theory. It is part of the strategy for winning cases and gives judges and juries considerable room to make choices.

## APPLYING THE LAW

Once the facts have been settled, courts are supposed to apply the appropriate law to produce the desired remedy. Applying the law, however, is extremely complex. As discussed in the first chapter, there is no single source of law. Instead, lawyers and judges are faced with many different sources that they can apply to a particular factual situation. They also are expected to follow certain procedures to apply various types of law to cases.

Major sources of law include precedents (previous court decisions), statutes (acts of legislatures), administrative (executive) rules, and constitutions. How these are used in cases can be understood more easily by looking at the procedures that judges are expected to go through to produce a decision. These include following the rule of precedent (*stare decisis*), interpreting the language of law, and determining the intentions of the lawmakers.

### The Rule of Precedent

A precedent is a judicial decision made in the past that relates in some way to a current case. The rule of precedent, or *stare decisis*, means that judges are expected to rely on similar past court decisions as the basis for deciding new ones. By applying established principles found in previous cases to current situations, judges promote legal stability and continuity.

Repeated application and restatement of the same rules by many judges presumably settles the law and permits people to safely get on with their activities, knowing their conduct is within the law. This is important, because people need to know what the law requires when they make agreements to buy and sell, write wills, contemplate divorce, etc. Their lawyers are supposed to be able to advise them what the law says.

**Legal Reasoning**  In legal theory, judges select particular precedents through legal reasoning.[3] When a case comes up for decision, a judge is supposed to search for similar cases decided in the past, dutifully noting the basis of the past decision and converting it into a more general principle of law that can be applied to the current case. Through the constant process of comparing old cases with the new ones, judges are said to find legal rules that govern the outcome of most conflicts brought to court. Legal reasoning permits some changes in the rules as they are used over the years, but the rules still are expected to remain visibly intact.

The rule of precedent serves as a kind of judicial brake, keeping judges within fairly narrow limits of the existing, stabilizing law. Following precedent also keeps judges within the limits of their traditional governmental role. By following precedent, judges defer to the lawmaking power of legislatures and content themselves to merely interpreting and applying the rules as they find them.

On the surface, the rule of precedent is very appealing, for it seems to provide certainty in the law and predictability about what judges will do. But the rule of precedent is not a precise guide for explaining how judges decide cases.

**New Situations**   While precedent is designed to preserve continuity, it cannot always cover all situations. Judges frequently must alter past principles to fit current conditions. Sometimes the social distance between a past case and a current problem is so great that a precedent has to be stretched very far to make it fit a current issue. Often, there are no prior decisions that apply.

For instance, during the 1800s, America had very little statutory law concerning property and contracts, rules of negligence, personal and commercial liability, and insurance. Judges either adapted old legal rules or made up new ones in order to decide cases that came before them.

Often many similar disputes come to courts before a legislature passes a law that sets up rules for settling conflicts. For example, millions of claims between landlords and tenants and between real estate developers and buyers of condominiums flooded the state courts before legislatures enacted special landlord-tenant and condominium laws. Even so, new laws rarely cover all situations perfectly, so judges still have to develop their own ways of resolving specific disputes.

**Judges Disagree** Another problem is that judges do not agree on what is a controlling precedent. The evidence for this is clear in the decisions of the U.S. Supreme Court and other appellate courts throughout the nation in which judges frequently dissent from the majority decision and often write their own opinions expressing their reasons for not going along. Both the majority and the dissenters are able to locate cases that relate to the current case. Even when judges do not dissent, there is ample evidence that judges on appellate courts often disagree on what the decision should be. But how can they all be right if precedent is supposed to dictate the outcome of current cases?

Since judges have been making decisions in the United States for over 200 years, there are thousands of previous cases that could be cited as precedents. In a country with fifty semiautonomous states and a national court system too, the odds are very high that many legal situations have been decided in a number of different ways.[4] Similar plaintiffs and defendants have won or lost, not as a result of a national system of law, but because thousands of judges in many different social and political environments see things differently. All of these cases are potential precedents.[5]

There are no restrictions on which cases can be used as precedents. Judges may select recent cases from their own states or districts, or they can use decisions made by judges years ago and miles away. Moreover, although many cases involve similar subjects, the facts in each particular case always are different, and judges have the power to decide for themselves which facts are relevant to their current case, which facts they should ignore, and even which cases provide more convincing support for their decision. Judges also may have personal pet precedents, which they use in certain types of cases.

And, finally, judges may reject all precedents in favor of their attraction to other law. Box 8.1, "Missouri Rules against the Right to Die," illustrates that even when the direction of precedent is fairly clear, judges' decisions may hinge on other criteria which justify different policies.[6]

**Vague Criteria** Although legal theorists generally emphasize the importance of precedent and legal reasoning in decision making, they are vague on the criteria judges should use to select precedents. Most admit that the process is much more complex than simply comparing the facts in cases.[7] Judges often have to be creative in applying old cases to new ones or seeing the way that the solution to old problems bears on new situations. It really does not matter very much what a former judge in a past case thought was important, but what contemporary judges coping with new problems believe is important or unimportant in previous cases. Judges may have to use their intuition or their best guess or hunch about which precedent to use.[8]

This point of view emphasizes the importance of the past, but it becomes very fuzzy when translated into a usable guide for judicial action. When judges

---

**BOX 8.1**

MISSOURI RULES AGAINST THE RIGHT TO DIE

Since 1976, state supreme courts have grappled with the rights of patients or their families and guardians to require doctors and medical institutions to withdraw life-sustaining treatment in hopeless cases. These are cases where the patient cannot be cured, and treatment, including feeding tubes, merely postpones death, often with intense suffering.

Since then, a dozen courts have ruled in many cases that patients have the right to refuse unwanted treatment, and that others may act on behalf of patients who have not and currently cannot communicate their wishes, such as those who are in a permanently unconscious vegetative state. Each year, new courts cited the growing volume of precedents to support their own right to die rulings.

But in 1988, the Missouri Supreme Court ruled that the parents of a permanently unconscious young woman injured in an automobile accident had no right to order the withdrawal of her feeding tube, which might have kept her alive for decades (*Cruzan v. Harmon*). Like other courts, the Missouri court cited every previous right-to-die case, but rejected all of them as wrongly decided.

Instead, the court relied on Missouri's living-will statute that contained a pro-life preamble. Since the young woman had not made her wishes known clearly and absolutely concerning medical care, she had no right to have the artificial feeding withdrawn. The court ruled that the state had an interest in preserving her life.

The U.S. Supreme Court affirmed the Missouri decision, stating that the states had the right to require written evidence of a patient's wishes regarding medical treatment, but it also indicated that its decision was limited to Missouri and that other states could have their own rules, including those which did not require written evidence. Therefore, not only is Missouri's judicial policy law, but contrary judicial rulings in other states based on other precedents also are valid.

---

themselves are asked how they select precedents, they provide a wide variety of methods, but none that specifies what a judge actually does. Some judges say they select precedents where the facts are similar or which offer suitable legal principles. Some select only contemporary cases; others say they simply use the best ones. However, a few judges say they select precedents that support what they want to accomplish in a current case.[9]

**Strategies**    There are a variety of legal techniques judges use to counter the arguments of other judges that particular precedents are controlling in a case or require a particular decision. Many previous decisions are based on a number of legal principles, so current judges always can say that parts of previous court opinions are *obiter dicta*. These are judicial statements in opinions that are not considered crucial to previous judicial reasoning. So labeled, they can be ignored.

Judges also may cite opposing precedents but then *distinguish* them from the current case, usually by explaining that the facts are too dissimilar to make the precedent relevant. Judges also may try to limit the impact of contrary precedents by declaring that their principles are unimportant or not binding except in certain situations, such as those in (or not in) the current case.[10] Like the rule of *stare decisis*, justifications for selecting or ignoring precedents also are part of the legal approach to decision making and permit a wide range of behavior.

Following precedent is firmly established in legal theory and it is an important part of a judge's role, but it does not tell us very much about what a judge does to decide cases. There are many old cases, and judges are free to determine for themselves which ones they will use to support their decisions. Therefore, precedent cannot predict the outcome of current cases, since each judge uses precedents as he or she sees fit and will not necessarily agree with the judge sitting close by or working in the adjoining courtroom.

### The Language of Law

In addition to following court decisions as potential precedents, judges frequently are required to interpret the meaning of statutes, administrative regulations, and state and national constitutions as well as private legal documents, such as contracts, wills, divorce agreements, and others. The state and national governments enact thousands of new laws and regulations every year, so the opportunities and demand for courts to interpret the meaning of the law is large and increasing. It often is a difficult and controversial task.

**Plain Meaning**   Analyzing the language of law involves several specific legal approaches. One is to look simply at the so-called plain meaning of words or what is common or usual language usage. The idea here is not much different from looking up words in a dictionary to get the correct definition. For some jurists, discovering the correct meaning does not appear difficult, for it apparently leaps out to the trained judicial eye. This view probably was expressed best by Justice Owen J. Roberts in a 1936 Supreme Court decision:

> When an act of Congress is appropriately challenged in the courts as not conforming to the constitutional mandate, the judicial branch . . . has only one duty, to lay the article of the Constitution which is invoked beside the statute which is challenged and to decide whether the latter squares with the former. . . .[11]

Despite Justice Roberts's optimism, a quick look at a college edition dictionary or a thesaurus of words and phrases reveals that English often is an elusive language with lots of different meanings for many words and ideas. Linguists often debate correct language usage, and when "legal linguists" with much to gain or lose tackle language in a court case, the opposing sides will give judges considerably different suggestions for what particular words and phrases mean. As in the selection of precedents, the meaning attached to words is likely to differ according to what each side wants the words to mean.

*Constitution*   Conflict over the meaning of words is seen most clearly in the interpretation of the national Constitution. For a document so important and basic to American government, the Constitution is extremely short. It merely outlines the scope and powers of government, the roles of the three branches of government, and individual freedoms. Only a few aspects of government are described fully. Most of the amendments added over the years also are very broad statements of policy designed to cover many different circumstances.

A major reason the Constitution is so brief and general is that it involved many political compromises made at the Constitutional Convention among many state delegates who could not agree on much about the new national government.

With vague and general terms and phrases, it is no wonder that people interpret the Constitution in many different ways and that there always are debate and controversy over how it should be applied to specific cases. There are about as many examples where the words in the Constitution have meant different things to different people as there are court cases. A few examples make the point.

Several recent justices of the U.S. Supreme Court have maintained that constitutional guarantees of free speech mean exactly what the words say: that Congress shall pass *no* law which infringes on the right to free speech. Most other justices have said, however, that free speech is not an *absolute* right, but can be limited or regulated to protect national security or to preserve our system of government.[12]

In 1896, the provision for equal protection of the laws found in the Fourteenth Amendment justified a racial policy of separate but equal facilities for blacks and whites (*Plessy v. Ferguson*), but in 1954 the U.S. Supreme Court decided that separate but equal was inherently unequal and that equal protection required integration (*Brown v. Board*).

Former Chief Justice Warren Burger explained his 1986 dissent in favor of some state regulation of abortion by claiming he would not have voted in favor of *Roe v. Wade* in 1973 if he had known the Court would later interpret that ruling as meaning abortion on demand.[13]

The language of the Constitution and of legal history may seem clear until it is applied to a particular political issue. Then, individuals on all sides begin to attach different meanings to the law to support their political position. Judges do this, too. Although some judges insist that law is clear and easily understood by a trained and experienced lawyer or judge, the reality is that law can have many different meanings. Interpreting the law is not a science, but is part of a judge's personal orientation. Consequently, the meaning of words is not so plain or clear that it can account for the way judges decide particular cases.

**Statutes**  Similar kinds of political issues emerge in defining the meaning of statutes. Statutes usually are much longer and detailed than constitutional clauses and give lawyers and judges many opportunities to examine and interpret words, phrases, and paragraphs. Many statutes are the result of political compromises, and the words and phrases are intentionally vague. But judges have to decide what the language means when they get a case.

Learned Hand, a well-known federal judge, has described the interpretation of legislation as "an act of *creative imagination*. . . . That is what most of our work is and to me it remains. . . . an undertaking of delightful uncertainty."[14] From this view, the plain meaning to one judge will not be so plain to another.

The meaning of statutes is often debated on appellate courts. In the 1930s, for example, the U.S. Supreme Court ruled that a federal motor vehicle theft law did not apply to airplanes, since the act only listed examples of ground transportation. It may seem reasonable and logical to apply the same law to any form of stolen vehicle, but since the law was "clear" it did not apply to airplanes. Likewise, a federal court of appeals overturned a criminal conviction for the interstate shipment of obscene phonograph records because the statute in question did not mention records. The Supreme Court disagreed, however, arguing that the *intent* of the law should not be undermined by too rigid concern with the meaning of the words.

The Supreme Court once delayed completion of a major Tennessee Valley Authority project that threatened the extinction of a small, rare fish. The majority said the Endangered Species Act clearly stated that no funds could be expended for projects that endangered rare animal species. Other justices disagreed, however.[15] The clear language was not always so clear to them.

Interpreting the meaning of statutes is not limited to vague words and phrases debated by appellate courts. Some statutes are intentionally general to permit application to different circumstances and to allow judges to make their own best guess in each case. Often, legislatures cannot agree on specific remedies for particular problems and pass the buck to courts. As discussed earlier, state criminal codes often permit sentences for particular crimes to range from probation to many years in state prison and for certain criminal behavior to be labeled as various specific crimes. Judges and prosecutors have considerable leeway to apply the law as they see fit, and judges' sentences often vary widely even though they rely on the same criminal laws.

In many civil cases, such as divorce, personal injury suits, and even contract violations, judges and jurors have to rely on their own sense of equity or right and wrong to reach a decision, because statutes do not require a particular result or because there are no statutes which govern the situation. For example, a contract between a city and a garbage collection company permitted the company to collect garbage outside the city limits. But the city grew a little every year by annexing county land, and it insisted on taking over garbage collection in the new area. The garbage company sued, claiming that the term "city limits" meant the boundaries when the contract was signed; the city claimed that city limits meant the current city limits. You be the judge.

**Strict Construction**   Closely related to evaluating the meaning of words is the idea of strict construction, which means that judges are supposed to stick very closely to the literal meaning of the words in the Constitution and to avoid judicial lawmaking. Under strict construction, courts should avoid making decisions that extend the scope and power of government beyond that described in the Constitution. Strict construction, however, is not primarily a legal concept, but is part of a political strategy to create a veneer of legalism for selective attacks on judges who make decisions that particular groups do not like. During his campaign for the presidency, for example, Richard Nixon pledged to appoint judges to the federal courts who would be strict construction. His definition of strict construction meant judges who were tough on "crime in the streets," which became a not-so-subtle code for commonplace crime committed by poor blacks.

Similarly, southerners and others often have supported strict construction as part of their opposition to court-ordered desegregation. Since neither education nor race relations is mentioned in the Constitution, strict constructionists argue that courts do not have the authority to require integration, busing, affirmative action, or other programs opposed by local citizens.

Any group that opposes a particular judicial decision is likely to use strict construction to justify its opposition. Though it often has been used by conservatives to attack the Supreme Court, strict construction could be used by anyone who objects to a particular ruling. News reporters, for example, who object to judicial restrictions of their coverage of court cases or their attempts to protect confidential sources of information sometimes protest that the Constitution guarantees *absolute* freedom of the press and that strict construction should be used to protect that freedom. Many judges disagree, however, and believe that freedom of the press must be limited, particularly when it runs into claims for a fair trial, which also is guaranteed by the Constitution.

### Intentions of the Lawmakers

Since the language of law often is unclear, or the apparent meaning is unacceptable, judges often look "behind" statutes or constitutions to try to discover the intent of the authors. The idea here is that while the language itself may be unclear, the process of creating the law may reveal what constitution makers or legislators had in mind when the law was debated, drafted, and voted on by a legislative assembly. This background material provides more information to judges than the written law alone and may give them guidance in making decisions about the meaning of the law.

**Framers of the Constitution**   But the search for intentions runs immediately into problems. This is especially so for the national Constitution and the goals of the framers. First, there are no official records of the debates, nor is there even a running history of exactly what took place at the Constitutional Convention. The only written records are the memoirs of a few notables written years after the close of the convention and the Federalist Papers, written by Alexander Hamilton and other supporters of a strong, centralized national government. While they provide some glimpses about the convention and the ideas behind the Constitution, they are neither a complete nor an unbiased report.

Many delegates to the convention did not stay for the whole time and many disagreed with various provisions. Finally, the Constitution is full of compromises and general policies designed to gather the widest amount of support so that a new federal government could be formed. It was not expected to please everyone or to fit everyone's intentions about what the new government would look like and how it would work.[16]

There is an age-old question that judges pose concerning the intent of the framers that is supposed to help them decide cases: What would the framers have done if they had to decide this case? It is an attractive, reverent question, but it does not get us very far. The founders had no crystal ball and were no better at anticipating the future than we are today. It is safe to say that they never thought or even dreamed about our current society and our problems.

To obtain guidance from their intentions as a solution to current issues is fantasy. A judge who thinks about the early days of the Constitution is inevitably imagining what the framers might have had in mind.

Box 8.2, "What Did the Framers Intend?," illustrates that the perspectives officials have of the Constitution may vary according to their background,

---

**BOX 8.2**

**WHAT DID THE FRAMERS INTEND?**

Former Attorney General and arch conservative Edwin Meese of the Reagan administration has objected to liberals on the Supreme Court using their personal policy preferences to expand the rights of criminal defendants through broad Constitutional interpretation. He insists judges should follow the original intentions of the framers. In his view, expansive Supreme Court decisions violate the Constitution and they should not be considered the law of the land.

Those who disagree with a Supreme Court decision have the responsibility to propose contrary statutes as alternatives to public policy. They need not defer to the Court.

But noted legal scholar, Leonard W. Levy, concludes that theory concerning the search for the intentions of the framers reverses the actual judicial process. Supporters of the theory maintain that:

... decisions of the Court ... [are] reached as a result of a judicial search for Framers' intent, 'whereas, in fact, the intent discovered by the Court is most likely to be determined by the conclusion that the Court wishes to reach. . . .' If we could ascertain original intent, . . . cases would not arise concerning that intent. They arise because the intent is and likely will remain uncertain. . . . The more one looks at a jurisprudence of original intent, the more it seems politically motivated as a disguise for political objectives."

Researchers at the Library of Congress recently discovered an original unpublished draft of the Bill of Rights written by Roger Sherman of Connecticut, one of the framers of the Constitution. Historians had long believed that Sherman opposed the Bill of Rights, but now that proves to be incorrect.

Other documents discovered earlier also show that many changes were made between the early and final drafts of the Constitution. The final version of the Bill of Rights uses broader and more universal language and ignored other proposed amendments because they were too controversial.

The chief of the library's manuscript division says the discovery shows how little we really know about the intentions of the framers. ". . .[T]o try to recover original intent from records that are nonexistent or not faithful to actual proceedings may be an impossible . . . assignment [in interpretation]".

experience, and political attitudes and objectives, and that new discoveries cast doubt on our ability to know original intent.[17]

**Legislative History**  Discovering the intentions of a modern legislature is much easier than searching for the motivations of the framers of the Constitution, but it still does not lead judges to a single path of decision making. In some instances, there is too little information about legislative history to give lawyers and judges a clear picture of what occurred before a bill was signed and what legislators had in mind. This occurs in many states where legislatures do not have large and experienced research staffs or efficient techniques for taking down and storing legislative records. Sometimes there is no legislative history. When the legislative evidence is sketchy or missing, judges have to make the best guess they can.

*New Situations*  This problem sometimes confronts judges who have to deal with old state laws or where new social conditions have occurred that a previous legislature could not or did not anticipate. Judges in different states often reason to different conclusions in similar kinds of cases.

For instance, state laws controlling the selection of jurors have been treated differently. In the 1800s, many states had laws requiring that jurors be selected from the list of registered voters. The effect of these laws was to guarantee that only men could serve on juries, since women were not permitted to vote. However, after women received the vote in 1920 through the Nineteenth Amendment to the Constitution, some women began to demand the right to serve on juries. Many local governments refused and women sued. Certain state supreme courts reasoned that since only men had the right to vote when jury laws were enacted, legislators must have meant that only men could serve on juries. However, other state supreme courts dealing with identical laws reasoned that since state law said that *persons* who were registered to vote may serve on juries and women had received the right to vote (and were persons too!) the legislature must have intended to include new groups of people who became electors. Therefore, women in these states had the right to serve on juries if they were registered voters. These cases dealt with the same laws, but reached different conclusions about legislative intent.[18]

*Conflicting History*  While legislative history is sketchy in some states and in certain laws, a different problem for lawyers and judges is that there often is "too much" legislative history and it is impossible to obtain a clear picture of legislative objectives.

The major problem concerns where and how legislative intent can and should be found. Does it include the attitudes and votes of all of the members of the legislature or perhaps the majority that voted in favor of a bill? If so, are their votes an adequate indicator of their intentions or should legislators be interviewed to obtain their personal motivations? Interviews are theoretically possible for a current legislature, but what about a former legislature that has been out of existence for 2, 5, 10, or more years?

Perhaps the recorded debates or reports in newspapers can provide some insight into legislative intent. But many public speeches and statements by legislators have hidden political purposes, such as whipping up support or opposition to a bill, providing clues to the opposition for possible compromises, or showing political supporters that a legislator is on their side.

Legislators' intentions also often have very little bearing on a particular law being examined by a court. For instance, legislators sometimes logroll with each other or with governors and Presidents. They agree to support one bill in return for the passage of others that provide important benefits such as government spending on highways or public buildings in their districts or tax and business laws that benefit certain of their constituents. Often they know little about and are not especially interested in some of the laws they agree to support. In terms of making law, they have no intent.

*Compromise*   Since the full legislature is not active in creating all laws, most searches for legislative history and intent concentrate on smaller groups of legislators who spend much of their time in various legislative committees. Committees have the major responsibility for drafting bills involving particular subjects. Most legislatures have committees on education, transportation, commerce, corrections, judiciary, welfare, and others. Committees do research, hold public hearings on proposed legislation, write bills to be submitted to the full house, and recommend legislation to other legislators. It is common for most other legislators to go along with committee recommendations on major legislation.

Although committees are especially important in most legislation, a close look at committee history quickly reveals that the members of legislative committees have different impressions about what a bill will include and what it will accomplish. In order to produce a bill that most committee members and other legislative leaders will support, they frequently compromise their personal goals for a group product. In addition, since both houses of a legislature have to agree on a single law, conference committees representing each house often are appointed by legislative leaders to write a final version that both houses will vote to approve. Usually more compromise is required.

Since the intentions of individual legislators, committee members, leaders, and entire houses of the legislature often are not the same, which one should be considered the true legislative intent that judges use to decide cases?

The realistic answer is that there are many legislative intents that often find their way into compromise legislation, and they do not provide clear guidance on how specific conflicts in court cases should be decided.

Justice Antonin Scalia of the U.S. Supreme Court and several other federal judges maintain that legislative intent is impossible to uncover and that judges should only interpret the words in the statute. He maintains that intent is distorted by lobbyists, members of Congress, and legislative staff, who insert new materials into legislative committee reports to give a particular slant to the law. However, Democrats, who frequently control one or both houses of

Congress, worry that the new Republican judges want to ignore legislative intent in favor of their own personal views of what the law should be.[19]

## THE ROLE OF LAW IN JUDICIAL DECISION MAKING

The legal explanations of judicial decision making do not help us understand courts very well. Careful analysis of precedent, the meaning of words, and legislative intent all indicate that legal explanations are too general and open to so many interpretations that they cannot account for how judges make particular decisions. But law pervades the entire judicial process. If it does not explain decision making, what does it do?

### Rationalization

Some observers of the judicial process argue that law is mere window dressing or rationalization for judicial decisions. Since law is too general and imprecise to determine decisions, judges always have to use enormous personal discretion to do their job. Therefore, judicial decisions inevitably reflect judges' attitudes, or their policy goals, or some social factor that influences their thinking.

But the public expects judges to act in a legal way, so they package their decisions in appropriate legal wrappings to make them acceptable or legitimate. Judges could not get away with simply saying their decision is their best guess about how a dispute should be settled or that they believe a certain policy will be good for society. They must make the decision appear as though it is required by what they find in the law for it to be accepted and implemented. Consequently, judges write opinions that include numerous precedents and discussion of statutes, constitutions, and perhaps legal history. Although the references do not cause a particular decision, they support and justify it.

There certainly is some truth to this view, especially on appellate courts, which often have to decide cases that raise novel and unanticipated questions and where there is wide disagreement about how they ought to be handled. There often is no guidance other than a judge's personal values and best guess about what will work. But law is more than a judicial smokescreen. It affects how decisions are made and the scope of decisions.

### Limited Judicial Policymaking

Law is an important value that limits the content of most judicial policymaking. Most judges believe that law requires them to follow precedent and to defer to legislatures. There is no formal rule that prevents judges from aggressively making policy, as some judges do, but their views of the law and the legal process prevent most judges from going off in new directions. It is a self-imposed limitation on their perception of their proper judicial role.

For example, when cases come up questioning the constitutionality of a state law or a local ordinance or a decision of a governor or city council, most judges are likely to rule in favor of other government officials and to permit them to go ahead with their own policies. A court case often delays a government project while the case is being heard, but it usually does not permanently stop it.[20]

The rule of law also makes judges very slow to change their own precedents, and they do so only after they are firmly convinced that a new direction is needed. Even so, change likely occurs only after much time and many court cases have passed. For example, in 1986, the Supreme Court overturned a 1965 decision which made it difficult for black defendants to prove discrimination when blacks were dismissed from juries. The majority opinion noted that accumulating experience in lower court cases had shown that defendants faced "a crippling burden of proof" and that a new policy was necessary. The new policy, which limited prosecutors' use of peremptory challenges (Chapter 7), was welcomed by liberal organizations, but it had taken over 20 years to obtain the new ruling.

Judges also are likely to consult the judicial policy of other jurisdictions before making new decisions. For example, the state supreme courts of New Jersey, New York, and California, and a few others in highly populous, urban, and socially diverse states, have been judicial innovators for several decades. Other states tend to follow their lead, although some are much slower than others to give up old ways and a few in very conservative, rural states reject most outside influence.[21]

An example is judicial policy toward the liability of manufacturers for injuries caused by their products. In the early 1900s, it was practically impossible for an injured person to hold a manufacturer responsible for injuries unless clear negligence could be proved and the consumer had purchased the product directly from the manufacturer. Several supreme courts began to make exceptions to these rules in 1913, but shifts in most courts did not occur until after 1960, when the New Jersey Supreme Court stated that manufacturers created an implied warranty that their products were safe and that direct links between consumer and producer were unnecessary for liability. In 1963, the California Supreme Court adopted an even broader rule of strict liability that did not rely on warranties. In less than 10 years, twenty-three state supreme courts followed the New Jersey and California examples, and a few years later, nearly three-quarters of the states had similar rules.[22]

Many judges also believe their role requires them to select the narrowest possible basis for deciding a case. Rather than seeing a case as an opportunity to do something new and bold, they usually believe they should limit their impact on policy by disposing of issues on specific grounds that affect only the litigants in the case.

For example, a health club owner already convicted of running a house of prostitution argued before a state supreme court that he should not be prosecuted again for the same act under a state antiracketeering law, because it would violate constitutional protections against double jeopardy (two or more prosecutions for the same crime). He also argued that the racketeering law was unconstitutional, because it was too vague and broad, and constituted cruel and unusual punishment.

The court agreed with the double jeopardy claim, but refused to even consider whether the racketeering law was constitutional. The net effect of the decision was that the criminal defendant succeeded in stopping the second prosecution, but the antiracketeering law itself was ignored and allowed to stand and be used again by prosecutors in the future.[23]

## Proper Procedure and Legitimacy

The rule of law and legal methods have a long history and tradition and provide the foundation for contemporary courts as separate government institutions, free from extensive legislative and executive control. The legal culture also emphasizes the superiority of independent courts over legislatures or executive agencies for resolving disputes in an impartial way. Legislatures and executives are assumed to be riddled with partisanship, influenced by public opinion, and preoccupied with policymaking and political compromise. In contrast, courts are seen as havens for *equal treatment, fair and explicit procedure, and an impartial hearing.* Going to court sometimes is the only chance for fairness.

This is part of judicial lore and a major characteristic of our political system. Many people believe that getting justice depends a lot on who you are and how much money you have, but most people still look to courts as a place for as much impartiality and equal treatment as it is possible to get in an imperfect, human world. Specific legal rules may not explain specific court decisions, but the rule of law is an important symbol and a process that supports our relatively free and open political system.

Judicial procedure, with its emphasis on fair hearings and on the right to produce evidence and witnesses and to challenge the opposition, is so important in the United States that it increasingly has been applied to decision making in other parts of government, particularly agencies of the executive branch that have the job of translating general legislative policy into day-to-day government regulations. Businesses, individual taxpayers, government employees, and other citizens who receive government benefits are affected by various government rules. People dissatisfied with agency policy often have the right to a judicial-like hearing before an agency official. Many government agencies use special administrative law judges who are not regular employees of the agencies to hear disputes. Their decisions also may be appealed to the regular courts.

Courts and law also provide a way for individuals and governments to settle conflicts without violence or without relying exclusively on personal power. Laws do not prevent violence or even revolution, but for most people in the

United States law provides a relatively civilized, routine, safe, and available way to resolve disputes. Certainly using law and courts costs money and requires personal resolve and some knowledge and sophistication, but courts are widely available. Increasing use of other judicial-like methods such as mediation and arbitration also may make justice cheaper, more available, and more effective. These too are part of law and the legal process.

### Values

Finally, law and judicial decisions are part of the broader social system and a way for social values and beliefs to influence official decisions. Generally, law and judicial decisions reflect middle-class and business values, since judges, most other office holders, and politically active citizens are middle-class.

Most criminal laws and judicial activity emphasize violent crimes against property and persons, and much criminal law directed at victimless crime also reflects traditional middle-class morals. Courts also are constantly asked to apply laws in favor of property rights, contracts, and debt collections. Law reflects social values, affects the kinds of cases judges are asked to decide, and affects the typical solutions that are used.

### CONCLUSION

This chapter has examined the importance of law in judicial decision making. Major features include fact finding and applying the law, with particular emphasis on the rule of precedent, the language of law, and the intentions of lawmakers. There are problems with each of these approaches, however, because there often are numerous precedents, and language and intentions often are unclear or conflicting. Judges, lawyers, and jurors always have lots of room to decide for themselves what the law means.

Despite the shortcomings of law in explaining judicial decisions, law has a profound impact on courts. Most important, law gives shape to the judicial process and particular procedures for settling disputes. It also reflects our strong concern with opportunities for fair hearings and impartial decisions.

Judicial processes have been adapted and used in mediation and arbitration as well as other government agencies. We probably will continue to strive for more fairness and build on the judicial model to achieve it. Law also reflects dominant social and political values in judicial decisions. While these values are predominantly middle-class and conservative, the courts adapt to change, although slowly, and tend to incorporate social values into the law. Finally, law is important in shaping the role of courts in policymaking and largely limits innovative decision making.

The following chapter continues our concern with judicial decision making, but concentrates on social and political influences on courts and judges and how social scientists have tried to explain judicial decisions.

## SUGGESTIONS FOR ADDITIONAL READING

Bork, Robert H.: *The Tempting of America: The Political Seduction of the Law* (New York: Simon and Schuster, Inc., 1990). Former Court of Appeals judge and nominee to the Supreme Court Judge Robert H. Bork argues forcefully that courts are legal, not political, institutions. Judges must resist the temptation to do justice in individual cases, which often means ignoring the law, in order to maintain the legitimacy of legal institutions.

Cardozo, Benjamin N.: *The Nature of the Judicial Process* (New Haven: Yale University Press, 1921). In this legal classic, a famous legal scholar and Supreme Court justice explains the process of judicial decision making, emphasizing the major legal and social forces which judges take into account.

Frank, Jerome: *Courts on Trial* (Princeton: Princeton University Press, 1949). A noted federal judge explains the shortcomings of trials for finding the facts and other considerations that typically affect trial court decisions.

Levi, Edward: *An Introduction to Legal Reasoning* (Chicago: University of Chicago Press, 1949). Another legal classic, this is a basic introduction to the methods courts are believed to use in deciding cases and adapting precedents to current cases.

Llewellyn, Karl: *The Bramble Bush* (New York: Oceana Publications, 1951). The author examines the links between courts, formal law, and society, but also the limitations of the legal approach to understanding judicial decision making.

## NOTES

1 Interview with the author.
2 Jerome Frank, *Courts on Trial* (Princeton: Princeton University Press, 1949), chaps. 3 and 6.
3 Edward Levi, *An Introduction to Legal Reasoning* (Chicago: University of Chicago Press, 1949); Lief H. Carter, *Reason in Law* (Boston: Little, Brown and Co., 1979).
4 Karl N. Llewellyn, *The Bramble Bush* (New York: Oceana Publications, 1951), p. 35; "Remarks on the Theory of Appellate Decisions and the Rules or Canons about How Statutes Are to Be Construed," *Vanderbilt Law Review*, 3 (1950), 396.
5 Albert Tate, Jr., " 'Policy' in Judicial Decisions," *Louisiana Law Review*, 20 (1959), 62–63.
6 Henry R. Glick, *The Right to Die: Policy Innovation and Its Consequences* (New York: Columbia University Press, 1992).
7 Benjamin N. Cardozo, *The Nature of the Judicial Process* (New Haven: Yale University Press, 1921), pp. 20–21.
8 Levi, pp. 1–2; Roscoe Pound, "The Theory of Judicial Decision," *Harvard Law Review*, 36 (June 1923), 951.
9 Henry Robert Glick, *Supreme Courts in State Politics* (New York: Basic Books, Inc., 1971), p. 79.
10 Harold J. Spaeth, *Supreme Court Policy Making* (San Francisco: W. H. Freemaan and Co., 1979), pp. 55–63.
11 *U.S. v. Butler*, 297 US 1 (1936).

12 Lawrence Baum, *The Supreme Court* (Washington, D.C.: Congressional Quarterly Press, 1981), p. 112.

13 *Tallahassee Democrat*, June 12, 1986, p. 1.

14 Learned Hand, "Fifty Years of Federal Judicial Service," in Donald K. Carroll (ed.), *Handbook for Judges* (Chicago: American Judicature Society, 1961), p. 97. Italics added.

15 These cases are cited in Edgar Bodenheimer et al., *An Introduction to the Anglo-American Legal System* (St. Paul, Minn.: West Publishing Co., 1980), pp. 133–136.

16 William Anderson, *The Nation and the States: Rivals or Partners?* (Minneapolis: University of Minnesota Press, 1955).

17 *New York Times*, October 22, 1986, p. 1 and July 29, 1987, p. 1; Leonard W. Levy, *Original Intent and the Framers' Constitution* (New York: MacMillan Publishing Co., 1988), pp. 388–89, quoting Jacobus tenBroek, "Use by the United States Supreme Court of Extrinsic Aids in Constitutional Construction; the Intent Theory," *California Law Review* 27 (1939), 404–406; 410.

18 Bodenheimer et al., pp. 145–146.

19 *New York Times*, April 14, 1989, p. 19.

20 See, for example, Kenneth M. Dolbeare, *Trial Courts in Urban Politics* (New York: John Wiley & Sons, Inc., 1967), pp. 108–109.

21 Gregory A. Caldeira, "On the Reputation of State Supreme Courts," *Political Behavior*, 5 (1983), 83–108; Peter Harris, "Structural Change in the Communication of Precedent among State Supreme Courts, 1870–1970," *Social Networks*, 4 (1982), 201–212.

22 Lawrence Baum and Bradley C. Canon, "State Supreme Courts as Activists: New Doctrines in the Law of Torts," in Mary Cornelia Porter and G. Alan Tarr (eds.), *State Supreme Courts: Policymakers in the Federal System* (Westport, Conn.: Greenwood Press, 1982), pp. 83–108.

23 *St. Petersburg Times*, August 7, 1981, p. 2B.

# 9

## SOCIETY, POLITICS, AND DECISION MAKING

The political view of judicial decision making sees judges and courts as important parts of the broader political and social system. The bonds between judges and society influence decision making and motivate people to become involved in judicial politics.

For example, all methods for choosing judges involve some type of partisan or interest group politics. Some of the politicking is geared to rewarding friends and supporters with good jobs, but politicians and lawyers also know that judges have discretion and are influenced in decision making by their backgrounds, past experiences, and points of view. If lawyers really believed that the law was clear and impartial and that it dictated the decisions judges made in every case, they would not care who served on the courts. Any trained lawyer would do. But lawyers and politicians understand that it does matter who becomes a judge, and like choosing a jury for a trial, they use their best hunches to guess which candidates are likely to make the kinds of decisions they want.

### THE POLITICAL PERSPECTIVE

The study of judicial decision making has something in common with the guesses that politicians and lawyers make about judges. For instance, social scientists have worked to discover the influence that judges' political party affiliations and other personal background characteristics have on decisions. Like politicians, social scientists are interested in whether judges' attitudes toward major social issues and groups account for the way they decide cases. Sometimes judges' attitudes are obvious through their public statements, written opinions, or prior political activity, while at other times social scientists conclude that judges have strong attitudes toward issues in cases because of their remarkable consistency in deciding many similar types of cases.

Judges are likely to be influenced by other things as well. For instance, judges read the newspapers and are likely to be influenced by changes in public opinion in their own area and the nation. They also have to take account of new laws and developments in technology and the social life of the country. Therefore, the broad social context or environment that surrounds courts is apt to affect judges' decisions.

Judges on appellate courts also have to interact with other judges in order to produce a court decision. They may have to modify their own point of view in order to create a majority. As we already have discussed in plea bargaining, the decisions of trial judges are affected by interaction in courthouse work groups.

Much social science research assumes that since judges are "politicians in black robes," they will behave in about the same way as legislators or other officials. While judges have much in common with others, they also are likely to see themselves and their job as unique. How they see themselves, their relations with other people, and their work contributes to judges' conceptions of the judicial role. Judges see their role differently and there is some evidence it influences their decisions.

### Social Science

An important difference between the perspective of politicians, lawyers, and social scientists toward decision making is that politicians and lawyers usually are interested in one judge and often one decision at a time. When a vacancy occurs on a court, for example, all public attention rivets on the list of potential candidates and the kinds of personal backgrounds and attitudes that are believed to be critical for the successful nominee. Speculation also abounds about the kinds of decisions the nominee will make, especially in controversial cases such as abortion, integration, etc.

Social scientists share this personal interest too, but their research on decision making usually includes gathering information on many judges and many decisions in order to paint a much broader and complete picture of the social conditions or variables that influence judicial decision making.

For example, from many studies we can make some fairly reliable conclusions about when and why political party membership makes a difference in decision making. This is very different from drawing conclusions about all judges from our own personal knowledge about who was chosen for a judgeship in Texas, New York City, or Seattle. The factors that determine particular selections in particular cities are likely to be very different. We cannot generalize from one or two examples, and social science research tries to uncover general patterns of judicial behavior and the circumstances which affect judges' decisions.

**Core Influences**   There are four main sources of influence on judicial decision making that have been studied heavily by social scientists. They include
*judges' backgrounds and environments, judicial attitudes, the judicial role,
and group interaction among appellate judges.*

Although these are separate approaches, they always are related to each
other. For instance, a lawyer who has spent an entire life in one part of a state
and who is chosen as a judge for a local trial court is influenced by the past,
personal attitudes formed over the years, and the social and political environment that surrounds the court. As a lifelong resident of an area and as an
educated and informed member of the community, the lawyer cannot help but
be affected by the values of the local society, the views of other political elites,
and a personal point of view. Most research on judicial decision making has
been done on appellate courts, but some studies also show that trial judges are
affected by many similar factors.

## SOCIAL BACKGROUNDS AND ENVIRONMENTS

The study of judges' personal backgrounds assumes basically that people
behave according to who they are. Background characteristics reveal the kinds
of personal experiences and exposure that judges have had during their lives. In
turn, these lead them to develop certain outlooks or ways of seeing facts and
issues that are presented in court cases. The fact that a judge is a Democrat or a
Republican, or a born-again Protestant or an agnostic, or is young or old does
not mean much in itself. But such personal characteristics become important as
indicators or clues about life experiences and judges' perspectives toward cases.

Judges also work in particular environments. Sometimes, their territory is
very limited, such as part of a city or county or, in the case of federal district
judges, parts of an individual state. Some state appellate judges also have
jurisdiction over parts of a state, and even federal appeals judges decide cases
that come from a particular region of the country. Each of these areas has a
somewhat distinctive local flavor or culture that may affect a judge's perspective. More important, since judges often are products of the same environment
as their court, the link between their background and the local culture often is
very strong and has a clear effect on judicial decision making.

Of all of the social background effects, judges' political party affiliations and
local political cultures have the greatest impact. Sex and race differences and
public opinion affect some decisions, but they generally are less important.

### Political Party and Culture

The combined effect of judges' backgrounds and local environments is clearest
in the trial courts. Sometimes judges fit into their locale like a hand in a glove.
Appellate judges are more removed from state or local environments, but their
decisions also are shaped partly by these same influences.

**State Trial Courts**    A comparison of sentencing in criminal cases by Pittsburgh and Minneapolis trial judges illustrates the impact of local political parties and culture on the trial courts.

Pittsburgh judges consistently are more lenient than those in Minneapolis.[1] They give probation more often, give shorter jail terms, and do not punish defendants who reject plea bargains with stiffer trial sentences.

The best explanation for these differences lies in the judges' attitudes toward criminal defendants and their beliefs about the goals of the criminal justice process. In turn, their attitudes are linked to how judges are chosen and the particular types of lawyers that each city puts on the courts.

At the time of the study, Pittsburgh judges were elected on a partisan ballot and got their jobs through extremely active and close connections with the local Democratic party. Most of the judges had supported and campaigned for other candidates and had held other political and government jobs. The Pittsburgh bar association had practically no role in judicial selection.

Pittsburgh was an old industrial city with many different ethnic, religious, racial, and economic groups. Most of the trial judges have ethnic and lower-income backgrounds typical of those who make up the urban Democratic party. And, although the judges have achieved the high status of a trial judge, they were educated in the "school of hard knocks" on the way up. Many of them empathize with defendants appearing before them.

Interviews with the judges show that their attitudes reflect their background and experiences and that they have strong orientations to the local popular political culture. They believe that defendants deserve a break, that judges should stay close to the people and make decisions on practical rather than formal legalistic grounds, that probation gives a defendant a chance to straighten out, and that each defendant should be carefully evaluated as an individual who might be helped by the system. Justice is very personal in Pittsburgh.

Minneapolis is very different. Minneapolis has a much more homogeneous northern European white Protestant population and a tradition of bipartisan politics in the selection of judges. Instead of political parties having a major role, the bar association and local newspapers are more important in determining who becomes a candidate. Elections are very low-key.

The judges are middle-class, Protestant, and northern European, and are selected from business-oriented law practices, often from large firms. They rarely have had prior political or government experience and little or no previous contact with lower-income people. Their views also closely reflect the local legal culture. They reject the personal and folksy approach of the Pittsburgh judges and see courts as organizations to protect society.

The Minneapolis judges adopt a crime control perspective of the criminal courts, and while they acknowledge the role of rehabilitation in criminal justice, they are much more likely to emphasize deterrence, punishment, and strict standards. Few of them are critical of state prisons and police. Their trials are highly formal ceremonies.

There is little doubt that Minneapolis decisions differ from Pittsburgh decisions because of differences in the local political and legal cultures, the way judges are chosen for office, and the kinds of people each society selects as judges.

**Federal Trial Courts**    Political party and local culture also affect decision making in the federal trial courts. As explained in Chapter 4, most federal district judges are born and reared in their judicial districts or the same state, and senatorial courtesy often assures the appointment of local politicos who have extensive experience in state politics. Presidents also favor members of their own party, and the Reagan and Bush administrations, in particular, have established close links between party membership and conservative ideology.

Democratic judges generally are more liberal than Republican ones. Both groups take positions which parallel long-standing differences between the two political parties. The differences extend to decisions concerning which parties have the right or standing to sue as well as decisions concerning the merits of their claims once they are presented in a trial.

Democrats decide more often in favor of criminal defendants who claim their constitutional rights were violated by state courts or in state prisons, they are more favorable to claims of racial and sexual discrimination, and they are more likely to vote in favor of labor unions than businesses and to permit wider government regulation of business. The Democrats usually are more attuned to the interests of underdogs, whereas Republicans emphasize business values and the power of government to limit individual liberties.[2]

The party affiliation of a federal judge probably is the most important influence on decision making, but there are additional political forces that affect the size of the gap between Democratic and Republican judges. One influence in the policy consistency of the U.S. Supreme Court. When the Court adopts a clear policy position, judges of both parties are more likely to toe the line and their decisions do not differ very much. During the early 1960s, for example, the Supreme Court produced consistent liberal judicial policy on civil liberties and most federal district judges followed their lead. Differences between Republican and Democratic judges were slight.[3]

*Powerful Local Culture*    An important exception, however, and one which also illustrates the powerful pull of party and local environments, were federal judges in the deep south during the early 1960s. Southern federal judges often clung to segregation and refused to follow the Supreme Court's lead despite having their decisions repeatedly reversed on appeal.

The judges who were least likely to decide cases in favor of blacks were those who had been born and educated in their states, had once held various state political offices, and were members of the Democratic party and the Southern Baptist church, the dominant and all-white political and religious organizations in their region. Many of them had been raised in the era when segregation was taken for granted as part of southern life, and they could not conceive of major change. Their personal backgrounds and previous experiences and the local political and social climate were too strong for them to shift judicial gears.[4]

However, change gradually did occur as the Supreme Court continued to provide consistent liberal leadership during most of the 1960s and new, somewhat more liberal judges were appointed to the courts by Democratic Presidents Kennedy and Johnson. Nevertheless, southern federal judges still are somewhat less supportive of individual rights and equality. Of judges in all regions of the country, they are least likely to decide in favor of constitutional rights of criminal defendants and claims of women in sexual discrimination cases. They also have been reluctant to order busing to achieve racial integration of public schools in areas with large black populations.[5] The region and state-based senatorial courtesy still exert conservative influence. The appointment of additional conservative southern judges by President Bush is unlikely to change this pattern.

*Wider Party Gap*   As the U.S. Supreme Court has become more conservative due to the appointment of new conservative Republican justices, there has been a growing gap in the decisions of the federal district judges based on their political party affiliation and the identity of the Presidents who appointed them.

Democratic judges appointed by earlier Democratic administrations have tended to look to older Supreme Court precedents to support liberal decisions in civil liberties and the rights of criminal defendants, while newer Republican judges have relied on more recent conservative decisions of the Rehnquist Court. Presidents Reagan and Bush have appointed a majority of the judges currently serving on the federal courts, but many Democratic judges will retain their positions for years to come. Therefore, we probably will continue to see differences among district court judges based on their political party affiliations and the policies of the Presidents who appointed them.[6]

**Appellate Courts**   It seems reasonable to guess that social backgrounds and local environments would have the greatest impact on trial judges who have stayed close to home all their lives and whose views are constantly reinforced by local society. But social backgrounds affect appellate judges, too.

Although they leave home for a post on a higher court, appellate judges usually have spent much of their lives in one particular area and have accumulated many years of personal and political experience that continues to influence their behavior.

*Partisan States*   Politics in Michigan is about as partisan as it is possible to get in the United States. The two political parties are very competitive and closely linked to two major state interest groups. The Democratic party generally depends on the United Auto Workers and other unions for its main support; the Republicans largely represent the management side of the auto industry and other businesses. The health of the auto industry and conflict between labor and management probably are the most sensitive and heated issues in the state.

Michigan judges are officially elected on a nonpartisan ballot, but the nominees also are endorsed by state party conventions, which nearly always select strong party supporters for court vacancies. Despite the nonpartisan ballot, judicial candidates have openly campaigned as Democrats and Republicans and have been supported by their state party organization.[7]

Once on the state supreme court, judges have taken fairly predictable political positions, especially in cases that reflect conflict between the political parties and their interest group supporters—workers' compensation (injuries on the job) and unemployment compensation. During one period of intense party conflict, in nearly every case in which the judges disagreed on the outcome, all the Democratic judges voted together against all the Republican judges. The Democrats supported the worker and the Republicans voted for management.

But, Republican and Democratic judges frequently formed separate blocs on a number of other issues as well. The Democratic judges were more likely to vote in favor of criminal defendants seeking a new trial, in favor of government regulation of business, in favor of individuals suing business, and for broadening legal rules affecting divorce, child custody, and trust and estate matters. The Republican judges take the opposite and more conservative position in most of these cases. It is also interesting that all the Democratic judges resided in larger cities, while all the Republican judges had their homes in small towns.[8]

After the Democrats had obtained a clear majority on the court and were voting heavily in favor of labor, businesses also began to reduce the number of cases they appealed to the court in apparent anticipation of defeat at the hands of the Democratic judges.

*Less Partisan States*   In some states, party membership does not account for differences in judges' decisions, and Democratic judges vote with Republicans about as often as they vote with fellow party members. One explanation is that in some areas judicial selection is genuinely bipartisan and both political parties endorse the same candidates. The judges also do not have extensive prior careers in partisan politics.[9] Although they identify with a political party, they are not active partisans and may not see court issues as reflecting political party platforms or particular constituencies.

Many states lie between the extremes of having much or little party influence on decision making due to the mix of judges on individual courts. There are numerous courts which include a few judges who are heavily influenced by their party background and others who have had little interest and exposure to partisan politics.[10]

Additional studies of the U.S. Supreme Court, federal courts of appeals, and the state supreme courts consistently show that party is the most significant variable explaining judges' decisions. Democratic judges are more liberal in a wide range of cases. More than Republicans, they tend to decide in favor of criminal defendants seeking new trials, people injured in automobile and industrial accidents, advocates of civil liberties, government regulation of business, the person seeking a divorce, and debtors rather and creditors.[11] There are differences, however, based on local political traditions and cultures. This appears clearest in state supreme courts, which are embedded in distinctively different political systems.

### Race and Sex

Although a judge's political party affiliation is a crucial influence in decision making, recent increases in the number of nonwhite and female judges have led political commentators and social scientists to wonder if a judge's race or sex makes a difference in judicial decision making as well.

Some key questions are: will black and female judges be more forgiving in criminal cases or favor minority defendants; will they favor the rights of underdogs and the disadvantaged; will they be more inclined to vote for minority and women's rights in discrimination cases or in others that involve the status of minorities and women?

**Blacks**   Most of what we know about differences between black and white judges concerns their sentencing of black and white criminal defendants. There is some evidence that black judges are slightly more lenient than white judges toward black defendants whose crimes and criminal records are similar to those of white defendants.

But the differences are not very great, nor consistent from city to city, nor always in the direction we might expect.[12] In some cities, black judges are more evenhanded toward both black and white defendants, while white judges are somewhat tougher on blacks. In other cities, black judges are less likely to imprison black defendants, but the length of prison sentences for black and white defendants are similar. There is no evidence that black judges dismiss cases against blacks nor allow blacks to escape punishment for their crimes.

A reason that black and white judges are not as different as we might expect is that they both are recruited for the courts from a small group of politically eligible lawyers who have similar political experience, law school education, and middle-class backgrounds (Chapter 4). They are likely to have similar values toward crime and criminals.

**Women**   Studies of women on the criminal courts also show that female and male judges are more alike than different, although there are variations in certain types of cases.[13]

In one city, female judges were more likely to convict defendants of rape, but the sentences they imposed were more lenient than those of the male judges. However, female judges sentenced female defendants to prison significantly more often than their male colleagues and the sentences they imposed were longer. The male judges were paternalistic toward most female defendants, believing that a prison term was not an appropriate sentence for most women defendants.

There is some evidence that women judges are more supportive of women's rights. A survey of female judges found that nearly half labeled themselves as feminists, although nearly three-quarters of the male judges were at least sympathetic to more liberated roles for women. The judges also were asked to decide two simulated cases involving alimony for a woman's education and a name change to a woman's maiden name. Both male and female judges overwhelmingly supported the alimony, but men were less sure of the wisdom of allowing women to use their maiden name when they had children who would carry the father's name.

The sex and the attitudes of the judges were important in accounting for how they decided this case. But political party was important, too. Judges sympathetic to women's causes were three times as likely to be Democrats.[14] Therefore, knowing the sex of a judge is insufficient for predicting how cases involving women's rights will come out. Additional information on the judge's political party and his or her attitude is needed before we should place our bets.

There has been little investigation of sexual differences in other kinds of cases, but sex-related issues are not relevant in most litigation. Political party probably will be much more important since there are both liberal and conservative—as well as Democratic and Republican—men and women, and it always is possible to locate suitable judges with all shades of political ideology. Liberal, conservative, as well as middle-of-the-road female judges have been recruited to the state supreme courts.[15]

Although political party is the most important factor which influences judges' decisions, additional personal characteristics have some effect. Many studies indicate that Protestant judges are more conservative on most social issues than Catholic or Jewish judges. Religious minorities are more likely to identify with underdogs and tend to lean in their direction. Older judges, those with previous government experience, tend to favor the government in criminal cases and to take other conservative positions.[16]

## Limits of Social Backgrounds and Environment

**Major Finding**    The general conclusion that emerges from most background and environment studies is that Democratic, non-Protestant, younger judges with little previous government or judicial experience take the liberal or underdog position more often than other judges. A judge's race or sex has a minor influence.

Many court cases raise issues that reflect concerns typical of American politics and the stands that the political parties and major interest groups take. To varying degrees, judges identify with these groups and issues and see court cases in a certain social or political light. Judges' political party affiliation is the single most important background factor in decision making, but its role varies according to patterns of local politics.

Political party may be a "summary" variable that captures and reflects a wide variety of personal experience and focuses it on the issues in cases. Judges who have been especially active in politics are most sensitive to the social content of court cases and respond to them in terms of their previous experience and outlook. The impact of political party affiliation also is especially apparent in cases that raise the most sensitive and divisive party issues, particularly labor-management conflicts.

Discovering that party affiliation and other characteristics frequently lead to differences in judicial decisions is important, especially since the finding runs contrary to legal views of how judges decide cases. Personal backgrounds have an impact on decisions due to the social, economic, and political content of cases and judges' experiences, not law and legal training.

Despite this overall general discovery, however, backgrounds do not account for most of the differences in judges' decisions on most courts.[17] This means, for instance, that while there are differences overall between Democratic and Republican judges, many individual Democratic and Republican judges still vote together. We often find in social research that one variable or even a set of related factors cannot fully account for a particular behavior, such as judges' voting. Many factors contribute together to understanding how judges decide cases. Judges' backgrounds and local environments contribute part of the explanation.

*Unknown Characteristics*   One limitation of this research lies in the kind of background information used to account for judicial decisions. Research on judicial backgrounds generally gathers information that is readily available in published biographical directories. Judges usually list their major social, political, and legal affiliations, education, employment, and other similar data. This information has been extremely useful in dramatizing the links between backgrounds and decisions, but it does not tap all the relevant background information about judges.

Other information might also be useful to relate to decisions, but it is harder to get. Some of it probably is impossible to obtain, especially for large numbers of judges. For instance, certain psychologists believe that personalities are set by age 5 or so. It would be intriguing to know something about judges' very early socialization and child training experiences, whether they came from a strict or lenient home, the nature of mother/father-child relationships, cultural origins, etc. It might be very interesting to see if early childhood experiences are related to decisions in cases affecting the rights of criminals, divorce cases, or cases that pit the haves against the have-nots. But, except for the occasionally cooperative judge who might agree to a "political psychoanalysis," we probably cannot get much of this kind of data.[18]

## Public Opinion

From the legal perspective, public opinion is not supposed to have an effect on judges' decisions, and lifetime appointments are intended to assure the separation of courts and opinion. However, since judges, both appointed and elected, usually have been born and reared locally and recruited from a local political system, it seems likely that public opinion would have an effect, especially in issues that are locally visible and controversial.

In addition, as discussed earlier in regard to judicial administration, many judges seem to consider themselves independent judicial officials who represent local populations in the courts. Consequently, judges may feel that they ought to take local values into account.

Most evidence indicates that public opinion occasionally has an effect on highly visible and controversial decisions when public opinion is clear and closely related to a particular type of case. In contrast, there is very little evidence that public opinion has a routine influence on most judicial decisions. Most of the time, the public pays little attention to courts and generally knows little about the content of decisions, including those of the U.S. Supreme Court.[19]

**Trial Courts**　An unusual link between public opinion and trial court decisions in California illustrates the rare situation in which public opinion may influence judges' decisions.

Sentencing in marijuana cases often changed in severity shortly after a public referendum was held on reducing criminal penalties for personal use of marijuana.[20] Since county votes on the marijuana issue varied considerably, judges did not become uniformly lenient or harsh. Instead, judges who were lenient prior to the referendum sometimes became more severe if the local vote indicated that the population favored keeping the criminal penalties. Severe judges often became more lenient when the vote revealed that the local population was in favor of reducing the penalties. The research took into account the possible separate effect of prosecutors' sentencing recommendations as well as other factors that might influence the judges. Even with these considerations, the referendum vote still had an important and independent effect on sentencing.

Similar results occurred in studies of the sentencing decisions of federal district judges in draft evasion cases during the Vietnam war.[21] Even though federal judges are appointed for life and cannot lose their jobs to a hostile voting public, judges' decisions reflected changes in public opinion about the war. There was a close relationship between public opinions that U.S. involvement in Vietnam was a mistake and the tendency of judges to give probation rather than a jail sentence to draft evaders. Federal district courts in states that generally are more innovative and progressive in policymaking also were somewhat more likely to give lighter sentences.

In issues as visible and controversial as marijuana, the Vietnam war, and race relations, judges can easily become aware of local and national opinion through their contacts with local people, the news media, and an occasional poll. Judges also may develop similar points of view from the same information available to everyone else. Even though there is no direct pressure from local political groups, their decisions may coincide with local beliefs and other patterns of state and local politics.

*Routine Decisions*   Except for highly visible and controversial cases, there is little evidence that public opinion directly influences trial court decisions. People are unlikely to think very much about most divorce or insurance or contract cases or to have an opinion about how they ought to be decided.

But even on such a salient and controversial issue as crime, public opinion has no clear effect. A study of Florida's major trial courts revealed that public opinion concerning the seriousness of crime and citizens' fear of crime had no bearing on the type or length of criminal sentences. Curiously, in Miami and other large cities, where the public was extremely concerned with crime, sentencing actually was more lenient than in most other parts of the state.[22]

The reason public opinion probably has no general effect is that it is not sharply focused on specific types of cases or clearly communicated to the courts so that judges and prosecutors can take it into account. Judges also must respond to other more immediate pressures when they are sentencing defendants to jail. For example, in large cities, jail overcrowding and the repetitious flow of less-than-homicide crimes probably soften the seriousness of most crime in the eyes of judges and prosecutors.

**Appellate Courts**   Nearly all of the research concerning the effects of public opinion on appellate courts has been done on the U.S. Supreme Court. But one interesting study has suggested that at reelection time, state supreme court judges may reduce their normal level of dissents in highly controversial cases, such as involving the death penalty, if they believe their dissents would run contrary to public opinion.[23] Because death penalty cases are visible and controversial and a number of state supreme courts have many of them, it is possible that public opinion could have an occasional effect under these unusual circumstances.

Certainly, it appears that if judges make highly unpopular decisions in a string of visible death penalty or other cases, such as former Justice Rose Bird and her colleagues of the California Supreme Court (Chapter 4), there sometimes is retribution at the polls.

*U.S. Supreme Court*   Justices on the U.S. Supreme Court are appointed for life and are far removed from the routines of politics, so that there is good reason to doubt that the Court will be influenced by public opinion. Also, the rare occasions when the justices mention public opinion in their written opinions, it most often concerns the death penalty, and then they usually disapprove of public opinion as a basis for making decisions.[24] But other federal judges are also appointed for life, and there is some evidence that they respond to clear indicators of public opinion, so perhaps the Supreme Court does as well.

A key problem is finding clear evidence of public opinion. Few polls have been done before or after Supreme Court decisions, or that clearly measure public sentiment toward the precise issues that the Court decides. Much of the best research is based on matching scientific national polls to fewer than 200 decisions decided over several decades.[25]

But even in these cases, national public opinion is not uniform. When the Court announces decisions and pollsters set out with questions to gauge public approval, the public generally is divided, with some in favor and some against the decisions, and people often favor and oppose different decisions at the same time. Public opinion also changes rapidly and often seems inconsistent from one poll to the next. All of this makes it extremely difficult for the justices to respond to opinion in future similar cases, even if they were inclined to do so.

However, there is some evidence of a link between public opinion and the Court. The Supreme Court is more likely to overturn local or state policies that deviate from national public opinion. Overall, it has upheld 47 percent of local policies that were consistent with national public opinion, but only 34 percent that were not. However, this also means that the Supreme Court overturns many local policies regardless of the direction of public opinion. In addition, if public opinion runs contrary to a federal law involved in a case, the Court is more likely to declare it unconstitutional. The Supreme Court has held constitutional nearly 70 percent of all federal laws. It upheld 80 percent which were consistent with national public opinion, but slightly over 60 percent that were inconsistent with it.[26]

Although it appears that the Supreme Court and public opinion sometimes match, there may be reasons other than public influence for the similarities.[27] For example, the justices may respond to particular constituencies such as blacks, women, or corporations whose interests are involved in specific cases than to general and vague national public opinion. But public opinion might match the direction of the decision because the public also is sympathetic to these various interests. The justices also form their own views of controversial issues and these may parallel mass public opinion.

Overall, about 60 percent of Supreme Court decisions are consistent with national public opinion, but this is about the same level of public approval attained by the rest of the federal government.[28] The public usually supports or quietly accepts most policies, which may explain the apparent linkage between public opinion and judicial policy. There also is evidence that if the public thinks well of the rest of the government, it sometimes spills over into approval for the Court, even though most people have little knowledge of Court decisions.

In general, while national public opinion and Supreme Court decisions sometimes move in the same direction, social scientists have not yet identified a clear link or a mechanism by which public opinion has been shown to influence the Supreme Court.

While it is uncertain that public opinion influences the Supreme Court in the short run, it probably has an effect in the long run through Presidential elections. This is not the same as saying the Supreme Court follows the election returns, which implies shifts in decisions as voter preferences change. Rather, as new Presidents are elected in response to majority opinion, many of them make new court appointments that reflect their own policy priorities. In turn, the views of the new judges often reflect recent public opinion as well.

But if public opinion shifts sharply in the other direction and the incumbent party is voted out of office, the Supreme Court may be out of sync with the rest of society, at least until new people once again are appointed.

## JUDICIAL ATTITUDES

The study of judicial attitudes is closely related to background analysis, and in some research the two approaches are combined. After all, backgrounds are relevant to decision making only when they are kept alive in a judge's mind through current attitudes and behavior.

But attitudes are not the same as backgrounds. Backgrounds are a kind of social map that locates and highlights the major characteristics and affiliations in a judge's life. Some of them, such as political party affiliation and political activism, are important in decision making because they reflect a profound and long-lasting set of experiences that shape the way judges see the world.

Personal backgrounds may influence judicial attitudes, but attitudes are not mirror images of an individual's past. *Judicial attitudes are the personal orientations, beliefs, or views that judges have toward the issues, litigants, and the facts in court cases.* They may be influenced by a number of external forces as well as judges' personal observations and evaluations.

### High Impact

The influence of judicial attitudes on decisions probably is very high.[29] As we already have seen, law is too vague and varied and widely interpreted to be very useful in accounting for how particular decisions are reached. With wide discretion in decision making, it seems likely that attitudes would be crucial for determining particular rulings.

**Distinctive Positions**   The characteristics of judicial positions, especially on appellate courts, also make it probable that judges' personal attitudes have an important impact.

Researchers generally believe that most judges come to the bench with a set of attitudes toward the major issues they will have to decide. Most judges are likely to be middle-aged or older, with many personal, legal, political, and perhaps other judicial experience behind them. As active political and legal elites, they are likely to have thought about the major social issues. Judicial recruitment also often selects those with a particular point of view.

However, unlike many other politicians, most judges on most appellate courts do not seek higher political office. They are apt to decide cases according to their personal beliefs without worrying how their decisions will affect their political future or their old supporters. If judges have not already formed attitudes, they are likely to do so quickly as they are forced to make decisions. Inevitably, they will begin to compare their own views with those of other judges and to side with judges who agree with them.

**Case Focus**  Judicial attitudes probably are important in decision making also because the legal culture expects judges to concentrate on the issues in cases, not on the litigants or the groups they represent in society. Of course, legal culture expects judges to focus on law, but since law does not restrict judges' decisions very much, judges inevitably will apply their attitudes to the issues. By the time a case gets to an appellate court, especially the U.S. Supreme Court, the litigants generally have refined their dispute in order to focus the judges' attention on one major issue they want to have resolved. However, even in trial courts, judges often boil cases down to one or a few central issues such as the seriousness of a crime and a defendant's prior record.

*The central hypothesis of the attitude approach is that judges see cases as raising important social, economic, or political issues, and they respond to them mainly in terms of their own attitudes or beliefs about how they should be resolved.*

Although the special characteristics of judicial positions make it likely that attitudes influence decisions, the persuasiveness of this approach rests mainly on its research methods and the consistent and precise results that it has produced. Therefore, it is necessary to understand the core research techniques used in the attitude approach to decision making.

### Attitudes and Votes

Attitude research looks mainly at how appellate judges vote in many cases. As in the background studies, researchers hypothesize that certain groups of cases (landlord-tenant, divorce, labor-management, crime, etc.) raise similar issues and that judges are sensitive to the social meaning or the main issues in a conflict. The research does not concentrate very much on what judges say in written opinions to explain or justify their decisions. The facts are used only to classify cases according to the type of conflict involved.

Most research also uses only cases in which dissents occur, since cases decided unanimously reveal no obvious differences in judges' votes and no way to see differences in their attitudes. This limits the research method to the U.S. Supreme Court and a few federal and state appellate courts where there are enough cases decided with split decisions to provide a sizable set of data. The patterns of decision making that emerge from these cases provide the basis for determining the existence and nature of judicial attitudes.

**Separating Cause and Effect**  The study of judicial attitudes presents a special problem. When social scientists want to explain certain behavior, they usually tie the actions being studied to various other separate or independent information about the people and events involved. For instance, judicial decision making is the behavior we want to explain and understand. In social science terms, it is *dependent* upon various *independent* contributing causes, such as judges' personal backgrounds.

Decisions are found in published casebooks or courthouse files, and information about backgrounds is available in various biographical sources. These two variables are related to each other through various statistical procedures. In order to link attitudes to decisions, we also ought to have an independent source of information about judges' views toward the issues they have to decide. This is the problem.[30]

Most research on judicial attitudes includes no separate or independent information about judges' thoughts or beliefs that can be related to their decisions. This is due partly to the expense and difficulty in obtaining interviews with judges. But it also reflects the reluctance of researchers to ask judges directly about their political and social beliefs.

Most attitude research deals with the U.S. Supreme Court, and no researcher has been able to obtain in-depth, attitude interviews with the justices. Interviewing has been done with other state and federal judges, but it is practically impossible to ask judges about their specific attitudes toward particular issues and people involved in court cases.

Part of the mystique of justice is that judges are objective arbiters of the law, not mere humans with opinions and values that affect their behavior. So, most judges rarely make speeches, grant interviews to the news media, or answer direct questions from social scientists about issues that will come up in court. Some judges even become upset when interviewers ask if judges *have* attitudes (regardless of their specific content), because the question implies that judges are something other than oracles of the law.

This problem is evident too in judicial confirmation hearings where some U.S. senators usually try to get prospective Supreme Court justices to reveal how they would deal with certain highly controversial issues. More than most other political appointees, justices politely skirt the questions and claim they cannot respond to questions about potential litigation, or even that they have no attitudes, as occurred with Justice Thomas when he insisted at his hearings that he had not thought about nor discussed abortion.

**Inferring Attitudes**   Since it is difficult to obtain plentiful and precise information about what judges think on the issues or the litigants appearing before them, we have to infer it in other ways and from other data. The only plentiful and widely available data are judges' decisions. But critics argue that using judges' decisions for information about their attitudes violates scientific method, because the decisions are the behavior we are trying to explain. Decisions cannot be used for information about the cause *and* the effect.

Using decisions this way is somewhat like saying that the reason a child is taller than before is because it has grown. We have simply said the same thing twice. This criticism is technically correct, but the attitude approach still is persuasive mainly because the *patterns* of judges' decision making often are very clear and consistent.

The attitude approach uses court cases as though they were questions in an opinion survey. A group of cases involving similar issues, such as all criminal appeals involving constitutional rights, all free speech cases, or others, serves as a group of "questions" involving the same basic or underlying value or theme to which the judges have to respond (decide). Although each case involves the same general subject, the particular demand raised in each case is different and requires judges to compare their own attitudes (consciously or unconsciously) with what the litigants want.

Some cases require a very low commitment to a particular value in order to generate a vote for it, while others ask judges to have much more support in order to cast a favorable vote. For instance, reversing the criminal conviction of a person arrested for quietly distributing leaflets on the sidewalk probably does not require a very high level of support for the value of free speech. The right to distribute leaflets in that manner probably is not seriously questioned by most judges in our society, and we might expect them to set the defendant free quickly.

But a case in which a defendant not only is distributing leaflets but is shouting, uttering obscenities, and urging an angry crowd to march through the streets is a different situation. Some judges believe that this kind of speech constitutes a threat to peace and public safety, and they would not permit it. They would vote against the value of free speech in this case because it requires a greater level of support for the value or principle than they have. Others believe, however, that there should be no restrictions whatever on speech and that it is the responsibility of the police to maintain order if it becomes necessary but not to stifle speech in advance. They would vote in favor of free speech in this and most other cases because they strongly support the value.

### Votes and Scales

Using a technique called *cumulative scaling*, it is possible to determine the pattern of judicial support for a major value raised in a set of cases. We may conclude that we have a scale of judges' attitudes if the votes in a set of cases range consistently from low to high levels of support among the judges.

A scale gives us a picture of the level of support of each judge and shows us how far the judges will go for a particular value. For example, some judges are "liberals" who will support practically any claim for free speech; others are "conservatives" who rarely vote to extend the right to free speech; while others are "moderates" who fall somewhere in the middle. On the other hand, if there is no pattern and judges' votes seem to be cast at random, we would have to conclude that we do not have a scale and that judges are not responding to an underlying theme or dimension that the researcher believed would be important.

Scales may be constructed for any policy area that a researcher believes would tap a dominant attitude among the justices. Usually, similar types of cases are included in one scale, such as a series of related civil liberties and political equality issues including rights of criminal defendants, freedom of speech, press, and religion, right to privacy, abortion, and racial and sexual discrimination. Although these cases deal with many different concerns, they all relate to the rights of citizens and government control of freedom.

Other scales include various economic questions such as labor-management disputes, government regulation of business, taxation, employee injury, and environmental protection. All these issues concern the economic power of underdogs and upperdogs and the power of government to regulate the economy. Generally, nearly all the Supreme Court's litigation can be included in these two scales.

**A Supreme Court Example**   A typical judicial attitude scale for the Supreme Court is presented in Table 9.1. The names of the justices are listed across the top from left to right, and the cases are listed vertically at the left side. The pluses and the minuses in the diagram are the positive and negative votes cast by each justice. The score at the right summarizes the size of the majority and how the case came out. The percentage of liberal votes cast by each justice is listed at the bottom.

The cases and the justices are placed in the diagram to produce a continuum of support for the central value presented by the cases. The justice who supports the value most is on the far left side, and the justice who votes in favor least often is on the right side. The cases also are arranged according to the number of positive votes.

We shall assume that this scale involves issues of "political freedom" (rights of criminal defendants, freedom of speech, press, and religion, and other civil liberties), but it could be a scale of economic issues as well. The first five cases at the very top of the scale are "easy," and nearly all the justices support the value to the level it is presented in these few cases. The last two cases are the "toughest," since they require justices to support the freedom issues strongly and only one justice will go that far.

Like most scales, this one is not perfect, for there are a number of votes that are not consistent with the justices' overall voting pattern. Several justices have votes "out of place," since occasionally conservative justices voted with the liberals in some of these cases. This suggests that occasionally the justices see something in cases that the others do not believe is important, or that they are not looking at the political freedom issue in these few cases.

*Court Divisions*   In this scale, Justice Thurgood Marshall is the strongest supporter of the freedom issue since he voted for it in all cases, followed by Justices Harry Blackmun and John Paul Stevens. Until Justice William Brennan was replaced in 1990 by Justice David Souter, who usually joins the conservatives, Justice Brennan frequently was as liberal as Justice Marshall,

**TABLE 9-1**
SCALE OF JUSTICES' VOTES IN CASES INVOLVING ISSUES OF "FREEDOM"

| Cases | Ma | Bl | Stv | So | Sc | O'C | Wh | Ke | Re | Size of Majority | Liberal (L) Or Conservative (C) |
|---|---|---|---|---|---|---|---|---|---|---|---|
| 2725 | + | + | + | + | − | + | + | + | + | 8-1 | L |
| 4210 | + | + | + | + | + | + | + | + | − | 8-1 | L |
| 4367 | + | + | + | + | + | + | + | − | − | 7-2 | L |
| 2475 | + | + | + | + | + | + | + | − | − | 7-2 | L |
| 3963 | + | + | + | + | − | + | + | + | − | 7-2 | L |
| 3888 | + | + | + | + | + | − | − | − | − | 5-4 | L |
| 3746 | + | + | + | + | + | − | − | − | − | 5-4 | L |
| 3632 | + | + | + | − | − | − | − | + | − | 5-4 | C |
| 4561 | + | + | + | + | − | − | − | − | − | 5-4 | C |
| 4210 | + | + | + | − | − | + | − | − | − | 5-4 | C |
| 2748 | + | + | + | − | − | − | − | − | − | 6-3 | C |
| 2831 | + | + | + | − | − | − | − | − | − | 6-3 | C |
| 2643 | + | − | + | − | + | − | − | − | − | 6-3 | C |
| 3293 | + | + | − | − | + | − | − | − | − | 6-3 | C |
| 3349 | + | + | + | − | − | − | − | − | − | 6-3 | C |
| 3742 | + | + | + | − | − | − | − | − | − | 6-3 | C |
| 2897 | + | + | + | − | − | − | − | − | − | 6-3 | C |
| 4673 | + | + | + | − | − | − | − | − | − | 6-3 | C |
| 2132 | + | + | − | − | − | − | − | − | − | 7-2 | C |
| 2282 | + | + | − | − | − | − | − | − | − | 7-2 | C |
| 2163 | + | + | − | − | − | − | − | − | − | 7-2 | C |
| 3205 | + | + | − | − | − | − | − | − | − | 7-2 | C |
| 2798 | + | − | − | − | − | − | − | − | − | 8-1 | C |
| 2291 | + | − | − | − | − | − | − | − | − | 8-1 | C |
| 3771 | + | − | − | − | − | − | − | − | − | 8-1 | C |
| % Liberal votes | 100 | 84 | 68 | 32 | 28 | 24 | 20 | 16 | 4 | | |

*Note:* Numbers under "Cases" are docket numbers. Under "Justices," Ma = Marshall, Bl = Blackmun, Stv = Stevens, So = Souter, Sc = Scalia; O'C = O'Connor, Wh = White, Ke = Kennedy, Re = Rehnquist.

and he sometimes would have been located to the left of Justice Marshall on the scale.

Justice Clarence Thomas is not included on this scale since he participated in few cases involving the freedom issue in 1991–1992. However, he did participate in 18 cases during this period in which the Supreme Court was divided. The issues included government regulation of the economy, defendants' and prisoners' rights, taxation, immigration, and others. In 12 cases he voted with the conservative majority and in three others he dissented with conservative justices (83 percent of the total). Only once did he vote with a majority that included Justices Blackmun and Stevens, who became the only two liberals after Justice Thomas replaced Justice Marshall. Justice Thomas also dissented alone in one case and dissented once with one of the liberals. There is little doubt that he will be a reliable member of the conservative majority.

The conservative majority is composed of Chief Justice William Rehnquist on the far right, joined by Justices Anthony M. Kennedy, Byron White, Sandra D. O'Conner, Antonin Scalia, David H. Souter, and Clarence Thomas. Most of them decide in the liberal direction only rarely. Although the conservatives occupy different positions from right to left, there are not huge differences among them. Some are more liberal than others on certain issues, and they may trade places with each other in the rankings from term to term. Justices O'Conner and Kennedy, for example, sometimes move closer to the left. But all can be expected to vote in the conservative direction most of the time.

It is ironic that Justice Kennedy votes heavily with the conservative justices since at his confirmation hearings he successfully presented himself as moderate and open to many points of view. He was viewed as much more moderate and temperate than Robert Bork, whom Kennedy replaced when Bork's nomination was rejected. But if Bork had been confirmed, he probably would have voted much the same way as Justice Kennedy. The replacement of Bork with Kennedy probably has not made much difference on the decisions reached by the Supreme Court.

The importance of votes and divisions on the Supreme Court is clearest in the 5-4 splits, in which a single vote could change the majority. In the most recent terms of the Supreme Court, approximately 25 percent of the cases were decided by this close vote. In nearly all of them, the conservatives held their majority together.[31] Conservative majorities composed of Justices Rehnquist, Kennedy, Scalia, O'Conner, and White produced several of the most controversial civil rights rulings in decades, which made it much more difficult for minorities to prove employment discrimination. These decisions prompted interest groups and Democrats and moderate Republicans in Congress to enact legislation which would change federal law so that the Supreme Court decisions no longer would apply.

Box 9.1, "Five-to-Four Majorities," illustrates controversial 5-4 decisions in the 1990 term of the Supreme Court, and indicates that conservatives prevailed most of the time.

*Attitude Change*   Occasionally, justices change their attitudes during their tenure on the Supreme Court. But change is rare. Neither Chief Justice Rehnquist nor Justices Kennedy and Scalia on the right were likely to trade positions with Justices Marshall, Blackmun, or Stevens. But a few others have shifted. For example, Justice Byron White used to be more in the middle of the Court, and he has voted both with the liberals and the conservatives in the past.[32] He often was a swing vote that could shift a majority to the liberal side, but with the new conservatives on the Court, he seems to have gravitated clearly into the conservative camp. Justice Harry Blackmun also started out as a conservative, frequently aligned on the right with his boyhood friend, former Chief Justice Warren Burger. The two became known as the "Minnesota Twins." But his views have changed over the years, putting him on the liberal side most of the time. The occasional shift in a justice's attitudes also indicates that prior

---

**BOX 9.1**

FIVE-TO-FOUR MAJORITIES

• Ruled against business practices that forced women of child bearing age from hazardous, but high-paying jobs (**liberal**: Marshall, Blackmun, Stevens, O'Conner, and Souter)

• Overturned a Florida death sentence because the state supreme court had ignored relevant evidence (**liberal**: O'Conner, Souter, Marshall, Stevens, and Blackmun)

• Allowed criminal convictions to stand even though produced by "harmless" coerced confessions (**conservative**: Rehnquist, Kennedy, Scalia, Souter, O'Conner)

• Permitted holding suspects up to forty-eight hours before preliminary hearings (**conservative**: Rehnquist, Kennedy, Souter, O'Conner, White)

• Upheld the constitutionality of mandatory life sentences for first-time drug offenders (**conservative**: Rehnquisrt, Kennedy, Scalia, Souter, O'Conner)

• Upheld as constitutional federal rules against abortion counseling at family planning centers funded in part with federal funds (**conservative**: Rehnquist, Kennedy, Scalia, Souter, White)

• Upheld the constitutionality of local ordinances banning nude dancing as not violating free speech and expression (**conservative**: Rehnquist, Kennedy, Scalia, Souter, White)

• Rejected prisoners' claims of poor prison conditions unless intentional indifference were shown by prison administration (**conservative**: Rehnquist, Kennedy, Scalia, Souter, O'Conner)

---

background and previous voting record is not always a foolproof predictor of how he or she will vote in the future.

### Consistent Attitudes

Most justices have a consistent liberal or conservative approach to Supreme Court cases. A liberal justice opposes government limitations on private rights and favors extending political freedom and opportunities. However, liberals support government regulation of business and economic underdogs in order to provide economic benefits for the have-nots. Conservatives believe that government should control individual liberty and limit freedom to preserve order but should not regulate business or adopt policies to aid economic underdogs. These two positions are similar to traditional liberal Democratic and conservative Republican party policies.

**Other Courts**   Similar kinds of studies have been done on other courts and they produce similar results. However, the types of cases included are somewhat different. The work of the U.S. Supreme Court is distinctive. It includes many more cases involving civil liberties and government regulation of the economy than are found in any other court. Most state supreme courts, for instance, have many more personal and individual conflicts such as divorce, insurance, property disputes, contracts, debt collections, etc.

Nevertheless, judges on state courts have attitudes that are relevant to the kinds of cases they are asked to decide. One researcher combined many typical state cases into one group that he labeled the *sympathy scale*, because all the cases involved people who had been injured or harmed in some way or pitted an upperdog against an underdog. Cases included in the sympathy scale were motor vehicle accidents, negligence, employee injury and unemployment compensation, insurance coverage, fraud, and criminal appeals.

As anticipated, the cases did tap an underlying theme. A few judges (usually with liberal Democratic backgrounds) were very sympathetic to underdogs, while Republicans almost always voted against criminal defendants and in favor of businesses.[33]

**Speaking Out of Court**   Although most attitude research relies heavily on case votes for information, it sometimes is possible to obtain additional information that corroborates the effect of attitudes on decisions. Some judges have had extensive political careers, and a few have made enough speeches or statements to the news media to reveal their feelings and beliefs about issues that come before their court. When this occurs, their stated attitudes and their decisions probably will go in the same direction.

Sometimes judges also write dissenting opinions in which they vehemently disagree with the majority and bare intensely held personal beliefs.[34] For instance, a judge who almost always votes against granting a new trial to criminal defendants may express personal attitudes by writing about fear of crime, threats to public order, and the decline of morality rather than precedent, statutes, and constitutions.

Other evidence about judicial attitudes sometimes can be found in the published memoirs of judges or their private papers and memoranda. However, this information usually is available after a judge has left the court and cannot be used for studying a current set of decisions.

Repeated success with cumulative scaling is very persuasive evidence that judges respond to issues in cases in terms of their views of American society and politics. If we combine attitude research with the studies of judges' backgrounds and their local environments, we begin to understand the links between a judge's upbringing and surroundings, adult experiences, recruitment to the courts, and attitudes toward litigation. Judicial decision making definitely is part of the political process, and it has much in common with other forms of political decision making.

### Limits of Judicial Attitudes

The combination of background and attitude research is the dominant mode of analyzing judicial decision making, and it is easy to go too far and conclude that it explains all judicial behavior. This would be an error. Several features of attitude research indicate that additional explanations for decision making are necessary.

It is fairly easy to conclude that judges who are located at the extremes of a judicial scale definitely are affected by their attitudes. They almost always vote in favor or against particular core values presented in cases. They stand out clearly as flaming liberals or staunch conservatives. Judges on the ends of judicial scales also sometimes are more outspoken than others because they feel strongly about their beliefs.

But judges in the middle of judicial scales are neither clear liberals nor conservatives. Researchers label them moderates because they will only go "so far" in support of a particular value and they take no extreme positions. While they may have a point of view about certain issues, they probably do not feel strongly. This also suggests that they may be influenced by other factors, such as persuasion by other judges or their own law clerks who may have a stronger point of view, or by special circumstances or sets of facts in particular cases.[35]

In addition, as will be discussed shortly, judges may have a view of how they *ought* to behave as judicial decision makers (judicial role) that is more important to them than their attitudes toward caases.

The U.S. Supreme Court almost always is faced with weighty issues in which innovative decision making always is possible and judges' attitudes are likely influences. However, most other courts deal with many more mundane and routine disputes in which most appellants lose in unanimous decisions. Many of these cases probably are uninteresting and do not arouse much judicial passion.

Judges may not even be especially interested in the details of certain problems such as state insurance law and do not have attitudes about how disputes should be resolved. Sometimes, judges on state appellate courts defer to other judges with more expertise who decide the cases alone, with the other judges simply going along.

Even when a few judges dissent, we cannot automatically conclude that all the judges in the majority have an opposing attitude. They may believe dissents are undesirable or they may go along for other reasons. As a consequence, we have to consider other explanations for judicial behavior where backgrounds or attitude theory do not quite fill the bill.

## JUDICIAL ROLE

Judicial role refers to the special position that judges occupy and *expectations* that they and other people have about how judges *ought* to behave. The sum total of a judge's role includes his or her interactions with all other people in other roles who are involved in the work of the courts. Therefore, the judicial role is complex and all-inclusive, since it relates to all of a judge's activities on the bench as well as visible personal behavior off the bench.

The role of a trial judge, for example, includes behavior in plea bargaining (relationship with police, defense lawyers, prosecutors, and defendants), conduct of trials (relationships with jurors, lawyers, defendants, spectators, and the news media), obligations to keep up with workload (relationships with court clerks, assistants, and perhaps a chief administrative judge), and personal conduct in public (relationships with other political and social elites, the news media, and, indirectly, the general public).[36]

A judge's concept of role is different from attitudes toward issues in cases, and the two may conflict. For example, a judge may personally believe that criminal defendants should receive every constitutional protection provided by the courts but also that appeals not filed correctly must be dismissed in order to preserve judicial decorum and authority. A judge's decision in a case in which his or her attitudes and role concepts conflict may depend on how strongly both values are felt.

Most of us take certain parts of the judicial role for granted, and there is little disagreement on what constitutes proper judicial conduct. For instance, judges and most other people probably agree that judges should stay away from racetracks and pool halls and other politicians. Judges also should not make a lot of public speeches. In general, judges should stay out of public view and always act calmly and moderately. Most judges appear to conform to these widely accepted notions of the judicial role. They keep to themselves most of the time and they promote a public image of personal detachment and objectivity. Judges are fond of saying that they must be like Caesar's wife—above suspicion, meaning that they have to be and appear as pure as possible.

### Decision-Making Roles

The aspect of the judicial role studied most often in relation to decision making is whether or not judges believe they should make law when they decide cases.

Traditional legal theory sees judges as *law interpreters* who decide cases by applying the existing law, precedents, and known legal principles to specific disputes. Supporters of this view often point to the separation of powers, which maintains that legislatures make the law, executive officials carry out the law, and judges interpret the meaning of law. This also means that judges should consciously limit themselves to avoid substituting judicial wisdom for the rightful power of legislatures to make policy.

Opponents of this traditional perspective argue that judges, especially on appellate courts, frequently have to be *lawmakers*, because the written law is unclear or contradictory or does not cover all possible situations and because legislative intent is impossible to identify.

Sharp differences in the way that appellate judges see their roles as decision makers is illustrated by the statements of state supreme court judges given in interviews about the judicial role. Judges who adopt the traditional law interpreter view assert:

> We can only act in one way: that is to be solely interpreters of the law. The moment he steps out of the role of interpreter, he violates the Constitution which separates the legislature and the executive from the judiciary.

The United States Supreme Court and other state courts too have set themselves up as some sort of super-Congress and they interpret the Constitution to mean what they think it should say. That's a violation of the separation of powers.

But other judges see their role differently, arguing that judges inevitably make law:

That whole idea about whether a judge makes law or whether he found what the law always was by looking somewhere up in the blue is not true. Judges always made law and always will. . . . In interpreting you're trying to give answers to problems that were not considered by the legislature and you try to guess what the legislature would have thought had they thought about the problem. But you get away from this quickly. What do you do when you get a question like this? You can't send it back to the legislature for a decision. . . . The question comes up and you decide it.[37]

More than half of all judges adopt the law interpreter approach with about one-quarter more taking a position midway between the law-interpreters and the law-makers. Judges in this group are called *pragmatists* or *realists* because they believe that on occasion they have opportunities or requirements to make law, but that most cases are routine and can be based on available law.[38] A slightly greater number of federal than state judges take the pragmatist or realist views, possibly because they have more opportunities to make innovative decisions.

### Roles and Attitudes

In order to determine how role concepts tie into judicial decision making, judges also have been asked to describe their basic political orientations prior to their appointment to their court. Some research has discovered that role orientations and political views run closely together. Judges who see their role as interpreting law tend to label themselves political conservatives, and judges adopting the lawmaker view describe themselves as liberals. Pragmatists include both liberals and conservatives.

Decisions in cases also tend to parallel judges' descriptions of themselves, but the differences among the three groups are not very great. Federal judges who are lawmakers tend to make a larger number of liberal decisions, especially regarding the rights of criminal defendants, but in other types of cases (employee and personal injury, labor-management, etc.) the differences are not large.[39]

Earlier research on state supreme court judges found no differences in the decisions of lawmakers and law interpreters and concluded that lawmaking did not automatically imply liberal decision making. Adopting the lawmaker orientation suggests a willingness to innovative or an awareness that judges do not receive adequate guidance from the existing law, not that particular court policies will be liberal or conservative.[40]

**A Unique Quality?**    These role studies present two possible interpretations of the importance of role concepts in decision making. One is that judges' role concepts are fancy masquerades for political attitudes, similar to other legal statements that judges include in written opinions to justify their decisions. Since it is less acceptable for judges than other politicians to have a policy point of view, judges hide their beliefs behind a legal-like definition of their role that will be more acceptable to the public.

The other is that roles are different from attitudes and have a separate effect on decision making. For instance, judges who adopt the lawmaker view appear to be somewhat more willing to seize the initiative in decision making and to innovate more frequently. Both points of view may be correct, depending on *how strongly* judges hold their beliefs and role concepts.

**Masquerade**    The possibility that a judge's view of role is a masquerade for political attitudes is demonstrated through several studies of the career of Justice Felix Frankfurter, an associate justice of the U.S. Supreme Court from 1939 to 1962. Appointed by President Franklin D. Roosevelt, Frankfurter strongly supported the New Deal and publicly opposed Supreme Court decisions of the early 1930s that declared many new provisions of the New Deal unconstitutional.

Justice Frankfurter also was a strong advocate of *judicial restraint*, which has much in common with the law interpreter role. Both views maintain that judges ought to defer to legislatures as the source of law. This philosophy reinforced his strong support for the substance of the New Deal, which was created by a very popular President and his congressional supporters.

Frankfurter also supported civil liberties, but his belief in judicial restraint required judges to permit government to limit civil liberties in certain circumstances.

Political scientists have put Justice Frankfurter's defense of judicial restraint to a careful test: if Frankfurter were consistent in his support for judicial restraint, he would permit government regulation of the economy as well as limitations on civil liberties. Voting against government would mean the justice was substituting judicial values and policy for those created by the elected agencies of government.

When economic regulation and civil liberties cases over several years are examined, it is clear in the economic cases that Justice Frankfurter voted for and against the government an equal number of times. Thus, the justice did not follow his own rules of judicial restraint consistently or even most of the time. However, when the cases are further subdivided into those in which the government regulated business and others when it regulated labor, a clearer pattern emerged. Justice Frankfurter voted over 90 percent of the time to permit government regulation of labor unions, but voted for the government in only one-third of the cases where it sought to regulate business. He also voted against civil liberties both when judicial restraint was an issue and when it was absent.[41]

Justice Frankfurter was fairly consistent (and conservative) on the civil liberties and economic dimensions, but not consistent on the judicial restraint dimension. The consistent antilabor, probusiness, and anti-civil liberites votes make it clear that Justice Frankfurter's judicial attitudes, not his role concepts, determined his decisions.

***Interaction of Roles and Attitudes***    The example of a single justice does not provide conclusive evidence about the effects of role concepts and judicial attitudes or lead us to the conclusion that attitudes are more important than roles in decision making. Other research suggests that role concepts and attitudes work together for many judges.

These findings come from a survey of state trial judges and their decisions in many criminal cases.[42] Judges were asked several specific questions about their political attitudes and role concepts. Their responses were related to their decisions to determine whether attitudes or role concepts or both factors had an effect on sentencing.

The study found that neither attitudes nor role concepts had much impact by themselves, but that judges who believed that political attitudes were a legitimate part of decision making were more likely than other judges to make decisions that were clearly related to their attitudes. By contrast, judges who felt that personal attitudes had no place in decision making seemed to block them from their decisions.

Nearly identical results were obtained in a study of state intermediate appellate judges. Neither role orientations concerning judicial lawmaking and law interpreting nor political attitudes by themselves predicted judges' decisions in granting criminal defendants new trials. However, judges who identified themselves as liberals *and* lawmakers were more likely than conservative lawmakers to overturn convictions. Liberal and conservative law interpreters overturned fewer but the same percentage of convictions.[43]

It does not appear that judicial role orientations were masquerades à la Frankfurter in either of these studies. Instead, the interaction of roles and attitudes help to explain judges' approaches to cases. Liberal and conservative lawmakers on appellate courts are more likely than law interpreters to act on their attitudes—as are trial judges who accept the role of attitudes and other factors in sentencing criminal defendants.

## Many Influences

Measuring the influence of several factors at the same time in decision making, such as roles and attitudes, has the potential of providing a much more accurate and complete description of judicial decision making. A broader view that includes elements from all approaches probably can tell us much more about the forces that affect judicial decision making than a single one.

For example, a recent study of the U.S. Supreme Court found that it was possible to substantially account for differences in support for the rights of criminal defendants by including four variables: the justice's political party affiliation (background), their previous voting patterns (stability of attitudes), the political party of the sitting President (an indirect indicator of current public opinion), and the proportion of criminal cases on the docket (policy priorities of the Court). All of these independent variables are derived from different theories about what makes the justices decide cases differently. But all of them combined are more powerful explanations than each of them separately.[44]

## APPELLATE COURTS AS SMALL GROUPS

An important feature of appellate courts is that judges are members of a group and interact with each other to produce a group product. Multimember or collegial appellate courts were created partly in the belief that several heads are better than one, so it seems reasonable to believe also that judges will consult with each other to reach decisions.

The small group approach assumes that the kind of interaction judges have with each other influences decision making. More precisely, most small group research hypothesizes that judges are interested in influencing the decisions of their court and in being on the winning side as often as possible. Therefore, they develop strategies to build winning coalitions and to have their views included in majority opinions.

### Groups and Individuals

This idea seems reasonable enough, but the small group approach conflicts with other approaches to decision making, which assume that personal attributes of judges largely determine decisions. Even the legal approach emphasizes a judge's personal responsibility to evaluate the facts and the law and to decide cases consistent with personal views. Many judges even resent suggestions by other judges concerning how they should decide cases.

The actual work of many courts also encourages individual decision making. The federal courts of appeals, state intermediate appellate courts, and some state supreme courts are required to hear thousands of appeals each year. Judges consider many cases to be unimportant and routine, and they take very little time to affirm the trial courts. Majority opinions may be assigned to judges through rotation or expertise before or without discussion of the issues. The assumption on the courts is that individual judges will make the decisions for the entire court and the other judges will support them. Some state intermediate appellate courts publish very few of their opinions, and judges do not review what their colleagues write before giving their own tacit approval. Weekly conferences are rushed, with only a few minutes given to any individual case. A judge describes a conference this way:

> And I say, "That's my case. Blah, blah, blah—any questions? No questions. Okay, we can go on to the next case." Obviously the close cases, the interesting cases, are

talked about a bit more, but there aren't a hell of a lot of those and we don't have enough time for those we do get.[45]

Except for the interaction among judges to spread the workload and to obtain formal approval for each other's opinions, there seems to be very little group involvement in the creation of decisions. Whatever factors influence decisions in these cases probably hinge on the personal attributes of the individual judges.

**Constructive Interaction?**   The relative luxury of group discussion, consideration of tentative opinions, and careful evaluation of alternative legal arguments and policies probably is reserved for supreme courts in states with intermediate appellate courts, the U.S. Supreme Court, and some of the work of the federal courts of appeals.

These courts have more time and get a larger proportion of unconventional cases. However, even on these courts personal interaction may not be as common as it might first appear or have much of an effect on determining who wins and loses. Shortly after joining the Supreme Court, Justice Scalia described the judicial conference in the U.S. Supreme Court this way:

> Not very much conferencing goes on. . . . [I have been] surprised and disappointd at how little interplay there is between the various Justices. . . . In fact, to call our discussion of a case a conference is really something of a misnomer. It's much more a statement of the views of each of the nine Justices, after which the totals are added and the case is assigned. [My own remarks] hardly ever seemed to influence anyone because people did not change their votes in response to my contrary views.[46]

Some appellate judges are extreme individualists who do not care much what other judges think and are unwilling to compromise or consider other points of view. Sometimes these judges appear as frequent lone dissenters who vote their conscience or their attitudes regardless of the views of the other members.[47] They sometimes write stinging dissents to let off steam, and they get a reputation for being personally abrasive and sarcastic to the other judges. Individualists may wind up with the majority because their personal views coincide with those of other judges, but that does not mean they interact in any meaningful way to help produce the majority opinion.

### Voting Change

The small group approach does not deny that some judges are extreme loners, but it maintains that generally there is much interaction and change (fluidity) between the votes cast at the conference when a case is discussed for the first time and the final vote.[48] Moreover, since the attitude studies rely only on the final published vote for information about the decision, they cannot take into account the activity that goes on in the time taken to write opinions and to solidify a majority.

During this period, judges try to influence each other to modify or switch their votes or to rewrite their opinions. Analysis of the private papers of former Supreme Court justices as well as Woodward and Armstrong's *The Brethren*, an insider's view of a recent Supreme Court, reveal a flurry of intense activity on the Court between the first and final votes.

However, cumulative scales of the final votes also indicate that personal attitudes, not group activity, are responsible for decisions. It does not look at if both theories can be right.

This conflict has been investigated for the Supreme Court through a careful comparison of the first and the final published votes.[49] Determining how much and the type of voting change that occurs between the first conference and the final tally can give us a much better picture of how much switching is due to group interaction. The findings are interesting and enlightening.

First, vote shifts occurred in about 60 percent of all cases, which confirms other observations that much activity takes place between the first and final votes. However, most voting changes occurred when judges who were in the minority or who had not participated in the first vote decided to join with the original majority. Judges who shifted tended to be ideologically located between the majority and minority blocs.[50] But, in all votes in all cases, judges switched positions only 9 percent of the time.

Most important, these voting changes were able to reverse the initial decision in only 14 percent of the cases. In these few cases, the first tentative majority lost one or two members and the original minority won out. There was no evidence that more vote switching took place in highly controversial or so-called landmark cases than in others that received less political or legal attention.

**Functions of Opinions** This research has been repeated for many different terms of the Supreme Court and reaches generally similar conclusions.[51] It strongly indicates that the activity between the first and final votes does not often affect which side wins or loses. Surely the justices must be aware of how little change occurs, and we might wonder why they do more than simply vote and write opinions. The answer lies partly in the need for group harmony and the legal and political significance of court opinions to the justices as statements of judicial policy.

Even though personal interaction may not switch many votes, it helps to produce a comfortable work environment. For example, former Chief Jusutice Earl Warren once compared the U.S. Supreme Court to a marriage in which couples and judges both have to adjust to and accommodate each other in order to avoid daily squabbling.[52]

Many appellate judges have their offices in the same building and they work there all day. At a minimum, they must hear cases together and discuss them as a group. They also may meet for lunch and are apt to see each other during the day to chat or compare ideas on pending cases. Good personal relations make for more pleasant work. However, various Court observers wonder if good personal relations operate on many appellate courts today, especially the U.S. Supreme Court, where caustic comments fly among the justices.

Social warmth, of course, is only part of the answer. Judges on higher appellate courts are likely to interact extensively in decision making because they see their written opinions as important sources of law and policy. Judges are not only interested in the final vote, but are heavily concerned with the kind of message they can send to lower court judges, lawyers, and other public officials about how disputes should be resolved. In their opinions judges explain the conditions under which legal abortions should be permitted, what is an acceptable affirmative action employment program, or when the federal government may condemn private property for a public project, etc.

Generally, the only way policies can be communicated to others is through one written majority opinion. Therefore, while judges may make up their minds early about which side they are on, there still are various alternatives about exactly what should go into the majority opinion, or into a group dissent. Since most judges have a point of view, they are likely to try to influence their colleagues to see the case their way.

Judges who write opinions for the majority also are likely to pay attention to the wishes and attitudes of their fellow judges in order to hold their majority together. This is important in occasional close cases where one defection could shift the majority to the other side, but it seems to affect judges with comfortable margins of support as well.[53]

There may be several reasons for this. First, some judges believe that the larger the majority, the more impact a decision is likely to have as public policy. For example, chief judges may strongly urge the members of the court not to dissent in highly controversial civil rights or religious freedom cases so that a decision has the maximum legal and political impact. Since one group or another in society is likely to oppose a decision regardless of which way the court goes, dissents give ammunition to those who would challenge the court's authority and legitimacy to make decisions. A unanimous court makes it appear that all the judges give their full support to the decision, thereby strengthening the court's power and authority.

There also is some evidence that judges find safety in numbers and are more willing to make controversial decisions if they have solid support from other judges on the court. Judges in groups share the heat and the responsibility.[54] Majority opinion writers like heavy majorities to maintain their reputation. If a majority opinion is harshly criticized in a dissent, it may create an image of incompetence or foolishness that judges would like to avoid.

### Group Dynamics

Interviews with judges and careful analysis of the personal papers of justices of the U.S. Supreme Court reveal that certain personal attributes are important in increasing a judge's influence on his colleagues and that courts use several techniques for dealing with disagreement.[55]

**Personal Attributes**   An important personal characteristic is a *congenial personality*. Some judges are smooth political types in the sense that they know how to make others feel good, worthy, and powerful. This probably does not switch many votes on any court, but it keeps the channels of communication open among judges and creates opportunities for judges who may disagree with each other to continue to consider each other's points of views. By contrast, judges who are abrupt, condescending to others, hostile, superior, angry, or extreme repel other judges so that even if they have something important to say, other judges are not likely to pay them much attention.

For example, despite his reputation as an eminent legal scholar and experienced government troubleshooter, Justice Felix Frankfurter apparently had little influence on his fellow justices because he expected much deference and great respect. Justices are unlikely to be overawed by their colleagues, however, and they did not give Frankfurter his expected due. Frankfurter also was acid-tongued and rough on justices whose written opinions and ideas conflicted with his own.[56]

Some judges are influential because they are perceived to have superior *intellectual abilities*. Judges on one state supreme court, for example, agreed that their chief justice was very influential in decision making because he had a "mind like a steel trap." He always could go right to the essence of an issue and make the solution seem clear and obvious to the others. Intellectual skills rank very high for judges as sources of influence.[57] This reflects the nature of high appellate court decision making in which judges and their law clerks spend most of their time alone researching and comparing precedents, studying statutes and other sources of law, and writing and commenting on opinions.

However, U.S. Supreme Court justices occasionally disparage each other's intellectual abilities as they disagree with the other justice's written opinions.

The current justices sometimes are very sharp with each other in their written opinions. Criticism flows to and from liberals and conservatives but also within the dominant conservative faction. Even though the same group of justices frequently votes together, solidarity does not always signify close and warm personal relationships. A former law clerk recently explained that the clerks are like ambassadors between the justices' chambers. Says another, ". . . [T]he Justices have learned to run a Court quite well without talking to one another."[58]

**Exerting Influence**   Personal attributes and capabilities help a judge to deal with colleagues and probably affect his or her own level of influence on a court, but there also are particular techniques that judges use to exert influence. They can be grouped into three main categories: persuasion, compromise, and voting.

*Persuasion and Compromise*   Persuasion is an attempt to get another judge to abandon a position and to join with others. Persuasion may be directed to judges who have not yet made up their minds about which side to support or to judges who have made up their minds but are uncertain about the wording of opinions or the legal basis for the decision. A pleasing personality and, especially, sharp intellectual skills are important in persuasion because a judge has to approach others through the force of ideas and thinking in order to get them to change their position.

Compromise, or bargaining, involves give-and-take among judges in which they agree to sacrifice parts of their opinions or perhaps certain ideas in return for assurances of support. Judges sometimes threaten to write dissents or separate concurrences if the majority opinion writer will not alter an opinion to remove objectionable sections. Judges defect from the majority relatively rarely, but the possibility always is present and the majority opinion writer has to keep the possibility in mind.

On many state supreme courts there are few dissents, so it does not appear that the threat of a dissent is a practical problem for the majority. However, judges still bargain and compromise because they think it is an important part of their role. Many believe that dissents are undesirable and that the court should work together as a unit. Bargaining and compromise are ways to maintain group solidarity, harmony, and friendship.[59]

*Voting* Voting is the third technique for asserting influence, and it may be used with persuasion and compromise as part of the decision-making process. For instance, the justices of the U.S. Supreme Court and many other appellate courts usually vote after discussion at their weekly conference in order to determine the tentative majority and to assign the writing of opinions. Persuasion and compromise come afterward as part of hammering out a final decision. Voting also may have an impact on later negotiations. If dissents are cast at the conference, the majority opinion writer has a clear picture of who is on which side and the points of view that may have to be accommodated before work on the opinion begins. Removing some of the dissents is part of the goal of the writer of the majority opinion.

The U.S. Supreme Court occasionally has avoided voting in order to prevent cleavages from becoming clear and difficult to overcome in certain controversial cases. Former Chief Justice Earl Warren has revealed that the justices agreed not to vote in *Brown v. Board of Education* in order to prevent them from becoming "polarized" and permanently dividing the court. No dissents were cast at the conference even though the justices did not initially agree on a decision. By avoiding explicit positions, the Supreme Court ultimately was able to produce a unanimous decision that put all nine justices behind the ruling.[60]

On some courts, voting seems to take priority over other techniques. Occasionally, the level of personal conflict is so great that the judges usually are unable to reach decisions any other way. Conference discussions are hostile or unproductive and the judges *have* to vote to get a decision. They allow the tally to determine the outcome of the case.

We do not have enough information to know why certain styles of decision making predominate on different courts. One guess is that the amount of social and economic diversity and political conflict which surrounds a court affects appellate decision making. Federal appellate and state supreme courts located in largely urban states with many different groups represented in the population are likely to produce judges from both political parties with different outlooks on public policy. Some judges are likely to have had extensive careers in state partisan politics and are used to political combat and disagreement. They probably do not mind a little conflict on the court as well. Voting may be a necessary way of resolving their differences. It also is clear that courts in these states generally produce more dissents. The order of voting by seniority and the role of the chief justice also probably have some influence.[61]

### Special Influence of the Chief Justice

The Chief Justice of the U.S. Supreme Court, and of many other appellate courts, has special influence. He or she has both formal and informal powers, but they all stem from the justice's official position as the "first among equals" on the court. In addition to the discuss list, described in Chapter 7, chief justices are influential in opinion assignment and serving as leaders of their court.

**Opinion Assignment**   If the Chief Justice is in the early voting majority, he has the power to assign the writing of majority opinions. The job may be given to anyone in the majority, and the Chief Justice often reserves certain cases for himself.[62]

In closely divided cases, the Chief Justice probably would assign the opinion to a moderate who could hold the majority together. Sometimes opinions will be assigned to judges who agree closely with the Chief Justice, assuring that the majority opinion will reflect the Chief Justice's views. At the same time, the Chief Justice has to be sure that the workload is fairly evenly distributed among all the judges.[63]

In many of the states where opinion writing is rotated, the chief justice cannot influence the content of opinions through the assignment process. Often state chief justices have only certain administrative or housekeeping duties and obtain their positions through seniority. Being chief justice in these states does not carry very much additional formal power.

**Leadership**   In addition to these formal powers, the chief justice of any appellate court has an opportunity to become the informal leader of the court. A leadership role is not guaranteed, but the prestige of the formal position gives the chief justice a special chance to be assertive. Social scientists have identified two forms of leadership that are important in small groups such as appellate courts. These are *social and task leadership*.[64]

Social leadership refers to skills at managing interpersonal conflict and tension. On an appellate court with judges who have persistent attitudes and exceptional personal ability, and who think highly of themselves, a social leader is important for developing and maintaining a climate of harmony and goodwill despite major differences of opinion. Task leadership involves managing the work of the court to be certain that cases are decided efficiently and that backlogs are prevented.

The presence of social and task leadership makes a difference on the work of appellate courts and the feelings judges have toward their job. With both forms of leadership present the work gets done quickly and judges are extremely satisfied with their job and relations with the other members. Conflict continues to exist, of course, but social leadership keeps it friendly and good-natured and the judges feel like members of a team. The production of decisions also is high.

Without social and task leadership, personal conflicts frequently flare up into lifetime personal feuds and there is a lot of sniping among the judges. Deciding cases takes much longer, the judges are unhappy about their work, and the production of decisions is lower.

Sometimes, a chief justice is able to be both task and social leader and has the greatest influence of any judge on the court. Often, however, a chief justice is good at one form of leadership but not the other. Sometimes a senior associate justice emerges as an effective coleader in maintaining cordial social relations or helps to move the court along to get the work done.

The leadership abilities of Chief Justices varies. Since the 1920s, Chief Justices William H. Taft (1920s), Charles E. Hughes (1930s), and Earl Warren (1950s and 1960s) were the most effective leaders. Taft was a very effective social leader, and Hughes and Warren were both social and task leaders. The other justices seem to have been very pleased and comfortable in their work during the tenure of these three Chief Justices.

Chief Justice Harlan F. Stone (early 1940s) was unable to follow Hughes's strong leadership role, and former Chief Justice Warren E. Burger seemed to be less able than his predecessor, Earl Warren. Both Stone and Burger experienced more than the usual discord on their Courts.[65]

Chief Justice William Rehnquist is reputed to be more skilled at getting along well with the other justices, including the liberals at the other end of the judicial scale.[66]

While social and task leadership are important in affecting the *style* of decision making and the *efficiency* of a court, there is no link between leadership and specific decisions. The other judges still are likely to hold relatively permanent sets of attitudes that direct their behavior most of the time. On the other hand, a skillful chief justice may be especially persuasive in borderline cases and can influence the content of majority opinions. On some courts, the chief justice may be the main source of intellectual guidance as well as the social and task leader and has enormous personal influence.

## CONCLUSION

This chapter has examined the political perspective of judicial decision making. Instead of looking at cases as legal problems, political scientists view cases as containing various social and economic issues. Since judges have so much discretion to focus on facts, interpret law, and assign different meanings to precedent, they will respond to cases according to psychological, social, and political forces similar to those that affect other political decision makers.

The major sets of influences on judicial decision making include judges' backgrounds, local environments, judges' attitudes, perceptions of the judicial role, and small group interaction. Each of these contributes something to our understanding of judicial decision making and convincingly establishes the work of courts as an integral part of the political process.

So far, the combination of backgrounds, local environments, and attitudes offers the most compelling explanation of judicial decision making. Small group interaction is important in forging the content of written opinions that contain policy messages, but it does not appear that group interaction changes many judicial minds about which side to support in a case. The addition of role analysis and other factors have the potential of producing a comprehensive theory of judicial behavior.

Although there is a great need to refine and expand research techniques to account for many differences in decision making, it is clear that the political approach as a whole provides a much more realistic answer about decision making than relying on law as an explanation for judicial behavior.

## SUGGESTIONS FOR ADDITIONAL READING

Lee Epstein, Thomas G. Walker, and William J. Dixon: "The Supreme Court and Criminal Justice Disputes: A Neo-Institutional Perspective," *American Journal of Political Science*, 33 (1989), 825–841. This article analyzes the importance of several variables from a number of theories of decision making as a way of increasing our understanding of the forces that affect judicial decisions. The authors maintain that social scientists need to adopt a broad institutional view of courts, rather than focus exclusively on judges as decision makers.

James L. Gibson: "Decision Making in Appellate Courts," in John B. Gates and Charles A. Johnson, (eds.), *The American Courts: A Critical Assessment* (Washington, D.C.: CQ Press, 1991). This is an overview of various approaches to judicial decision making and proposals for linking different approaches and theories.

James L. Gibson: "The Role Concept in Judicial Research," *Law and Policy Quarterly*, 3 (1981), 291–308. An overview and analysis of the use of role theory in decision making research.

Thomas R. Marshall: *Public Opinion and the Supreme Court* (Boston: Unwin Hyman, 1989). The most complete work linking public opinion to the U.S. Supreme Court.

C. Neal Tate: "Personal Attributes as Explanations of Supreme Court Justices Decision Making," in Henry R. Glick, (ed.), *Courts in American Politics*, (New York: McGraw-Hill Publishing Company, 1990). This is an examination of the impact of the background characteristics of Supreme Court Justices on decision making. Tate argues that background characteristics are a good substitute for judicial attitudes, which are difficult to document.

## NOTES

1 The following is based on Martin A. Levin, *Urban Politics and the Criminal Courts* (Chicago: University of Chicago Press, 1977).

2 C. K. Rowland and Robert A. Carp, "A Longitudinal Study of Party Effects on Federal District Court Policy Propensities," *American Journal of Political Science*, 24 (1980), 291–305; Richard C. Feiock, "Support for Business in the Federal District Courts," *American Politics Quarterly*, 17 (1989), 96–104; C. K. Rowland and Bridget Jeffrey Todd, "Where You Stand Depends on Who Sits: Platform Promises and Judicial Gatekeeping in the Federal District Courts," *Journal of Politics*, 53 (1991), 175–185.

3 C. K. Rowland, Robert A. Carp, and Ronald A. Stidham, "Judges' Policy Choices and the Value Basis of Judicial Appointments," *Journal of Politics*, 46 (1984), 886–902.

4 Kenneth N. Vines, "Federal District Judges and Race Relations Cases in the South," *Journal of Politics*, 26 (1964), 337–357; for additional examples of differences among courts based on local environments, see: Lettie McSpadden Wenner and Lee E. Dutter, "Contextual Influences on Court Outomes," *Western Political Quarterly*, 41 (1988), 115–134.

5 Michael W. Giles and Thomas G. Walker, "Judicial Policy-Making and Southern School Segregation," *Journal of Politics*, 37 (1975), 917–936; Ronald A. Stidham, Robert A. Carp, and C. K. Rowland, "Women's Rights before the Federal Courts," *American Politics Quarterly*, 11 (1983), 205–214; Rowland, Carp, and Stidham, pp. 886–902.

6 Rowland and Carp, pp. 291–305.

7 S. Sidney Ulmer. "The Political Party Variable in the Michigan Supreme Court," *Journal of Public Law*, 11 (1962), 352–362; Glendon Schubert, *Quantitative Analysis of Judicial Behavior* (Glencoe, Ill.: The Free Press, 1959), pp. 129–142.

8 Malcolm M. Feeley, "Another Look at the 'Party Variable' in Judicial Decision-Making: An Analysis of the Michigan Supreme Court," *Polity*, 4 (1971), 91–104.

9 David W. Adamany, "The Party Variable in Judges' Voting: Conceptual Notes and a Case Study," *American Political Science Review*, 63 (1969), 57–73.

10 Philip L. Dubois, *From Ballot to Bench* (Austin: University of Texas Press, 1980), chap. 6.

11 S. Sidney Ulmer, "Social Background as an Indicator to the Votes of Supreme Court Justices in Criminal Cases: 1947-1956 Terms," *American Journal of Political Science*, 17 (1973), 622–630; C. Neal Tate, "Personal Attribute Models of the Voting Behavior of U.S. Supreme Court Justices: Liberalism in Civil Liberties and Economic Decisions, 1946-1978," *American Political Science Review*, 75 (1981), 355–367; Stuart S. Nagel, "Political Party Affiliation and Judges' Decisions," *American Political Science Review*, 60 (1961), 843–850; "Ethnic Affiliations and Judicial Propensities," *Journal of Politics*, 24 (1962), 92–100; Sheldon Goldman, "Voting Behavior on the United States Courts of Appeals Revisited," *American Political Science Review*, 69 (1975), 491–506; Jon Gottschall, "Carter's Judicial Appointments: The Influence of Affirmative Action and Merit Selection on Voting on the U.S. Courts of Appeals," *Judicature*, 67 (1983), 165–173; C. Neal Tate, "Personal Attributes as Explanations of Supreme Court Justices' Decision Making," in Henry R. Glick, ed., *Courts in American Politics* (New York: McGraw-Hill Publishing Co., 1990), pp. 266–275.

12 Cassia Spohn, "The Sentencing Decisions of Black and White Judges: Expected and Unexpected Similarities," *Law and Society Review*, 24 (1990), 1197–1216; Susan Welch, Michael Combs, and John Gruhl, "Do Black Judges Make a Difference?" *American Journal of Political Science*, 32 (1988), 126–136; see also Thomas G. Walker and Deborah J. Barrow, "The Diversification of the Federal Bench: Policy and Process Ramifications," *Journal of Politics*, 47 (1985), 596–616.

13 John Gruhl, Cassia Spohn, and Susan Welch, "Women as Policymakers: The Case of Trial Judges," *American Journal of Political Science*, 25 (1981), 308–322.

14 Beverly Cook, "Will Women Judges Make a Difference in Women's Legal Rights? A Prediction from Attitudes and Simulated Behaviour," in Margherita Rendel (ed.), *Women, Power and Political Systems* (The Netherlands: Croom Helm, 1981), pp. 216–237.

15 David W. Allen and Diane E. Wall, "The Behavior of Women State Supreme Court Justices: Are they Tokens or Outsiders?" *Justice System Journal*, 12 (1987), 232–245.

16 See references in footnote 11.

17 Don Bowen, "The Explanation of Judicial Voting Behavior from Sociological Characteristics of Judges" (unpublished Ph.D. dissertation, Yale University, 1965); Joel Grossman, "Social Backgrounds and Judicial Decision-Making," *Harvard Law Review*, 79 (1966), 1551–1564.

18 In-depth psychological data are hard to obtain, but several ideas about the influence of backgrounds on personality and personality on decision making can be found in some judicial literature. See, for example, Burton Atkins, Lenore Alpert, and Robert Ziller, "Personality Theory and Judging," *Law and Policy Quarterly*, 2 (April 1980), 189–220, and H. M. Hirsch, *The Enigma of Felix Frankfurter* (New York: Basic Books, Inc., 1981). See also Harold Lasswell, *Power and Personality* (New York: W. W. Norton Co., 1948).

19 Thomas R. Marshall, "The Supreme Court as an Opinion Leader," *American Politics Quarterly*, 15 (1987), 147–168.

20 James H. Kuklinski and John E. Stanga, "Political Participation and Government Responsiveness: The Behavior of California Superior Courts," *American Political Science Review*, 73 (December 1979), 1090–1099.

21 Beverly Blair Cook, "Public Opinion and Federal Judicial Policy," *American Journal of Political Science*, 21 (August 1977), 567–599; "Judicial Policy: Change over Time," *American Journal of Political Science*, 23 (February 1979), 208–214; Glen T. Broach et al., "State Political Culture and Sentence Severity in Federal District Courts," *Criminology*, 16 (November 1978), 373–382; Herbert M. Kritzer, "Political Correlates of the Behavior of Federal District Judges: A 'Best Case' Analysis," *Journal of Politics*, 40 (1978), 25–58; "Federal Judges and Their Political Environments: The Influence of Public Opinion," *American Journal of Political Science*, 23 (February 1979), 194–207.

22 George W. Pruet, Jr., and Henry R. Glick, "Social Environment, Public Opinion, and Judicial Policymaking," *American Politics Quarterly*, 14 (1986), 5–33.

23 Melinda Gann Hall, "Constituent Influence in State Supreme Courts: Conceptual Notes and a Case Study," *Journal of Politics*, 49 (1987), 1117–1124.

24 Thomas R. Marshall, "Public Opinion and the Rehnquist Court," *Judicature*, 74 (1991), 322–329.

25 Thomas R. Marshall, *Public Opinion and the Supreme Court* (Boston: Unwin Hyman, 1989).

26 Thomas R. Marshall, "Public Opinion, Representation and the Modern Supreme Court," *American Politics Quarterly*, 16 (1988), 296–316.
27 Gregory A. Caldeira, "Courts and Public Opinion," in John B. Gates and Charles A. Johnson, *The American Courts: A Critical Assessment* (Washington, D.C.: Congressional Quarterly Press, 1991).
28 Marshall, 1988.
29 On these and related points, see Glendon Schubert, *The Judicial Mind* (Evanston, Ill.: Northwestern University Press, 1965); Schubert, *The Judicial Mind Revisited* (New York: Oxford University Press, 1974); Spaeth, especially chaps. 5 and 6.
30 Theodore L. Becker, *Political Behavioralism and Modern Jurisprudence* (Chicago: Rand McNally & Company, 1964), chap. 1.
31 "Statistics," *Harvard Law Review*, 103, (198), 394 and 104 (1990), 362.
32 Bob Woodward and Scott Armstrong, *The Brethren* (New York: Avon Books, 1979), pp. 257, 302–303, 521, and 528; *The New York Times*, March 8, 1986, p. 10.
33 Daryl R. Fair, "An Experimental Application of Scalogram Analysis to State Supreme Court Decisions," *Wisconsin Law Review*, 2 (1967), 449–467.
34 David J. Danelski, "Conflict and its Resolution in the Supreme Court," *Journal of Conflict Resolution*, 11 (1967), 72–73; Henry Robert Glick, *Supreme Courts in State Politics* (New York: Basic Books, Inc., 1971), pp. 96–99; and David J. Danelski, "Values as Variables in Judicial Decision-Making," *Vanderbilt Law Review*, 19 (1966), 721–740.
35 Fred Kort, "Quantitative Analysis of Fact-Patterns in Cases and their Impact on Judicial Decisions," *Harvard Law Review*, 79 (1966), 1595–1603; Jeffrey A. Segal, "Supreme Court Justices as Human Decision Makers: An Individual-Level Analysis of the Search and Seizure Cases," *Journal of Politics*, 48 (1986), 938–55; Kevin T. McGuire, "Obscenity, Libertarian Values, and Decision Making in the Supreme Court," *American Politics Quarterly*, 18 (1990), 47–67.
36 The literature on judicial roles is summarized well in Charles H. Sheldon, *The American Judicial Process: Models and Approaches* (New York: Dodd, Mead and Co., 1974), pp. 83–98.
37 Glick, pp. 39–41.
38 J. Woodford Howard, Jr., "Role Perceptions and Behavior on Three U.S. Courts of Appeals," *Journal of Politics*, 39 (1977), 916–938; John T. Wold, "Political Orientations, Social Backgrounds, and Role Perceptions of State Supreme Court Judges," *Western Political Quarterly*, 27 (1974), 239–248; Glick, chap. 2.
39 Howard, "Role Perceptions and Behavior. . . ."
40 Glick, p. 50; Harold J. Spaeth and Michael F. Altfeld, "Felix Frankfurter, Judicial Activism, and Voting Conflict on the Warren Court," in Sheldon Goldman and Charles M. Lamb (eds.), *Judicial Conflict and Consensus* (Lexington: University Press of Kentucky, 1986), pp. 87–114.
41 Harold Spaeth, "The Judicial Restraint of Mr. Justice Frankfurter: Myth or Reality," *Midwest Journal of Political Science*, 8 (1962), 22–38; Joel B. Grossman, "Role Playing and the Analysis of Judicial Behavior: The Case of Mr. Justice Frankfurter," *Journal of Public Law*, 11 (1962), 285–309.
42 James L. Gibson, "Judges' Role Orientations, Attitudes and Decisions: An Interactive Model," *American Political Science Review*, 72 (1978), 911–924.
43 John M. Scheb, Thomas D. Ungs, and Allison L. Hays, "Judicial Role Orientations, Attitudes and Decision Making: A Research Note," *Western Political Quarterly*, 42 (1989), 427–435.

**44** Lee Epstein, Thomas G. Walker, and William J. Dixon, "The Supreme Court and Criminal Justice Disputes: A Neo-Institutional Perspective," *American Journal of Political Science*, 33 (1989), 825–841.

**45** John T. Wold, "Going through the Motions," *Judicature*, 62 (1978), 64.

**46** *New York Times*, February 22, 1988, p. 18.

**47** For a discussion related to this point, see Gregory J. Rathjen, "An Analysis of Separate Opinion Writing Behavior as Dissonance Reduction," *American Politics Quarterly*, 2 (1974), 393–411.

**48** J. Woodford Howard, Jr., "On the Fluidity of Judicial Choice," *American Political Science Review*, 62 (1968), 43–57; Walter F. Murphy, *Elements of Judicial Strategy* (Chicago: University of Chicago Press, 1964).

**49** Saul Brenner, "Fluidity on the United States Supreme Court: A Reexamination," *American Journal of Political Science*, 24 (1980), 526–535.

**50** Timothy M. Hagle and Harold J. Spaeth, "Voting Fluidity and the Attitudinal Model of Supreme Court Decision Making," *Western Political Quarterly*, 44 (1991), 119–128.

**51** Saul Brenner, "Fluidity on the Supreme Court: 1956–1967," *American Journal of Political Science*, 26 (1982), 388–390; "Ideological Voting on the U.S. Supreme Court: A Comparison of the Original Vote on the Merits with the Final Vote," *Jurimetrics Journal*, 22 (1982), 287–292.

**52** "A Conversation with Chief Justice Earl Warren," in Sheldon Goldman and Austin Sarat (eds.), *American Court Systems* (San Francisco: W. H. Freeman and Co., 1978), p. 520.

**53** Saul Brenner, "Minimum Winning Coalitions on the U.S. Supreme Court," *American Politics Quarterly*, 7 (1979), 384–392.

**54** Sheldon Goldman and Thomas P. Jahnige, *The Federal Courts as a Political System*, 2d ed. (New York: Harper & Row, Publishers, Inc., 1976), p. 190.

**55** Murphy, Glick, chap. 5; Howard, "The Fluidity of Judicial Choice."

**56** Hirsch, chaps. 5 and 6.

**57** Glick, p. 113; Woodward and Armstrong, *passim*.

**58** *New York Times*, July 28, 1989, p. 21.

**59** Edward N. Beiser, "The Rhode Island Supreme Court: A Well-Integrated Political System," *Law and Society Review*, 8 (1974), 167–186.

**60** "A Conversation with Chief Justice Earl Warren," p. 521.

**61** Glick, pp. 90–93. See also John W. Patterson and Gregory J. Rathjen, "Background Diversity and State Supreme Court Behavior," *Polity*, 8 (1976), 610–622; Donald R. Songer, "Factors Affecting Variation in Rates and Dissent in the U.S. Courts of Appeals," in Goldman and Lamb, pp. 117–138, and Henry R. Glick and George W. Pruet, Jr., "Dissent in State Supreme Courts: Patterns and Correlates of Conflict," in Goldman and Lamb, pp. 199–214; Paul Brace and Melinda Gann Hall, "Neo-Institutionalism and Dissent in State Supreme Courts," *Journal of Politics*, 52 (1990), 54–70.

**62** Elliot E. Slotnick, "The Chief Justice and Self-Assignment of Majority Opinions: A Research Note," *Western Political Quarterly*, 31 (1978), 219–225.

**63** David W. Rohde, "Policy Goals, Strategic Choice and Majority Opinion Assignments in the U.S. Supreme Court," *Midwest Journal of Political Science*, 16 (1972), 652–682; Gregory James Rathjen, "Policy Goals, Strategic Choice and Majority Opinion Assignments on the U.S. Supreme Court: A Replication," *American Jour-*

*nal of Political Science*, 18 (1974), 713–724; Elliot E. Slotnick, "The Equality Principle and Majority Opinion Assignment on the United States Supreme Court," *Polity*, 12 (1979), 318–332; Elliot E. Slotnick, "Who Speaks for the Court? Majority Opinion Assignment from Taft to Burger," *American Journal of Political Science*, 23 (1979), 60–77; Harold J. Spaeth, "Distributive Justice: Majority Opinion Assignments in the Burger Court," *Judicature*, 67 (1984), 299–304.

64 David J. Danelski, "The Influence of the Chief Justice in the Decisional Process of the Supreme Court," *American Court Systems,* pp. 506–519.

65 Danelski, "The Influence of the Chief Justice . . ."; Goldman and Jahnige, pp. 185–189; Woodward and Armstrong, *passim.*

66 *Wall Street Journal*, June 18, 1986, p. 1.

# 10

# JUDICIAL POLICYMAKING

Besides settling disputes, court decisions often make judicial policy. There is no single or best definition of policymaking, but most people have in mind something more than a decision in a typical court case or other routine government action, such as processing applications for welfare or running the drivers' license bureau.

A working definition of policymaking is *government action that is directed at solving or coping with social, economic, or political problems.*[1] In this sense, judicial policymaking is broader or more comprehensive than day-to-day decision making that disposes of individual personal disputes and cases of crime. Policymaking deals with the broader significance of judicial decisions.

How we look at judicial policymaking is important, because it affects our understanding of the role of courts in American government and the significance we attach to different types of court decisions. There also is much debate in the United States over whether courts ought to make policy and the ability that courts have to solve social problems. Americans take many problems to court, and as society becomes more complex and technically sophisticated, courts are constantly confronted with new and thornier issues. How courts deal with them is an important part of judicial policymaking.

All courts do not make policy in the same way. We have to distinguish the policymaking activity of trial and appellate courts and consider the special role of the U.S. Supreme Court as a national policymaker. Examples of court policymaking and the content of contemporary judicial policies also will help to complete our understanding of courts in policymaking.

## COURTS AS POLICYMAKERS

### Appellate Courts

The picture that comes to mind most often when we think of judicial policy-making is an announcement of the U.S. Supreme Court in a single case that raises new, unusual, and controversial issues. For example, the school integration policy announced in *Brown v. Board of Education* (1954) is one of the most visible and important judicial policies in a century. It contained the most sweeping judicial statement about race relations and provided the basis for other decisions that limited racial discrimination in other areas of American life.

Many other individual cases also clearly qualify as judicial policies. Decisions broadening the constitutional rights of criminal defendants, decisions that limit the power of the states to regulate abortion or to use the death penalty, are good examples of highly visible judicial policies.

**Key Characteristics**   Supreme Court policies contained in a single case often grab our attention like claps of thunder, but appellate decisions have a number of important characteristics that make them stand out as judicial policies. In fact, the special features of appellate decisions have largely shaped the way that social scientists think about judicial policymaking.

*Guidance*   First, appellate decisions are expected to provide guidance to lower appellate and trial courts when they confront similar issues in the future. Therefore, a single appellate judicial policy can have an impact on hundreds or thousands of cases involving similar conflicts that enter the courts later on. In addition, if an appellate court repeatedly reverses a lower court in the same policy area, such as defendants' access to lawyers, or racial discrimination, it repeatedly sends a message to lower court judges that conflicts should be resolved differently.

Publicity about new decisions also communicates court policies to police departments and other officials. Sometimes Supreme Court policies attract a great deal of attention because several cases involving similar issues, such as the death penalty, reach the Court about the same time and the Court decides all of them with the same opinion. As we saw earlier, many organized interest groups actively support litigation and shape their appeals to provide judges with opportunities to make general policy statements that will affect many people throughout the country.

*Written Opinions*   Another important feature of appellate policymaking is that policy is communicated most often through written court opinions. Trial judges rarely write opinions explaining their decisions. When they do, they usually concentrate on the particular facts in the case before them. Their legal orders also are designed to carry out their decision in one case only. Therefore, it is more difficult to see a judicial policy in most trial court decisions. Written appellate opinions give us much more information than trial verdicts.

Majority opinion writers usually summarize the key facts in the case and the legal and social background of the controversy. A court's policy is found in the judges' written evaluation of the issues and the legal arguments made by both sides. By accepting or rejecting their lawyers' view, and often producing new legal interpretations of their own, judges indicate their approach to a problem.

Usually, judicial policies are general statements of how problems should be resolved, but occasionally judges list particular rules that should be followed in the future. The clarity and detail of policies vary, but we always get a much better idea of what judges have in mind in written appellate opinions than without them.

*Planning*   Appellate courts receive most attention in discussions of judicial policymaking also because appellate decision making is believed to involve conscious and rational planning. Unlike busy trial courts, many appellate judges have time to examine various angles to a case. They can think about the basis and development of the conflict, consider how the case fits into current policy, and carefully make decisions that seem to produce the best solutions. Judges may consider several alternatives before selecting one plan. Appellate policymaking involves an intentional search for solutions.

Legal training emphasizes logic and rationality, so it seems likely that even if judges decide according to their attitudes, the process of reaching decisions still will involve conscious evaluation of the issues. In addition, appellate judges spend much energy persuading their colleagues and compromising on written opinions, which requires conscious and considered decision making. Finally, judges sometimes worry how their opinions will be read and applied by others, so many of them pay close attention to creating policies that will accomplish their goals.

*Government Targets*   Finally, appellate courts receive as much attention as policymakers because many of their decisions are directed at the policies of other government officials. This magnifies the significance of judicial policy, because it affects the strategies other government officials develop to deal with social problems. There are many appellate decisions that affect other government policies, such as appeals by criminals who claim that their rights were violated by police or trial judges, government regulation of business and labor, zoning decisions of local governments, tax cases, school desegregation, state regulation of abortion, and many others.

### Trial Courts

It is more difficult to see trial courts as policymakers. Nearly all trial cases focus on specific facts and litigants, and trial decisions are aimed at resolving particular disputes. Trial judges handle hundreds or thousands of seemingly routine cases every year, probably with little opportunity to think about the overall impact of their decisions and how they contribute to solving any local problem. Few trial judges think of themselves as policymakers, whereas appellate judges often distinguish between their role in making law from the more routine case-by-case approach of the trial courts.

There are two points of view about the significance of trial courts as policy makers. The traditional perspective is that trial courts enforce local norms and values and have a small policymaking role. A more contemporary view is that trial courts also make policy, but most often in ways which are distinctive from appellate courts. Both views will be presented.

**Norm Enforcement**    Traditionally, many social scientists viewed trial courts as norm enforcers in routine civil and criminal cases.[2] This means that trial judges concentrate on individual cases and apply local values, customs, or state law to their decisions.

For example, state law provides a range of punishments for particular crimes. Judges are obliged to stay within the legal range, and the particular sentences they select are likely to conform to widely held or locally dominant views about how criminals ought to be punished. Even when there is little statutory law, as in divorce and other family matters, judges are believed to apply community standards to their decisions. In this view, most trial courts do not innovate, nor do judges usually have any long-range plan or conscious strategy in mind as they make decisions. Their decisions also rarely provide guidance to other courts. Consequently, *trial judges rarely make policy*.

*Separate Functions*    The main advantage of this view is that it helps to distinguish the work of trial and appellate courts. For instance, trial judges routinely approve plea bargains and negotiated settlements in civil cases, and supervise trials, whereas appellate judges make decisions without juries and explain the basis of their decisions in written opinions.

Policymaking and norm enforcement also distinguish the social significance of courts. On the one hand, appellate courts make decisions that broadly affect and guide society, while trial courts deal with more narrow problems that concern people directly and individually. Through norm enforcement, trial courts perform an important public service of meeting heavy citizen demand for authoritative settlement of disputes.

*Trial Court Innovation*    Although there are differences between appellate and trial courts, viewing trial courts as norm enforcers is much too limited for two main reasons. First, as will be discussed shortly, the content of many routine trial court decisions often reveal patterns that form a distinctive policy. Second, trial courts also have some opportunities to make innovative decisions. These are not precedents in the legal sense because they are not binding on other courts, but they provide examples to other judges for how they might deal with new and thorny problems. An example of innovation discussed in Chapter 7 is the sentencing decisions of trial judges as alternatives to imprisonment.

Box 10.1, "Innovation in Trial Courts," further illustrates unusual recent cases that have required both federal and state trial judges to develop novel solutions to new as well as old problems.

No day goes by that a trial judge somewhere in the country does not get a new and unusual case and is forced to make a controversial decision. In many

---

**BOX 10.1**

INNOVATION IN TRIAL COURTS

**Federal district courts**

• In Kansas City, Missouri, a federal district judge ordered the city school district to raise local property taxes in order to pay for school improvements he previously had ordered to attract white students back to the public schools.

• A Los Angeles federal district judge ruled that district boundaries for the county board of commissioners violate the Federal Voting Rights Act by discriminating against Hispanics.

• In Louisiana, a federal district judge ruled that the federal government may require Gulf Coast shrimpers to use turtle-saving devices on their nets.

• In order to end overcrowding, federal district court judges in two-thirds of the states have ordered state prisons not to admit new prisoners.

• A Pennsylvania federal district judge declared unconstitutional provisions of the state's restrictive abortion law which required a woman to first inform her husband of her plans to have an abortion and to listen to a state-prepared talk by her doctor about the risks and benefits of abortion and childbirth. (This law was largely upheld by the U.S. Supreme Court.)

• Federal judges in Georgia and Minnesota have blocked their states from enforcing laws which required minors to notify their parents before having an abortion. (The Supreme Court has overturned the lower federal court ruling in Minnesota and upheld the state law.)

• A federal district judge in Texas has held the state in contempt for failing to improve conditions at its facilities for the mentally retarded.

**State trial courts**

• A Kansas trial judge has sought to guarantee a patient's confidentiality by ordering the patient's doctors not to inform his former wife that the patient had tested positive for the AIDS virus.

• A Tennessee trial judge gave custody of seven frozen embryos of a divorcing couple to the wife, who had donated the eggs.

• A New York state trial judge authorized a husband to demand an abortion for his comatose wife on the chance the procedure might save her life.

• In Indiana, a juvenile court judge ordered an 18-year-old woman not to have an abortion because it violated the paternity rights of her boyfriend. In a similar case, a Utah judge refused to block an abortion at the request of the woman's estranged husband.

• A New Jersey trial judge awarded the father custody of a child produced through a biological surrogate mother, ending all claims by the surrogate who later contested the adoption. The judge openly acknowledged that he was making new law since no state statute or prior judicial ruling applied to this situation.

• In New Jersey, a state trial judge ruled that Atlantic City casinos can be held liable for the gambling losses of drunken customers who are plied with free liquor by the gambling establishments.

---

cases, no matter which way a judge decides, the ruling will make news, because the subject matter of the case is different from run-of-the-mill judicial business.

These trial decisions have many characteristics similar to appellate decisions. The judges undoubtedly are aware of the seriousness of the issues involved, give careful consideration to alternative policies, and sometimes write opinions explaining their decisions and orders. These decisions also affect other government policy, they often rest on interpretation of the U.S. Constitution, and affect important local problems.

Nevertheless, controversial cases still are the exception, not the rule, in the trial courts. On the whole, trial judges make many more routine decisions than innovative or unusual ones.

**Cumulative Policymaking**  Although trial courts deal with many seemingly unimportant cases, they give trial judges an opportunity to make policy in a different way. The idea of cumulative policymaking is an alternative to viewing trial courts as norm enforcers.[3]

With their heavy caseloads, trial judges make decisions on the same subjects over and over again throughout the year, and they often adopt a consistent point of view in dealing with certain conflicts. This puts a distinctive judicial mark on the management of local problems. This can be viewed as cumulative judicial policymaking, because it builds up over time through decisions in many similar cases. Appellate courts also make cumulative policies, since not all their decisions are innovative or announce new solutions to problems.

*Social Significance*  The concept of cumulative policymaking has certain advantages over norm enforcement. First, if we conclude that trial courts enforce norms while appellate courts make policy, we tend to dismiss trial courts as litigation factories where judges crank out decisions by automatically applying local standards of proper conduct. The concept of trial court norm enforcement leads most people to focus on appellate courts as the only important judicial institutions.

Norm enforcement also implies that each trial decision is a separate event with no social significance beyond the immediate parties to the dispute. However, cumulative policymaking sees sets of trial decisions as socially significant judicial decisions and makes us more sensitive to the impact of trial courts in society.

*Few Clear Norms*  Norm enforcement also underestimates the importance of judges' values or attitudes in decision making and oversimplifies the way that norms influence decisions. As we saw in the previous chapter, there is no automatic or regular way that local opinions, values, or morals are communicated to judges. An occasional poll may influence judges' decisions in certain highly visible and controversial cases, such as possession of marijuana, but that certainly is not the routine way that judges make decisions.

In many cases, such as industrial accidents, contract disputes, patents, and others, it is doubtful that most people have relevant norms or that their values determine how they would act, say as a juror, in a specific case. Norms found in law also usually are vague and require judges to decide for themselves how to settle specific disputes. Finally, in a large city, there are no universally held community norms or standards. Judges always have to choose, and they usually act according to their own values or they are affected by other members of local courthouse work groups.

By adding a cumulative dimension to the usual descriptions of judicial policymaking, we have a much broader concept of the policymaking role of courts. In this broader perspective, we are not particularly concerned whether judges are consciously aware of their behavior or have a particular intent in mind when they make decisions. Rationality also is not a prerequisite of policymaking. Instead, *cumulative policymaking is found in the consistency of judges' decisions, not in what judges are thinking*.

**Sentencing**   Examples of cumulative policymaking are all around us. Judges who routinely dismiss criminal charges or give very lenient sentences to youthful marijuana smokers arrested at a rock concert or at a college football game exhibit a local judicial policy concerning how courts should deal with certain categories of crime. Not many years ago, judges in most states rarely sentenced drunk drivers to jail, despite state laws permitting 1- or 2-year prison terms. But recently, due partly to organized interest groups such as Mothers Against Drunk Drivers. Some judges are beginning to get tough.[4]

Occasionally, judges' sentencing policies become so clear judges are known by their nicknames, such as "Hanging Harry"—Judge Harry Lee Coe III of Tampa, Florida.[5] As mentioned earlier, appellate courts also make cumulative policy in otherwise routine cases, such as the reversal of every death sentence by the New Jersey Supreme Court for a decade between 1982 and 1991.[6] This pattern of decisions is nearly identical to those of the California Supreme Court under former Chief Justice Rose Bird.

Consistent patterns of lenient and harsh sentences or reversals of death sentences are illustrations of cumulative policymaking. It is easy to say that these decisions simply reflect local community norms, but the nagging question is *whose* norms—all parents, middle-class parents, college students, insurance companies, the police, religious fundamentalists, auto accident victims, state legislators?

Another example concerns sentencing of black and poor criminal defendants. Many citizens and social scientists have thought that white judges and juries are biased and treat blacks and the poor more harshly. Some also believe that a judicial policy of harshness is part of a strategy to preserve middle-class dominance and a smoothly running judicial system.[7]

There has been much research to discover if, when, and how often discrimination occurs. If judges generally sentence blacks and the poor more harshly, we could conclude that they have a judicial policy of dealing differently with blacks and whites.

A careful examination of much social science research suggests that assumptions of racial and social class sentencing have been exaggerated.[8] When previous convictions and type of offense are taken into account, sentencing differences based on race and social status become extremely small. There is no general policy of discrimination. In fact, we could conclude that there is a general policy of even-handedness in most sentencing. (These studies do not deal with the issue that most defendants are poor and that many are black.)

Important exceptions occur, however, in capital cases. Several studies found that in the southern states, blacks found guilty of raping white women or killing whites received the death penalty significantly more often than whites convicted of any rape or murder. Studies on sentencing in nonsouthern states found that the poor (not only blacks) faced the death penalty more often in various capital cases.

The importance of the death penalty in capital cases as local cumulative judicial policy is emphasized when we recall that the Supreme Court suspended executions in 1972 because it found that the *pattern* of death sentences was unequal and discriminatory in the United States. Whether discrimination was an intentional policy or not, the Supreme Court ruled that it must be replaced with a policy of fairness and equality.

*Family Law* Another illustration of cumulative policymaking is found in court decisions in family law. There is a widespread judicial policy in the United States against jailing fathers who do not pay required child support, despite numerous court appearances and judicial warnings. Studies show that men often quit paying child support a short time after their divorce and original court orders.

Despite the persistent efforts of a few mothers to take their former spouses to civil court and occasional criminal cases brought by prosecutors, very few fathers end up in jail. Judges give many reasons for not sending fathers to jail. Some say that it is impossible to earn a living while in jail. Judges also have no independent way of finding out if delinquent fathers can afford to make payments, especially since many court cases pit poor mothers against poor fathers. Regardless of the justifications, judicial policy is to warn and persuade, but not to jail, fathers.

Sometimes community norms seem so strong and consistent that it is very tempting to conclude that judges simply follow the force of social custom. But this obscures more than it reveals about judicial behavior. For example, judges almost always have awarded custody of children in divorce cases to the mothers. Some states also have had laws stating that mothers should be given special preference by judges. However, some states have changed their laws so that neither parent has a formal legal edge in child custody cases.[10] Nevertheless, state judges continue to award custody to mothers in most cases. That is the cumulative judicial policy regarding child custody.

However, there also are signs of change from many different quarters of the political system. The United States Internal Revenue Service has begun to apply income tax refunds to past due child support when delinquent fathers have been identified by state welfare offices. Judges in a few states have set aside an entire court day once a month for hearing only child support cases, and they sometimes sentence dozens of deadbeat dads to county jail in a single morning.

Policy toward child custody also is changing. Mothers continue to receive custody of their children in over 90 percent of divorces because both parents agree, but state law and judicial policy increasingly provide for alternatives. Over half the states have changed their laws to provide for possible joint custody, which sometimes means that children live part of each year with a different parent. There is evidence that when both parents demand full custody and cannot settle out of court, judges also are inclined to favor fathers who can demonstrate that they are better able to provide for their children.[11]

These changes are in the news and appear at judicial conferences where judges exchange ideas and methods for dealing with certain types of cases. The women's political movement receives much media attention, but men's organizations also have been formed in recent years to press their side of the family law debate. Judges cannot help but become aware of changes in society and in other courts, and cumulative judicial policy in family law probably will take some new directions in the near future.

## TRENDS IN JUDICIAL POLICYMAKING

Mention judicial policymaking and a federal judge ruling on civil rights springs to mind. Many people seem to believe that judicial policymaking started with the Supreme Court in the 1950s under the leadership of liberal Chief Justice Earl Warren. That is when the Court began to make new decisions in civil rights and criminal law. Until then, it seems, the Supreme Court performed a more "normal" judicial function of interpreting and applying the Constitution.

But the picture of judicial policymaking is more complex than this. *Courts in America always have made policy.* The issues and problems have changed as the country developed from a simple society to a large industrial nation, but courts always have had to interpret law in new ways or to develop new rules when law did not exist.

### Early Policymaking

There are many examples of judicial policymaking throughout American history.[12] With independence, the new thirteen states theoretically were free to choose whatever law they preferred. However, since the states had no other legal experience, they adapted and used English law, regardless of their hostile feelings toward the British.

English law meant *common law*, which is made by judges through individual court decisions. Starting with independence, American judges decided for themselves how the law should be applied to their cases. In fact, since common law emphasizes judicial power, many early judges viewed legislative lawmaking as an interference with judicial authority, and early courts often competed with legislatures for the last word in state policy.

**Necessary Innovation**   In the early days of the nation, judges often believed that serving on state supreme courts was more prestigious than any position other than President, so the state courts had many famous innovative judges who were willing to create new policy. James Kent, a New York judge famous for his judicial opinions and innovative ways, explained the opportunities and needs of judging in early America:

> I took the court as if it had been a new institution, and never before known in the United States. I had nothing to guide me, and was left to assume . . . powers and jurisdiction as I thought applicable. . . . I saw where justice lay, and the moral sense decided the court half the time. . . . *I most always found principles suited to my view of the case.*[13]

Judicial innovation affected most areas of law, including contracts, early government regulation of corporations, and even marriage. State judges in the early 1800s, for example, broadly interpreted common law marriage in order to bestow legitimacy on thousands of marriages (and births) that had not been performed by clergy. Many early settlers despised the English church and American clergy were not very plentiful, so judges did some fancy judicial footwork to convey social and legal approval to many households.

State courts interpreted and applied new state laws on property, trusts, wills, estates, divorce, business, and transportation. All of these once were new areas of American law. State courts also adopted the power of judicial review and frequently declared acts of state legislatures unconstitutional. Many of these decisions voided laws that failed to meet the rigid requirements of detailed state constitutions, but others reflected judges' beliefs in laissez faire, the view that business should be free from any governmental regulation. These views were common in the 1800s and were reflected in judicial policy.

Early Supreme Court cases most clearly illustrate the importance of judicial policymaking in shaping the nation. *Marbury v. Madison*, 1803 (Supreme Court review of Congress), *Martin v. Hunter's Lessee*, 1816 (Supreme Court review of state courts), *McCulloch v. Maryland*, 1819 (supremacy of national law), and *Gibbons v. Ogden*, 1824 (federal regulation of interstate commerce) were fundamental national decisions that helped to define the character of the federal system, the power of the national government, and the emphasis that commerce and development were to receive in the United States.

None of these areas of policy was settled or routine law; they were brand-new policies created by the Supreme Court through its interpretation of the new Constitution. Their overall impact on American government and society equals or exceeds the controversial decisions made by the Supreme Court today.

## Regulation of Business

Compared with many other areas of law, court policy toward business and government regulation of the economy has had a profound and lasting impact on American society. The importance of judicial policy in this area can hardly be overemphasized, since the development and organization of business affects the type and level of employment, the overall standard of living of the country, the growth of cities, and other social behavior.

**Laissez Faire**   In the early 1800s, a few states had constitutions and statutes that severely limited business organization and activities, and some state courts reinforced them. However, after the Civil War, commerce increased quickly as people moved west. Trade, manufacturing, transportation, and cities grew, and corporations and larger business ventures became common. Gradually, courts joined the tide of promoting business growth. They interpreted corporate powers broadly and declared unconstitutional various state laws designed to regulate big business or impose other limitations, such as laws restricting child labor and the maximum hours an employee could be required to work in one day or week.

*Toward the end of the 1800s, the Supreme Court generally prevented government regulation of business by applying the Fourteenth Amendment of the Constitution to corporations.* The Thirteenth, Fourteenth, and Fifteenth Amendments were adopted shortly after the Civil War and were designed to grant citizenship to the former slaves and to give blacks the same protections of law provided other citizens. However, state courts and the Supreme Court used the "due process of law" and "equal protection of the laws" phrases to protect business corporations from government regulation.

Under this interpretation, corporations were viewed as persons and government regulation was interference with due process. Many state courts also relied on various state laws to stymie government involvement in economic regulation. On the whole, courts either acquiesced in the development of big business or helped the process along by preventing legislatures and executive officials from creating their own policies that would have limited or regulated business growth and activity.

**Modern Regulation**   The crash of the stock market in 1929 and the depression of the 1930s quickly undermined the prestige and glamor of big business and began the process of increased government regulation as well as the growth of national social welfare programs designed to help the poor.

For a time, the Supreme Court resisted this change. During the early years of the New Deal, the Supreme Court declared unconstitutional many new laws that involved the government in economic recovery and regulation. But the Supreme Court was out of phase with the very popular Democratic President Franklin D. Roosevelt and the Democratic-controlled Congress. The justices of the Supreme Court had been appointed to office years earlier, and a majority still were attuned to old policies that favored an unregulated economy.[14]

The conflict between liberal laws bumping into the conservative Supreme Court led to a major confrontation between President Roosevelt and the justices. The President asked Congress to approve a new court appointment system in which he could appoint a new justice for every sitting justice who was over age 75 up to a maximum court membership of fifteen justices.

This famous "court packing" plan was designed to give President Roosevelt control of the Court by loading it with his own appointees, all of whom presumably would share his policy goals. But, like many other court reforms, this was a drastic change in a cherished institution, and even President Roosevelt's supporters in Congress refused to support it.

Although the court packing plan failed, the justices responded to the unusually clear political message that the Supreme Court was out of date. By 1937, one of the conservatives, Justice Owen J. Roberts, shifted his vote to the liberal side, creating a narrow but historic 5 to 4 split that supported the New Deal.

Since the late 1930s, the Supreme Court generally has taken a liberal position toward federal regulation of the economy and rarely has declared economic legislation enacted by Congress unconstitutional. It still has been important in economic cases, however, often by requiring government agencies to follow proper procedures in implementing government policy and interpreting regulatory statutes. It has not had much impact, though, on the power of the government to become involved in economic life.

Since the 1970s, the Supreme Court has been dominated by conservative justices who have viewed economic regulation somewhat more unfavorably than in previous years. Nevertheless, the Supreme Court has endorsed the power of federal and state governments to tax and regulate business practices through a wide variety of laws and agencies.

The most important restatement of the power of the federal government to regulate the national economy, even at the possible expense of individual state interests, is a 1985 Supreme Court decision that held that only Congress and the political process may determine the extent of federal economic regulation (*Garcia v. San Antonio Metropolitan Transit Authority*). However, if business regulation by the states does not interfere with national regulation, the states too are free to regulate economic and business relationships within their borders.[15]

In the broad overview, government regulation of the economy is here to stay with only modest changes in a liberal or conservative direction as Presidents and justices come and go.

Most state courts also generally side with state governments in upholding the power of administrative agencies to regulate economic activity. The odds are good that an appeal brought against state government by an individual citizen, business, or other group will be decided in favor of the government's right to regulate professions and grant licenses, regulate pollution, make zoning decisions, or take other action that affects the economy.

## Individual Rights

Rather than conflict over the economy, the most controversial judicial policy today concerns the rights of individuals. Cases involving individual rights include racial, sexual, and age discrimination; freedom of speech, press, and religion; rights to privacy; equal political representation; the rights of criminal defendants; and fair judicial and administrative procedure.

These cases all have something in common, since they concern the position of the individual in the political and legal systems. As we saw in the preceding chapter, judges generally respond to these issues in the same way, voting either for the individual in most cases or in favor of government limitations of private rights.

**Early Limited Rights**  Generally, until the mid-1930s and the beginning of World War II, courts supported government limitations on private rights and permitted private discrimination. In particular, courts usually upheld criminal convictions of individuals who had asserted their right to free speech and to press for socialism and other unpopular causes. Governments prevented the American Communist party from publishing political propaganda, and Communists were barred from holding office in labor unions. Segregation also was accepted.

The police also were free from judicial regulation, and poor criminal defendants had no access to free legal assistance in most cases or protection against police pressure and arbitrary search and seizure for evidence. Schools freely mixed education and religion, and many local governments demanded that businesses close on Sunday, banned the sale of books they considered obscene, and required employees to take loyalty or religious oaths as conditions of employment.

*Passive Courts*  Judges usually did not create these restrictive views of freedom and civil rights, but they also did little to prevent other people and government officials and institutions from limiting freedom. Criminal defendants and other unpopular litigants who protested government power and private discrimination generally lost in court. The right to speak out and to publish, practice religion, use public facilities, and attend neighborhood schools depended more heavily on a person's race, religion, and local goodwill than on explicit legal rules designed to apply equally to everyone.

**World War II**  The rise of Nazi Germany and fascism in Europe and the beginning of World War II made many Americans more sensitive to the value of free speech and individual rights, and this affected Supreme Court policy as well. In addition, after enduring years of opposition from conservatives on the Supreme Court, President Franklin Roosevelt was able to begin making judicial appointments in 1937. In a few years, he made a total of nine appointments, more than any President other than George Washington, and most of the new justices were more liberal.

With some exceptions, the new justices were able to shift Supreme Court policy toward greater political freedom and individual rights. However, after 1945, America became preoccupied with the Cold War and the fear of communist subversion, and the Supreme Court temporarily backtracked on political freedom. When McCarthyism faded in the late 1950s, the Supreme Court, under Chief Justice Earl Warren, became an even stronger supporter of civil liberties and civil rights.[16]

For many years the Supreme Court generally was alone in adopting more liberal policies. Some federal judges and a few state supreme courts quickly followed the early lead of the Supreme Court, but many other American judges and public officials either resisted this shift in judicial policy or interpreted Supreme Court policy so narrowly that it had limited effects on local policy.

The role of the Supreme Court and other courts in civil liberties and civil rights policy has been a gradual one. For instance, the fight for civil rights has been going on since the Civil War, and blacks have continually looked for access to some level or part of government and allies among whites who would support equal rights. The NAACP was organized in 1911 and worked for years to achieve its later victories. In addition, the Supreme Court and a few other state and federal courts ruled against segregation in particular settings, such as southern attempts to keep blacks from voting in Democratic party primary elections (1944), racial restrictions on housing (1948), or segregation of state university law schools (1950). Nevertheless, *Brown v. Board* stands out as the major symbol of the modern era of Supreme Court policy toward the broad field of individual rights.

While the movement toward civil rights has been gradual, the major judicial innovations have been made since the 1950s. Court decisions established national policy in civil liberties and civil rights and set the stage for later Supreme Court decisions in the 1970s and 1980s. Even though the current Supreme Court majority is more conservative, the Warren Court has had a lasting impact by establishing a much broader and proindividual interpretation of political rights in the United States than had ever existed before.

**Rights for All**    Race relations policy is especially important, because it marks the real beginning of racial integration and a chance for blacks to achieve equal rights. These cases are significant also, however, because they stimulated other groups in the United States to think explicitly about their own status in American society and to view courts as likely locations to make political demands.

There is a link, for example, between the early struggle for black civil rights and more recent demands of students to challenge arbitrary dress codes or to publish what they like in a student newspaper. The struggle for black civil rights also is related to the women's political movement and to demands of prison inmates and of patients in mental hospitals who protest crowded facilities and poor living conditions.

The main legal vehicle for most contemporary civil rights and civil liberties policies in the Fourteenth Amendment, which guarantees due process of law and equal protection of law. These are the same provisions used by the Supreme Court in the 1800s to prevent government from interfering with the rights of business. Today, the amendment is applied to individual citizens.

*New Limits*    Since the 1970s, Supreme Court policy in civil rights and civil liberties has become more conservative as new justices appointed by Republican Presidents Richard Nixon, Gerald Ford, Ronald Reagan, and George

Bush have replaced the Warren Court liberals, but most of the early decisions in race relations, the rights of criminal defendants, and others have remained largely intact.

However, the recent appointment of additional conservatives to the Supreme Court probably signals a more fundamental shift to the right. In many decisions involving job discrimination, busing to achieve racial integration in the public schools, and abortion, the Supreme Court has overruled or substantially reduced the coverage of previous Supreme Court policies.

One of the most controversial is the Court's decision in *Wards Cove Packing Company, Inc. v. Atonio* (1989) in which the Supreme Court overruled a Supreme Court precedent from the 1970s that prohibited unintentional discrimination, particularly tests unrelated to job performance that tended to screen out blacks. In the *Wards Cove* decision, the Supreme Court put the burden of proof on the employee rather than the employer in proving that such tests were not a necessary part of company operations, something that most employees will find difficult to do.

However, after two years of partisan conflict between liberal Democrats and moderate Republicans on one side and conservative Republicans and President Bush on the other, Congress and the President have compromised on a new civil rights law which will substantially eliminate the impact of *Wards Cove* and other Court decisions. Consequently, even though the Supreme Court limited civil rights, it has not had the last word.

In school desegregation, the Supreme Court has ruled that busing may be abandoned in particular school districts where it appears that school boards have done everything "practicable" to end discrimination. In abortion, the Supreme Court has upheld certain restrictive state laws that make it difficult for women to obtain an abortion. *Roe v. Wade*, the 1973 decision that granted the fundamental right to obtain an abortion, has survived to the early 1990s, partly because Justice Sandra D. O'Conner is reluctant to abandon it, but with a heavy conservative majority now on the court, a national constitutional right to an abortion is being weakened.

Another example of modification of liberal Supreme Court policies concerns the use of evidence at a criminal trial. In 1961, the Supreme Court ruled that evidence the police seized improperly, such as without a valid search warrant, could not be used in state court (*Mapp v. Ohio*). This is called the *exclusionary rule*. (The rule had applied to federal courts for many years.)

The rule has been criticized on many counts. Some people believe it interferes with police investigations, encourages police to lie about their methods, or is ineffective in reducing police misbehavior while releasing many obvious criminals. In the 1970s, the Supreme Court chipped away at the rule by limiting its use in particular circumstances. The Court has not explicitly overruled previous judicial policy, but it has interpreted its application more narrowly. The net result is that it has upheld more criminal convictions when the appeal is based on police violations in obtaining evidence.

The current Court also has made it easier for police to obtain and use confessions, eased the power to search automobiles and airplanes and personal belongings without a judge's warrant, and made it more difficult for prisoners to appeal to the federal courts.

Although the Supreme Court is moving in the conservative direction, national judicial policy overall still is more supportive of the individual in society than in any period prior to the 1950s. Nevertheless, the new conservative Supreme Court probably will not support the development of new policies designed to enlarge civil rights or increase the individual's rights to challenge government authority.

### Local Judicial Policies

There are many other judicial policies that are largely unaffected by Supreme Court decisions. Most cases involve no constitutional issues and are settled entirely according to federal or state laws or the personal evaluations of judges concerning what is equitable, fair, or reasonable. Even when Supreme Court policy might be relevant, such as in criminal cases, most defendants never raise constitutional claims or their legal motions are quickly dismissed as flimsy attempts to have their cases dismissed.

This does not mean that trial and appellate judges ignore Supreme Court decisions, but they do not consider them relevant to most of their cases. Also, many types of conflicts, such as divorce, landlord-tenant disputes, or creditor-debtor conflicts, have not been tackled by the Supreme Court. Therefore, local judicial policies must be distinguished from Supreme Court policy.

**Criminal Justice**   Local criminal justice policy is very different from the image we often get by looking only at the Supreme Court. For example, increasing the legal rights of criminal defendants has not altered the overwhelming odds of conviction. The chances are good that defendants have lawyers early in the judicial process and that their attorneys consider the possibility of police violations of their rights, all in accordance with Supreme Court policy, but very few defendants "get off" because local trial judges decide that their rights actually were violated. The exclusionary rule concerning improperly obtained evidence is rarely raised by defendants, and it probably accounts for only 1 or 2 percent of all dismissals in the criminal courts.

Defendants' rights receive a great deal of attention in the news and they are important in establishing national standards of how criminal justice ought to operate, but in the daily grind of cases, most defendants are willing to confess and plead guilty to get their cases settled. They are not interested in constitutional issues.[17] Therefore, if prosecutors or police decide to press charges, local judicial policy almost always results in a conviction. Those who are set free escape a jail sentence because prosecutors decide not to proceed, not because judges invoke the Constitution to protect defendants.

Another feature of criminal justice policy is that the criminal justice system concentrates heavily on the poor and the down-and-out and disproportionately on blacks. Sentences are fairly equal for similar crimes and criminal records within individual cities, but since few middle-class or white-collar criminals are apprehended or prosecuted anywhere, criminal justice policy means punishment for the poor.[18]

There often are large differences among cities on how judges deal with criminals. For example, a study of three large cities revealed that Baltimore judges sentenced defendants to prison up to twice as often as Chicago and Detroit judges. Lengths of prison sentences also varied considerably, with Detroit judges giving the shortest sentences. Pittsburgh and Minneapolis judges also treat defendants very differently.[19] Information on sentencing policy is not available for more than a handful of American cities, but the chances appear good that there is a great deal of variation in the way that local courts treat crime.

**Economic Disputes**   In local economic disputes, the haves come out ahead. Most economic conflicts pit business or government organizations against individual defendants (Chapter 5). The organizations usually come to collect debts or to obtain compliance with a contract, rental agreement, or a government regulation. The organizations also are repeat players who are experienced in using the courts, can more easily afford to hire attorneys, and are not personally or emotionally involved in the dispute. Their cases are likely to be part of regular business or government activity.

Local judicial policy normally agrees with plaintiff claims, and reinforces property rights and governmental authority. The rate of plaintiff victories is very high. Generally, plaintiffs win no less than 75 percent of their cases, but in most cities and towns, plaintiffs win well over 85 or 90 percent of their cases.[20] Many of these are by default, because defendants do not show up in court, but even in contested cases, plaintiffs do very well, winning two-thirds or more of their cases.

Usually, trial judges consider only the narrow issues involved in economic disputes. For example, they want to know if the defendant signed a loan or sales agreement and is behind on payments, or if a tenant has not been paying rent on time. Broader and more basic questions concerning possibly confusing legal language in contracts or rental agreements or the willingness of businesses to extend credit to people who are poor financial risks usually do not come up in local court cases.

By considering only the limited issues in an immediate case, cumulative judicial policy generally reinforces the economic system and the different status and power that groups have in America. Although there is much government regulation, the American economy is based on private ownership and the profit motive, and business has accumulated enormous wealth, power, and sophistication. Judges sometimes influence some of the rules about *how* the economic game is played, but they rarely affect the basic character of the game.

Generally, groups with wealth, status, and success come to court to press their claims and they leave court with additional victories.

**Other Issues**   Although the overwhelming majority of criminal and economic cases do not raise issues of constitutional rights, constitutional issues do arise in the states. Cases concerning discrimination, defendants' rights, abortion, and others frequently occur as a result of state and local government action, and some of them reach the U.S. Supreme Court.

As discussed earlier, most state courts decide these cases in a conservative direction, but several innovative and liberal state supreme courts, for example, in New Jersey, New York, California, Alaska, and a few other states, have interpreted state constitutions in ways that are more favorable to individual rights than U.S. Supreme Court decisions. Several governors and state legislatures also are considering seeking protection from a possible reversal or weakening of *Roe v. Wade* by suggesting that the right to an abortion be included in state constitutions.

Former Justice William J. Brennan frequently has urged the state supreme courts to rely on state constitutions rather than U.S. Supreme Court precedents as a basis for expanding individual rights.[21] As the U.S. Supreme Court shifts further to the right, liberal supreme court decisions at least in certain states increasingly will become a political counter to conservative national judicial policy.

## JUDICIAL ACTIVISM AND RESTRAINT

This chapter maintains that judges always have made policy because they always have been required to cope with social problems. Some judges have eagerly created new policies, but even when judges stick closely to old ways of deciding cases, they make policy by supporting the status quo. No matter what the specific content of judicial decisions is, judges make policy.

Nevertheless, many people continue to disagree whether judges *ought* to make policy in their decisions or *should* limit themselves to interpreting and applying the law. The debate over judicial policymaking often is discussed in terms of "judicial activism" and "judicial restraint." There are several ways that these terms are defined.[22]

### Overturning Precedent

One view of judicial activism is that it is any judicial decision that changes past patterns of judicial policy or precedent. For instance, a decision that requires that juvenile offenders receive the same constitutional protections as adult criminals would be an activist decision, because it differs substantially from previous judicial decisions that have permitted state officials to treat juveniles in a paternalistic way and to deny them routine access to lawyers and court procedures common in adult court.

However, this view of activism can become confusing, for after a certain period of time, repeated decisions giving juveniles the same rights as adults may become routine. These later decisions could be called an exercise of judicial restraint, because trial courts follow the now established judicial policy toward juveniles. However, people who oppose the policy might continue to brand it as new and improper and, therefore, a sign of judicial activism.

**Incremental Change**   Sometimes the degree of court departure from past judicial policy is not very clear, so we have a difficult time classifying particular judicial policies as either activist or restrained. For example, in the 1960s, the Supreme Court agreed for the first time to hear a case involving legislative reapportionment (the drawing of district lines to determine patterns of representation in the states). At the time, this was a very innovative and activist decision, because a prior Supreme Court had said these cases involved political rather than legal issues and had refused to consider them. When the Supreme Court announced its one-person, one-vote rule, it upset years of unequal representation in the states.

The Supreme Court still gets cases involving apportionment. It has followed the basic requirements of the one-person, one-vote rule, but it also has permitted slight deviations from absolute voter equality in the size of legislative districts. Redistricting to guarantee minorities an impact on elections also has become a recent judicial issue.

It is difficult to understand these decisions in terms of activism and restraint, since the current Supreme Court generally conforms to what was once a very unusual and activist decision, but it also has changed a little from previous judicial standards. Is the current court activist, restrained, or a little of each? It is hard to say.

### Declaring Legislation Unconstitutional

The most widely used definition of judicial activism is judicial review: courts are activist when they declare acts of a legislature unconstitutional.[23] By contrast, courts are restrained when they defer to legislatures, although even in this view courts may declare laws invalid when these laws blatantly contradict constitutions.

Judicial reversal of legislation is not common, but is stands out as the clearest and most dramatic form of activism, for courts declare decisively and absolutely that a law is invalid because it violates the higher law of a state or the national constitution.

This definition of activism and restraint was the one used by Justice Felix Frankfurter to justify his progovernment decisions. He said he believed that courts ought to defer to the people's agencies of popular government (restraint) even if judges disagreed with the content of their decisions.

Recent critics of the Supreme Court and other federal courts frequently use this argument, too.[24] In their view, the judiciary has gobbled up powers that should be left to the other branches of government. They believe that the Constitution or certain amendments, particularly the Fourteenth, were not intended to give the courts so much influence in policymaking.

**Frequency of Judicial Review**   Table 10.1 summarizes the activity of the U.S. Supreme Court and the fifty state supreme courts in declaring legislation unconstitutional.

*Supreme Court*   The Supreme Court has declared relatively few federal laws unconstitutional, but it has been much more active regarding the states. It has overturned nearly ten times as many state laws as it has federal laws. Throughout history, the Supreme Court has been inclined to declare state laws unconstitutional when they run contrary to national public opinion (Chapter 9) and when state political party majorities and ideologies are opposite the party affiliations of a majority of the Supreme Court.[25] The Supreme Court also has been much more active in judicial review in the last several decades than during any previous period. Of all laws and ordinances declared unconstitutional, more than 40 percent were overturned since the stormy 1960s.

*State Supreme Courts*   State supreme courts also are active in reviewing state legislation. Complete historical information is unavailable for the states, but in one 5-year period, state supreme courts heard nearly 3250 cases in which state statutes were challenged as being unconstitutional and they overturned nearly 600 of them. Together, the fifty state supreme courts declare about

**TABLE 10-1**
JUDICIAL REVERSAL OF LEGISLATION

| U.S. Supreme Court | |
|---|---|
| Federal laws declared unconstitutional, 1803–1989 | 125 |
| Number and percent since 1960 | 54  (43%) |
| Average number per year since 1960 | 1.8 |
| State and local laws declared unconstitutional | 1194 |
| Number and percent since 1960 | 510  (43%) |
| Average number per year since 1960 | 17 |
| **State Supreme Courts** | |
| State laws challenged as unconstitutional, 1981–85 | 3248 |
| State laws declared unconstitutional, 1981–85 | 591  (18%) |
| Average number per year | 118 |
| Average number per year per court | 2.4 |

*Source:* Derived from *The Constitution of the United States: Analysis and Interpretation, 1990 Supplement* (Washington D.C.: U.S. Government Printing Office, 1991); David Adamany, "The Supreme Court," in *The American Courts: A Critical Assessment,* John B. Gates and Charles A. Johnson eds. (Washington, D.C.: CQ Press, 1991), p. 6; Lawrence Baum, *The Supreme Court* (Washington, D.C.: CQ Press, 1989), 3d ed., pp. 177 and 180; and Craig F. Emmert, "Judicial Review in State Supreme Courts: Opportunity and Activism," paper presented at the annual meeting of the Midwest Political Science Association, Chicago, April 13–16, 1988.

seven times as many state laws unconstitutional as does the U.S. Supreme Court. In terms of their relations with their respective legislatures, the state supreme courts declare about the same number of acts of state legislatures unconstitutional each year as the U.S. Supreme Court declares acts of Congress unconstitutional.

The combined figures for all fifty states conceal differences among them. Some of the states have many opportunities to exercise judicial review. In the 5-year period noted above, Georgia ranked first with 165 cases in which state laws were challenged as unconstitutional. It overturned twenty-five laws or about 15 percent. Washington state had eighty laws challenged and overturned twenty-nine, or 36 percent of them. By contrast, North Carolina had only thirty-four challenged laws, and the supreme court overturned only one law.

The key factors that account for differences among the state supreme courts in overturning legislation are caseloads, the length of state constitutions, and judicial control over the supreme court docket. Heavy caseloads and long and complicated constitutions—found mostly in the southern states—provide more supreme court cases and create more opportunities to challenge state laws. But in nonsouthern states, where constitutions tend to be shorter, courts that have substantial discretion over their caseloads appear more likely to select cases in which they will probably overturn a state law.

**Constitutional Duty**  Although appellate courts declare legislation unconstitutional, there are problems with equating judicial review with activism. Courts long have had the power to interpret constitutions and hold legislation up to the standard of that higher law. Therefore, judges could veto legislation and say "the constitution made them do it," and deny that they were substituting their own policy preferences for those of the legislature.

It also is possible that when they declare a statute unconstitutional, judges could be following their own previous judicial policy. Such action would satisfy the other definition of judicial restraint. This is what occurred in the 1930s when the conservative Supreme Court fought the New Deal. The justices had not done anything very innovative. They simply had followed decades of previous judicial decisions that had favored business and limited the scope and power of government to regulate the economy. Moreover, the justices maintained that they were only following the Constitution. In the Court's view, it was behaving in a perfectly restrained way, but to Congress, the President, and much of the public, it was behaving in a very activist way by stalling much-needed New Deal programs Congress had the right to enact.

### Policy Conflict

The most useful way to understand discussions and disagreement over judicial activism and restraint is in terms of policy conflict between courts and the other branches of government.[26] From this point of view, it does not matter how judges and legislators justify their behavior. It is only necessary to look at the concrete substance of judicial decisions and compare it to the content of policy made by legislatures or governors and Presidents.

If judicial policy conflicts with the policy of the other branches of government, courts will be *perceived* by most people as being activist no matter what judges say they are doing. Therefore, the behavior of the Supreme Court in the early days of the New Deal as well as the policies of the Warren Court in civil rights and civil liberties would be defined as activist. This is true even though the 1930s Court insisted it was following judicial precedent (restraint) and the Warren Court clearly made numerous innovative decisions.

The Burger Court of the 1970s and early 1980s was perceived as restrained by some because its decisions generally were less innovative and more conservative than those of the Warren Court. But many staunch conservatives viewed the Supreme Court and other federal courts then as extremely activist, because their decisions were more liberal than policies favored by President Reagan and conservatives in Congress. Now, the Supreme Court is chipping away further at earlier liberal decisions. To liberals, this is judicial activism, but conservatives see the Court as restrained, restoring the proper political balance and adhering to the "true" meaning of the Constitution.

Viewing activism and restraint as the degree of political conflict and consensus between courts and other branches of government clarifies the political battles that often rage over judicial policymaking. Opponents use the terminology of judicial activism and restraint as a more legitimate and refined way of attacking the Court, but the real conflict is about the content of judicial decisions and how they relate to the policies of the other parts of the government.

Liberals generally support a liberal court, while conservatives criticize it. This means there is no absolute standard to evaluate judicial activism and restraint. Taking one position or the other relates closely to the particular policies an individual prefers. An activist court is perceived as good for society if it makes decisions an individual favors, while opponents object because the court abandons tradition and their view of the proper judicial function.

## COURTS AS PROBLEM SOLVERS

Although judges always have made policy, their approach to policymaking has varied. Most judges have been and continue to be passive. They issue general orders and rely on litigants to comply voluntarily. Recently, however, some judges have become more assertive and controlling. Their decisions have created additional controversy about the proper role of courts and whether judges are becoming too powerful. This section focuses on the methods of judicial policymaking and the debate over the capabilities and right of courts to try to solve contemporary problems.

## Methods of Judicial Problem Solving

**Traditional Methods**   Most judicial policymaking relies on two main strategies that we shall call *judicial stopping power* and *general legal orders*. Both of these are limited methods of judicial policymaking.

*Stopping Power*   Most judicial decisions concentrate on stopping behavior that interferes with individual rights or ending other private behavior or governmental policies that judges believe are improper. For example, in the 1930s the U.S. Supreme Court stopped New Deal laws from being put into effect. The justices provided no alternative economic solutions of their own. Many of the civil rights decisions in the early years of the Warren Court also stopped government-sanctioned discrimination against blacks in the southern states.

Stopping actions can be found in numerous policies. For instance, citizens who are unable to persuade their city council not to build a new garbage dump in their section of town may persuade a judge to order the city to stop construction at least until a judicial hearing can be held. A judge might stop the planned merger between two corporations because of a belief that their combined activities will result in a restraint of trade. Judges also may order labor unions to stop harassing other employees who wish to go to work or stop anti-abortion protestors from blocking the entrance to clinics. These decisions are important policies so far as they go because they benefit certain groups, but they are limited ways of solving problems. They stop behavior, but do not offer other solutions to conflicts.

*Legal Orders*   In addition to stopping actions, judges often issue very loose or general orders to litigants to comply with a judicial policy. A judicial order at the end of a written opinion may be something like: "Take action which is not inconsistent with this decision." That leaves a great deal of room for the parties in the case to decide for themselves what they should do. For example, the Supreme Court decision that requires that poor criminal defendants be provided with lawyers (*Gideon v. Wainwright*, 1963) does not specify exactly how that must be done. Local governments have leeway to determine how lawyers shall be provided and how much and by whom they will be paid. Many states created public defenders' offices, while others used volunteer lawyers or a rotational system among local attorneys.

Early decisions to integrate particular schools usually permitted local school boards to create an integration plan themselves rather than have a judge outline in detail how integration would be achieved. Many court cases give litigants options to determine how they will translate a general judicial rule into concrete local action.

**Assertive Policies**   In the past 15 to 20 years, some judges have become dissatisfied with the limited impact of stopping power and general legal orders and have sought new ways to affect the behavior of litigants. This is not a new form of policymaking, but an extension of recent judicial decisions. Recent policies differ mainly in the number and detail of requirements that judges impose on litigants and the amount of supervision that is necessary after a decision is made to see that the policy is carried out. Some judges remain involved in a dispute long after the case has been decided and personally monitor the actions of litigants.

These assertive decisions involve the courts more deeply in problem solving and also make the role of courts more controversial. For example, for many years most state laws have provided only for small fines (under $1000) to be imposed on industrial polluters. Many companies found it simpler and cheaper to plead no contest (guilty without admitting it) and to pay the fine rather than take difficult and expensive steps to end pollution.

In time, some judges became frustrated by their inability to do anything about the basic problem of pollution. Instead of accepting no contest pleas and payment of fines, a few judges put companies on criminal probation and gave them a few months to change their industrial procedures to eliminate or reduce pollution. Judges would appoint someone to visit the offending factory to see what the company was doing to comply with the court. Therefore, in addition to determining legal liability, *judges become administrators* who supervise the implementation of their own policy.[27] As additional curbs on business violations, the federal courts recently have issued new sentencing guidelines for punishing more severely those corporate officials responsible for illegal activities.

Similar changes have occurred in other areas of judicial policy. Many judges decided that achieving racial integration required more aggressive strategies, such as busing children from one area to another to ensure greater racial balance in the schools. These decisions have a big impact on other local school policies, because extra busing is expensive. Some school boards have had to drop other school activities in order to pay for it.

In a similar way, providing equal legal opportunity to get a job has been supplemented by permitting or requiring employers or schools to reserve a certain number of spaces for minorities who are not able to compete scholastically with eligible whites due to past discrimination. These affirmative action decisions are designed to overcome the effects of past discrimination and to give blacks and other groups positive assistance in climbing the social and economic ladder.

Boxes 10.2 and 10.3, "Assertive Policymaking in a Texas Federal District Court" and "Federal Courts and the Environment" illustrate the more assertive and far-reaching decisions that some judges are making today.[28] Their decisions may affect a wide variety of policy areas where judges previously adopted a "hands-off" attitude and allowed other state and local officials to run programs with little judicial involvement.

### Why More Assertive Policies?

There are a number of reasons why some judges have become more assertive in policymaking.

---

**BOX 10.2**

ASSERTIVE POLICYMAKING IN A TEXAS FEDERAL DISTRICT COURT

For 18 years, Justice William Wayne Justice has made decisions conservatives hate and liberals love. The judge receives lots of hate mail and many Texas politicians wish Congress would impeach him. His most controversial and far-reaching decisions include:

• Declaring the state's prison system unconstitutional because overcrowding and terrible living conditions constituted cruel and unusual punishment. His required reforms have been estimated to cost Texas over $1 billion. He recently held the state in contempt for not making the improvements he had ordered.

• Requiring desegregation in schools throughout the state in a single decision.

• Holding various plans to reapportion the state legislature unconstitutional because they discriminate against nonwhites.

• Requiring a public school to add two black cheerleaders because selection processes excluded black students.

• Forcing a high school to abandon their "Dixie" fight song.

• Rejecting the state's bilingual education program as discriminatory.

---

**BOX 10.3**

FEDERAL COURTS AND THE ENVIRONMENT

Cases challenging the U.S. Forest Service's timber-selling program have reached an all-time high—540 cases in a single year, double the number the year before. Environmentalists explain that there are adequate federal laws to protect the environment, but the Interior Department under President Bush refuses to apply them as Congress intended.

The cases are leading judges to determine how much land needs to be set aside from logging in order to save the rare Spotted Owl, balancing the reestablishment of wolves in the Rocky Mountains with the interests of local cattle herders, and other issues. Much of the logging activity in the Pacific Northwest has been stopped by court injunction while judges review wildlife management proposals.

A spokesperson for the secretary of the interior has said: "When you have a judge interpreting the Endangered Species Act the way some of them are doing now, in essence the judge is acting as the Secretary of the Interior."

---

**Expanded Rights**   First, the change probably reflects the impact of several decades of federal judicial innovation in individual rights. Federal judges have shown themselves over the past 30 years to be more receptive to the constitutional claims of underdogs than the state courts or any other part of government. The early success of civil rights groups in the federal courts undoubtedly has spurred others to take their grievances to the federal level as well.

In addition, there often is no other basis to challenge the action of a state or local government. For example, school or job placement tests may be legal under state law, and are usually supported by state judges. The only way to challenge them as discriminatory is to expand the issue into questions of fairness or justice that fit under a broad interpretation of the Constitution.

Federal judges are used to getting cases like these and seem more inclined to take a broader view of many issues. Some federal judges also are very independent of local opinion and groups and quickly establish a reputation as mavericks who will create new solutions to old problems.

Earlier judicial policies also provide a springboard for new policies. For instance, while there is no "natural" or inevitable link between past civil rights decisions and affirmative action, it is not difficult for a judge who is sympathetic with the problems of blacks and other groups to decide that something more than a stopping action or vague orders is needed to achieve equality. White flight to the suburbs has created many segregated urban school systems because few white children are left in many urban neighborhoods. A judge who believes that integration ought to be achieved may decide on busing or permit the construction of public housing for the poor in certain parts of a city to accomplish these goals. These decisions are "starting actions" that require governments to take positive steps to make integration more of a reality.

**Technology**    Aggressive judicial policies also are likely because technological change occurs rapidly. There constantly are new problems and developments that create conflicts that wind up in court. Whether they like it or not, judges now will have to contend with new issues, such as patents on gene splicing, safety of nuclear energy, use of new scientific crime lab techniques in trials, determining legal death in comatose patients, etc. Cases often come to court before legislatures deal with these issues, and judges have to act on their own. The newness of the issues will lead to more innovative decisions.

Sometimes old and new technology collide, creating new problems for the courts to resolve. For instance, a new area of litigation is "toxic torts," which are cases begun by consumers, factory workers, and others who believe they have been injured by products, such as cigarettes or weed killers, or chemicals in the workplace, such as asbestos. But unlike catching a hit-and-run driver, it has been very difficult to place responsibility for long-delayed injuries caused by materials that have been manufactured, distributed, sold, and used by different businesses and individuals.

But new technology constantly increases our ability to link cause and effect, and injured litigants increasingly demand that judges and juries find ways to compensate people for these modern maladies. Such cases constantly provide opportunities for new assertive and innovative judicial policies.

**Business Regulation**    Finally, assertive judicial policymaking grows out of continued government regulation of business and economic life.

There are many general state and federal laws that give regulatory agencies enormous power to write specific rules for regulating most aspects of the economy. There often are disagreements between businesses and government on what these rules mean and how they should be applied.

For example, any time the federal government makes substantial changes in the income tax laws, such as during the Reagan administration, there are many unanswered questions about how the Internal Revenue Service will interpret the law in individual and business tax disputes. Many of these conflicts will end up in court. Other examples are government regulations designed to balance business interests with those of the environment, as already described in the box "Federal Courts and the Environment."

### Limitations of Judicial Policymaking

Recent court innovation has led many people to question whether courts have the *ability or capacity* to make basic and far-reaching policies.[29] They argue that it is one thing for judges to grant limited grievances and claims or to stop behavior that interferes with equal rights. It is another matter for judges to order fundamental and expensive changes and to take charge of school systems or state hospitals to be sure judicial policies are adopted.

Making and implementing basic policy requires substantial expertise and investigative procedures not found in courts. Moreover, they argue that spending decisions should be made by legislatures. Consequently, many people have concluded that judges should leave these basic and complicated policies to legislatures and to executive branches, where they traditionally have belonged.

Concern about *judicial capacity* to make policy is different from conflicts over the legal *right* of courts to make policy. The right of judges to make policy usually is a partisan issue, with court critics and supporters disagreeing about the substance of individual judicial decisions. Judicial capacity to make policy involves the basic organization and behavior in the judicial process and whether it helps or hinders judges to be effective policymakers.

There are a number of limitations on judicial policymaking that lead many observers to doubt judicial capacity. Most of these limitations contrast judicial policymaking with the opportunities and powers of legislators and executives to make and carry out government programs.

The limitations always have applied to courts, but they are even more relevant today due to the increased tendency of some judges to create many more innovative and far-reaching solutions to social problems. Limitations generally can be viewed as involving the limited scope of judicial policymaking and the varied impact that policies are likely to have on society.

**Scope**   Judicial policymaking usually has a narrower scope than legislative or executive policy. For example, courts do not create, develop, or pay for basic programs such as public schools, welfare systems, and highways. Judges do not create space programs or spend billions of dollars to send vehicles to the planets. Judges do not decide to fight a war or to give foreign aid. Judges also are not responsible for increases and decreases in taxes or for government bureaucracies hired to carry out government programs. Basic government programs are made and paid for by Congress, state legislatures, local boards and councils, and the executive branch—not the courts.

Court cases frequently involve public schools, welfare, and other issues, even occasionally foreign policy, as in passport or draft cases, but the cases almost always concern narrow issues and how particular programs are administered and whether they discriminate against various groups. Court decisions also sometimes cost governments money if procedures have to change, but courts rarely have much effect on the basic structure, financing, and impact of most government programs.

*Isolated Decisions*   Critics of recent judicial policymaking complain that since judges do not focus on the "big picture" of policymaking, they cannot appreciate the effect that their isolated decisions have on other government programs. Requiring busing or improved prison conditions requires additional state money or possible shifts in expenditures from other equally valuable programs. Judges have no overall responsibility for collecting taxes and balancing budgets, and they act irresponsibly by ordering government spending in specialized areas.

The nature of litigation also isolates judicial policy. Courts are passive and dependent policymakers. They cannot initiate any policy on their own, but have to wait for others to "invite" courts to become involved by bringing cases to them. Also, since litigants and their lawyers shape the issues, judges have to link their decisions to the particular circumstances raised in each concrete case. Judges do not have the freedom of a legislature to shape the content of their own policies. Judicial policymaking also starts late, after much conflict already has taken place and other solutions have been tried or considered. Judicial policy often is designed to clean up the messes created by others. Critics lament that this is a poor way to solve problems.

*Limited Information*   Judges also have limited information for making decisions. Descriptions of judicial decision making often picture judges as wise people who carefully weigh and consider many aspects of a case before choosing the best solution. But judges usually have to rely on the information litigants give them. Most of it is legal lore, which cannot take into account the social and economic consequences of a dispute. When litigants refer to scientific research, they also are likely to provide only information that supports their side. A litigant's finances and their lawyers' ability to present complex technical data also are not equal, so we cannot assume that the "fight theory" will produce truth or even adequate information.

Most judges also have only legal and clerical assistants, not social scientists, engineers, or other analysts who might be able to provide additional information. An exception is the power of federal judges to appoint expert witnesses who provide information to the judge. But only one or two experts usually are used in a particular case, and no such witnesses are employed in most cases.

The information that courts obtain also is limited by the views that judges have of proper judicial procedure. Many judges do not believe that courts ought to obtain information that is not provided by the opposing lawyers. They also believe judges should evaluate the merits of each side only as presented through regular testimony. But other judges sometimes are frustrated by the limited information provided in most cases.

For example, a state supreme court judge recalled the difficulty his court had in obtaining adequate data in a confusing criminal case involving the insanity plea. The judges could not decide how to sort out the vague and competing notions of insanity or determine how they should permit the insanity defense to be used. The judge said he would telephone a psychiatrist friend to get his advice. The other judges quickly objected, however, because it opened the decision-making process to outsiders and brought in information in an informal and unconventional way. The lawyers in the case also could not review the information or present legal arguments about it.[30]

Most appellate court data gathering is haphazard, unplanned, and of unknown quality. It also is likely to vary widely with individual judges and courts. It is not a systematic way of providing courts with information that they need to make a well-informed evaluation of a case and to produce a general policy to be followed by others. The information issue is important in a wide variety of litigation. Cases involving the technology, capabilities, and costs of pollution control, medical technology, education administration, and many others require expertise and information that few judges have firsthand or that litigants can be relied on to provide.

*No Planning*  The passive and dependent nature of judicial policymaking also makes it very difficult for judges to plan or develop comprehensive policy that will effectively cover a broad range of problems. Even if judges have some power to select cases, such as on the U.S. Supreme Court, they cannot fully control their own agenda. Courts get a wide variety of issues that come to them in no special order. The issues simply come up as they are appealed and judges have to decide them. Consequently, several months or years may pass between cases that deal with closely related issues. Instead of proceeding in a comprehensive way or in a straight line to accomplish specific policy objectives, judges often make policy by bits and pieces that are not necessarily part of any well-conceived or overall plan. There are many stops and starts and gaps and holes in the patchwork of judicial policies.

After a period of time goes by, lawyers and social scientists often look back over a set of cases involving similar issues to try to find the common logic or theme of judicial policy as it evolves from case to case. But very imaginative thinking often is required to see how all the cases fit together. Often the membership of a court changes so that new judges have decided the most recent cases. At other times, judges on the same court refer to different precedents or sets of facts that they say are controlling in their decisions.

This problem is illustrated by the history of obscenity cases brought to the U.S. Supreme Court since the late 1950s. Until then, obscenity was not protected by American courts as part of free speech, and local governments were free to limit the sale and possession of sexual literature, movies, etc., as they saw fit. Beginning in 1957, the Supreme Court began to question unlimited local control by devising certain tests or rules to guide local police and prosecutors in determining what was obscene. The cases involved arrests and prosecution for obscenity violations. However, the justices never agreed on a clear definition of obscenity, and their various rules, often revised from case to case, were so vague that they did little to affect prosecutions for selling or possessing obscene material. Later, several justices favored abandoning the idea of devising rules of any sort, but most justices continued to try to clarify judicial rules and said they would review cases individually according to Supreme Court guidelines.

During the late 1960s and early 1970s the membership of the Supreme Court changed and a majority of liberal justices who had favored broader interpretations of free speech became the minority. The conservative majority continued to try to define obscenity and favored some form of government limitations on its *sale*. However, in 1969, the Supreme Court also declared unconstitutional a Georgia law that made *possession* of obscenity a crime (*Stanley v. Georgia*). The Supreme Court recently has permitted local officials to seize videocassettes of obscene movies and to use zoning laws to control the location of businesses that sell obscene materials. However, it also has rejected as a violation of free speech local laws that define pornography as discrimination against women.[31]

While obscenity cases mostly dealt with similar issues, the Supreme Court has provided no firm or coherent policy or set of guidelines for local government other than a tendency to agree that local governments have a legitimate interest in regulating the sale and distribution of obscenity in some way. How regulation is to be achieved has been and continues to be unclear.

**Impact** In addition to problems stemming from the limited scope of judicial policymaking, judges usually cannot oversee the impact or effect of their decisions. They also cannot change their minds and call a decision back in order to change it. The only way courts can make new or different decisions is if similar cases come up later. Although it is rare, courts occasionally reverse an earlier ruling. In contrast, a legislature can take up an issue again whenever it wishes and change the law, and executive officials can modify their rules as they implement policy on a continuing basis. The few judges who have attempted to oversee how their policies are implemented are the exception, and even they cannot act as administrators in every important case. They have to use their energies and time on a few issues, meaning that other cases will receive no follow-up review whatever.

Appellate judges also cannot effectively monitor how trial judges use appellate policies in other cases that receive little publicity. For instance, a state supreme court that interprets rules of divorce very liberally in one symbolic case has no capacity whatever to find out whether its rules are applied or ignored in each county or district court. There simply are too many divorce cases and few of them become visible to anyone other than the litigants.

*Unclear Policies* Judicial policies often have limited impact because they are unclear. The obscenity cases are good examples of unclear judicial policies. Another is the Supreme Court's 1972 ruling on the constitutionality of the death penalty (*Furman v. Georgia*). The court ruled that the way the death penalty was applied was unconstitutional because it was arbitrarily and inconsistently imposed. In particular, it tended to discriminate against blacks and the poor.

However, the justices did not agree on which facts were the most important ones or the goals the Court ought to achieve. The majority opinion simply suspended executions. It was a short *per curiam* (no one judge claimed authorship), and each of the five justices who voted in the majority wrote a separate concurring opinion expressing a different point of view about the death penalty. Each of the dissenters also wrote a separate dissent. It is difficult to find a court policy in this case or to be sure what the justices had in mind. The decision was interpreted to mean that the states should revise their death penalty statutes to prevent discrimination, but there was little guidance provided concerning how they should do it.

Producing clear judicial policies presents a difficult problem, especially for appellate courts. Appellate courts usually want to create rules or guidelines that will apply to many different circumstances that may come to trial. However, if they provide a specific set of rules and criteria for future decision making, many trial court judges may decide that the specific rules do not apply to most cases with slightly different circumstances. On the other hand, if the rules are very vague and all-inclusive, trial judges are free to interpret the rules as they like. Consequently, many judges try to balance the need for general and specific rules.

For example, in the 1973 abortion decision (*Roe v. Wade*), the Supreme Court was fairly specific but not conclusive about abortion policy. The Court stated specifically that abortion was a private and personal decision of the mother during the first three months of pregnancy but that government could limit abortion after that period except when it threatened the life or health of the mother. However, even with these specific statements, determining when and how pregnancy affects a woman's health and how abortion may be limited has been interpreted in a number of ways. If judges disagree with the way their policies are put into effect by other judges or they object to what legislatures and governors or Presidents do to limit the right to an abortion, there is nothing they can do about it unless a very similar case comes up soon again to give them another opportunity to make another formal decision.

Since 1973 there have been more than a dozen opportunities for the Supreme Court to rule on various new state restrictions on the right to an abortion. The issues have included restrictions on facilities that may perform abortions (rejected), the power of husbands and parents to veto a woman's abortion decision (approved and rejected), obligations of the states and federal government to pay for abortions (exemption granted), obligations of doctors to consult with parents of very young women desiring abortions (approved), and state requirements that doctors explain the abortion technique and advise women of the condition of the fetus (approved and rejected).

***Dependence on Others*** Judges also are dependent upon others to implement their policies. They cannot do it themselves. Usually, judges rely on voluntary compliance that occurs because people believe courts have the legitimate authority to make decisions and people ought to follow them. However, some judicial policies, such as those involving civil rights or religion in the public schools, are extremely controversial and are resisted by many citizens and public officials. Failure to win political support for court policies or the reluctance of officials to use force to implement judicial orders can undermine the effectiveness of judicial policy. (The issue of compliance will be discussed in the next chapter.)

Judges sometimes produce vague or muddled policies on purpose in order to get the greatest amount of voluntary compliance and to give local officials plenty of room to maneuver on how court policies will be put into effect. This occurs in many cases. The most famous example of this type of decision is the second decision in *Brown v. Board of Education* (1955), in which the Supreme Court stated how school integration should be implemented nationwide. Instead of calling for an immediate end to all segregation in the public schools or creating specific procedures for integration, the Supreme Court said its decision should be implemented with "all deliberate speed" and that individual segregation issues should be handled in separate court cases in the federal districts where schools were located. This language permitted local officials and federal judges to interpret deliberate speed as they wished. A few districts integrated quickly, but many managed to create strategies that postponed desegregation for years.

## An Evaluation of Courts as Problem Solvers

The limitations of judicial policymaking make courts seem much too handicapped to be very effective. However, this view of judicial policymaking contrasts courts with an *ideal model* of policymaking in the other branches of government, not with a close examination of how the other branches actually make policy. For instance, when we say that courts receive limited or biased information or that they cannot produce comprehensive plans, we imply that legislatures and the executive branch have these powers and use them effectively. But that is not necessarily true. *Many limitations of judicial policymaking are not exclusively court problems, but are limitations of the policymaking process of all of government.* Several illustrations will help to clarify this broader issue.

**Ineffective Legislatures**    People concerned about judicial policymaking frequently believe that state legislatures and Congress are the locations where policy ought to be made. But for years state legislatures and Congress have been criticized for being very ineffective policymakers. Presidents and governors initiate policy most of the time and set the policy agenda for legislatures to consider. Legislatures are not rubber stamps, but they typically respond to initiatives from the executive branch. Many observers believe legislatures are not capable of developing policy on their own.

State legislatures, in particular, come under heavy criticism for not being up to the task of policymaking.[32] Most state legislatures meet for very short sessions once each year or every other year. Many legislators have little or no previous experience in politics and are paid very little for their legislative work. Therefore, they must spend much of their time on private business. The states also give individual legislators little clerical assistance or office space to do their legislative work. They usually are on their own and have to rely on others for advice and information.

Some state legislatures also have very small staffs to do research or to advise legislative leaders on policy. There is little comprehensive planning and evaluation, and most programs are based on previous policies and patterns of spending over the years. Most observers also conclude that private interest groups have enormous advantages in most state legislatures due partly to legislative inability to collect independent information and the lack of political party competition in many of the states. There also is a high turnover of state legislators because of dissatisfaction with the job, not because of tough election competition for their seats.

Congress does not have the severe problems of state legislatures in staffing, office space, and overall professionalism. Congress is in session almost all year, and it has much better ways to gather its own information. But Congress has been criticized for abdicating its responsibilities in policymaking to the executive branch.[33]

Congress usually enacts very general laws and budgets that permit the executive branch wide latitude in carrying out programs. A federal law usually establishes an agency and gives it money and staff, but states only in general terms what activities it is to pursue. It is up to the agency itself to write the specific rules that translate policy into action. Some experienced members of Congress (and state legislators) are experts in particular areas of public policy and can match wits with anyone in the executive branch. But most legislators know little about the details of most policies and cannot effectively review the behavior of executive agencies and lobbyists.

*Reaction Not Proaction*   Expert or not, legislatures, like courts, often deal with problems late in the game, after considerable social or physical damage has been done. Problems are not tackled until considerable interest group or general public concern requires that "something be done."

Moreover, understanding what is involved in coping with a problem often is tremendously complex for anyone—government official, private expert, or average citizen.[34] For instance, air and water pollution have been problems in some cities for at least 75 years. However, most of the states and the federal government did not begin to deal with this problem until the late 1960s. Today, polluting acid rain is an international problem, since industry in the northern United States and Canada both pollute the atmosphere. The two countries disagree on the source of pollution and what to do about it.

Similar confusion often exists in major social policies too, with little agreement, for example, on the causes of crime and poverty and how to reduce them, or on definitions of pornography and what, if anything, to do about the sale of obscene materials. Since legislators often cannot agree among themselves or with governors and Presidents, they often produce vague compromises that permit a wide range of possible action or that pass on the responsibility of making more concrete and difficult decisions to executive officials—*and to courts*.

**Interest Groups**    Federal policymaking also has been characterized as being overly dependent on private interest groups. The rules that executive agencies create to regulate business, for example, often are written in cooperation with business lobbyists, and the regulations often are favorable to particular industries. Congressional committees often go along.[35]

Many basic federal programs enacted over the past 50 years sometimes are seen as reflecting the successful lobbying of business, labor, farm, and various social groups in the federal government. Federal spending provides programs for everyone who clamors the loudest for a piece of the government pie. Many interest groups are so successful that the views of a regulating agency become so narrow they are identical with the policy views of the group they are supposed to regulate. Narrowness is a problem for courts, too, but they at least always have two and often more sides to each issue. Reformers would like to see Congress assert itself by writing more specific laws that do not give the executive side so much discretion to interpret and use the law as it sees fit.[36]

**Judicial Capacity or Policy Conflict?**    We cannot build up judicial policymaking by tearing down the other branches of government, and that is not the purpose of this short review of legislative and executive policymaking. Instead, this overview is designed to balance criticism of the courts in policymaking. Many of the problems that have been singled out as distinctly judicial problems are not unique to the courts, but are wider and more general aspects of American politics and government.

In addition, many of the criticisms directed at legislatures and the executive branch, particularly the dominance that private interest groups have in government, are just as severe and contrary to ideal models of policymaking as any aimed at the courts. Improving the effectiveness of government requires greater coverage than simply appealing to judges to back off.

Although some people seem genuinely concerned about the capacity of courts to make policy, it seems that *most criticism of judicial capacity really masks opposition to particular policies*. It is a variation of the activism-restraint or lawmaker-law interpreter debates. Court supporters and opponents usually line up according to the particular substantive policies they prefer.

For instance, those who question the capacity of courts to supervise pollution control usually are conservatives who want to spend less, or who want to cut the federal budget, or who favor less regulation of business. Environmentalists, however, support the courts and the decisions. Busing to achieve racial integration often is portrayed as unpopular with everyone, but the harshest critics are conservatives who always have been lukewarm or hostile to civil rights. Spending money on prisons and state mental hospitals never has been very popular in the states, and it accounts for only a few percent of the total of all state money spent on all government programs. Increasing state expenditures in this area would not be a large increase in any state's budget, but it is not something state officials want to do, especially during periodic economic recessions as occurred in the beginning of the 1980s and 1990s. The greatest critics also are those who have never been especially fond of civil rights or social welfare programs. But liberal politicians, civil rights organizations, and inmates support these decisions and do not question judicial capacity to make policy. They see the decisions as essential to protect human rights. If legislatures refuse to act, courts should, in their view.

Courts will continue to get these and other cases because various groups refuse to accept inaction or defeat by legislatures and executives. They look to the courts as another chance to get what they want or believe is right. Those who are successful in the courts will continue to praise them as important contributors to policymaking; those who object to court decisions will continue to attack the courts as going beyond their proper function. In other words, judicial policymaking, including the capacity of courts to make policy, is an issue that will be fought out in the ongoing political process.

### CONCLUSION

There is no single view of courts as policymakers. Many people readily agree that appellate courts make policy because of their ability to announce novel solutions to social problems in individual cases. However, this chapter also discusses how trial courts make policy in the routine cases they decide every day. Both the visible and innovative role of appellate courts and the more subtle, cumulative role of the trial courts emphasize the influence that both levels have in governing. Moreover, both kinds of policymaking have occurred throughout American history, because courts always have been required to deal with unsettled issues.

There is considerable debate over whether courts should make policy. The traditional view is that courts ought to be restrained or only interpret the law. However, conceptions of activism and restraint are extremely vague and contradictory, and mean different things to many people. Debate about activism and restraint also is linked to support and opposition to particular decisions. Whenever courts make decisions that run contrary to the beliefs or policies of certain legislators, executives, or a vocal part of the public, courts will seem to be activist to someone. Even the more detached concern with judicial capacity to make policy usually appears to be a fancy cover for criticizing recent judicial decisions.

In a country as large and varied and as changing as the United States, we cannot expect widespread agreement on the merits of many judicial decisions. Groups that seek and benefit from new decisions and those that long for the status quo will always wind up on the opposite sides of the debate about judicial policymaking. The concepts and examples in this chapter should provide a guide for understanding the role of courts in making policy and the political debate that often rages about judicial decisions.

## SUGGESTIONS FOR ADDITIONAL READING

Cannon, Mark W., and David M. O'Brien, eds.: *Views from the Bench: The Judiciary and Constitutional Politics* (Chatham, N.J.: Chatham House, 1985). Based on the views of trial and appellate judges about the role of courts, this book includes contrasting perspectives about judicial policymaking, including discussions of interpreting the Constitution and judicial activism and restraint.

Fisher, Louis: *Constitutional Dialogues: Interpretation as Political Process* (Princeton: Princeton University Press, 1988). More than a study of the Supreme Court, this political history and analysis links the power and role of the Supreme Court to other political institutions, and sees constitutional law as a political process involving much more than the Supreme Court having the last word on defining the law.

Gates, John B., and Charles A. Johnson, eds.: *The American Courts: A Critical Assessment* (Washington, D.C.: CQ Press, 1991), "Part I: Judicial Policy Making: An Overview." This section includes five chapters on the U.S. Supreme Court, federal Circuit Courts of Appeals, federal District Courts, state supreme courts, and local trial courts, which examine the role of each of these courts in making policy, but also suggest new ways for studying judicial policymaking.

Halpern, Stephen C., and Charles M. Lamb, eds.: *Supreme Court Activism and Restraint* (Lexington, Mass.: Lexington Books, 1982). Includes fifteen essays on historical and normative as well as political behavior perspectives on the meaning of judicial activism and restraint.

Spaeth, Harold J.: *Supreme Court Policy Making* (San Francisco: W. H. Freeman and Co., 1979). Although this book does not cover the current Supreme Court, it is rich in concepts and presents a clear explanation of the important role of the Supreme Court in national policymaking. Chapters 1 and 7, in particular, focus on understanding the Supreme Court as a policymaking institution.

## NOTES

1 For a helpful discussion of various views of judicial policymaking, see Richard S. Wells and Joel B. Grossman, "The Concept of Judicial Policy-Making," *Journal of Public Law*, 15 (1966), 286–307.
2 The concept of norm enforcement is discussed in Herbert Jacob, *Justice in America*, 4th ed. (Boston: Little, Brown and Co., 1983), chap. 2. See also Joel B. Grossman and Richard S. Wells, *Constitutional Law and Judicial Policy Making*, 2d ed. (New York: John Wiley & Sons, Inc., 1980), pp. 36–42; Sheldon Goldman and Thomas P. Jahnige, *The Federal Courts as a Political System*, 3d ed. (New York: Harper & Row, Publishers, Inc., 1985), pp. 191–192.
3 Henry Robert Glick and Kenneth N. Vines, *State Court Systems* (Englewood Cliffs, N.J.: Prentice-Hall, Inc., 1973), pp. 97–103; Henry R. Glick, *Courts, Politics and Justice* (New York: McGraw-Hill Book Co., 1983), pp. 278–281. See also Lynn Mather, "Policy Making in State Trial Courts," in *The American Courts: A Critical Assessment*, ed. John B. Gates and Charles A. Johnson (Washington, D.C.: CQ Press, 1991), pp. 119–157.
4 Joseph W. Little, "An Empirical Description of Administration of Justice in Drunk Driving Cases," *Law and Society Review*, 7 (Spring 1973), 473–492; *Newsweek*, September 13, 1982, pp. 34–39.

5 *St. Petersburg Times*, May 24, 1991, p. 1B.

6 *New York Times*, January 25, 1991, p. A10.

7 See, for example, Richard Quinney, *The Social Reality of Crime* (Boston: Little, Brown and Co., 1970), and *Critique of Legal Order* (Boston: Little, Brown and Co., 1973).

8 John Hagan, "Extra-Legal Attributes and Criminal Sentencing: An Assessment of a Sociological Viewpoint," *Law and Society Review*, 8 (Spring 1974), 357–383; Theodore G. Chiricos and Gordon P. Waldo, "Socioeconomic Status and Criminal Sentencing: An Empirical Assessment of a Conflict Proposition," *American Sociological Review*, 40 (December 1975), 753–772; James L. Gibson, "Race as a Determinant of Criminal Sentencing: A Methodological Critique and a Case Study," *Law and Society Review*, 12 (1978), 455; and Cassia Spohn et al., "The Effect of Race on Sentencing: A Re-examination of an Unsettled Question," *Law and Society Review*, 16 (1981–82), 71–88; Michael L. Radelet, "Racial Characteristics and the Imposition of the Death Penalty," *American Sociological Review*, 48 (1981), 918.

9 Stuart S. Nagel and Lenore J. Weitzman, "Women as Litigants," *The Hastings Law Journal*, 23 (November 1971), 190. See, generally, Norma Juliet Wikler, "Equal Treatment for Men and Women in the Courts," *Judicature*, 64 (November 1980), 202–209.

10 Wikler, pp. 206–207.

11 *Newsweek*, January 10, 1983, pp. 42–48; *Tallahassee Democrat*, December 2, 1984, p. 1; *The New York Times*, December 5, 1982, p. 54; March 16, 1986, p. 17; and April 6, 1986; and Phyllis Chesler, *Mothers on Trial: The Battle for Children and Custody* (New York: McGraw-Hill Book Company, 1985).

12 The following discussion relies generally on Lawrence M. Friedman, *A History of American Law* (New York: Simon and Schuster, 1973), especially pp. 96–98, 118–120, 180.

13 William Kent, *Memoirs and Letters of James Kent* (1898), quoted in Friedman, p. 119. Italics added.

14 See Robert A. Dahl, "Decision-Making in a Democracy: The Supreme Court as a National Policy-Maker," *Journal of Public Law*, 6 (1958), 286–287; Richard Funston, "The Supreme Court and Critical Elections," *American Political Science Review*, 69 (1975), 800, 802.

15 Sheldon Goldman, *Constitutional Law: Cases and Essays* (New York: Harper-Collins Publishers, Inc., 1991), p. 322.

16 *Ibid.*, chap. 3.

17 There is a great deal of research support for the unimportance of constitutional issues in most criminal cases. See, for example, David W. Neubauer, *Criminal Justice in Middle America* (Morristown, N.J.: General Learning Press, 1974), pp. 140–142 and 167; Stephen L. Wasby, *The Impact of the United States Supreme Court* (Homewood, Ill.: The Dorsey Press, 1970), chap. 5.

18 James Eisenstein and Herbert Jacob, *Felony Justice* (Boston: Little, Brown and Co., 1977), p. 302.

19 *Ibid.*, pp. 290–292. Also, Martin Levin, *Urban Politics and the Criminal Courts* (Chicago: University of Chicago Press, 1977).

20 Lawrence M. Friedman and Robert V. Percival, "A Tale of Two Courts: Litigation in Alameda and San Benito Counties," *Law and Society Review*, 10 (Winter 1976), 284–285; Barbara Yngvesson and Patricia Hennessey, "Small Claims, Complex Disputes: A Review of the Small Claims Literature," *Law and Society Review*, 9

(Winter 1975), 244; Austin Sarat, "Alternatives in Dispute Processing: Litigation in a Small Claims Court," *Law and Society Review*, 10 (Spring 1976), 364.

21 Elder Witt, "State Supreme Courts: Tilting the Balance Toward Change," *Governing* (August 1988), 30–38; *New York Times*, December 19, 1986, p. 12.

22 Glendon Schubert, *Judicial Policy Making* (Glenview, Ill.: Scott, Foresman and Co., 1974), pp. 209–213.

23 Sheldon Goldman and Thomas P. Jahnige, *The Federal Courts as a Political System* (New York: Harper & Row, Publishers, Inc., 1976), pp. 206–207. For additional discussion of the concepts of activism and restraint, see Bradley C. Canon, "A Framework for the Analysis of Judicial Activism," in Stephen C. Halpern and Charles M. Lamb (eds.), *Supreme Court Activism and Restraint* (Lexington, Mass.: Lexington Books, 1982), pp. 385–419.

24 See Raoul Berger, *Government by Judiciary* (Cambridge, Mass.: Harvard University Press, 1977).

25 John B. Gates, "Partisan Realignment, Unconstitutional State Policies, and the U.S. Supreme Court, 1837–1964," *American Journal of Political Science* 31 (1987), 259–280. See also Lee Epstein and Karen O'Conner, "States and the U.S. Supreme Court: An Examination of Litigation Outcomes," *Social Science Quarterly* 69 (1988), 660–674.

26 This view is presented by Schubert in *Judicial Policy Making*, pp. 209–213.

27 Christopher D. Stone, *Where the Law Ends* (New York: Harper & Row, Publishers, Inc., 1975), p. 184.

28 *Newsweek*, March 1, 1982, pp. 53–54; *The New York Times*, November 21, 1982, p. 16; January 6, 1987, p. 7; May 1, 1990, p. A10.

29 See, for example, Donald L. Horowitz, *The Courts and Social Policy* (Washington: The Brookings Institution, 1977).

30 Based on interviews with state supreme court judges.

31 *The New York Times*, February 25, 26, and 27, 1986, p. 1; April 23, 1986, p. 7.

32 For discussions of the policymaking role of state legislatures and governors, see Thomas R. Dye, *Politics in States and Communities*, 4th ed. (Englewood Cliffs, N.J.: Prentice-Hall, Inc., 1981), chaps. 5 and 6; Samuel C. Patterson, "American State Legislatures and Public Policy," Sarah McCally Morehouse, "The Governor as Political Leader," in Herbert Jacob and Kenneth N. Vines (eds.), *Politics in the American States*, 3d ed. (Boston: Little, Brown and Co., 1976), chaps. 4 and 5.

33 See the essays in David B. Truman (ed.), *The Congress and America's Future* (Englewood Cliffs, N.J.: Prentice-Hall, Inc., 1965); James L. Sundquist, *The Decline and Resurgence of Congress* (Washington, D.C.: The Brookings Institution, 1981).

34 Stone, chap. 11.

35 Roger H. Davidson, "Breaking Up Those 'Cozy Triangles': An Impossible Dream?" in Susan Welsh and John Peters (eds.), *Legislative Reform and Public Policy* (New York: Praeger, 1977), pp. 30–53.

36 Theodore J. Lowi, *The End of Liberalism*, 2d ed. (New York: W. W. Norton Co., 1979).

# 11

# THE IMPACT OF
# JUDICIAL POLICY

Many people assume that court decisions are put into effect as a natural outcome of cases, but nothing happens automatically in the judicial process. The previous chapter explained, for example, that judges have very few tools to guarantee that their decisions will be followed by litigants or by other officials. Judges make decisions that fly out into society, and other people see and use them in forming their own solutions to problems. Therefore, the impact of judicial policies depends heavily on the links between courts, other political officials, and society.

This chapter looks at several major parts of the impact of judicial policies. First, it reviews how social scientists think about impact. Then, it examines how judicial decisions are communicated and who is listening to courts. The final part of the chapter surveys what other judges and public officials do with judicial policies and how judicial decisions are applied to particular circumstances.

Another part of judicial impact concerns the broader and longer-term effects of judicial policy on society. The issues here go beyond the immediate reactions of lower court judges and other officials and deal with the general consequences of judicial policy on American society. The final chapter of the book looks at a number of policy areas in order to assess the broader role of courts.

## SCOPE AND MEANING OF IMPACT

Most of what we know about the impact of judicial decisions concerns appellate courts, especially the policies of the U.S. Supreme Court. This is consistent with the special attention that social scientists and legal scholars always have given the highest appellate courts as the major sources of judicial policy. In addition, impact research has concentrated heavily on a few very controversial and "very public" policies, especially prayer and Bible reading in the public schools, the rights of criminal defendants, and school desegregation. We do not know as much about the effects of less visible decisions.

### Terms and Concepts

Judicial impact covers considerable ground. It may include any behavior or activity that is *a response to a judicial decision*. Social scientists use several different terms and concepts in analyzing the effect of judicial policies.

**Compliance**   A major concept is compliance.[1] The central idea in compliance is that litigants and government officials are obligated to carry out court decisions. Following judicial rules is compliance; refusing to abide by judicial orders is noncompliance or evasion. The news media also frequently refer to compliance, for example, when school administrators or other officials talk about their behavior as being "in compliance" with judicial orders.

Compliance and noncompliance are relatively clear-cut labels for responses to judicial policy, and they probably can account for some behavior. Most judicial rules and orders in trial and intermediate appellate courts are specific, and there are not many ways that they can be interpreted. It also is possible for people to interpret many Supreme Court decisions along the lines envisioned by the justices. For instance, the U.S. Supreme Court has made several decisions that have banned Bible reading and prayer in the public schools. State supreme courts that later decided similar cases followed Supreme Court policy 85 percent of the time.[2]

*Many Officials*   It may seem reasonable to conclude that if compliance is the rule in highly controversial cases, people generally comply with all judicial policies. But this may be a risky assumption, because putting judicial policy into effect often depends on more than one person or organization. While some people support judicial policy and comply, others may resist.

For example, although state supreme court judges generally followed the prayer and Bible reading decisions, many local school officials did not. In addition, compliance with broad judicial policies often depends upon gradual changes in society, such as changing public attitudes toward religious minorities, race relations, or other deeply held beliefs. There also are many invisible judicial policies that attract little public interest or news coverage and where compliance may be easier to avoid because no one is paying much attention to them.

**Policy Implementation**   There are many circumstances where the compliance and noncompliance labels hide many different responses to judicial policies. A more accurate view, but one that also is more complex, is to look at the way judicial policy is carried out as various forms of policy implementation.[3]

Not all policies are so clear that litigants, other judges, and public officials know precisely how they are supposed to act. Vague decisions, concerning such issues as desegregation, obscenity, the death penalty, and others seem to invite numerous interpretations. Those who agree with what they believe is the spirit or intent of a decision often try to implement it as fully as possible. Those opposed often ignore the ruling or apply it very narrowly. Still others may be confused or indifferent about what judges require, and they interpret judicial policies differently, according to what they think the judges had in mind.

The particular way people apply a judicial decision is not strictly compliance or noncompliance, because the original judicial policy permits discretion. Moreover, since few government decisions are contested in court and few trial decisions are appealed, there always are many interpretations and applications of judicial policy throughout the country.

A related problem with the compliance and noncompliance labels is that other officials and the public sometimes ignore or defy court policy in the short run, but gradually comply over the long term. For example, Supreme Court policy to desegregate the schools was heavily resisted in the south, but with continuous demands from civil rights organizations and additional judicial and other federal pressure, old policies and patterns of segregation gradually disappeared. Consequently, whether or not there is compliance with judicial policy often depends on when you look.

## COMMUNICATION OF JUDICIAL DECISIONS

Before judicial decisions can have an impact, they have to be heard and included in someone's perceptions and thinking about judicial policy. Therefore, the process of communicating judicial policies is a crucial part of what happens to them. There are three major elements to judicial communications: *who is listening* to court decisions and their roles in applying them in society, *how judicial decisions are communicated*, and *the effectiveness of judicial communications*.[4]

### Who's Listening?

Litigants naturally are interested in judicial decisions, since they are directly affected. However, most analysis of judicial impact does not concern litigants, but the effects of major court policies on larger groups of people. The individual litigants usually are quickly forgotten, while the policy content of a decision lives on.

**Judges and Government Administrators**   Lower court judges and various government administrators are the main audiences for most appellate decisions.

Judges react to decisions because they are obligated to interpret and apply higher court policy to their own decision making. In terms of the U.S. Supreme Court, all other judges in the United States are obligated to follow Supreme

Court policy. In a similar way, state trial and intermediate appellate courts are expected to follow the decisions of their own state supreme court.

Opportunities for interpreting and applying appellate court policies abound, since over the years, courts make many decisions in most areas of policy. In addition, some appellate decisions are vague and some are decided by different judges with conflicting attitudes. Also, some decisions receive much attention while others are more obscure and are rarely noticed. But all of them are potential precedents that can be used in future decision making. *How other judges use appellate policies is a prime issue in judicial impact.*

Various government officials also are potential audiences for particular judicial policies, depending upon the subject of the case and its relevance to their own responsibilities. For example, decisions regarding prayer in the public schools mostly concern state and local school officials. Police departments are affected by decisions regarding the rights of criminal defendants; prison administrators are affected by judicial policy on prison living conditions; and so on.

The impact of judicial decisions on government administrators usually is not as broad as it is for lower court judges. Judges always are expected to apply the principles of higher judicial policy to similar cases, but government administrators are not necessarily affected by cases in which they are not directly involved. For example, a federal appeals court that finds Texas prison conditions so bad they constitute cruel and unusual punishment does not automatically apply to Louisiana and Mississippi even though they are in the same federal judicial circuit.

***Powerful Implementers***   The responses of lower court judges and government administrators to judicial policies are very important for three main reasons. First, *these officials are responsible* for implementing most decisions. Second, judicial decisions do not filter down and change society automatically. Lower court judges and state and local officials are important *go-betweens or agents* who translate and apply judicial decisions to specific circumstances affecting the public. They also often have a continuous role in certain policies.

For instance, the place of religion in the public schools has been a controversial issue, especially since the 1950s. Then, state and local officials had to respond to U.S. Supreme Court decisions that prohibited religious teachers from coming into the public schools to teach religion. In the 1960s, the Supreme Court banned prayer and Bible reading in the classroom. More recently, the issues concern moments of silence for personal prayer, whether local schools may permit student religious organizations to use school facilities for religious services and meetings, and prayer at other school functions, such as sporting events and graduation. However local administrators decide to implement court policies, they are the important agents who determine what happens to judicial policy throughout the nation.

Finally, administrators are *opinion leaders* who often make public statements about judicial policy or communicate their own interpretations to others further down the line of administrative command. Teachers take their cues from principals and they in turn from superintendents. Police officers often depend on sergeants, captains, and perhaps legal advisers in police departments to tell them how they should proceed.

The importance of administrators as opinion leaders and supervisors is illustrated by the implementation of the prayer and Bible reading decisions. As we shall see, most school officials ignored or evaded the decisions and allowed local policy to continue as before. But leaders also can change direction. A new school superintendent moved into a conservative midwestern community where feelings ran heavily against the Supreme Court. However, the new administrator believed the Supreme Court decision was a proper one, and he immediately ordered school principals to stop devotional exercises. They followed his rule at once.

The superintendent was successful partly because subordinates follow their leader but also because other leading citizens believed that, despite their distaste for this particular policy, the Supreme Court had the legitimate authority to make decisions and the Court must be obeyed.[5] However, had the superintendent ignored the Supreme Court, it is likely that religion in the schools would have gone on as before since few citizens would have demanded a change.

**Political and Social Elites**   In addition to judges and government administrators, other elites respond to judicial policies. One group is other official elites. These are government officials who are not directly responsible for implementing judicial policy but who have attitudes that influence public opinion and other official decisions.

For example, the burden of making desegregation work usually falls on federal district judges and local school administrators. However, mayors, governors, state legislators, members of Congress, and Presidents often make public statements reported in the news media about the wisdom of integration, busing, or public obligations to obey the Supreme Court. When public officials loudly condemn judicial decisions, it does not encourage compliance. In contrast, their support sometimes gives judicial policy a boost.

In addition to official elites, various social and economic elites also may affect the implementation of judicial policy. These are people who rarely hold public office, but who are especially active in politics, and their opinions "count" more heavily with public officials. These are people with college and graduate educations, larger incomes, the owners of major businesses, or certain high-status professional people, such as wealthy lawyers, doctors, and others. They frequently join civic groups devoted to civic improvement and political reform. In small cities and rural areas, there often is a small group of active middle-class businesspeople who organize behind particular candidates, contribute to campaigns, and expect to be heard on major issues. Their opinions also often influence how judicial policies are implemented by local governments. In larger cities, there are many more competing elites whose views may be taken into account by city officials.

**Consumers**   Another audience for judicial policies are various groups of consumers. These are people who are affected by a judicial decision because they have something in common with the litigants in cases or they are in situations that are affected by changes in policy. For example, many black and white schoolchildren and their parents are affected by school integration; all criminal defendants are affected by decisions in constitutional rights cases; many women and doctors are concerned with abortion decisions; etc.

Few individuals have much effect on how judicial policies are implemented, but they still are important for two major reasons. First, social scientists and politicians often want to know how groups of people are helped or hindered by judicial policy. Second, various groups of consumers often organize into active interest groups that lobby for change or protest and demonstrate for or against particular judicial policies.

## How Decisions Are Communicated

People learn about judicial decisions in a number of ways. Some of them are through *cases and opinions* that technically are available to anyone, but that are used mostly by judges and lawyers. Other methods of communication are through *government channels*, and the *mass media* and *other publications*.

**Court Opinions**   A court order of a trial court or the written opinion of an appellate court is the most direct way of finding out what is in judicial decisions. Court orders are written after a trial and are filed in the courthouse along with other case documents. But, since trial decisions are not considered precedents, few judges, lawyers, or other people bother to collect the outcomes of trials.

Written opinions of appellate courts are much more available and are more important. Opinions often can be obtained immediately after a decision and are distributed to anyone who wants a copy, such as interested lawyers or news reporters (such as in *slip opinions* distributed by the Supreme Court). The West Publishing Company also gathers the written opinions of state and federal intermediate appeals and supreme courts and publishes them in volumes of cases called *reporters*. These can be found row after row in the libraries of law schools and state supreme courts, and in other public libraries in larger cities.

All decisions of the U.S. Supreme Court are available to the public almost immediately through *U.S. Law Week*, a paperback journal that appears in subscribing libraries a week or so after the opinions are announced. It also includes selected cases from the federal courts of appeals and the district courts. Decisions of many state appellate courts are available in similar publications.

Indexes of court cases, such as *Shepard's Citations* and various others, help judges and legal researchers locate cases on particular subjects and in certain courts. The *Index to Legal Periodicals* organizes and lists articles in numerous legal journals, and it can be found in most large public or university libraries. Journal articles often contain descriptions and legal analyses of various judicial decisions.

**Reversals and Remands**    In addition to written appellate opinions that are used as precedents, communications between appellate and trial courts in particular cases occur in reversals and remands. A reversal occurs when an appeals court substantially disagrees with a lower court decision. A decision to reverse is accompanied by an appellate court order to dismiss the case or acquit the defendant. In a reversal, the legal relationship between the parties is the same as before the case was begun and the trial court is not required to take any additional action.

A remand modifies a trial or lower court decision and sends the case back for a new trial or a new court order that takes the appellate ruling into account. When a case is remanded, the lower court must take some additional action.

For example, remands occur frequently in criminal cases when an appellate court overturns a conviction because of a particular legal error, such as improperly admitted evidence, coerced confessions, or improper instructions to a jury. Instead of turning the criminal loose, the appellate court calls for a new trial with a new jury and without the tainted evidence or the confession, or with improved jury instructions. However, prosecutors sometimes decline to try a case again and defendants are set free.

In civil cases, appellate courts sometimes decide that a trial judge improperly dismissed a suit or issued an improper order. The appellate opinion often orders a change in the order in a way that is "not inconsistent with this opinion."

Remands occasionally create intense political conflict among courts in controversial cases when lower court judges want to avoid appellate policy and stick with their original decisions. Even when remands seem clear to others, lower court judges sometimes find ways of "not believing what they hear." For example, many southern civil rights cases in the 1950s and 1960s did not produce immediate integration despite remands from the Supreme Court and the federal courts of appeal, because certain southern federal district and state supreme court judges interpreted remands in ways that avoided integration. Usually, additional appeals and more specific remands were necessary to change a lower court's decision.

*Contempt of Court*    "I'll hold you in contempt!"—shouts an angry judge, leaning forward from his raised bench, gavel in hand, ready to reprimand an obstinate lawyer or his client. Such is the stuff of television dramas, but the use of contempt, which involves jail sentences or fines, is extremely rare. Nevertheless, courts occasionally threaten contempt of court when others continue to balk at judicial orders.

A citation for contempt occurs in two general situations: when a lower-court judge repeatedly fails to follow remands and clear instructions from an appellate court; when government officials or private citizens refuse to carry out the direct orders of a trial judge. Holding a person in contempt is the ultimate judicial weapon because it results in costly penalties.

An illustration of the use of contempt in a lengthy conflict involving stubborn local officials who refused to follow a judge's direct order is described in Box 11.1, "Housing Desegregation in Yonkers."[6]

**Government Officials**   Court cases are used mostly by judges and lawyers who are concerned with how specific court orders should be put into effect and how precedents apply to future cases. Other government administrators often are not trained lawyers, are not especially interested in the details of court opinions, and have other administrative responsibilities that get most of their attention. They are less likely to study carefully or even to read most judicial opinions. Still, many of them are affected by judicial policy and they often want or need to know what is the "bottom line" of a judicial decision. They rely on other government officials for information and advice.

There are several ways administrators can obtain information through government channels. For example, a school board or superintendent wondering how to comply with rulings about religion in the schools could contact the state attorney general or the state department of education. One of the main jobs of the state attorney general is to issue *advisory opinions* to state and local government agencies. Opinions may include information about the meaning of appellate court rulings and the attorney general's view about how they ought to be implemented.

The state department of education and other major government agencies also employ lawyers who keep up with appellate court decisions and give legal advice within their agency. They frequently interpret the meanings of opinions and may give advice to state and local officials and furnish copies of relevant opinions. However, since government officials must request this information, it does not come to them automatically.

Police departments might obtain information about cases from the prosecuting attorney; however, the prosecutor usually does not think of serving as "lawyer-to-the-police." The attorney might give information if requested, but usually there is not a continuous flow of legal information between the two departments. Some big-city police departments employ lawyers, but most others have no systematic way of getting legal information.

**Mass Media**   Most people, including government officials, police, and the general public, usually learn about judicial policy through the mass media. The most complete and informative sources are big-city newspapers that cover national news and the Supreme Court with their own reporters, such as the *New York Times, Washington Post,* and *Los Angeles Times.* These newspapers are used heavily as sources of world and national news outside their immediate vicinity. Other newspapers rely heavily on reporting services such as the Associated Press (AP) for national news.

**BOX 11.1**

**HOUSING DESEGREGATION IN YONKERS**

After five years of litigation, the city of Yonkers, adjacent to New York City, was found guilty in federal district court of four decades of deliberate housing and education discrimination, and city officials agreed to build new public housing and schools in mostly white neighborhoods. But they did not act on their promise.

In the summer of 1988, federal district Judge Leonard B. Sand finally ordered the city council to begin planning new housing or face contempt citations, fines, and possible imprisonment. The judge began fines against the city at $100 for the first day, to be doubled every day thereafter. City councilmen who voted against complying with the court would be fined personally $500 daily until they agreed to comply.

The mayor urged the council to go along, but four of the seven refused. The vice-mayor boasted he would go to jail for 20 years, if necessary, to avoid integrated housing. Confronting the entire city council in his courtroom, the judge promptly held the city and the four councilmen in contempt. The judge also ordered the city council to meet at least once each week to reconsider its action. The promised fines would bankrupt the city within twenty-two days.

New events occurred rapidly. The city began paying the fines, and indicated that it could afford eighteen days worth or the city's entire cash reserve of $26 million. But it also asked the federal court of appeals to reverse Judge Sand's contempt ruling. At the same time, New York Governor Mario Cuomo put pressure on the city by publicly threatening to remove city officials for improper conduct. Moody's Investors Services, an investor's guide, suspended its ratings of Yonkers municipal bonds, signaling to the financial markets that investing in Yonkers had become very risky. A state board took temporary control of the city's finances.

The court of appeals suspended Judge Sand's ruling for three weeks until it could decide the case, but the court only modified his ruling by capping the fines at $1 million per day, which extended the day the city would go bankrupt. The four city councilmen who were paying personal fines appealed to the U.S. Supreme Court, which gave the

National newsmagazines such as *Newsweek, Time,* and *U.S. News and World Report* include stories about the Supreme Court and occasionally other state and federal courts. Their stories usually are longer and provide more background than most of those that appear in local newspapers. However, the newsmagazines do not have the space to reprint all or even major sections of written opinions, and they report on few cases.

Television and radio news is the most abbreviated. A half-hour national news program or even special reports cannot provide in-depth analysis of Supreme Court decisions or news of other courts. Usually they provide only short blurbs about the parties to the case and the conflict, and very short statements about what immediate action the court decision requires.

More news about the courts can be found in a variety of specialized publications for particular audiences. For instance, police and sheriff's departments, criminologists, prison administrators, and others interested in criminal law have association newsletters and many research journals that often include summaries and analyses of recent cases. Employee associations also provide information about pertinent court cases. For example, members of teachers' unions receive publications that often include articles on court decisions that

**BOX 11.1 continued**

case rare expedited service. In September, the Supreme Court ruled that the fines against the city councilmen were improper, but it affirmed the fines against the city. Judge Sand immediately met with city officials to resolve the dispute, but the councilmen refused to budge.

By September the city was paying fines of $1 million per day, and the state board managing the city's finances planned to lay off city employees and shut down city services. By early November, the city would be out of business.

This financial impact turned the tide against the city council. Fearing the loss of their jobs and basic services such as garbage collection and police protection as well as the economic ruin of the city and the value of their homes, even the strongest opponents to public housing began to call for the city to reach a settlement with Judge Sand.

Two city councilmen agreed to switch their votes if Judge Sand would reduce the amount of public housing required, but the judge replied that he would consider modifications only after the council voted to comply

with his order. Within a few days, one councilman switched his vote, saying the city had done all it could.

Despite the change in the vote, which produced a majority of the city council now in favor of compliance, the conflict did not end. Judge Sand changed one of the locations for public housing, but the city commission again refused to accept the plan. In October, the judge again threatened contempt if the city did not buy the land for the project. Later, in November, a group of Yonkers citizens sued the city council for $166 million for wasting city money in a doomed battle against the court order.

A year later, in 1989, Judge Sand ordered Yonkers to spend an additional $24 million to build new schools required to end education discrimination in the city. In early 1990, the Supreme Court issued a written opinion supporting its earlier decision against the city. However, because the Court had rescinded their personal fines, several city councilmen claimed victory and vowed to continue to seek ways to fight court orders for integrated public housing and new schools.

affect teacher-pupil relations, teachers' rights in dealing with administrators, and other issues that affect the public schools.

### The Effectiveness of Communications

Although there are many channels of communication, potential audiences do not necessarily use the same sources, nor do they get the same meaning from communications. Communications can have a number of different effects, depending upon the message and how it is transmitted. The results often fall far short of what we might expect if we envision a direct line between a clear sender and an attentive listener. There are several problems with judicial communications.

**Judicial Ambiguity**    A major problem is that judicial messages sometimes are so unclear that practically any meaning can be derived from written opinions.[7] Consequently, judicial impact depends upon what people hear or *choose* to hear. A good example is the Supreme Court's call in *Brown v. Board* for integration "with all deliberate speed" (1955). The opinion stressed that the lower federal courts should be patient and rely on school boards to develop plans for integration. The opinion produced different responses. A few judges put the emphasis on *speed* and moved quickly toward integration, but most judges and other local officials chose *"to deliberate."*

The 1973 *Roe v. Wade* decision granted the right to abortion, but also included an ambiguous invitation for government to regulate abortion. The years following that decision have produced a wide range of government limitations and more Supreme Court decisions to clarify what government may and may not do to limit this right.

Ambiguity also occurs when judges produce decisions with many concurring and dissenting opinions which express somewhat different views than the majority opinion. Lower court judges who are not thrilled with the decision may find ideas and phrases in these other opinions which allow them to go their own way. Ambiguity also is present in judicial policy when a court has made many decisions in the same policy area, such as the obscenity cases.[8] It often is unclear exactly what the Supreme Court wants other officials to do.

Since many government administrators, the public, and even lower court judges do not pay close attention to every Supreme Court decision, it is not surprising that policy implementation often is different from what the justices of the Supreme Court probably had in mind in a particular decision.

Ambiguity is more likely in general appellate rules, but trial judges also sometimes are not very clear about what litigants are supposed to do after a decision. For example, a divorce decree may state that visits between children and the parent without custody are to be decided by the parents "in the best interest of the children." Statements like this are designed to permit a variety of options as family circumstances change, but they also invite many interpretations, some of which end up in court again.

*Intentionally Broad*    General and ambiguous judicial policies are not judicial accidents. Appellate judges often create general rules intentionally, because they cannot agree on anything more specific but also because they are afraid that people will not or cannot comply if their rules are too precise and demanding in a situation requiring substantial social change. Appellate judges also like to see wide adoption of their rules, so they have to be general to govern many different circumstances.

**Limited and Loaded Reporting**    Few judges and lawyers have time to study most appellate opinions. Instead, they concentrate on law that is directly connected with their own current cases. Also, few judges and lawyers outside of large cities have access to a complete set of appellate decisions, since it is expensive to keep federal and state appellate cases current. People outside the legal system are even less likely to use the volumes of decisions, even if they have access to a law library.

Newspapers also have serious limitations. First, newspapers selectively report cases, and few decisions of most appellate courts, including the U.S. Supreme Court, receive any news attention. Explosive national and international events also usually crowd out almost any court decision for news space.

Reporting on courts also sometimes is inaccurate or loaded in a certain direction. Very few reporters are trained lawyers, and they sometimes gloss over important differences among similar cases or fail to explain a decision correctly. Many Washington and state capital reporters are responsible for covering more than just the courts, and they get spread thin.

Most news stories about court decisions also emphasize reactions to decisions. Instead of in-depth analysis of legal opinions to explain what the judges said, the mass media prefer more personal human interest items that readers can identify with, such as interviews with officials who have to implement the policy or public reactions from interest group advocates or "the man in the street."

Sometimes news headlines, followed by shallow stories, stimulate emotional reactions rather than clear thinking about judicial policy ("Court Overturns Conviction of Rapist Murderer" or "High Court Orders Busing" or "Court Rules Against God").

*Getting the Message*   Despite distortions and omissions of the mass media, some cases receive very wide publicity, and it should be possible for most people at least to obtain the gist of some decisions, especially those that directly affect their own rights or livelihood. But this does not seem to occur. A survey of bookstore owners in a dozen states found that only 15 percent were well informed about Supreme Court policy on obscenity and only 10 percent had heard of specific Supreme Court decisions that related to their right to sell erotic literature. Their decisions to stock sexual literature bore no relation to Supreme Court cases or to decisions of their own state supreme courts, which varied widely in toleration of obscene literature.[9]

Surveys of the general population also consistently show that most people have heard of a few major and very controversial policies, but are unfamiliar with most areas of law or specific cases.[10] Therefore, even if newspapers and other media were to become more comprehensive and accurate in their reporting of Supreme Court and other judicial news, it is unlikely that many more people would become better informed.

**Decentralized Government**   The decentralized structure of American government also interferes with effective communications and cooperation. First, the branches and levels of government that are expected to carry out judicial policy often *fail to work together*. Federal, state, and local officials are elected or appointed by different constituencies, and they often try to avoid becoming involved in controversial and unpopular policies created by each other. They also compete for control of public policy. Even by giving legal advice, state officials may appear to take on partial responsibility for implementing unpopular decisions, such as banning religion in the public schools.

Besides lack of cooperation, *courts are not always clear about who is responsible* for carrying out judicial policies. References to school systems, police departments, hospitals, etc., do not designate particular people who are supposed to be listening and to act, and they confuse implementation.

For instance, who is supposed to improve county jail conditions—the sheriff, the jailer, the state department of corrections, the legislature, the county commission? Each of them often is partly responsible for how jails are run. County and state governments both contribute to paying for jails. Sheriffs usually are responsible for administering them day to day through the jailer, but state departments of corrections often have the power to set minimum state standards permitted by state legislatures. Since improvements always cost money and are controversial, these officials and parts of government frequently point the finger of responsibility at each other. Unless judges tell specific individuals to carry out judicial policy, it often is easy for government administrators to duck judicial policy.

Finally, communications and cooperation among levels of government also are hindered because state officials have *no clear authority* to require local governments or particular agencies, such as school systems, to comply with judicial policy. For example, with a few exceptions, desegregation has involved individual school districts, not entire state systems. Consequently, obtaining compliance with an appellate court policy often requires local groups to sue local officials in local courts, hoping that judges will adopt the spirit of an appellate ruling. However, judicial systems also are decentralized and appellate courts have little coercive power over local courts.

## POLICY IMPLEMENTATION

What do citizens and officials do with the information they obtain about judicial policy? Who is supposed to act, and what influences them to follow the lead of an appellate court or to resist it? What political strategies do they use to implement judicial policy? Most policy implementation falls on local judges and government administrators, but legislators and chief executives often have well-publicized opinions about controversial decisions that may influence others. Consequently, implementation of judicial policy often involves the interactions of many local, state, and national elites.

### Judges and Government Administrators

Lower court judges and government administrators frequently are cross-pressured on controversial issues. They get demands for integration as well as opposition to busing and demands for improved prison and jail conditions, but also anger and resentment from police, legislators, and the public toward criminals. What determines their responses?

**Clarity and Simplicity**   Many researchers have believed that the clarity and simplicity of judicial policies makes an important difference in implementation. When judicial policies are clearly communicated, other judges and officials have little discretion. They have to apply them as the appellate court intended. But when decisions are vague or ambiguous, officials read or hear different messages.

Decisions that affect very narrow and specific aspects of law are not controversial, and do not cost much if any money are likely to be followed closely and quickly. For example, a decision requiring that state hospitals provide a hearing for psychiatric patients within one day of their confinement was followed quickly by judges and state officials, and the legislature quickly changed state law to make it consistent with the court decision.[11]

**Attitudes, Backgrounds, and Environments**    Most socially significant judicial policies are not as narrow, clear, or precise as that involving the psychiatric hearing, but, as discussed earlier, it still is possible for lower court judges and government administrators to understand the basic purpose of an appellate court policy, if they really want to know and find ways to carry out the spirit of the law.

But broad language allows officials to interpret and use appellate court decisions in different ways, if they wish. For example, there is little doubt that the Supreme Court in the 1950s intended to achieve school integration, but many southern officials chose to interpret the policy to permit delay and resistence. In 1973, the Supreme Court granted the right to an abortion and allowed legislatures to regulate it, but many states consistently sought to make it very difficult to exercise that right.

Consequently, more important than clarity of decisions are the attitudes and backgrounds of lower court judges and government administrators and the impact of local social and political environments—the same factors which are important in shaping other judicial decisions.

Judges and other officials often are homegrown products of their state or community and share many of the same values as other local people (Chapter 9). In many controversial areas of judicial policy, they are likely to take local values into account in translating appellate decisions. Trial judges sometimes resist local pressures and opinion, but other elected officials often view themselves as *representatives* and are more likely to be sensitive to local feelings, customs, and clear political demands to avoid unpopular judicial policy.

**Strategies of Implementation**    Judges and other officials adopt certain strategies to implement judicial policy and justify their responses to appellate courts.

*Distinguish or Generalize the Facts*    The most common one is to distinguish or generalize the facts in cases. For example, some judges stay on the lookout for any due process violations in criminal cases, while others limit Supreme Court policy to circumstances that are identical to the original Supreme Court case.[12]

A study of five state supreme courts found that all of them endorsed the U.S. Supreme Court's clear and explicit policy in the famous *Miranda* decision (requiring the police to read a suspect his rights). However, state courts distinguished their criminal cases according to subjective judgements about when a suspect actually is in custody (on the street, in a police cruiser, or in the station) or how the state must demonstrate that a suspect had waived his rights and submitted to questioning. In other words, the interpretation of factual differences determined whether constitutional protections were applied in the cases.

Some courts generalized the facts and used the ruling broadly to benefit many defendants, but others restricted application of the rule so that few defendants obtained the benefits of the Supreme Court decision. In three of the five states, defendants won more of their cases after than before *Miranda*, but in one state there was no difference and in the other defendants lost substantially more often.[13]

In a similar way, a workers' compensation board may interpret an employee injury case so narrowly that only employees with a job and an injury identical to that contained in the appellate case are entitled to compensation, or they can broadly interpret decisions to apply to many workers injured or made ill on the job.[14]

*Cover Similar Disputes*   Another strategy is to expand or narrow the application of judicial policy to similar types of disputes. For instance, years ago, judges often refused to apply *Brown v. Board* to public transportation, parks, and other public facilities because Brown dealt with education. But other judges, who strongly favored integration, argued that the principle of desegregation was more important than the education context and that desegregation should be applied to all public facilities. Government administrators often adopt similar tactics. For example, suits against particular county jails for poor living conditions often are not applied to all jails in the state even though their problems are very similar.

*Ignore Precedents*   A third strategy, particularly for less visible lower court judges, is to ignore precedents. For example, some local judges have ignored Supreme Court policy granting to juvenile offenders constitutional rights similar to those guaranteed to adult defendants. They continue to treat juveniles in a paternalistic way, but one that also denies them the right to consult with an attorney and other protections from self-incrimination.

The abundance of decisions made by liberal and conservative Supreme Court majorities over the past thirty years in many controversial policies, including rights of criminal defendants, civil rights, abortion and others, presents judges with many precedents they might use or ignore in their own cases.

*Criticize Courts*   Judges and other officials frequently combine strategies to resist judicial policies with criticism of appellate courts. The U.S. Supreme Court, in particular, has been criticized by state judges and other state and local officials for protecting the rights of criminal defendants, restricting religion in the public schools, and permitting abortion and busing and affirmative action. Any group or official who strongly disagrees with a judicial decision may attack a court for exceeding its authority, being too activist, being a policymaker, or even being immoral.

As a general rule, when an appellate court policy requires substantial change in local social arrangements, behavior, customs, or beliefs, lower court judges and local government administrators are likely to avoid direct application of court policy to their own local area. For example, federal judges are reluctant to order busing when it will result in a huge influx of black schoolchildren into newly integrated public schools. They are more likely to agree to busing when black children will be well under half of a school's population.[15]

*Multiple Strategies*   Official reactions to judicial decisions and strategies of implementation are closely intertwined. We can see how they operate together in Boxes 11.2 and 11.3, "The Rise and Fall of Defendants' Rights"[16] and "The Storm over Prayer in the Public Schools."[17]

### Legislatures

Appellate courts affect legislatures by declaring legislative acts unconstitutional (judicial review) and by interpreting the meaning of statutes. Political conflict between courts and legislatures is most dramatic and clear through judicial review because a court clearly and decisively declares a law null and void.

**Overturning Acts of Congress**   The U.S. Supreme Court has overturned some very important national laws, including early child labor laws, the federal income tax, and much early New Deal legislation. In 1970, the Supreme Court overturned part of the Voting Rights Act that gave the right to vote to 18- to 21-year-olds in state and local elections (*Oregon v. Mitchell*). Congress immediately introduced an amendment that ensured that right to vote, and it was ratified by the states in about six months. In 1989, the Supreme Court declared unconstitutional the Flag Protection Act, passed quickly by Congress in reaction to the burning of the American flag by political protestors. But, despite a popular presidential promise to amend the Constitution to protect the flag from intentional destruction, Congress was unable to garner the votes.

Although some very important or controversial national policies have been declared unconstitutional by the Supreme Court, the confrontation between the Supreme Court and Congress through judicial review generally is overstated. At least one-third of federal laws declared unconstitutional were overturned more than 8 years after they were first enacted, so there often was no direct confrontation between the Court and the Congress that had passed the law.[18]

Also, probably about one-third of Supreme Court reversals of federal law do not affect fundamental policies vital to the nation. In many cases, there is *no visible reaction* from Congress to Supreme Court reversals because they are much less crucial than other pressing problems.

**Overturning State Legislation**   However, the Supreme Court has a substantial effect on state and local policy through judicial review. In particular, individual rights regulated by state and local governments are heavily reviewed by the Supreme Court. Over 500 laws have been overturned since 1960, nearly 200 more than between 1900 and 1930, when the Supreme Court declared much state regulation of business unconstitutional.[19]

**BOX 11.2**

THE RISE AND FALL
OF DEFENDANTS' RIGHTS

Prior to the 1960s, police were free to question defendants when and for however long they wished and poor defendants had no right to an attorney. Confessions were admitted as evidence in criminal courts with little concern about how they had been obtained.

In *Gideon v. Wainwright* (1963), the Supreme Court ruled that poor defendants had the right to a paid attorney. The decision had little effect since most defendants were ignorant of their right to request an attorney and they were not advised of this right. Government also provided few funds to pay for court-appointed lawyers.

The following year, in *Escobedo v. Illinois*, the Supreme Court ruled that defendants must be allowed to consult with an attorney if they ask to do so. But the new policy said nothing about when defendants could talk to a lawyer and when police could question them. The decision was vague and general and had no effect. Lower courts continued to ignore defendants' rights.

Conservatives assailed the Warren Court for being soft on crime, while liberals urged the Court to clarify defendants' rights in order to compel the police and lower courts to comply with the intent of Supreme Court policy.

*Miranda v. Arizona* in 1966 clearly spelled out that everyone in police custody must be advised that they have a right to remain silent, that any statements can and will be used in court against them, that they have the right to an attorney during any interrogation, and that if they are too poor to obtain a lawyer, the trial judge will appoint one.

All state courts complied with this new clear policy and required police to "Mirandize" defendants or have convictions overturned on appeal. However, most courts limited the policy's application by not applying it to defendants already convicted and applying it to new cases only if defendants

objected to Miranda violations during their trial. Other factual differences in cases also limited its application. The Supreme Court was attacked again by conservatives who claimed the Court was handcuffing the police. Miranda was a major target of candidate Richard Nixon in the 1968 presidential election campaign.

Since the 1970s, following the appointment of new conservative Republican justices to replace retiring liberals, the Supreme Court has narrowed the circumstances for excluding a defendant's statements to the police. However, the Court has not overruled Miranda, and it has reaffirmed its importance especially when a defendant asserts his or her right to an attorney and refuses to answer police questions.

But not all coerced confessions are illegal any longer. The Supreme Court recently has ruled that if a defendant would have been convicted on the basis of other evidence submitted at the trial, the coerced confession is "harmless error." It also permits planted jailhouse informants to persuade suspects to talk about their crimes. The Supreme Court also has broadened police power to search vehicles without a warrant.

Most state supreme courts follow the Supreme Court's conservative line, but several, from Pennsylvania to Utah and Michigan to California, have used their own state constitutions to protect the rights of criminal defendants beyond what is required by the U.S. Supreme Court.

In the nearly three decades since Miranda, police departments throughout the United States learned to routinely issue warnings to criminal defendants, and new recruits accepted it as part of standard police procedure. But recent decisions of the Rehnquist Supreme Court are substantially eroding the impact of Miranda and other decisions that protected criminal defendants from excessive government power. It is likely that the police and the courts in most states will once again relax constitutional standards in gathering and using evidence and confessions.

---

**BOX 11.3**

THE STORM OVER PRAYER
IN THE PUBLIC SCHOOLS

In 1962 and 1963, the Supreme Court decided in *Engle v. Vitale* and *Abington
Township School District v. Schempp* that
prayer and Bible reading in the public
schools were unconstitutional as a violation
of separation of church and state. But the
decisions were muddled because several
justices added that religion was important in
America and an appropriate subject for
study in the schools. The Court also did not
specify which officials should implement the
new policy.

Federal officials did nothing. In 25 percent of the states, state school superintendents announced that all devotional
exercises should cease. Surveys showed
that, with the state taking the heat, all local
school districts complied.

In the remaining states, state and local
officials, supported by Protestant religious
organizations, defied the Supreme Court or
remained silent despite their full understanding of the new policies.

When religion and the schools became a
local issue, some officials incorrectly interpreted the decisions as requiring religion in
the public schools. Others satisfied local beliefs by distinguishing the specific prayers
contained in the Supreme Court cases from
their own practices or allowing teachers to
decide for themselves to conduct devo-
tionals or to excuse objecting students from
religious exercises. However, for all practical
purposes, little changed.

Faced with continued demands to remove prayer from the classroom, but unwilling to abandon religion completely, many
states changed their laws to require a moment of silence at the beginning of the

school day to be used for personal prayer.
However, in a 1985 case from Alabama, the
Supreme Court ruled that this also violated
the Constitution, but state laws which permit
a moment of silence for unspecified purposes were not affected.

While the case was traveling through the
federal courts, Alabama Governor Fob
James was threatened with contempt of
court for urging school teachers to defy a
federal district court order which suspended
the state law.

Most cases develop in the deep south
where religion and education always have
been closely intertwined and where state officials are very reluctant to risk offending
what they believe is public opinion hostile to
the new rulings.

Recently, a federal court of appeals refused to allow Protestant fundamentalists to
remove their children from public schools
because the parents objected to textbooks.
The Supreme Court also has declared unconstitutional a Louisiana law requiring the
teaching of creation wherever evolution was
part of the science curriculum, arguing that
the law clearly is intended to endorse religion (*Edwards v. Aquillard*, 1987). But the
Supreme Court has allowed religious clubs
to use school facilities for after-hours meetings, the same privilege enjoyed by other
extracurricular student groups. New cases
involving prayer at school functions such as
graduation and sports events are on the judicial agenda.

Justices Rehnquist and Scalia dissented
in favor of the Louisiana creation-science
law. They have since been joined by other
conservatives who probably share their
views, making it possible that the Supreme
Court will allow religious teachings and symbols to reestablish themselves in the public
schools.

---

State judges usually have been conservative on constitutional rights and do
not innovate very much. Therefore, many state supreme court cases have been
taken to the U.S. Supreme Court.

In a recent year, the Supreme Court overturned eighteen state laws and local
ordinances. These rulings included the inequality of property tax assessments,
sales tax exemptions for religious organizations, state flag burning laws, state

limitations on abortion, special contract awards to minorities, discrimination in the conduct of elections, a state prohibition on publishing the name of a rape victim, and defendants' rights. Additional cases concerned conflicts between state laws and federal patents, residency requirements for admission to the bar, price fixing, and others.

Although members of Congress are not directly involved in these cases, the issues are so controversial and important to many Americans that they often speak out on Supreme Court policy and sometimes propose national legislation that affects these policies. Supreme Court review of state policies attracts more attention and is more controversial than other judicial issues.

**Judicial Review in the State**    State supreme courts also review state legislation. State constitutions are very long and contain many specific rules that often are contrary to new state laws. In fact, the constant interplay between detailed state constitutions, new legislation, and judicial review leads to even longer and more specific constitutions, which, in turn, increases state judicial power.

State supreme courts have overturned thousands of state laws. Table 11.1 summarizes the major types of cases involving judicial review, percent heard, and percent overturned by state supreme courts. The major categories are criminal (constitutional rights and application of state criminal laws), economic regulation (government regulation of businesses and professions), various private disputes, civil rights and civil liberties, and disputes among government agencies.

The specific issues concern state bar association regulations, prison administration, welfare, mental hospitals, marriage and divorce, adoption and child custody, zoning, campaigns and elections, private property rights, police behavior, sentencing, and others—all areas of policy traditionally regulated by state government.[20]

The table shows that although many cases concern the rights of criminal

**TABLE 11-1**
JUDICIAL REVIEW CASES IN THE STATES

| Type of case (N = 3248) | Percent heard | Percent overturned |
|---|---|---|
| Criminal | 41 | 9 |
| Economic regulation | 24 | 23 |
| Private disputes | 15 | 23 |
| Civil rights/liberties | 8 | 34 |
| Intergovernmental | 8 | 39 |
| Other | 4 | —* |

Note: * Not reported.
Source: Adapted from Craig Emmert, "Judicial Review in State Supreme Courts: Opportunities and Activism." Paper presented at the annual meeting of the Midwest Political Science Association, Chicago, April 13–16, 1988.

defendants and other criminal laws, courts declare few challenged laws unconstitutional. However, state courts declare unconstitutional approximately one-quarter to nearly two-fifths of other types of laws. Laws involving disputes between government agencies are most likely to be overturned. There is little evidence that state legislatures react to most of these decisions, which means that the laws are allowed to die.

**Interpretation**   Courts have a more frequent, but usually much more subtle and indirect, effect on legislatures through interpretation of statutory law.[21] When a court interprets a law, it technically is left intact, but the real meaning is shaped by judges as they apply it to particular cases. But judicial interpretation of legislation is not likely to create many political confrontations for several reasons.

First, many state and federal laws are interpreted by courts every day, and it is impossible for Congress and state legislatures to keep up with decisions. Second, many laws are as ambiguous as judicial policy. Often, few members or factions in a legislature agree on what a law was intended to accomplish, and they are even less likely to agree on a response to what the courts do with them. Statutory interpretation also often is complex and hinges on certain phrases or parts of a statute. Finally, most laws interpreted in court cases are not earth-shattering policies, and few legislators pay close attention to them. Judicial interpretation also often involves old legislation, and legislators always are more preoccupied with the present.

**Reactions in Congress and State Legislatures**   There are four main ways that legislatures respond to judicial decisions: *do nothing; write new laws; propose constitutional amendments;* and *criticize the courts*. The responses vary somewhat according to the type of decision a court makes.

*Do Nothing*   The most common reaction to *judicial interpretation of statutes* is to do nothing. In a few cases, legislatures accept court decisions and change laws to take them into account, but in over 95 percent of all Supreme Court decisions, Congress takes no action to revise the law, either to evade decisions or to incorporate judicial policy into new legislation.[22] State legislatures also rarely revise particular judicial decisions.

*New Laws*   Legislative reaction to decisions that *declare laws unconstitutional* is more mixed. Again, the prevailing pattern is to do nothing, but legislatures frequently write new laws. Over American history, Congress has rewritten as many as one-half of the laws voided by the Supreme Court, but evidence since the 1950s shows that the Congress is much less likely now to revise Supreme Court policy,[23] probably because there is less agreement in Congress on how to respond.

Internal conflict often is a sufficient hurdle preventing Congress from enacting new law, but the ability of Congress to prevail over the Supreme Court also is influenced by the power of the President to veto acts of Congress. A recent example of an attempt by Congress to reverse the Supreme Court is found in

Box 11.4, "Supreme Court, Congress, and the President Battle Over Civil Rights."[24]

*Constitutional Amendment* State legislatures often cannot save a law by writing up a modified version with hopes for a supreme court change of heart (or membership). Judges might even be sympathetic to the need for new laws, but detailed constitutions hamstring everyone. Therefore, the only way to enact some laws is through constitutional amendment.

Constitutions are amended frequently in the states, but very infrequently at the federal level. State constitutions are relatively easy to amend. In most of the states, a two-thirds majority of both houses of the legislature proposes amendments that must be approved by a majority of voters. In many states, voters are asked to vote on a long list of detailed amendments to the state constitution every year. State constitutions also are not so revered as the national Constitution, since they are amended so often and occasionally are revised completely. About three-quarters of proposed amendments are approved.[25]

Amending the federal Constitution is much more difficult. It can be done in several ways, but the most likely is for two-thirds of the members of both houses of Congress to approve a proposed amendment. Then it must be approved by the legislatures of three-fourths of the states. It is not easy to find that much agreement on fundamental policies. The Constitution has only twenty-six amendments, unlike hundreds in many of the states.

A few of the amendments were enacted in response to particular Supreme Court decisions that rejected important congressional decisions. In addition to the Twenty-sixth, the Eleventh (limiting the right of citizens to sue state government), the Fourteenth (citizenship for blacks and guarantees of their civil rights), and the Sixteenth (the federal income tax) were adopted in response to particular judicial decisions. Dozens of other amendments have been proposed for various reasons but were unable to attract sufficient support in Congress or in the states. Recently, various members of congress have proposed amendments prohibiting abortion, busing, and flag burning, or permitting prayer in the public schools, but they are unlikely to get very far, because opinion is heavily divided on these and other similar issues.

*Criticism* Members of Congress and state legislatures sometimes react to judicial decisions by heavily criticizing courts or judges for particular decisions. In Congress, committees hold public hearings on criminal justice, abortion, prayer, and other issues. Interest group advocates who agree with legislative critics have been invited to testify about their beliefs and the harm they feel has been done by the Supreme Court.

Legislative criticism allows representatives to let off steam and to cater to voters. But sometimes their criticism takes the form of vengeful legislation to limit or punish a court. Congress and the states have proposed laws limiting judicial review, the jurisdiction of the courts, and changing judicial procedure. Very few of these have passed, however, because legislators usually cannot agree on them. For every court detractor there usually is one or more legisla-

## SUPREME COURT, CONGRESS, AND THE PRESIDENT BATTLE OVER CIVIL RIGHTS

With its conservative majority firmly in place, the U.S. Supreme Court in 1989 made six civil rights decisions that weakened affirmative action programs and made it more difficult for individuals to sue employers and government officials over charges of racial and sexual discrimination and harrassment. These decisions reversed one Supreme Court precedent, declared one local ordinance unconstitutional, and reinterpreted Congressional laws and Supreme Court decisions.

Civil rights organizations quickly lobbied Congress to enact a new law that would restore prior civil rights policies. Liberal Democrats, headed by Senator Edward Kennedy, and moderate Republicans, led by Senator John Danforth, proposed a civil rights law that would eliminate the impact of three of the six decisions. Congress passed the law in 1990, but President Bush vetoed it, claiming the law would lead employers to hire minorities by set quotas in order to protect themselves from job discrimination suits, even though the law disclaimed using quotas in hiring. Democrats countered that the quota claim was a campaign ploy to whip up working class support for Republican candidates in the 1990 elections. Congress was unable to override the veto.

A similar civil rights bill was passed by Congress in 1991, but this time both sides compromised. Democrats and moderate Republicans in Congress were concerned that President Bush would again veto the bill. The President was reported to be unwilling to continue to fight with the moderate faction of his own party and feared the possibility that Congress might override the veto. Possibly the thinly veiled racist gubernatorial campaign of David Duke, a former Ku Klux Klansman and newly minted Republican Louisiana state legislator, and the Senate sexual harrassment hearings of Justice Clarence Thomas also encouraged the President to settle the civil rights conflict. Many large corporations also withdrew or softened their opposition to the bill out of concern for unfavorable publicity.

By compromising, both sides could claim victory and take political credit for a good law. The President asserted that he had beaten the Democrats on quotas while the Democrats responded that the President finally had decided not to use race as a political issue.

The new law included stronger language prohibiting hiring by quotas, but it also contained most of the provisions of the vetoed 1990 bill. Most important, it restored a 1971 Supreme Court policy requiring that in cases of job discrimination, *employers* must prove that qualifications or tests which resulted in unequal hiring were job related and necessary for business purposes. The 1989 Supreme Court decision had put the burden on *employees* to prove job requirements were *not* necessary, a requirement most employees could not satisfy because they had little information about business.

The bill also made it easier for individuals to sue for back pay and damages for many forms of discrimination and harrassment on the job and it set dollar limits for damage awards. Finally, the bill made it difficult for employees to sue to reopen affirmative action hiring agreements reached years ago by workers and employers.

The impact of this conflict among the three branches of government is uncertain. First, the Supreme Court's decision that declared unconstitutional a city ordinance requiring that minority contractors be given 30 percent of the dollar amount of city building contracts was not targeted by the new law. Reports are that many federal courts are following this decison (*Richmond v. Croson*) and minority set-aside programs are being removed or voluntarily abolished by many local governments. Second, President Bush continued to indicate his opposition to hiring quotas and affirmative action and sent contradictory signals to federal agencies about using affirmative action. Third, labor lawyers and others disagree whether to expect a new wave of job discrimination suits now that it has become easier to prove discrimination and collect damages. Others believe that businesses will improve their antidiscrimination policies to prevent lawsuits. Finally, with a sympathetic Supreme Court, local governments, businesses, and conservative organizations can be expected to continue to seek reversals of civil rights policies that make it easier to hold officials and companies liable for discrimination.

tors who defend judicial decisions. So, it is difficult for legislatures to get back at the judges.[26]

The number of laws passed that curb the courts is very small, but intense and prolonged criticism provides alternative leadership for other people who want to evade judicial decisions. People may reason that if state legislators, members of Congress, and other prominent politicians disagree with court decisions, why should local school officials and citizens comply?

There also is some evidence that courts sometimes retreat a little with heavy legislative opposition. FDR's court-packing plan finally persuaded the Supreme Court to approve New Deal laws, and the Warren Court softened its support for free speech in the late 1950s, although it held fast on integration and defendants' rights.

## Presidents and Governors

"Mr. Justice Marshall has made his decision. Now let him enforce it." These famous angry words, reportedly exclaimed by President Andrew Jackson, create the impression that Presidents and the Supreme Court often are at odds and that Presidents willfully disobey Supreme Court decisions. But this exaggerates and overdramatizes relations between courts and chief executives.

The decision that upset Andrew Jackson was not a direct court order requiring him to comply with a judicial decision. Instead, President Jackson was declining to use military force to require the state of Georgia to implement a Supreme Court decision recognizing certain Indian rights. Jackson (and most pioneers) hated Indians and bitterly resented the decision. Presumably, Jackson also did not want to become embroiled in a local problem and especially wanted to avoid controversy over using the army to support an unpopular decision.

Andrew Jackson's reaction illustrates two of three situations in which chief executives respond to judicial decisions. First, like legislators, Presidents and governors frequently attempt to influence public opinion by publicly endorsing or opposing court rulings which affect broad or sensitive policies. They publicly express their own points of view and encourage others to follow or ignore court decisions. Second, they can decide whether to use the power of the federal or state government to help implement judicial policy. Third, chief executives and their high level appointees sometimes are directly involved in cases and they are required to respond to direct judicial orders to take a particular action. Like most other officials, they usually comply.

**Opinion Leadership**    Chief executives are in strategically ideal positions to provide opinion leadership for policy implementation. Presidents and governors are the most visible figures in national and state politics, and they command more news attention than any other official. Since the early days of radio and especially television, chief executives frequently have "gone over the heads" of legislatures and courts to appeal directly to citizens. Direct appeals to voters through the mass media also can influence legislators who may believe that a persuasive President or governor can sway the public.

President Franklin Roosevelt frequently appealed directly to citizens through his famous "fireside chats" over the radio. He used one of these to criticize the Supreme Court severely for not pulling with the President and Congress toward economic recovery and to urge the public and Congress to support his plan to enlarge the Supreme Court.[27]

President Dwight Eisenhower never gunned for the Supreme Court, but he was forever evasive and lukewarm about school desegregation and never urged the public to support *Brown v. Board*. President John F. Kennedy played a different role regarding school prayer. He said people could comply with both the Court and their beliefs by praying privately and at places other than the public schools.

The most continuous and concerted attack on the Supreme Court since the 1930s was carried on by Richard Nixon. His Presidential campaigns included a strong dose of anti-Court rhetoric when he complained about "crime in the streets" and liberal judicial decisions that "handcuffed" the police. Nixon also opposed busing for school integration and proposed new legislation that would prohibit it.[28] However, his plan was not adopted by Congress.

President Reagan publicly disagreed with the Supreme Court on busing, prayer in the public schools, abortion, affirmative action, and the rights of criminal defendants. Since conservative Republican justices became a firm majority by the end of the 1980s, President Bush has had little reason to complain about Supreme Court decisions.

**Executive Power**   Besides trying to lead public opinion, Presidents can influence the implementation of judicial policies through their control of executive power. Just like Andrew Jackson, who refused to pressure Georgia, other Presidents have stayed out of local conflicts as much as possible or refused federal assistance to promote compliance.

When a Boston high school was integrated through busing in 1975, angry parents, white students, and other demonstrators threatened buses and black students. Mayor Kevin White asked President Gerald Ford to order federal troops to help overworked police, but the President replied that busing in Boston was a local problem that should be handled by local officials. President Reagan's Justice Department also refused to endorse busing for integrating public schools. During the Yonkers public housing crisis, Governor Mario Cuomo threatened city officials with removal, but he took no action against them.

*Challenges to Judicial Authority*   Although Presidents are reluctant to become involved in local implementation of judicial policy, they sometimes feel they must use federal power when state or local officials refuse to comply with clear and direct judicial orders.

Although he personally did not favor integration, President Eisenhower ordered federal troops to Little Rock, Arkansas, in 1957 when Governor Orval

Faubus openly defied a federal court order to integrate the local high school by calling out the national guard to prevent black students from entering. President Kennedy also used federal troops to integrate the University of Mississippi in 1962.

President Eisenhower's responses to integration reflect the two attitudes that many political elites have about judicial policy: They personally may object to the content of particular decisions, but they also believe strongly that courts must be obeyed. Executive support for clear judicial orders is an important ultimate weapon in securing compliance with judicial policy.

There are not many instances where state or federal police coercion is necessary to implement judicial policies. Most public officials accept court authority and comply with direct orders. In other judicial policies that allow for leeway and interpretation, most officials make at least some change in policy that allows them to claim compliance. Whenever officials seem willing to go along with judicial policy, even in very small steps, judges usually are generous and take a wait-and-see attitude about how judicial policy is going to be implemented.

**Judicial Orders**   Presidents and governors, or their appointees, sometimes are directly involved in cases and receive clear judicial orders. They too almost always obey.

Although chief executives obtain their formal power from constitutions, their real authority rests mainly on the perceptions that others have of them, and the willingness of others to carry out policy and to lend support in the future. Part of this support is based on the executive branch as one of the three legitimate arms of government which also upholds the law and the Constitution. Therefore, the chief's image depends on a willingness to abide by the law and judicial decisions.

A President or governor who refuses to accept a clear judicial order is an "outlaw" who risks undermining his or her own legitimacy. Consequently, there are few instances in which chief executives openly and continually defy clear judicial orders.[29]

A famous example of executive compliance is the steel mill decision of President Truman in 1952. A strike had shut down the steel mills during the Korean war, and the President seized the mills to keep them operating. In *Youngstown Sheet and Tube Co. v. Sawyer*, the Supreme Court ordered the President to remove federal control from the mills and he immediately complied.

*Watergate*   A more recent and dramatic confrontation between courts and the President is the Watergate conspiracy and the White House tapes decisions that led to Richard Nixon's resignation in 1973.[30]

The Watergate investigation concerned a burglary at the headquarters of the Democratic National Committee carried out by people connected with the Republican party and Richard Nixon's previous presidential campaign. During the investigation, witnesses testified that President Nixon had recorded conversations in the Oval Office, and the special Watergate prosecutor demanded the tapes as evidence. Nixon refused, claiming absolute executive privilege, and his lawyers asked federal District Judge John J. Sirica to order the tapes withheld. The judge refused and Nixon appealed to the Court of Appeals, which quickly affirmed Judge Sirica.

Nixon vowed to take the case to the Supreme Court and said he would only obey a definitive ruling. But Nixon's advisers believed he would lose at the Supreme Court, and he decided not to appeal. Instead, the President offered an edited summary of the tapes, but this was unacceptable to the prosecutor, and Judge Sirica also did not back down. Nixon finally released the tapes.

The prosecutor quickly asked for more tapes and the same confrontation was repeated. Nixon again appealed to the Court of Appeals, but he also filed a petition of *certiorari* asking the Supreme Court to hear the case on a rare expedited basis. Believing the case was a national emergency and that Nixon probably was using a weak argument of executive privilege to shield the tapes, the justices voted to hear the case right away.

The justices quickly understood that they needed to meet Nixon's challenge to produce a definitive ruling in a single unanimous opinion. Dissents and concurrences would only detract from the decision and give the President room to interpret the Supreme Court's ruling in his favor.

After oral argument, the justices agreed that the President had no absolute power of executive privilege and that the tapes were necessary evidence for a criminal trial. After much negotiation and compromise, the Court produced a unanimous opinion with no loopholes. It clearly required the President to turn over the tapes.

Nixon saw no alternative. His credibility and legitimacy were gone and impeachment lay aheaad. He complied with the Supreme Court ruling. The recordings showed that Nixon had actively participated in plans to cover up the Watergate break-ins, and he quickly resigned.

## CONCLUSION

Although direct judicial orders usually are obeyed, an important point is that impact is not merely compliance or noncompliance with decisions. Judicial policy often is unclear and is interpreted and used differently by many people, frequently to suit their own political goals. Therefore, impact is better understood as various forms of policy implementation.

Judicial policy implementation often is hampered by the flow of communications. Courts are more remote than other political institutions. They communicate through formal legal channels that are unfamiliar to most nonlawyers. Moreover, judicial policy is not automatically transmitted to lower court judges, lawyers, or other public officials. It is merely available through published court opinions and news coverage. Although judges and others are expected to be aware of appellate court policy, not everyone is.

Consequently, it is important to understand who is listening to judicial policy and what they understand it to mean. Most people obtain their information from the news media, and the messages often are garbled in transmission or in the way that people hear them.

The reactions of local officials are especially important, since they often are the ones who must apply most judicial decisions. Most lower court judges and other public officials have their own attitudes and beliefs about visible and controversial Supreme Court policies, and many are concerned about how the decisions will sell at home. If they perceive that the local public and other elites are hostile to a new judicial policy, they probably will use a number of strategies to limit its effects when they are confronted with similar cases and issues. Therefore, understanding the impact of judicial policy requires substantial examination of how other political and social elites treat pronouncements of the courts.

Many judicial policies have little immediate impact, but with repeated demands for action and new decisions which reinforce earlier ones, judicial decisions gradually get through. The police create procedures to advise defendants of their rights and issue guidelines for obtaining evidence. Integration of the schools took a long time, but many schools did become integrated.

A remaining question concerns the broader and long-term effects of judicial policy on society. For example, although the Supreme Court permits abortion, what effect have the decisions had on the availability of abortion and the policies of doctors and hospitals? Although the police read defendants their rights, what effect does this have on getting convictions and protecting defendants from police pressure to confess? These are some of the issues that remain to be discussed in the final chapter, which assesses the role of courts in American society.

## SUGGESTIONS FOR ADDITIONAL READING

Canon, Bradley C.: "Courts and Policy: Compliance, Implementation and Impact," in John B. Gates and Charles A. Johnson (eds.), *The American Courts: A Critical Assessment* (Washington, D.C.: CQ Press, 1991), chap. 17. This chapter examines various theories used in the study of judicial impact and areas for future research, and has a good bibliography of existing studies.

Dolbeare, Kenneth M., and Phillip E. Hammond: *The School Prayer Decisions: From Court Policy to Local Practice* (Chicago: University of Chicago Press, 1971). Although an early study of the impact of judicial decisions, this book provides rich detail on the perceptions and reactions of local officials to a controversial policy.

Johnson, Charles A., and Bradley C. Canon: *Judicial Policies: Implementation and Impact* (Washington, D.C.: CQ Press, 1984). This is the most comprehensive treatment of the impact of judicial decisions. It develops new theory and provides many illustrations of the ways that judicial policies are communicated and employed.

## NOTES

**1** See, generally, Stephen L. Wasby, *The Impact of the United States Supreme Court: Some Perspectives* (Homewood, Ill.: The Dorsey Press, 1970), especially pp. 27–30.

**2** G. Alan Tarr, *Judicial Impact and State Supreme Courts* (Lexington, Mass.: Lexington Books, 1977), p. 54.

**3** Lawrence Baum, "Judicial Impact as a Form of Policy Implementation," in John A. Gardiner (ed.), *Public Law and Public Policy* (New York: Praeger Publishers, 1977), chap. 7; Bradley C. Canon, "Courts and Policy: Compliance, Implementation and Impact," in John B. Gates and Charles A. Johnson (eds.), *The American Courts: A Critical Assessment* (Washington, D.C.: CQ Press, 1991), chap. 17.

**4** This section relies on Charles A. Johnson, "The Implementation and Impact of Judicial Policies: A Heuristic Model," in *Public Law and Public Policy*, chap. 6; Wasby, pp. 83–89; and Charles A. Johnson and Bradley C. Canon, *Judicial Policies: Implementation and Impact* (Washington, D.C.: CQ Press, 1984).

**5** Richard M. Johnson, *The Dynamics of Compliance* (Evanston, Ill.: Northwestern University Press, 1967), pp. 106–116 and 124.

**6** Based on numerous articles in the *New York Times*, 1988 to 1991.

**7** Lawrence Baum, "Implementation of Judicial Decisions," *American Politics Quarterly*, 4 (January 1976), 92.

**8** Johnson and Canon, pp. 49–54.

**9** James P. Levine, "Constitutional Law and Obscene Literature: An Investigation of Bookseller Censorship Practices," in Theodore L. Becker and Malcolm M. Feeley (eds.), *The Impact of Supreme Court Decisions*, 2d ed. (New York: Oxford University Press, 1973), pp. 119–138.

**10** Kenneth M. Dolbeare, "The Public Views the Supreme Court," in Herbert Jacob (ed.), *Politics and the Federal Courts* (Boston: Little, Brown and Co., 1967), chap. 12; John H. Kessel, "Public Perceptions of the Supreme Court," *Midwest Journal of Political Science*, 10 (May 1966), 167–191; Kenneth Dolbeare, "The Supreme Court and the States: From Abstract Doctrine to Local Behavioral Conformity," *The Impact of Supreme Court Decisions*, pp. 202–209.

**11** Kathryn Moss, "The Catalytic Effect of a Federal Court Decision on a State Legislature," *Law and Society Review* 19 (1985), 147–157.

**12** Walter F. Murphy, "Lower Court Checks on Supreme Court Power," *American Political Science Review*, 53 (December 1959), 1017–1031.

**13** Donald R. Songer, "Alternative Approaches to the Study of Judicial Impact," *American Politics Quarterly*, 16 (1988), 425–144.

**14** Charles A. Johnson, "Judicial Decisions and Organization Change: Some Theoretical and Empirical Notes on State Court Decisions and State Administrative Agencies," *Law and Society Review*, 14 (Fall 1979), 27–56. See also, Traciel V. Reid, "Judicial Policy-Making and Implementation: An Empirical Examination," *Western Political Quarterly*, 41 (1988), 509–527; Charles A. Johnson, "Law, Politics and Judicial Decision Making: Lower Federal Court Uses of Supreme Court Decisions," *Law and Society Review*, 21 (1987), 325–340.

**15** Johnson and Canon, p. 65.

**16** Neil T. Romans, "The Role of State Supreme Courts in Judicial Policy-Making: *Escobedo*, *Miranda* and the Use of Judicial Impact Analysis," *Western Political Quarterly*, 27 (March 1974), 38–59; Bradley C. Canon, "Organizational Contumacy in the Transmission of Judicial Policies: The *Mapp, Escobedo, Miranda* and *Gault* Cases," *Villanova Law Review*, 20 (November 1974), 58–77; Charles A. Johnson, "Do Lower Courts Anticipate Changes in Supreme Court Policies?" *Law and Policy Quarterly*, 3 (January 1981), 55–68; D. Wilkes, "The New Federalism in Criminal Procedure: State Court Evasion of the Burger Court," *Kentucky Law Journal*, 62 (1974), 421–451; *The New York Times*, May 19, 1982, p. 1; Congressional Reporting Service Review, September, 1991, 1–28.

17 Kenneth M. Dolbeare and Phillip E. Hammond, *The School Prayer Decisions: From Court Policy to Local Practice* (Chicago: University of Chicago Press, 1971), p. 35; Robert H. Birkby, "The Supreme Court and the Bible Belt: Tennessee Reaction to the 'Schempp Decision.'" *Midwest Journal of Political Science*, 10 (August 1966), 304–315; Dolbeare and Hammond, chaps. 5 and 6; Richard M. Johnson, chap. 6; Congressional Reporting Service Review, September 1991, 1–28.

18 Robert A. Dahl, "Decision-Making in a Democracy: The Supreme Court as a National Policy-Maker," *Journal of Public Law*, 6 (1958), 285; Jonathan D. Casper, "The Supreme Court and National Policy-Making," *American Political Science Review*, 69 (1975), 53.

19 Lawrence Baum, *The Supreme Court* (Washington, D.C.: Press, 3d ed., 1989), p. 177. See also Robert J. Harris, "Judicial Review: Vagaries and Varieties," *Journal of Politics*, 38 (August 1976), 183–184.

20 Susan P. Fino, "Unconstitutional Inequality: Judicial Review under State Equal Protection" (paper presented at the Annual Meeting of the American Political Science Association, New Orleans, La., August 29–September 1, 1985); Johnson and Canon, pp. 237–240.

21 Casper, 56.

22 Baum, p. 199.

23 Casper, p. 53.

24 Information was derived from the *New York Times*, 1989 to 1991. The cases involved in this conflict are: *City of Richmond v. J. A. Croson Co.*, 109 S. Ct. 706 (1989); *Wards Cove Packing Co., Inc. v. Atonio*, 109 S. Ct. 2115 (1989); *Martin v. Wilks*, 109 S. Ct. 2180 (1989); *Patterson v. McLean Credit Union*, 109 S. Ct. 2362 (1989); *Jett v. Dallas Independent School District*, 109 S. Ct. 2702 (1989); *Lorance v. AT and T Technologies, Inc.*, 109 S. Ct. 2261 (1989).

25 Thomas R. Dye, *Politics in States and Communities*, 5th ed. (Englewood Cliffs, N.J.: Prentice-Hall, Inc., 1981), pp. 43–46.

26 Stuart S. Nagel, "Court-Curbing Periods in American History," *Vanderbilt Law Review*, 3 (June 1965), 925–944.

27 Becker and Feeley (eds), pp. 39–42.

28 *Ibid.*, pp. 43–47.

29 Baum, *The Supreme Court*, p. 208.

30 Bob Woodward and Scott Armstrong, *The Brethren* (New York: Avon Books, 1979), pp. 339–412.

# 12

---

# COURTS AND SOCIAL CHANGE

---

The previous chapter examined how judicial policies are communicated to others in the political system and how public officials respond and implement them. Often, judicial policies seem to have very limited effect because other officials ignore them or interpret and apply them in ways that maintain old ways of doing things.

But measuring the impact of judicial policy depends on when you look and on what else is happening in the larger political system. It often takes years and the actions of other officials before judicial policies have an intended effect, especially policies which require sweeping changes in social values and behavior, such as racial integration or school prayer. This chapter examines the broader and long-term role of courts in changing patterns of social behavior in the United States.

## PERSPECTIVES ON CHANGE

Three perspectives on the ability of the courts to affect society are: *legal independence; social determinism*; and *socio-legal interaction*.

### Legal Independence

The traditional view is that courts are unique and independent institutions, with law as a distinctive set of rules. Law imposes standards for conduct and rules of procedure for dealing with disputes. The judicial role is to discover and apply the law to disputes that come before the courts.

**419**

Most important in this perspective, *law is stable and endures social change*. Law and judicial decisions do alter, but only a little, and only in response to major social evolution occurring over the very long haul. But even then, law is unwilling to give up its old principles and rules, and courts adhere closely to guidelines for the past. New legal principles are logical and natural outgrowths of past ones. The essence of legal independence is that courts pronounce and enforce legal rules, but law is not substantially affected by social change, nor does it contribute much to society.

This traditional view was nurtured in the United States mainly through the creation of university law schools in the late 1800s (Chapter 3). There probably are some law professors and judges who hold this extreme view today, but it is not the prevailing way for understanding the role of courts in society. Rapid social change, social science research, as well as enterprising news reporters have uncovered too many ways in which courts and law are intimately connected to politics and society for this view to be dominant today.

### Social Determinism

A second view held by many politicians and social scientists is that courts and law are very much affected by social change, but that judicial decisions do not have much effect in the opposite direction; they doubt that courts can do much to change society. They often believe that fundamental changes have to occur in the hearts and minds of people before much of anything significant occurs. For example, during the early days of the civil rights movements in the 1950s, President Eisenhower believed that school desegregation was a *moral* problem and that government could not do much about it.

Many social scientists also are inclined to conclude that law only reflects changes that already have occurred or that law registers the winners of a particular political conflict. Laws and specific rules contained in official decisions are only the vehicles for carrying out policies already reached as a result of politics.

Much research also demonstrates that the decisions of state and local governments to spend money on major policies such as education, highways, welfare, and others are heavily determined by social and economic conditions such as urbanization, median family income, the structure of federal grants, and similar influences. Law almost never appears as an important consideration.

**Bridge Building**   Law professor Lawrence M. Friedman has offered an imaginative analogy of bridge building as a way of understanding this view of law and policy.[1] Two communities on the opposite banks of a wide river want a better method for gaining access to each other for trade and social interaction than the old ferryboat, which has become too small for the growing population and for carrying modern vehicles and manufactured goods. The people lobby their leaders, who agree to levy taxes and advertise for construction bids. The new bridge satisfies many local demands for a better way for getting across the river.

The bridge is like a new law or judicial decision. It is a result of political demands for a new method for dealing with an irksome problem or a widely recognized social need. Bridges can be built and used wherever they are needed or wanted.

*Courts as Bridge Builders*    The analogy works especially well for courts. Courts are the most passive lawmaking institutions and always must wait for demands to reach them in the form of cases before they can build new bridges. However, most judges view themselves as law interpreters, not lawmakers, and are reluctant to build new bridges, preferring only to settle "traffic accidents" that occur on the existing ones. But when demands become strong and clear enough or when other courts have started to build new bridges, other judges frequently get on the bandwagon.

The reactive role of courts in the face of changing social demands and new situations applies even to the most far-reaching Supreme Court decisions. The Supreme Court did not create the civil rights movement or demands for equality or for safe, legal abortions. These had been growing by bits and pieces throughout the country for decades.

Following World War II, the Supreme Court responded and gradually gave support for social equality and individual rights. However, courts also may dismantle or modify new bridges. The current conservative Supreme Court majority has not torn down many bridges by overturning old precedents, but it has limited traffic by narrowly interpreting and applying old decisions to new situations.

## Socio-Legal Interaction

Judicial response to social change and demands for new policy is only one part of the judicial impact equation. A third perspective is that *judicial policies also promote social change*. In the analogy of the bridge, once a bridge is in place, it begins to have new and unanticipated effects on society. The bridge promotes additional traffic, and communities on both sides of the bridge grow. New generations take the bridge for granted and would be shocked and outraged if the bridge were removed and no new means for getting across the river put in its place. In time, the once new bridge might become overcrowded and additional lanes might have to be added or new bridges constructed farther upstream as the communities swell and spread out.

Judicial bridges work in roughly similar ways. Court decisions in civil rights required other officials to pay attention to demands for equality, and while change often was painfully slow and frustrating, other federal officials began to support and supplement judicial policies in order to further integration. As new cases with new situations come before the courts, *judicial policy frequently expands and requires additional social change*.

Some federal courts also have constructed more elaborate judicial bridges than many litigants expected. For example, innovative judges have required cross-city busing in order to achieve school integration and have required state and local governments to spend money to improve jails, prisons, and state hospitals. Decisions requiring that poor defendants be provided with attorneys also led state and local governments to create and fund public defender programs.

People become accustomed to new judicial policies and take them into account in their behavior. The police became more careful about warning defendants of their rights, and affirmative action programs designed to promote the hiring of racial minorities are in place in dozens of cities, most of them produced voluntarily by organizations representing minority workers and city government.

Despite strong opposition from the Reagan administration, until the late 1980s the Supreme Court had endorsed affirmative action. However, many white workers claim that affirmative action produces reverse discrimination in hiring and promotion, and they recently have tried to dismantle that bridge. In 1989, with conservatives firmly in control, the Supreme Court permitted whites to sue to reopen old affirmative action agreements. But, as described in the previous chapter, Congress blocked that decision by enacting a new civil rights law. Older affirmative action programs are still in place. However, social conflict on these and other controversial policies continues.

**Social Complexity**   The effect of judicial policy on society is not easy to separate from other influences. Society does not sit still, quietly awaiting new judicial policy. Life goes on with an enormous number and variety of relationships and centers of influence. Legislatures and executives continue to make decisions and people continue to press competing claims in government. Technology takes giant leaps, and business creates new products and processes that change our lives and produce new problems and issues. Social change also builds on itself, often in ways that defy easy explanation and understanding. Therefore, it usually is inaccurate to attribute change to a single source.

*Judicial Responsibility*   Blaming or praising courts for what occurs in society usually oversimplifies and distorts reality. For example, some politicians often see a direct cause and effect between liberal judicial decisions and crime rates or a general decline in morality. Others believe that eliminating prayers and bible reading from the public schools has contributed to social disintegration. Still others credit the courts for creating civil rights.

But there is much more going on in society that might contribute to crime and other social problems. More frequent and deeper economic recessions and high unemployment, the dissolution of families, disruptive population shifts to other states, the widespread availability of handguns, drug abuse, and even sexual violence in movies are a few other likely sources of trouble.

Although there are many problems in explaining the role of courts in social change, understanding judicial impact requires trying to find out what difference judicial decisions make on society. This chapter concludes with a brief overview of the effects of judicial policy in race relations, the rights of criminal defendants, and women's rights.

A key element in these and other policies is the continuing interplay among demands for judicial action, court decisions, the effect of judicial policy, further social change, and additional political action and litigation. There rarely is a final resolution of conflict; instead, there is continuing political and social behavior that temporarily deals with particular problems.

## RACE RELATIONS

The cornerstone of modern civil rights policies is *Brown v. Board of Education* (1954). Until then, the Supreme Court allowed racial segregation through the separate-but-equal doctrine contained in *Plessy v. Ferguson* (1896). So long as public facilities provided blacks were equal to those furnished whites, the races could be kept separate.

### Public Education

Following World War II, the Supreme Court whittled away at separate but equal by repeatedly finding that separate facilities, most often in public schools and universities, were not equal, but the Court did not abandon this policy and require racial integration until 1954.

In that year, the Supreme Court stated that separate facilities were inherently unequal and that black children suffered from segregation. It overturned its old policy, and school segregation imposed by state law no longer was legal. It called for integration "with all deliberate speed," a vague and general principle for obtaining change. Since the only states that required segregation through law were the states of the old Confederacy and the border states, the new judicial policy was aimed at the south.

**Resistance and Demands**    During the decade following *Brown v. Board*, only about 2 percent of black schoolchildren in the south attended school with whites. Texas led the list with 5 percent integration.[2] Most state and local public officials, from governors down to school boards, were hostile to the idea of integration and often created ingenious ways to avoid it, sometimes going to the extreme of closing public schools and giving public financial aid to students to attend private, segregated schools. Even some federal judges did not welcome the ruling and failed to order any local integration, preferring time to take its own course.

The decade from 1954 to 1964 was a period of resistance and violence, and of arrest and sometimes murder of civil rights demonstrators. But it also was a period of increased black demands and demonstrations for equality and appellate federal court decisions which struck down attempts to circumvent integration. The courts also expanded the principle of school integration to cover a full range of public facilities, from drinking fountains and washrooms to restaurants and motels.

Despite repeated judicial decisions for integration, the southern states did not begin to substantially integrate public schools and other facilities until additional federal policy with a bigger bite began to have an effect. The courts could order integration but had no enforcement power. Occasional acts of outright defiance led Presidents to send in federal troops or marshals, but this could only be done a few times before the image of a police state began to appear, and Presidents naturally were reluctant to bring back images of federal military occupation and the Civil War. More subtle but still effective measures were available.

**The 1964 Civil Rights Act**   A crucial change occurred with the enactment of the Civil Rights Act of 1964. Both Democratic President Lyndon Johnson and the Democratic controlled Congress decided to get behind civil rights in a major way. They were affected by a number of factors, including additional civil rights litigation in the federal courts, continuous demands from blacks for racial equality, and the assassination of President John F. Kennedy in 1963 in Dallas. President Kennedy had proposed the law, and his successor saw it as a monument to the dead President. The combination of the assassination following a decade of protest and litigation provided a sad but unequaled opportunity to get the law enacted.

The new law outlawed discrimination in voter registration procedures, segregation in any area of public accommodation including motels, restaurants, places of entertainment, etc., and discrimination among large employers and labor unions, and it instructed federal agencies to end discrimination in all programs receiving federal financial aid.

*Impact of Federal Aid*   The federal aid portion of the law had a direct impact on southern public schools. The U.S. Office of Education required the submission of desegregation plans in order for schools to keep federal aid. A failure to comply would lead to a curtailment of federal funds.

The lion's share of money for public schools comes from state and local sources. The federal government contributes no more than 10 percent of the total, but it is directed to special programs such as improving science, language, and mathematics training, provision of instructional materials, and special assistance to schools located in especially poor areas. A cutoff of these funds might not cripple a public school, but it would damage particular areas of the curriculum and stretch already thin state and local resources.

Not coincidentally, the largest federal school aid program was enacted by Congress in 1965, the year after the Civil Rights Act was passed. Therefore, a cutoff of federal money would mean that public schools would be giving up a much bigger piece of federal money than ever before.

The carrot-and-stick approach had more effect than prior judicial decisions. Many school districts resisted integration until the early 1970s, but since few or no blacks had ever attended school with whites, any desegregation seemed dramatic. By 1966, the year after the new federal education act was passed, southern schools were 12 percent integrated; by 1970, about one-quarter of black schoolchildren went to school with whites; and by the 1980s, over 80 percent of southern black schoolchildren went to integrated schools. However, the percentage has declined slightly to around 70 percent.[3]

**Busing**    *Brown v. Board* and the Civil Rights Act did not solve the puzzle of integration. *Brown* required the end of law-imposed segregation, which frequently resulted in black schoolchildren being taken out of their neighborhoods to attend segregated schools. The decision did not address the problem that many schools, especially in large cities, are segregated because people of different races live in substantially different parts of the city. Instead of legally imposed segregation, this is de facto segregation caused by segregated, but not government-enforced, residence patterns. However, school officials sometimes make this form of segregation worse by drawing school district boundaries in ways that grouped whites and blacks in different schools.

Solving this problem required a new approach: busing children within school districts to create a more even racial balance in the schools. Busing was approved by the U.S. Supreme Court in 1971, when it ruled that southern school districts must get rid of all remnants of the dual school system and that busing was a tool that the federal district courts could use to accomplish that goal (*Swann v. Charlotte-Mecklenburg Board of Education*).

*Northern States*    Since then, busing has been applied in the north as well, where school segregation is even more severe due to substantial residential segregation. In large urban, industrial states such as Illinois, Pennsylvania, Michigan, New York, New Jersey, and others, about half of all black schoolchildren attended segregated schools.

Many federal district judges ordered school districts to use busing to achieve integration. However, the Supreme Court limited the impact of busing in 1974 by ruling that it may not be imposed on school districts that have not been found to discriminate against blacks (*Milliken v. Bradley*). In the Milliken case, only the school district of Detroit had been shown to promote segregation, but the lower federal courts had ordered busing *between* Detroit and suburban school districts, because Detroit had too few white students to create an equal racial balance in the city's schools.

The decision limits possible desegregation in northern cities, since many of them, including Washington, D.C., have a very large percentage of black students and busing within the city school district cannot substantially reduce racial segregation.

Procedures to integrate urban schools received additional support by the Supreme Court in 1990, when it ruled that federal district judges may order local school officials to raise property taxes to pay the costs of busing or other plans, such as placing magnet schools (those with attractive special programs) in black neighborhoods to attract whites. Judges may not levy taxes them-selves, but they may block state laws which prevent local school districts from raising taxes (*Missouri v. Jenkins*).

The effects and desirability of busing are still hotly debated. The Reagan administration in various amici curiae briefs asked the Supreme Court to end busing, but the Court refused, reasserting that busing is a suitable lever in the struggle to integrate the nation's schools.

However, toward the end of the 1980s, parents and school boards began to argue that local schools should be permitted to end busing when further integration cannot be achieved. In 1986, the Supreme Court gave some support to this view when it refused to review a federal court of appeals decision allowing Norfolk, Virginia to abandon busing of elementary school children. School officials and white parents had successfully argued that busing was weakening parental involvement in the public schools and that whites were fleeing the school system. But, blacks argued that an end to busing meant a return to de facto segregation.

Federal judges throughout the country have disagreed on this issue and some have refused to permit school boards to end busing. But, in 1991, the U.S. Supreme Court confirmed the Norfolk policy for the nation. In a case from Oklahoma City, it ruled that when school segregation is a result of persistent voluntary housing patterns (i.e., not created nor enforced by govern-ment) and school boards have done everything "practicable" to eliminate segregation, they may be released from previous desegregation orders (*Board of Education of Oklahoma City v. Dowell*). However, the Court left it for federal district court judges to determine when local efforts to achieve integra-tion have been satisfactory.

**Effects of Integration**    School integration has had a number of social effects. Segregated education was believed harmful, especially for blacks whose schools were never equal to those for whites. Black schools often were old, in poor condition, and with few modern and important facilities such as chemistry labs, or even enough textbooks, paper, pencils, and chalk. Black teachers, however well-intentioned, often were poorly trained. Black children usually came from poor families where books and education had never had much of a chance, so there were few opportunities for them to break out of a cycle of poverty. Going to school with whites was intended to provide the best public education available for everyone.

In the 1960s, desegregation of neighborhood schools seemed to make a big difference on the school performance of black children. Blacks who attended integrated schools did better than blacks with similar social and economic backgrounds who attended segregated schools.[4] However, busing often alien-ates white families in homogeneous white neighborhoods, who become angry when their children are required to attend inner-city schools. There also is less evidence that black children who are bused to school with whites perform much better than before.[5]

The size of black student enrollments also seems to affect the success of school integration. When black students comprise 30 percent or more of the student body, white parents begin to withdraw their children from the public schools at a faster rate. Consequently, as public schools become more segregated, the rate of additional segregation increases and racial isolation worsens.[6]

Despite busing and magnet schools, substantial school integration probably can only occur with housing integration, with whites and blacks attending schools near their homes. But, despite the federal Civil Rights Act of 1968, which outlaws discrimination in housing, most blacks are too poor to buy homes in integrated neighborhoods, and private discrimination makes substantial housing integration unlikely.

Since the Supreme Court also has permitted school districts to stop busing when little additional integration can be achieved, it is likely that de facto segregation of the public schools will increase.

## Voting Rights

Although school integration has not been fully obtained and is declining in many cities, the early school decisions have stimulated other civil rights policies. As mentioned earlier, the Civil Rights Act of 1964 did more than authorize federal agencies to cut off aid to segregated schools. It required equalization of voter registration procedures, banned discrimination in public accommodations, and took early steps to ban all forms of discrimination in employment.

The Voting Rights Act of 1965 authorized the U.S. Attorney General to send federal voter registrars to southern counties that clearly discriminated against blacks, and required states and counties that had discriminated to submit proposed changes in election laws to the federal government for approval. As a result, many blacks were registered to vote for the first time. Now, the percentage of blacks who are registered to vote is just a few percentage points lower than white registration.

**Discriminatory Results**   The Voting Rights Act has been extended several times. The 1982 Voter Rights Act allowed individuals to sue state and local governments if they believe that election procedures and the drawing of district boundaries consistently deny minorities a chance to elect candidates of their choice. Therefore, the earlier ban against intentional discrimination has been joined by prohibiting unintentional discriminatory results or effects. This policy has been supported by the Supreme Court. It has applied the law mostly to legislative and city elections, but, as discussed in Chapter 4, state officials also have been required to redraw judicial districts to give minorities a chance to elect judges they prefer.

**Increased Participation**   Minorities have vastly increased their participation in American politics as a result of the Voting Rights Acts and related judicial decisions. Over 7000 blacks hold public office throughout the United States, including over 400 in state legislatures, more than two dozen in the House of Representatives, over 300 mayors, including mayors of Atlanta, Los Angeles, and New York City, and the nation's first black governor in Virginia.[7] Jesse Jackson also ran a plausible campaign for President in 1988, winning Presidential primaries in Alabama, Georgia, Louisiana, Mississippi, and Virginia—states where blacks could not vote in 1965. Virginia's Governor Douglass Wilder also campaigned briefly for the 1992 Democratic Presidential nomination.

With occasional exceptions, racism as a campaign strategy also has dramatically decreased, including in the south, since both white and black candidates often need black support to win. Blacks are elected most often when black voters are in the majority, but white candidates also guard against alienating blacks whose votes can make a difference. Election politics also spills over into other issues. For example, as discussed in Chapter 4, southern U.S. Senators were especially concerned about alienating blacks in the Bork and Thomas nominations to the U.S. Supreme Court.

Black politicians can do little on their own to improve conditions for blacks. But their presence and status in all levels of government symbolizes the accomplishments of the black middle class and provides legitimate official positions for blacks to focus attention on civil rights and economic and other policies to help the poor.

### Affirmative Action

Demands for integration have gone beyond school desegregation and voting rights. The Civil Rights Act of 1964 is a comprehensive law that also banned discrimination in employment. Ending this form of bias received a huge boost when the executive branch of the federal government adopted affirmative action programs to implement the employment provisions of the Civil Rights Act.

Affirmative action emphasizes hiring blacks and other minorities and women who have suffered from discrimination. This often means giving blacks preference for jobs and training programs over some whites who are more qualified. The Supreme Court also has dealt with affirmative action.

**Early Cases**   In *Regents of the University of California v. Bakke* (1978), the Supreme Court decided that a special and separate admissions program for minority students was unconstitutional, because it discriminated against whites. However, the justices added that ensuring ethnic diversity in a university is a worthy goal and that the regents could consider the race or ethnic origin of its applicants in an informal weighting system that might benefit some students as they are compared with all other applicants. However, the Court held against strict quotas.

The following year, the Supreme Court decided *United Steelworkers v. Weber*, which seemed to move in the opposite direction from Bakke. Like Allan Bakke, who was refused admission to medical school, Brian Weber was excluded from a special job-training program in which half the seats were reserved for blacks who previously had been almost totally excluded from better jobs. Weber claimed his civil rights were violated under provisions of the 1964 Civil Rights Act, which prohibits job discrimination based on race.

The Supreme Court disagreed, but was extremely vague in explaining its policy toward affirmative action. The Court stated only that voluntary programs developed by unions and employers to erase earlier effects of discrimination did not violate the law.

In 1980, the year after *Weber*, the Supreme Court also approved a 1977 federal law that requires that 10 percent of state and local building projects funded with federal money must be set aside for minority-owned businesses (*Fullilove v. Klutznick*).

**Goals or Quotas**    Affirmative action is very controversial. Presidents Reagan and Bush have argued that affirmative action results in hiring quotas and discrimination against white workers. The conservative Rehnquist Supreme Court also has cooled toward affirmative action, but Democrats and moderate Republicans in Congress have continued to support affirmative action as a way of redressing past discrimination and providing minorities with employment opportunities.

In 1986, the Supreme Court ruled that the city of Cleveland may enter into an agreement, approved by a local federal district judge, to end a history of discrimination by hiring and promoting black fire fighters at the possible expense of better-qualified whites. White fire fighters and the Reagan administration in an amicus brief argued unsuccessfully that federal courts should order an end to discrimination only when particular individuals could prove that they had been the victims of discrimination (*Fire fighters v. City of Cleveland*).

In a similar decision announced the same day, the Court upheld a federal district judge who had ordered a labor union that persistently refused to comply with court orders, to obtain a precise goal of having 29.23 percent minority membership by the following year. This percentage is equal to the percentage of the nonwhite labor pool in the industry. Judges also would be permitted to intervene in membership procedures, if necessary, to accomplish this requirement.

The majority claimed this was only a goal, but the conservative dissenters, led by Justice Rehnquist, said it was a quota that was not permitted by law and had not been approved in earlier Supreme Court cases (*Sheet Metal Workers v. Equal Employment Opportunity Commission*).

In 1989, the Supreme Court majority, now led by Chief Justice Rehnquist, ruled that new employees may sue to reopen early affirmative action agreements (*Martin v. Wilks*), but Congress stifled that policy in the 1991 Civil Rights Act. Older affirmative action agreements still are in place.

**Uncertain Future**    The Supreme Court decisions toward affirmative action and job qualifications are not as far-reaching as *Brown v. Board*. The Supreme Court has only approved affirmative action started by others. It has not required it nationwide. The decision in Bakke also was only a *stopping action* that banned a particular affirmative action program.

The impact of affirmative action also depends heavily on the President and the executive branch and private business, labor, universities, and local governments initiating affirmative action programs on their own. President Bush is not a strong supporter of affirmative action, and both his administration and the Supreme Court have sent signals that encourage conservatives to oppose new affirmative action agreements.

Despite the Bakke decision, affirmative action has not had a revolutionary impact on higher education. Box 12.1, "A Decade after Bakke," demonstrates that forces other than court decisions are more important in determining integration in the nation's universities and professional schools.[8]

---

**BOX 12.1**

A DECADE AFTER BAKKE

After successfully suing to be admitted to the University of California at Davis Medical School, Allan Bakke completed his studies and is an anesthesiologist in Rochester, Minnesota. But his famous Supreme Court case has not fundamentally affected minority university enrollments.

The percentage of blacks enrolled in law and medical school is about the same as before Bakke—about 5 or 6 percent of the total, although some more blacks are enrolled in other graduate and professional schools. A hurdle to substantial integration is that black undergraduate enrollments have been nearly level at about 1 million. But the percentage of blacks who graduate from college within six years of receiving their high school diplomas is about half that for whites, or about 10 percent, which further shrinks the pool of students for graduate and professional schools.

Since affirmative action often is a voluntary or permissive policy, integration depends heavily on the recruitment policies of individual schools. Since many minority students are poor and cannot afford the fees for professional school, they are heavily dependent on grants and loans. But student loans are less available now than several years ago, and the Bush administration recently prohibited grants supported by federal funds from being designated solely for minorities.

An obstacle to integration at undergraduate schools is that black colleges traditionally have heavily recruited minority students and offered grants. Harvard leads the nation in attracting black merit scholars, but predominately black Florida A and M University is second. Some blacks prefer to study where they will be socially comfortable, and some fear the prospect of being isolated at a large state university located in a small, white rural community.

## The Economic Effects of Civil Rights

The civil rights movement and judicial and other federal policy has produced more than equal rights for nonwhites. It also has improved their economic and social condition in many areas of American life.

The percentage of blacks completing high school has increased from 20 percent in 1960 to approximately 65 percent in 1989. The white graduation rate is just under 80 percent. Hispanic graduation rates have increased as well, but lag behind the others at just over 50 percent. The percentage of black doctors, teachers, managers, and clerical workers also has nearly doubled since 1960, but it has leveled off during the 1980s. The percentage of blacks employed as domestic workers and farm laborers continues to decline, but the rate for Hispanics has increased sharply.[9]

The federal Labor Department also found that minority employment in businesses which have affirmative action plans is two-thirds higher than in businesses without them and that nonwhites are much more likely to be promoted under affirmative action programs than without them. Affirmative action appears to be achieving the results that the courts envisioned.[10]

**Deep Divisions**    The picture certainly is not all positive, however. Civil rights organizations lament the inferior economic position of blacks in the United States. Some blacks have significantly improved their economic circumstances. Since 1970, black households earning over $50,000 have doubled to over 11 percent, but black households with incomes under $5000 have increased from 10 percent to nearly 15 percent. White households earning more than $50,000 have increased from 18 to 25 percent but white households earning less than $5000 have remained nearly constant. The number of whites living below the government-designated poverty line has increased nearly 20 percent since 1970, but the increase for blacks is over 40 percent. Overall, close to one-third of blacks live in poverty compared with less than 10 percent of whites. Over 40 percent of black households with children are headed by women compared with 13 percent for whites, and their incomes are far below those of whites.

There also now seems to be a permanent underclass of very poor blacks concentrated in the worst areas of large cities, where pervasive poverty and welfare dependance, drugs, crime, misery, and hostility reign. There seems little hope that their economic and educational prospects will be improved in the near future.[11]

Despite the ups and downs of civil rights policy, the general social, economic, and political status of blacks and other minorities has improved greatly since the 1950s. Perhaps the most fundamental change is that blacks no longer are shunned in the United States as nonpersons or treated generally as third-class citizens. Certainly, much prejudice and discrimination still exist, but much less so than before. However, economic and social gaps between whites and blacks persist and judicial policy alone probably can do little to change that.

## RIGHTS OF CRIMINAL DEFENDANTS

The major innovations in the rights of criminal defendants also were made by the Warren Court in the 1960s and 1970s. The decisions covered a number of specific rights, but they all have had mixed effects on society. Several of the decisions were vague and provided no specific guidelines for police. Others required specific changes in police conduct, but have had *little practical effect on defendants*. Many Warren Court decisions also have been limited by conservatives on the Burger and Rehnquist Courts.

### Search and Seizure

The decision with the most uneven effects probably is *Mapp v. Ohio* (1961), which concerns the use of illegally seized evidence at a trial. The Fourth Amendment to the Constitution requires probable cause that a crime has occurred and the issuing of warrants to permit police to search individuals, houses, and personal possessions. In an earlier case, the Supreme Court had ruled that Fourth Amendment protections were part of due process guaranteed by the Fourteenth Amendment, which the states had to follow.

The Mapp decision specifically required the *states* to exclude from trials evidence that had been seized illegally by the police (*exclusionary rule*). But the Supreme Court did not spell out how the Mapp decision should be translated into practical rules for the police. The basis for probable cause, what the police had to do to get warrants, and variations in circumstances that affect decisions to search were left unclear. Police and lower court judges were left on their own.

**Reactions to Mapp**  Some big-city police departments tried to develop explicit internal standards and procedures to guide police, but many smaller cities either ignored Mapp or provided little or no help for the police.[12] Consequently, implementation varied tremendously around the nation. If Mapp were faithfully implemented, it was expected to reduce arrests in cases involving concealed evidence, such as weapons, drugs, and gambling paraphernalia.

A survey of nineteen cities after Mapp showed that it seemed to reduce arrests significantly in six cities, had a slight affect in ten cities, but had no effect in five others. In a few cities that implemented the spirit of Mapp, the number of search warrants issued by local judges increased from nearly zero to several thousand each year.[13] But even in complying cities, police and judges often were confused about what they were required to do and many violations of the right to privacy occurred.[14]

**Limiting Mapp**  The modest effects of Mapp have been reduced still further by search and seizure decisions of the Burger and Rehnquist Supreme Courts. From about 1970 to the present, the Supreme Court in dozens of cases has changed the meaning of a legal search and seizure and limited the application of the exclusionary rule to certain parts of the judicial process.

Requirements for determining what is probable cause were reduced, consent to search automobiles was generously interpreted in favor of the police, and police were permitted to detain the occupants of a home while property was being searched.

Also damaging to Mapp is a decision that evidence seized illegally could be used to challenge a defendant's testimony on cross-examination. The Supreme Court also has ruled that even when judges or magistrates make an error in granting a search warrant and police are unaware of the error and act "reasonably," the illegally seized evidence can be used in court.

**The Rehnquist Court** By the late 1980s and early 1990s, the Rehnquist Supreme Court had limited Mapp even further. It has permitted police to do a sweeping inventory search of private possessions found in automobiles and to open closed containers. If drugs, weapons, or other illegal items are found in the process of a general search, an individual can be charged for illegal possession. Searches of automobile junkyards, garbage stacked outside the home, fields where marijuana is suspected, flyovers in small planes and helicopters, and searches of barns to detect marijuana plants all have been allowed without warrants. Probation officers also have been permitted to search a probationer's home without a warrant if there are reasonable grounds for finding prohibited items. Setting up roadblocks to check all drivers for drunk driving also has been allowed, but selective stopping of particular cars was not approved. Federal law enforcement officials also do not need a search warrant to search the foreign homes of nonresident aliens with no connections to the United States. This 1990 case was most relevant to the Manual Noriega drug trial in Miami.

More directly invasive to the individual, the Rehnquist Court has upheld mandatory drug testing of officers of the U.S. Customs Service and railroad employees without requiring probable cause to suspect drug use or search warrants. Routine drug testing for both sets of employees was considered necessary to guarantee safety on the job, and, in the case of the customs officers, a way to ensure integrity (*National Treasury Employees Union v. Von Raab* (1989) and *Skinner v. Railway Labor Executives Association* (1989).

State and local governments have instituted mandatory drug testing policies for police, firefighters and others engaged in dangerous and critical occupations. Some governors proposed mandatory drug testing for all state employees, but opponents criticize these plans as currying to public fear of crime and demands that government solve the drug problem.

**Aftermath** Since Mapp was never popular with most judges and police, it seems likely that recent Supreme Court decisions that reduce its protections send a clear message to local officials to relax whatever standards they reluctantly had created.

Nevertheless, search and seizure rules have little practical effect on most criminal cases. Although about 10 percent of criminal defendants in federal courts ask for suppression of evidence at their trials, judges almost never grant their requests and evidence is excluded in only a little more than 1 percent of criminal cases. It is unlikely that state judges are any more generous.[15]

## Right to Counsel

Several landmark constitutional decisions form the foundation for the rights of criminal defendant to have access to lawyers. They are: *Gideon v. Wainwright* (1963); *Miranda v. Arizona* (1966); and *In re Gault* (1967). Gideon required that poor defendants be provided with counsel. Miranda went further and required that police clearly inform individuals in custody of certain specific rights: the right to remain silent; a warning that anything the suspect says can and will be used against the individual; the right to consult with a lawyer and the right to have a lawyer present at interrogation, and if the suspect cannot afford a lawyer, that one will be provided. Gault required that juvenile defendants receive certain rights provided adult offenders, particularly the right to counsel.

**Impact**   The greatest impact of Gideon was to require state and local governments to furnish lawyers to poor defendants, and many states began their public defender programs after this decision. But since poor defendants had to request a lawyer, it did not have as much effect as many people expected.

Miranda changed that, however, and police throughout the country began to use "Miranda cards," which they routinely pulled out and read to defendants. Miranda warnings have become commonplace, especially in large cities where police departments are more professional and likely to examine Supreme Court rulings. Police in smaller towns and rural areas, however, probably are less consistent in following Miranda.

*Miranda*   Police and trial judges are inclined to follow the clear requirements of Miranda, but the way the rules *actually* are carried out probably does not benefit most defendants. This is especially true since most police believed Miranda handicapped the police.[16] Most police whip out their Miranda cards and hurriedly read the four rights to defendants at the moment of arrest and as the handcuffs are being snapped shut. Police usually do not explain what they are saying, and rarely repeat the warnings or make certain a defendant really has understood what he or she is being told. The tension, jostling, and confusion that often occur with an arrest is not a "good learning environment."

Bewildered or angry suspects are not likely to fully comprehend the meaning and importance of a rushed and wooden reading of their rights, even if they say they understand. Police and prosecutors also sometimes ignore the warnings after they are read and quickly ask suspects if they want to make a voluntary statement. Police also interpret the timing for reading an individual his or her rights differently. For instance, many read the card right away, but others reason that if they do not try to talk to a defendant on the way to the station, they do not have to read the Miranda rights at all or until later on, perhaps after a defendant has started talking.

The total environment of the criminal justice process also undermines the potential effects of Miranda. Stable courtroom work groups encourage settling cases quickly through plea bargaining and defendants believe they get lighter sentences by cooperating, so few refuse to talk (Chapter 6). Many defendants, especially those accused of misdemeanors, do not even bother to request lawyers and plead guilty very early in the process.

*Gault* The practical effects of Gault on juveniles are even less than the impact of Gideon and Miranda. Most juvenile court judges, prosecutors, and public defenders view their roles as "helpers" to steer juveniles away from becoming career criminals and to encourage them to recognize their wrongs and personal shortcomings as the first step toward rehabilitation. Assumptions of guilt are common, but there is little talk of plea bargaining or proving a case in court. Juveniles are simply encouraged to admit their errors.[17]

When Gault was decided, judges in many juvenile courts either failed to warn juveniles or their parents of their constitutional rights or they rushed through them in a rough and angry way and quickly moved on to the case. Some parents only received a formal notice of their child's rights through the mail, and there was no emphasis on using them in court.[18]

Juvenile courts in larger cities often have special public defenders assigned full time to juvenile court, but they also provide no real defense. They usually make a pitch for the child and recommend probation, parental supervision, or light penalties. Since most defendants and their parents are poor, uneducated, and unsophisticated in the ways of the court, they almost never contest regular court operations and cases are settled quickly.

**Limiting Miranda** The Supreme Court has also limited the impact of the Miranda warnings. In *Harris v. New York* (1971), the Supreme Court permitted prosecutors to use statements made without Miranda warnings during a trial to challenge the credibility of a defendant's testimony on the stand. This is similar to its policy permitting illegally seized evidence to be used in court for the same purpose.

In 1980, the Supreme Court decided that a defendant's silence also could be used as evidence to challenge a defense (*Jenkins v. Anderson*). It also decided that conversation between police in the presence of a defendant shortly after arrest that leads the defendant to provide evidence against himself or herself does not qualify as interrogation and could be used in court (*Rhode Island v. Innis*). In similar cases, the Supreme Court ruled that Miranda had not been violated when suspects were not officially in custody but made incriminating statements without the Miranda warnings, or when defendants had confessed first, been read their Miranda rights later, but waived those rights and confessed again.

During the early 1980s, however, the Supreme Court also expanded the right to counsel to include misdemeanor cases that result in a jail sentence and to include the right to counsel for one appeal. Importantly, the Court also ruled that when a defendant asserts the right to counsel but not the right to silence, the police cannot continue to question the suspect until his or her attorney is present.

However, a major shift in Supreme Court policy toward Miranda occurred in 1984, when the Court ruled that when public safety is threatened, the police may question suspects without prior Miranda warnings (*New York v. Quarles*). In this case, police apprehended an unarmed suspect at gunpoint after a short chase, but before being read his rights, police asked and the suspect revealed the location of his hidden gun. The Court stated that such a rapidly changing or ". . . kaleidoscopic situation . . . where spontaneity rather than adherence to a police manual is necessarily the order of the day . . . ," an exception to Miranda is in order.[19]

The dissenting justices in this case found nothing unique in the way that the suspect had been apprehended and placed in custody and concluded that his hidden gun posed no danger. They disagreed that a public safety exception to Miranda was necessary.

Few recent cases have affected the interpretation of Miranda as much as Quarles, but the Supreme Court also has ruled against defendants in later cases who claimed their Miranda rights have been violated. The Court has allowed the voluntary confession of a mentally ill suspect, did not allow suspects to exclude all or particular statements made after voluntarily waiving their rights, and accepted as evidence a videotape of a suspected drunk driver even though he had not been read his rights. The Court also ruled that a defendant—given a reduced sentence in return for his testimony against others—was not subject to double jeopardy after he refused to testify in a second trial and the bargained sentence was withdrawn.

**Increased Police Power**  As explained in Chapter 10, neither the Burger nor Rehnquist Supreme Courts have overruled Miranda, Mapp, or other landmark cases concerning the rights of criminal defendants. They have only *distinguished* recent cases from the older precedents.

However, these distinctions have weakened the older decisions and given police, prosecutors, and local judges much more freedom to use evidence and testimony in trials that previously would have been excluded. One political scientist has concluded that the decision in Quarles marks the end of Miranda protection since police can apply the public safety rule to any policing situation.[20]

Legislators and governors in several states also have proposed amending state constitutions to weaken rigorous state exclusionary rules. The amendments would make state rules consistent with recent conservative Supreme Court decisions.

The other decisions broadening defendants' rights probably will not have a very significant impact on most defendants. Extending the right to counsel to misdemeanors probably is not very important, since the large majority of minor cases end with guilty pleas. Access to lawyers for appeals increases the potential for more appeals, but only a small minority of defendants go to trial in the first place and most lose on appeal. Since the criminal courts emphasize plea bargains, the right of prosecutors to use statements in court made without the Miranda warnings will increase their bargaining power over defendants.

## Death Penalty

Along with Mapp and Miranda, the death penalty is one of the most controversial criminal justice issues. The Eighth Amendment to the Constitution forbids "cruel and unusual punishment," and these terms have been used almost exclusively to oppose the death penalty. However, a large majority of Americans favor the death penalty, nearly three-quarters of the states use it, and state judges who have consistently overturned death sentences have been strongly criticized or have even lost their jobs. It is unlikely that the death penalty will be abolished in the forseeable future.

**Unfair Application**   Decisions of the Warren Court gave death row inmates various opportunities to challenge their convictions and sentences, and few people were executed. In 1972, the Supreme Court ruled that the *way* the death penalty was administered by the states constituted cruel and unusual punishment (*Furman v. Georgia*). The death penalty was imposed unfairly and unevenly on similar kinds of defendants convicted of similar kinds of crimes.

But instead of banning the death penalty outright, the Court allowed the states to rewrite their death penalty statutes in order to make the imposition of the sentence more equal. The Court believed that the best way of ensuring fairness was to separate the trial from sentencing. Once a person has been convicted, a separate hearing would determine other relevant, aggravating, and mitigating circumstances surrounding the crime and the defendant.

The states rewrote their death penalty statutes to make them more fair and equitable, and limited to the most horrendous crimes. Nevertheless, these new laws also were challenged. In 1976, the Supreme Court combined five death penalty cases from the southern states to rule on the constitutionality of the new state laws (*Gregg v. Georgia*).

Once again, the Court did not ban the death penalty as unconstitutional. It stated that the death penalty has long been accepted in the United States and the framers of the Constitution did not believe it was cruel and unusual punishment. The Court also ruled that state laws that provided ways for considering additional circumstances relevant to the crime and the criminal were constitutional because they removed the capricious and arbitrary way that the death penalty had been imposed in the past. This requirement has been restated in subsequent death penalty cases. The Court did not consider an additional argument that the prosecutor's unlimited discretion to seek the death penalty for different defendants continued to produce erratic and arbitrary sentencing (Chapter 6).

**Limiting Appeals**   Executions have resumed in the United States since 1976, but previous constitutional protections continued to give death row inmates many opportunities to appeal, and some cases have taken years or even a decade or more to get through the courts. Each death row inmate has a strong incentive to appeal, of course, and the odds of reversing a death sentence make appeals worthwhile. The federal courts have overturned about 40 percent of death sentences.[21]

In the 1980s, however, frustration with drug-related crime has hardened attitudes toward defendants. As discussed earlier, Chief Justice Rehnquist and others have sought ways to decrease a convict's opportunities to appeal a sentence in the federal courts.

In 1991, the Supreme Court limited the right to appeal to the federal courts if an inmate had not used all available state remedies. Also, the House of Representatives and the Senate passed separate anti-crime bills that included a federal death penalty for major drug dealers, and limited the opportunity of death row inmates to file appeals in the federal courts after their opportunities to appeal in the states had been exhausted. Liberals tried to include a provision allowing appeals based on racial bias, but this received little support. The bills also would have allowed the use of improperly seized evidence if the police acted in "good faith," and included various gun control provisions.

But President Bush, believing that opportunities to appeal still were too liberal, threatened to veto the bill and Congress abandoned it. Perhaps President Bush is counting on the Supreme Court majority to continue to narrow the rights of criminal defendants. In contrast, liberals fear that state courts often do not give adequate attention to requirements for a fair trial and police procedures and want to retain the opportunity to appeal to the federal courts.[22]

**Few Exceptions**    The Supreme Court also has considered additional death penalty cases. In 1976, the Supreme Court banned the death penalty for rape. Recently, the Court has ruled that imposing the death penalty on defendants under age 16, on the mentally retarded, or the insane is cruel and unusual punishment, but that 16- or 17-year-olds were not automatically exempt, depending on mitigating and aggravating circumstances.

However, as discussed earlier, in 1987, the Court also rejected statistical evidence that the death penalty was disproportionately imposed on blacks. Defendants still must show that the penalty had been imposed in an unfair and capricious way in their own cases (*McClesky v. Kemp*). The Court also has changed earlier policy by allowing the death penalty to be imposed on accomplices who did not do the actual killing. The Supreme Court also has not allowed new constitutional protections concerning the death penalty to be applied retroactively to defendants convicted of crimes before the new Court decisions were made. But the Supreme Court rejected the use of evidence of the impact of a crime on the victim or victim's family at the sentencing stage of a case as possibly prejudicial to the defendant.

Overall, recent Supreme Court policies heavily limit the opportunities of convicted murderers to fight the death penalty and other defendants from using the federal courts to seek protection under the Constitution.

## WOMEN'S RIGHTS

For most of U.S. history, women have been dependent on and "protected" by men. Paternalism translated into public policies which denied women the right to vote and to enter various professions, including the practice of law (Chapter 3). During the nineteenth century, married women, in particular, had few property or other rights and were treated as children.

Many limitations on women have persisted.[23] For instance, in 1948, the Supreme Court, citing social etiquette, upheld a Michigan law that permitted only the wives or daughters of bar owners to obtain bartender licenses. All other women were excluded. In 1961, the Warren Supreme Court, famous for its liberal racial and defendants' rights policies, upheld a Florida law that removed women from registration lists used for jury selection. The case involved a woman convicted by an all-male jury of murdering her husband. This policy was not reversed until 1975.

Women have not shared the historical fate of blacks who were isolated from whites and generally relegated to a lower-class existence. Women always were integral parts of family units, but they also had distinctive roles which gave men the upper hand and underscored the common belief that a woman's place is in the home. However, changing social values are reflected in automobile bumper stickers which read "A woman's place is in the house . . . and in the senate."

Substantial changes in women's rights did not occur until the 1970s. They involve three general areas: *economic discrimination, sex role differences*, and *abortion*.

### Economic Discrimination

The revolution in civil rights is partly responsible for making women more aware of their own limited position in society, but other social forces were at work as well. By the 1960s, many more females, especially married women, were working and well-educated women were increasingly dissatisfied with being shunted into traditional female jobs as secretaries, nurses, primary school teachers, and similar positions. Divorce rates also increased rapidly in the mid- to late 1960s. Women were out of the home and wanted a more equal opportunity to make it in the marketplace.[24] Approximately 45 percent of the labor force is composed of women.[25]

**The 1964 Civil Rights Act**    The first major shift in policy was not a Supreme Court decision but the 1964 Civil Rights Act. Title VII of the Civil Rights Act prohibited discrimination on the basis of race, color, religion, sex, or national origin in all aspects of employment, including hiring, pay, and promotions. Title VI of the law called for eliminating discrimination in all programs and activities receiving federal aid.

These two sections of the Civil Rights Act were beneficial to blacks and also provided an opportunity for women to break into employment traditionally held by men and to claim equal treatment on the job. Women could look forward to becoming doctors, lawyers, fire fighters, and construction workers.

Including sex discrimination in the bill—which was aimed mainly at ending racial discrimination—was done by southern legislators who hoped it would make the bill so unpalatable that most legislators would vote against it. Regardless of the intent of the legislation, however, it provided a new legal bridge for women to pursue new economic opportunities.

*Affirmative Action*    Significant implementation of the law was accomplished through affirmative action programs which required government agencies, government contractors, and larger private employers to hire women for jobs traditionally held by men. The effect of affirmative action on women's economic opportunities probably is greater than its effects on nonwhites since many white females possess college and advanced degrees and, given new opportunities, are in a better position to put them to use. Based on its earlier decision in the *Weber* case, which allowed affirmative action agreements, in 1987, the Supreme Court gave similar support to programs benefitting women (*Johnson v. Transportation Agency, Santa Clara County, California*).

**Other Laws**    Congress also has enacted additional laws important to women. In 1964, Congress enacted the Age Discrimination Act, which protected workers from age discrimination on the job. In 1974, it passed the Federal Equal Credit Opportunity Act, which prohibits sex discrimination in lending money. It voided policies which prevented married women from borrowing money separately from their husbands. In 1978, Congress banned employment discrimination on the basis of pregnancy and required disability and health insurance plans to cover pregnant employees. This bill was in response to a 1976 Supreme Court decision which did not require pregnancy coverage in disability insurance plans.

In 1984, Congress guaranteed the right of employees (such as pregnant women) to leave and return to their jobs without losing pension rights and increased the rights of spouses to receive pension benefits if their partners died before attaining retirement age, a provision especially beneficial to women. However, state governments were not required to pay unemployment compensation to new mothers when their previous employers refused to reinstate them. In the same year Congress made it easier for women to collect court-ordered child support. All of these laws benefit millions of women.

**Court Decisions**    The Supreme Court has not been the leader in equal rights for women, and there is no sexual counterpart to *Brown v. Board* which fundamentally alters the traditional position of women in America. In women's rights, the 1964 Civil Rights Act preceded a change in judicial policy. However, through interpreting federal legislation and overturning restrictive state laws, the Supreme Court has removed additional limitations on women's economic rights. These decisions generally reinforce more sweeping action taken in the 1970s by Congress and the executive branch.

The first significant decision was in 1971, when the Supreme Court overturned a state law that gave preference to men as executors of estates, a law that reflected traditional assumptions that men were more experienced and adept than women at managing money (*Reed v. Reed*). The Court stated that governments must have compelling justifications for distinguishing between men and women. In 1973, the Supreme Court overruled military policy that made it more difficult for female than male members of the military to obtain dependents' benefits and PX privileges for their spouses (*Frontiero v. Richardson*).

*Job Discrimination*   The Court also has required equal pension and health insurance benefits for men and women; ruled that temporary absence during pregnancy does not require female employees to give up seniority rights; that state laws which require employers to grant unpaid maternity leaves are constitutional; and it has held that women may sue employers for discrimination without first proving that they have been denied equal pay for equal work, a provision of a 1973 law. As discussed in Chapter 3, the court also has ruled that the 1964 Civil Rights Act applies to law firms, permitting female lawyers to sue for job discrimination. The Court also has banned formerly all-male social clubs, such as the Jaycees, Rotary and the New York Athletic Club from excluding women because the clubs are places where informal business discussions and deal making take place. To exclude women deprives them of equal access to business opportunities (*Board of Directors of Rotary International v. Rotary Club*, 1987 and *New York State Club Association v. City of New York*, 1988).

However, not all decisions have gone in favor of women. Recall that the Rehnquist Supreme Court interpreted the civil rights laws in ways which made it more difficult for women to challenge a company's seniority system as discriminatory and for women to sue for job discrimination. The civil rights law passed by Congress in 1991 reversed these decisions, but advocates of civil rights in general cannot expect much support from the current Supreme Court.

**Changing Attitudes**   Although women have benefited from federal policy, change also is due to new social attitudes and leadership, such as President Carter's and various governors' pledges to appoint women to high political office and the commitments of law firms and other employers to hire women for nontraditional jobs. The change in public attitudes concerning sexual equality is dramatic. In 1945, 60 percent of the public believed that women should not work if their husbands could support them. By 1980, 60 percent held the opposite view, and 80 percent of people under age 30 believed married women should work regardless of family circumstances.[26]

*Equal Rights Amendment*   Widespread support for more liberated roles for women also is reflected in the near passage of the Equal Rights Amendment in 1982. The proposed amemdment stated: "Equality of rights under the law shall not be denied or abridged by the United States or by any state on account of sex." Although the amendment was three states short of the thirty-eight needed for ratification, the extent of support for the amendment reflects how much attitudes toward equal rights for women had changed since the early 1960s. Most of the states that failed to ratify were in the south, a region which responds conservatively to social change.

**Economic Effects**  As mentioned earlier, affirmative action policies are largely responsible for most changes in women's work. Judicial policy reinforces the trend. Women still predominate in traditional areas, such as domestic service, secretarial work, nursing, etc., but they also are a growing and significant number in formerly mostly male occupations.

From 1970 to 1989, the proportion of women in the work force rose from 38 to 45 percent. However, women increased their presence in mathematical and computer science jobs from 15 percent of the total in 1970 to 36 percent in 1989. The percentage of female social scientists and urban planners rose from less than one-quarter in 1970 to nearly 50 percent in 1980.[27] The number of female lawyers has nearly tripled during the past decade—up from 5 to 15 percent of the total.

Although women have made considerable progress getting into new occupations, women still do not make nearly as much money as men. Female employees sometimes are paid less than men for the same work, but the difference is due mostly to women still being employed in traditional female jobs that always have been valued less and rewarded at a much lower level.

## Sex Role Differences

Although it generally is illegal to discriminate on the basis of gender, the Supreme Court has agreed that sex role differences sometimes justify different policies for men and women. However, attitudes change about what are genuine sex role differences, and judicial and other policies change with it.

**Educational Opportunities**  Women have not faced the same hurdles as blacks in obtaining an education. Sex discrimination occurs in more subtle ways, such as housing rules on college campuses, funding of athletic programs, and the recruitment and pay for female faculty. In 1972, Congress banned discrimination in most aspects of education, including admissions, housing rules, financial aid, faculty and staff recruitment, and pay and athletic programs. As in the 1964 Civil Rights Act, Congress put teeth into the law by authorizing the cutoff of federal aid to educational institutions that discriminate.

The Supreme Court endorsed this law, but has limited its impact by authorizing the cutoff of federal funds only for particular programs at the schools that discriminate. Consequently, if only an athletic program is found to be discriminatory, the school would not lose federal funds for other activities, such as scientific research (*Grove City College v. Bell*, 1984).

Civil rights organizations and others claimed that this decision had a much broader impact than on sex discrimination because the principle was expanded to permit widespread discrimination against blacks, the handicapped, and the elderly at many colleges and other institutions receiving federal aid. Just as they did in 1991, they lobbied Congress to enact a new federal law to void the Supreme Court decision. The main opponents to the new law were Protestant fundamentalists who believed the law would require equal treatment of homosexuals, which they strongly repudiated.

In 1988, Congress voted overwhelmingly to restore the previous policy of cutting off all federal aid to any institution which discriminated, even if the discrimination was limited to one particular program or activity. President Reagan vetoed the law, but Congress had the votes to override the veto.[28]

**Employment Opportunities**    A complex aspect of discrimination concerns forbidding pregnant women from taking certain jobs that may be harmful to the woman and/or her fetus. In 1982, Johnson Controls, Inc., a manufacturer of batteries, began to prohibit women from working in assignments where they might be exposed to high levels of lead, believing that it could harm a fetus that might be carried by a female employee. All women, unless they had documented proof that they were unable to bear a child, were automatically excluded from this work. Men were not screened or excluded. However, these jobs also were among the best paying ones, and women objected that they had no access to them whether or not they were pregnant or even planned to have a child. One employee who became a litigant had been surgically sterilized in order to get one of the higher paying, but risky, jobs.

The federal court of appeals had ruled that because the policy was designed to protect an unborn child, sex discrimination was not involved. But the Supreme Court ruled in 1991 that the Pregnancy Discrimination Act, passed in 1978, stipulated that unless pregnant women are unable to perform a task, they must be treated like other employees. In addition, even though Johnson Controls had not intended to discriminate, since the job classification was based on gender and childbearing ability, not on actual fertility or pregnancy, the policy *resulted* in discrimination on the basis of gender. The Court declared that women have the right to choose for themselves whether to work in potentially hazardous jobs (*Automobile Workers v. Johnson Controls*).

**Other Policies**    In 1976, the Supreme Court voided an Oklahoma law which prohibited the selling of weak 3.2 beer to males under the age of 21 but permitted females over 18 to obtain the beverage. The state's logic was that young men are much more reckless than young women. However, the Court ruled that despite differences in automobile accident and drunk driving arrest rates, few men or women overall are involved in these mishaps and the distinction between the sexes was not a reasonable one (*Craig v. Boren*, 1976).

However, the Court has found some laws reasonable which distinguish between men and women. In 1981, The Court upheld a California criminal law that made it illegal for a male to have sexual intercourse with a consenting

female under the age of 18 (statutory rape) but did not hold the female crimi-
nally responsible. The Court ruled that the law had a reasonable purpose of
preventing teenage pregnancy and was based on inherent sex differences since
only females can become pregnant. However, Justices Brennan, Marshall, and
White dissented, pointing out that there was no evidence such laws were
effective and that thirty-seven other states had gender-neutral rape laws
(*Michael M. v. Superior Court of Sonoma County*, 1981).

The Court also held in 1981 that the military registration law which required
only men to register for a possible military draft did not discriminate. The Court
reasoned that legislative intent was to facilitate the raising of a *combat* army,
and since other laws explicitly made women ineligible for combat, the law was
a reasonable governmental policy (*Rostker v. Goldberg*, 1981).

However, while not officially assigned to combat, women increasingly
perform important and dangerous support roles for the military, such as in the
Mideast war against Iraq, where several were killed or injured. Female pilots
flying military support planes, such as refueling transports, also are likely to
be hurt or killed in the future. These roles blur the distinction between
combat and military support, and Congressional and Supreme Court policy
may be forced to change as a result of the gradually changing role of women
in the military.

## Abortion

The most controversial issue in women's rights—and probably the nation—is
abortion. New laws and judicial decisions which enable women to become
doctors or to put on hard hats or join city garbage crews are controversial and
are resented by some males, but abortion divides the nation and generates
intense political conflict.

The right to choose abortion runs head on into traditional moral beliefs about
the sanctity of life and abortion as murder. No matter what policies governments produce, they are bound to be controversial and unsettled for many
years to come. On this issue, the Supreme Court, as well as Congress, the
President, and the states are squarely in the middle of the battle.

*Roe v. Wade* **(1973)**   In 1973, the Court ruled that a woman has a constitutional right to privacy that protects a personal choice to have an abortion in
consultation with her personal physician. A fetus was determined not to be
viable during the first three months of pregnancy when the abortion procedure
is relatively safe. Therefore, the state could *not* interfere with a woman's
abortion decision.

During the second three months, however, abortion becomes medically
more risky and government could regulate abortions, such as requiring them to
be performed in hospitals. During the final three months fetuses often are
viable, and the state may prohibit abortion except when the mother's life or
health are threatened. *Roe v. Wade* overturned state laws that outlawed abor-

tion, but it left open numerous special circumstances for limiting abortion. The vote was a by a wide margin of 7 to 2. Only Justices Rehnquist and White dissented.

The decision produced a storm of protest equal in force and vehemence to any directed at previous Supreme Court decisions. Many prolife groups assumed Roe would unleash a wave of abortions, which they opposed as legalized murder. Some antiabortion extremists resorted to violent protest and intimidation of doctors, nurses, and patients, and there were several dozen abortion clinic bombings during the early 1980s. Violent protests continued into the 1990s. Certain members of Congress and others urged a constitutional amendment prohibiting abortion, and antiabortion groups began to lobby state legislatures for laws that would heavily limit the right to an abortion.

**Legislative and Judicial Conflict**   Most legislatures responded to Roe. Congress limited federal Medicaid payments, which assist the medical needs of the poor, to abortions only when the health of the mother was threatened. A majority of states also enacted laws limiting the right to an abortion. As discussed in Chapter 10, many of these new laws became the subject of litigation, and the Supreme Court has granted some limitations but rejected others.

The Court has approved federal and state laws limiting payment for abortions (*Maher v. Roe*, 1977 and *Harris v. McRae*, 1980), but, until the late 1980s, it did not endorse state restrictions which make it difficult emotionally or financially for women to obtain an abortion, such as waiting periods and requiring that all abortions between three and six months of gestation be done in hospitals, rather than women's clinics (*City of Akron v. Akron Center for Reproductive Health*, 1983 and *Planned Parenthood, Kansas City, Missouri v. Ashcroft*, 1983).

Justices Brennan, Marshall, and Blackmun dissented in all the abortion funding cases, arguing that the laws attempted to evade the broad right to an abortion contained in *Roe v. Wade*, and predicted that a cutoff in federal assistance would prevent mainly poor women from obtaining abortions. Those who could afford to pay their own way would have little difficulty in obtaining an abortion.

In 1986, the Supreme Court rejected a Pennsylvania abortion statute that imposed major psychological burdens on women and reaffirmed the basic right to an abortion (*Thornburgh v. American College of Obstetricians*). Pennsylvania required that a woman seeking an abortion be given printed or verbal information including the unknown physical and psychological effects of abortion and the medical risks involved, the likely age and viability of the fetus, that state benefits are available for child birth and care, and that fathers are required to provide child support. The woman had to sign that she had received the information. The Court viewed these requirements as overbearing and improper state efforts to dissuade a woman from exercising her right to obtain an abortion.

As in other cases involving controversial social issues, the Reagan administration filed an amicus brief in which it explicitly asked the Court to overrule *Roe v. Wade*. Although it was unsuccessful, the majority which supported the abortion decision had shrunk to five justices. Pro-choice advocates feared that the replacement of any of the majority with new conservative justices could lead to a fundamental reexamination of the right to abortion.

**Supreme Court Shifts**   With the appointment of Justice Kennedy in 1988, President Reagan had achieved a conservative majority on the Supreme Court which was much more inclined to limit the right to an abortion (Chief Justice Rehnquist and Justices Kennedy, O'Connor, Scalia, and White). The later addition of Justices Souter and Thomas provide likely additional conservative votes, and pro-life organizations believed they had a good chance of obtaining a reversal of *Roe v. Wade*.

The Supreme Court has not abandoned the right to choose abortion, but like their narrow interpretation of other liberal precedents, the new majority has substantially limited this right and fostered limited opportunities to obtain an abortion. An early indicator of the shift occurred in 1988 when the Supreme Court upheld a federal law that provided money to religious organizations which counseled teen-age girls to abstain from sex and avoid abortion (*Bowen v. Kendrick*). However, the Court also found that these groups engaged in religious teachings, which were forbidden by the doctrine of separation of church and state. The vote was 5 to 4.

*Approving Restrictions*   A year later, in a more basic shift in direction, the same majority upheld a Missouri law that contained much heavier restrictions than those found in earlier state laws that the former liberal majority had rejected. The statute focuses on the rights of the unborn fetus rather than on women's rights and raises additional issues of free speech. The case was so controversial that an estimated 300,000 people demonstrated outside the Supreme Court days before the Court was to hear the case.

The Missouri law contains a preamble stating that life begins at conception, prohibits the use of public hospitals or other public facilities and employees from performing abortions, prohibits public funding for abortion counseling, and requires that physicians determine the viability of the fetus estimated to be more than twenty weeks in gestation. Public employees also are forbidden from speaking about abortion in public facilities. The Court found that these provisions did not conflict with *Roe v. Wade*, which permits the states to regulate abortion after the first trimester (*Webster v. Reproductive Health Services*).

Justices Blackmun, Brennan, and Marshall dissented and termed the majority's opinion fundamentally damaging to the right to an abortion and an effective reversal of *Roe v. Wade*. In their view, it resurrected again the specter of illegal and dangerous abortions and forecast more restrictive Supreme Court decisions to come. Justice Scalia, who was a member of the majority, agreed that the decision had effectively overruled Roe but that the Court should have done so explicitly.

The Court continued on its restrictive path in 1990, when it approved several state laws requiring women under age 18 to notify one or both parents of their plans to have an abortion, including divorced parents and those who may never have lived with the young woman. A Minnesota statute required notification of both parents but allows a judge to approve an abortion in place of the parents if the judge determines that the young woman is mature and capable of giving informed consent. The Court was split on these various provisions, and Justice O'Conner was unwilling to endorse the most restrictive limits. The Court approved of statutes requiring notification of one parent, but required the option of seeking a judge's approval if states required that both parents be notified (*Hodgson v. Minnesota* and *Ohio v. Akron Center for Reproductive Health*).

But, in 1992, in a Pennsylvania case widely expected to doom *Roe v. Wade*, the Supreme Court by a 5-4 vote again upheld the right to an abortion but continued to approve restrictions, including requiring a woman to listen to a presentation persuasive against abortion, delaying the abortion for twenty-four hours after the presentation, and requiring a teenager to obtain the consent of one parent or a judge. The Court rejected requiring a married woman to inform her husband of her intent to have an abortion (*Planned Parenthood v. Casey*). Surprising to many, the majority upholding Roe included conservative Justices O'Connor, Kennedy, and Souter, and Justices Blackmun and Stevens. Justices Rehnquist, Scalia, White, and Thomas dissented and would have overturned Roe.

**Complex and Continuous Conflict**    Political conflict surrounding abortion is complex and constant, and it includes much more activity than just Supreme Court decisions. It involves all levels of government, public opinion, and many interest groups in a continuous interplay of competing demands for influence in abortion policy. This whirl of activity is portrayed in a chronology of recent major events in Box 12.2, "Politics and Abortion."[29] Just as in other controversial policies, there is no end to this conflict in sight. Regardless how the Supreme Court rules in the future, those in favor and those against the right to choose abortion will continue to try to influence governmental policy.

**Access to Abortions**    The number of legal abortions performed after *Roe v. Wade* increased at a steady rate from about 650,000 per year in 1972 to 1½ million by 1978, where it remains today.[30] The decision undoubtedly provided opportunities for abortion that did not exist in states which banned nearly all abortions.

The abortion decisions have had medical consequences as well. Medical experts have determined that the number of illegal abortions has declined from about ¾ million in 1969 to around 10,000 in the early 1980s. Certainly more

**BOX 12.2**

ABORTION RIGHTS AND POLITICS

• *August 1987*: President Reagan announces that the administration will draft new rules prohibiting federal money from funding family planning clinics that provide abortion counseling.

• *August 1987*: A Minnesota law, which requires women under age 18 to notify both parents or obtain a judge's permission for an abortion, is declared unconstitutional by a federal district judge.

• *September 1987*: A federal district judge bars Georgia from enforcing a law requiring minors to notify their parents before obtaining abortions.

• *December 1987*: The U.S. Supreme Court deadlocks 4–4 (Justice Kennedy's confirmation was pending), and rejects an Illinois law requiring minors to notify their parents before obtaining an abortion.

• *January 1988*: Medical researchers announce that it is possible for a woman who is pregnant with more than one fetus to abort some while allowing the rest to proceed to birth. The development suggests new issues in the abortion conflict.

• *February 1988*: A federal district judge in Denver blocks enforcement of new Reagan administration rules withholding federal funds from clinics which do abortion counseling.

• *March 1988*: The Reagan administration postpones plans to end federal funding of clinics that counsel abortion after a federal district judge issues a nationwide injunction blocking the rules.

• *June 1988*: Florida enacts a law requiring minors to obtain their parents' or a judge's consent to an abortion.

• *June 1988*: The U.S. Supreme Court upholds a federal law permitting federal funds to go to religious groups who counsel teenaged girls to abstain from sexual relations and avoid abortion.

• *July 1988*: The U.S. Senate approves Medicaid payments for abortions in cases of rape or incest. It is the first expansion of federal policy since 1981. Action in the House of Representatives is pending.

• *August 1988*: A federal court of appeals reverses the district court and upholds Minnesota's restrictive abortion law.

• *November 1988*: Pro-life groups claim that the election of President George Bush signals the appointment of additional conservatives to the Supreme Court and enough votes to overturn *Roe v. Wade*.

• *January 1989*: The U.S. Supreme Court grants certiorari to a case involving Missouri's severely restrictive abortion law.

• *April 1989*: Hundreds of thousands of demonstrators march in Washington, D.C., days before the Supreme Court is to hear arguments in the Missouri case.

• *April 1989*: Researchers say medicine is unable to extend the survival of fetuses born before twenty-three or twenty-four weeks of pregnancy. Opponents to abortion have wanted viability to be established much earlier to justify prohibiting abortions that occur early in pregnancy.

• *July 1989*: The Supreme Court upholds Missouri's restrictive abortion law. Abortion rights advocates say the decision is a disaster. Randall Terry, head of Operation Rescue, a radical antiabortion group, expects new restrictive state laws.

• *July 1989*: The Louisiana legislature recommends that state district attorneys enforce criminal abortion laws enacted prior to *Roe v. Wade*.

• *October 1989*: Relying on a state constitutional right to privacy, the Florida supreme court declares unconstitutional a state law requiring teenage girls to obtain their parents' consent to an abortion. Florida's pro-life Governor Bob Martinez vows to submit new legislation in a special legislative session.

• *October 1989*: The Florida legislature refuses to consider the governor's and other abortion proposals. Polls show 60 percent of Floridians oppose strict limits on abortion. Thousands demonstrate in front of the capitol. Restrictive abortion bills also were defeated in Michigan and Minnesota, but enacted in South Carolina and Pennsylvania.

• *October 1989*: The U.S. House of Representatives votes to allow federal Medicaid policy to pay for abortions in the case of

**BOX 12.2 continued**

incest or rape. Many representatives perceive their constituents are pro-choice. Nevertheless, the bill is largely symbolic because few women seek abortion for these reasons. Gubernatorial candidates in various states make gains in the polls by taking a pro-choice stance.

• *November 1989*: Less than two weeks before a case was scheduled for oral argument before the U.S. Supreme Court, Illinois agrees to discard state regulations requiring abortion clinics to be equipped and staffed like hospital operating rooms. Abortion rights groups are pleased to settle the case because it was a possible vehicle for the Supreme Court to overturn *Roe v. Wade*.

• *January 1990*: A federal district judge rejects another restrictive Pennsylvania abortion law.

• *March 1990*: The Republican controlled Idaho legislature restricts the right to abortion only to cases of rape, incest, severe fetal deformity, and threats to the physical health of the mother. However, Democratic governor Cecil Andrus vetoes the bill. The territory of Guam prohibits abortion except when a woman's life is threatened, but the law was immediately placed under a judicial restraining order.

• *March 1990*: The Maryland legislature is unable to agree to a new abortion bill.

• *April 1990*: Connecticut becomes the first state to make abortion a legal right under state law. It would protect the right to an abortion even if Roe were overruled.

• *June 1990*: The U.S. Supreme Court upholds a Minnesota and other laws requiring teenaged girls to obtain their parents' or a judge's consent to an abortion.

• *August 1990*: A federal district judge declares unconstitutional several provisions of another Pennsylvania law that heavily restricts access to abortion. In addition to other provisions, the law required a woman to obtain her husband's consent.

• *May 1991*: The U.S. Supreme Court upholds Reagan administration rules prohibiting federal funds from going to family planning clinics that provide abortion counseling. Planned Parenthood Federation of America announces plans to lobby Congress to reverse the decision.

• *August 1991*: Approximately 100 abortion opponents are arrested in Wichita, Kansas, after defying a federal district judge's injunction against blocking the entrance to abortion clinics.

• *October 1991*: A federal court of appeals reverses the federal district judge in the most recent Pennsylvania case. However, the appeals court rejects that portion of the law requiring a woman to obtain her husband's consent to an abortion. Other restrictions were allowed and pro-choice groups said the decision effectively overrules Roe.

• *November 1991*: Abortion rights groups hope the Supreme Court will review the Pennsylvania statute, even if it overturns Roe, hoping the decision will damage President Bush's chances for re-election in 1992.

• *November 1991*: The U.S. Congress restores federal funds to clinics which counsel abortion. However, President Bush vetoes the bill and the House is twelve votes short of being able to override it. The restrictions stand.

• *January 1992*: The U.S. Supreme Court grants certiorari in the latest Pennsylvania case. The Pennsylvania law, largely upheld by a federal court of appeals, requires: prior notification of the husband; a 24-hour waiting period; minors to notify one parent; and doctors to provide information about the risk of abortion, the stage of development of the fetus, and alternatives to abortion. The Court is widely expected to uphold most of these restrictions.

• *April 1992*: Kansas Governor Joan Finney signs an abortion law that requires a minor to notify one parent, an eight-hour waiting period, and, if the fetus is capable of living outside the womb, bars abortion unless the mother's life is threatened.

• *April 1992*: Operation Rescue stages protests at abortion clinics throughout Buffalo, New York, but is unable to force their closure or stop abortions.

• *June 1992*: The U.S. Supreme Court upholds most of Pennsylvania's abortion restrictions, but does not overturn Roe.

women have had the benefit of improved health care and greater safety through legalized abortion. The cost of obtaining abortions also has gone down, health care has improved, and the number of abortion clinics unrelated to hospitals has grown.[31] But pro-choice advocates fear a return to unsafe illegal abortions since many state restrictions have been approved by the Supreme Court.

*Is Roe Responsible?*   It is difficult to fix the responsibility for increased abortions solely on the Supreme Court, because New York, Hawaii, Alaska, and Washington state had enacted liberal abortion laws prior to *Roe v. Wade*. New York also did not require state residence in order for an individual to obtain an abortion, and many women who could afford it went to New York.

Also, the rate of increase in abortions was higher *before* the 1973 Court decision than afterward. From 1970 to mid-1972, abortions increased over 300 percent. From mid-1972 to 1975, the number of abortions increased to over 1 million per year, but the rate of increase was reduced to 60 percent. The leveling off in the annual rate of abortion probably is unconnected to the politics of abortion but reflects the increasing age of the baby-boomers and a decrease in the number of young women in the population, the group most likely to have abortions. It also may indicate greater use of contraception and sterilization.[32]

The huge number of illegal abortions prior to *Roe v. Wade* also strongly suggests that the Supreme Court did not create the public demand for abortion. It already existed. The Court made it possible for many women who otherwise would have obtained illegal and possibly dangerous abortions to find safe and legal alternatives.

But, since the number of illegal abortions prior to Roe was even higher than the number of legal abortions performed following the decision, it is questionable if the Court generated any new demand for abortion. Later increases may be due as much to advertising of services by women's rights groups and to greater acceptance of abortion as more women openly obtained them and abortion was discussed in the news, TV talk shows, and women's magazines.

**New Technology and Attitudes**   Changes in medical technology also are beginning to affect abortion procedures and attitudes. When *Roe v. Wade* was decided, medical science often was able to keep premature babies alive if they were born in the last trimester of pregnancy or about the twenty-eighth week. New procedures decreased this to the twenty-sixth, then to the twenty-fourth and possibly the twenty-third week. This is during the second trimester of pregnancy, when the Supreme Court said that abortion was legal but could be restricted in certain ways.

Estimates are that 90 percent of abortions are performed during the first trimester, but others are performed later because young or poor mothers often postpone the decision. Some doctors and other medical personnel are becoming uncomfortable with the legality of abortion during a period when fetuses can survive outside the womb and become healthy children.

*Social Pressure*   But divided public opinion and pro-life demonstrations and boycotts also have made some doctors uncomfortable about routinely performing abortions, especially in conservative and rural areas, where they are likely to be visible to many people in their community. Many doctors probably perform occasional abortions for their private patients, but do not offer abortions in clinics or generally as part of their obstetric specialty. In northern Minnesota, for example, one abortion clinic is available for twenty-four rural counties, but the doctor flies in from Duluth because no local physicians will perform the procedure. Only a half-dozen doctors in Montana and none in Alaska report they perform abortions. Young and poor women find it most difficult to travel to larger communities to obtain abortions.

Some doctors also report they fear their regular patients will stay away and their incomes will suffer if they become known as abortion doctors. Even in large cities, those who offer this service are shunned by their colleagues and considered second class physicians. Comments made by pro-choice friends in jest, such as "Still killing babies this late in the afternoon?" make doctors cringe, withdraw from their associates, and feel guilty about performing abortions.[33]

Staff doctors and administrators also determine whether to allow abortions in their local hospitals. In the years immediately following *Roe v. Wade*, more hospitals liberalized than restricted their policies to permit elective abortions as well as those needed to safeguard a woman's physical health. The policies depended much more on the attitudes and values of hospital personnel than on local community values, demands for services, or state law.[34] Recently, some hospitals, again mostly those in rural areas, have changed their policies to prohibit abortions.

Although federal courts and the U.S. Supreme Court contribute to abortion policy, the availability of abortions under *Roe v. Wade* probably has been determined more by social and political values that surround the abortion issue. But the Supreme Court will continue to determine how free the states are to restrict the right to abortion. If *Roe v. Wade* is overturned, or further eroded by subsequent interpretations of Roe or reliance on more recent precedents that sanction state restrictions, access to abortion will decrease further. Doctors and hospitals and clinics will become less able to offer abortions without risking criminal penalties. But abortion rights advocates and their opponents will not abandon the fight and abortion will be on the political agenda for years to come.

## CONCLUSION

When courts announce new and momentous decisions, our expectations sometimes rise very quickly. Many individuals and interest groups hope for immediate implementation of what they believe the court had in mind, while others fear terrible consequences of new policies. This is similar to our expectations of newly elected Presidents and governors, who promise so much immediate change during their campaigns. But, in a short while we sometimes realize that nothing much has changed or that the promises cannot be achieved, at least in the short run, and we become disappointed or cynical.

But we have to realize that neither the Supreme Court nor the President has so much power that either one can dramatically change traditional values and beliefs or decades of customary social and political behavior. Substantial change often takes a very long time and courts have little control over it.

Judicial policy does not move in a single straight path. A current Supreme Court often modifies earlier policies, and lower court judges and other officials move in a number of different directions. Judicial decisions also stimulate additional litigation and lawmaking that may either support, modify, or undermine previous judicial policy. The process of litigation, judicial policymaking, impact on various audiences, social change, other lawmaking, and more litigation is a continuous political process with no single goal or end in sight.

We also cannot expect courts to solve major social problems. For a long time, the federal courts were the only hope for blacks seeking equal rights, but they did not get much more than hope until Congress and the President put additional teeth into the law. Still, full equality does not exist in America. Fundamental social change requires money, new ideas, new attitudes and beliefs, shifts in lifestyles, and probably more. We cannot realistically blame courts for not accomplishing more, and we should not give them all the credit for changes we might favor.

Courts have important effects on society *so far as their structure and resources permit*. They are courts, after all, not legislatures, Presidents, or police. They do not command the army, nor do they have administrators who will do their bidding. But, even vague and general judicial policies have some long-term impact on society. This is a big accomplishment, since the major power of courts is their right to make legal decisions that most of us feel compelled to obey and since so many other changes occur in society after judges make their rules.

## SUGGESTIONS FOR ADDITIONAL READING

Abraham, Henry J.: *Freedom and the Court: Civil Rights and Liberties in the United States* (New York: Oxford University Press, 1988). A political and legal history emphasizing freedom of religion, rights of criminal defendants, and political and racial equality and Supreme Court policies.

Cashman, Sean Dennis: *African-Americans and the Quest for Civil Rights, 1900–1990* (New York: New York University Press, 1991). A political history of civil rights and social change in the United States.

Friedman, Lawrence M.: *American Law* (New York: W.W. Norton and Co., 1984). An overview of the history of American law with emphasis on the interaction of social change and the development of new law.

Friedman, Lawrence M.: *Total Justice* (New York: Russell Sage Foundation, 1985). An analysis of the revolution in civil rights and due process and the explosion of law in modern society. New demands for more law are due to general social expectations for justice and compensation for personal loss.

Hall, Kermit L.: *The Magic Mirror: Law in American History* (New York: Oxford University Press, 1988). A history of law and social interaction from the colonial period to modern America.

Slonim, Shlomo, ed.: *The Constitutional Bases of Political and Social Change in the United States* (New York: Praeger, 1990). Nineteen essays by law professors, judges, and political scientists on the Constitution and social change, including religious freedom, minority rights, and individual liberties.

Tribe, Laurence H.: *Abortion: The Clash of Absolutes* (New York: W.W. Norton and Co., 1990). A description and analysis of the web of law, politics, sex, medicine, and morality in the abortion issue.

## NOTES

**1** Lawrence M. Friedman, *American Law* (New York: W.W. Norton and Co., 1984), pp. 255–256.

**2** Harrell R. Rodgers, Jr., and Charles S. Bullock III, *Law and Social Change* (New York: McGraw-Hill Book Company, 1972), p. 75.

**3** Charles S. Bullock III and Harrell R. Rodgers, Jr., *Racial Equality in America* (Pacific Palisades, Calif.: Goodyear Publishing Co., 1975), pp. 3–50. A good summary of major changes in the status and rights of blacks is available in Thomas R. Dye, *Politics in States and Communities*, 5th ed. (Englewood Cliffs, N.J.: Prentice-Hall, Inc., 1985), chap. 13; 7th ed., 1991, chap. 14.

**4** James S. Coleman, *Equality of Educational Opportunity* (Washington, D.C.: Government Printing Office, 1966).

**5** Dye, 5th ed., p. 384.

**6** *Ibid.*, pp. 385–386.

**7** *New York Times*, February 29, 1988, p. 13; Dye, 7th ed., 1991, p. 99; *Statistical Abstract of the United States*, 1991, Tables 4 and 7.

**8** *New York Times*, July 12, 1988; *Statistical Abstract*, 1991, Figure 4.2 and Table 261; John Gruhl and Susan Welch, "The Impact of the Bakke Decision on Minority Enrollment in Medical and Law Schools," *Social Science Quarterly*, (September 1990), 458–473.

**9** *Statistical Abstract*, 1991, Figure 4.2 and Table 652.

**10** *The New York Times*, June 19, 1983, p. 12.

**11** *New York Times*, February 29, 1988, p. 13; *Statistical Abstract*, 1991, Table 721.

**12** Wasby, *The Impact of the United States Supreme Court*, pp. 162–169.

**13** Bradley C. Canon, "Testing the Effectiveness of Civil Liberties Policies at the State and Federal Levels: The Case of the Exclusionary Rule," *American Politics Quarterly*, 5 (January 1977), 57–82.

**14** Wasby, *The Impact of the United States Supreme Court*, p. 164.

**15** Research by the federal government cited in Yale Kamisar, "The Warren Court (Was It Really So Defense-Minded?), The Burger Court (Is It Really So Prosecution-

Oriented?), and Police Investigatory Practices,'' in Vincent Blasi (ed.), *The Burger Court: The Counter-Revolution That Wasn't* (New Haven: Yale University Press, 1983), p. 81.

16 Neal Milner, "Comparative Analysis of Patterns of Compliance with Supreme Court Decisions: *Miranda* and the Police in Four Communities,'' *Law and Society Review*, 5 (August 1970), p. 126.

17 Henry R. Glick, "The Judicial 'Firm': A Useful Model for Understanding Decision-Making in a Juvenile Court,'' *Judicature*, 7 (February 1980), 328–337.

18 Norman Lefstein et al., "In Search of Juvenile Justice: *Gault* and Its Implementation,'' *Law and Society Review*, 3 (May 1969), 491–562.

19 467 U.S. 649 (1984). Cited in Sheldon Goldman, *Constitutional Law* 2 ed. (New York: HarperCollins, Publishers, 1991), p. 630.

20 Goldman, p. 579.

21 *Tallahassee Democrat*, June 9, 1991, p. 1A.

22 *New York Times*, October 23, 1991, p. A1 and November 27, 1991, pp. A1 and A7.

23 David L. Kirp et al., *Gender Justice* (Chicago: University of Chicago Press, 1986), pp. 104 and 120.

24 Charles A. Johnson and Bradley C. Canon, *Judicial Policymaking: Implementation and Impact* (Washington, D.C.: Congressional Quarterly Press, 1984), pp. 211–262.

25 *Statistical Abstract*, 1991, Table 656.

26 Kirp et al., p. 141.

27 *Statistical Abstract*, 1991, Table 652.

28 *New York Times*, March 3, 1988, p. 1; March 22, 1988, p. 1; March 23, 1988, p. 1.

29 *New York Times*, 1987 to 1992; *The Nation*, October 30, 1989, p. 1; *Newsweek*, April 2, 1990, p. 39; *Time*, October 23, 1989, p. 35 and April 2, 1990, p. 22.

30 Susan B. Hansen, "State Implications of Supreme Court Decisions: Abortion Rates Since *Roe v. Wade*,'' *Journal of Politics*, 42 (May 1980), 376; *Newsweek*, January 14, 1985, pp. 20–30; *Statistical Abstract*, 1991, Table 102.

31 Johnson and Canon, p. 9.

32 *Statistical Abstract*, 1991, Table 747.

33 *New York Times*, July 11, 1989, p. 1 and January 8, 1990, p. 1.

34 Jon R. Bond and Charles A. Johnson, "Implementing a Permissive Policy: Hospital Abortion Services after *Roe v. Wade*,'' *American Journal of Political Science* 26 (February, 1982), 1–24.

# INDEX